EERDMANS' HANDBOOK TO
THE WORLD'S RELIGIONS

Consulting Editors

R. Pierce Beaver   Emeritus Professor of Mission
University of Chicago, USA

Dr Jan Bergman   Professor of the History of Religions
Uppsala University, Sweden

Dr Myrtle S. Langley   Head of Practical Theology and Missiology
Trinity College, Bristol, England

Dr theol. Wulf Metz   Professor at the Fachhochschule
Munich, Germany

Dr Arild Romarheim   Lecturer in World Religions
The Free Faculty of Theology
Oslo, Norway

Professor Andrew Walls   Head of the Department of Religious Studies
University of Aberdeen, Scotland

Dr Robert Withycombe   Librarian, St Mark's Library and Theological Institute
Canberra, Australia

Canon R.W.F. Wootton   Formerly Leicester Diocesan Chaplain for Community Relations
Leicester, England

Copyright © 1982 Lion Publishing

Published by
Lion Publishing
Icknield Way, Tring, Herts, England

First American edition 1982
Reprinted 1983
William B. Eerdmans Publishing Company
255 Jefferson Ave. SE, Grand Rapids, Michigan
49503

ISBN 0-8028-3563-5

Printed and bound in Hong Kong
by Mandarin Offset International (HK) Ltd.

EERDMANS' HANDBOOK TO
THE WORLD'S
RELIGIONS

WM. B. EERDMANS
PUBLISHING CO.
Grand Rapids, Michigan

Contents

Preface

As far back as we can go, even before the earliest written records, there is evidence that religion was a key aspect of life. The mystery of birth and death, the challenge of life itself, has always moved mankind to reach out to something – someone – beyond, in search of meaning. 'No one', it has been said, 'can understand mankind without understanding the faiths of humanity.'

This book is intended to present the reader with a comprehensive, clear and stimulating introduction and guide to the world's religions, from man's earliest forms of worship to the present day.

After setting the scene and discussing the origins of religion the Handbook describes the ancient religions – Egypt, Greece, Rome, the Norse gods . . . Primal religions today are illustrated with a series of case-studies from many parts of the world. On the major Eastern and world religions, articles give information on the history, scriptures, worship, beliefs and practices of the various faiths.

More than fifty specialist authors from many different countries have contributed to the Handbook. They write from a Christian concern to describe each faith 'as it is', presenting different viewpoints clearly and objectively so that they speak for themselves. As reporters, they have no wish to erect images of a religion which they then knock down; nor do they try to cover up facts which an insider may not want brought out into the light of day.

In the section on Christianity, there has been a real attempt to be equally dispassionate! If conviction shows through, however, it is because there can never be total objectivity when it comes to deeply-held matters of belief. Different religious faiths cannot be put on the supermarket shelves and one labelled 'best buy'. So the section title puts a question: is Christianity in fact a 'religion' at all, or does it claim more, to be the fulfilment of religion?

The evidence is presented. The response – whether the faiths of mankind are being studied simply from academic interest or as part of a deep personal search – must be left to the reader.

Contributors

Oxford, Ohio, USA. *African Religions*; *The Luba Epic*.

The Rev. Robert Brow, Rector of St James' Church, Kingston, Ontario, Canada. *Origins of Religion.*

John Allan, former Head of Religious Education, Hreod Burna School, Swindon, Wilts, England; Director of Training, British Youth for Christ. *A Fusion of Religion: Syncretism.*

Professor Sir Norman Anderson, formerly Professor of Oriental Studies and Director of the Institute of Advanced Legal Studies, London University. *The Law of Islam*; *The Future of Islam.*

Dr George Bankes, Assistant Keeper of Ethnology, The Manchester Museum, Manchester, England. *Land of the Aztecs and Incas: America before Columbus.*

Dr Robert Banks, Visiting Fellow, Department of History, Faculty of Arts, Australian National University, Canberra. *The Covenant*; *Torah and Mishnah*; *The God Who Speaks*; *Competing Ideologies Today: Communism.*

Dr Axel-Ivar Berglund, Lecturer in Missiology and Cultural Anthropology, Uppsala University, Sweden. *Primal Religions, Case-study 10: The Zulus.*

Dr John Berthrong, Lecturer at the Centre for Religious Studies, Toronto University, Canada. *Sages and Immortals: Chinese Religions.*

Dr Barbara M. Boal, Lecturer in Primal Religions, Selly Oak Colleges, Birmingham, England. *Primal Religions, Case-study 1: Asia*; *Cao-Dai and Hoa-Hao.*

Newell S. Booth, Jr., Professor of Religions, Miami University,

The Rev. Colin Buchanan, Principal, St John's Theological College, Bramcote, Nottingham, England. *Christian Worship.*

Chua Wee Hian, General Secretary, International Fellowship of Evangelical Students. *The Worship of Ancestors*; *Community of a Common Life.*

Harvie M. Conn, Associate Professor of Missions and Apologetics, Westminster Theological Seminary, Philadelphia PA, USA. *Primal Religions, Case-study 2: Korea.*

Dr Geoffrey Cowling, Senior Lecturer in History, Macquarie University, North Ryde, New South Wales, Australia. *Story of a Nation* (Judaism); *Developments in Judaism*; *Moses*; *Ezra*; *Theodore Herzl.*

The Rev. Dr Clyde Curry Smith, Professor of Ancient History and Religion, University of Wisconsin, River Falls, USA. *The Ancient Religions of Greece and Rome.*

The Rev. Douglas Davies, Lecturer, Department of Theology, Nottingham University, England. *The Study of Religion*; *Myths and Symbols*; *Religion of the Gurus: The Sikh Faith.*

Richard H. Drummond, Professor of Ecumenical Mission and History of Religions, University of Dubuque, Theological Seminary, Dubuque, Iowa, USA. *Gautama The Buddha in His Setting*; *The Buddha's Teaching.*

The Rev. William H. Edwards, Pitjanjatjara Area Chaplain, Uniting Church in Australia. *The Aborigines.*

The Rev. Dr R.T. France, Senior Lecturer in New Testament Studies, London Bible College. *Jesus*; *The Bible.*

Dr Raymond Hammer, Director, Bible Reading Fellowship. *The Eternal Teaching: Hinduism*; *Roots: The Development of Hindu Religion*; *Approaches to Truth: The Great Interpreters*; *Concepts of Hinduism*; *Hindu Worship and the Festivals*; *Men and Movements*; *Escape from Life?*; *Karma and Dharma: Hindu Ethics*; *Hinduism Outside India.*

The Rev. C. D. Harley, Lecturer in Old Testament and Jewish Studies, All Nations Christian College, Ware, Herts, England. *Chosen People: Judaism*; *Life in a Jewish Family.*

Antony J. Harrop, United Bible Societies Distribution Adviser in South Asia. *A Day in the Life of a Muslim Family.*

Dr John R. Hinnells, Lecturer in Comparative Religion, Manchester University, England. *The Cosmic Battle: Zoroastrianism*; *Mithraism: Cult of the Bull*; *Courage and Faith: The Parsis.*

Leslie Hoggarth, Lector in the Centre for Latin American Linguistic Studies, St Andrews University, Scotland. *Primal Religions, Case-study 12: The Andes.*

Dr Åke Hultkrantz, Professor in the History of Religions, Stockholm University, Sweden. *Religion Before History*; *Nomads of the Steppes.*

The Rev. James Irwin, Dean of Maori and Polynesian Studies, Theological Hall, Knox College,

Presbyterian Church of New Zealand. *Primal Religions, Case-study 7: The Maoris.*

Dr David Kerr, Director of the Centre for the Study of Islam and Christian Muslim Relations, Selly Oak Colleges, Birmingham, England. *The Worship of Islam*; *The Unity and Variety in Islam.*

The Rev. Christopher Lamb, BCMS/CMS Other Faiths Theological Project, Birmingham, England. *The Claim to be Unique.*

Dr Myrtle S. Langley, Head of Practical Theology and Missiology, Trinity College, Bristol, England. *Respect for All Life: Jainism.*

Robert D. Linder, Professor of History, Kansas State University, Manhattan, Kansas, USA. *The Future of Christianity.*

Dr Carl Loeliger, Senior Lecturer in Religious Studies, History Department, University of Papua New Guinea. *Primal Religions, Case-study 4: Melanesia*; *New Myths: The Cargo Cults.*

I. Howard Marshall, Professor of New Testament Exegesis, Aberdeen University, Scotland. *Christian Beliefs.*

Dr Theol. Wulf Metz, Professor at the Fachhochschule, Munich, Germany. *The Enlightened One: Buddhism*; *The Buddhist Lands*; *One Goal, Many Paths*; *Buddha – Just a Good Hindu?*; *From Memory to Writing*; *The Appeal of Buddhism in the West.*

A.R. Millard, Rankin Senior Lecturer in Hebrew and Ancient Semitic Languages, Liverpool University, England. *Cradle of Civilization: The Ancient Near East.*

Wm. Montgomery Watt, formerly Professor of Arabic,

Edinburgh University, Scotland. *The Way of the Prophet* (Islam).

J.W.E. Newbery, Professor Emeritus (Native Studies), University of Sudbury, Canada. *Primal Religions, Case-study 11: North American Indians.*

Dr Michael Pye, Lecturer in the History of Religions, Leeds University, England. *A Tapestry of Traditions: Japanese Religions.*

The Rev. A.D. Rogers, Principal Lecturer in Theology and Religion, Dorset Institute of Higher Education, England. *Primal Religions, Case-study 8: Madagascar.*

John Ruffle, Keeper of Archaeology, Ethnography and Birmingham History, Birmingham City Museums and Art Gallery, England. *Ancient Egypt: Land of the Priest-King*; *Egyptian Temples: Houses of Power.*

Joan E. Rule, Senior Lecturer in English, Dauli Teachers' College, Papua New Guinea. *Primal Religions, Case-study 5: The Foe of Papua New Guinea.*

The Rev. Michael Sadgrove, Vice-Principal, Salisbury and Wells Theological College, England. *The Christian Life*; *Branches of the Church.*

The Rev. Dr Werner Schilling, Lecturer in Foreign Religions and Missiology, Free Theological Academies, West Germany. *Unity and Peace: The Baha'i Faith*; *Persecution of the Baha'is.*

Lothar Schmalfuss, Director of Studies, the University, Neubiberg, Germany. *Muhammad*; *Science, Art and Culture in Islam.*

Eric J. Sharpe, Professor of Religious Studies, University of Sydney, Australia. *Six Major Figures in Religious Studies.*

The Rev. Dr Anthony C. Thiselton, Senior Lecturer in Biblical Studies, Sheffield University, England. *Competing Ideologies Today: Existentialism.*

Angela Tilby, Producer, Religious Programmes, BBC Television, England. *Part Seven: Rapid Fact-finder* (joint author with Dr John-David Yule).

Dr A.R. Tippett, Research Fellow, St Mark's Library, Canberra, Australia. *Primal Religions, Case-study 3: Oceania.*

Dr Harold W. Turner, Director, Project for the Study of New Religious Movements in Primal Societies, Aberdeen University, Scotland. *Holy Places, Sacred Calendars*; *World of the Spirits*; *Christianity and the Primal Religions.*

Professor Andrew Walls, Head of the Department of Religious Studies, Aberdeen University, Scotland. *The Old Gods: Religions of Northern Europe.*

J. Christy Wilson, Jr, Professor of World Evangelization, Gordon-Conwell Theological Seminary, South Hamilton, Massachusetts, USA. *The Qur'an.*

Marvin R. Wilson, Ockenga Professor of Biblical Studies and Chairman of the Department of Biblical Studies, Gordon College, Wenham, Massachusetts, USA. *Branches of Judaism*; *The Influence of Judaism.*

Dr Edwin M. Yamauchi, Professor and Director of Graduate Studies, History Department, Miami University, Oxford, USA. *Secret Knowledge: The Gnostics*; *The Mandaeans: Gnostic Survivors*; *Faith of Light and Darkness: the Manichaeans.*

The Rev. Dr John-David Yule, Assistant Curate of St Andrew's Church, Cherry Hinton, Cambs, England. *Part Seven: Rapid Fact-finder* (joint author with Angela Tilby).

Part One

The Development of Religion

The Study of Religion

Douglas Davies

Every adult male Muslim is required to make the pilgrimage to Mecca once in his lifetime. These pilgrims are setting out from Aswan.

What is religion? There have been many definitions. Some have simply described it as 'belief in spiritual beings'. Others have attempted more comprehensive definitions in terms of beliefs or a description of practices.

Some of the different approaches to religion are as follows:

● **Anthropologists** describe religious beliefs and practices as they find them in living communities. Religion helps to unite people in a shared experience and explanation of life. It provides a pattern of human behaviour, often in response to the hazards of life.

● **Sociologists** stress the social dimension of religious ideas. Religion provides an agreed way of looking at the world. It gives the individual a sense of purpose and meaning.

● **Historians** describe religion in terms of events resulting from beliefs; **theologians** are concerned with the beliefs themselves, the question of whether they are true or false, and with people's response to them.

The different approaches are valid in different ways and within their own limitations. The basic difference is that of standpoint: there is the way of the believer and the way of the scholar.

The believer

Theology is the term usually given to the study of one's own religion. It is concerned with the meaning of the doctrines which have developed over the years, with the way doctrine is derived from *scriptures*, and the interpretation of the scriptures. This often leads to the formation of different schools of tradition and to sectarian divisions within major religions.

It also leads to the application of this knowledge to ordinary behaviour —*ethics*—and to special acts of worship—*liturgy*.

These are the names used of Christian theology, but similar strands can be found in other world religions.

Theology, then, is the study of a religion from the inside. It assumes that the faith is true. Then it seeks to explore it more fully, and often attempts to relate that faith to changing world situations. Theology is always grounded in a religious tradition.

The scholar

The 'scholarly approach' to religion means a neutral, non-committed form of study. It looks at the form of a religion: it does not ask whether it is true.

The phrase 'scholarly approach' is deceptive if it means that religious people cannot adopt an intellectual approach to religious things. Very often they can and do. But the scholarly, objective or scientific perspective is one which emphasizes the outward and visible aspects of a religion, even when this means describing the nature of people's religious experiences, rather than pinpointing the great issues of truth and awareness of God as felt by the believer himself. It is possible for the religious person to speak in one context as a believer about the intimate things of his religion, and in another as a scholar about the way his fellow-believers see things.

What, then, are the different methods scholars have adopted in studying the whole subject of religion? And what are the key ideas that will help us understand the 'scholarly approach'?

Reductionism

The different approaches are not, of course, mutually exclusive. In fact each method of study can add to our total picture.

This is in contrast to the 'reductionism' of some approaches which try to explain everything in terms of one theory. Religion is 'nothing but' economic, sexual or evolutionary drives.

For instance, Marx explained religion in economic terms. Freud explained it in sexual terms. Some nineteenth-century anthropologists explained it simply in terms of evolution.

The anthropologists

Anthropology is the study of human behaviour: religion as a pattern of behaviour can be observed like any other human activity.

As a discipline it has added enormously to what we know of peoples throughout the world, particularly the more primitive tribes. Anthropologists from the last century on have been particularly keen to study such tribes because they were interested to relate the new science to the theory of evolution.

Evolution

The work of Charles Darwin provided scholars with the kind of theoretical explanation of religion which had not been present in the eighteenth-century arguments of philos-

'No-one can understand mankind without understanding the faiths of humanity. Sometimes naive, sometimes penetratingly noble, sometimes crude, sometimes subtle, sometimes cruel, sometimes suffused by an overpowering gentleness and love, sometimes world-affirming, sometimes negating the world, sometimes inward-looking, sometimes universalistic and missionary minded, sometimes shallow and often profound—religion has permeated human life since early and obscure times.'

Ninian Smart, *Religious Experience*

ophers such as G.W.F. Hegel and J.G. Herder.

Instead of abstract ideas of progress and development, scholars such as E.B. Tylor, J.G. Frazer and W. Robertson Smith, whose works spanned the period between 1870 and 1920, sought to identify specific periods through which man had passed, by characterizing the beliefs held during these successive eras. They named these stages of religious life according to their own, largely speculative, theory of the dominant concern present in each one.

Often religion was said to cease to be significant once science replaced it as a stage in human thought. This was a characteristic argument of Sir J.G. Frazer, whose book *The Golden Bough* is still in print even though it is more a work of speculation than of fact.

Functionalism

The twentieth century saw a marked difference of approach to the study of religion, and in particular the question of the development of religion changed its form. Instead of asking the evolutionary question of how religion first originated, anthropologists chose to ask what function was served by religion in each particular society where it occurred. The anthropologist E.E. Evans-Pritchard expressed this neatly, saying that 'religion is what religion does'. Bronislaw Malinowski (1884–1942) abandoned the historical dimension, preferring to study intensively the role played by religion in the Trobriand Island community where, as an Austrian citizen, he was interned during World War I.

Malinowski believed that there were scientific laws of culture and that they could also be applied to religion. The individual biological needs of food, shelter, sex and security could also be viewed as social needs which people provide for corporately through economic, political, kinship and religious institutions. Magic was useful because it brought one man into a leadership position during times of crisis in society. It made some sort of positive action possible and thereby pre-

vented chaotic behaviour. Religion along with magic provided the basic integrating force in society, for it was the response to the human desire for survival. Magic, performed in the face of natural calamity, provided a psychological support for people's fear. Much of this theory resulted from Malinowski's observation of primitive society, but as his private diaries show—published long after his death—his own fears of loneliness, the dark, and of death probably guided the way he constructed his theory of religion.

Structuralism

After the 1950s, anthropologists turned their attention more to the role of religion as an expression of the structure of the ideas, values and beliefs of a society. They drew a picture of the relationships which existed between doctrines. They asked how people argued, how they organized their beliefs, and what was the inner logical pattern of a religion.

For example, village Buddhists escape painful experiences by means of exorcists: how do they square this with the Buddhist ideal which denies the validity of such exorcism? Or how do Christian groups relate their beliefs about everyday life to the concept of the Trinity? This structuralist approach draws attention to the organization of human thought, and to the way man brings an ordered pattern to his complex world. For instance, the French anthropologist Claude Levi-Strauss has studied the question of how this works out in the case of myths.

The psychologists

Whereas in the nineteenth century scholars were happy to combine anthropological ideas with those concerning the human mind, in the twentieth century the mind has been singled out for special attention by the psychologists. Sigmund Freud drew heavily from evolutionary anthropology, especially from William Robertson Smith's famous *Lectures on the Religion of the Semites* (1889), but his wish was to show how the underlying power of the human

Hindus bathe in the sacred rivers such as the Ganges, to wash away pollution, both physical and spiritual.

mind, grounded in a kind of sexual energy called the libido, ascribed to a god-figure attitude which originated in the child's relationship with his human father.

Projection

This introduces a major concept in religious studies: that of 'projection', a term which embraces not only the psychological approach of Freud but also the earlier philosophical argument of Feuerbach (1804–72), who claimed that statements about God were really to be understood as statements about man. Man had tended to construct ideas of God and then to look at them as though they had a reality of their own. For a proper understanding of theology one should reverse this process and interpret religious doctrine in human terms. Feuerbach influenced Marx and Engels, and thereby the rise of communist society and its view of religion as an outmoded way of interpreting life.

Freud also decided that religious positions were no longer useful to man, as his book *The Future of an Illusion* (1927) clearly showed: here projection is seen as illusion, the human mind leading man away from truth and reality, and therefore to be deplored.

The psychologist William James adopted a rather more positive attitude to the role of religion. In *The Varieties of Religious Experience* (1902), he gave a full description of religious experiences possessed by various people, comparing and contrasting what he called 'the religion of healthy-mindedness' with that of 'the sick soul'.

For James, religion was of value in helping man to live a positive and courageous life. It was seen as ultimately about the fact that there is something wrong with us, and with ways of saving us from that wrongness. In other words, religion helps man to accept himself and his life-condition rather than falling prey to the infirmities of his life. All this is of positive advantage to man, so that James did not see religion as an illusion with no real future as Freud thought it to be.

The sociologists

The discipline of sociology also developed rapidly in the early twentieth century. Here too the idea of projection was of great significance, particularly for Emile Durkheim (1858–1917). His famous study of *The Elementary Forms of the Religious Life* owed much to the same lectures by Robertson Smith which had also influenced Freud. It presupposed an evolutionary approach to religion, but did not accept the view that religious ideas were simply misleading products of the human mind. Here Durkheim as a sociologist parted company both with the psychology of Freud and the speculative anthropology of Frazer. Durkheim was convinced that there was something real in religion, and that man was not deceiving himself. In identifying the reality underlying religious behaviour he also parted company with theological explanations, for the reality influencing religion, he came to believe, is society itself.

Durkheim was as preoccupied with the idea of society as Freud was with the unconscious mind: he believed that there was a different sort of reality at work in social groups from that in individual lives. Society could be studied much as botanists studied plants. Religion was the human activity which spoke about social reality while using words about gods.

In one sense Durkheim was adopting a similar outlook to Feuerbach—that man merely seems to believe in and to speak about God, while really talking about his own social group without realizing it. But for Durkheim, who did not believe in a God who exists in his own right and independently of man, society is such an important thing that it can completely fill the place of God. Society is there before I am born and exists after my death. It gives me ideas and language to think and speak with. It protects me and makes me feel worthy of life. So, despite the fact that man projects all these ideas onto a god-figure, the ideas themselves are true, and what is more, they are necessary if society is to be held together as a moral community.

Six Major Figures in Religious Studies

Eric Sharpe

FRIEDRICH MAX MÜLLER (1823–1900)

Often called 'the father of comparative religion', Friedrich Max Müller was the son of a German Romantic poet. He studied in Leipzig and in Paris, where he began his first major work, a monumental edition of the Sanskrit text of the *Rig Veda*, published in four volumes between 1849 and 1862. He settled in England in 1846, and spent most of the remainder of his life in Oxford, becoming Professor of Comparative Philology in 1868. A prolific writer, his later books included *Comparative Mythology* (1856), *Introduction to the Science of Religion* (1873), *India, What can it teach us?* (1883), and many other works, including three series of Gifford Lectures and two volumes of personal reminiscences. He was also responsible for editing the fifty-volume series of *Sacred Books of the East*—still an invaluable source for the study of religion.

Max Müller brought the religions of the world for the first time to the notice of the English-speaking public, interpreted to the West the ancient and modern religions of India, in a vital, if sometimes idiosyncratic, way. His theories that religion arose through the personification of natural phenomena have, on the other hand, been wholly superseded.

EDWARD BURNETT TYLOR (1832–1917)

In its early years, the study of comparative religion was much concerned with the origin and evolution of religion as a universal human phenomenon. E. B. Tylor, who in 1896 became Britain's first professor of anthropology, in the 1860s coined the term 'animism' to describe what he believed to be the earliest stage in this evolutionary process, a simple 'belief in spiritual beings'. Tylor studied in Mexico; this visit resulted in his first book, *Anahuac* (1861). He subsequently published *Researches into the Early History of Mankind* (1865), and his most important work, *Primitive Culture* (1871), in which the 'animism' theory is clearly stated. Briefly, it is that early man's experiences of dream and trance led him first to a belief in a separate 'soul' (*anima*) in himself, and later to postulate the existence of surviving souls (ghosts), and of many such 'souls' in animals, plants, the atmosphere, etc. Out of this belief in souls or spirits, there eventually developed belief in gods.

As an evolutionary theory, it is of very little value, but it does represent accurately the way in which primal (and other) peoples look on the unseen world. Tylor's example, as well as providing for the first time a way of understanding religion at a basic level, served to point anthropology along a path which it still to some extent follows.

WILLIAM JAMES (1842–1910)

William James, the brother of the celebrated American novelist Henry James, was chiefly responsible, in the years around the turn of the century, for popularizing the new subject of the psychology of religion. His book *The Varieties of Religious Experience* (1902) is a classic, and still widely read today. Trained in medicine, he taught both physiology and psychology at Harvard as early as the 1870s, and in 1890 published a celebrated textbook, *The Principles of Psychology*. Most of his other books, including *The Will to Believe* (1896), *Pragmatism* (1907) and *Human Immortality* (1908), were originally courses of lectures.

In his *Varieties* he drew many valuable distinctions between types of religious experience, the best-known being that between the optimistic 'religion of healthy-mindedness' (typified by Christian Science) and the pessimistic 'religion of the sick soul' (traditional Calvinism). He also had much to say on mysticism, and discussed 'altered states of consciousness' many years before the subject became fashionable. He came from a Swedenborgian background, and his own religion was an indistinct theism, far removed from orthodox Christianity. Although he is still worth reading, his approach was too individualistic, and he had little to say about the corporate aspects of religion. His methods, too, were seriously called in question by the depth-psychologists (Freud, Jung and their followers), and are hardly applicable today.

WILLIAM ROBERTSON SMITH (1846–94)

Robertson Smith, best known for his magisterial book *Lectures on the Religion of the Semites* (1889), was a minister of the Free Church of Scotland. In 1870 he became Professor of Old Testament Studies at the Free Church College in Aberdeen. In the early 1880s he was dismissed from his chair for 'unscriptural' teaching, and in 1883 was elected Professor of Arabic at Cambridge. A liberal evangelical, he was responsible for bringing together traditional philological study of the Bible and the new insights of anthropology.

He first visited North Africa in 1879, and was impressed by the existence of 'totemism' among the Sinai Bedouin: this resulted in his first major work, *Kinship and Marriage in Early Arabia* (1885). In his later *Lectures*, he concentrated on the concept of sacrifice, which he saw less as a legal transaction than as a practical means of establishing communion with deity. He also recognized that in religion, custom and ritual are often more significant than systems of belief, and that it is vitally important that the student be an accurate and sympathetic observer of the practical side of religion. His influence was widespread: he inspired J. G. Frazer to study totemism, and was a forerunner of the sociological study of religion – for which reason he, almost alone among his contemporaries, is still respected among sociologists and anthropologists. Despite his brush with ecclesiastical authority, he remained warmly evangelical in his personal beliefs.

NATHAN SÖDERBLOM (1866–1931)

The link between comparative religion and Christian theology was firmly established in the early part of the twentieth century by a group of scholars of whom Nathan Söderblom was perhaps the most outstanding. Born the son of a Lutheran country minister in Sweden, from 1894 to 1901 he was Swedish legation pastor in Paris; in 1901 he became Professor of Comparative Religion in Uppsala, and remained in this post until his elevation to the archbishopric of Uppsala in 1914, a post he occupied until his death in 1931. His scholarly work spanned many fields, among them Iranian studies, Luther studies, mysticism, Catholic modernism and general comparative religion.

Though few of his many books were translated into English, his Gifford Lectures *The Living God* (published posthumously in 1931) were widely read in their day. He endeavoured to locate historical Protestantism within Christianity, and Christianity within the religions of the world. He drew valuable distinctions between 'mystical' and 'revealed' forms of religion, and later between two forms of mysticism, 'mysticism of personality' (Paul, Luther) and 'mysticism of the infinite' (Indian religion). As well as this academic work, Söderblom made an invaluable contribution to twentieth-century Christianity as one of the fathers of the ecumenical movement.

RUDOLF OTTO (1869–1937)

Educated at Erlangen and Göttingen, most of Otto's career was spent in teaching posts at Göttingen, Breslau and Marburg. After early work in Luther studies, he turned his attention to the philosophy and psychology of religion, and after 1911 to the study of Indian religions. His best-known and most important work, *The Idea of the Holy*, first appeared in German in 1917, and in English in 1923. In it, he attempted to show that religion begins with 'the sense of the numinous', that is, of a mysteriously 'other' deity both fearsome and fascinating (*numen* = deity). This book became a religious classic.

His later Indian studies included *Mysticism East and West* (1932) and *India's Religion of Grace* (1930), and a critical edition of the *Bhagavad Gita* (*The Original Gita*, 1939). In 1921, convinced of the importance of living, inter-religious dialogue, he inaugurated the Inter-Religious League, which was not a success. In his last years his internationalism caused him to fall foul of the Nazi government in Germany, and he died in 1937.

Otto's most lasting contribution to the study of religion lay in his insistence on the importance of immediate, non-rational experience to any estimate of the nature of religion. Although *The Idea of the Holy* was not always well understood, it spoke directly to the mind of the twentieth century, and helped lay the foundations for much later work in the area of personal religious experience and of mysticism.

The nineteenth-century interest in anthropology was aroused by expeditions such as Charles Darwin's world voyage on board HMS Beagle.

The positive function of religion was something taken up by the sociologist Max Weber (1864–1920) who sought to show how religious ideas influenced the active social life of a group. His famous study of *The Protestant Ethic and the Spirit of Capitalism* sought to show how the Calvinist idea of predestination led believers to adopt an earnest and rational life in which they endeavoured to fulfil their calling as good stewards of God's grace. This led to the situation in which commerce and industry could develop rapidly, with maximum investment of capital and minimum loss of energy by those responsible for production of goods. Religious ideas thus motivate man's action in the world, rather than—as Marx claimed—providing an anaesthetic for worldly life.

Religion as phenomenon

'Phenomenology' differs from the previous approaches by concerning itself neither with the historical origin of religion nor with the function of a religion in contemporary situations. It sets out to classify the phenomena that are associated with religious traditions: objects, rituals, doctrines, or feelings. Each phenomenologist identifies what he thinks is the essence of these phenomena, and sets about describing their influence upon man.

Gerardus van der Leeuw (1890–1950) was among the most distinguished of phenomenologists of religion. For him, power is the source and underlying essence of all religion; it is manifested in many ways, from the idea of man in Melanesian religion to the awe and wonder experienced in the world religions. His phenomenology is a description of the many ways in which 'man conducts himself in his relation to power'. Salvation comes about when the source of power is possessed or attained.

A person's religious experience cannot, of course, be observed by someone else. The phenomenologist can only see the consequences of people's experience. So phenomenology cannot deal with questions of truth. It can only describe what can be seen by an outside observer.

The historical approach

Mircea Eliade was born in Bucharest in 1907, and has worked and taught in many parts of the world. He is the best-known and most influential representative of the study of the history of religions. It is difficult to distinguish clearly between historians and phenomenologists of religion because their perspectives are similar. So while Eliade seeks to discover how religions have developed through their historical phases, his major concern is with the idea of the 'holy'.

A Buddhist believer kneels before images of the Buddha in a shrine in Kampuchea.

The enormous Hindu Wat at Angkor, Kampuchea, is almost a mile square. Surrounded by a vast cloister and moat, the central shrine represents the hub of the universe.

What are the various ways in which mankind becomes aware of the holy? His task leads him to discuss 'hierophanies'—the ways in which the sacred is manifested—including sacred places and persons.

For instance, Jesus Christ was said to be the supreme hierophany because in him the sacred, which normally belongs to a realm totally different from our own, is manifested in something belonging entirely to our world, his human nature. Eliade believes that the Western world has allowed its ability to perceive the sacred to wither, and that the task of the history of religions is to help it to regain this sense of the holy within its materialistic life.

Eliade resembles Rudolf Otto (1869–1937) whose famous book *The Idea of the Holy* asserted that the central reality of true religion lies in a sense of the magnetic and awe-inspiring nature of the source of religious experience. Some critics argue that this approach, which does not question the existence of a divinity but rather seems to presuppose the existence of a supernatural realm, has sought to foster religion rather than to be a dispassionate study. Historians and phenomenologists may reply that they seek only to avoid reductionism and to treat the evidence with the seriousness it deserves and in a method appropriate to it.

Comparative linguistics

In 1888, the same year that Smith gave the Burnett Lectures on *The Religion of the Semites*, Friedrich Max Müller delivered the Gifford Lectures entitled *Natural Religion*. Müller told how he became entranced as a young man with the idea of translating the sacred texts of India, how his early work in the 'science of language' led him to a study of mythology and finally to 'the science of religion'. Religion is that mental state which 'enables man to apprehend the Infinite under different names', and the science of religion is the attempt to retrace the development of the names given to the gods.

Müller's study of religion is thus a study of language. For instance, the Latin *deus*, the Sanskrit *deva*, and the Greek *theos* are related and refer to the idea of brightness. He is usually remembered for his notion of the 'disease of language': the description given to something actually becomes its name, and then is imbued with a nature all of its own. It is as though man forgets that he has given a name to something, and comes to believe that it has a reality and power in itself, as in the case of the bright sun becoming a deity in its own right. Müller's work has been largely forgotten in the West, but he is still recalled in India as the man who opened up the study of Eastern texts and stimulated an entire generation of later scholars of comparative religion. He laid the solid foundation of attempting to classify and order the vast amount of material in a systematic way.

Theory of meaning

In place of the evolutionary approach to religion inherited from the nineteenth century, there is now emerging another idea which may well provide an integrating theory for the study of religion. This approach stresses man's drive to establish a meaningful world of thought and life. It avoids all simple cause-and-effect arguments, and encourages us to look at the complex inter-relationships which exist between man and his environment.

We might call this approach the 'theory of meaning'. It is much more concerned with what religion does for people now, than with how religion might have originated in the past. It sees each man as one partner involved in an extensive series of communications with others, receiving feedback from them and changing his own outlook in the process. This model of meaning further emphasizes the dynamic nature of religion and of religious experience.

Holy Places, Sacred Calendars

Harold Turner

The places where the gods are revealed or act, and the times when they do so, are central to religious experience.

The place of a vision, healing, miracle or sign tends to be set aside as a special holy space where the gods may be expected to act again. This may begin as a mere cleared circle in the grass, where people come with prayers and offerings. Symbolic objects representing the divinity, altars for the offerings and sacrifices, and buildings to protect both images and altars and to serve as a 'house for the god' may then be added. As the shrine is elaborated it may become a vast temple space with massive structures.

Such sacred places have a symbolic significance. They may be regarded as the 'centre of the world' or 'navel of the earth', as the meeting-place between the gods and men, and the earthly replica of the heavenly realms. The inner cell where the image rests is the 'most holy place', often followed by a series of courts, with degrees of lesser holiness, to the entrances.

Ascent from the earthly to the heavenly realm is symbolized by vertical features—massive stairways, sacred pillars or trees, and sanctuaries on holy mountains. Similar ideas may attach to sacred caves, groves, healing wells, mysterious rock formations, or the tombs of saints or martyrs. Since divine power is more accessible at sanctuaries, these become places of pilgrimage.

The synagogues, churches and mosques of Judaism, Christianity and Islam, however, should be seen as meeting-places for the worshippers, not as sacred dwelling-places for God. They may have a historical or devotional value. But they do not possess a special 'holiness' because God is more active there than anywhere else.

Distance in time separates people from the divine creative acts of the past. In many religions this is overcome by regular recital of sacred myths, retelling what the gods did in creating the world, giving the land, and showing how to make fire, to hunt, farm, build and live together. The recital brings these foundation events to life again. Similarly periodic rituals re-enact and so renew the actions of the gods.

Together myths and rites make up great religious ceremonies which are timed by the rhythms of the seasons or of the heavenly bodies. The most basic is the new year renewal rite when both human and earthly vitalities, which have been used up, corrupted or attacked by evil forces, are purified and given fresh life from the spirit world.

Calendars first developed as schedules telling when to be ready for the next renewal of divine blessing or power.

Calendars, however, could not tell the right time to secure divine blessing on activities such as building a new village, making war, trading, travel, marrying or anything else of special importance.

For these, diviners sought to read the signs of divine approval in the position of the stars (astrology), the flight of birds, by casting lots, consulting oracles, and in many other ways. Divination is therefore important where people feel totally dependent on gods who do not otherwise disclose their will.

Religions with scriptures, such as Judaism, Christianity and Islam, have other means of revelation, and at their best have opposed divination. On the other hand, they have their calendars of times for renewal, whether in daily devotions, weekly worship or annual renewals of experience of the divine blessing.

The Cycle of the Years

One year does not move directly into the next. Each year dies and is buried, returning to the time of origins, before history, to be renewed and brought back to life as the new year.

THE TIME OF ORIGINS

renewal — YEAR 1

renewal — YEAR 2

renewal — YEAR 3

renewal — YEAR 4

Ritual renewal of the new year — YEAR 5

Australian aborigines believe that before the time of man, spirits moved over the earth. Landmarks such as rock outcrops are marks of the spirits. This rock represents a mythical water-serpent who opened up water-holes.

The Golden Pavilion at Kyoto in Japan was built as a garden house. After its owner's death its great beauty led to its use as a Zen temple.

Religion Before History

Åke Hultkrantz

Evidence from archaeology

Most religions are known to us through written sources. 'Prehistoric' means that we are dealing with the time before recorded history; that is, before there were written records about myths, rituals and beliefs. Writing was developed in the ancient civilizations of the Near East, China and Middle America. The literate era started about 3000 BC in the Old World, and shortly after the birth of Christ in the New World. For the sake of convenience we may designate all religions before 3000 BC as prehistoric.

Non-religious man?

The question of the origins of religion will not concern us here. Earlier evolutionists thought that there had been an original non-religious phase in human history. Their information has, however, proved to be false. All we can say is that some groups, for example the Maasai in Kenya, appear to lack a belief in life after death.

Some students of religion consider that man's religious consciousness was born during the time when man first appeared. Others find traces of 'religious' behaviour even in the animal kingdom. Despite some startling progress in animal-behaviour studies (ethology) and the study of ancient man (palaeoanthropology), nothing certain can be said about these alternatives. All that we know is that some early human cultures seem to have contained traces of religious orientation.

Archaeological finds

The main difficulty in any approach to prehistoric religion lies, of course, in the absence of written sources from this extensive period in the history of mankind. The prehistorian is referred to silent survivals of the past: bone materials, stone arrangements, rough stone figures, rock drawings and similar materials. Such objects are difficult to decipher. For example, it is difficult to tell whether a Danish bog find from the Iron Age—be it a well-preserved human body or a golden dish—was used as a gift of offering or not, since there are no documents from that time to illuminate what really happened. (Some modern archaeologists even question whether Denmark, or even Scandinavia, had a religion during the Bronze Age!) We shall never know for certain what the people of those days thought.

However, there are means to come closer to an understanding of at least some general ideas of those distant times. Let us first see how the prehistoric source materials can be classified. The difficulty of such a classification is obvious: we cannot know if a particular type of artifact—an axe, say, or a wagon—ever had a ritual purpose. Nevertheless, a survey of materials which seem to qualify as connected with religion calls for a division along the following lines:
- burial places and burial finds;
- deposition of offerings;
- representations of deities, spirits and cultic figures (carved idols, reliefs, rock paintings, rock drawings, etc.);
- remains of constructions with religious associations, such as altars, temples, or foundations of world pillars.

Archaeologists usually point out that this material can be interpreted only by analogy. The prehistoric material must be placed in a context which may suggest its original meaning. Of course, all such conclusions are hypothetical. The history of prehistoric research has seen a succession of interpretations. The methods of archaeological reconstruction have become more refined, comparisons with the world of the science of the peoples of mankind (ethnology) more restricted in scope, and ecological perspectives more decisive. Nevertheless, much of our reconstruction of prehistoric religion remains guesswork. Almost every interpretation of beliefs can be and has been contested.

Prehistoric versus historic

The prehistoric era of religion stretches from the beginning of mankind—probably about two or three million years ago—until approximately 3000 BC. During all this time religious knowledge was transmitted through the spoken word (beliefs and myths) and through imitative behaviour (rituals). This somewhat restricted how much knowledge could be accumulated—although it is amazing how much tribal keepers of oral traditions are able to memorize.

In many prehistoric societies the fight for subsistence may likewise have precluded the growth of sophisticated religious thought (although there are examples of primal societies with a good deal of leisure time at their disposal). We therefore find some basic differences between representatives of preliterate and literate religions; for instance, the former value repetition in myth and ritual, the latter develop dogma and may go in for intricate speculations.

The perspective of society

The main differences between prehistoric and historic religions are, however, that the former are organized around the perspectives of the hunter, food-gatherer, fisherman or early farmer, whereas historic religions on the other hand, represent the world-view of the developed civilizations, beginning with Egypt, Mesopotamia and China. In other words, prehistoric religions were at home in small-scale, tribal societies where family or kin-groups meant more than other forms of social organization, and where the influence of

natural forces had a tremendous impact on daily life and religion. Such primitive societies still linger on today, and it is possible to link the types of these societies with prehistoric periods.

The first period is the Palaeolithic, or Old Stone Age, during which people were hunters, food-gatherers and fishermen. Latter-day hunting societies have been organized along similar lines, and the patterns of their religions are probably reminiscent of those of Palaeolithic times.

Farmers and herdsmen

The Palaeolithic was followed by the Neolithic, or New Stone Age, about 10,000 BC. This was the time when many hunters turned into primitive farmers. In the following millennia pastoral nomadism developed out of this agriculture in places where the cultivated lands met the grass-lands and deserts. The world of the farmers and herdsmen is still with us. There is every reason to expect that their religious practices resemble those of their prehistoric predecessors.

These analogies between past and present are very rough and ready. Ecological, technological, social and historical differences may cast doubts upon their validity. But they do give us certain clues on which to base our interpretation.

Lower Palaeolithic religion

It is extremely difficult to tell from the finds at our disposal what religion was like during the long period called the Early or Lower Palaeolithic (before 30,000 BC). This was the time of the pre-human members of the family of man, the early hominids such as *Australopithecus africanus*, *Homo habilis* (2,500,000 BC), *Homo erectus* (1,600,000 BC) and *Homo neanderthalensis* (100,000–30,000 BC). Originating

in Africa, perhaps—only Africa has the earliest skeletons and a continuous succession of species—the hominids spread to Europe (where they appeared before 1,000,000 BC) and to Asia; Peking man and Sangiran man in Indonesia were both representatives of *Homo erectus*.

The beginnings of culture

We have some information about the modest cultural achievements of early man. For instance, we know that two-and-a-half million years ago groups of hominids in East Africa used choppers, scrapers and other stone utensils that they had shaped themselves. They practised division of labour between the sexes, and food-sharing.

However, their religious ideas, if any, are unknown to us. This is what we might expect, for the cultural capacity of early man was crude and he did not express clear religious ideas that can be recognized as such by today's archaeologists. We have neither burials, drawings, nor stone monuments to guide our search. However, the tool-making of these early individuals suggests that they had creative intelligence and therefore, very possibly, a form of religion.

Peking man

Many prehistorians have assumed that Peking man, who lived about half a million years ago, had some concept of religion or magic. In his cave near Chou Kou Tien he assembled human skulls which were broken at the *foramen magnum*. This gives easy access to the brain, and it would seem that Peking man extracted and ate the brain. If this was the case (we can never be sure, of course), the motive was religious or magical rather than for food, for Peking man had many animals to hunt. Such cannibalism, when practised in present-day primal societies, usually implies the incorporation of the dead man's vigour and power.

This is a most hypothetical interpretation, and, unfortunately, practically all finds from the Lower Palaeolithic that lend themselves to a religious interpretation are subject to the same difficulty.

Take, for instance, the discoveries of circles of mammoth skulls in Russia and the Ukraine. We are familiar with similar skull arrangements from North America in historical times, the circles of buffalo skulls on the plains which were important in worship. However, the Palaeolithic mammoth skulls *may* have served as weights on the tent-cloths instead of stones. In several instances there are bone circles surrounding fire-places, and in these cases a religious purpose is probably out of the question.

Neanderthal man
Almost all the early remains that may have religious significance are associated with Neanderthal man and the last 50,000 years of the Lower Palaeolithic—the so-called Mousterian period.

Neanderthal man buried his dead with proper ceremonies, and he seems to have believed in some kind of life after death. In the cave of Shanidar, northern Iraq, a dead person was buried under a heap of stones, resting on a bed of many flowers. At Techik Tach in Turkestan, a child was buried surrounded by five pairs of horns of the mountain goat, apparently placed in a circle. A cave at Monte Circeo in Italy contains a human skull within a small circle of stones; here is one of the so-called 'skull burials' that continue throughout the Palaeolithic period.

Grave gifts are common in many instances (for example, at La Chapelle-aux-Saints in France). Towards the end of the Mousterian period the dead were buried in a contracted position ('flexed burials') and painted with red ochre. Both these measures may reflect a belief in a future life: a return to the womb

This limestone fertility figure, discovered in Karpathos, dates from around 3,500 BC.

of Mother Earth, a continued existence in another world through the red 'blood'. Studies of certain modern peoples support these interpretations, but others are of course possible.

From this time also we have evidence of sacred objects: round fossils and pieces of iron pyrites. One round fossil from Tata, Hungary, is engraved with two lines, forming a cross; this could be the first clear evidence of the idea of a quartered universe, a concept widely represented in both Old and New World cosmology.

Bear worship
Even in recent times some Arctic peoples have worshipped bears. It is quite possible that similar religious beliefs were represented in Central Europe (France, Switzerland and Italy) in Mousterian times. Thus, in the Drachenloch Cave in Switzerland, bear skulls have been found enclosed in a stone coffin covered by stone slabs. This looks like a regular bear burial. Some reputable scholars today (Koby, Leroi-Gourhan, Kurtén) insist, however, that the bears in question—

they are cave-bears—had died a natural death in their winter lairs. The apparent burial chests would then be due to natural rockfall from the ceiling of the cave. This is a plausible explanation, but the 'cultic' interpretation seems no less plausible. Finds from Dordogne (in France) and Weimar (in Germany) suggest deliberate burial of bears—brown bears in these cases.

The main idea behind bear ceremonialism is that the dead animal will return to life, or persuade its relatives to make themselves available to the hunter, provided it has received a correct burial. The pattern of burial has been taken from human burials.

Modern man
Neanderthal man belonged to Europe, the Middle East, North Africa and northern Asia. He was slowly replaced by another species, *Homo sapiens*, our own direct ancestors, who had already spread over the continents before the end of the Lower Palaeolithic: Siberian mongoloid peoples entered the New World as early as 60,000 years ago, or perhaps even earlier, and Australia received its population from Indonesia more than 30,000 years ago. This is of some importance for our reconstruction of religious history. It means that the main structures of American and Australian hunting religions go back to the Lower Palaeolithic. And it may even imply that the totemism and high-god beliefs both appearing in these religions are just as old.

Upper Palaeolithic religion
At the beginning of the Upper Palaeolithic period about 30,000 years ago, Neanderthal man had left the scene in Europe and modern man, *Homo sapiens*, took over. The main periods were the Aurignacian (from 30,000 BC),

the Solutrean (from 20,000 BC) and the Magdalenian (15,000–10,000 BC). It is now that the religious patterns, which we could glimpse in earlier periods, take a more discernible form. The world-view is still that of hunting peoples, but it varies in different parts of Eurasia. The religious developments in Africa, southern Asia, Australia and America are as yet hidden from us.

The burial customs give evidence of a clear belief in life after death. For example, in some caves near Menton in south-east France some 'flexed' skeletons were found, stained with iron oxide, adorned with rows of pierced shells and bracelets, and equipped with quartzite tools and flint knives. Skeletons from Italy to Russia testify that the dead were buried with their most precious property. No doubt, they were thought to take it with them to another world.

The mother-goddess

It is from this time that the famous sculptured 'Venus'-figurines in ivory, bone and stone appear (Gravettian period, 25,000 BC). They are distributed from France to eastern Siberia, and the best-known of them all is the Venus from Willendorf in Austria. They all have characteristic, distorted features: the parts of the body which serve sexual and child-bearing functions—the breasts, the hips, the buttocks, the private parts—are excessively enlarged, whereas little attention is paid to the face, the arms and the legs.

It has been suggested that these fat-rumped (steatopygous) figures are just representatives of mortal women, portrayed in the fashion of the time. This is scarcely probable, however. The emphasis on the sexual parts shows very clearly that these Venuses were supposed to represent deities of fertility, growth and fruitfulness. Here we have for the first time real representations of a deity, the mother-goddess, conceived as one or many.

There is a seemingly puzzling question here. How could the mother-goddess, forerunner of Ishtar, Cybele and Artemis, be such a prominent divinity in a hunting culture? The answer is simple. In recently-studied northern Eurasian cultures, the

Magnificent cave-paintings have been discovered in several sites in southern France, dating from before 10,000 BC. Was this simply the self-expression of man the hunter-gatherer? Or were these caves used (as has been suggested) for 'religious' purposes.

women had similar birth goddesses protecting them during pregnancy and childbirth. Many Siberian tribes believed in a mother of the wild animals, a mistress who protects the wild creatures she has given life to. We also know that women played a very important role during the Stone Age as mothers, housekeepers and gatherers of roots and berries.

Do these figurines prove that the concept of a male god was introduced later than the concept of a goddess? Such a conclusion seems unwarranted. Before the emergence of the Middle Eastern city-states, the Supreme Being was never represented in art as far as we can tell. As a diffuse sky-god he was not easy to picture.

We know that bull-roarers have been used to imitate the voice of the Supreme Being, or the voices of dead ancestors, in some modern primal hunting religions (in Australia, South Africa, Brazil and California). Some perforated, ornate stone slabs that have been found in Upper Palaeolithic caves may have been bull-roarers symbolizing the presence of the Supreme God, or other supernatural beings. However, this is far from certain.

Cave paintings

The most telling artistic creations from the Upper Palaeolithic are the engravings and paintings on cave walls. They first appear in the Aurignacian period, but receive their full development in the Magdalenian. Their focus is in southern France and northernmost Spain. The most famous and most numerous rock-paintings stem from 15,000 to 11,000 BC; this is the time of the caves of Dordogne (Lascaux), Ariège (Niaux, Les Trois-Frères, Montespan) and northern Spain (Altamira).

Four-fifths of the figures are animals, and of these most are horses and bisons, the hoofed fauna of the frost-bitten plains. Reindeer occur only at a late stage, at the same time as the glaciers made their last push forward. The composition of the beautiful, realistic animal scenes has been interpreted in various ways. In spite of some recent speculations in another direction, it seems quite reasonable to believe that the animals refer to hunting ritual and hunting magic. Hunting was the major occupation of Palaeolithic man, and ceremonies to secure a successful hunt were most certainly part of the hunting craft, just as they have been among traditional hunters up to the present day.

Only 4 per cent of the pictured animals show arrows (or wounds resulting from arrows). Does this mean that they cannot be associated with hunting magic? Not necessarily. Among primal peoples hunting ceremonies are often very complicated, and real magic—indicating the anticipation of success in the hunt—is only part of a wider pattern. The mere representation of an animal form may lead to the kill—so it was believed.

Why did this animal ceremonialism take place in caves, often in the depths of scarcely accessible inner chambers? We do not know, but it may, perhaps, have something to do with the fact that in widespread tales, recorded even in this century, the animals are supposed originally to have come from underground, or to have once been secluded in caves.

Some wall scenes depict human beings in animal disguise. They may represent ritual performers, perhaps magicians or ritual dancers, or maybe mythical beings. Well-known is the 'sorcerer' of the cave Les Trois-Frères: a picture of a human being with reindeer antlers, long beard, bear's paws and a horse's tail. He has been interpreted as a shaman or a god of the cave, but his position in the picture over a great number of animals makes it more likely that he was a lord of the animals, a master of the game.

All these interpretations are of course tentative. There is a host of pictures which do not easily lend themselves to interpretation, such as pictographs of headless animals (there is even a sculpture of a bear without a head), of women dancing around a phallic man, and so on. However, such representations strengthen the general impression that Upper Palaeolithic European religion was concerned with the animals and sexual fertility — natural targets in a religion chiefly concerned with hunting. We can say the same about animal ceremonialism in Siberia in the same era: reindeer skeletons were carefully buried in anatomical order. Such hunting rites have survived in this area into the twentieth century. As in the bear rites, the aim has been to restore the animal to a new life, in this world or hereafter.

From the end of the Palaeolithic, or the Mesolithic, we have evidence of what appear to have been sacrifices to the supernatural rulers of the reindeer in northern Germany. Reindeer were submerged in a lake close to present-day Hamburg, and weighted down with stones. It is less likely that these reindeer were caches for the hunters, as has been suggested.

Neolithic religion

The Neolithic is, strictly speaking, the period when objects of stone were no longer chipped but ground and polished. More important, this is the age, from about 10,000 BC, when man went over to producing rather than hunting or gathering his own food. The population of the world was probably then around 10 million people. The climate had changed—the melting of the ice was in full flux—and the warmer weather made new inventions in subsistence possible.

Farming and village life

Agriculture was born, possibly as a consequence of the gathering of seeds by the women. This new way of life made it possible for a rapidly-growing population to settle in one place—to live in villages, and to practise pottery-making and weaving. Village life had a tremendous impact on religion, and so had the new food sources, the products of agriculture (or horticulture, as primitive agriculture is sometimes called).

The Neolithic period provides us with archaeological materials from the whole world. There are at least three independent centres where farming began. One is the Middle East, more specifically the mountain slopes of the Fertile Crescent. Wheat and corn were cultivated here, and dogs and goats were domesticated. The taming of animals slowly developed into pastoral nomadism on the outskirts of the area. In the north where the grasslands were wide and open, horse riding was introduced in about 900 BC.

Another centre of agriculture was south-east Asia, homeland of the cultivation of root-crops such as yams. Close by, in Assam, rice was introduced as a staple food that quickly spread to China and the surrounding areas.

A third centre was Central America, where the cultivation of maize began around 5000 BC.

The religions of the Neolithic peoples were closely adapted to these three agricultural civilizations and spread with them. When pastoral nomadism appeared on the scene a new profile of religion was formed that changed the course of world religions.

Death and burial

If we now concentrate on the west Asian–Mediterranean Neolithic religions, it is easy to see how the archaeological finds fit in with this picture. People lived in villages and similar settlements; outside these, true cemeteries have been found (although in some cases the bodies were buried under the floors of the houses). Graves were provided with gifts and offerings, such as beads, shells, utensils like ivory combs, and female figurines—perhaps symbolizing servants for the next life, or protective goddesses.

The closer we come to the time of the developed civilizations, the more differentiated are the burials according to rank or class. Social distinctions (stratification) developed as the political organization based on kinship was succeeded by one based on territory, and a surplus of products made it possible for some men to become relatively rich and important. This development was reflected in the burial customs. 'Inhumation' was now common: man was interred in the ground like the grain, to arise again in another world. Coffins became more commonly used as time went by. Towards the end of Neolithic, cremation was practised here and there, perhaps associated with a more spiritual view of the afterlife.

In some early Neolithic burials the heads of the dead were removed and placed in a circle, facing the centre. This seems to be the last survival of an old Palaeolithic tradition. The beliefs behind this arrangement are hidden from us. Perhaps the circle as a symbol of the universe had something to do with it.

Male and female

Many female sculptures, fat-rumped and violin-shaped figures in bone, clay and terracotta, testify to the prominence of fertility cults. Figurines from Romania (5000 BC) show a mother with her child, later a favourite motif in the Egyptian and Christian religions. In some places there are also phallic statuettes, most certainly representing the male companion of the fertility goddess. The female statuettes are, however, in the majority, no doubt reflecting the elevated position of the woman, and so also the goddess, in a matrilinear agrarian society. The functions of the mother-goddess were now adapted to farming needs: she appeared as goddess of earth and vegetation.

Other fertility divinities were also portrayed, sometimes through animal masks, sometimes in sculpture. Serpentines around the goddess hint that she was a snake-goddess; in later Cretan culture the goddess raises her hands holding snakes. The snake was a fertility symbol in historical times in Europe, the Middle East, India and China (as the dragon).

Another divinity is probably represented in the bull effigies with human masks in the Balkan area. The cult of the bull, symbol of fertility, seems to have been distributed over the Mediterranean and Middle Eastern world. In historical times, it became associated with gods like Baal and Dionysus, with the supernatural master of the bull figures in Zoroastrian religion, and Mithra is represented as killing the bull to rejuvenate the world. The bull-fights in south-western Europe are probably reminiscences of ancient rituals in the worship of the bull-cult.

Priests and temples

This was the time when a form of priesthood evolved and temples of wood, stone and clay became common. The casual sacrificial places of the earlier nomadic hunting culture were succeeded by large buildings for divine service. Here were kept altars, vessels, inscribed objects, vases with paintings of ritual scenes, sculptures in clay and, later on, copper and gold. All these were used in the rituals.

In the Ukraine and surrounding areas archaeologists have found remains of temples, and clay models of temples. For instance, in the southern Bug Valley, now in Soviet Moldavia, Russian prehistorians have discovered a temple at Sabatinovka dating from about 5000 BC. Built of wattle-and-daub, it occupied about seventy square metres. Its big rectangular room, with a floor plastered with clay, contained at the back a clay altar, upon which sixteen female figurines were found. They had large buttocks and were seated on horn-backed stools. Beside the altar was a chair of clay, perhaps intended for the high priest.

European and west Asian Neolithic developments are paralleled in east Asia, and are definitely connected with the Chinese Neolithic period. But the developments in south-east Asia are more difficult to follow. In America the fertility religion of the horticulturists was simply a transfer of the hunter's conceptual world to the planter's; agrarian rituals did not vary basically from hunting rituals in post-Columbian eastern North America. However, some mythological motifs connected with the 'maize mother' point to communications with Indonesia. In large areas of agricultural America the Neolithic period continued until the arrival of Columbus, and even beyond this date.

Megalithic monuments

Towards the end of the Neolithic era structures composed of large stones, or megaliths, were erected in Europe. Perhaps most of them were burial structures: the striking tombs (dolmens) consisting of a large, flat stone supported on uprights, and the passage graves, found on the islands and shores of the Mediterranean and Western Europe. However, beside the megalithic tombs there are also huge stones in alignment, or menhirs, as at Carnac in Brittany. Their purpose is hidden from us; perhaps they marked ritual procession routes. Some large constructions, such as the Hal Tarxien stone buildings in Malta, were evidently temples. Chalk sculptures found in them show realistic human features and some kind of gowns, and may represent gods and goddesses and their priests.

Other megalithic structures give the impression of having had astronomical functions. Perhaps they helped to determine the calendar and the agricultural seasons, always important to the farmer. Stonehenge, on Salisbury Plain in England, for instance, has a circle of sarsen stones; certain stones line up with the sunrise at midsummer. Whatever calendar purpose Stonehenge had, it was also a place of worship. Fertility-gods and goddesses were probably worshipped here, as has been suggested by archaeologists.

Megalithic monuments have been found from Britain in the west to Assam in the east, and reached south-east Asia, Polynesia and—according to some scholars—even the New World. Certainly, the Egyptian pyramids and the Maya pyramids in Yucatan do resemble each other, and in both cases they served as burial chambers. All over Eurasia and America, astronomers and prehistorians have identified stone constructions as observatories and megalithic calendars. If this is true, it is almost certain that astronomy was pursued within the frame of religious and ceremonial interests.

The great civilizations

The megalithic monuments are, like the Bronze-Age finds that date from approximately the same time, stepping stones to the era of the great civilizations, or 'high cultures'. The latter started on the river plains in Egypt, Mesopotamia and other Near Eastern areas around 3000 BC. They introduce the age of history, that is, of writing. Living in towns, central political power, large economic surpluses and strict class differentiation are the characteristics of these new kingdoms. In the religious sphere they are distinguished by sacred kings, a priestly hierarchy, developed ritual, hecatombs of blood-sacrifices and imposing temple buildings. Their religious world is populated by great gods and goddesses (usually arranged in hierarchical order under a supreme god); their realm of the dead is stratified.

We have come a long way from the simple stone arrangements of the Palaeolithic peoples. Despite the 'Neolithic revolution', it is a continuous road that leads from the simple beliefs of Palaeolithic hunting groups to the polytheism of the great ancient kingdoms.

The Megalithic monument of Stonehenge dates from the early Bronze Age. It is thought to have been used for astrological and religious purposes.

Origins of Religion

Robert Brow

What was the first religion of man? Answers to this question differ widely and depend very much on what view is taken of man's origin. Those who go to the early chapters of the Bible as their source point out that religion was not invented, evolved or discovered by man: from the day of his creation man knew the one Creator-God who had made him, and from the time of his fall man worshipped this God through sacrifice. Monotheism and the practice of animal sacrifice—these, they say, are clearly shown by the Bible to be the twin characteristics of original religion. God was God, and sinful man could not approach him in his own righteousness.

In support of this view it is often pointed out that the most ancient literature of the Greeks, the Egyptians, the Chinese, the Hindus, and the traditions of many races agree that the first men brought animals to represent and substitute for them in their worship of God. As we shall see, there came a time when Buddha in India, Confucius in China, and the Greek philosophers reacted against the animal sacrifices of a corrupt priesthood, and the main non-Christian world religions were built on other premisses. At this stage, however, we are not concerned with the merits or demerits of animal sacrifice. What we are discussing is basically a matter of history, and obviously the evidence provided by the ancient documents of the Bible about man's original religion must be taken seriously.

Evolution of religion

There is, however, another answer to the question which denies all this. It starts with the view that man evolved from a pre-simian ancestor. Since animals have no religion, there must have been, it is said, a long ascent through apish chatter and fear of the dark unknown to what Bouquet calls 'animatism', a 'belief in a vague, potent, terrifying inscrutable force'.

Animatism developed into 'animism', the spirit-fearing religion of most isolated tribal people. Then came the polytheism immortalized in the Greek mythologies. Israel's glory, so this summary of the development of religion suggests, was that she was able to narrow down the many gods of the surrounding nations to one tribal god. And eventually the one Creator-God of the Hebrew prophets, together with the philosophical monotheism of Plato, paved the way for higher religion.

This answer has held the field among many scholars since Darwin. Evolution was regarded as proved, and it was attractive to infer the evolution of religion from it. The only problem was how to fit the Bible into this scheme. This was neatly solved, however, by Wellhausen's documentary hypothesis which rearranged the Old Testament scriptures in line with the evolution of religion theory.

Wellhausen's reconstruction has now, however, been discredited. And we also have examples of monotheism and elaborate priestly religion from long before the time of Abraham. The theory of the upward evolution of religion is therefore being restated to push the emergence of monotheism back into the shadows of prehistory. Led by Wilhelm Schmidt of Vienna, anthropologists have shown that the religion of the hundreds of isolated tribes in the world today is not primitive in the sense of being original. The tribes have a memory of a 'high god', a benign creator-father-god, who is no longer worshipped because he is not feared. Instead of offering sacrifice to him, they concern themselves with the pressing problems of how to appease the vicious spirits of the jungle. The threats of the medicine man are more strident than the still, small voice of the father-god.

We see, then, that the evolution of religion from animatism can no longer be assumed as axiomatic and that some anthropologists now suggest that monotheism may be more naturally primitive as a world-view than animism. Their research suggests that tribes are not animistic because they have continued unchanged since the dawn of history. Rather, the evidence indicates degeneration from a true knowledge of God. Isolation from prophets and religious books has ensnared them into sacrificial bribery to placate the spirits instead of joyous sacrificial meals in the presence of the Creator.

So the evidence of history brings us back to reconsider the biblical answer. This, as we have seen, states that the first man was created in the image of God; he was a monotheist; and he practised animal sacrifice. But now, you may ask, can this be squared with evolution, the apish chatter, the cave-men, and the images of hundreds of textbooks?

Evidence

Let us first remove some misconceptions and clear the ground a little to enable us to look again at man's early

religious history. Even if it were conclusively proved that God created man by some process of mutations and selection, it would not follow that the process was a chance one. The Christian insists that, whatever methods were used—and the scientists should be encouraged to find out what they were—God planned the creation of man and he carried it out in accordance with his own purposes.

Science's function is to describe processes, but it cannot pronounce on the purpose of things. Physicists and biologists have a right to say that in looking at matter and life scientifically, no evident purpose is discovered. They overstep their limits if they go on to require faith in pure chance as opposed to faith in a creator. In any decision which may have to be made between faith in God or in 'blind chance', the science of evolution is strictly neutral, and cannot be anything else.

As scientists recognize their limitations, it is also important for Christians not to go beyond what is written in the first book of the Bible. Genesis man is not defined in terms of bone structure, or brain-size, tool-using, agriculture, social organization, or even artistic ability. Adam is the first creature who can talk back to his Creator, worship him, and choose among alternative ideologies. Any previous hominids, cave dwellers, Neanderthals, etc., who might have walked upright for thousands or millions of years, were by this definition animals who did not have what was required to make them in the image of God.

Sacrifice

According to the Bible, the first true man is a monotheist, and when he falls into sin, he seeks restoration through animal sacrifice. The theory of the evolution of religion suggests that man is an animal taking a long time to become divine. The Bible describes a human couple made in the image of God, who degenerated into what we are now. The question at issue is the real nature of man, not the names of Adam and Eve.

There is one more piece of ground to clear before we begin our dig down through the mound of religious history. Even though we may accept that early man was a monotheist and practised animal sacrifice, we should not expect prehistory to give us any proof of this type of religion. Whether animals were sacrificed to God or not cannot be known from their bones. God required altars to be of earth or uncut stones, whereas elaborate altars indicate a developed priestly system. Since earth crumbles and stones are used in building, most of the early altars will be unrecognizable even if they are found.

Nor does the true monotheist use idols or images. Idolatry always indicates that monotheism has degenerated into polytheistic confusion. The fact that the dead were buried in various ways does not affect the evidence either way. We should not therefore expect any evidence of religion till it is well past the original stage. By the time a professional priesthood develops, and temples, idols and elaborate altars leave their archaeological evidence, literature has begun and we are on surer ground.

Ancient literature

As we consider some of the evidence which illustrates the biblical view of the origin of religion, it would be foolish to claim the case is proved. Since we have no way of examining the religion of the first true man, and actually true religion is never examinable, the matter is unlikely ever to be proved either way. All we can do is to show that an original monotheism gives an explanation of many historical facts which are very intractable on the evolution of religion hypothesis.

If we could look down on the ancient world in about 1500 BC, we would see ordinary men and women still offering animal sacrifice as their normal way of approaching God or the gods. The earliest literature of India, the Sanskrit *Vedas*, picture the nomadic Aryan tribes who fought their way eastwards across the Indus and Ganges plains. The head of the tribe offered animal sacrifice with the same simplicity as Abraham.

When they settled in India, the Aryans developed a regular priesthood, and the *Vedas* are the hymns which the priests chanted as the sacrificial smoke ascended to God. The hymns address God under various names such as 'the sun', 'the heavenly one' and 'the storm', but the interesting thing is that, whatever name they gave to God, they worshipped him as the supreme ruler of the universe. This practice is called henotheism. God has several names just as Christians today have several names for God, but the names do not indicate different gods. They are different facets of one God.

Henotheism changes into polytheism when the names of God are so personified that various gods are separated, and they begin to disagree and fight among themselves. The later Vedic literature has certainly become polytheistic by, say, 1000 BC but the earliest Aryans must have been monotheists.

Gods and myths

The original Creator-God of the Aryans was known among all the Indo-European nations. His first name was Dyaus Pitar ('divine father') which is the same as the Greek Zeus Pater, the Latin Jupiter or Deus, the early German Tiu or Ziu, and Norse Tyr. Another name was 'the heavenly one' (Sanskrit *varuna*, Greek *ouranos*), or 'the friend' (Sanskrit *mitra*, Persian *mithra*). By metaphor and simile other names were added. God is called 'the sun', 'the powerful one' 'the guardian of order'. The sacred fire (Sanskrit *agni*, Latin *ignis*, Greek *hagnos*), common to all early sacrificial worship, had a peculiar fascination and was soon endowed with divine qualities.

Gradually story-tellers embellished their tales with love and jealousy and war and drunkenness, and so the mythologies appeared. The earth became God's bride, attracted worship to herself as 'the queen of heaven', and added sex to worship in her fertility cults. Where there are no written scriptures, and no prophet to apply God's truth, degeneration into polytheism is the rule of religion. Even the great monotheistic relig ions, Judaism, Islam and the Christian church, all give evidence that a pure monotheism can quickly be corrupted. The emergence of mythological polytheism among the Greeks and Aryans is proof of the inventiveness of the bards, but no evidence against a primitive monotheism.

The early Semites of Babylonia, Assyria, Syria and Phoenicia also practised animal sacrifice in their approach to God. Instead of adding mythological families and friends and enemies to the Creator, the Semites tended to nationalize him into a tribal deity. He was the one who helped the nation in war. The Babylonian Bel vied with the Syrian Rimmon, while the prophets of Israel had to keep pointing out that there could be only one Creator-God, not Ammon's Molech, and Moab's Chemosh, and Israel's Yahweh as one among many.

Israel was always monotheistic, though she was often tempted to think of the Lord as a lord among many local lords (Canaanite Baal meant 'lord' or 'husband'). Much has been written about the names of God, but whether he was called Elohim ('the mighty one') or Yahweh ('he was, he is, he will be') or Adhonay ('the Lord'), he was One. A thousand years later Muhammad proclaimed the same truth about Allah, though in Islam also 'the One' has many names. It is interesting that Islam, true to its Semitic origin, considered Allah as the conquering Arab tribal god.

Cities and science

The Semites were not the first rulers of the Middle East. An interesting people called the Sumerians had a city-state civilization which flourished before 2500 BC. They were related to the Indus Valley people of north India, whose great cities flourished till they were ousted by the invading Aryans about 1500 BC. Little is known about the religion of the Indus Valley people as their script has not yet been deciphered but, like the Sumerians, they were already polytheists. Sumerian gods lied and fought and lusted against each other resulting in a gradual decadence and collapse of their civili-

zation. They were an easy prey to Semites in the west, and invading Aryans in India, just as a later Hindu polytheism was conquered by Islam in the eleventh century AD.

We cannot prove the Sumerians were originally monotheists before their decadence into crude polytheism, but it could be argued that their science and civilization was the product of a time when they knew An, the one Creator-God of heaven. It is a fact of history that polytheism has always weakened a nation, whereas monotheism invigorates and unifies.

Case-histories

If this interpretation of history is

The sacrifice of animals to the gods still plays an important part in Hinduism.

correct, then it is obvious that some of the Semites and Indo-Europeans must have retained a monotheistic faith when other nations had already long degenerated into polytheism. The Egyptian priesthood, for example, continued the practice of animal sacrifice, but polytheism predominated until Akhenaten reinstated a kind of monotheism for a few years. The Minoan civilization of Crete also had animal sacrifice at the centre of its religion, but a degenerate view of the gods is evident before its overthrow.

The earliest religious history of China is very hard to study. The Chinese script, not being phonetic, gives us no linguistic clues to the names of God. In the sixth century BC the joint attack of Taoism and Confucianism virtually obliterated the ancient Chinese priestly and sacrificial worship. We can dimly trace, however, the supreme sky-god who was worshipped as Shang-ti or Hao-Tien. He was approached through the Kiao, Hsian and Hsien sacrifices. These were offered in the open air and, like the biblical sacrifices, included killing an animal, sprinkling its blood, and burning the carcass on an altar. In spite of successive waves of Taoism, Confucianism, Buddhism and early Christianity, Chinese sacrificial worship continued in temples here and there until the communists took over.

So the case for an original monotheism and worship through animal sacrifice, with subsequent degeneration into polytheism, is by no means proved. But it is certainly much easier to fit it into the recurring cycles of history than a gradual upward evolution of religion. Where documented case-histories are available, as among the early Aryans and Hebrews, the evidence for degeneration is strong.

The whole of biblical history, and the subsequent history of the Christian church, illustrates that God reveals himself as Creator, provides a way of forgiveness and fellowship through sacrifice, and all sacrifices have their meaning and fulfilment in the death of Jesus Christ. The Bible and church history also furnish many tragic illustrations of man's inveterate desire to add deities which are less demanding, and turn sacrifice or the communion service into a bribe to force God's hand.

Priests and priestcraft

Why was the emergence of priestcraft as an institution common to ancient India, China, Egypt, classical Greece and Rome, many other civilizations, and even the medieval Christian church?

First we must try to picture worship based on animal sacrifice in its simplest form. To modern man the very idea of animal sacrifice conjures up revolting images of dark, superstitious rites and gory victims. It is important to realize that before the rise of Jainism and Buddhism in the sixth century BC men were meat-eaters, as they still are in most parts of the world. If animals are to be eaten, they have to be killed, and most races have agreed that the blood should be drained out from the carcass. This happens in our Western civilization in thousands of slaughterhouses. We turn away our eyes, but for early man each 'sacrifice' had a spiritual significance. When we read of thousands of animals being sacrificed by Solomon, we could simply paraphrase 'he gave a big feast for all the people'. In both Greek and Hebrew the same word is used for sacrifice and killing animals.

The important thing about animal sacrifice in the Bible is that God used the joyous occasions of eating meat as visual aids to teach spiritual truths. There is nothing more primitive or obnoxious about attaching spiritual truths to animal sacrifice than to bread and wine. The animal sacrifices looked forward to Christ's death and resurrection just as the Christian communion services look back. That a wide variety of spiritual meanings was attached to animal sacrifice is evident from the Old Testament books of Exodus, Leviticus and Numbers. These various rites can be seen as different facets of the death of Christ and the same facets of his death are now expressed in the communion service or eucharist.

Myths and Symbols

Douglas Davies

If we had just heard a moving piece of music, we would find it strange if someone asked us whether the music were true or false. Music, we might reply, is neither true nor false. To ask such a question is inappropriate. Most people know that music can, as it were, speak to them even though no words are used. In fact, some of the great symphonies can affect us almost more deeply than any number of words, while choral works such as Handel's *Messiah* can produce an effect greater than the text alone could ever do.

As with music so with people. The question of what someone 'means' to you cannot fully be answered by saying that he is your husband or she is your wife, because there are always unspoken levels of intuition, feeling and emotion built into relationships. The question of 'meaning' must always be seen to concern these dimensions as well as the more obviously factual ones.

Myths

Myths take many forms depending on the culture in which they are found. But their function is always that of pinpointing vital issues and values in the life of the society concerned. They often dramatize those profound issues of life and death, of how man came into being and of what his life is really about, of how he should conduct himself as a citizen or husband, as a creature of God or as a farmer, and so on.

Myths are not scientific or sociological theories about these issues. They are the outcome of the way a nation or group has pondered the great questions. Their function is not merely to provide a theory of life which can be taken or left at will; they serve to compel a response from man. We might speak of myths as bridges between the intellect and emotion, between the mind and heart—and in this, myths are like music. They both express an idea and trigger off our response to it.

Sometimes myths can form an extensive series, interlinking with each other and encompassing many aspects of life, as has been shown for the Dogon people of the River Niger in West Africa. On the other hand, they may serve merely as partial accounts of problems such as the hatred between men and snakes, or the reason for the particular shape of a mountain.

One problem in our understanding of myths lies in the fact that Western religions—Judaism, Christianity and Islam—are very concerned with history. They have founders and see their history as God's own doing. This strong emphasis upon actual events differs from the Eastern approach to religion, which emphasizes the consciousness of the individual. Hinduism and Buddhism possess a different approach to history, and hence also to science.

In the West, the search for facts in science is like the search for facts in history, but both these endeavours differ from the search for religious experience in the present. In the West, history and science have come to function as a framework within which religious experiences are found and interpreted, and one consequence of this is that myths have been stripped of their power to evoke human responses to religious ideas.

The eminent historian of religion, Mircea Eliade, has sought to restore this missing sense of the sacred to Western man by helping him to understand the true nature of myths. The secularized Westerner has lost the sense of the sacred, and is trying to compensate, as Eliade sees it, by means of science fiction, supernatural literature and films. One may, of course, keep a firm sense of history and science without seeking to destroy the mythical appreciation of ideas and beliefs.

Symbols

Religious symbols help believers to understand their faith in quite profound ways. Like myths, they serve to unite the intellect and the emotions for the task of discipleship. Symbols also integrate the social and personal dimensions of religion, enabling an individual to share certain commonly-held beliefs expressed by symbols, while also giving him freedom to read his own private meaning into them.

We live the whole of our life in a world of symbols. The daily smiles and grimaces, handshakes and greetings, as well as the more readily acknowledged status symbols of large cars or houses—all these communicate messages about ourselves to others.

To clarify the meaning of symbols, it will help if we distinguish between the terms 'symbol' and 'sign'. There is a certain arbitrariness about signs, so that the word 'table', which signifies an object of furniture with a flat top supported on legs, could be swapped for another sound without any difficulty. So the Germans call it *Tisch* and the Welsh *bwrdd*.

A symbol, by contrast, is more intimately involved in that to which it refers. It participates in what it symbolizes, and cannot easily be swapped for another symbol. Nor can it be explained in words and still carry the same power. For example, a kiss is a symbol of affection and love; it not only signifies these feelings in some abstract way: it actually demonstrates them. In this sense a symbol can be a thought in action.

Religious symbols share these general characteristics, but are often even more intensely powerful, because they enshrine and express the highest values and relationships of life. The cross of Christ, the sacred books of Muslim and Sikh, the sacred cow of Hindus, or the silent, seated Buddha—all these command the allegiance of millions of religious men and women. If such symbols are attacked or desecrated, an intense reaction is felt by the faithful, which shows us how deeply symbols are embedded in the emotional life of believers.

The power of symbols lies in this ability to unite fellow-believers into a community. It provides a focal point of faith and action, while also making possible a degree of personal understanding which those outside may not share.

In many primitive societies the shared aspect of symbols is important as a unifying principle of life. Blood, for example, may be symbolic of life, strength, fatherhood, or of the family and kinship group itself. In Christianity it expresses life poured out in death, the self-sacrificial love of Christ who died for human sin. It may even be true that the colour red can so easily serve as a symbol of danger because of its deeper biological association with life and death.

Symbols serve as triggers of commitment in religions. They enshrine the teachings and express them in a tangible way. So the sacraments of baptism and the Lord's Supper in Christianity bring the believer into a practical relationship with the otherwise abstract ideas of repentance and forgiveness. Man can hardly live without symbols because he always needs something to motivate his life; it is as though abstract ideas need to be set within a symbol before men can be impelled to act upon them. When any attempt is made to turn symbols into bare statements of truth, this vital trigger of the emotions can easily be lost.

In Bali the myths and legends of Hinduism are re-enacted each year in dramatic dances. Here Hanuman the monkey-god had come to help the prince Rama rescue his wife from the demon-king Ravana. Behind is the Barong, a friendly dragon.

Even before Moses we find four aspects of sacrifice which were common knowledge to the Hebrew patriarchs, the Aryans of India, the ancient Greeks, and probably many other races.

● The most common was the sacrificial *fellowship meal*, whenever men sat down to eat joyfully before God.

● An extension of this was the idea of a *covenant*, based on eating together, witnessed by the blood of the animal. The covenant might be between two men or tribes, or between men and God.

● Then there were occasional whole burnt offerings, usually presented by a king or patriarch to indicate *worship, consecration, or thanksgiving to God*.

● And when there was known sin, or a flagrant breaking of the moral order, a *sin offering* or expiatory sacrifice was required.

The earliest sacrificial worship was conducted by the head of the family or tribe. In settled conditions the development of a regular priesthood was inevitable, especially with the growth of cities and the increasing pomp of a royal court. There were dangers, but nothing inherently wrong, in having a full-time or even a hereditary priesthood. Moses appointed his own brother Aaron as the head of a hereditary, exclusive line of priests. His own tribe, the Levites, became full-time attendants on the service of God, and were supported by the tithes of the other tribes.

Similarly in the settled conditions of city life, the building of permanent facilities for sacrificial worship was acceptable to God. A temple with altars for large numbers of people, together with the attendant buildings, was required in the reign of Solomon. It is interesting, however, that the argument of the New Testament letter to the Hebrews goes back to the mobile tabernacle rather than the elaborate temple. There were certainly great dangers in the use of temple and elaborate altars, as there were in the development of a full-time priesthood, and the prophets constantly had to fight priestly rapacity and the misconceptions of the people. Where there were no

prophets, priesthood and temple worship always degenerated into the ugliness of priestcraft.

Ritual

The clearest documented account of this degeneration appears in the history of the Brahmin priesthood of India. The earliest group of Vedic hymns called the *Rig Veda* were first collected in an oral form, say about 1500 BC, as the Aryan tribes were invading north-western India. The collection may have been the work of the first regular priests. At this time sacrifice could still be offered by any Aryan, and priesthood was by inclination, probably on a part-time basis. Under settled conditions the power of the priests tended to increase. They suggested that unless the right sacrifices were offered the gods would be displeased, and therefore only highly trained priests could learn the prayers and rituals which were necessary.

Some specialization began, and a school of singing priests (Udgatri) arose who chanted the special hymns for each sacrificial occasion. Their collection of 1,225 hymns (the *Sama Veda*) were all from the *Rig Veda*, except for seventy-five new ones. Then a third book called the *Yajur Veda* was produced by a class of priests who did the actual offering of sacrifice. Their collection was mainly the ritual formulae muttered in a low voice during the various stages of the sacrifice.

Thus by about 900 BC there were at least three groups of priests with their own special duties and training schools. The priests had leisure to study and teach, and knowledge brought power. It was only natural that the priestly schools should produce notes and commentaries on their books (the same kind of thing happens today). The material is called *Brahmanas*, which includes explanation of the hymns, the rituals of sacrifice and the duties of the priests. The study of this material produced an elaborate scholasticism.

By the time of the *Brahmanas* (about 800–700 BC), the Brahmins had become a hereditary priesthood in charge of all sacrificial duties, for which they were paid fees by the people. The Brahmins were now suggesting that by the right sacrifices, which they alone could offer, they could procure the favours of the gods, various temporal blessings, and a good place in heaven. Gods, men, governments, all were under priestly control.

Priestcraft and magic

About the same time as the *Brahmanas*, a fourth *Veda* was compiled called the *Atharva Veda*. Because of its lateness and the low ethical quality of its contents, this *Veda* is still not recognized in some parts of south India. The *Atharva Veda* has 6,000 stanzas, of which 1,200 are taken from the *Rig Veda*. Most of the remaining stanzas consist of charms and incantations for magical purposes. This shows how easily priestcraft degenerates into magic. Once sacrifice becomes a meritorious act which forces God to give blessings, it can be used to obtain benefits for oneself and harm for one's enemies. Obviously we are now only one stage removed from the medicine man. He still uses sacrifice, but it is directed to spirits instead of to God, and all ethical or worship content has disappeared.

The progress of modern cultural anthropology indicates that virtually all primal tribes still use animal sacrifice, and there is growing evidence to show that their sacrificial practices are a degeneration from one of the ancient priesthoods, just as those are a degeneration from the original religion of man.

As we shall see, there were great movements of revolt against priestcraft in the sixth and fifth centuries BC. The resulting great world religions and the rise of Christianity largely obliterated animal sacrifice as a significant stream in the history of religion. Before leaving the subject, however, we must note how prevalent priestcraft was in all civilizations, and how it even threatened to throttle the Christian church.

The essence of priestcraft is the rise of a group of people who claim to control access to God, and who suggest that the offering of sacrifice is a meritorious act which forces God to grant favours. Priestcraft always takes away the joy of worship. It stifles individual piety, truth and justice, and divorces morality from religion. Its tragedy is that it forces honest and true men to fight against God, since God appears to be the ally of the priests. This explains the strange alliance of poets, philosophers, Marxists, continental freemasons, humanists, pietists, university students, and the middle-class conscience against that 'opium'.

Government and religion

Many learned treatises have described early religion before 3000 BC, but without written records such dogmatism is guesswork based on less than one per cent of the evidence. If all our modern books were destroyed, what would an archaeologist be able to make of our religion from our ruins and graves? A creator-god worshipped through animal sacrifice leaves no archaeological evidence. We must therefore confine ourselves to civilizations which have left written documents.

The most ancient religion accessible in a deciphered script is that of Sumer. Hundreds of documents list sacrifices to the gods at the temples of Ur, Nippur and other cities. By about 2500 BC we know that the city temples had acquired vast lands, and there was a fierce rivalry between the priests and the government. Already Enlil, the god of creation, had been joined by numerous other gods who lied, lusted and fought against each other. A corrupt priestcraft serving degenerate gods heralded the overthrow of this city-state civilization by Semites from Babylonia.

The Babylonians also had an elaborate priesthood with vast temples and hordes of temple servants. The main difference was that the priests were mostly of the royal family, and the supreme head was a priest-king. This may reflect the original nomadic practice of having the head of the tribe act as priest. For the Babylonians the supreme god was An (who corresponded to the Semitic El, Hebrew Elohim and Arabic Allah), but many extra divinities were absorbed from the conquered Sumerians.

Where the priesthood is a department of state and the high priest is also king, the running battle between government and religion is avoided. It is also possible that the vicious effects of priestcraft are tempered by the need to maintain an ordered government. On the other hand, when religion has become a department of government, a seeker after the city of God, like Abraham, has no alternative but to leave. The Bible pictures Abraham as a man who abandoned the city-state religion of Ur to follow and serve God. Wherever he stopped, he built an altar of uncut stones and worshipped with the primitive simplicity of animal sacrifice.

Priesthood

In Egypt we find the priesthood of the sun-god Re overshadowing the king from about 2400 BC. This was followed by a revolt of the barons who divided Egypt into a collection of warring states, and brought the priests under control. After the expulsion of the Hyksos in about 1570 BC, Egypt attained her greatest political power. The secret was that, instead of one powerful priesthood, there were several (the priesthoods of Amun, Ptah, and Re) which the pharaohs played off against each other. That the priesthood had degenerated to magic not far removed from the medicine man is evidenced both from Egyptian records and from the account of the Exodus in the Bible.

The early religion of Crete may be clarified when the linear A script is deciphered. We know from Greek sources, however, that it was centred on the sacrifice of a bull and was attended by a priesthood. The earliest Greek epics describe animal sacrifice on numerous occasions, very similar to the worship of Abraham in Palestine and the Aryans in India. The Greek priesthood was weakened by being attached to a particular deity at a particular shrine and none other. The priesthood was not necessarily hereditary, and no intellectual qualifications nor elaborate teaching were required. The priesthood was often laughed at, but its scattered weakness meant that the Greek thinkers never engaged the ancient religion in open battle. The supreme place of Zeus indicates that before the inventive period of Greek mythology, the creator was worshipped through animal sacrifice as among the other Indo-European nations.

The only other ancient priesthoods of which we have written evidence before 500 BC are the Persians and the Chinese. Zoroaster of Persia and Confucius of China were contemporaries, and they both proclaimed ethical religions in opposition to the degenerate priesthood and polytheism which existed before them. We know as little about the Magi priesthood of Persia as about the Wu priesthood of China. Both practised animal sacrifice, presumably without any ethical content, and both failed to satisfy the questions of thinking men. As we shall see, Zoroaster and Confucius were part of a great movement of freedom for the human mind from priestcraft in the sixth century BC. Its importance for world history may be compared with that of the Renaissance and Reformation in Europe 2,000 years later.

Passing over the many other priesthoods, such as the Roman Flamens, who sacrificed white lambs on the ides of the month, the Aztecs, who offered human victims, and the Nordics and Germans, whose altars were overthrown by the early Christian missionaries, we must briefly mention the phenomenon of the emergence of the vast system of medieval priestcraft within Christendom. The New Testament letter to the Hebrews makes it clear that all the Old Testament sacrifices were fulfilled in Jesus Christ. From the death of Christ onwards there could be no more animal sacrifices looking forward to the cross; the bread and wine of the communion service were to look back.

But just as the true meaning of animal sacrifice always tended to be transformed into a meritorious act which had merit in itself and forced God to be gracious, so with the com-

Religions of the World

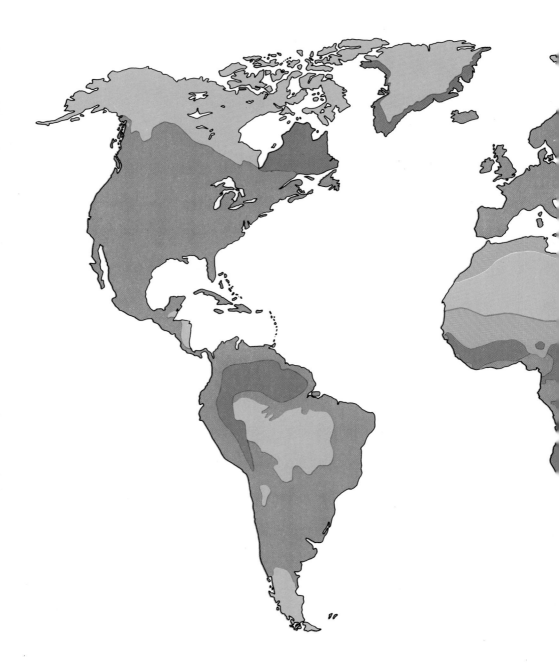

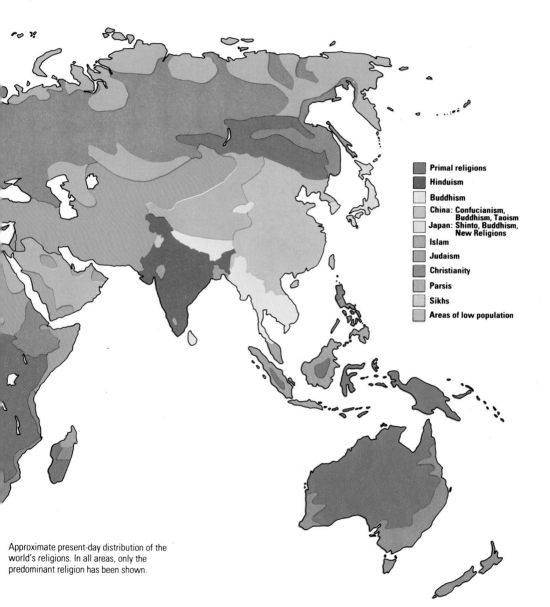

Primal religions

Hinduism

Buddhism

**China: Confucianism,
Buddhism, Taoism**

**Japan: Shinto, Buddhism,
New Religions**

Islam

Judaism

Christianity

Parsis

Sikhs

Areas of low population

Approximate present-day distribution of the
world's religions. In all areas, only the
predominant religion has been shown.

munion service. Then, gradually, it was suggested that without a properly ordained priest a communion service was not valid. Meanwhile the services became more elaborate and required special training. By the end of the Middle Ages all the characteristics of priestcraft were evident.

The sixth-century revolt

In the sixth century BC there was a tidal wave of revolt against the priestcraft of the ancient world. This wave shattered the power of the old religions, though their cults continued to exist as backwaters for centuries. Seven world religions appeared within fifty years of each other and all continue to this day: Zoroastrianism, Judaism, Buddhism, Jainism, Confucianism, Vedanta Monism, Taoism.

The wave seems to have had its origin in Persia. Zoroaster's actual teaching remains obscure. Scholars are still discussing whether he was a dualist or a monotheist. Some have given him a very early date, but the most likely seems to be some time in the first half of the sixth century. He must certainly have influenced Cyrus, who overthrew the Babylonian Empire in 539 BC, and sent the first group of Jews back to Palestine to rebuild their temple. By the time the temple was completed in 516 BC, four religious giants in India and China, Buddha, Mahavira (founder of Jainism), Confucius and Lao-Tse, had dared to question the authority of the Brahmin and Chinese priests. Socrates (470–399 BC) came at least a hundred years after Zoroaster, but he was preceded by Pythagoras (flourished about 530 BC), who first brought the new ideas of the sixth-century religious revolt into Greece.

The first causes of this great movement are probably as complex as the Renaissance and Reformation in Europe 2,000 years later. One obvious possible source is the preaching of Isaiah (about 740 BC onwards) and the other eighth-century prophets of Israel, with the refrain from Jeremiah and Ezekiel a century or so later. Certainly we can find most of the ethical emphases of Zoroaster, Buddha (about 563–483 BC), Mahavira (599–527 BC) and Confucius (551–479 BC) in the great prophets.

It is hard to believe that the prophets were heard by no one else but Israel and Judah. Isaiah's language was intelligible without translation in cities all over the Fertile Crescent. The transmission of religious ideas, especially when they were so revolutionary, would be exceedingly rapid. By the time it takes us to write and publish a book, the ancient world would have gossiped the ideas far more extensively. The number of major cities from Athens to China were comparatively few, and all were cosmopolitan with several languages spoken by the various national groups who lived there. Religious teachers and their disciples travelled constantly and, most important of all, people had the time and interest to listen to them.

The revolt in India

Whatever the cause of the tidal wave, the actual force of its impact can be seen most clearly in India. The sequence of the *Vedas*, and *Brahmanas*, the *Upanishads*, and the writings of the early Buddhists and Jains give us a picture of what happened with a clarity which is unequalled except in the Bible. From a study of the sixth-century revolt in India, we can postulate with some degree of certainty what must have happened in other parts of the ancient world.

As we have seen, Indian life was dominated by the Brahmin priests. From the primitive simplicity of animal sacrifice 1,000 years before, they had developed an elaborate system of ritual. Specialization into various schools with their own literature, the leisure to study, and access to weighty books, all enabled them to increase their hold on the common people. They, and they only, could offer sacrifice, and their sacrifices and magical prayers were so powerful that men and even gods had to submit to them. Economically their rapacious demands had become intolerable. For every occasion of birth, puberty, marriage, war, death, or transgression of the ritual laws, the

Brahmins demanded *dakshina* (money gifts).

All these might have been tolerated, but when they insisted on interfering in politics, the pressure of discontent among the second caste of warriors, nobles and kings increased till a revolt was inevitable. The actual spark may or may not have come from Israel via Persia, but it is significant that the revolt was simultaneous in both India and China. It took several different forms.

Atheism

Some of the warrior caste became atheists (*charvakas*). They said that since God did not exist, the whole system of priests, sacrifices and the mumbo-jumbo Vedic prayers was all nonsense. The first recorded example of true atheism is in Jerusalem, 'The fool says in his heart, "There is no God" ' (Psalm 14:1). It is interesting that the second should be a vigorous group of atheists in India five centuries before Christ.

Of course, in the ancient world it was impossible just to declare atheism. The atheist had to state his way to salvation. Since there is no God, what must man do? The answer that the *charvakas* gave was that the only good that man knows is happiness, so the highest good was to do what made one truly happy. In this modern opinion they preceded the Epicureans of Greece by two centuries and our atheists by twenty-four.

Buddhism

Buddha, who lived around 563–483 BC, was a prince of this second or warrior caste. The first written accounts of his life are at least two hundred years after his death, and scholars agree that the two main forms of Buddhism existing today have moved far from their founder's teachings. Certain facts, however, do seem established. The tradition is that he was shocked into seeking the meaning of life by the sight of a leper, an old man and a corpse. He practised austerities for many years till he attained the illumination he was seeking. He certainly knew about the

Hindu priests still carry out the age-old rituals of the Vedic scriptures. Chanting hymns in Sanskrit, these priests are performing a fire ritual to ensure a good harvest.

religion offered by the Brahmin priests, and rejected this decisively. He seems to have been an atheist, or at least to have abandoned the usual worship of the gods. He had no time for animal sacrifice, Brahmin priests, or even the caste system.

Buddha's doctrine was simple and down to earth. The cause of all unhappiness is desire. The lust for power, success, money, sex, comfort and other bodily pleasures causes all the ills of life. Salvation (*nirvana*) is therefore the losing of all desire. It is not necessary to become a hermit or stop doing the necessities of life, but it is essential to have no passion in doing them. The practising Buddhist tends as a result to develop a quiet, serene type of personality, but the desire for the good of others and the passion for social justice is eradicated along with the desires for self. Jesus expected us to love our neighbours as ourselves. Buddha denied love for self so that practical love for others was also lost. The main sects of Buddhism vary enormously in their basic practices and philosophy, and they will be looked at in their own section. Here we have only noted that Buddha fits exactly into his time and the movement of revolt against priest craft that swept the ancient world.

Ethicism

A contemporary of Buddha, also a prince of the warrior caste, was Vardhamana Mahavira (599–527 BC). His reaction against the amorality of priestcraft was to stress the need for good deeds. Priests and sacrifices and even God were unnecessary, since this world had an inbuilt, ruthless moral order which automatically rewarded goodness and punished evil. Salvation was therefore attained by destroying the evil of one's heart through doing good. The details of his philosophical system, called Jainism, were only recorded nearly 1,000 years later, and are held by a small fraction of the people of India.

An interesting fact is that Mahavira's ethical system for the first time required vegetarianism to the extent that no animal life was to be harmed. Jainism gave to India the word *ahimsa* (no-harming), which was taken up and used with a very different meaning by Gandhi. Originally it was connected with the sacredness of all animal and insect life, which is very hard to practise in the modern world, though it was professed by Albert Schweitzer in Africa.

If we omit the inclusion of respect for animal life as part of his system of ethics, it is obvious that Mahavira's 'way' was similar to that of his predecessor Zoroaster in Persia, and his contemporary Confucius (551–479 BC) in China. All three were first and foremost preachers of ethics. The desire to do what is right and good, quite apart from any doctrines about God, is a recurring theme in the history of philosophy. Aristotle (384–322 BC) and the Stoics of Greece, the high-principled Chinese, Roman and English 'gentleman', the modern humanist, and many liberal Jews, adhere to this religious genus. I have called ethicism a type of religion because it has a 'way' enforced by a real conscience, and an experience of feeling right or righteous. Whether or not God exists, the devotee has an assurance that all is and will be well. There are many examples of this kind of thinking in nineteenth- and twentieth-century modernism in the West.

Monism

We have looked briefly at three types of revolt against an intolerable priestcraft. They all agreed in their rejection of animal sacrifice, the priests who controlled it and even the God to whom the sacrifices were directed. Because of this direct attack on Brahmanism and the caste system, the three forms of revolt were excommunicated from Hinduism for over 2,000 years. Now that the Brahmins have found other ways of establishing their position through education and the key positions in India, Buddhism, Jainism and even atheism have been readmitted as accepted paths within Hinduism. Protestantism has also come perilously close to including ethicism and even atheism as acceptable 'ways' within the Christian fold.

We must now look at a fourth kind

of revolt, which is philosophically far more important, and may in this century become the main threat to Christian theism. Monism is a type of thinking which first appeared in the Hindu *Upanishads* (teachings for a disciple). Over 200 of these writings exist. The main group belongs to our period in the sixth century BC, although some are much later additions.

The writers of the *Upanishads* did not seek to banish the gods and priests and sacrifices, but offered a parallel and deeper way of union with the absolute. The sacrifices are spiritualized, and God is given a new meaning. He is no longer a theistic Creator, but the absolute, the deepest self, ultimate reality, or what modern writers call 'the ground of all being'. Priests and sacrifices were suitable for the uninitiated, but the true monist had a direct access to the absolute which bypassed the need for ritual. The discipline developed to attain this union with the absolute was called yoga. It is still widely practised in India, and is now being vigorously propagated in the West.

The extensive literature of Hinduism describes the various types of monism in the greatest detail. Our task here is to note that this type of religion has appeared again and again in the history of the world. The four main monistic positions can be set out as follows, though there are refinements and sub-divisions for each of these:

Pantheism
- Absolute pantheism: Everything there is is God.
- Modified pantheism: God is the reality or principle behind nature.

Vedanta
- Modified monism: God is to nature as soul is to body.
- Absolute monism: Only God is reality. All else is imagination.

The Chinese teacher Lao-Tse (born about 550 or 600 BC) was a contemporary of Confucius, and obviously belongs to the same wave of revolt against priestcraft. He insisted on freedom from elaborate ritual and regulations. He rejected the man-made restraints typical of ethicism, so that Confucius found him incomprehensible. Positively he recommended conformity to the way (Tao) of the universe. Of the four kinds of monism, Taoism would appear to have been closer to pantheism or modified pantheism than to the typical Vedanta type of Hindu monism. Instead of a stress on meditation, it was more a seeking to be natural, or at one with the course of nature. But in any case, Taoism was certainly monistic as opposed to the ancient theism and polytheism of China.

Monism and Christianity

Monism has since had a long history, not least in Christianity. After the powerful attack from the direction of Gnosticism in the second century, the Christian church had to face a monistic counter-attack from the Neo-Platonists in the third century. Plotinus (about 205–269) made a journey to the East and returned with an arsenal of monistic ideas against

Confucius, the Buddha and Lao-tzu were all teachers who reacted against the 'priestcraft' of their time. This scene shows an imaginary meeting between them.

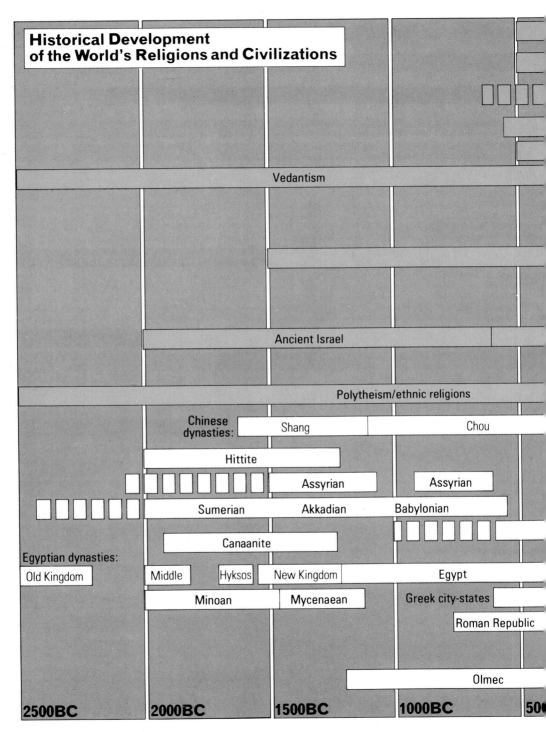

Historical Development of the World's Religions and Civilizations

Vedantism

Ancient Israel

Polytheism/ethnic religions

| Chinese dynasties: | Shang | Chou |

Hittite

Assyrian   Assyrian

Sumerian   Akkadian   Babylonian

Canaanite

Egyptian dynasties:

Old Kingdom   Middle   Hyksos   New Kingdom   Egypt

Minoan   Mycenaean   Greek city-states

Roman Republic

Olmec

| 2500BC | 2000BC | 1500BC | 1000BC | 50(|

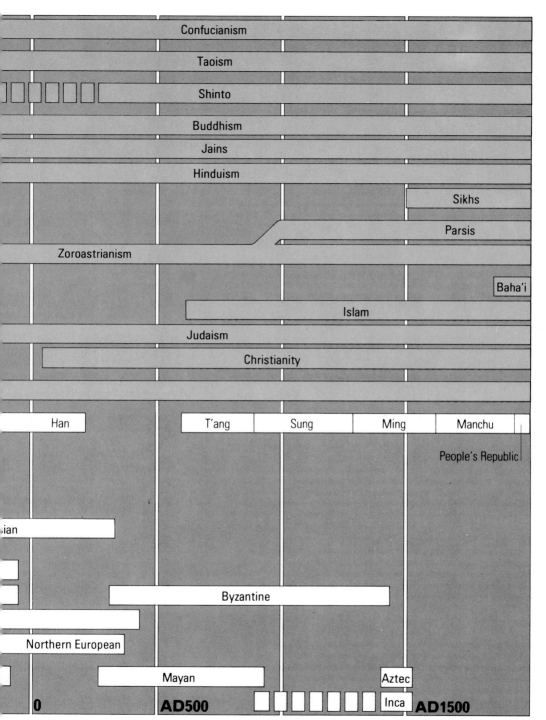

Confucianism

Taoism

Shinto

Buddhism

Jains

Hinduism

Sikhs

Parsis

Zoroastrianism

Baha'i

Islam

Judaism

Christianity

Han T'ang Sung Ming Manchu

People's Republic

...ian

Byzantine

Northern European

Mayan

Aztec

Inca

0 AD500 AD1500

the rapidly-growing Christian church in the Roman Empire. To claim the Greek philosophical heritage he included some ideas from Plato, but his system of contemplation was identical with the yoga of Hindu monism.

Plotinus failed to rally the Roman Empire against Jesus Christ, but he was rediscovered and introduced through the back door many centuries later. An Italian philosopher, Giordano Bruno (1548–1600), represented the first Western monistic reaction to medieval priestcraft, and his pantheism influenced the Jew Spinoza (1632–77). Meanwhile many of the mystics had been influenced by Neo-Platonism through a forgery attributed to Dionysius the Areopagite. Most of the readers of *Pseudo-Dionysius* thought that they were still Christians, but their piety had become strangely Hindu, and one of them, Eckhart (about 1260–1327), was nearly condemned for heresy.

Philosophical monism entered the German church through Johann Fichte (1762–1814), who is described as an ethical monist. He was dismissed from the University of Jena for atheism in 1799, but was later appointed to the University of Berlin. Through G.W.F. Hegel (1770–1831) one wing of the idealists became the true materialists like Feuerbach (1804–72) and Karl Marx

(1818–83). Friedrich Schelling (1775–1854) led a group who had a less materialistic view of reality which was closer to the Hindu Vedanta type of monism. Another wing was championed by Schleiermacher (1768–1834), who tried to show that true Christianity is in fact a kind of monism.

The renewed invasion of Eastern religious ideas in our own day by Hindu gurus, Zen masters and Tibetan rituals, is evidence that the struggle of alternative religions and ideologies is as strong as ever.

The chart (below) shows the main religious systems preached in the sixth century BC and the later developments classified under them. Priestcraft was a degeneration from the original religion of man. Atheism, Buddhism, ethicism and monism are the four possible reactions of a thinking man against it, and all are at least twenty-five centuries old.

Obviously all five of these options are very much with us today. Christianity contradicts the major premiss of each of them and offers salvation from outside ourselves altogether, so it is not dependent on our own stumbling attempts at happiness or spiritual fulfilment. But that must be the subject of a later section.

Religious systems sixth century BC and their later developments

Ritualism	Atheism	Buddhism	Ethicism	Monism
Salvation by right ritual	*Salvation by doing what makes you happy*	*Salvation by losing all desire*	*Salvation by right actions*	*Salvation by union with the Absolute*
Brahmanism	Charvakas	Buddhism	Zoroastrianism	Taoism
Priestcraft	Epicureans	Monasticism	Jainism	Neo-Platonists
	Atheists		Confucianism	Spinoza
	Existentialists		Aristotle	Sufis
			Stoics	Idealism
			Humanists	Unity
			Liberal Judaism	

Part Two
Ancient Religions

Land of the Aztecs and Incas: America before Columbus

George Bankes

'Pre-Columbian' America is a term generally applied to Middle and South America before its conquest by the Spaniards in the sixteenth century AD. The native inhabitants of this area were all American Indians.

In much of Middle America, now mainly the modern states of Mexico and Guatemala, and the central

America before Columbus

Chichen Itza

THE AZTECS AD 1519

Tenochtitlan

Teotihuacan

THE MAYA AD 300 - 900

THE MOCHE 6th century AD

Pachacamac

Cuzco
Tiahuanaco

THE INCAS AD 1525

Andes, largely modern Peru and highland Bolivia, high cultures with polytheistic religions developed. In both areas, however, there were two levels of religion. The common people had their local shrines at which offerings were made. But there were also the organized state religion with temples and systematic theologies.

What we know about these religions comes from archaeology, contemporary native documents such as the Aztec and Maya codices, and Spanish accounts. The origins of formalized religions in both Mexico and Peru can be traced back to temple structures with associated cults as early as 1200 BC.

Middle America
Sacred jaguar: the Olmecs

Between about 1200 and 100 BC a people, called the Olmecs by archaeologists, lived on the Gulf Coast of Mexico. They built ceremonial centres such as La Venta which were carefully planned temple communities. At La Venta a group of buildings was arranged symmetrically along one axis. At the south end was a clay pyramid, shaped like a fluted cone.

Olmec religion seems to have centred around the jaguar in various guises. At La Venta three identical mosaic pavements, made from blocks of green serpentine, were discovered

The city at San Juan Teotihuacan in Mexico was for centuries the metropolis of Central America. The enormous pyramids of the Sun and of the Moon were probably built in the Mayan period.

Each was laid out in the form of a stylized jaguar face, and as soon as it was finished it was covered up. These could have been some kind of offering to the beast.

On the lid of a stone coffin, or sarcophagus, at La Venta a jaguar mask is depicted with feathers for eyebrows and a forked tongue of the type only found in snakes. This seems to show him as part bird and part snake, suggesting that he may be the ancestor of the Mexican god Quetzalcoatl, usually shown as a plumed serpent. It also suggests that in Olmec times different animals were combined to form one god, which is an idea basic to Middle American deities.

The Olmec jaguar could also assume human characteristics. A carving from the site of Potrero Nuevo shows his union with a woman. This act was believed to have produced a race of creatures half human and half jaguar. The human element is generally childish, with a paunch and stubby limbs. Onto this are grafted the jaguar characteristics: fangs, sometimes claws, and a snarling mouth turned down at the corners. The heads are often cleft at the top. These hybrid creatures were probably deities, possibly of fertility.

The Maya

Successors to the Olmecs were the Maya, a Middle American people who lived in the semi-tropical rain forest of the Guatemalan department of El Peten and the adjacent parts of Mexico and Belize. The Maya developed an elaborate state religion based on ceremonial centres or cities containing temples. Alongside this existed a native folk religion. The earliest temples were being built about 200 BC at Tikal and Uaxactun. However, it was during the 'Classic Period', between AD 300 and 900, that Maya culture and religion fully developed. After AD 900 the state religion largely collapsed, though the folk one has partially survived.

Maya religion was—and still is—a contract between man and his gods. The gods helped man in his work and provided him with his food. In return they expected payment which usually had to be in advance. Prayer was directed towards material ends such as obtaining rain to make the crops grow.

Before an important ceremony there seems to have been little difference, except in scale, between the preparations in the village and those at the ceremonial centre or city. Before all ceremonies there had to be sexual continence, fasting and usually confession. Continence involved sleeping apart from wives for a specified period. If this was not carried out, both the ceremony and the guilty person might be endangered. In antiquity the body was painted black, the colour of unmarried men, during fasting.

Sacrifices in many forms played an important part in Maya religion. They could consist of one's own blood or that of human or animal victims. Also produce such as maize might be offered. Human sacrifice involved extracting the heart while the living victim was held down by the arms and legs. The rain-gods preferred small offerings, such as miniature corn grindstones, and in the case of human sacrifice the preferred victims were children.

In Maya theology there was no general assembly of gods. Maya deities usually only wanted recognition in the form of frequent offerings. Few of them were human in form, and most showed a blending of human and animal features. For example, the all-important Chacs or rain gods are shown in the Maya codices as long-nosed gods with snake features. In addition, gods like the Chacs were conceived of in fours, each one being associated with a compass direction and a colour. For example, there was one Chac for the east with the colour red.

These gods of the Maya had a dual character: both benevolent and malevolent. Also there was a sexual duality. The Chacs are generally masculine, but one is sometimes shown as female. The Maya indiscriminately marshalled their gods in large categories, and a god could belong to two diametrically-opposed groups. The sun-god was mainly a sky-god, as one would expect. However, at night he passed through the underworld on his way eastward from the point of sunset to that of sunrise. During this passage he became one of the nine lords of the night and the underworld.

The great city of Teotihuacan

Teotihuacan was a large city that flourished in the Valley of Mexico at much the same time as the Maya zenith, between AD 300 and 700. To judge from the number and size of the temples at Teotihuacan it appears to have been a theocracy. The city seems to have fallen to outside invaders about AD 700.

On Teotihuacan's temple walls, religious symbolism features strong-

ly. The rain-god, called Tlaloc or 'he who makes things grow', is frequently depicted, suggesting that he was held in great esteem. One fresco shows him with a spectacle-like mask over his face and fangs protruding from his mouth. The other deity who features prominently at Teotihuacan is Quetzalcoatl. He can be seen on a temple façade bearing his name, where he is surrounded by sea shells and snail shells. He may have represented the waters of the earth.

The Toltecs

The Toltecs were a coalition of nations in north-central Mexico. They established their capital at Tula, about fifty miles/eighty kilometres

The mythological figure Quetzalcoatl appears in many pre-Columbian religions. He is often represented as a plumed serpent, as in this carving from the Toltec city of Chichen Itza.

north of Mexico City, about AD 980.

The fifth ruler of the Toltecs, the semi-legendary Ce Acatl, was a priest-king who took the name of the god Quetzalcoatl. Soon after his accession he was expelled by devotees of the god Tezcatlipoca and migrated with his followers to Yucatan where he founded Chichen Itza. The two principal Toltec pyramids, the Castillo at Chichen Itza and the Temple of the Morning Star at Tula, illustrate how religious life had changed since the collapse of the theocracy at Teotihuacan. At the foot of the stairway of each pyramid was a large colonnaded hall. Here warriors could gather together at religious festivals to use their own altar platforms and sacrificial stones. Theocracy had been largely superseded by militarism.

Among the Toltecs Quetzalcoatl became a sky symbol instead of one of water. Another Toltec deity was a combination of the eagle and jaguar, representing the earthly warrior caste. The latter had the duty of feeding the sun and morning star with the hearts and blood of sacrificial victims.

Aztec religion traced several important elements back to Toltec times. Both Toltec and Aztec religion displayed a close connection between kingship and warriorhood on the one hand and fire, the sun and the morning star on the other. Also the Toltec method of human sacrifice was continued by the Aztecs. The victim was held down on a low stone block, his chest opened with a knife and the heart torn out.

Religion of the Sun: the Aztecs

The Aztecs migrated into the Valley of Mexico in the late twelfth century and founded their capital city of Tenochtitlan about AD 1370. However, they did not start their political expansion until after AD 1430.

The Aztecs believed that two primordial beings originated everything, including the gods. They were Ometecuhtli, 'Lord of the Duality', and Omeciuatl, 'Lady of the Duality'. They lived at the summit of the world in the thirteenth heaven. These two produced all the gods and also all mankind. However, by the time of the Spanish Conquest, the two primordial beings had largely been pushed into the background by a crowd of younger and more active gods.

The Aztecs believed that the gods in their turn created the earth. The most important act in this creation was the birth of the sun. The sun is supposed to have been born at Teotihuacan through the self-sacrifice of a little leprous god. The remaining gods followed his example of sacrifice to provide the blood needed to set the sun moving across the sky.

In order to keep the sun moving on its course it had to be fed every day with human blood. The Aztecs regarded sacrifice as a sacred duty towards the sun. Without this the life of the world would stop. Therefore constant human sacrifices—mainly of war captives—had to be provided. It is thought that more than 20,000 were slain each year.

There was a strong solar element in Aztec religion. Huitzilopochtli, the tribal god of the Aztecs, personified the sun at its height. He was the god of the warriors. In contrast there was the rain-god Tlaloc, who was the supreme god of the peasants. Tlaloc was rated equal with Huitzilopochtli, and their high priests were equal in status. This clearly shows how Aztec religion combined both ancient and modern elements in the form of the old rain-god and the later tribal one.

Aztec warriors who were sacrificed or died in battle were believed to join the sun in the sky for four years. Afterwards they were reincarnated as humming-birds. When the peasants died they went to Tlalocan—a lush tropical paradise. Those who did not get to either of these places went to Mictlan, a cold, twilit underworld.

Central Andes

Chavin

Between 1200 and 400 BC a cult connected with the worship of a feline animal spread over northern, central and part of southern Peru. It appears to have emanated from a stone-built temple at Chavin de

Huantar in the north Peruvian highlands.

The temple at Chavin is riddled with interior galleries. Some of these contained offerings of fine pottery, guinea-pigs and llamas as well as sea shells. In the oldest part of the temple is a gallery containing a tall sculptured standing stone. Carved on this is a stylized feline—probably a jaguar—in human form. Snakes represent the eyebrows and hair. The upturned lips of this creature have earned it the name 'The Smiling God'.

Another version of the Chavin feline is the 'Staff God'. This is a standing feline figure with a large rectangular head and outstretched arms, holding a sort of staff in each hand. The fingers and toes have claws, while snakes represent the hair. This could have been a nature-god who was thought to live up in the sky with the eagles and hawks also carved on pillars at Chavin.

The Moche
The Moche people revived the Chavin feline cult on the coast of north Peru during the first millennium AD. They made many pots showing fanged humans, often with snake belts. Frequently they are depicted fighting a monster, part human and part animal, which they generally defeat. Human prisoners were sacrificed to these fanged beings. There seem to have been a number of other animal deities, such as one which was part owl and part human. The moon also was probably an important deity.

Tiahuanaco
The ruins of the city of Tiahuanaco are on the eastern side of Lake Titicaca, just in present-day Bolivia. Most of the buildings there are ceremonial and were erected during the period AD 200–500, when the city's influence was widespread.

The principal deity of Tiahuanaco appears to have been a standing figure carved on a monolithic gateway. In each hand he holds a vertical staff with eagle-headed appendages. His radiating head-dress includes six puma heads. From his belt hang a

row of trophy heads suggesting human sacrifice. This figure could represent Viracocha, the creator god of Inca mythology.

The Chimu
The Chimu established a kingdom on the coast of north Peru between AD 1200 and their conquest by the Incas in the 1460s. Their greatest divinity was the moon. She was believed to be more powerful than the sun since she appeared by both day and night. The sun was believed to be an inferior supernatural being. Several constellations were highly regarded; Fur or the Pleiades was the patron of agriculture. The sea (Ni) was also very important. White maize flour and red ochre were offered to Ni with prayers for fish and protection against drowning. The feline cult of earlier times appears to have largely died out by this period.

The Incas—an empire built on sacrifice
The Incas first established themselves in the Cuzco area about AD 1200. However, their conquest of highland and coastal Peru was not completed until about AD 1470, by which time their empire covered some 400,000 square miles/a million square kilometres.

In the Inca Empire there were numerous local shrines which were allowed to exist alongside the state religion. Some of these were of great antiquity and a few, like the oracle at Pachacamac, were noted for their pronouncements. There were numerous Inca shrines round Cuzco which ranged from natural features such as hills to temple buildings.

The Inca state religion was largely concerned with organization, particularly that of the food supply, and ritual, rather than with mysticism and spirituality. Divination was essential before taking any action. Nearly every religious rite was accompanied by sacrifices. These were usually of maize beer, food or llamas, but were occasionally of virgins or children.

The Inca emperor Pachacuti instituted the worship of a creator-god called Viracocha (or Huiracocha).

Viracocha created the sun, moon, other supernatural beings and all mankind. He was the theoretical source of all divine power, and had supernatural beings like the sun to help administer his creation.

The cult of the sun was very important to the Incas. He was thought of as a male god, Inti, who protected and matured the crops. Sun temples were established along with fields to support the religious officials. These temples also housed the images of all the other sky-gods like the thunder-god who was the servant and messenger of the sun.

In contrast to many Middle American peoples, the Incas and their predecessors had a widespread ancestor cult. Elaborate offerings including food and drink were placed with the dead. The mummies of Inca emperors were preserved in their palaces and brought out at festivals.

After death the Incas believed that virtuous people went to live in the 'upper world' (*Janaq Pacha*) which was rather like earth. Sinners went to the 'lower world' (*Uku Pacha*) where they were cold and only had stones to eat.

The Spanish conquest

At the height of its political power and cultural achievements, the Inca Empire was destroyed by the Spanish invasion of 1532. Their ruler was deposed and killed, and within fifty years the last vestige of Inca resistance had ceased. Roman Catholic Christianity, imposed by force, displaced the old religion officially. However, it lingered on among the people, and some of its features are still recognizable in present-day Indian beliefs.

Human sacrifice was central to the religion of the Aztecs and, to a lesser extent, of the Incas. This altar is in the ancient Inca city of Macchu Picchu.

Cradle of Civilization: the Ancient Near East

Alan Millard

The wheel and writing originated in the Near East; so too did many other inventions basic to Greek, Roman and modern Western civilization. It is also, of course, the region in which Judaism and Christianity began. In modern terms it embraces western Iran, Iraq, Turkey, Syria, Lebanon, Jordan, Israel and northern Arabia.

In parts of this region the basic cereals—barley, emmer and wheat—grew wild. The animals that could be domesticated most easily roamed there, and the climate followed a regular pattern. Raw materials of every sort were ready to hand: reeds in the rivers, timber in the hills, stones that could be chipped into tools, copper for smelting and casting.

After the last Ice Age, about 10,000 BC man began to settle in the Near East, developing agriculture and metallurgy. Varying natural resources caused development in different ways. Some areas grew richer than others, some were more self-sufficient than others. The whole area depended upon the weather for its prosperity. If there was too little rain in the winter, the soil would become too dry for the crops to grow, there would be little pasture for the animals, and man would starve. Too much rain could bring disastrous floods; too much sunshine could dry up the water supplies and burn the plants. It is not surprising that man's earliest religious beliefs, so far as we can trace them in this region, were concerned with survival, with the powers of the weather, the growth of crops, and the breeding of man and animals.

Over the period from 3000 BC to 500 BC, many different cultures rose and fell in the Near East. Some are well-known to us because their ruined temples and palaces have been explored, their writings deciphered and read. Others are little known because their major cities have not been found or uncovered, or none of their records survive. Thousands of written texts are available to us from the culture of the Babylonians, many informing us about their religion. On the other hand, for the Philistines we have no more than the incidental information given in the Old Testament, and the ruins of a single small temple. The Babylonian culture was the most ancient and the most influential, affecting the whole of the Near East in some way at some time.

The first empires: ancient Mesopotamia

Mesopotamia is the Greek name (meaning 'between the rivers') for the land of the Tigris and Euphrates rivers, the area now ruled by Iraq and Syria. To the north the mountains of Turkey and to the east the Zagros range loom over the plains. On the west the steppe country reaches out to the Arabian Desert, while the two great rivers drain through marshes and lagoons to the Persian Gulf in the south.

Mesopotamia was a region, therefore, that had no easily defensible frontiers. It was open to invasion and infiltration from each direction. Throughout historical times we learn of fierce hill-folk making raids from the east, and of hungry desert herdsmen overrunning the fertile lands from the west and south. This process began as soon as man realized the possibilities of cultivating the rich soil and harvesting the fish of the rivers. The northern part of Mesopotamia receives enough rain each year for farmers to grow grain and find pasture for their flocks. Men have lived in the hills and near the rivers since the Neolithic age, about 12,000 years ago.

The south, ancient Babylonia, depends upon artificial irrigation by drawing the water from the rivers and carefully controlling it, in order to grow any crops. It appears that this skill was put into practice there about 5000 BC. From then onwards we can trace a steady development of settled life until we find great cities flourishing by the rivers and canals at the end of the fourth millennium BC. From these cities traders and colonists spread up the Euphrates into Syria, eastwards into Persia, and south down the Persian Gulf, carrying with them the inventions and ideas of their culture.

Amongst these was one of man's greatest inventions, writing. Without wide-ranging written documents, relatively little can be learned about the life and religion of a long-dead society. The objects surviving from an ancient religion can be misunderstood very easily without the precise information that written texts can give. It was apparently the need to organize and administer the large settlements and their vital irrigation systems that stimulated the development of writing in Babylonia, and, at the same time—possibly by imitation—in Egypt.

The Sumerians

The Babylonian cuneiform writing on clay tablets was produced for the dominant people of the south, the Sumerians. Their religious beliefs are the earliest we can learn about in

The Civilizations of the Ancient Near East

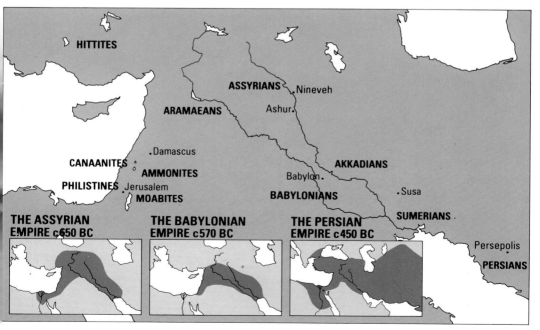

This clay tablet from Ugarit, written in cuneiform script, is a listing of fields with the owners' names.

This clay tablet from Ugarit, written in cuneiform script, is a listing of fields with the owners' names.

Mesopotamia, but it is impossible to be sure that any feature is purely Sumerian because the land was always inhabited by a mixture of races. Indeed, apart from their language, there is very little that can be called distinctively Sumerian.

In Uruk, the city of about 3000 BC best known from excavations by archaeologists and from the earliest texts, there were two main temples. One was for Anu, the supreme god, the king of heaven; the other was for Inanna, the great mother, goddess of fertility, love and war. Inanna was, undoubtedly, the principle of life men had worshipped from time immemorial, the goddess found depicted on paintings, carved in stone and modelled in clay in almost every prehistoric dwelling-place.

At Uruk the temples employed large numbers of people, and owned large estates. Beside the farmers and herdsmen who tilled their land, there were craftsmen making fine objects for use in the temple services, weavers making clothes for the sacred statues and for the priests, and scribes keeping check on all the temple affairs. The priests had an important place in city life, the high priest sometimes being the king of the city. This seems to have been the normal structure of temple life in the Babylonian cities for many centuries.

Records of temple business from about 2300 BC show at least 1,200 people in the employ of a temple in one city, a temple that was dedicated to an unimportant goddess.

Each major city in the south was the centre for worship of a particular deity. During the third millennium BC, beside Anu and Inanna at Uruk, there were Enlil, lord of the atmosphere, who was worshipped at Nippur, and was, next to Anu, the chief of the gods; Enki, ruler of the fresh waters that come from beneath the earth, who had his shrine at Eridu; the sun-god, Utu, whose home was at Larsa; and the moon-god, Nanna, who lived at Ur. In some places the chief deity was simply called 'Lord of the City X'.

Ancient theologians organized the relationships between the gods and goddesses. Each principal god had a family and servants, and they were honoured with temples and chapels also. Enlil's son, Ninurta, was lord of Lagash, for example. The less important deities had shrines inside the larger temples, but they were also revered in small shrines set amongst the houses of the citizens.

The temples dominated the cities. When a temple grew old, or was thought to be too small, a new one was built, often on top of the ruins of the previous one. Over the years, the temples came to be set up above the houses round about on the platforms that covered the earlier buildings. Stone is scarce in Babylonia, so the temples were built of mud-bricks, giving them a very solid appearance. The most important part was the holy room where the statue of the god stood. Each day the statue had to be washed, dressed and fed. The clothes and food were supplied by the worshippers as offerings, or drawn from the wealth of the temple. Store-rooms around the temple courtyard held reserves of all sorts, and items that could be exchanged for goods the temple needed. There were also houses for the priests. The holy room always seems to have been enclosed. The statue was not visible to everyone entering the temple, only to those permitted to enter the innermost part.

Myths of the gods

From 3000 to 2000 BC Sumerian culture continued to flourish. Poets of those centuries told stories about the gods, probably setting them to music. Some of these myths survive, a few in copies made about 2500 BC, many in copies of around 1700 BC.

The gods of the Sumerians were the powers of nature as revealed in the world. So the sun-god was the sun and the power within it. Just as human activities are limited, so were the gods each restricted to their own sphere. The myths show the gods acting in their own positions. They fight to hold their places against evil powers that want to break down their ordered way of life, they quarrel over their areas of influence, they engage in trickery and show every kind of human emotion and vice.

Like most people, the Sumerians asked why the world existed, why man was made. Several myths give answers. In one, Enlil separated the heaven from the earth. On the earth he made a hoe to break the soil. Out of the hole made by his hoe sprang man, like a plant. Another myth tells how Enki and the mother-goddess created man. The gods were tired of the work they had to do, tilling the ground and digging canals to grow the crops for their food. Enki had the idea of making a clay figure which the mother-goddess would bring to birth. This was done, resulting in man. Ever since, man has had to work the ground in order to grow food for the gods and for himself.

The myth goes on to tell how the god and goddess drank too much beer in their celebration afterwards. They quarrelled, and the goddess boasted she could spoil their creation. Enki challenged her, boasting that he could find a place for any creature she made. The goddess produced all sorts of cripples and freaks, but Enki found each a place in society. So the story not only explained why man was made, but also offered a reason for the existence of the deformed.

Another topic the poets took up was the story of Dumuzi, later known as Tammuz. He was a shepherd who wooed and married the goddess Inanna. Afterwards, Dumuzi was carried off to the world of the dead. There is more than one version of the story. In the clearest, Dumuzi was the substitute provided by his wife who had dared to enter the realm of the dead in order to obtain her release. In other versions Dumuzi was captured by police from the underworld. There follows in all the stories great lamenting for the dead god, and attempts to restore him to life. The idea that he did rise from the dead is hard to find in the Sumerian texts. It is very likely that the story arose from the cycle of nature when the fresh growth of spring dies in the summer heat. Certainly the story was significant for the Sumerians. In many cities it was retold each year as the king performed a symbolic marriage with a priestess in a rite aimed at securing prosperity for the year.

The Akkadian Empire

During the third millennium BC Semitic peoples settled in Babylonia in increasing numbers. They mixed with the Sumerians, adopting their culture and their writing. From 2300 BC they came to dominate Mesopotamia when Sargon of Akkad set up the first Semitic empire, ruling all the lands from the Persian Gulf through Syria to the Mediterranean.

This was a time of high artistic achievement, and probably the time when the Sumerian stories began to be put into the Semitic language we call Akkadian. Semitic compositions, too, were recorded in writing. These Semites identified some of their gods with the Sumerian ones. Thus Anu was equated with El, the chief god; Inanna with Ishtar; Enki was known as Ea, a name that seems to mean 'living'; and the sun and moon became Shamash and Sin. It can be argued that El was at first the name of a single, unique god, and that an original monotheism developed into polytheism, but this is very doubtful.

Sargon's dynasty fell to mountain raiders, then a new line of kings arose, at Ur. There they built a magnificent temple-tower (*ziggurat*) for the moon-god, which still rises over the ruins. More invaders ended Ur's rule, and made the Semitic

Akkadian or Babylonian language the normal one, ending the use of Sumerian outside of the schools.

It was in the schools that many of the Sumerian myths were copied out as writing exercises alongside a growing number of tales in Akkadian. Some of these were new compositions, some were new forms of the ancient Sumerian stories.

The Gilgamesh epic

The most famous are those that tell of the great King Gilgamesh. He had ruled Uruk, there is now evidence to suggest, about 2700 BC. Somehow he had captured the story-tellers' imaginations, and become a legendary figure. In Sumerian there are several separate stories about him; in Akkadian there is one long epic. Its basic theme is the problem of man's mortality. Gilgamesh did many great deeds, but he was forced to recognize that he would die one day. He set out on a quest to gain immortality. After many adventures, he came to the place where there lived an old man, the Babylonian equivalent of the biblical Noah. This man, Ut-napishtim, was the only mortal who had won immortality. But Gilgamesh was disappointed, for the man was incredibly old and lay on his back doing nothing. Perhaps immortality was not so good after all!

He told Gilgamesh how he had reached his state. The gods had created mankind, but man disturbed

This is a modern reconstruction of the Ninmah Shrine, one of the magnificent temples of ancient Babylon.

them by his noise. Unable to quell the noise, the gods decided to destroy mankind by a great flood. Enki, who had made man in the first place, warned his particular devotee and told him to build a large boat in which he might escape. When the flood came, Ut-napishtim, his family and a variety of animals were safe. After the flood, the ship grounded on a mountain in the north-east of Mesopotamia, and the gods rewarded Ut-napishtim with immortality. But Gilgamesh could not have that experience.

Ut-napishtim told him how to get a plant that might make him young again. Gilgamesh found it, and was taking it home to Uruk to test on an old man, when he put it on the ground while he had a swim. A snake ate it, and went away sloughing its skin. The power of the plant was proved, but there was no other, and Gilgamesh could only go home with the thought that his noble deeds would live long after his death.

This story summarizes the basic outlook of the Babylonians. For them, life on earth was the main concern, life after death was a vague and shadowy concept. They thought of the world of the dead as a place of dust and gloom. Yet it was necessary for the dead to be properly buried; for if not, they would return to haunt their relatives. Offerings were made for the dead, too, partly to keep their memories alive.

Omens: the fingers of the gods

The present life of man was entirely under the control of the gods. To have success or a happy life, it was essential to keep the gods in a good humour. There were special days of festival when the worshippers would attend ceremonies at the temple, or carry the statues through the streets. There were sacrifices that could be made to show devotion or ask for help. An ordinary man could not simply walk into the presence of a great god. He had to be introduced by a servant. This is the scene engraved on the cylinder seals current during the Third Dynasty of Ur and following centuries. The owner of the seal would identify himself with the

figure on it, and pray for the god's blessing. But the gods were unpredictable. The Babylonian could hope, but he could have no assurance of divine favour. This led to the development of another aspect of Babylonian religion which is not yet extinct, the taking of omens.

The Babylonians, and the Sumerians before them, believed they could find out about the future from all sorts of strange happenings. In the birth of monstrosities, in the movements of animals, in the shapes of cracks in the wall, or of oil poured into a cup of water, they saw the fingers of the gods pointing to the future. If a man wanted to marry, or a king to go to war, the omens would be consulted. One common way was to examine the liver of a sacrificed animal. If the form was exactly as it had been once before then the events that followed on that occasion, if good, would suggest it was a good omen; or if bad, that the proposed action should not be taken.

A special class of priests was trained to take and interpret the omens, and they built up an enormous encyclopedia about them. In watching the stars they learned a lot about them, and became able to predict eclipses and to correct the calendar. They also originated fortune-telling by astrology.

The Assyrian Empire

In northern Mesopotamia the state of Assyria grew strong about 1400 BC, and, after an interval, became the dominant power in the Near East from 900 to 612 BC. The Assyrian kings tried to copy the Babylonians, whose culture was much older. They worshipped the same gods, but the chief, identified with Enlil, was Ashur, the god after whom the land was named. When the Assyrians went to war, it was at Ashur's command they marched, it was to defend or extend his frontiers they fought, and it was for his glory they conquered other states. Of course, it was the king on whom all the glory actually fell, and the disgrace in defeat.

When the Assyrians conquered other lands, they did not interfere in the local religion, and, if the people

The Babylonians made models of demons from clay. They were hung in doorways or buried under doorsteps to ward off evil.

were submissive, they allowed them to continue their own customs. If they revolted, then their gods might be taken away captive, to be set in the Assyrian temples. Usually they were respected, and were sometimes returned when a once-rebellious land was made to submit.

The Babylonians

The Assyrians fell to the Babylonians or Chaldeans, of whom Nebuchadnezzar is the most famous ruler. He rebuilt Babylon and the great temple of Marduk, the patron god of the city. Marduk had risen to prominence under Hammurabi of Babylon in about 1750 BC, and was popular when Babylon's power was greatest. It was in his honour that the Babylonian creation story was written.

This describes the beginning of the world, when all was sea. The gods born by the sea disturbed her, and she planned to destroy them. They chose a champion to fight her lieutenant, but he failed. Another was chosen and failed. Then Marduk, a god of no importance, offered a plan, and succeeded. His prize was the kingship of the gods. His gift to the gods was the creation of man, with the aid of his father Enki-Ea, to do the work they so disliked. The poem ends with a long list of Marduk's powers. By the time of Nebuchadnezzar there were some theologians who tried to explain all the gods as

The Babylonian answer to the quest for immortality was given by a divine 'barmaid' to the hero Gilgamesh:

Gilgamesh said: 'O barmaid, let me not see the death I constantly fear.'

The barmaid said to him, to Gilgamesh: 'Gilgamesh, where are you wandering to? You will not find the life you seek. When the gods made mankind, They set death aside for men, But they kept life in their own hands. So, Gilgamesh, do you fill your belly, Be happy day and night, Take pleasure every day, Day and night dance and play. Wear clean clothes, Wash your head, bathe in water, Attend to the child who holds your hand, Let your wife be happy with you. This is what man's lot is.'

aspects of one god, Marduk or another, in an attempt to reduce the diversity of the gods to some sort of order, perhaps from a feeling that there could not be so great a variety of powers ruling the world.

The Persians who conquered Babylon kept the local religion alive, and in a few centres it flickered on until the first century AD. Some of the gods and goddesses continued to be worshipped by local people until the coming of Islam to Iraq.

Canaan: gods of nature

Canaan was the name for Palestine from about 1800 to 1200 BC. The people living there were a mixture of races, basically Semitic, with close relatives in Syria to the north. After Israel took control of the land, by about 1100 BC, some of the Canaanites maintained separate states in the north, in the area the Greeks called Phoenicia (modern Lebanon). Their culture and religion continued to flourish there, and influenced the people who occupied neighbouring lands.

Temples, religious objects and inscriptions that have been unearthed tell us something about the religion of the Canaanites and Phoenicians. Other information is given by Hebrew, Greek and Latin books. Ancient Israel was warned to avoid all contact with Canaanite religion, in fact, to wipe all traces of it from the land in which they were to settle (Exodus 23).

Canaanite temples

Excavations have uncovered remains of many small temples in the towns of Canaan. They were single rooms with a niche opposite the doorway where a statue of the deity might stand. Other rooms in front of, or beside the shrine could be for the priests or for storage. In a few cases, the thickness of the walls suggests there was an upper storey, and models in pottery show that some temples had towers. Presumably these were for special rites, perhaps for the worship of the sun or the stars.

Where the temple had a courtyard,

This pillared Canaanite temple is in Byblos in Lebanon. The stone trough in the foreground would have been used for sacrifices, sometimes of humans.

it is likely that the worshippers stood there while the priests alone entered the sanctuary. A large altar may have stood in the courtyard, with a smaller one inside the building. Animal bones suggest the animals commonly sacrificed were lambs and kids, and at one place piglets had been slaughtered. Liquid offerings of wine and oil were made, and incense was burned.

In some temples stone pillars stood as memorials to the dead. Other pillars were symbols of the gods. They were objects of worship which were covered with fine cloth, and carried in procession for the faithful to see. Their ancient name, *bethel*, 'house of god', suggests that the god was supposed to live in them.

Statues of gods and goddesses were carved in stone or wood, or moulded in metal. They were overlaid with gold, dressed in expensive clothes, and decorated with valuable jewellery given by the devotees. They have not survived, but there are many small bronze figures that are still to be seen, and they are probably copies of the larger images that stood in the temples. These small ones were made for the worshipper to offer at the temple, or to use in private devotions at home. When new, most of them were probably plated with gold or silver. The most common figures are cheap pottery representations of a naked female, thought to be the mother-goddess, giver of fertility. They were used as charms.

War, love and power

To the north of ancient Canaan, but sharing much of the same culture, lay the merchant city of Ugarit. Excavations there since 1929 have yielded a lot of information about the local religion. In particular, clay tablets, written about 1300 BC, have added an important dimension to our understanding of Canaanite thought, a dimension that could not be obtained from the material remains alone.

These texts from Ugarit contain stories about the gods, and instructions about their worship. We learn that the Canaanite gods were like many others of the Ancient Near East. They were the powers of the

Babylonian worshippers hoped to relieve their troubles by prayers in which they confessed their faults and praised their gods, although they usually speak in very general terms, often saying that man cannot really understand what he should do.

Part of a prayer to Marduk:

'Warrior Marduk, whose anger is like a flood, Whose forgiveness is like a loving father's, I am sleepless through speaking but not being heard, I am depressed from calling but receiving no answer. This has made my heart grow weak, And made me bent like an old man. Great lord, Marduk, forgiving god, Who among all kinds of men, Can understand his nature? Who has not been at fault, who is there who has not sinned? Who can know the way of a god? O that I were careful not to sin, O that I would seek the places of life always! Mankind is set by the gods on a hapless course, To endure what the gods inflict upon him. If I, your servant, have sinned, If I have passed the divine bounds, What I did in my youth, forget it, whatever it was, And absolve my fault, remove my wrong, Lighten my troubles, relieve my distress ... Warrior Marduk, let me live to sing your praise!'

natural world. At their head was El, whose name means simply 'god'. He was the father of gods and of men. His wife was Asherah, the mother-goddess. El appears in some of the myths as an old man, too old to act effectively, bullied by his wife and his children. In one story he is shown in a drunken stupor; in another he marries two girls who bear him two sons, Dawn and Dusk.

El had a daughter, Anat. She personified war. One poem tells how she slaughtered the people of a city, tied their heads to her waist, and waded up to her thighs in their blood, laughing with joy. Anat was also the goddess of love, and is described in some stories as the lover of her brother Baal. He was the best-known of the Canaanite gods. His name means 'master' or 'lord', and he was actually the god of the weather, Hadad, 'the thunderer'. The texts of Ugarit tell how Baal fought and conquered Yam, the sea, with Anat's help. She also helped him in his fight against Mot, god of death. Although Anat ground Mot like corn, he recovered to live in unresolved tension with the other gods. Some interpret this long myth as an explanation of the cycle of nature through the seasons, others as an account of recurrent famine, and yet others as a parable about death.

Baal's control of the seasonal rain made him popular. There is a vivid account of the effect his presumed absence had in 1 Kings 18 in the Bible. There the priests of Baal implore him to end the drought that had hit the land. Crying to him to send rain, his frenzied servants gashed themselves with swords and spears in a display of devotion.

Other gods

Other gods and goddesses whom the Canaanites worshipped include Shapash, the sun-goddess, Yarikh, the moon-god, and his wife Nikkal. There was Reshef, the god who shot his arrows of plague and illness into men; Eshmun, the healer; Kothar-and-Khasis, the divine craftsman. Each city had its chief deity who was often called 'master' (*baal*) or 'mistress' (*baalat*) of the place. At Tyre

the city-god was Melqart, meaning 'king of the city'. There were many minor gods and goddesses, the spirits of hills, springs and rivers, who are now forgotten.

One of them is known because his cult existed in Roman times. He was Adonis, whose name also means 'lord'. A legend tells how the goddess Astarte fell in love with the young hunter Adonis, but her husband was jealous and, disguised as a wild boar, killed the hunter. Each year at a certain time, a river that runs from the Lebanon into the sea at Byblos turns red with the blood of Adonis, and all the women mourn for him. No doubt this is one of many local cults that were practised by the Canaanites. The Canaanite religion was not exclusive; foreign gods were taken into the pantheon, identified with Canaanite gods, or worshipped beside them.

Beliefs of the common man

It is difficult to discover what the ordinary man believed, or how he worshipped. In offering sacrifices, the person could share in the meat at a cultic banquet with the priest and the god, the sacrifice being a sign of devotion, the payment of a vow, or an offering for pardon. Beside the chief gods there were many spirits and demons who had to be placated or warded off. Dead relatives, too, required regular commemoration to prevent their ghosts from haunting the living.

The priests in major temples had many colleagues serving small shrines on hill-tops, the 'high places', mentioned in the Bible, and in every town and village. These men, and others, cast spells and forecast the future, telling the anxious inquirer if it was a lucky day for a business venture, a war or a wedding. Divination was a skill Canaanites learned with the help of Babylonian manuals, and applied in every possible way.

According to Hebrew and Greek writings, popular worship included ritual prostitution and other excesses. Child sacrifice was believed by the Romans to be a custom of the Phoenicians, and the people of Israel were instructed not to 'pass their children through fire to Molech', another form, apparently, of infant sacrifice (see, for example, Leviticus 18:21). Remains of such offerings have come to light in the ruins of Carthage in North Africa. At a small shrine near Amman in Jordan, burnt human bones were buried in the floor in considerable quantity. The majority of the bones belonged to children. The archaeologists cannot determine whether these were the remains of children sacrificed to a deity, or of children who had died naturally and who had been cremated. Such uncertainty often attends archaeological discoveries.

A happier side of Canaanite religion can be seen in the titles 'merciful' and 'gracious' applied to El. The main impression, however, is of gods and goddesses who were imagined as wilful and capricious, just like their human followers. Whatever a Canaanite might do, he could not be sure of divine approval or blessing, for he could not know his gods.

The gods of the nations

At the same time as the Israelites took control of Canaan, other peoples were settling in adjacent lands. Along the coast, in the south-west of Palestine, were the Philistines; eastwards, across the Jordan, were Edomites, Moabites and Ammonites, while the Aramaeans occupied Syria to the north.

The religions of all but the Aramaeans are little known, for these people have left us very few inscriptions, and their cities have not been extensively explored. The Bible speaks of Chemosh as the national god of Moab, and a little more can be discovered about him from the famous Moabite Stone. This inscription, engraved about 830 BC, describes Chemosh in much the same way as the God of Israel is depicted; he is angry with his land, so hands it over to an enemy, then he gives relief, and the enemy is defeated. Booty and captives were dedicated to him by the victorious king of Moab, Mesha, who set up the stone in a temple of Chemosh at Dibon. When under attack, another king of Moab

sacrificed his son in a bid to arouse Chemosh's aid (2 Kings 3:27). It was to Moab that the seer Balaam was brought to curse Israel (Numbers 22).

Clay figures of humans and animals, and especially of the 'mother-goddess' type, are found in Moab, Edom and Ammon, just as in Canaan and Israel. From the little known of Moabite religion, similarities with Canaanite beliefs are evident, although the position of Chemosh as a national god is more like the position of Israel's deity. It is reasonable to assume that Edomite and Ammonite religions, of which even less is known, were very like the Moabite one. Edom's national god was Qaus, and his name formed part of personal names borne by Edomites (such as Qaus-gabbar, 'Qaus is mighty').

In Ammon (the name is preserved in modern Amman) the people worshipped Milcom. He may be identified with the Molech to whom Canaanites offered children. As for the Philistines, the Old Testament suggests that they adopted Canaanite gods (Dagon, Judges 16:21ff; Baal-zebub, 2 Kings 1:2), and a small temple uncovered at Tel Aviv is similar in design and furnishings to Canaanite shrines, except that it contained Philistine pottery.

The Aramaeans

The Aramaeans of Syria also absorbed the religion of the people of the land. Hadad was revered as the chief god of Damascus, with the added title Ramman or Rimmon, 'Thunderer'. He was also called 'Lord of heaven' (Baal-shamen). Beside him was his consort Athtar. El continued to have worshippers, who gave him the title 'Creator of heaven and earth'. The 'Queen of heaven' was a name for the mother-goddess.

In course of time, these Semitic deities were identified with Greek and then with Roman gods, and some took over the attributes of others. Under the Roman Empire, magnificent temples were built for the gods at the main centres, and some still stand, most notably at Baalbek in Lebanon. There Baal-shamen was equated with Zeus and

The fertility-god Baal was worshipped in Canaan.

groups, the highest being the priests of Bel. They presided at the sacred meals following sacrifices. This was an ancient practice, followed by the Canaanites, when the priests, the offerers and the gods were all thought to eat and drink together. Wealthy citizens gave funds for the banquets to be held regularly, expecting to gain merit thereby. Admission was by small clay tokens bearing suitable pictures and inscriptions. As elsewhere in the Ancient Near East, the people of Palmyra buried their dead with care, recording their names so that their memory might not be lost.

Sun and storm: the Hittites

From about 2000 BC until 1200 BC most of the area of modern Turkey was controlled by an Indo-European people. They are called the Hittites, although the name really belonged to another, non-Indo-European, group. A third people, the Hurrians, possibly related to the modern Armenians, mixed with the Hittites and influenced their religion and culture from 1450 BC. After the end of Hittite power, the language and religious beliefs continued for a long time in parts of Turkey, being known to writers of the Roman period.

The country is mountainous, each town being distinct. As a result, each town had its own god or goddess, usually the deified elements, the sun, storm, and so forth, whom the citizens worshipped in the main temple of the place. A Hittite myth makes clear how the gods depended upon their human servants: when a disaster befell the land, the gods were starving because the sacrifices were interrupted. All sorts of other powers claimed attention: the spirits of earth, of grain, of fire, of seeing, of hearing. Magic spells were recited to win their aid or ward off their evil.

At the capital city, Hattusha, modern Bogazköy, the king led the cult of the storm-god and the sun-goddess, the national deities. The king was both high priest and deputy of the storm-god, and high priest of all the other gods. He was expected to attend the major annual festival of

Jupiter, as the sun-god, while the goddess Atargatis, a fusion of Athtar and Anat, became Venus.

At Palmyra, the caravan city between Damascus and the Euphrates, a powerful state existed during the first century BC and the first three centuries AD. Baal-shamen was important there, in addition to a triad of local deities, Bol, or Bel, Yarihbol, and Aglibol, the last two being the sun and the moon. Appropriately for a trading city, Gad, 'good luck', was prominent, too. The great temple of Bel still stands, its size and extensive outbuildings showing the wealth of the city and the number of staff employed in the cult.

The priests were organized in

each god in that god's city. Elaborate rituals were performed to ensure that he was cultically pure for such occasions. If the king did not attend, or committed some other error, a catastrophe could overtake the land. This is seen in a series of prayers offered by a king for relief from a plague that affected the land. The king discovered that certain actions of the past were wrong, and tried to put them right. His confession reads in part:

'Weather god of Hatti, my Lord, and you gods, my lords: It is the case that (men) are sinful. My father too has sinned by transgressing against the word of the weather god of Hatti, my lord. But I have sinned in nothing. Now it is (true) that the father's sin falls on the son. So the sin of my father has also fallen upon me.

See, now I have confessed it to the weather god of Hatti, my lord, and to the gods, my lords: it is so, we have done it. Now because I have confessed my father's sin, may the mind of the weather god, my lord, and the gods, my lords, again be pacified! Again be graciously inclined towards me, and drive the plague away from the Hatti land once again. And may the few who are left to offer thick bread and wine no longer continue to die.'

The causes of divine anger might be petty, as when the god's robe was worn out, or significant, the breaking of an oath. They could be discovered only by asking the god to give a sign through an omen of some sort. Only in such ways could man learn the mind of the gods, and hope to gain their goodwill.

Ancient Egypt: Land of the Priest-King

John Ruffle

The magnificent pyramids at Giza, outside Cairo, have stood for four-and-a-half thousand years.

Ancient Egypt is the name given to the civilization in the lower reaches of the Nile Valley, from about 3100 BC to 30 BC, when the Romans occupied Egypt. It covers periods of strength such as the Old Kingdom (about 2700–2200 BC), when a line of powerful rulers left their pyramids as monuments, the Middle Kingdom (about 2000–1800 BC), another time of strong central government with influence amongst Egypt's neighbours, and the New Kingdom (about 1550–1225 BC), when Egypt was one of the dominant countries of the Near East. It also covers periods of weak-

ness when Egypt was torn by internal strife and occupied by foreign powers.

Obviously such changes in political strength and economic fortunes over 3,000 years meant that philosophical and religious attitudes also changed, but there are enough consistent features for us to be able to talk about Egyptian religion as a whole.

Naked figures

Writing was not practised in Egypt until about 3100 BC, when a single central government was established. What we know about Egyptian religion before then, therefore, has to be deduced from objects found by archaeologists. These take us back another 2,000 to 3,000 years and mainly consist of amulets, usually connected with hunting or fertility. Animal tusks worn as pendants were probably intended to protect the hunter and make him successful; earthenware figures of naked women were meant to ensure plenty of healthy children.

Some pictures painted on pots, or scratched onto rocks, seem to suggest religious rituals, but without a written explanation it is impossible to understand them fully. Sometimes they seem to refer to ceremonies or figures that we recognize from later periods, and it is fairly safe to assume that the basic beliefs and practices did not greatly change in the historical period.

Animal-headed gods

The gods of ancient Egypt—as they are represented in the temples and tombs—present a bewildering complexity of strange forms, half animals, half men. In fact we know very little about Egyptian religious beliefs, since there are no studies of Egyptian theology made by the ancient Egyptians themselves.

Many of the Egyptian gods represented strong forces in the natural world. Egypt's prosperity depended on the daily reappearance of the sun and the annual flooding of the river, and these natural forces (with others) were thought of as gods needing to be cajoled and encouraged by sacrifice

and worship. The Egyptians often portrayed them as animals. For example, they chose the hawk, which flies high in the sky, as a representation of the sun; and the cobra, which was often found basking on the hot threshing floors, as a symbol of the harvest goddess.

At an early stage other characteristics were associated with some of the gods. The ibis-headed god, Thoth, was thought of as the god of scribes and writing; Khnum, the ram-headed deity, was considered the creator of men on his potter's wheel, and so on. How these special attributes came to be given to particular deities is not clear, but they seem to be established in these roles at an early date.

The gods were often associated with particular cities. This probably dates back into the prehistoric period when Egypt was a series of individual communities. As these came together into larger political units, so their local deities gradually became important in the nation as a whole. For example, the god Amun from the city of Thebes was a kind of national god, protecting and leading the whole nation for a time during the New Kingdom while Thebes was the home city of the ruling family.

This was not exclusive, however. The town-folk of other communities would continue to worship their own local god or they would feel free to pray to any other god who might offer special favours. So a scribe who hailed from Denderah might accompany the king to the temple of Amun at Thebes after some notable victory, but would pay his respects to Hathor whilst at Denderah. He would also pray to Thoth, the god with a special interest in writing, for help in his career.

There are also references to 'God' or 'The God', who seems to have been an unnamed universal divine power who controlled the universe and upheld good against evil.

The 'reform' of Akhenaten

For a short while, from about 1375 to 1350 BC, there was an attempt to impose a form of monotheism. The Pharaoh Amenophis IV, who is vari-

The solid-gold death-mask of the young King Tutankhamun.

The Egyptian king acted as an intermediary between gods and people. This relief shows the hawk-god, Horus, speaking with King Ptolemy.

Wealthy Egyptian women dressed luxuriously in fine linen. They wore elaborate jewellery and used an array of cosmetics.

ously described as a visionary or a lunatic, gradually built up the worship of the Aten, or the sun's disk, until he was the only god whose worship was tolerated. The other gods were proscribed, their temples closed, their priesthoods disbanded and their names erased from all monuments where they could be found. The worship of Amun, in particular, was strongly attacked. The Aten was regarded as the source of all life. This gift of life was passed to the king, who changed his name to Akhenaten (which means 'the one who is beneficial to the Aten'), and to his family and thence to the people.

This 'reform' probably had some political cause, such as an attempt to stabilize and unite the nation, but was also influenced by Akhenaten's bizarre personality. It was apparently not popular; the priests would certainly have been against it since it deprived them of their living, and it survived only briefly after Akhenaten's death. The power of the priests of Amun could not so easily be destroyed. This period was exceptional, since normally the gods seemed happy to exist side by side even when ideas claimed on their behalf appear contradictory.

Other gods

As well as the 'mainstream' gods, other deities were adopted by the Egyptians. Some private individuals who had distinguished themselves in

some way were deified. Imhotep, for instance, a vizier of King Djoser (about 2680 BC) who also wrote a medical treatise and a wisdom book and was credited with the building of the first pyramid—he appears to have been an early Leonardo da Vinci—was worshipped as a minor deity who had special power to heal the sick. His cult was especially popular during the period of Greek influence in Egypt in the first three centuries BC.

The king or pharaoh was also thought of as a god; he was referred to as 'The Good God', but it was a restricted idea of divinity because he was, plainly, mortal. Very few rulers actually had a statue placed in the temple shrine as an object of worship. The fact that the king could be both god and priest is an indication of some of the contradictions of Egyptian religion.

Sacred animals

Animals too form an interesting aspect of Egyptian religion. The actual practice varied according to the place and the time. In some cases all the animals of one species were regarded as sacred, and they were mummified and buried in huge numbers: baboons, crocodiles, ibises, and even cats and dogs, received this treatment on occasions. In other cases one individual animal was singled out as the incarnation of a god. There were several places where a particular bull was selected, perhaps because it had some distinctive markings, and was then taken into the temple, pampered throughout its life and mummified and ceremonially interred at death.

Well-travelled gods! festivals and services

The festivals and daily services in the temples show that the Egyptians thought of their gods as having the same needs and instincts as themselves. The day began with a ritual in which the god was wakened by a choir. The night attire was then removed from the image of the god, which was washed, dressed and offered food and drink. After this the god might be called upon to receive

visitors, deliver oracles or undertake some other duties. We may assume that his behaviour and his decisions would reflect the views and wishes of the priests who could claim to interpret them on his behalf. He would receive other offerings of food during the day, and eventually be put to bed for the night in his shrine.

The daily routine was broken by festivals. Some were short, involving only a special offering or a procession inside the temple. Others involved long journeys by river to the temple of another god. Amun, for example, went by boat from his great national temple at Karnak to the smaller shrine at Luxor which was regarded as his private home, where he stayed for several days with his consort Mut and then returned along the processional way. Hathor travelled nearly 100 miles by boat from Denderah on her annual visit to the temple of Horus at Edfu.

The festivals which involved processions along the river or in the town were treated as holidays by the people, who lined the route to cheer and wave at the god's shrine. Some travelled on long pilgrimages to attend. One writer records 700,000 pilgrims gathering for a festival. Some festivals we know only by name; it is intriguing to try to imagine what happened on The Day of Smelling Onions!

The actual images of the gods that were the centre of this worship have not survived. They may have been of stone or fine metal, probably richly ornamented. At festivals they were carried (hidden from public gaze) in ornate wooden shrines in a large model boat which was borne on the shoulders of several bearers. For the river journeys they travelled in special boats built of wood but shaped to resemble the early reed boats, a reminder that these festivals had their origin in very early times.

The priest who performed all the religious ceremonies was in theory the king. All the temple reliefs show him making the offerings, but in fact of course they would be made by his deputies. The priesthood was at first a duty taken on by the local dignitaries working according to a roster, but gradually a professional priesthood was set up. At certain periods when the king was weak, the high priest of Amun or another major god was the real ruler of Egypt.

In addition to the high priest there was a whole range of other clergy with carefully graded ranks and titles. Women also served as priestesses, and of course there were numerous other people in the temple service, ranging from choristers and librarians to cooks and gardeners.

Born from water

There is no ancient Egyptian sacred book, equivalent to the Bible or Qur'an, which was accepted as a revelation of divine truth. The Egyptians had their myths like those of the ancient Greeks. The Egyptian myths told the story of the relationships between the gods, but very few have survived intact. All we have are short scattered references which can sometimes be pieced together to tell the whole story, though we cannot be sure that we have it correct.

Various creation myths abounded, for example. The Egyptians generally imagined the universe as originally filled with water, from which a hill arose on which life began. This was no doubt derived from what they observed each year as the Nile flood subsided. Thereafter the stories become extremely complex. Different gods were thought to have somehow emerged from the hill or the water, and in various ways to have created other gods. Many of the great temples were claimed to be built on this primeval hill.

An interesting claim was advanced by the priests of Memphis on behalf of their god Ptah. They declared that he was the great god who somehow was also the great watery universe from which the other gods were born, their acts of creation being simply the carrying out of his will.

As well as the myths there are prayers and hymns to the gods, which read very much like the Old Testament psalms. Books of wisdom are also known, which, rather like the biblical book of Proverbs, range from practical and moral advice to

Egyptian Temples: Houses of Power

John Ruffle

The outward appearance of an Egyptian temple was not particularly elegant. To us, whose ideas are perhaps coloured by Gothic cathedrals or even Greek temples, they appear more like power stations than temples. This in fact reflects their purpose. They were less concerned with telling people outside about the majesty and power of the god to whom they were dedicated, and more concerned with the ritual that went on inside. This ritual was intended to ensure that the gods would continue their favour towards Egypt, and it was therefore the prime consideration in the design of the building.

The plan of the temple

The two main types of temple were the cult temple, dedicated to a particular god, usually the principal god of the city or area, and the funerary temple, dedicated to the memory of a dead king who was treated as a god. To all intents and purposes the plans of these two types were the same.

The temple was thought of as the house of the god and its plan was similar to the plans of the houses of nobles and officials. These usually consisted of a number of reception rooms leading to the private family rooms and ultimately to the owner's bedroom. In the temples the same types of room were used, with large courts and halls corresponding to the reception room, and the shrine corresponding to the main bedroom. The main difference was that the rooms of the temple were laid out in a straight line so that processions could pass from the main gate to the sanctuary without awkward bends.

Some temples were in use for several hundreds of years and were extended and altered, demolished and rebuilt during that time, but the same general arrangement was followed throughout. Even those cut in the rock cliffs of Nubia, like the temples of Ramesses II at Abu Simbel, kept to the same basic plan. A few exceptions occurred, as when for example two deities of equal rank occupied the same temple at Kom Ombo; a double aisle and twin shrines were provided.

The temples represented Egypt in miniature. The great monumental entrance was similar in shape to the hieroglyph which stood for the horizon or limits of the country. On the outside walls of this gate we see the king destroying his foreign enemies. Inside, the halls were decorated as huge thickets, the floors painted to represent water, and the ceilings painted with stars. Egyptian architects did not use vaulting, so the flat stone blocks that formed the ceilings had to be supported by closely arranged pillars which were based on plant shapes, usually with papyrus or lotus capitals.

Ritual protection of the temple

As far as possible the temple was cut off from the outside world to protect its ritual purity. At the foundation ceremony, a pit was filled with clean sand containing magic amulets which warded off any evil influence that might attack from below. The corners of the building were further protected by foundation deposits, consisting of animal sacrifices, groups of model tools and other items. A high wall protected the temple estate, and the building itself was erected within another wall and an ambulatory or corridor which formed a further protective layer around it.

Elaborate precautions were even taken to remove rain-water from the roof, with a complex series of channels and huge gargoyles. The shrine itself was often constructed as a separate building within the main temple, complete with its own roof. So it was again separated from contact with the world outside.

Within the main building various rooms were set aside for special purposes. There would be a library for the papyrus rolls with the ritual texts, a vestry for the special clothing and store-rooms for the chalices, censors and other vessels used in the rituals. Often, in addition to the main god who occupied the central shrine, there were other gods, perhaps members of his family who shared the temple. Their images were kept in smaller shrines built around the central shrine in the sanctuary area.

Deepening mystery

The walls of the temple were decorated with relief carvings of scenes from the temple rituals. The words that were recited at the ritual were also inscribed on the walls. From the position of these carvings within the temple it is sometimes possible to tell the uses of the different rooms. These carvings were not just a large-scale service-book; the ceremony that was performed when the completed building was formally presented to the god included an *Opening of the Mouth* ritual by which all these carvings were given life and everlasting effectiveness. So the mere portrayal of the ritual supposedly guaranteed that it would continue for ever, even if the priests ceased to perform it.

As the worshippers moved from the temple entrance to the sanctuary the air of mystery gradually deepened. The size of the rooms was reduced in stages, the roof level came lower and the floor was stepped up. Daylight was also gradually excluded. From the open court one passed to courts lit by a clerestory or openings in the first wall which was sometimes only constructed half-way to the roof; the innermost rooms were completely cut off from daylight. Even today some temples are visited by the light of oil lamps, and it is easy to imagine how the flickering, leaping light of torches playing on the richly-painted figures and hieroglyphs on the walls must have combined with the singing and incense to create a feeling of awe and wonder in the worshippers.

The roof of the temple was also important. Some ceremonies, involving, for instance, the union of the divine image with the sun, were performed there. Special stairs with shallow steps were used so that the image of the god could be carried up to the roof in a small portable shrine. Small roof-top chapels were built for these ceremonies.

Shrines

Outside the main building of the temple, but within the enclosure wall, were many other buildings. These may still be seen in some temples such as Karnak and Denderah. There are small shrines and chapels, often including one where a divine marriage and birth ritual was enacted. There was also housing for the priests, slaughter-yards and bakehouses where offerings were prepared, a well that provided holy water, and a sacred lake on which other rituals would be performed, rather like medieval mystery plays.

The bulky stone construction of the temples has meant that, along with the pyramids and rock-cut tombs, they have survived the passage of the years. Long after their original use was superseded, many provided refuge for later inhabitants such as Christian monks, and even whole village communities.

The temple at Luxor.

1. The ankh *amulet was the symbol of life triumphant over death. 2. The entrance to the temple at Dendera. 3. The hawk-headed god Horus in a tomb-painting. 4. Outside the temple complex at Luxor. 5. The terrace temple of Queen Hatchepsut near Thebes. 6. Inside the temple at Luxor. 7. A processional avenue at Karnak, flanked by ram-headed sphinxes.*

The Egyptians believed in judgement after death, when a person's soul was weighed in a balance by the gods.

general theological reflections on the nature of life.

There are also many magical spells, which may be counted as religious since they invoke the gods and try to persuade them to give help and protection from all sorts of evils.

Living and dying well

Several of the wisdom books encourage their readers to live according to a moral and ethical code of personal piety. They urge this partly because it is the way to earn respect from one's fellows, partly beause it is pleasing to 'the god'.

Living a good life was thought to be a way of ensuring a safe passage to the afterlife. There are many representations of a judgement scene in which the dead man's heart is weighed in a balance against a feather which represents Truth. The result was recorded by Thoth, the scribe of the gods, in the presence of Osiris, and those who failed were destroyed for ever. This judgement was not, however, a great incentive to piety, since the result could be influenced by correctly reciting an incantation in which the man denied that he had ever committed a whole range of sins.

Journey to the next world

The Egyptians seem always to have had a belief in an afterlife. The very earliest tombs contain items of food and equipment, and later on the decoration of the tombs tells us how the Egyptians thought such a life would be. Generally it was thought to be similar to this world but better, with successful hunting and harvests, rich banquets and pretty girls.

The idea went through various stages of development. At first it was thought that the king would spend his afterlife alongside the sun-god Re on his daily journey across the heavens. Soon, however, his future became linked with the god Osiris, and each king in turn as he died became identified with him. Gradually this privilege was extended, first to the nobles and later to all classes, so that each man on his death somehow became identified with Osiris.

The story of Osiris himself was not recorded in full until the Greek writer Plutarch (about AD 100) recounted how the good king Osiris was murdered by his jealous brother Seth. With the help of his wife Isis and other gods, Osiris eventually became the ruler of the afterworld and a symbol of continued life after death. There are several references to the story in Egyptian literature which make it clear that there were differing versions of this account.

The journey to the afterworld was fraught with difficulty. All sorts of obstacles lay in the way, and demons were ready at every turn to seize the traveller. A successful journey was assured by possession of a papyrus roll containing a series of incantations which could be recited to allow the dead man to pass when an obstacle or demon was encountered. These books are usually called *The Book of the Dead*, although there are several different titles. Copies were placed in the tomb with the dead man for his use, or at different periods they were inscribed inside the coffin or on the tomb walls.

It was, of course, plain to the Egyptians that the physical body remained in this world and that it was the dead man's spirit that passed on. They thought that this spirit needed the body as a kind of base, and for this reason they made elaborate attempts to preserve the body by mummification. It was particularly serious if a body was lost at sea or destroyed by fire, although in extreme cases a statue or portrait of the departed might serve as a substitute.

The funeral service included a ceremony called *The Opening of the Mouth* in which the mouth and other openings of the body were magically treated to ensure that the dead man might continue to use his body to feed, see, hear and so on. The same ceremony performed over statues and paintings endowed them with a form of life in the afterworld.

The Gods of Ancient Egypt

AMUN
King of the gods, patron deity of the pharaohs. Later identified with the sun-god Amun-Re.

ANUBIS
God of the dead, guardian of tombs and cemeteries.

ATEN
The sun. For a short time became the chief and only god.

HATHOR
Sky-goddess. Later became the cow-goddess, goddess of love and dance, lady of the underworld and mistress of the stars.

HORUS
God of Lower Egypt. The sky-god.

ISIS
Queen of the gods, the great mother-goddess. Corn-goddess and fertility-goddess.

KHNUM
Old Egyptian god of the Upper Nile. Creator of gods, men and waters.

THOTH
Moon-god. Later the god of learning and wisdom, the inventor of writing.

OSIRIS
Fertility and vegetation-god. Later became supreme god of Egypt with Re and king of the dead.

SEBEK
Water-god. Sometimes the personification of evil and death.

PTAH
God of the dead. Creator and fertility-god.

SETH
God of storms. Violent and dangerous, he was the murderer of Osiris.

RE
Sun-god, the great state-god of ancient Egypt. King of the gods, father of mankind and protector of kings.

The Cosmic Battle: Zoroastrianism

John Hinnells

The story of Zoroastrianism begins in the third millennium BC with the Indo-Europeans. Somewhere to the east of Europe about 3000 BC a group of tribes began to split up. Some travelled south and settled in Greece and Rome, others went north and settled in Scandinavia, and others went east to Persia (now Iran) and India. It is because of this common descent that the ancient languages of these countries have a similar pattern.

The important group for Zoroastrian studies is the third one which settled in India and Persia. These people are called the 'Indo-Iranians' by scholars. They referred to themselves as the 'Aryas' (Aryans), 'the noble ones'. They travelled eastwards in two main waves. The first, in approximately 2000 BC, passed through northern Persia leaving only a few settlers there, with the main body carrying on into north-west India where they gradually over-threw the Indus Valley civilization. The second wave of Indo-Iranians settled in Persia about 1500 BC.

Natural powers

The religion of the Indo-Iranians provides the background to Zoroastrianism just as ancient Israelite religion does to Christianity. The Indo-Iranians were nomads, travelling from pasture to pasture on foot with their herds, not staying long enough to build temples, travelling light so that they did not have statues of the gods.

Theirs was a religion of the mountain-top, with the dome of the sky for their temple, using the ordinary household fire as the focus for their ritual offerings. Their imagery was drawn from wind and storm, from sun and rain. Their gods were not thought of in human form, but as the forces which surround man—the gods of True Speech and Hospitality, of Contract and Victory. Their demons were similarly abstract: Wrath and Greed, the Lie and Pro-crastination. The world was full of spirits that man must treat with cau-tion, and make the due offerings so that they might not be angry. The peasants had no real hope of life after death: the sunlit paradise was only for men of power and wealth, priests and princes.

The prophet Zoroaster

Zoroaster is the name by which the West knows the prophet of ancient Persia, more correctly called Zarathushtra. It was usual to date him about 600 BC, but the evidence of language is persuading more scholars nowadays to date him about 1500 BC, which means that he lived when Persia was emerging from the Stone Age. This would make him the first of the great prophets of the world's religions.

Zoroaster's life

Zoroaster was a descendant of the first wave of Indo-Iranians. His people had become settled agriculturalists who were threatened by the second wave of Indo-Iranian settlers. We know little of the prophet's life. He was a priest (interestingly, the only one of the great prophets who was); he was married and had several children.

At the age of thirty he had the first of a series of visions which inspired him to preach a new message. His teaching was at first rejected, and he suffered persecution, being forced to leave his home. It took ten years before he made his first convert, his cousin. Then his message found favour with a local king, Vishtasp, and Zoroaster's religion became the official teaching of a small kingdom somewhere in north-east Persia, in what is now part of the southern USSR (the precise location is not known). Zoroaster's religion in time spread throughout Persia and became the official religion of what was, for 1,000 years, one of the major world empires.

Zoroaster's teaching

Zoroastrians believe that their prophet is the one chosen by God to receive his unique revelation. This is contained in seventeen hymns, the *Gathas*. Obviously the prophet gave more teaching than this, but all that has survived is a fragment cast into verse-form to help memorize the words in an age and region where writing was unknown. These hymns are now the central part of a major act of worship (*yasna*).

The great choice

Perhaps *the* characteristic feature of Zoroaster's teaching is his emphasis on personal religion, inspired presumably by his conviction that God had called him and appeared to him personally. All men (and women, both sexes have the same duties in Zoroastrianism) have a personal responsibility to choose between good and evil. On the basis of their exercise of their free-will, men will be judged in the hereafter. Those whose good thoughts, words and deeds out-weigh the evil will go to heaven, regardless of their social status; those whose evil thoughts, words and deeds outweigh the good will go to hell, again regardless of their social status. This moral democracy offended the established priests and princes who had considered paradise their sole preserve.

A similar prophetic emphasis can be seen in the badge Zoroaster took for the religion. For the Indo-Iranians a sacred cord was the symbol of priesthood, as it still is with the Brahmins in India. Zoroaster made this and a sacred shirt (made of white cotton rather like a vest) the symbolic armour which all believers should wear at all times after initiation, to remind them of the battle they must fight against evil.

Good and evil

God, Zoroaster taught, was the wholly Good Creator of all things, of sun, moon and stars, of the spiritual and material worlds, of man and beast. The Wise Lord (Ahura Mazda) is the bountiful sovereign, the friend not only of Zoroaster but of all men.

He is in no way responsible for evil in the world; this comes from the Destructive Spirit (Angra Mainyu) whose nature is violent and destructive. It was he who created the demons, who rules in hell and who has opposed God from the beginning. In Zoroastrianism the 'Devil' is

Modern Zoroastrian tradition identifies this as the symbol of man's spiritual self.

not a fallen angel, for that would make the Good Creator ultimately responsible for evil—an inconceivable idea for Zoroastrians. The world is the battleground in which the forces of good and evil do battle. The world and man were created by God to aid him in this battle.

He also created a number of heavenly beings. Foremost among them were the Bounteous Immortals (Amesha Spentas), the sons and daughters of God, as they became known. In some ways they resemble the Christian idea of archangels (which belief some scholars think was influenced by Zoroastrianism). But like the gods of the Indo-Iranians there is an important abstract dimension to their nature, as their names show. They are: Good Mind (Vohu Manah); Righteousness (Asha); Devotion (Armaiti); Dominion (Kshathra); Wholeness and Immortality (Haurvatat and Ameretat). These are not only heavenly beings, they are also ideals to which the righteous should aspire. So by sharing in the good mind, by a life of devotion and righteousness, man shares in God's dominion and attains wholeness and immortality.

Each of the Bounteous Immortals is thought to protect, and be represented by, one of the six creations which together constitute the Good Creation of God: cattle, fire, earth, metal, water and plants. At important acts of worship, a representative of each creation and therefore of the Bounteous Immortal, is present so that the earthly and heavenly worlds are both symbolically present. The seventh creation is man himself, the representative of God, and present at the rite in the person of the priest.

Zoroaster taught that the world was essentially good, but spoiled at present by the attacks of evil. He looked forward to the day when the battle with evil would reach its climax, when good would triumph and the world would be restored to the perfect state its Creator gave it. At the last the dead will be raised and judged, the wicked will go to hell, and the righteous dwell with God in perfection for eternity.

Persepolis was the chief royal palace of the Achaemenid kings.

The spread of Zoroastrianism

The first 1,000 years after the death of the prophet are shrouded in mystery. There simply are not the sources to reconstruct Zoroastrianism's early history. It appears to have spread across the Persian plateau largely through the movements of tribes and through tribal battles. The Medes came to power in western Persia in the seventh century BC, and the Persians in the sixth century. By that time Zoroastrianism was evidently a power in the land.

The Persian Empire

Persia really emerges into the light of history in 559 BC when Cyrus ascended the throne of a small Persian kingdom called Anshan in the southwest of the country. In 550 he seized the throne of the Medes, then captured the fabulously wealthy king of Lydia in distant Anatolia (modern Turkey). Then in 539 the mighty Babylonian Empire capitulated before him. So in twenty years he rose from being the ruler of a petty kingdom to emperor over what was then the world's largest empire.

In capturing Babylon, Cyrus liberated the Jews from their exile, an act which the biblical book of Isaiah ascribes to the powerful guidance of God, who specially chose Cyrus to accomplish his purposes. No other foreign king is spoken of in such glowing terms in the Bible. Cyrus established for himself a considerable and widespread reputation for tolerance and justice. The dynasty which ruled Persia after him—the Achaemenids (named after a legendary ancestor)—continued to uphold these ideals. It also spread Zoroastrianism throughout the realm.

The people largely responsible for its propagation were the Magi, the priestly tribe of the Medes who continued in office throughout all periods of the Zoroastrian history of Persia. The Magi acted as royal chaplains, and travelled with all important delegations, whether on military or diplomatic missions. They also lived in the many Persian settlements in various parts of the empire. So when

Matthew's Gospel refers to wise men (Magi) visiting the infant Jesus, his readers would know well the significance of that. The later Christian legend that they were kings is wrong.

Alexander 'the vandal'

The Achaemenid Empire was brought to an end by Alexander in 331 BC. In Persian history he is not known as 'Alexander the Great' but rather 'Alexander the vandal', because he killed priests and burned down the royal palace of Persepolis. He said he wanted to unite the cultures of Persia and Greece, but he and his successors, the Seleucids, are remembered as the foreign interlopers who intruded into Persian life.

The Parthian Empire

A native Persian dynasty gradually expelled Seleucid power from the land in the middle of the second century BC. They are known as the Parthians, because of the region in Persia from which they came. They did not bring an advanced technology with them from this remote region, so in the early part of their rule they took over certain Hellenistic features such as coin-types and some architectural styles. But their own feudal Persian culture is better reflected in the surviving minstrel tales and epic legends. It was during the Parthian period that the first moves were made to collect together the ancient traditions which made up the Zoroastrian holy book, the *Avesta*.

The Parthians have not received the attention they deserve, mainly because the archaeological and written sources are so few. Yet they ruled Persia for about 400 years, with an empire as large as that of their more famous Achaemenid forebears, stretching at times from north India to what is now Turkey. They were the largest power to confront the might of Rome. They had good relations with Israel; invading the land in 40 BC, they deposed the hated Herod and put a Jew in his place. The Romans returned two years later and restored Herod.

It is interesting to speculate how different history would have been if

Israel, at the time of Jesus, had been under the sway of the tolerant Parthians instead of the widely-hated Romans. What is not generally realized is that at the time of Jesus, the Parthians had made Zoroastrianism the most powerful religion of the then-known world.

'Church and state'
In AD 224 the ruler of a province in the south-west of Persia rebelled against the Parthians. The new dynasty was named after a legendary ancestor, Sasan. The Sasanians ruled Persia until the Muslim invasion in the seventh century. They left behind a wealth of material splendour and a number of writings, creating the impression that this was the most glorious epoch in the history of Zoroastrian Persia.

The high priest was a major power behind the throne, determining much of imperial policy. After Constantine and his successors made Christianity the official religion of the Roman Empire, providing a religious basis for its unity, a comparable unity was necessary in the major Eastern empire. Zoroastrianism had always stressed the unity of church and state, and this was developed to the full in Sasanian times.

The Islamic conquest
The Arab armies of the new Muslim religion entered Persia in AD 633, only one year after the death of Muhammad. At first they came for booty, but later battles were aimed at permanent conquest. The intention was primarily to enforce submission to the rule of Islam. In theory religions which the Muslim authorities recognized as 'people of a book', that is, those who had received a revelation from God (mainly Jews and Christians), were allowed to continue their religion, subject only to the imposition of an extra tax.

But the position of Zoroastrianism as a religion of a book was less clear, and as the new world empire took hold, the position of Zoroastrians in their own land became increasingly threatened. Education, promotion, equality before the law, all were denied to the followers of Zoroaster. Gradually they were forced to retreat into the obscurity of desert villages. So the religion of the land became associated with poverty and backwardness.

Persecution
Zoroastrians, as the oppressed poor, were often the subjects of vicious attacks from Muslim 'bully boys'. Even in the twentieth century under the protective Pahlavi dynasty, 'infidel-baiting' was common in the remote villages far from official gaze. Because dogs are holy animals to Zoroastrians, one favoured approach was to hack a dog to pieces and throw the remains into the yard of a devout Zoroastrian house. Any Zoroastrian venturing alone into a Muslim quarter could expect verbal and often physical abuse.

Persecution, oppression, poverty, injustice, isolation—these have been the conditions which Zoroastrians have faced in their own land for over 1,300 years of Muslim rule. It is an enormous tribute to their courage, determination and faith that there are any followers of Zoroaster left in present-day Iran. There are a few in the cities, but the majority continue to shelter in the villages of the Yazdi plain. Altogether there are about 17,000 still following the religion of ancient Persia.

The Parsis
The main base of the religion today, in numerical terms, is in India, among the Parsis. In the tenth century AD a small band of the faithful set out to seek a new land of religious freedom, preferring to leave Persia rather than give up the religion of their forefathers. In India they have lived in peace and security, in time even achieving a position of wealth and power which they used to campaign for and support their co-religionists back in the homeland.

Zoroastrian beliefs
The tenth century was not only the time when the 'Pilgrim Fathers' of Zoroastrianism set out for India, it was also a time of literary activity

among the Zoroastrians of Persia. A number of texts were produced to encourage, inspire and instruct the faithful in the contemporary language known as Pahlavi or Middle Persian. The holy book, the *Avesta*, was in a language which only a few learned priests understood. Translations, summaries and explanations were produced, as well as defences of the faith against Muslim, Christian and Hindu teachings. Although they were written in the ninth and tenth centuries, they can be taken as the definitive statements of traditional Zoroastrian thought. These Middle Persian texts codify, elaborate and systematize the teaching of Zoroaster himself, from which they stem.

Creation

The Middle Persian forms of the names of God and the 'Devil', ancient Ahura Mazda and Angra Mainyu, are Ohrmazd and Ahriman. Ohrmazd, it is taught, dwells on high in perfect goodness and light whereas Ahriman dwells from eternity in darkness below in the abyss. Battle between these two primal spirits was inevitable, so Ohrmazd created the heavenly and material worlds to aid him in the battle. First he created the heavenly beings, then the world in purely spiritual form, that is, invisible and intangible. In Zoroastrian belief the material world is not evil or corrupt, rather it is the visible, tangible manifestation of the spiritual creation. It is the creation of God, therefore it is good.

The essential characteristics of evil are violence, chaos and the will to destroy. When Ahriman saw the Good Creation of God, he tried to destroy it, afflicting it with misery, suffering, disease and death. None of these evils, therefore, came from God, nor were they part of his plan for creation. They are unnatural afflictions wrought by a wholly independent 'Devil' who seeks to ruin the perfection of the divine creation.

In the myth of creation it is said that Ahriman defiled all parts of creation: the ordered creation was afflicted with chaos; the round, flat earth was shaken so that valleys were opened up, and mountains raised; the sun was dislodged from its ideal noonday position; fire was afflicted with smoke; the archetypal man and bull were afflicted with suffering and death. Ahriman was apparently triumphant. Then a miracle occurred: the dying bull and man emitted sperm; from the bull's seed grew cattle, from man's came a plant whose leaves grew, separated and formed the first human couple. In Zoroastrian thought man is literally at one with his environment.

The cosmic battle

Then Ahriman sought to escape from the world, but found he was trapped within it. Thus the cosmic battle between good and evil is now fought out in the arena of world history. For the first 3,000 years after Ahriman's attack, the two forces were reasonably evenly balanced in what is known as 'the period of mixture' (that is, of good and evil). Then the prophet Zoroaster was born. With the revelation of the Good Religion the defeat of Ahriman was assured. From this time on, the defeat of evil began.

But in Zoroastrian thought it does not come suddenly and unexpectedly like a thief in the night, it is a further 3,000-year conflict as Ahriman makes a desperate bid to destroy all that is good. This final fling is in vain. At 1,000-year intervals three saviours are born: each born of a virgin who had been impregnated with the prophet's seed preserved in a lake where the maidens bathed. They are, therefore, of the line of the prophet, though born of a virgin. A part of the evil creation is destroyed by each of them, until the third saviour raises the dead and introduces the last judgement. From this, men will return to heaven and hell for a limited period before they re-emerge to pass through a stream of molten metal—the final ordeal before all men dwell in total perfection with Ohrmazd.

During these cataclysmic events the heavenly forces will have been engaged in the final battle with the demonic powers, finally overcoming them. The molten metal which had already restored the earth to its original state by reducing mountains and filling up the valleys, and which finally tested men, now fills up hell. So Ahriman is rendered powerless for eternity. For the first time Ohrmazd becomes all-powerful. Evil is wiped out. So, in the myth, the earth ascends to the moon, the heaven descends to the moon—neither is done away with. Zoroastrians do not speak of 'the end of the world', for that would be the end of what God made. Instead they look forward to the 'renovation of creation', the time when heaven and earth join together to make what is literally the best of both worlds.

Man's nature and destiny

In Zoroastrian thought man faces two judgements. One comes after death when his thoughts, words and deeds are weighed in the balances. If good outweighs evil, then man's own conscience guides him across the Bridge of the Separator (Chinvat Bridge) to heaven. If evil predominates then his conscience leads him trembling to the bridge from which he falls into the abyss of hell. The second judgement is after the resurrection.

Whereas Christianity has no explanation for the belief in two judgements, Zoroastrianism has. Man has two sides to his being, the physical and the spiritual. Both are the creations of God. Man must be judged, rewarded or punished in both aspects of his being. The first judgement after death is evidently one in the spirit because the body can be seen to remain on earth. But hell is not eternal in Zoroastrian belief. The purpose of punishment, they believe, must be corrective. However 'eternal' is defined—whether as everlasting or absolute—eternal hell cannot involve corrective punishment. In hell, Zoroastrians believe, the punishment is made to fit the crime, so a cruel ruler who tortures or starves his people is himself tortured and starved in hell. But at the resurrection all men return from heaven or hell to face their second judgement, this time in the body; and again they return to heaven or hell as appropriate so that they may be physically rewarded or corrected.

The purpose is that the whole man, body and soul, should be so corrected that he may dwell, in the perfection of his united being, with God. Man is a divine creation, intended to be a fellow-worker with God; his final destiny must be with God. During his earthly life he has complete free-will to act as he chooses, to support the forces of good or evil. He can live contrary to his nature, but he cannot, in eternal terms, change that nature. Through judgement, heaven and hell, he is corrected and rewarded, for his part in the great battle between good and evil.

This rock relief is at Naqsh-i Rustam, the 'valley of the kings' near the palace of Persepolis. The Sasanian monarch Shapur I (c. AD 242–273) rides in triumph and majesty before the kneeling figure of his defeated Roman enemy. Like their Achaemenid and Parthian forbears, the Sasanian monarchs ruled over an empire stretching from India to the shores of the Mediterranean. For over 1,000 years, Zoroastrian Iran was the major power in the known world.

Body and soul

Man's foremost duty is to make his body the dwelling-place of the Bounteous Immortals; as we have seen, his life is to be determined by the Good Mind of Righteousness and Devotion directed towards divine Dominion, Wholeness and Immortality—and to reject the demons such as Violence, Greed and the Lie. He should seek to reflect the bounteous, creative spirit of God and reject the negative path.

In doing this he must keep the spiritual and material sides of his nature in balance. So man has a religious duty to expand God's material creation as well as to support his spiritual creation. He should get married and have children; he should seek to expand his herds and the natural environment through agriculture. To remain celibate is sinfully to refrain from this duty. On the other hand, man should not abuse the divine gift of marriage through lechery. In Zoroastrian belief a monk is as great a sinner as a lecher—both deny what God wills. Similarly man should not fast so that the spirit is exalted over the body, nor should he be gluttonous and exalt the body over the soul. The health of body and soul are interdependent and should be cared for equally.

The world is God's Good Creation, and it is man's religious duty to care for and enjoy that creation, for Zoroastrians believe that 'misery drives away the divine'. There is no belief here that man is a spiritual self imprisoned in an alien material universe, as there is in some religions. Indeed, it is practically the reverse— the 'Devil' is a spiritual being trapped in what is to him an alien good universe. The spirit of happiness permeates not only Zoroastrian ethics, but also their rituals, which are described in the section on the Parsis.

The sacred fire, symbol of Ahura Mazda, is nowadays housed in fire temples. Originally, Zoroastrian worship was conducted in the open air, but a temple cult was introduced in Achaemenid times and received lavish royal patronage.

If evil is associated with death and decay in the material world, then man has a duty to avoid contact with any matter that aids these evils. Dirt, rotting and dead matter are places where death, and therefore evil, is present. The housewife cleaning the home, rites associated with birth, marriage and death, standards of personal hygiene—all are concerned with the great cosmic battle between good and evil. In this way man, the fellow-worker with Ohrmazd, seeks to wipe out evil and restore the world to its God-created perfection.

Personal responsibility

Zoroastrianism is a religion which is concerned with the *Good* God, the *Good* Creation and the *goodness* of man. The term its followers often use of it is 'The Good Religion'. It has no doctrine of original sin, nor of one man dying to save all. Every man is responsible for his own part in the cosmic battle, and for his own destiny. It is a religion of stalwart determination—which is perhaps what has enabled it to survive for so long, despite a millennium of oppression.

Mithraism: Cult of the Bull

John Hinnells

Mithra is perhaps unique in history in that he is one god who has been worshipped in four different religions. He appears in Hinduism and Zoroastrianism because both derive from the Indo-Iranian religion of which Mithra was a part, and in Manichaeism because of the form that religion took in Persia.

The Romans

A basic question scholars cannot answer with certainty is what is the relationship of those forms of Mithra worship with the Roman cult of Mithras. It used to be assumed that the Romans took over the Persian form, but increasingly scholars argue that the Roman cult was a new Western religion with a veneer of Persian and oriental learning to make it appeal to the many people in the empire who were fascinated by Eastern cults.

The earliest reference to the Roman Mithras is by the poet Statius who died in AD 96. The earliest-known temples were built in the mid-second century, and building continued until the fifth century. Temples are found as far apart as Wales in the west, Hadrian's Wall in northern England, Dura on the Euphrates, and Alexandria in Egypt. The areas of greatest concentration are the city of Rome and its port of Ostia, and the frontier regions of the empire, especially along the Danube and Rhine rivers.

The army appears to have provided the greatest number of recruits, but traders and officials were also members of the cult. Both military and civilian initiates were of a respected social class, inscriptions suggesting a fairly high proportion of centurions and officers. The portrait of a Mithraist in one temple shows a clean-shaven, very respectable young man. The male is significant—women were excluded from the cult.

Statues and temples

There are enormous problems in reconstructing what the Mithraists believed and did. No text written by a Mithraist has survived, only the comments of outside observers, mainly Christians, who (with the possible exception of the Neo-Platonist Porphyry) were generally biased and ignorant. There is no Mithraic 'Prayer Book' that we know of. So the main source of information is the products of archaeology, silent stones and stereotyped inscriptions dedicating a statue or temple. Religious iconography is notoriously difficult to interpret, and this is especially true in the case of Mithraism.

Mithraic temples were generally small and built to resemble a cave, in imitation of what they thought was the 'world cave' which Mithras had created, with the vault of the sky spanning the earth. On each side of a central aisle were benches on which the initiates reclined. At the end opposite the entrance was a main cult relief, usually carved in stone in the round, though in Italy some painted scenes are found. Often, in the central aisle and near the main relief, were set small altars on which incense was burned.

The bull-slaying scene

The theme of the main cult relief was virtually always Mithras slaying a bull. This act was represented with remarkable consistency of detail. The god generally puts his left knee on the bull's back, keeping his right foot on the creature's hoof, pulls back its head with his left hand and stabs it with his right. A dog leaps towards the blood from the wound, as does a snake, while a scorpion grasps the bull's genitals. At either side of the main scene are two torchbearers, one with a raised torch, the other a lowered torch. How to interpret this scene without any explanatory texts is a real problem. It used to be thought a variation of the Zoroastrian creation myth; only here it is not the 'Devil', but Mithras, who takes the first life, from which all creation proceeds. But this has been shown to be unlikely—if not impossible.

The view most scholars favour nowadays is that the scene has to be understood in astrological terms, because so many of the symbols can be interpreted astrologically—snake (*hydra*), dog (*canis*), bull (*taurus*), scorpion (*scorpio*), to list only a few. Precisely what is being depicted astrologically we still do not know—perhaps the date at which the cult started, or when it was thought creation had taken place.

Ascent of the soul

Each community of believers was divided into seven grades of initiation. In ascending order these were: Raven, Bride, Soldier, Lion, Persian, Runner of the sun, and Father. Progression through the grades was thought to reflect the spiritual ascent of the soul through the planetary spheres which bind it to the material world. The Father was a man of piety and wisdom, rather ascetic and in charge of the discipline in each group. It is reasonable to suppose that with progression through the grades, the initiate was taught deeper levels of spiritual learning, so that the cult relief may have had more than one interpretation.

Each grade clearly had a different cultic function. The main ritual which we know of is a feast enjoyed by the members in imitation of a meal shared by Mithras and Sol (the sun) over the body of the slain bull. One ritual which Mithraists did *not* practise, but which many popular books say they did, was the 'taurobolium'. This was a known rite in Roman religion where an initiate entered a pit over which a bull's throat was cut, and the initiate washed himself in and drank the blood. Mithraic temples were far too small to get a bull in, and presumably they did not want to. Clearly the act of slaying the bull was one which only the god could perform, even though the initiates could imitate the ritual meal which

Statues from temples to Mithras show the god slaying a bull.

followed. One inscription refers to Mithras saving his followers by the shedding of eternal blood, so it was he alone who could save them. They shared in this salvation through the meal (of bread and wine, apparently) and through a lifetime's personal discipline as each person progressed up the spiritual ladder of the seven grades.

Destroyed

Mithraism died out largely because of the success of Christianity. Christians had a special hatred of Mithras— Tertullian described Mithraism as a devilish imitation of what he believed was the true religion. Whenever Christians could break into a Mithraic temple they destroyed it and the reliefs with axes. But at least one Mithraic practice survived—25 December is celebrated in various cultures as the birth-day of a new sun. Mithraists used the date to celebrate the birth of Mithras, and Christians took it over for the celebration of Jesus' birth.

The Ancient Religions of Greece and Rome

Clyde Curry Smith

The ancient history of Greece covers some 6,000 years or more of development from the first permanent settlement based upon grain agriculture until Greece was absorbed by Rome. Within this immense period, only the last 2,000 years at most are definitely Greek by language.

The ancient history of Rome, by contrast, begins in the eighth century BC and extends into the fifth century AD, and the Latin language is present over that whole span.

For our beginning we must look at the environment of that great inland sea—the Mediterranean basin. This large, deep trench is bordered by mountainous folds. An earthquake and volcanic belt along its whole length is the fundamental feature with which man here has always had to contend. And that vital force was seen as centred in the sea. So we meet the sea-god Poseidon: the one who both 'embraces the earth' and 'shakes' it, as Homer would say.

Five larger islands define the sub-basins of the Mediterranean: Sicily (which divides the whole), Sardinia and Corsica, Crete (which separates off the Aegean) and Cyprus.

The rugged Mediterranean coastlands offered little good land for the development of civilization. It was the sea itself which became a major force in Mediterranean development. The seaways meant transport and profit in trade (and booty in piracy), relying only on the stars and fair winds—those unpredictable elements which provided the context for man's religious response.

Hence, the wanderers—the Greek word for 'planet' means 'wanderer'—in the sky were understood by the wanderers upon the sea to be those greater forces which guided them. Thus in Greek (and Latin) we meet: Zeus (Jupiter), Aphrodite (Venus), Ares (Mars), Hermes (Mercury), and Khronos (Saturn). They, along with the sun and moon, defined times and seasons, regulating human life and its economic base.

The Aegean basin

When the south-eastern mountain ranges, which originally connected the Balkan and Anatolian peninsulas, were shattered, the Aegean was formed, its main island chains being the tops of the earlier mountains.

For the Aegean region as a whole there has been no essential climatic change since prehistoric times. Only about one-tenth of the land area was level enough to be cultivable. Vegetation depends on elevation, latitude and coastal influence, but it is also under human control. One of the major effects the human agriculturalists had on the landscape was the progressive removal of woodland. In its place came the cereal grains, wheat and barley, personified by Demeter (Ceres), the Lady who nourished all.

Prehistoric religion in Greece

Because of its mountainous condition, the Greek mainland shows fewer and less spectacular examples of human presence during the long Palaeolithic period than the steppes of Eurasia. Yet its forests and scrublands were home to hunters' game, and it was open to entrance by land passage through Macedonia into the Thessalian plains or through Epeiros into the Ionian islands.

The known burial practices of Neanderthal man throughout Eurasian sites are not yet documented specifically in the Aegean basin. Their response to the mystery of birth is also not known, unless it lay in the so-called 'Venuses' (exaggerated female figurines). Otherwise we can at best describe their technological skills and assembled tool-kits, their domestic construction and hunting prowess, from skeletal debris and collections of tools of some 70,000 years ago, found since 1960 at Petralona in Macedonia and at Pantanassa in Epeiros.

The oldest farming village known is Nea Nikomedia in Macedonia, dating from before the end of the seventh millennium BC.

When barley and wheat entered the larger European and Mediterranean worlds, they were accompanied by those who understood their cultivation. These people's way of thinking included observing the seasonal cycle, and its ritual correlation with preparing, planting, weeding and harvesting, or breeding, pasturing, tending and milking. In this we see the base for *all* later development of religious ideas.

The impact of the Neolithic agricultural transformation can best be measured by the shift in population density from, at most, one person to every ten square miles under hunting and gathering conditions, to ten to one hundred persons per square mile under farming conditions. The Aegean basin never had enough space; population growth was always a critical factor, leading to social instability which produced migrations and the practice of killing unwanted children by exposure.

The Parthenon in Athens was sacred to the city's patron goddess, Athena Parthenos.

This rich Mycenaean funeral mask is known as the mask of Agamemnon. According to Homer, Agamemnon was the leader of the Greeks in the siege of Troy.

Minoan-Mycenaean civilizations

The new technology which completed the thrust towards civilization was development in metal-working. Gold and silver had previously been used as rare ornaments. But now (3000–2000 BC) the discovery of how to reduce metals and produce alloys—especially of copper with tin—made it possible to make tools much stronger than the old stone ones, so that tougher lands could now be cleared and ploughed.

The crafts of smiths became economically competitive. They also introduced a rich source of analogy and myth in speaking about the creative process. The stone-workers' skill was turned towards architecture and sculpture, the potters' craft diverted towards aesthetic expression. In their place the moulding and hammering—often noisy and dirty—and extraction by fire of strong and glistening metals from apparently fragile and earth-like ores, became the significant imagery for the vital forces and dimensions of life which were to dominate the new age.

The early Bronze Age

Metal technology yielded specialized craftsmen, a new group set apart from the routine of village-farming life with its industries of pottery and weaving. The technology itself required a religious rhythm for the reduction of the metal from the ore, just as much as the secret lore related to the firing, alloying, casting or hammering processes.

For the earliest phase of the Bronze Age on the Greek mainland, objects of religious significance are minimal. There is much better evidence from the group of islands called the Cyclades. Best-known of all Cycladic objects are the marble figurines. The two most common are the elongated female (frequently highlighted with red and gold paint, standing erect, with just the nose represented on the head, arms crossed below the breasts, occasionally pregnant) and the abbreviated 'fiddle-shaped' version, which emphasizes only the necklace and the sexually-explicit features. We also know of a few nude males in a posture similar to that of the females, a few seated figures playing the lyre or pipes, and some animal-shaped terracottas. Although the figurines are usually less than twelve inches (thirty centimetres) tall, several life-sized examples exist. These were broken at the neck and knee to fit into the grave, and may well have stood elsewhere before burial. These Cycladic graves may themselves imitate a house or house-shrine.

The Middle Bronze Age, which roughly coincides with the first half of the second millennium (2000–1550 BC), seems to be an era of human reshuffling. Indo-European language groups appear not only in Anatolia (the Hittites) and the Aegean (the Greeks) but also in a great segment of the Eurasian continent, from India in the south-east to the Hebrides in the north-west.

The Middle Helladic period of the mainland was marked by the arrival of the first of several waves of

'Greeks', who were the ancestors of the Late Bronze Age Mycenaeans. The sites that archaeologists have investigated reveal the poverty both of towns (again without walls) and of shallow graves (without goods).

For the remainder of the Middle Bronze Age on the mainland there was no significant architecture. It was therefore very surprising when the Shaft Grave circles were discovered on the high citadel (*acropolis*) of Mycenae. Their gold treasures indicate the presence of aristocratic sea-going warriors who had amassed considerable wealth in portable loot.

Over these same centuries, from Crete, there is evidence of royal palace complexes. The palace rulers are said to be 'theocratic', because excavations have revealed no separate structures which can be called 'religious'.

The Minoans seem to have worshipped bulls and sacrificed them. There were 'bull-leapers', who performed dangerous acrobatics over a bull for religious purposes. This is often portrayed in wall-paintings, seals and the minor arts, bronze and terracotta. These ceremonial games took place in the large central courts of the palaces.

The palaces also contained 'pillar crypts', decorated with the double-headed axe, the chief Minoan religious symbol, possibly from its use in animal sacrifices. (The word 'labyrinth' comes from *labrys*, the Lydian for double-axe.) The double-axe was a woodsman's tool rather than a weapon. Actual examples have been found, with other carpentry tools.

Storage magazines were sometimes connected with the pillar crypts. In the floor of one at Knossos were 'temple repositories' containing faience figurines handling snakes. Snakes were used as house-guardians and so became the sacred animal of the household-goddess.

Minoan seals portraying cult-scenes are another important source for our knowledge of Minoan religion.

Citadels of the Mycenaeans

The Minoan epoch came to an end disastrously, probably when the vol-

The double axe was a religious symbol for the Minoans. It may have been used in animal sacrifice.

canic island of Thera erupted with extreme violence in about 1450 BC. This was documented fully at Kato Zakro. Of the palaces, neither Phaistos nor Mallia were to recover. Knossos alone, though in less grand fashion, was to be rebuilt, apparently by others. The old Minoan people had to desert their ash-covered valleys. The few who survived did so on isolated hills in the mountainous and western districts of the island.

The Late Bronze Age or Late Helladic era belongs to the Mycenaeans, both on the mainland and the islands, including Crete. The Middle Bronze mainland had been dominated by Minoan cultural influence, but as the Late Bronze Age began we find the *tholos* tomb builders. There are no surviving indications of the dwellings of these aristocratic warrior-rulers, though they may well have been built on the sites on which the Mycenaean palaces were to appear. The *tholos* tombs were underground beehive-shaped vaults, entered by way of a long, gently-sloping tunnel, and topped by an earth mound.

The principal grave goods were those of the warrior entombed. Minor objects show fishes, animals and birds, heroic figures doing battle with fellows or heraldic creatures, and female figures, in Minoan style, bare-breasted, tending domestic animals or plants. The gold cups from the Vapheio grave have scenes of netting and mating of great bulls.

'There is a land
called Crete in the
midst of the wine-
dark sea, a fair
country and fertile,
seagirt, and there are
many peoples,
innumerable; there
are ninety cities . . .
and there is Knossos,
the great city, the
place where Minos
was king for nine-
year periods, and
conversed with great
Zeus.'

Odyssey 19.172–174,
178–179

The Mycenaean palace complexes are neither towns nor houses, but fortified centres for developing valley communities. What most distinguishes these complexes from their Minoan predecessors is their location on high citadels, and their massive fortification walls. Five major sites on the mainland are known: Thebes, under the modern city; Athens, levelled for the fifth-century *acropolis*; Tiryns and Pylos, both well-preserved; and Mycenae, the best example, though part of the palace itself has collapsed down the slope. From Mycenae the civilization takes the name 'Mycenaean'.

The new ingredient in the Late Bronze Age is the earliest written texts, in a script called 'Linear B'. This was deciphered in 1952 and shown to be an archaic form of Greek.

The Linear B texts give a wholly new dimension to investigation. To date, tablets have been found only at Knossos, Pylos, Mycenae and Thebes. They include inventory lists of people and their occupations, livestock and agricultural produce, land ownership with some usage, textiles, vessels, furniture, metals and military equipment, and a grouping defined as 'proportional tribute and ritual offerings'.

It seems that commodities could serve as either tribute or offering, and that these were assessed seasonally according to fixed schedules, that receipts varied from assessments, and, most important of all, that there were functionaries of all sorts, as well as deities known by name or title. Poseidon is of considerable importance, as is 'the Lady' of different places. Zeus, Hera, Ares, Hermes, Athena, Artemis, Dionysus, and a few other classical deities are named. Among the great variety of functionaries which made up this administrative complex a 'priestess' or 'priest' is very occasionally mentioned.

The epics of Homer

There is a gap at the end of the Bronze Age, with the destruction of the Mycenaean world. The palace bureaucracies disappeared. Migrants and invaders worked the land on both sides of the Aegean basin. Some peoples simply survived the transition, to pass on in their own time. It is impossible to document which tribes were descended from old or new or intermixed inhabitants, though that must have been one of the functions of the great interest in genealogy.

Pottery remains from this period are very few. We have nothing which documents the religious response to reality—nothing, that is, except the 'epic interlude': the unsurpassed poetry of Homer, regarded by many later Greeks almost as sacred scripture.

The epic language is peculiar in that it was apparently not a spoken dialect, nor equivalent to any of the historic dialects found in inscriptions or subsequent literature. It was, however, designed to be recited.

The nearly 28,000 lines of Homer which form the *Odyssey* and the slightly longer *Iliad*, constitute the surviving bulk of this epic form with its strict metre.

The Homeric gods

The gods are portrayed in essentially human terms, but they do not grow old, and they are immortal. The gods have power (*daimon*) to change their appearance, size and attributes beyond the bounds of the human form they may take.

Their awesome status causes man to feel dread, fear, shame, or reverence. In response man feels impelled to pray, to entreat, to praise, take an oath, make sacrifice of a victim, or pour out a libation of wine. Many of these activities can be tied quite naturally to daily domestic routine. The communication between god and man may be direct or via an intermediary (including the god in disguise as human friend), or by a dream. The gods may be consulted through an agent accomplished in the art of divining, most commonly through birds or the interpretation of dreams. Lightning, thunder or falling stars may also serve as omens. And places where there was an oracle, such as Dodona with its great oak-tree at which people list ened for the voice of Zeus, played a lesser role.

Life in Homer takes on some specific burden which humans must bear, sometimes even the delusion with which the gods affect them. The human characters tend to explain the course of events as the destiny imposed by the gods—even if, as Helen says to Hector, 'so that hereafter we shall be made into things of song for the men of the future'. With gifts and prayers these gods may be implored to change the situation. The god might sometimes do so, or might merely turn his head away in rejection. For these gods—even Zeus himself—are equally bound by fate. Whatever else may be granted, humans are not permitted to escape death, which is their final destiny. Within that framework all phenomena, religious as well as otherwise, are set. Although the gods manipulate human actions, they neither make nor change human nature.

The heroes

Heroes seek honour, glory and renown, believing that to obtain these is of much greater worth than life itself.

The burial of the dead is of great importance. They require that last honour, even though their souls go forth immediately to the underworld (Hades), lest they become the god's curse upon the living. In Homer, the funeral would seem to include cremation (if that of a warrior, dressed in his full armour) and some kind of interment of the burned remains accompanied by lamentations. A mound was heaped over the grave, with a stone indicating the dead man's profession.

Anger of the gods

The other side of heroic life is an overbearing, presumptuous pride, violence and transgression. Although it cannot be shown that in any final sense, other than death, recompense is required for sin, there nevertheless are hints at some larger levels of justice and decency which the gods love in preference to cruelty, or to excessive glorification over slain men. Since fate determines all, the anger of the gods, like the anger of men towards one another, must work out its destined course. Yet their full destructive anger may be averted by means of prayer, libation (a poured-out drink offering), and sacrifice. The gods may be offended by perverse judgements, refusal or neglect of funeral rites, brutal conduct in a host's home, and murder of a guest. Ultimately, the values of the society are vindicated by the gods.

The writings of Hesiod

Hesiod's *Theogony* does not provide us with much insight into religious belief. Much of *Works and Days* provides specific seasonal information concerning work, especially agricultural, which needs to be done. Similarly, much concerns the ritual for domestic necessities, or the omen-like significance of days in the month. Pithy words of wisdom and matters of general behaviour constitute the basic ingredients of the rest, with several famous parables as illustration. The poem concludes: 'But that man is fortunate and blessed who, knowing all these matters, simply works, blameless towards immortals, watching all bird-signs, and avoiding wrong-doing.' The path of religious duty is not neglecting what ought to be done, and avoiding what ought not to be done.

Temple and city-state

The Mycenaean age ended in destructive violence brought about by human efforts around 1100 BC and, with it, not only palace and palace art but also the Linear B script pass into obscurity. The archaic phase of classical Greece opens on a new world with the coming of alphabetic writing. The fundamental factor is a devastating decline in total population. Whereas some 320 inhabited sites are known from the thirteenth century BC, many of them large centres, only forty are known from the eleventh century, and all of these are small.

What remained intact through that major alteration, was a legacy of technology in the mundane matters of mixed farming, building, carpentry, boat-building, spinning, weaving, pottery and metallurgy. The simultaneous shift from bronze to iron carried with it the 'hateful strife of evil war', rather than healthy competition among hard-working neighbours.

Greece was divided among the Hellenes into at least twelve separate regions, and the Greek language into five major linguistic blocks. It is not surprising that Greece consisted ultimately of no fewer than 158 independent city-states. Most were quite small (some fifty to a hundred square miles on average), and were incapable of sustaining a total population above 10,000. By colonial expansion even more city-states were founded throughout the greater Mediterranean basin.

Their history is one of warring states achieving from time to time a truce which enabled them to translate their hostility into competitive athletics at the four great Panhellenic festivals. According to tradition, the Olympic games began in 776 BC. The Pythian, Isthmian and Nemean games began not more than two centuries later. On the Anatolian side of the Aegean, the Panionian festival dedicated to Poseidon was celebrated by another cluster of twelve Greek city-states, just as Attic Greeks combined annually for the Panathenaia dedicated to the goddess Athena, patroness of Athens, on her birthday.

Festivals required proper facilities. In the earlier era separate 'houses for cult images' did not exist. When separate temples were invented after the catastrophic transition, three sources were drawn on: the oval country hut, the throne and hearth chamber abstracted from the Mycenaean palace, and the elongated house of rulers of the period 900–700 BC. The first type has as its example the earliest known temple, dedicated to Hera Akraia at Perachora, built by the beginning of the eighth century BC.

By the sixth century BC, to use Lewis Mumford's words, 'a new god had captured the Acropolis, and had, by an imperceptible passage, merged with the original deity'. What he had in mind was the city (*polis*) itself. Just as ordinary men insinuated themselves by warfare into the political life, so the city assembly (*ekklesia*) insinuated itself into what religious structure was still considered relevant. This humanizing transition is evidenced by the development in sculpture of the perfected human form, as well as by contemporary inscriptions and decrees.

Yet several major groups remained outside the pale of citizenship-participation: the children, the large cluster of slaves descended from suppressed indigenous inhabitants or taken captive in war, and also the resident aliens.

This means that not more than one fifth of the total population in fact functioned politically, and hence religiously. Those who were excluded from the official cult of the city sought an alternative expression of their religious nature.

Official city religion is clearly manifest in the very layout and architecture of the city. The lofty citadel (*acropolis*) which had been the Mycenaean fortress and palatial residence was now abandoned—left for the gods alone. The new city lies within the plains whose agriculture supports its economy. The centre of life is the market-place (*agora*), whose purpose reveals that economics is central to this renewed urban life, and whose architecture reflects the necessity for public access. Although public inscriptions bear witness of dedication and piety to the official religion, no gods dwell there. At some distance from the city centre, or perhaps on the old *acropolis*, decorative and elaborate temples were created and maintained, with more than a hint that a major function was as treasury for the wealth of the city.

The growth of temples typifies this new era of the growth of the city-state and of law and order. The decorative arts were used to portray mythical events that expressed this sense of order. Victory over the great uncivilized forces was personified in the victory of lapiths against centaurs, or of their legendary ancestors against amazons. The final form of Greek mythology is the end product of the creative formation of the Greek city-states. Their nature is also reflected in the temple architecture with its basic patterns or 'orders'.

At the individual level of society, from the Geometric period onwards come marker-stones (*stela*), especially those set up at graves. Thus names and titles, genealogies and deeds enter into history. Objects of all kinds were dedicated to the gods, but the funeral *stele* is fully human.

Temple styles

The history of temple styles is summarized in three successive 'orders': Doric, Ionic and Corinthian. The columns of these orders are increasingly elaborate and more highly embellished. As Gisela Richter has stated: 'A central hall was provided with a columned porch, practically always in front and often also at the back; pilasters terminated the side walls of the central hall. Rows of columns were placed in front, at the back, and sometimes all around to form a colonnade; occasionally col-

umns were added also in the interior to support the roof.' The pitched roof created triangular space at each end, the pediment, which came to be decorated often with a central mythological theme for the particular temple.

Even the largest temples are quite small: few exceed thirty metres (one hundred feet) in over-all width, nor much more than twice that in length. The inner hall, being open only in one direction, could not have allowed easy access to many people at once. Clearly the major purpose was to provide a space for the great statue of the god who was worshipped.

Painting and sculpture

Vase-painting styles developed from the earlier black-figure to red-figure techniques. Athenian examples dominate both varieties. Some shapes in the black-figure style were exclusively intended for ritual use: as grave-offerings, or for other uses at funerals, or for use in marriage ceremonies.

Although the illustration focussed

Greek architecture flourished in the sixth century BC. This temple at Hatra is exceptionally well preserved.

'I am Demeter the
honoured, the
greatest benefit and
joy to undying gods
and to mortals. But
come now, let all the
people build me a
great temple and
beneath it an altar
under the steep walls
of the city, above
Kallikhoron, on the
rising hill. I myself
shall introduce rites
so that later You may
propitiate my mind
by their right
performance.'

Homeric *Hymn to
Demeter* 268–274

on a god or myth, that is no guarantee of explicit religiousness. The world of vase-painting is basically secular, reflecting the structure of the city-state. Yet, as well as maenads—the ecstatic female followers of Dionysus—with their attendant satyrs, with the onset of the red-figure phase, women of all sorts, increasingly in domestic scenes, are more often portrayed.

Temples are rare in these paintings; but altars with sacrifice are often shown. The deities invoked are rarely to be seen, and the attendants cannot be distinguished from those in domestic life. Since there was no explicit ceremony, marriage processionals indicate that event. Funerals show chiefly the laying out of the body, the women mourning—only the men approaching in ritual gesture. The strange phenomenon of the *herm*—that human-headed, otherwise unhewn pillar, in the form of an erect penis, which stood everywhere throughout the city, outside the doors of ordinary houses—is illustrated in scenes beginning with its carving to the perfunctory act of worship made by passers-by. Similarly, the phallus-bearing celebrants in some revelry, often dedicated to Dionysus, are commonplace. Erotic scenes, both hetero- and homosexual, were considered appropriate subjects even on votive and funeral plaques.

The Greek world-view

Although the fifth century BC has often been interpreted as a crucial age for human civilization, its achievements were built on the whole period from the time of Homer. The boundary is not only the turn of a century, but the life and death of one man, Socrates (469–399 BC).

Before Socrates it was thought that all things were made out of one or more of the four basic ingredients: air, earth, fire and water. The one fully preserved example of pre-Socratic cultural inquiry is Herodotus (about 490–430), who divided the known world into five intellectual components. The Greek was set over against the Egyptian, Libyan, Scythian and Persian, collectively considered as 'barbarian'—that is, incapable of Greek language and hence of civilized Greek thought. Pre-Socratic understanding turned on the assumed relationship between nature and custom, but this broke down in the crisis which accompanied the destructive half-century of war among the Greek city-states.

The literary response to the Peloponnesian war is provided by two groups of Athenian writings. The first consists of plays, cast in metrical poetry. These portray the actions of the gods in relation to men, especially in the growing horror of a world at war. Beginning with the self-esteem which all Greeks shared from their common resistance to the Persian invasions, all the cherished assumptions of Greek society were questioned by Aeschylus (525–456), Sophocles (497–405) and Euripides (485–406), as Athens, whose democracy had become imperialistic in regard to its allies, struggled with Sparta, whose militaristic regime championed the freedom of the other city-states.

The second (prose) grouping came to be called 'Sophist'. They taught rhetoric, 'the art of persuasion'. The major surviving fifth-century author in whose work these ingredients are found is Thucydides (about 455–400).

Both analyses, poetic and prose, arrive at the role of the irrational in human affairs, and particularly in power politics. For in both Thucydides and Euripides, we are introduced to the pathology of human nature under stress. Human affairs cannot ultimately be blamed on the gods, though perhaps some fortune or necessity controls the mysterious past which has produced the present disastrous situations at both the urban and the individual levels. When human nature is aroused to do something—anything—it is not possible to turn it aside, either by law or fear of punishment. Consequences cannot be anticipated. This somewhat sceptical approach was accompanied by a sense that the Olympian gods were remote—and scarcely model examples of ethical behaviour.

The Hellenistic world-state

The ridicule of the gods in the plays of Aristophanes (about 450–385) received no apparent criticism at the time, although dedications to the gods continued to be made in the state's official inscriptions. But after the defeat of Athens in the war, the trumped-up charges against Socrates were said to be: not acknowledging the gods worshipped by the state, and introducing new divinities or an educational atheism which served to corrupt the young men from their attitudes as good citizens.

It is less than clear what, in their own times, either Plato (about 429–347) or Aristotle (384–322) contributed to religious thought. Aristotle's treatise format has a greater precision than Plato's dialogues. His discussion of fundamental substance as the basic constituent of reality served the growing sense of the nature of God, so that *Metaphysics* contains reference to the 'unmoved-mover'—God—as First Cause.

By the fifth century there was an unprecedented enlargement of religious vocabulary. From Herodotus comes a word for 'religious observance', almost 'religion' itself, and a verb 'to observe religiously' or to worship, to *do* religion. In contrast, by the time of Theophrastos (371–287), a word was in common use whose meaning, 'fear of' or 'reverence for' divinity, already had such negative overtones that it could designate the 'superstitious' man. Interestingly, the era produced no words for 'believing in' gods.

Rulers who became gods

Hellenization was taking place even before the advent of Alexander the Great (356–323), though it was his conquest of the vast Persian Empire in the east which brought the process to fruition. Alexander founded some seventy cities on the Greek pattern, mostly named after himself, 'Alexandria'. With easy transport and communication within the empire, Greek being the common language, Hellenization opened up the Mediterranean world to Eastern influences, including religious beliefs. This era was one of conspicuous luxury among the rich and powerful, while inflated prices and lower wages were the lot of the poor.

At the very top of the society were the Hellenized rulers, who declared themselves to be divine. Alexander, whose heroic deeds could not be doubted, was believed to have been received among the gods on his death, like Heracles before him. This soon degenerated into automatic deification for the king.

Even the Athenians, in response to their 'liberation' in 307 BC by the Macedonian king, Demetrios Poliorketes (336–283; 'sacker of cities'), hailed him Saviour and Benefactor, incorporating him and his father into the city-cult, with an annually-elected priesthood whose name was placed at the head of their decrees and contracts.

In a hymn by Duris of Samos (about 340–260), this 'liberating' Demetrios could be integrated with Demeter and her local solemn processional 'mysteries', identified with the offspring of Poseidon (the mightiest of the gods) and Aphrodite, and even prayed to under the assurance that while: 'the other gods are either far away or have no ears, or are not, or pay not the slightest heed to us; you we see face to face, not in wood and not in stone, but verily and in truth'!

Mysteries and healing cults

The specific technical term 'the mysteries' first occurs in Herodotus and the tragedians, though their usage had clearly grown out of urban ceremonial and temple festivals. It is amazing that 'the mysteries' were successfully kept such a close-lipped secret by all who referred to them, whether initiates or not. By Hellenistic times, however, the process of initiation was open to all Greek-speaking people not ritually impure who could afford the initiation fee.

Ultimately, *the* mysteries, meaning those primarily of Eleusis near Athens (commonly called 'Greater') must be said to lie in the initiate to whom something real is revealed, rather than in the ritual act or paraphernalia. The total complex included: 'things said', 'things shown' and 'things performed'.

Initiation promised happiness, perhaps simply in a glorious vision of the god. Although at first no particular good life was implied beyond death, the mystery religions were highly syncretistic and tended to absorb Eastern myths which hinted that this happiness continued into an afterlife, perhaps by a unification with the gods or by a deification of the human. But no kind of group association followed, and no moral demands were required for this bliss—except purity at the cult and silence ever after on 'the mysteries'.

The mythological and ritual complex at Eleusis, involving the goddess Demeter and her daughter, was tied to cereal grain. The processional and festival celebration, which was the context for initiation, took place in September–October—the ploughing season. Unlike other Greek temples, the one at Eleusis was meant for a large gathering and could hold up to 10,000 people.

Another cult, involving Dionysus, was tied to wine-making. Celebration of the country Dionysia began with the picking of the grapes and the initial pressing. The following month, festivities shifted to the sanctuary within the city. During the classical period, comedies ('revelling songs') could be performed there and then. By late winter, the wine in vats had clarified and the sediments had

Delphi was the site of the most important Greek oracle. The oracles were generally consulted on personal matters.

settled. In early spring came the ceremony at which the new wine was first tasted, offered to the god, then consumed by officiants from a sanctuary in the marshes.

The city Dionysia was celebrated in March–April. It shows a toning-down under urban control of the excesses of the rural activities, though phallic processions out from the walls to a shrine used only once a year, then back into Athens, remained an ingredient. This was the season for the complex cycles of plays—three tragedies and a satyr-play, as well as another series of comedies.

The word of the god

Herodotus tells us that the most ancient oracular site in all Greece, and the only one in his time, was that at Dodona with its great oak-tree. Preserved inscriptions of questions asked of the oracle at Dodona reveal concern for health, including successful pregnancies. There were also oracles in Amphiaraus and Trophonius. In each case some kind of earth-fault or warm spring provide the context for belief in a divine presence and a cultic sacrifice. After this the inquirer, sleeping at the spot, received by dream an appropriate response to his inquiry. Individuals brought their own private concerns; officials consulted about matters of state.

A vase-painting of the famous oracle at Delphi shows the priestess (called the Pythia) without mystery, as a woman seated on a tripod. The 615 responses known from Delphi are made up of contemporary enquiries and those which are set in Homeric times but recalled by later writers. The contemporary enquiries relate mainly to matters of worship, law, custom or sacrifice. The latter relate to personal affairs whose fulfilment is usually neither explicitly religious nor political. The oracles were chiefly designed to give simple commands on religious matters. Their use by states in matters of political importance was rare. Individuals were chiefly concerned for healing or good fortune.

Divine healing: Asclepios

The temple-cult of Asclepios, the god of healing, was set up principally in times of great need, expecially by city-states threatened by disease. It thrived because rich people who were healed rewarded the cult with wealth, though payment was not required from the poor. It became the most widespread of all the newer cults, with important centres at Pergamon and Corinth as well as Epidauros and Kos.

Apart from the environment of cleanliness and pure air, a combination of exercise, cold baths, rest, herbal prescriptions and diet were employed, along with dreams induced by suggestion. The god was believed to visit the supplicant as he slept.

The rites at Samothrace were open to men and women, children, slave and free. There were both public and private aspects. Initiation took candidates through several levels. The first stage was performed in the *anaktoron*, divided into a main hall, which even the uninitiated could enter, plus an inner sanctum. The higher stage was performed in a separate building, the *hieron*. This was an assembly hall, with benches along the side wall for spectators. An inscription at the entrance in Greek and Latin proclaimed 'the uninitiated may not enter here'. Initiates undressed and, as shown in a relief of Demeter pouring water over a naked man, underwent a ritual bathing, before receiving a purple garment. The initiate proceeded to the central area of the hall, and pledged ultimate secrecy before a sacred hearth on which small animals were offered.

At a much later (Roman) stage, in the second century AD, the structure underwent remodelling to accompany a dramatic change in the ceremonies. The apse was restructured so that one could descend into a crypt beneath. The space above was separated from that below by a grating. Over this a bull or goat was slaughtered, so that the one beneath—initiate or priest—was drenched in its blood.

The great Roman goddess Juno was associated with women, the moon and hunting. She was often identified with the Greek goddess Hera.

Mars was the Roman god of war, first in importance after Jupiter.

The Gods of Ancient Greece and Rome

The ancient Greeks had a very precise understanding of their gods, including their family histories and their characters. The gods lived on Mt Olympus, ruled by Zeus. The gods of ancient Rome, by contrast, were not clearly defined. But when the Romans conquered Greece, they took over the Greek gods, giving them new names and identifying them with their own gods.

Greek name
    Roman name

ARES
    MARS

The violent and quarrelsome god of war.

APHRODITE
    VENUS

The goddess of love, beauty and fertility.

APOLLO

The god of flocks and herds, archery, music, prophecy and medicine. As Phoebus, 'the bright one', he was also the sun-god.

ARTEMIS
    DIANA

The goddess of hunting, fertility and childbirth.

ASCLEPIOS
    AESCULAPIUS

The god of healing. His staff coiled with snakes is still the symbol of medicine.

ATHENA
    MINERVA

The goddess of war and handicrafts.

Neptune, the Roman god of the sea, was identified with the Greek god Poseidon.

Mercury, the equivalent of the Greek Hermes, was god of trade and merchandise and also messenger of the other gods.

Greek name
Roman name

DEMETER
CERES
The goddess of corn and crops.

DIONYSUS
BACCHUS
Associated with the underworld, and with crops, fruit and wine. Worship of Dionysus involved ecstatic dances and orgies.

HEPHAESTUS
VULCAN
The god of fire, especially volcanoes and the blacksmith's forge. Also patron of crafts.

HERA
JUNO
Wife of Zeus. The patroness of marriage, childbirth and women.

HERMES
MERCURY
The messenger of the gods. Also god of merchants and traders.

HESTIA
VESTA
The goddess of the hearth, the home and the family. Also the goddess of the city of Rome.

POSEIDON
NEPTUNE
First called the 'earthshaker', the causer of earthquakes, but later identified as god of the sea.

ZEUS
JUPITER
The father of gods and men, though not the creator-god. Also god of the sky and weather.

Syncretism in Egypt

Two cults from Egypt provide an interesting illustration of further syncretism with the Ancient Near East. The cult of Serapis was created in Egypt under the Ptolemies as an intentional fusion of the Greek mysteries with the native Egyptian cult of Osiris, a funerary deity. The name itself was a compound of Osiris and Apis, the sacred bull. Serapis became a manifestation of the one god. Attached to his cult-centres were functionaries who proclaimed the power and mighty deeds of the god.

The second cult is that of Isis, originally the personification of the pharaoh's throne. In the ancient myth she became important as the king's divine mother in whose lap he sat, a 'madonna-and-child' image. She also became associated with the royal succession myth of Osiris and Horus, in which she was a deliverer.

Under the impact of Hellenistic syncretism these two cults of Isis and Serapis may be brought together. These deities had the power of deliverance from war, prison, pain, wandering, shipwreck, even death; and were believed to guide mankind, for they saw the manifold deeds of both the wicked and the just. They were expected to grant to the righteous, where such righteousness is individual virtue, appropriate sacrifice, and a share of blessings received.

The Western enigma

As the Greek world entered the Iron Age, the loosely-knit Etruscan confederation of twelve fortified cities in north-west Italy shared a Late Bronze culture. The Etruscans imitated both Greek vases and Near Eastern bronzes, and blended their themes. Greek and Eastern gods and myths were also absorbed and blended.

The Etruscans, like the Greeks, adapted the Semitic alphabet for inscriptions, notably on tombs. The later Roman tradition, with access to Etruscan religious writings now lost, credited the Etruscans with being 'a people who above all others were distinguished by their devotion to religious practices'.

'Go proclaim to the Romans it is heaven's will that my Rome shall be capital of the world; accordingly they must cherish soldierliness, and they must be assured, and transmit to posterity the assurance, that no human power can withstand Roman arms.'

Romulus in *Livius* 1.16

The Roman Republican expansion

Rome—the beginnings

Historically, the event which marked the beginning of actual Roman achievement was the sacking of the city of Rome in 387 BC by those same marauding Gauls who helped eliminate the Etruscans. Until then the central Mediterranean had suffered rivalry among the Greeks of Magna Graecia in southern Italy, the Phoenicians centred on Carthage, and the Etruscans. The conflict focussed on Sicily. It was the disruption of this balance of power which permitted Rome to move swiftly, deploying the sword, founding colonies and building roads, to bring all Italy south of the Po under their rule within a century.

The extension of Roman citizenship to the conquered peoples redefined the relation between old adversaries. A new world power was created, charged with the religious spirit of *Roma*. To the original twelve Etruscan and thirty Latin cities, this expansion added a further 350 towns south of the Apennines and another eighty in the Po Valley, all under the dominion of Rome.

The historical character of Rome, which took shape in the centuries between the two sackings of the city—by Gauls in 387 BC and by Goths in AD 410—is best described on two levels: the social institutions on which the structure of urban life rests, and the buildings, known to archaeology, in which the structure was contained. At the first level the focus of attention is on the army, the law, the populace and the religion. The architectural needs of each caused the city's buildings to be erected. Nothing was planned, it simply grew.

Religion of hearth and field and city

Just as the myth of Rome as *the* city of cities was to dominate the political aspect of Roman self-understanding, so the myth of their own religiousness was to dominate their personal and cultic insights. Cicero (106–43) put it clearly: 'If we compare ourselves with other peoples, in various things we appear equal or even inferior, except that of religion, meaning the worship of the gods, in which we are by far superior.' 'Religion' (*religio*) is a Latin concept; there was no exact equivalent in Greek.

Latin authors could speak of a person as having a 'religious nature free of superstition'; or affirm that 'it is proper to be religious but not to be superstitious', contrasting the positive and negative elements of belief. On the other hand, the late Republic came to be sceptical of older religious forms still practised. Authors, with the bondage of religious duties in mind, could affirm that religion is that from which the soul (Lucretius), or oneself and one's household (Livius), ought to be freed.

The documented evidence provides little knowledge of early Roman domestic religion. The structure of the laws, especially those relating to women and marriage, children and inheritance, bears out the links of household and hearth, with paternal domination expressed in religious custom and ritual. The 'Twelve Tables', the oldest law code, are strictly civil.

To the Romans, gods were functions. Irrespective of what myths might have been attached to a particular deity, the Roman concern was to assign the precise office, so that the office rather than the older personification received appropriate worship. Agricultural deities could simply define the basic processes: Vervactor (first ploughing, or digging up stubble), Redarator (second ploughing), Imporcitor (cross-ploughing), Insitor (seeding), Obarator (covering of seeds), Occator (harrowing), Sarritor (hoeing), Subruncinator (weeding), Messor (harvesting), Convector (transporting), Conditor (storing), Promitor (utilizing). In a similar vein the ancient 'Calendar of Numa' details the days of each month on which business or assemblies might (or might not) be conducted, as well as the great variety of festivals.

The houses at Pompei, buried following the erruption of Vesuvius in AD 79 show vividly the domestic, social and religious life of a Roman city.

The gods in their temples were attended by their own priests. The ordinary people had little to do with them except at religious festivals, when animals would be brought as sacrifices.

The communal religion was related to the basic agricultural economy, and so was dependent upon the Etruscans and others, for Rome developed too late to foster more than the mythology of her own creation. This religion was primarily that of the state, with the city personified as the chief deity. The Romans were aware of the need to accept some foreign gods, especially Greek, into their state-cult, and they modified these deities to fit their functional need. Livius (59 BC–AD 17) claims that the first celebration in Rome of a public offering of a sacred meal to images of Greek deities placed on couches (*lectisternium*) took place in 399 BC. To justify the adoption of foreign gods, the Romans claimed to confuse foreign deities with their own.

Three of the oldest deities—Jupiter, Juno and Minerva—were worshipped in an impressively large temple on the Capitoline hill. They are thus known as the 'Capitoline Triad'. The temple was dedicated to Jupiter the Best and Greatest (*Jupiter Optimus Maximus*): his was the central hall of worship, flanked by those of Juno and Minerva to the right and left.

Other deities followed in the remaining centuries BC in response to various communal needs or crises, such as the cult of Aesculapius (Greek Asclepios) to overcome pestilence in 293–291, or that of the Cybele to counteract Hannibal's military threat in 204. At the turn of the era, Augustus (63 BC–AD 14) could still be described as one who 'treated with great respect such foreign rites as were ancient and well-established, but held the rest in contempt'. That distinction of old versus new in matters of religion was characteristic. Conservatism was maintained by the high priest, *pontifex maximus*; openmindedness was fostered by the *viri sacris faciundis*, religious officials who were responsible for the introduction of a new idea precisely when it was most appropriate.

Foreign elements could be brought into Rome; and equally, those already present might be suppressed or

Beliefs and philosophy

driven out. Hence the official Senate decree of 7 October, 186 BC, which severely limited the celebrations of the Bacchanalia and the number of its followers. This applied not only to Rome but also to its allies, and arose from the supposed threat of societies which meet in secret or conduct secret rites.

Among legitimate groupings within Rome were various associations of pontiffs, augurs and auspices; flamens or special priests for individual gods; and the vestal virgins.

If we explore the relation of domestic with communal religion in Rome, the observation made as early as 1911 by W.W. Fowler remains most pertinent: 'In no other ancient State that we know of did the citizen so entirely resign the regulation of all his dealings with the State's gods to the constituted authorities set over him. His obligatory part in the religious ritual of the State was simply *nil*, and all his religious duty on days of religious importance was to abstain from civil business and to make no disturbance.'

Beliefs and philosophy

Marcus Tullius Cicero wrote *On the Nature of the Gods* in 45 BC in the form of a dialogue among several of the intellectual positions of his day: Sceptic, Epicurean and Stoic. Two important traditions are absent: the Peripatetic (if the Stoics were really different from Aristotle as he was by then understood) and the Cynic position which was merely described.

The importance of the various positions lies simply in the fact that religion until then had no explicit intellectual content. It hinged exclusively on ritual: right doing, not right thinking, and certainly not yet right believing. For until the first century

'... there are many things in philosophy which have not yet been satisfactorily explained, particularly that most obscure and most difficult question concerning the nature of the gods, which is so extremely important both for a knowledge of the human soul and also for the regulation of religion.'

Cicero, *The Nature of the Gods* 1.1

The Romans used charms to ward off evil. These bronze hands are covered with magic symbols.

The later Roman emperors were considered to be divine. This cameo shows the Emperor Augustus being crowned as he sits beside the goddess Roma.

BC the vocabulary of belief was hardly coined. The value of this practical religion can be quite bluntly stated: 'Men describe Jupiter as best and greatest not because he makes us just or temperate or wise, but because he makes us healthy, rich and prosperous.'

For the relatively few who were caught up in the discussion or could read, or for the larger audience to whom the philosophical views were preached by itinerants, there began that transformation by which religion came to mean an intellectual consideration of god, gods and the world. The several philosophies ask essentially three questions: 'What is the nature of the world?' 'How do I know the world?' 'How am I to live in the world?' Although theologically they produced different systems in response, they began with similar assumptions in answer to these questions:

● Matter is the sole reality.
● Senses are the sole source of knowledge.
● Being untroubled and undisturbed

is the nature of happiness or pleasure.

The Epicurean position was that gods exist but they have no concern for the world. The Stoic position was that the world is ruled by a divine rationality (*logos*), manifest as fate and providence, and closely related to human reason. Scepticism was a by-product of the Platonic Academy, sharing in the common assumptions. Its appeal was to the one who 'suspends judgement about things that are either good or bad by nature, or that are to be practised or not practised, and in so doing he resists the dogmatic tendency and follows without strong convictions either way the observances of everyday life', achieving thereby the desired untroubled state. Cynics are 'dog-like' (*kunikos*) because they substitute for a system a way of life blatantly rejecting all imposed values. They identified the ideal life with that of nature. Taking nothing but the beggar's knapsack and staff, delighting in flouting all standards of decency, they wandered about with a minimum of food or shelter, though often functioning as missionaries by preaching on the street corners.

Empire—
the Roman world

When Vergil (70–19 BC) wrote the *Aeneid* to honour the emperor Augustus by linking him with Rome's past, Augustus not only restored the hut of Romulus, but—with due conservative propriety and patience—absorbed into himself the whole religious tradition of the city by assuming the office of high priest. A temple of Roma and Augustus at Ostia expresses the result. Throughout the time of the empire, even the older gods of the state cult, with the exception of the major deities—Jupiter, Juno and Minerva—gave way to the increasingly dominant cult of the imperial house.

Deification Roman style

Republican Rome, even with its dictators, had avoided constitutionally the absolute rule of Hellenistic kings. A precedent was set by the Roman Senate on the assassination of Julius Caesar in 44 BC, when he was enrolled among the gods. The deification of his successor, Augustus, had been demanded in parts of the empire, especially in the east, while Augustus was still alive, and divine honours were accorded him in some places. Though the Senate's action in proclaiming Augustus divine followed the precedent, Tiberius (42 BC–AD 37), who succeeded him, stoutly resisted deification, and so much angered the Senate that he was not even acclaimed as a god upon his death. Thereafter, apart from Nero and the three unsuccessful military contenders for his position, all the early emperors received a place among the gods: even Gaius Caligula (AD 12–41), who had assumed it for himself while living, and Domitian (AD 51–96), who did likewise, though without reaffirmation by the Senate.

From the days of Augustus oaths of allegiance to the emperor were required from the Roman businessmen making money in the provinces. These show him as already

'son of a god' and express loyalty not only to him but 'to his children and descendants'. From the coronation of Caligula, the oath includes Augustus between 'Zeus the Saviour' and 'the holy Virgin of our city' (Athena Polias). Such oaths were engraved in bronze (at the oath-takers' expense) and mounted for all to see.

The religious mix of imperial Rome

The disastrous eruption of Vesuvius began on the morning of 24 August, AD 79, and by evening had buried the two flourishing cities of Pompeii and Herculaneum and the coastal resort of Stabiae. Martial asserted that 'even for gods this was going too far'. Many other cities of the ancient Mediterranean world have been destroyed and buried, but none so completely preserved in the process.

The religious evidence from Pompeii is of two principal forms. There are buildings: both official buildings, innumerable domestic shrines and wayside altars. We also have works of art, especially frescos, and inscriptions of all sorts, including graffiti and even papyri.

Family cults flourished. Nearly every house and workshop had its private shrine (*lararium*), normally housing busts of ancestors and other traditional household gods (the *Lares* and *Penates*). The simple rites at these shrines were part of daily life and under the care of the paternal head of the household, and would have included rituals for important family events such as the coming of age of the heir. Many plaques and statues have been found, representing various minor deities—Faunus, Silvanus, Flora, Priapus and so on. They are largely concerned with fruitfulness and reproduction, plenty and gain. Wreaths of fruit, or horns of plenty (*cornucopiae*) were commonplace. So too was the phallus, either alone or gigantically displayed on a little deity, often with scales to weigh its fullness.

Official cults were more elaborate but their remains are fewer. Pompeii had ten temples, but three had been wrecked in the earlier earthquake of AD 62 and were still unrepaired at the

'It is hard to say whether the birthday of the most divine Caesar is more joyful or more advantageous; we may rightly regard it as like the beginning of all things, if not in the world of nature, yet in advantage. There is nothing that was decaying and declining to unfortunate state that he did not restore, and he gave a fresh appearance to the whole universe, which would have been content to accept its own ruin if there had not been born the universal blessing of all— Caesar Augustus. The birthday of the god was the beginning of the good news (*evangelion*) to the world on account of him.'

Roman Proconsul to Provincial Assembly of Asia, 9 BC

Secret Knowledge: the Gnostics

Edwin Yamauchi

The Gnostics were followers of a variety of religious movements in the early Christian centuries which stressed salvation through 'secret knowledge' (*gnosis*). We know about these movements, known as Gnosticism, through the writings of the church fathers of the second century, who viewed the various Gnostic groups as heretical perversions of Christianity.

Another source of information, though admittedly very late, is the writings from the Mandaeans. The Mandaeans, who live in present-day Iraq and Iran, are the sole surviving remnants of the ancient Gnostics.

In 1945 a priceless cache of twelve Coptic codices was found at Nag Hammadi in Upper Egypt. The collection, which was deposited about AD 400, contains fifty-three treatises, including both Christian and non-Christian Gnostic texts.

Pre-Christian Gnosticism

As a result of these discoveries, modern scholars see Gnosticism as a religious phenomenon which may have been quite independent of Christianity. There is as yet no clear agreement about when or how it originated.

In spite of the lack of clear and early evidences, some scholars, such as R. Bultmann, have assumed a pre-Christian origin of Gnosticism. Bultmann explained the Prologue to the Gospel of John as the revision of an originally Gnostic document. Such a reconstruction is extremely speculative.

The safest conclusion from the available evidence is that Gnosticism existed in rudimentary form at the end of the first century AD. It is altogether hazardous to read back the fully-developed Gnosticism of the second century AD into earlier texts.

Spirits and demons

In clearly Gnostic systems there is a sharp dualism—an opposition between a transcendent God and an ignorant 'demiurge' or creator (who is often a caricature of God in the Old Testament). The material creation is viewed as evil. Sparks of divinity, however, have been encapsulated in the bodies of certain 'spiritual' individuals destined for salvation.

These 'spiritual' persons are ignorant of their celestial origins. God sends down to them a redeemer, often a Christ who merely seems to be human, to bring them salvation in the form of *gnosis*. Thus awakened, the 'spiritual' escape from the prison of their bodies at death and traverse the planetary spheres of hostile demons to be reunited with God.

Since salvation is not dependent upon faith or works but upon the knowledge of one's 'spiritual' nature, some Gnostics indulged in extremely licentious behaviour. Most Gnostics, however, took a radically ascetic attitude towards sex and marriage, deeming the creation of woman the source of evil, and the procreation of children to be but the multiplication of souls in bondage to the powers of darkness.

The Mandaeans: Gnostic Survivors

Edwin Yamauchi

The 15,000 or more Mandaeans who live in southern Iraq and Iran are the sole surviving remnants of ancient Gnosticism. Their texts, which are written in an eastern Aramaic dialect known as Mandaic, are an important source of Gnostic teachings.

The oldest texts are lead amulets from about the third century AD, followed by magic bowls from about AD 600. The important religious manuscripts are not older than the sixteenth century, with most coming from the eighteenth and nineteenth centuries.

Knowledge of life

The most important work, the *Ginza*, relates the creation of the universe and the fate of the soul after death. The *Johannesbuch* reveals that the Mandaeans venerate John the Baptist. They regard Jesus, however, as a false prophet. The *Haran Gawaita* gives us a legendary account of their alleged migration from Palestine.

In their dualistic world-view, it is Ptahil who creates the world with the aid of the evil Ruha, 'Spirit'. Manda d-Haiye, 'Gnosis (Knowledge) of Life', reveals himself to man as an incarnation of three heavenly spirits (*uthras*). At death the soul of the Mandaean leaves behind his 'stinking' body and ascends to the world of light.

The Mandaeans observe elaborate rituals. The *masbuta* is a magically purifying rite of baptism. At death a sacramental meal (*masiqta*) is celebrated to assist the soul in its journey to the world of light. The Mandaeans have a highly-developed code of ethics, including a stress upon marriage and children which is quite unique among Gnostics.

Many scholars have argued for a pre-Christian origin of the Mandaeans from Palestine. The objective evidence, however, does not prove that Mandaeism existed earlier than the second century AD.

time of their burial. One had been converted to the use of a private association; two were dedicated to the imperial cult, one to the most recently enrolled member, Vespasian (AD 9–79), who died just one month before the eruption, and the other to Fortuna Augusta. Graffiti bear out the people's nonchalant attitude towards this cult: 'Augustus Caesar's mother was only a woman!' Of the remaining four temples, only that dedicated to the cult of triune Isis, her consort Serapis and their divine child Harpocrates showed the signs of prosperity coming from popular support. Wall-size frescos indicate the religious life within this sanctuary as conducted by its white-robed, shaven-headed priests.

Apart from the buildings designed for religious use, we have the houses of rich and poor, in which were displayed not only wealth and varying aesthetic taste and styles, but also frescos or mosaics of religious themes. The most important of these is the sixty-roomed 'Villa of the Mysteries': one room presents on three walls twenty-nine figures nearly life-size, subdivided into ten group scenes, acting out a complex Bacchic ritual. This was entirely a woman's rite. It is impossible to say what place this great house or its spectacular scene played within the religious life of the city—perhaps somewhere in between the few great temples and the numerous little shrines.

The preserved ruins of Ostia, the port of Rome, show a different array within this religious mix, including (by the third century AD) not less than fifteen Mithraea—shrines devoted to Mithras (see *Mithraism*).

Philosophical religion

Roman religion was thus a complex mixture from varied sources. Later in the third century AD the mix was to receive a more systematic treatment blending the religious and philosophical elements into a form of Neo-Platonism. Plotinus (205–269) was its founder, and Porphyry (232–305) his expositor. This revived Platonism was a blend of elements from the traditions of Plato himself, Pythagoras, Aristotle, and the Stoics. World-

mind, World-soul and Nature are the descending levels of reality between the Ultimate One, which is the ground of existence and the source of values, and Bare Matter. All these ingredients lie within human nature, whose purpose is to achieve unification in a kind of ecstatic union with the One. This rare union was believed to occur as a result of prolonged effort of the will and understanding. Plotinus makes little explicit reference to religious ritual or particular gods, though the writings of his followers do contain hymns to certain gods. The result is the philosophical equivalent of the 'mysteries'.

A crutch for a tottering state

Of the thirty-five Roman emperors from AD 192 to 284, only three reigned for more than ten years, and only one died a natural death. All the others died of unnatural causes at the hands of troops or counter-claimants, after a reign of less than a year in at least twelve cases. Consequently, few of these imperial figures lived long enough or died in such a way as to receive deification. Most of the emperors, even the stronger ones, preferred to rule under the aegis of some greater deity, since they had perceived that to be declared divine themselves hardly secured them a long life. The most important such god is Aurelianus' choice: *Sol Invictus*, the Unconquered Sun.

It was a mere matter of time before the one resilient religion would be imposed upon the state. This took place in the 'Edict of Milan' issued in 313, jointly by Licinius and Constantine. Christian worship, like any other, was allowed to take place freely; and the Christian church, alone among the competitive cults, was singled out for 'compensation from our benevolence'. It was its organization that gave it an edge over all alternatives, from the authorities' viewpoint, for Christianity, as Arnold Toynbee has said, 'was singular in building up for itself a world-wide administrative organization, instead of letting each local group of converts go its own way'.

'Hence it is that throughout wide empires, provinces, and towns, we see each people having its own individual rites and worshipping the local gods ... but the Romans one and all.'

Minucius Felix, *Octavius* 6.23

The end of antiquity

The remoulding of the Roman Empire as Christian in all senses took more than a century, though Theodosius I had proscribed other religions by AD 381. The old forms, however, lingered on in several ways. Initially 'pagan' (*paganus*) had meant a rural in contrast to an urban dweller, and Christianity had made little headway in the former environment before it became the state religion. By this later date, the term came to designate civilians in general, over against soldiers, and thus took on its 'religious' connotation.

Several remnants of the older religion survived for a while. The short-reigned Julian (361–363), a philosopher like Marcus Aurelius, was the last non-Christian emperor. Symmachus, as prefect of the city in 382, could address to the Western emperor Gratian a passionate plea, upon the removal of the altar of victory from the assembly hall of the Senate, not to terminate all those 'ancestral customs' which 'promote the status of the public worship which has proved an advantage to the state for so long a time'. Rome itself, however, was becoming less advantageous as the capital. Once it had proved vulnerable to Visigothic assault in 410, it was but a matter of time before the imperial government was withdrawn to a safer location.

The sacking of the city after 800 years precipitated a crisis of ideas for a state newly allied to the Christian religion. Augustine of Hippo (391–430) in his *City of God*, carefully sifted all the religiousness of the ancient city and its empire; what was worthwhile was baptized into Christ, the rest was to be put aside for ever. The city, now greatly reduced in dignity and size, became the Christian Rome. Its bishop became the sole remaining officer of rank when the imperial government of the West was transferred north to Ravenna, and then in 476 when the Western empire itself ceased to exist. Rome's change of hands is well illustrated when its bishop, Leo the Great, in office from 440 to 461, assumed the defunct urban title of *pontifex maximus* ('Supreme Pontiff'). The Christian church was the final successor to the ancient religion which was the city, and in such terms the primacy of the church at Rome came to be declared.

Faith of Light and Darkness: the Manichaeans

Edwin Yamauchi

Mani (AD 216–276), a Persian prophet born in Mesopotamia, established a dualistic religion which he claimed was the final, universal revelation.

The Prophet Mani

In 1970 the discovery of a tiny Greek parchment, the Cologne Codex, confirmed Arabic traditions that Mani was raised among the Elchasaites, a Jewish-Christian baptist group. When he was twenty-four, Mani spoke against the water baptisms of the Elchasaites and preached instead salvation by secret knowledge (*gnosis*).

Mani preached in Mesopotamia, Persia and even India. He enjoyed the patronage of Shapur I, a Sasanian (Persian) king. Shapur's son, Bahram I, however, persecuted Mani. After being bound in chains for twenty-six days, Mani died in prison.

Mani, who was a gifted painter, composed a picture-book to propagate his faith among the illiterate. He also wrote seven works, including *The Shapurakan*, dedicated to King Shapur, and *The Living Gospel*, which proclaimed Mani as the Paraclete foretold by Christ. Though we have but few of the earliest texts in Syriac and in Middle Persian, we have thousands of pages of Coptic Manichaean texts which were found in Egypt in 1930. Another later collection of Manichaean texts (eighth and ninth centuries AD) comes from Chinese Turkestan.

Light and Darkness

Mani taught that there were two independent principles, Light and Darkness. In the first epoch Light and Darkness were separate; in the second they were intermingled; and in this the final epoch they were to be separated once more.

Christ is sent to liberate the particles of light in men. Perfected Manichaeans must persevere through ascetic practices until death, when their particles of light will rise up in the Column of Glory (the Milky Way) to paradise.

The Manichaeans were sharply divided between an elite circle known as 'the chosen' (*electi*), and the mass of laymen known as 'hearers' (*auditores*). The 'hearers' lived the lives of ordinary citizens. They offered daily gifts of fruit, cucumbers and melons—which were believed to possess a great deal of light—to the elect.

The Manichaeans were zealous missionaries who carried their faith to Africa, to Europe and even to China. They posed a threat to the Christian church in the fourth century, and numbered among their 'hearers' Augustine before his conversion. They bequeathed some of their dualistic beliefs to heretical groups which flourished in Europe in the Middle Ages, such as the Paulicians, the Bogomils and the Albigenses.

The Old Gods: Religions of Northern Europe

Andrew Walls

The religion of the Northern peoples underlies all modern European life and thought. Northern Europe has been significant in Christian history for its peoples began to embrace the Christian faith in substantial numbers in a period when the faith was losing its hold in some other areas. But to much of the Northern world the faith came late and penetrated slowly. Gaul (modern France) and Spain, nearer to the early Christian Mediterranean heartlands, were long in seeing the rapid conversion movements that had marked those heartlands with their inheritance of Greek and Roman. In Britain the penetration was slower still; the adoption of Christianity by some Celtic peoples was speedily submerged under successive waves of Germanic newcomers.

Not until AD 960 was there a breakthrough in Denmark; later still in Norway, Iceland and Orkney; not until the early twelfth century in Sweden. And thoughts and ways associated with the old life remained for centuries—perhaps still remain—in uneasy tension with biblical religion. The ancient 'primal' religions of the West have been part of modern Europe's unconscious formation, and occasionally come to the surface—as when Nazi Germany artificially revived Teutonic mythology, and gave it a new meaning.

The Northern peoples

Two groups of Northern peoples who dominated the land north of the Mediterranean civilization concern us here, the Celtic and the Germanic. The original home of the Celtic peoples seems to have been in what is now Bavaria. By about 300 BC they had spread out eastward and westward in a vast arc from Ireland to Anatolia. Caesar's Gauls and, if not Paul's Galatians, then at least their neighbours, were Celtic. Successive migrations covered the British Isles. Roman power conquered many of these tribes, and assimilated them in varying degrees to Roman culture; others remained untouched.

The 2,000-year-old 'Tollund man' was discovered in a peat bog in Denmark. He had been ritually strangled, probably as a sacrifice to the goddess of fertility.

Race and language

For centuries Celtic pressure kept the
Germanic peoples to Northern lands.
Romans, indeed, were often somewhat hazy as to the distinction between these barbarian peoples. But as
Roman power declined, that of the
various Germanic peoples increased,
and the Dark Ages saw their vast
expansion. Our concern lies especially with the peoples of Germany
(who expanded into Celtic Britain)
and those of Scandinavia, famous for
their enterprising voyages, their
settlements in harsh conditions
and their unquenchable predatory
instincts. In race, language and
the structure of their religion these
peoples were related, though we
know more details of the religion
of the Scandinavian than of the
German peoples.

Both the Celtic and the Germanic
complexes belonged to the Indo-
European language group, which
also includes Greek, Latin and Sanskrit; and some scholars (such as
Dumézil) have discerned a common
structure in the religion between
Celtic, Germanic, Roman, Greek,
old Persian and Vedic religion in
which godhead appears in threefold
form. However this may be in principle, the actual worship of one group
could strike another as strange and
exotic, as we know from Roman
accounts of Gauls and Germans.

Our knowledge, very fragmentary
and incomplete, comes from four
main sources:

Early writers

Writers such as Polybius, Caesar and
Tacitus give accounts for readers in
civilized Mediterranean lands of the
way of life of certain 'barbarian'
peoples who were or had been
Rome's enemies. They often write in
the manner of nineteenth-century
anthropological writers, their accent
on the quaintness of their subjects
tinged with some wistful admiration
for these 'noble savages'. Naturally
they tend to translate into terms they
think their readers will understand,
but from comparison with the other
sources they come out reasonably
well.

Myths and folk tales

Stories of the 'other-world' were preserved by oral tradition and written
down in the Christian period. The
Scandinavian myths, preserved in
Iceland (where Christianity was
established in AD 1000) by a writer of
genius, Snorri Sturluson (died in
1264), and reflected in other sagas
and poems (notably the vivid but
tantalizing *Voluspà*) give the fullest
account we have of the belief-system
of any ancient preliterate people; but
even here we must beware of taking
everything as of equal value or as
reflecting the same religious setting.

Some of the best-known stories,
such as the adventures of Thor, dressed as a bride trying to get his

*The splendid prow of
a Viking ship.*

hammer back, are probably not myths at all, but stories for entertainment belonging to a period when belief in the old gods was losing its hold: no one mocks the one who has the power of life and death. The rich Celtic literature is even harder to interpret, for the stories have been divorced from the original religious context altogether, and been preserved through a long period of Christian oral transmission, so that their religious significance has to be pieced together by hints and analogies and comparison.

Christian missionaries

Sometimes Christian writers tell us, usually incidentally, something of the old religion: its survival or its ways of thought. For instance, the correspondence of the English missionary Boniface (680–755) who worked in Frisia, or of the historian Bede writing when Christianity was the dominant faith in England, are full of hints—but only hints, for the Christian writers were rarely interested in the old religion for its own sake—indeed, it revolted them. Occasionally one gets an eyewitness description: most vividly, perhaps, that of Adam of Bremen of the old Swedish religion.

Archaeological finds

This source of material is constantly increasing, and has immensely deepened our knowledge of religious practice. It is, of course, notoriously hard to interpret with assurance, but can be effectively used in combination with the literary sources.

In assessing all the sources it must be remembered that we are dealing with a period of many centuries, and seeing much of that vast period through material collected still later. The religions of primal, preliterate societies have histories just as Christianity, Islam or Buddhism have—they change and develop, and appear in various guises. It is thus perilous to generalize from one place or period to another. This said, the degree of consistency across our fragmentary sources is remarkable.

The Celts: worshippers of the horned god

The history of the Celts before their contact with the Roman Empire is particularly obscure, and their religion hard to interpret. Celtic peculiarities mentioned by classical writers correspond with details revealed by archaeology, but may have been misunderstood. For instance, Lucian of Samosata, the satirist, describes an old man in skins leading adoring disciples by chains attached to his tongue. This was interpreted for him by a Hellenized Celt as representing the Herculean strength of eloquence; how does this connect with the Gaulish coins and Irish stories which depict chains from a head or mouth with severed heads attached?

Julius Caesar's account of the Gauls he fought (*Gallic War* 6.14) is based on personal acquaintance: but when he says that the Gauls worship Mercury above all gods, while keeping appropriate worship for Apollo, Mars, Jupiter and Minerva, we may suspect that he is imposing a framework he knew on something he did not fully understand.

The inscriptions in Britain and Gaul show Romanized expressions of Celtic religion: Celts who are using some of the language or images or divine names of the Romans, or perhaps Roman soldiers keeping on the right side of the local gods. The Irish and Welsh stories come from a still later period, when the old gods had been formally abandoned. It is clear, however, that some of the strange figures in the stories are in fact the old divine beings described in human form.

Local gods

As we have seen, Caesar assumed the Gallic Celts worshipped the same gods as the Romans, though under different names. 'Of these deities', he says, 'they have almost the same idea as all other nations.' Certainly some inscriptions show the imagery associated with the Roman gods Mercury, Mars and Silvanus. But while many divine names—Cocidius, Nodons, Braciaca and others—appear in in-

A Viking helmet from the Sutton Hoo treasure in Britain shows both the rich culture and the warlike nature of the northern peoples.

scriptions, no single name appears so consistently as to suggest his universal worship. Clearly local names were used at local shrines for deities associated particularly with those places. In Romanized areas these gods might be linked with the Roman deities whose functions theirs most nearly resembled.

Cernunnos: The Horned One

The most widely distributed Celtic divine symbol is of a god with horns. There are signs of an antlered god amongst the Bronze Age predecessors of the historic Celts, and in many parts of the Celtic world and in many periods one can find symbols of the stag, or a horned naked god with phallus erect (a common fertility symbol in many cultures), or a serpent with a ram's head. The symbols range from crude scrawls to the beautiful artistry of the Gundestrup bowl. One inscription seems to identify the antlered god as 'Cernunnos', perhaps meaning 'The Horned One'.

That the Horned One is a symbol of fertility is not open to doubt; but some of the Romanized inscriptions clearly make him also a warrior-god, a Celtic Mars. Such indications raise the question of whether the Celts 'departmentalized' the universe under different divinities, or whether their devotion tended to be directed to a divinity associated with a particular place or people, but manifesting himself in various ways as fertility or war predominated in their concerns.

The Horned One sometimes has a consort; and 'Earth Mothers' clearly played a part in worship. The forceful female figures of some of the Irish stories are doubtless memories of them—mysterious, vigorous, beautiful and consuming. They are often represented (and again the stories have similar features) in groups of three.

A High God

Did the Celts have a High God? No trace of such a cult can be found among the physical remains; yet a modern observer might visit hundreds of African peoples where the High God is recognized and see no material sign of his worship.

In the Irish stories concerning the mighty figure of Dagda one can trace, in reduced, humanized form, something of a great divinity of the past, who cannot be seen as simply a fertility or a warrior symbol. Yet the name is found only in the stories. Perhaps the stories of Dagda are a pointer to a more enlarged concept of divinity than one would receive from archaeology alone; and perhaps Celtic concepts were either more comprehensive or less tidy than Roman writers imagined.

Human sacrifice

Water-sources—wells and springs, and the sources of rivers necessary to fertility of the soil and the support of life—seem to have been favourite centres of Celtic worship, and shafts and pits found at such places were presumably used in sacrifice. Some elaborate pre-Roman structures have been found at Entremont and Roquepertuse, for instance, but in general early sanctuaries would have seen simple. In the Roman period temples on the Roman pattern occur, sometimes enclosing thermal springs. Several classical writers speak of Celtic worship being conducted in sacred groves.

The feature of Celtic religion that most impressed Roman writers was its violence and prevalence of human sacrifice. Possibly they exaggerated, as observers often exaggerate exotic features; none the less, there is plenty of other evidence in their favour.

The human head had a significance we cannot fully fathom. It is central to the great early sanctuaries at Entremont and Roquepertuse, the latter full of niches for heads, and the severed head is perhaps the most widespread feature in all Celtic imagery. Just a hint of what the head cult must have meant in the old religion is given in the Welsh *Mabinogion*, where the companions of Bendigeid Vran, having removed his head, enjoy eighty gloriously happy years, known as 'the Entertaining of the Noble Head', and 'it was not more irksome to them having the head with them than if Bendigeid Vran had been with them himself'.

Ancestor-cult is suggested both by the signs of worship at grave mounds and Caesar's insistence that the Gauls claim common descent from a deity, otherwise unattested, that he refers to as Dis Pater.

Life after death

The evidence of the graves with carefully-chosen grave goods points to some emphasis on the afterlife. Caesar speaks as though the Gauls believed in transmigration of souls. Some have thought that he simply means shape-changing, as practised by the shamans of the older peoples of Central Europe; but Irish stories such as that of the rebirth of Etain may suggest that Caesar's words should be taken seriously. At any rate, he had noted something about Celtic belief in the afterlife which to a Roman seemed strange.

The Druids

All the classical writers were impressed by the Druids, the Celtic religious functionaries. When Strabo speaks of them as students of moral philosophy he is probably idealizing: their role in sacrifice, divination and liturgy ('they commit to memory immense amounts of poetry', says Caesar) is better attested.

The possible links of Celtic tradition with that of Vedic India remain tantalizingly speculative. After the Christian triumph in Celtic lands residual beliefs were diverted, some local divinities became identified as evil spirits, some others, with their healing cults, perhaps being merged into Christian saints.

The Germanic peoples: mortal gods

The Roman historian Tacitus, about AD 98, describing the *Germani* of his day, is very conscious of the gulf between them and 'civilized man' in Roman society, but betrays envy of their vigour and simplicity. Like other Romans, he is most conscious of the militancy of the Germans, their proneness to battle, the constant flowing of blood; but he admires the austere family morality of a chaste and essentially monogamous people.

Like other Roman writers, he identifies the Germanic gods with what he assumes to be their Roman equivalents, and detects a triad of Mercury (the god most venerated), Mars and Hercules at the heart of Germanic devotion. He also notes the cult of a female deity, which he believes to be imported and identifies with that of Isis. Hercules is elaborately invoked before battle, and the war god presides over the administration of justice. With some surprise, Tacitus notes that it is the priests who prescribe the punishment of offenders.

Divination practices, he observes, are similar to the Roman, but include strange practices such as those associated with horses. And women have something of 'holiness and prophecy' about them which gives them some influence in German society, though he does not elaborate on this 'prophetic' function.

German deities

The triad noted by Tacitus was presumably Wotan, Tiwaz and Thor. The Germanic peoples were essentially polytheistic, and many divine names are known. Nevertheless, over the millennium and more which separates Tacitus from the Icelandic writer Snorri Sturluson and the observer of late Swedish paganism, Adam of Bremen, three, or sometimes four, divine names tend to be mentioned as though they summed up the Germanic divine world. Two

The richly-carved 'Franks casket' shows many scenes from Norse mythology. These are the three norns, who watered and tended Yggdrasil, the tree of life.

are constant: the divinity known by the Southern peoples as Wotan or Woden (whose name is perpetuated in the calendar as Wednesday) and by the Norse peoples as Odin; and the thunder-deity Thor, who has left his name as Thursday.

In early accounts Tiwaz (of Tuesday) the legislator divinity, is crucial, but in the Norse literature his successor Tyr plays a rather marginal part. There, however, the fertility-god Frey (of Friday), with or without his female counterpart Freyja, is very prominent.

According to Sturluson, there are two groups of divinities, of differing origins, once at war but now united: the Aesir (including Odin and Thor) and the Vanir (including Frey). While some have followed Sturluson in seeing this as having a basis in historical fact, an Aesir-worshipping people vanquishing a Vanir-worshipping people but adopting something of their religion, others see the tension between the active, intervening deities (Aesir) and the maintaining, reproductive deities (Vanir) as funda-mental to all Germanic, and perhaps all Indo-European, religion.

Aristocratic Odin

Norse religion, of which (thanks to Snorri and the other saga-tellers) we know a little more than we do of related peoples like the Saxons, varied according to social divisions and preoccupations. The active cult of Odin was for leaders and warriors, for the Viking in fact. Odin gives victory—but, fickle and capricious, he is as likely to take it away again. Through the Valkyries he collects heroes for his great hall, Valhalla, where the days are spent in battle and the nights in feasting. He has one eye (for he surrendered one for a single drink of the spring of wisdom and understanding); he hung nine days and nights from the world-tree Yggdrasil, to learn how to read the hidden runes. A whole complex of ideas—wisdom, poetry, heroic war-fare, shape-changing, strangulation, death—belong to him, and the grim stories of ritual killings by noose and spear suggest something of early

The most spectacular feat performed by the god Thor was his encounter with the Midgard serpent which encircles the earth. Thor attempted to catch it from a fishing-boat.

forms of devotion to him.

For other people dependent on agriculture the fertility cult of Frey could not be neglected. Adam of Bremen tells us of this deity's mighty phallic image at Uppsala about 1070.

The hammer of 'Black Thor'

The most widespread devotion of all would seem to belong to Thor. At Uppsala his throne stood between that of Odin and that of Frey; and in the late Northern paganism 'Black Thor (from the colour of his images?) was above all the enemy of the 'White Christ'. His sign, the hammer, was used in weddings and as a protective act, rather as Christians used the sign of the cross; and, as archaeology reveals, Christians took a cross to the grave, when traditional pagans took a hammer.

Thor, like the Vedic Indra, is a thunder-god, full of chaotic energy and boundless power. And if princely leaders saw Odin as their patron, the ordinary man was more likely to seek a friend in Thor.

In many stories Thor is associated with Loki, a strange, ambivalent trickster figure. It is Loki who secures by a trick the death of Odin's son Balder, the fairest of the gods. The Balder myth is beautiful, but there is little sign that he was worshipped.

The doom of the gods

Nor is there any sign of a High God. In the chaos of divine energy, the worshipper chooses the divinity most likely to favour him. The gods themselves will pass away—for at some time there will fall the day of Ragnarök, the doom of the gods, when each will fall in mortal combat, and earth and mankind will perish with them. Then a new heaven and earth will arise, and Balder return from the dead, and the male and female creatures sheltering in the world-tree will people the new world. In the end, Yggdrasil, the self-renewing world-tree, must be greater than Odin, the great god, who hung in its branches to gain its secrets.

The Norse Gods

Aesir

The great gods who lived in Asgard

Vanir

Lesser gods, formerly at war with the Aesir, but later reconciled.

ODIN/WODEN/WOTAN
Father of all the gods and 'father of the slain'. God of war, worshipped especially by leaders and warriors.

THOR
'The thunderer', depicted as a great giant with a hammer. The strongest of the gods. God of fertility.

BALDER
'The bright one', the most beautiful of the gods. Son of Odin and Freyja.

LOKI
A mischievous god, the father of monsters. He brought harm to the gods, especially by causing the death of Balder.

NJORD
Ruler of the wind and sea.

FREY
Ruler of the rain and sun. God of fertility. Son of Njord.

FREYJA/FRIGG
Goddess of love and fertility. Consort of Odin, sister of Frey.

HEIMDALL
'The white god', watchman of the gods.

Valkyries

Odin's war-maidens. They chose warriors who died in battle to be received into Valhalla, the favourite home of Odin.

Nomads of the Steppes

Åke Hultkrantz

Some 3,000 years ago the wide steppes of southern Russia were sparsely populated by Indo-European peoples: the Cimmerians west of the Caspian Sea, the Persians east of it. The northern Persians, or Scythians, developed into horse-riding nomads about this time or soon afterwards.

This had tremendous historical consequences. Not only did they, in the seventh century BC overrun the Cimmerian lands, so that their territory stretched from present-day Romania to Turkestan; they also opened communications between East and West, so that religious ideas and art forms ('animal style') streamed over the open steppes. Long after the disappearance of the Scythians, this road to China constituted a major link between Western (Christian) and Eastern religious ideas. The famous silk route (from the first century AD) partly followed the same way.

The Greek historian Herodotus (fifth century BC) gives some interesting information on Scythian religion. The foremost divinities were the Sky Father, Papa, married to Mother Earth, Api. Among other deities, all apparently heavenly beings, were the fire- and war-gods. There were no images of the gods, altars or temples. The gods received animal sacrifices, usually horses. They were strangled, and their meat cooked over a fire that was made on their bones. A piece of the meat was thrown into the fire.

They had a war-god who was represented by an iron sword raised on a heap of brushwood. To him were sacrificed cattle and horses in large numbers, as well as prisoners of war; their blood was poured over the god's sword. Herodotus also mentions diviners, who, however, were killed when they were unsuccessful.

When a king died his corpse was carried around on a wagon among the tribes of his domain, followed by his wives and servants in a long procession. He was finally buried in a wooden chamber together with several court servants (who were strangled), his horses and some golden bowls. An enormous earth mound was heaped over the burial place. The bereaved cleansed themselves by entering a tent filled with steam from hemp seeds that had been thrown on red-hot stones.

This is the first description we have of a religion of the horse nomads. Its essentials fit in rather well with what we know of later religions among equestrian pastoralists. The pattern of horse nomadism spread to the Mongol and Turko-Tataric tribes to the east of the Scythian area and on the plateaux of central Asia. Here the war-like religion of the plains joined the traditional hunting religions with master-of-the-animals concepts and shamanism, and formed a new type of religion.

The Mongols: a sense of wonder

A good illustration of this kind of religion is offered by the Mongols of central Asia. From tribal beginnings in north-eastern Asia they ousted the Turkish peoples of Mongolia and then built up an empire that stretched from the Amur River to the Volga and beyond—the greatest empire the world had seen (thirteenth and fourteenth centuries AD). Their primitive beginnings, nomadic way of life and stratified patriarchal society were all reflected in their religion.

Tengri

The supreme god was Tengri, a name by which both the god and the blue sky were designated. Prayers were directed to him by lone supplicants bowing down on mountain-tops, and juniper incense was burned in his honour. Like other nomadic high gods Tengri was not represented by pictures. He did not create the world. In all of central Asia the beginning of the world was referred to two creators, one a good spirit (but not Tengri), the other a devil. This story of creation was diffused from Europe to North America and was sometimes combined with the flood myth, sometimes with the myth of a primeval sea.

'Tengri' is, however, also a word for everything 'heavenly', wonderful or marvellous, and for ninety-nine tengri gods that in particular protect the herds. For instance, Ataga tengri gives luck in horse-breeding, another tengri protects the cows, still another the yaks. Manaqan tengri is the guardian of the wild game.

Landmarks like mountains, lakes and rivers were worshipped. In particular the mountains inspired great awe. Passes and mountain-tops were residences of spirits, and whoever passed by had to propitiate these spirits by throwing a stone on a pile of rocks, a so-called *obo*. The ground was sacred, and libations were poured out for Mother Earth.

Genghis Khan

Dead princes and tribal ancestors had their own shrines. Chingis Khan—better known as Genghis Khan—the mighty ruler of the Mongols (died AD 1227), was considered to be of heavenly descent. A statue representing him was raised on a wagon in the military camp, and horses were dedicated to him. Sometimes he was mentioned as Tengri himself, sometimes as a culture-hero who had initiated all cultural and religious institutions. Offerings were also given to other deceased great princes by their descendants: most often horses were impaled above their graves. The Mongols of the Golden Horde in southern Russia suspended horse skins upon poles over the graves of their great leaders.

At the entrance of their tents the Mongols placed house idols (*ongons*) to whom they offered milk. These *ongons* were made of felt.

There was a 'fire mother' to whom butter was offered regularly. At the end of the year she also received a bone from a sheep, and ritual hymns were addressed to her. Fire was supposed to have cleansing power.

Shamanism

The tribal leaders were also shamans, that is, experts who cured diseases and who divined hidden knowledge while in a trance. Shamanism, a heritage from very ancient times, was strongly integrated with ancestor-worship—the shaman's guardian spirits were his ancestors—and con-

The Scythians were among the first peoples to excel at horsemanship.

centrated on the exorcism of evil spirits. Shamans performed many of the customary sacrifices.

Of the Mongol and Turkish tribes that invaded Europe during the first Christian millennium, the Huns were known for their belief in Tengri and the Magyars (Hungarians) for their high-god beliefs and their shamanism.

Slavic religions: gods of fear

From their ancient homes in Poland and White Russia the Slavs spread over Eastern Europe during the first millennium of the Christian era. They were organized in numerous tribes which, as time passed, formed themselves into larger groups. Of these only the western Slavs, formerly living east of the Elbe, and the Russians have left traces in the history of religions. What they believed is not at all clear, however, and interpretations differ widely among scholars.

Thunder-god

Thus, we can only guess what the religion of the Russians was like before the emergence of the Russian grand duchy in the ninth century. The most well-known god seems to have been Perun, a god of thunder and lightning, and apparently a Supreme Being.

His position was probably reinforced when in about 980 Vladimir the Great—of Viking descent—created two cultic centres for him, one in Kiev, the other in Novgorod. In Kiev, Perun was represented in wood on a hill outside the princely palace together with a few other gods. His image was adorned with a head of silver and a beard of bronze. Cattle and even human beings were sacrificed to this god. When in 988 Vladimir was baptised, the idol was dragged into the River Dnieper and the sacrificial grove destroyed. It is obvious that the cult of the thunder-god had developed under the influence of the cult of Thor in Scandinavia; Kiev was effectively a Viking colony.

Other Russian gods were Svarog and Dashbog, father and son, both representing the sun and the fire. The common element in their names, *bog* (compare the Indian *bhaga*), stands for 'richness' and also 'god'. Volos is mentioned as the god by whose name one swears solemn oaths. Perhaps he was a master of meadows and herds.

Vampires and werewolves

The folk beliefs in Russia, Poland and Yugoslavia have probably preserved traits of ancient Slavic religion. Best-known are the vampires, dead people who suck the blood of the living, and the werewolves, human beings transformed into wolves. *Rusalki* are maidens who have suffered premature death. Bogs are the abodes of *bagnik* and *bolotnik*, old and dirty men. Very commonly referred to are river-maidens, *vila*, seen as beautiful and cunning.

Western Slavic temples

In the western Slavic area the old religion continued until 1168 when the temple in Arkona on the River Rügen was destroyed by King Valdemar I of Denmark. Unlike the Russians the west Slavs built temples to their gods, probably very late, and possibly influenced by Germanic peoples. The temple clergy seem to have enjoyed high prestige. In Arkona, for instance, only the priest was allowed into the temple where he made libations and, at the harvest, sacrifices of meat. He also performed divination; for instance, he took omens from the movements of the white horse dedicated to the chief god, Svantevit ('the sacred lord').

The west-Slavic gods were very war-like and all-knowing. The latter quality was expressed by their statues having several heads or faces. Thus, Svantevit's huge image had four heads, two looking ahead, two looking backwards. Triglav in Stettin (modern Szczecin) had three heads, Rugievit at Garz on the Rügen one head with seven faces (and seven swords hanging from his belt), Porsevit at the same place had five heads, and so on. The idea of multi-headed gods is truly Slavic. Even in late

Chingis Khan was the greatest ruler of the Mongols. His empire stretched from the Caucasus mountains to the Indus river, from the Caspian Sea to Peking.

Serbian folklore there is a three-headed mysterious nightly rider, Trojan (probably called after Emperor Trajan).

The temples sometimes contained precious things. Triglav's statue was made of gold (but Svantevit's image in Arkona was a wooden idol, chopped up and put into the fire by the Christian king, Valdemar). In the temple belonging to the war-god Jarovit of Wolgast a shield was preserved which was brought forth every time they prayed for victory in battle. Sacred groves were next to the temples. In Stettin Triglav had a sacred oak with a spring beneath. The god Proven who was venerated at the site of Oldenburg (north of Eutin) owned a grove of sacred oaks surrounded by a wooden fence. Here the prince executed his justice in the middle of his subjects, just as the Germanic kings did under an oak.

Baltic religions: a late survival

The old religions of the Baltic peoples—the Latvians, Lithuanians and the now extinct ancient Prussians—lived on until very recent times. Thus, the sacred groves in Latvia were not felled until the eighteenth century, and the cult of Perkons (Perkunas in Lithuania), god of thunder and fertility, and closely related to the Slavic Perun, prevailed in Latvia until 1750. As a matter of fact, Lithuania did not turn Christian until the fifteenth century. Thus it was still possible to observe these indigenous religions until the end of the last century.

Baltic religions are of interest because they are supposed to have been very close to the original Indo-European religion in Persia and India. The heavenly god, Dievs, has his counterpart in the Indian Dyaus, and Perkunas is identical with the Indian Parjanya.

A characteristic feature of Baltic religions is that there are many female divinities (whereas Slavic religions are noted for their lack of goddesses). We find a host of 'mothers', among them Mother Earth (Zemes mate) and the Fire Mother (Uguns mate). The Sun (Saule in Latvia) is represented as a beautiful maiden with golden hair who rides in a wagon drawn by horses. Laima and Mara (St Mary) are important goddesses of fate, and guardians of human beings. Laima receives sacrifices of dogs, sheep and pigs and blesses the fields and the cattle.

Besides Dievs, who is thought of as a farmer with a family, there are other sky-gods, such as Usinsh. The latter is a god associated with the spring and is a patron of horses.

Among terrestrial gods should be mentioned the earth-god, Zemes dievs, who has developed into a lord of the farmstead, and the fertility-god Jumis, who is represented by a double ear of corn. Jumis is connected with the harvest feast in the autumn, when he is identified with the last sheaf of the cornfields.

Part Three
The Primal Religions

World of the Spirits

Harold Turner

When we hear of primitive superstitions, witchcraft and ju-ju, fetishism or mumbo-jumbo, we may think of tribal peoples with no real religion. In fact, many tribal peoples are much more religious than many modern Westerners. They live close to nature and sense its mysterious powers. They are at the mercy of natural disasters, storm and flood, famine disease, fire and earthquake, which are all seen as evil forces. They mee other peoples who are hostile, or fine evil people in their midst. Death i close and often comes tragicall early.

Tribal peoples therefore feel themselves defenceless, weak, surrounde

Primal religions in the world today

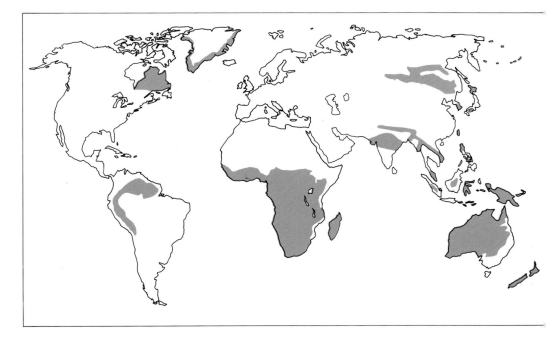

by evils, and unable to cope with life or to achieve the happiness we all long for. They readily become aware that an invisible, more-than-human power surrounds them, and develop their own religious systems to forge links with this power.

Ants before God

The religions of tribal peoples are therefore linked with real human needs, and have the hallmarks of true religion. They have a realistic view of life, a humble view of human nature, and a sense of depending on the spirit world. As the Nuer of the Sudan say, 'Man is like an ant before God.'

Many Westerners have despised tribal religions because the outward forms are different—no church buildings or Sunday services, no scriptures, hymn-books or creeds. Some have even claimed, like Charles Darwin in Patagonia, that such peoples have no religion at all. In a few cases this seems to be true; but most of the 200–300 million tribal peoples of the Americas, Africa, Asia and Oceania are very religious indeed. In the last 100 years, through close study by missionary scholars, anthropologists and others, we have come to understand these religious systems much better.

Superstitious mumbo-jumbo?

Most of the common terms for these religions are either offensive or inaccurate. People do not like their religion to be called heathen, savage, primitive or superstitious, and words such as animistic, pre-literate, traditional or ethnic are not accurate enough. The word 'superstition' should be kept for the few customs and beliefs that linger on after a religious system has collapsed, or has been replaced by another one. Religion must be carefully distinguished from magic, where people try to use spirit powers for their own selfish ends. Magic is a kind of religion in reverse. Since there are parts of the world where 'tribalism' is a bad word, it is not easy to speak even of tribal religions.

Some people are now using the word 'primal'. This means religions

The ancient religion of Tibet is called Bön. Like many primal religions, it considers that mountains such as Kangchenjunga, are the sacred abode of the gods.

that are *prior* to those we call the 'universal' religions. These include Christianity and the great Asian religions, which appeared later in history, usually have scriptures, and often see themselves as applying universally, to all peoples. Primal religions are not religions for all peoples, and so do not become missionary, as the universal religions often do. They are the religion of one tribe or people who realize that other peoples have their own gods and systems. The word primal also means *primary* or basic. Primal religions usually have the main basic features that belong to all religions.

The spirit world

Basic to primal religions is a belief in a spiritual world of powers or beings stronger than man himself. We are not alone in the universe. Behind ordinary things and daily events there is spirit power. Sometimes this is seen as a power running through everything, but specially concentrated in anything unusual or in any

special skill of a human being. This is called *mana*.

Often this power is seen in a host of spirits dwelling in all kinds of places, or just wandering about. Some of these spirits may be friendly to people and be thanked for their help with prayers and offerings; others may play tricks on them and be a nuisance; and others again may be evil spirits or demons, who are dangerous and must be avoided or placated. So we use 'animism', from the Latin for spirit. Such beliefs emphasize that we do not control everything, and that superior spiritual forces are also at work.

Some primal religions have another group of spirit powers we can call gods. These rule over some area of the world or of human life, such as hunting, farming, fighting or metal-working. For example, among the Yoruba people of Nigeria, Ogun is the god of both metal-working and war. These major gods often have temples or shrines, with special priests and festivals, and are much more important than the spirits.

At Lomé in Central Togo, a strange selection of stones, skulls and bones are on sale as fetishes. Spirits are believed to reside in the fetishes.

'High God', 'Sky-god'

Many primal religions have a single supreme god above all other powers. Sometimes he is even thought of as a universal God for all peoples. For instance, North American Indians think of the Great Spirit, and the New Zealand Maoris of Io. This God is usually the creator of all things. Sometimes he is concerned that people live moral lives, and deals with them through the lesser gods. At other times he is believed to have been angry with mankind and to have withdrawn from the world, or else he is so high and mysterious that he cannot possibly reach him. This 'High God' or 'Sky-god' may have no temples, priests, organized worship or sacrifices, and so he is easily missed by outsiders.

The living dead

Most tribal peoples also believe that the spirits of those who have died live on. These 'living dead' have dealings with those still living in this world. The living must honour these ancestral spirits, and can rely upon them to protect or guide, and also to take their prayers to the higher spirit powers. Sometimes this system is called 'ancestor-worship'; indeed, notable ancestors have been promoted to gods. But usually, these practices show a strong sense of the continuing presence of ancestors, who are honoured rather than worshipped, and who are remembered, at least for a few generations, as human beings, not gods.

Dreams and visions

Primal religions depend on myths rather than scriptures and creeds to learn about the spirit powers. Such myths relate the great things the spirit powers did in making the world and in giving people various natural resources and skills needed to sustain life—hunting, fishing, growing crops and making fire, pottery and houses. Myths are not fairy-tales, but long and often complicated stories containing a people's theology and philosophy of life. In them we can find a deep understanding of human nature and of basic human problems.

Individuals may also meet the spirit world through ecstasy or visions, by being possessed by a spirit which for a short while controls a person's behaviour and speaks through him, perhaps in a strange spirit language, and especially through dreams. When dreams are vivid or unusual, people ask others to help interpret what the spirit powers are saying to warn, command or reward.

Bringing in the New Year

Rituals are another way of communicating between the two worlds. Sometimes they are laid down in the ancient myths; the ritual and the myth together form a complex act of worship or a great festival. In such ceremonies, the stories in the myths may be acted out afresh so that people believe that they are sharing once again the full power of the gods, and renewing life from its origins.

Some of the most important rituals concern the New Year; the old, worn out and corrupted world is discarded and replaced by a renewed creation fresh from the gods, just as in the beginning. The ritual may include such ceremonies as putting out the old village fires that have been kept alight all year, and lighting a new fire for the next year by striking flint on stone, or using some other method the gods first taught to men. Although the ceremonies may also involve much merry-making, there is a deep religious awareness of the corruption and shortcomings of humans and their world, and of the need for regular renewal from the sources of life.

Killing for the gods

Prayers and offerings to the gods feature prominently in the rituals. Some of the prayers are both beautiful and deeply spiritual, and can be used in worship by the universal religions. Others tend to be rather self-centred, asking for prosperity and practical blessings. Not all peoples sacrifice to the gods, but many primal religions have well-defined systems listing the items to be given by killing, burning, pouring out or in other ways, or food to be shared with the god in a communion meal.

'Those who are dead are never gone:
They are there in the thickening shadow.
The dead are not under the earth:
They are in the tree that rustles,
They are in the wood that groans,
They are in the water that runs,
They are in the water that sleeps,
They are in the hut, they are in the crowd,
The dead are not dead.

Those who are dead are never gone,
They are in the breast of the woman,
They are in the child who is wailing,
And in the firebrand that flames.
The dead are not under the earth:
They are in the fire that is dying,
They are in the grasses that weep,
They are in the whimpering rocks,
They are in the forest, they are in the house,
The dead are not dead.'

From *Chants d'ombre Suivis de Hosties Noires*, ed. Leopold Senghor

Medicine men

To help with all these religious activities most primal religions have some kind of specialist, usually best called a 'medicine man'. He may perform the activities of a priest, medium, diviner, healer and herbalist, and shaman but not of a witch, sorcerer, or mere magician. Priests look after the shrines and organize the festivals; mediums become 'possessed' by the spirit power; diviners are skilled at interpreting omens or signs showing the will of the gods; healers may know useful techniques and remedies (such men first used quinine, cocaine, morphine and other drugs); shamans specialize in travel in trances to the world of the spirits to learn from its mysterie● Many of these tasks require lon● apprenticeships, but more impo● tantly a special gift at birth, or special divine call. Thus the go● keep the final control in their dea● ings with this world.

Although many primal religion● have collapsed under modern press ures in developing areas of the worl● others have persisted remarkably an● have adapted to change. They shoul● never be regarded as the childis● religions of primitive peoples, or th● crazy antics of savages dominated b● 'witch-doctors'. They are seriou● efforts by adult peoples to create an● preserve a spiritual system which ca● sustain them in both life and death●

A wooden figure for scaring away the 'devils of disease', from the Nicobar Islands, north of Sumatra.

Case-study 1: Asia

Barbara Boal

ecstatic trances to communicate with the spirits. They bring back instructions for correcting the erring community. They seek to restore harmony between man, the spirit world and everything created. This harmony is fundamental to their beliefs. Similar beliefs are held by the Ainus of northern Japan, the mountain peoples of Taiwan and, to some extent, the Hakka.

Nomadic groups

Many people think these nomadic groups are the descendants of Asia's ancient peoples and have preserved traditional ways down the ages. Today they live in small bands, usually in remote, forested hill-country, where they were probably pushed long ago by more highly organized immigrants. They include very small tribes in west-central and south India and in Chota Nagpur. The Andaman Islands are almost entirely inhabited by such peoples; they are also scattered in remote forest and swamp areas of coastal Kampuchea. Better known, perhaps, are the tiny minority groups of Semang-Negritoes and their neighbours, the Senoi, inhabiting the jungle hills of northern and central peninsular Malaysia; also the Aëtas-Negritoes of Luzon, Mindanao and Mindoro in the Philippines. Other hunter-gatherer groups can be found wandering in central Kalimantang (Borneo), the Celebes and eastern Sumatra.

Such groups may be made up of simply one elder and his family or several families. Scarcity of food dictates the smaller groups which, however much they roam, usually keep within their own boundaries. Food is always shared out equally—roots, tubers, leaves and fruits from the forest, possibly fish speared or trapped. Small game are hunted by bow-and-arrow except on the Malaysian peninsula, where Senoi blowgun and poisoned dart have also been adopted by the Semang.

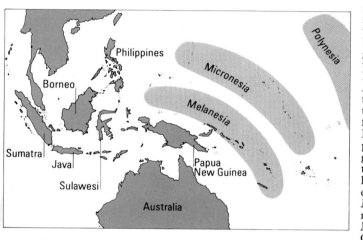

Asia and Oceania

Asian tribal peoples do not separate the sacred and secular. Their religious concepts are expressed in ritualized activities involving the community.

But these concepts and actions do not result from verbal 'beliefs'. In this they differ from 'religion' as we know it in the world's major faiths.

The key to understanding Asian tribal world-views is 'relationship': with gods and spirits; with fellow human beings; with nature.

These cannot be separated: they are parts of one whole. Each group has religious practices appropriate to themselves and their environment. But everywhere they seek to restore the good order that was created 'in the beginning'. So there is a great variety of belief among these tribal groups stretching across Asia and the neighbouring islands.

The spirits

Shamans dominate religion in Siberia. They believe in a high god, beyond all good and evil. Chosen by family then later by the spirits, male and female shamans enter rigorous training. Their souls leave the body by

When humans were sacrificed, the Konds used to place emblems beneath the sacrificial stakes. This is an emblem of the leopard clan, with its victim in its mouth.

everybody; for the person's soul has wandered out of the group and must be brought back. The shaman employs the power of certain herbs and plants disliked by the spirit world, to drive away the evil and call back the wandering soul.

Taboo

In cases of more serious illness, the whole group is involved in taboos and ritual observances, perhaps in days and nights of music and spirit-possessed dance. Finally, on receiving the blood sacrifice offered by the head of the house, the spirit is driven out. If the patient dies, another set of group taboos to do with pollution begins. Deaths, like births, are full of danger and the group must isolate itself both for its own safety and that of its neighbours. If any member breaks the taboo, terrifying tropical storms will follow. These come from a supreme god. But there is little idea of a hierarchy of spirit beings. The idea that spirits of the ancestors are present is vague and unwelcome. Safety and well-being depend on the unity and harmony of the

Land and ritual

Their home area of land and its produce appear to have great religious significance. However far they wander and set up temporary dwellings, they return repeatedly to the place they regard as their own. Many, such as the Malaysian Senoi hill-people—widely known as 'slave' (*Sakai*)—have changed to slash-and-burn cultivation for part of each year. They still live in very temporary shelters during food-collecting expeditions, but cultivation demands settled base camps for part of each year. It also sets up a different religious attitude to the land and to the

Each Bontoc village has its council platform. Under each large leaning-stone is buried at least one head from a former head-hunting expedition.

spirits.

The Senoi are surrounded by taboos and work restrictions as soon as they choose which trees to fell and fire to prepare a hill-plot. There is a series of rituals seeking the spirits' help in securing a good crop, until the final harvest celebration. These are performed by the whole tiny community. For instance, the whole group is in 'quarantine' on the first day of planting. Similarly, one person's sickness involves

living community.

Tribes with more complex social structures and more settled and advanced economic patterns develop a stronger pattern of rituals. These in turn demand ritual specialists for proper celebration. Nevertheless, there are still three levels of relationships. Though certain rites may be performed for the individual they still involve the wider community. The Konds are an example.

Human sacrifice

The Konds—or Kui, as they call themselves—live in the jungle-covered Eastern Ghats of Orissa, India, and number nearly a million. Traditionally they supported themselves by slash-and-burn hill-plots, and by hunting and gathering during the dry 'hungry season'. Paddy-cultivation has now steadily increased.

In 1835 the East India Company first encountered the Konds' human sacrifices to satisfy the earth's demands. Emphasizing the need for right relationships between man, the gods and the world, they felt that human sacrifice was needed for wholeness and fertility.

Earth-goddess

The creator-god, Bura, formed the earth-goddess, Tari, as his companion but found her sadly lacking in wifely attentions. She tried in vain to prevent his creating the world and man. All was paradise in the created world except for her growing jealousy. This led to a fierce conflict between the two. All the Konds except a small minority believed that the earth-goddess had won, though she let the creator keep second place. She taught man the arts of hunting, war and cultivating only in return for human sacrifice, her proper food.

Though now replaced by buffalo as victims, this ritual continues. Strips of flesh are hacked from the victim and buried in the village and in neighbouring villages to release her gift of fertility. Many villages were formerly at war. Brief, strict peace-pacts are therefore made for each annual stage of this three- or four-year ritual, ensuring co-operation for the set few days. In some areas it is still annually celebrated in each district, also at certain farming seasons or when the health of the people or its livestock is affected. This binds the people together as Konds, when otherwise the strongest unit is the lineage group.

A number of myths and dialogues show how the Konds tried to avoid the earth-goddess's demands:

'We will die rather than give you human beings!'

But breaking the relationship with her also involved breaking the relationship with the land—bringing drought and famine—and with mankind, bringing pestilence and death. Hence they always made them submit, as the means of re-creating harmony and well-being.

Kond rituals

The Konds try to use mystical powers in many other rituals to increase or restore relationship—and strength and well-being—in the district, village, kin-group or household. Rituals:

● **between the god, man and the land.** Many rituals follow the farming calendar, from ground preparation and sowing to reaping and threshing; also taboolifting rituals on hunting and gathering wild produce.

● **to seek the blessing and help of the ancestors.** Some of these matters involve other clans: such as marriage or the taking of a second wife, or the removal of an entire village with its ancestors, if problems and pestilences show the need.

● **to guard against loss of well-being through pollution.** Ritual impurity runs the full gamut from small household avoidances to incest, which pollutes the earth and everybody in the area.

The Konds follow a slash-and-burn agriculture. But the trees at the crown of the hill are left untouched out of reverence for the hill-god.

All births and deaths pollute, but most serious for the Konds are deaths before due time, by tiger-mauling, in childbirth, or by hanging, falling from a tree or drowning. These place the entire village in 'quarantine', traditionally for a month, but nowadays for a shorter period, while priest and people undergo daily purification rites.

● **to safeguard life.** The danger may come from high-ranking spirits: gods of the hill, of smallpox, of boundaries, of iron (war), or hunting. These are stronger than spirits of springs, trees and lesser hills. Offence against them rapidly brings disaster. Also lifedestroying is an overpowering belief in evil eye, sorcery and witchcraft. These powers, neutral in themselves, become evil and deeply feared when someone uses them against his fellow. This reverses Kond beliefs about community well-being. Counter-rituals by 'witch-detectives' may return the evil to its originator, but the victim may nevertheless fall sick or die.

One community

Seers communicate with the spirits through trances or divination to find out who caused the problem and why. Seers or priests perform the rituals, sacrificing cocks, goats, pigs or buffalo. A spirit-chosen keeper of the village's shrine-stones performs many annual purification rituals. Many villages also have groves sacred to the hill-god or guardian spirit. The household head is priest for ancestor rites and some look after bronze emblems—such as animals and reptiles or other household spirits.

The ancestors, the unborn and the living are all one community. The same daily activities continue in the shade-world. Death in old age with a full funeral gives the best hope of passing peacefully to the ancestors. The dead are also rehabilitated into the bereaved home in the form of a spider, found near the funeral pyre. Sudden death in the feared forms mentioned earlier rules out being accepted by the ancestors. This results in unbearable loneliness for the dangerous spirit. For the Konds, it is as necessary to live in community after death as before it. The manner of death, not good or evil behaviour in this life, decides the future life.

Village centres
The Bontocs and Kalingas of Mountain Province in north Luzon have some similarities to the Konds, but many striking differences. In north Luzon the north–south ranges rise well over 6,000 feet/1,828 metres, often in almost vertical paddy terraces.

For the Bontocs the village is the centre of life. Large villages are sub-divided, with councils meeting on raised stone platforms circled by large, upright stones. These serve as social, ritual and political centres. Head-hunting forays ritually began and ended there, and no elder could sit in council until he had buried a head under his leaning-stone, in this way adding his victim's power and wisdom to his own. Status is all-important. It may be inherited or achieved by great community feasts of many buffalo. The number of buffalo horns nailed above the donor's door proves to both spirits and men the size of the offering.

Several features are similar to the Konds. Women do not sit in council. But they have considerable voice in making decisions. There are separate dormitories for youths and girls, with visiting between them permitted before marriage. Childlessness proves that the spirits are ill-disposed and offends the ancestors, so is reason for divorce. Both peoples revere sacred groves. Both sexes may be seers and priests. The whole farming year has rituals showing constant struggle to win fertility from wilful spirits.

Omens
Unlike the Konds, the Bontoc emphasize omens. These are central to everything. The movements of birds, insects and natural phenomena, the entrails of animals, the silence or crow of a cock held by a priest, and many such 'trials' postpone major ritual celebrations or guide an individual. The Bontoc respect family pigs in their stone-built sties; Kond pigs are scavengers, sacrificed only in pollution rituals, and are taboo to women.

Ancestors are important to both peoples. But Bontocs do not cremate their dead. They ritually seat them in chairs for long periods before putting them in caves at the foot of ravines, where they are visited every year.

Since head-hunting was so important for Bontocs and their northern neighbours, the Kalingas, inter-village feuding was a way of life. Violent incidents are now avoided by their peace-pact system, much stronger than the Konds'. In every village respected elders have been appointed to arrange settlements by traditional methods.

For both Kalingas and Bontocs, religious ceremonies are bound up with status-feasting. A powerful liquor is distilled from fermented rice or sugar-cane and shared between ancestors and the living, or offered with chicken, pig or buffalo sacrifice to particularly feared mountain spirits. A family may run into debt for years or generations, slaughtering many buffalo to ward off disease by feasting both spirits and the village.

The high regard for old village councillors is dying as authority passes into the hands of younger, educated men. With it passes the way of life that held together ancient lore, religious ritual and the elders' responsibility for the well-being of their community.

A special platform is built for the priest to perform the buffalo sacrifices.

Case-study 2: Korea

Harvie Conn

Korea's traditional religion, Sinkyo, has been called 'the religion without a name'. It is not so much a structured set of uniform beliefs as a religious way of seeing the world and a person's sacred link with it. This used to be called 'animism'. Like all religions it has five 'magnetic points'.

● **I and the cosmos.** Man is in rhythm with the world. The forces of nature controlling life and death, fertility and sterility, become personified and god-like. This world is a religious arena inhabited by spirits of heaven and the soil, water and the trees.

● **I and the norm.** The myth of Tan'gun, legendary founder of Korea, underlines that sense of cosmic norm to which the Korean must conform. Ung, the son of heaven, changed a bear into a woman. The bear-woman could find no one to marry. Ung changed his form, married her and fathered her child, Tan'gun. The myth is remembered on 'opening of heaven day' (*Kaech'onjol*), an annual national holiday. Similar tales surround the archetypal tribal leaders, and mythical ancestors of present-day clan families.

● **I and destiny.** How do we reconcile the fact that we are active beings and also victims of fate or destiny? Borrowing from

Yin and Yang represent the interdependent female and male, negative and positive forces of life.

pre-Confucian roots, Sinkyo finds its answer in a cosmic pattern where heaven, man and nature make a harmony of opposites. These opposites complement each other. They are the great forces of the Yin and the Yang, non-being and being. The Yin is negative, passive, weak and destructive. The Yang is positive, active, strong and constructive. As they act and interact, harmony is achieved and recreated again and again. Our individuality comes from these opposites. The Yin is the female, mother, soft, dark, wet. The Yang is male, father, strong, hard, bright.

Out of these opposites comes the system called 'geomancy'. Where shall we live?, becomes a religious question of choosing a good house-site or grave-site in harmony with these opposites. The house or burial place, for instance, must be arranged in conformity to the cosmic workings of yin-yang and the harmony of the five elements: wood, metal, fire, water, earth. The interacting flow of these forces must not be disturbed.

● **I and salvation.** Since this harmony is often broken, Sinkyo must also meet man's craving for salvation. When the rice paddies are ploughed in the spring, a farmers' band pacifies the spirits of the earth with music and ritual. When the ridge-pole of a new house is raised, wine and food are thrown at it, while a member of the household chants, 'Please, Grandfather and Grandmother of the ridge-pole, bless us with good luck and long life, and many sons!'

Life is under a curse, a shadow darkening the cosmic harmony. The way back to 'paradise lost' is by ritual sacrifice. Throwing a stone on a simple altar keeps you from getting sore feet on a journey. Spitting on the altar is a sign of purification, and wards off evil spirits. Earth spirits must be satisfied before a corpse can be laid to rest. The 'sin' is not that of a personal violating of the will of a personal 'god' but the corporate breaking of cosmic unity.

The chief role in restoring unity is often played by the Mudang. Always a woman, her most important task is curing mental and physical disease. Like the shamans of Siberia, she also conducts communal sacrifice, assures the farmers of good crops, fishermen of safe journeys and a good catch. She will produce sons for a barren woman, recall the spirits of the dead after a funeral, or lead them to the kingdom of the blessed. She will pacify the spirits of those who die violent or tragic deaths. Her role is regarded as beneficial.

Sinkyo feels deep horror at the threat of death which destroys cosmic harmony. Some 2,000 years ago, it was common for Koreans to bury the dead with their personal belongings, including gold and silver.

With the growing influence of Confucianism on Korea from the third century AD, Sinkyo saw the spirit world in a new way. The Confucian concept of filial piety as the summit of all virtues strengthened, if it did not create, Korea's early ancestor-cult. Food was offered to kinsmen at death and at memorial times in the following years. They hoped the ancestor would favour the descendants.

● **I and the Supreme Being.** Koreans read about the gods in the great picture-book we call the cosmos. Among the spirits of nature, the spirit of heaven (Hananim or Hanunim) has a special place. Not a 'high god', remote and supreme, he is said to

bring sunlight and rain. Lightning, drought and other disasters are his judgement on the wicked. By his favour we live and breathe. When national disaster came, the king used to appeal to Hananim by confessing his own sins and those of his people. In some sense a 'heavenly father', Hananim was the grandfather of Tan'gun, the aboriginal hero of Korea.

Sinkyo and the new religious movements

As Korea was invaded by Confucianism, Buddhism and Christianity, Sinkyo did not shrink but was altered and strengthened. From Confucianism came the ethical codes surrounding the ancestor-cult. Taoism and neo-Confucianism strengthened the magical side of Sinkyo and its geomancy. From Buddhism came a stress on suffering and pain, now linked with healing and divining.

Sinkyo has also provided the

background for Korea's new religions. Chondogyo was founded in the mid-eighteenth century in reaction to the coming of Christianity. It reinforced man's sacred links with the universe. Sun Myung Moon, the Korean founder of the Unification Church, can be seen as the great link-man between the people and the spirit world.

When the rice-paddies are ploughed in the spring, the spirits of the earth are pacified by music and special rituals.

Case-study 3: Oceania

Alan Tippett

In Oceania beliefs range widely from a hierarchy of high gods to a host of vague spirit forces, forest imps, culture heroes, ancestor-gods and totemism. Some places emphasize religious experience, others formal rituals. Rituals, in turn, may range from a simple chant to a highly elaborate cult.

In Papua New Guinea many tribes were untouched by Western civilization until very recently. One such tribe is the Melpa.

The practitioner may be a simple all-purpose village priest, a healer (shaman), a diviner, a prophet or a complex priest-hood—or a sorcerer. The sorcerer is normally an anti-social individual. A village priest or curer may use counter-sorcery to defeat him.

Magic and religion are inter-twined, but quite different, with different goals and usually differ-ent practitioners. For example, many island communities threw over their old religion with its belief in a hierarchy of high gods, priesthoods and temples, and turned to Christianity. Yet they had trouble ridding themselves of sorcery and domestic magic.

Creation

Attitudes to creation vary widely. Some societies believe the earth always existed. Others have elab-orate creation myths and a sup-reme creator-god (or goddess). In many, however, he or she com-pleted creation and retired, and is not worshipped like the gods of the house and garden. Beside the creator-gods we often find de-partmental gods, such as the god of the sea, embodied, say, in the shark, who is approached at times of sea travel or fishing.

Spirits and totems

Spirits may always have existed or be ghosts—spirits of the dead who once existed on earth as people and have not been proper-ly despatched to the afterworld, or are disgruntled by unpleasant memories of earth. These are different from culture heroes, recent and remembered ancestor-gods for whom special rituals may be used to gain particular ends, or the living dead, who still belong to the lineage or clan.

Totemism is not found every-where and does not always mean the same thing. By totems we usually mean land creatures, water creatures, trees or plants, or even natural phenomena which are specially linked with the gods and the individual or group. Their fortunes are inter-woven by belief and symbolic ritual, and group survival depends on these sacred links. Totemism is hedged with taboos and learned by symbolic per-formances such as dances and chants. In some places totems are mainly linked with marriage pat-terns, but they may bear on war or even relationships with other people in the community.

Power and custom

There is a belief in a dynamic power for good or evil, *mana*, which depends on the intention of the person using it. This power is transmitted, controlled and encountered quite logically, and religious and magical rituals depend on it. *Mana* may be acti-vated by ritual or by accidental touch. Good health, long life, fertility, security, success, good harvests and trade depend on the right use of *mana*. Its misuse is dangerous; taboo is used for pro-tection.

Religion, and especially ritual, ties up with every stressful situa-tion or point of social, economic or political anxiety. It helps maintain balance in the group.

Ritual is also used in agricultural fertility rites, passing of the seasons, first-fruits, rites of passage (including funeral rites), ceremonial welcomes and farewells, trade exchanges, ceremonies before war and after victory, and (in pre-Christian times) in head-hunting, cannibalism, widow-strangling and other local customs.

Spiritual beings may or may not have a fixed living-place, but there is always a right place and way of approach for consulting or sacrifice. Gods and spirits may embody themselves in a myth, animal or person, or enter objects to be venerated or consulted. Sacred places are usually recognizable by rock formations, groves or buildings, and are protected by taboos.

Numerous waves of migration have contributed new religious features to Oceanic religion. For instance, in Fiji we find the snake-cults, ancestral cults and totemism. Frequently the names of the earlier gods of the land have been taken over by later invaders.

The dead
Probably all the Oceanic peoples believe in life after death, but views of the afterlife vary. For some there are different levels in the afterlife. In some, worthy ancestors in living memory may be made gods and called on to help in the areas where they once excelled—in war, magic, agriculture. Sometimes an ancestor has a strong cult backed by long genealogies and origin myths. Frequently the dead go to a place of waiting, or pass through a series of trials. In some places we find a 'place of the dead' for each village or district, which seems to clash with the wider idea of a 'heaven' for the whole tribe found in the same region.

Survival
How far primal religion survives today in Oceania is a moot point.

Kukailimoku is the Hawaiian god of war. This wooden statue stands over six feet high.

The Melpa have periodic pig-feasts when scores of pigs are slaughtered to fulfil the social and religious obligations of the group.

Much of the region is now Christianized, and the great religions of Tonga, Maoriland and Fiji have disappeared. Nevertheless, pockets of animism, magic and sorcery survive even in the urban centres of Oceania, and primal religion is still practised in the mountainous interiors of the larger islands. Rites associated with fishing, subsistence farming, barter and daily home life are still practised in western Melanesia, Papua New Guinea and West Irian.

Many forms of sorcery are still used and very much feared, even by educated persons; a person who knows how to counter sorcery is assured of a good livelihood in any town. Colonial governments prohibited cannibalism, head-hunting and other forms of ceremonial cruelty, undermining their basic religious belief, but primal religion has adjusted to such changes and often co-exists with some local form of Christianity.

Case-study 4: Melanesia

Carl Loeliger

Melanesia is the area of the Pacific Ocean from the western end of New Guinea (Irian Jaya) to Fiji in the east, from the northernmost islands of Papua New Guinea to New Caledonia in the south, and includes Irian Jaya, Papua New Guinea, the Torres Strait Islands, the Solomon Islands, the New Hebrides and New Caledonia. There are no fewer than 1,200 vernacular languages among its roughly 5 million inhabitants.

More than a century of close contact with foreign cultures and Christianity has changed Melanesian primal religion, but has not everywhere reduced its vitality and pervasiveness.

World-view

Melanesians make no distinction between the 'religious' and the 'secular', between the 'natural' and the 'supernatural'. Their religion can be seen as a particular view of the universe, and a set of relationships with it, including people, gods, spirits, ghosts, magical powers, totems, the land and features of the landscape, living creatures, trees, plants and all physical objects, all of which are in some sense potential sources of power.

Relationships with people and ancestral spirits are universally the most important, for at the centre of life is 'the community of men and spirits all of whom are alive'. This community, with membership of an extended family and links with a particular piece of land give a person identity and security, a reason for living, a sense of history and an approach to the future. All the rituals of birth, initiation into adult life, marriage and death are directed towards maintaining these links.

Melanesian primal religion aims at life, fertility, prosperity, harmony, control and balance in all relationships, particularly with men and spirits, and in this world rather than the next. However, as with many other religions, not all its activities match these ideals. Narrow concern with the clan, suspicions and hostility between and within groups, and in some areas between the sexes, have helped foster seemingly harsh and inhuman attitudes and practices.

Myths and stories

Melanesian primal religion features a range of migration stories, myths and other stories, legends, songs, prayers and incantations similar to that of any major religion. Parts are known only by initiated males, or by specialists or adult women. Especially sacred knowledge is restricted to elderly initiated people. There is a variety of creation stories, but little speculation about the origins and nature of the universe. Many people believe that important parts of culture—social, economic and political life—were created for, or given to, the people by gods.

Gods and spirits

Not all Melanesian peoples have believed in a god of the whole universe, or in a powerful god or gods, or that the god or gods are interested in human activities. But some believe gods to be creators who continue to care for the world. Many believe in a variety of spirit beings including evil 'ghosts', demons and witches (not widespread), many of which can harm or kill people. Ancestral spirits are important everywhere; some societies look forward to the return of the dead, others fear it. Some societies regard the spirits of the recent dead as dangerous; others think they are friendly towards the living. They believe that elaborate rituals in honour of the dead—mourning, food offerings, dances, exchanges of pigs, food and valuables—will ensure that the dead will protect the living. Where beliefs in totems occur, the totems—animals, birds, fish, trees, plants—are sometimes seen as ancestors, sometimes simply as emblems.

Ritual and magic

Rituals vary from simple acts linked with everyday activities (hunting, gardening, fishing) to complex rituals, festivals and festival cycles lasting days, weeks, even months and years. In the major activities initiated men take the central role; women and juniors have only minor roles. The pig figures in many of these rituals and festivals. Food, drink and sexual taboos accompany most important rituals. Some peoples believe rituals force the spirits or gods to act; others believe the gods are free to act as they will.

Magic has a place in most societies. The sorcerer is an important person in many Melanesian societies; deaths are often credited to his activity, since a death is usually regarded as being caused by someone. Every Melanesian society includes people with special ritual responsibilities, temporary, permanent or hereditary.

For Melanesians, sacred places can include features of the landscape, such as caves, pools, streams and rocks, but also manmade constructions varying from simple structures to large elaborate buildings such as the Sepik ancestral spirit houses.

Conduct

In some societies ethics and religion seem to have no connection; in others the spirits and gods are clearly concerned with behaviour. Ethical conduct is the particular interest of the god Datagaliwabe among the Huli people of the Southern Highlands of Papua New Guinea.

A carved image of the dead person stands guard over his rock tomb.

Toradja funeral celebrations can last for several months. At the climax dozens of sacred buffalos may be slaughtered.

The Toradja coffins are boat-shaped, like their houses.

The Toradja people from the highlands of Sulawesi were almost completely cut off from all outside civilization until the beginning of this century.

New Myths: The Cargo Cults

Carl Loeliger

New religious movements in Melanesia have become widely known since the Pacific War (1942–45) as 'cargo cults', a term often used to ridicule or condemn. This term and others have frequently led to a complete misunderstanding of these movements. Scholars justify use of the term by pointing to the term 'kago cult' in Melanesian Pidgin, and belief in the 'cargo myth (or story)' in about half the movements.

There were new religious movements in Melanesia before the modern colonial period, and there have been many in the colonial period, all with their main roots in Melanesian culture and primal religion. These movements use myths to justify changes and provide the dynamic for renewal.

A new era

Typically, somebody claims that, through a dream or vision, supernatural powers have told him that a messiah (sometimes) and the ancestors or spirits of the dead will soon return in ships, aeroplanes or trucks bringing huge supplies of manufactured goods. Their arrival will usher in a wonderful new era when Melanesians will have their identity, dignity and honour restored. Inequality, suffering and death will cease.

Sometimes the 'prophet', his associates and whole communities are seized by mass shaking fits, or fall into an ecstatic state. There may be slaughtering of pigs, harvesting or destruction of food crops and dispersal of wealth ready for the new life. Facilities to handle and store the new wealth may also be built. Graveyards get special attention, ready for the return of the ancestors. New, revived or modified rituals and customs may be announced for the faithful to follow.

The movement unites previously separated or hostile groups, although not everybody in an area always joins. Unlike primal religion, the new religious movement reaches beyond the clan and village. When the ancestors, wealth and new life fail to arrive, reasons are found, but the validity of the myth is not questioned. The movement may break out again at any time.

Characteristic features

The movements have characteristic features.
● Elements of primal religion;
● Christian elements;
● Belief in the return of the dead and sometimes in the coming of a messiah;
● Belief in the cargo myth;
● Belief that Melanesians will become whites and vice versa;
● Violence or threats against whites;
● Attempts to restore native political and economic control;
● Unifying separated groups.

No movement has all these features. The most widespread feature, belief in the cargo myth, appears in more than half; violence or threats to whites occur in less than half; belief in the coming of a messiah in only about one-sixth. But these movements possess an uncanny ability to survive and revive.

The movements have their roots in primal religion, even when biblical stories and Christian rituals are used. Colonial administration, European technology and culture, Christian missions and events such as the Pacific War have also influenced their rise. These movements may be traditional responses to difficulty. When Melanesians are unable to match outsiders' power and wealth, they turn to traditional means, myths and rituals to survive. They find it difficult to accept that an individual or group will not share power, goods, food and knowledge with others.

The shared life

Five major themes are found in the great variety of Melanesian myths:
● The division of humanity into two groups as a result of choices made by two original people;
● The two brothers who became separated, one being stupid or hostile (it is hoped they will meet and be reconciled and so will all people);
● A paradise lost due to the disobedience, stupidity or ingratitude of an individual or group;
● The turbulent end of the present world;
● The arrival of a legendary messiah with the ancestors and the ushering in of the new age.

Basic to all this is the shared life of men and spirits and the belief that all people belong to one family and are equal but, through some error or misfortune in the past, divisions and inequalities have arisen.

Feared by the government

These religious movements make converts beyond the village and clan, marking them off from primal religion. Their social, economic and political aspects have usually been obvious, and colonial and post-colonial administrations, missions and churches have feared them. Before the 1960s there were few 'secular' movements with political aims.

Whether or not they overtly express concern with 'cargo', the aim of the new religious movements is not merely wealth and prosperity but proper human relationships, liberation and the restoration of human rights, identity, dignity, respect and equality.

Case-study 5: The Foe of Papua New Guinea

Joan Rule

In the tribal religion of the Foe in the Southern Highlands of Papua New Guinea, the chief spirit is the 'Old One who is in the East' (*Ama'a Hai Ta'o*). Although he is the chief spirit, he is not the creator.

There are in addition three groups of spirits who live in fixed places:
- the evil things (*ma'ame gai*)
- the *hisare*
- the *hibu yii*.

Certain men in each village make a special relationship with one of these groups of spirits, and others pay them to make an offering on their behalf.

The evil things
The 'evil things' inhabit a clump of trees, a big rock or some unusual natural feature. For example, in about 1967, on a point of land on the south-eastern side of Lake Kutubu, in a swampy area of wild bamboo, a man named Igare from Gese village found a small area with red cordyline shrubs growing neatly. This, all agreed, must be a spirit house; so it was regarded as a place of the evil things. Men who made a relationship with the evil things, and who had the right spells for them, were in their favour and would not be harmed. But those who roused their anger would get swollen legs or a swollen stomach. Parents warned children against going near, for fear of disturbing them and making them angry. Children whose parents had garden-houses in the area had to be very careful not to make a noise near the dwelling-place of the evil things.

Further up the lake, some *hisare* spirits live. In the waters of the lake live a number of fearsome water spirits, the *guruka*. Men who make a relationship with the *hisare* spirits also make contact with these *guruka*. After the *hisare* men have danced with the *hisare* spirits, the *guruka* will come up from the water and dance around the *hisare* camp. They will bring cassowary's feathers or perhaps men's bones and present them to the *hisare* men, acting for the spirits. According to the gift, the following month a cassowary will be caught, a man will die, or some similarly appropriate event will occur.

Wandering spirits
Other spirit beings wander from place to place. The *soro* are spirits of the air who wander here and there at will, always on the lookout for some harm to do to humans. Children are afraid of the spirits of the air, being sure that they could carry them off or do dreadful things; but adults make it plain that they must work in company with the spirits who live within living men (*baisese*). A pair or group of *baisese* must work with at least one spirit of the air. If a man has an enemy, his spirit will go out, find another man's spirit, find a spirit of the air and then go to do damage. For example, in about 1960 a stone was thrown into a man's sleeping area. He realized that his spirit was leaving him, pressed into service by a fellow villager's spirit. He said, 'There'll be a man harmed at Hegeso village', naming the man. Two days later the man was dead.

Spirits of the dead
Most feared of all are the spirits of the dead. These include the spirits of men slain, mostly in inter-village fighting, and the spirits of those who have died from other causes. Both can cause harm and serious illness, entering into a person's body in the form of stones and wood which will cause death.

The spirits of the slain (*bauwabe*) are the most potent. These spirits live 'up above' and are always painted all over with red. A man who makes offerings to a spirit of the slain finds that his spirit appears to him in a dream or vision, guaranteeing success and help. But if a man and his kinsmen are enemies of a man who is slain, his spirit appearing to them means trouble. If a man has a bad ulcer or abdominal pain, this is clearly the work of the spirit of the slain.

The spirit of a man who has died in any other way goes 'east', but wanders back and hovers around, at least for a time. It can cause sickness, but not death. An exasperated mother may say to a child, 'If you don't stop, the spirit will come with a bamboo and leaves, collect your tears and drink them, and if they're sweet cause you lots of harm.'

Medicine men
Medicine men once claimed to be

able to 'suck' out the stones and sticks implanted by the spirits. They were paid in strings of cowries, or with a pig. This cult died a natural death. The prices charged were high, and the number of cures not impressive. At the local health centres, on the other hand, drugs such as penicillin and chloroquine produced dramatic cures free of charge.

The other answer is to pay someone to drive away the spirit causing the trouble.

Bamboo and sorcery

The sorcerer is greatly feared. In a group of two or three hundred people, complete and electric silence resulted as a well-known sorcerer produced a small bamboo of sorcery material bought from sorcerers in the west to produce the death of named men. Foe sorcerers have three main methods.

The first, 'hitting the skin with a stick', is the most potent; the man will die in one or two days. Sorcery material from the bamboo, generally a fine, white, powdery substance, touches the skin of the doomed man, either by means of a stick, or by being shaken on him while he is asleep. If it can be put into his bamboo of water or his food, it works just as well.

In the second method, pieces of the man's belongings—a fragment of his cane leg-band, or of the leaves or cloth covering his buttocks—are put in the bamboo of sorcery material which is placed in the fork of a tree, where it wears slowly away. Or it may be placed in a large ant-mound on a tree trunk, or in a small running stream. As the friction or the eating takes place, the man will sicken and die over a period of four or five months.

The third method, white sorcery, is done with a set of small white stones. The sorcerer obtains a tree gum, and says his spell as he rubs it into the stones. This also causes death.

Case-study 6: The Aborigines

W. H. Edwards

The first Europeans to observe the Australian Aborigines thought they had no religion. In fact spiritual beliefs are basic to daily life and social relationships.

At the time of European settlement, there were about 300,000 Aborigines belonging to about 270 language groups. Myths passed from one area to another, and all groups shared a common view of the world, although differing in beliefs and practices. For example, although no group believed in a high god, some emphasized spirit figures such as the Wandjina, seen in the cave art of the north-west, and Baiame, referred to in many of the stories from the south-east. In other areas no spirit figure was given such prominence. In the west and centre, circumcision was the main rite of initiation, but this had not spread to the east.

The Dreamtime

Rather than looking forward to a life after death, the Aborigines look back to an era known as the Dreamtime. In this period the landscape as we know it today received its shape. Ancestral beings such as kangaroo-men, emu-men, bowerbird-women and fig-men moved over the face of the earth. They hunted, fought, married, defecated, laughed and performed ceremonies. Their footprints and actions became the hills, waterholes, trees, caves, stars and other features of the landscape.

The central places of these stories are the totemic sites related to particular clans. These clans are regarded as descended from the ancestor beings. An old man can point to a rock said to be the fig-man and say: 'That is my grandfather'. The clan groups are responsible for looking after the sites, passing on the stories and performing the rituals. The major sites are considered sacred, and only men may visit them. Other sites can be visited by women and children. The activities of the ancestor beings in the Dreamtime set the pattern for human behaviour. Morality is a matter of conforming to these traditions.

Tracks of the ancestors

In some Aboriginal languages the same word is used for the Dreamtime and for the stories relating the events of that era. These stories reflect the peoples' nomadic existence. The countryside is criss-crossed with the supposed tracks of the ancestral beings. The stories of their journeys and deeds have passed down through the generations in the form of song-cycles, sung to complex rhythms. These myths are also related as stories.

The Aborigines had no priests and everyone was expected to perform a role in the ceremonies, but older men, skilled in recalling the stories and songs, were greatly respected. These men also guarded the special boards or stones on which were scratched patterns representing the stories. They were hidden in caves and brought out on ritual occasions, to recall and teach the stories. Symbolic markings painted on the walls of caves served the same purpose. The sites, the boards and rocks and some of the song-cycles and cave-paintings were all considered sacred, and to be seen or heard by men only.

Corroborees

The activities of the Dreamtime are re-enacted in ceremonies generally known as 'corroborees'. These usually consist of dancing, accompanied by the singing of the song-cycle. The painting of the body and preparation of the site are essential to the performance. Some corroborees are seen by everybody in the group; others are for men only. The women have their own songs and dances related to fertility cults and the roles of wife and mother.

Some of the ceremonies are related to the rites of passage For example, a male Aborigine becomes a man, not by reaching a certain age, but by undergoing initiatory rites such as circumcision. From this time the young man is introduced to the mysteries of the men's sacred life, learning their stories and songs, and being shown the sacred boards and sites. The youth undergoing this period of initiation is also referred to as sacred. The man who inflicts the wounds

At 'corroborees' Aborigines celebrate the events of the 'dreamtime' when primeval spirits formed the earth.

The Aborigines have their own unique art-forms, such as bark-painting.

on the young man must provide him with a wife from his own kin-group.

Food supply

Other ceremonies are known as increase rites. As hunters and gatherers, the Aborigines had no direct control over the supply of their food, by herding or cultivating. They tried to achieve some control by performing rites to increase the supply of a particular food, or to produce rain. This was done in various ways, by rubbing a special rock with a stone or red ochre, by cleaning a site, by letting blood from a vein onto sacred rocks or boards, or by performing special songs and dances.

Power

The series of Red Ochre rites passed from one group to another in the deserts of west and central Australia, and relate the myths to social control and discipline. Rocks linked with these stories are thought to have special power. People fear to offend this power, but by properly observing the rites the power can be gained by men. By continually performing the rites, men re-invest the sites with power, and are in turn empowered by them.

Aboriginal identity

For the Aborigines the enduring reality is spiritual. The Aboriginal man believes that the same spirit which lives in him lives also in the related totem animals and plants, in the rocks and water-

At many sites in Australia there are Aboriginal rock paintings. This one shows the Lightning Brothers, who perpetuate the rain. The Aborigines believe these to be self-portraits. Whenever the colours begin to fade they are ceremonially repainted.

holes, and in the stories and ceremonies. At death, the spirit is released from the body to return to a spiritual existence. Thus the Aborigine has links with all his surroundings, with all the members of his kin-group and of other groups in the neighbourhood, and with past and future generations. His beliefs help him to accept life's circumstances and to know that, despite the activities of evil spirits which bring death, sickness and natural disasters, he will be provided for and cared for.

Since Europeans entered Australia, many Aboriginal tribes have disappeared and others have lost all vestiges of the traditional life. Some groups in the north, west and centre have kept their traditional values, beliefs and ceremonies. In recent years, a return to traditional areas, a growth of Aboriginal identity, increasing economic independence and a change in government policies have led to an upsurge of traditional practices among some groups. But they tend to concentrate on certain aspects, such as man-making ceremonies, as other aspects are seen to be in conflict with other demands of present-day life.

Case-study 7: The Maoris

James Irwin

Maoris of New Zealand share some religious features with Polynesia (the triangle bounded by Hawaii, New Zealand and Easter Island). Their creation stories are very similar and they share a number of gods, although their roles and status differ.

Why the rain falls

Maori mythology tells of the first parents, Ranginui and Papatuanuku, who were locked in a deep embrace. As sons were born they were kept between the parents, and only allowed glimpses of light. The myth tells how the sons struggled to escape. After several abortive efforts, one son, Tane, placed his feet against Rangi, and his extended arms against Papa. Struggling fiercely, upside-down, and helped by his brothers, he forced his parents apart. Rangi became the sky, and Papa the earth—Sky Father and Earth Mother. The grief of their separation is seen in falling rain and rising mists.

Liberated in the world of light (*Te Aomarama*), the brothers fought for power. Tane became god of the forests, Tangaroa of the seas, Tumatauenga of war, Rongo of agriculture, and Whiro, the evil one, became ruler of the dark areas of life. Tawhirimatea stayed with his father, becoming god of winds and hurricanes.

The brothers were immortal. They formed a female from the earth, and Tane breathed into it life-giving force (*hauora*); woman entered the world. Tane named her Hinetitama and took her as his wife. Their offspring became the human race. These beings are called gods or 'powers' (*atua*).

Out of nothingness

Ancient Maori philosophers thought much about beginnings, and expressed their beliefs in chants. One tells of the time of nothingness (*Te Kore*); then, long ago, the time of potential being (*Te Korekore*), then deep darkness (*Te Po*). Finally darkness was defeated and the world of light (*Te Aomarama*) appeared. This chant goes back long before the coming of Europeans to New Zealand. From these ideas comes the Maori view of a three-tier universe: the sky (*Te Rangi*), world of light (*Te Aomarama*) and the great dark, the realm of the dead (*Te Po*).

Io was the ultimate source of all supernatural power (*mana*). He lived in the highest of twelve heavens, and had ultimate control of all events. Io was known only to carefully chosen initiates, trained in complete isolation. They offered suitable rituals in

Intricate carving on a Maori meeting-house represents the primeval parents of the Maoris. The history and customs of the Maoris are told in the paintings and carvings on the meeting-house.

isolated places, and never spoke of Io.

Mythical monsters

As well as the gods of the 'departments of life' Maoris recognized many other powers. Some were powers of particular tribes or territory; others were family gods, known as guardians (*kaitiaki*), who warned of danger or gave encouragement. Most tribes and sub-tribes had some object called a mythical monster for example a log, or floating mass of weeds. These were to be avoided as sacred (*tapu*) objects. Many were believed to lie in deep holes in rivers or lakes, and were sometimes considered good, sometimes dangerous.

Spirits (*wairua*) could be good or evil. A departed ancestor, not given a proper funeral and so not with his ancestors, became a wandering spirit, troubling his descendants until the rites were completed. The spirits of aborted foetuses were regarded as troublesome and malicious.

God-sticks for priests

The Maoris had no temples or altars, although special secluded places were used for certain rites. Sometimes large, roughly-carved stones were placed in a clearing in a forest. These were used by a seer (*tohunga matakite*) as a place for calling his particular god. The stones were not shrines or idols. They were places where the seer would place an offering and wait until the god agreed temporarily to inhabit the stone. 'God-sticks' were used in a similar way for agricultural rituals. Minor gods, who did not do what was expected of them, were abandoned.

Eating the war victims

Sacrifice did not feature largely in Maori religion, except for food offerings to pacify a god and to show respect. It was common to offer first-fruits of harvest to Rongo. The heart of the first person killed in war was offered to Tumatauenga and then, if he was a person of status, eaten by the victor to gain the spiritual power of the victim. When an important carved meeting-house was built, it was common for the body of a slave to be buried beneath the main pole.

The land used as the forecourt of a meeting-house was sacred when any gathering was held. Strict rules were observed. In death and mourning, the body was taken to the meeting-house to lie in state until the rituals were completed. This could last several days and nights, and all members of the extended family gathered. Among the Maoris, death was and is a public matter. When no rituals were taking place, the meeting-house became free from *tapu* but was still treated with respect.

If a baby sneezes...

Mauri is the life force in everyone and in certain talismans which symbolized what protected vitality, spiritual power, fertility, lands and forests. When babies sneezed at birth, it was a sign of their life force. Should someone's life force be destroyed, spiritual power would be lost and the person would soon die.

● Spiritual power is a gift from the god, and also refers to status and authority. It is powerful, and could harm individuals and communities.

● *Tapu* is the system of prohibitions warning of danger, and protecting individuals from uncontrolled spiritual power.

● *Noa* is being free from *tapu* restrictions. If *tapu* was breached, danger could only be cancelled by a purification rite (*Whakanoa*).

Maoris make up ten per cent of the population of New Zealand.

Rituals in running water

Ritual was very important to Maori people, and they emphasized the correct recital of *karakia*. Should a priest make a mistake in his incantation it was considered an ill-omen, followed by disaster.

In the rituals, water, fire and cooked food had special significance, as they could defeat evil. For special rituals, a priest would stand waist-deep in running water to protect himself from the forces he was calling up.

'Into the womb of Papa'

Maoris see the universe as sacred, so land is very important. It is to Earth Mother (Papatuanuku) that all men return at death. 'They are received into the womb of Papa.' Land is held by tribes and sub-tribes in trust for future generations and must be cared for as a man cares for his wife. Man gets from the land not only his food, but also his identity. To be without land is to be a nobody, literally worthless. To have land is to belong to the people, both alive and dead.

Waken gently!

Dreams and visions are seen as messages from the world of the spirit. A dream is usually told to a priest to have its meaning explained. It was believed that a person's spirit often left the body and travelled over wide areas during sleep. It was important to waken a sleeping person gently, to allow the spirit time to return to the body.

The last goodbye

Birth and death featured prominently in Maori religion. At birth, the father or a priest would recite a *karakia* to have supernatural power given to the child, especially the first-born. Then a feast was held. There were no rites of initiation, as the child was considered a full member of the tribe from birth.

The rituals of death were elaborate and long, and still feature prominently in Maori life. It is a time to express grief, to say farewell to the dead, to make final reconciliations, and to send the dead person's spirit to the ancient homeland (*Hawaiki*), where it is installed with ancestors. Final rituals return the living relatives to ordinary life, cleansed of grief and of the *tapu* of death. The mourning is public, and whenever possible the rites are carried out at the meeting-house, for the deceased belongs to the tribe, not to the individual family.

The concept of future reward or punishment is completely absent. The departed spirits go 'above' or 'below' and seem to live a life similar to that in this world. They can interact with the living members of the sub-tribe to which they belonged in life. The realm of the dead (*Rarohenga*) is guarded by Great Hine of the Dark (*Hinenuiotepo*), through whom all must pass to reach the underworld. Originally Hinenuiotepo was Hinetitama, who fled from her husband Tane who had breathed life into her.

Glossary of Maori Words

aitua	tragedy; disaster
ao	world
ariki	high chief
atua	supernatural powers; gods
ahurewa	sacred place (sometimes given as *tuaahu*)
Hawaiki	unknown ancient homeland of the Maori
Hinenuiotepo	guardian to the underworld
Hinetitama	first human being
hui	any gathering of Maori people
Io	supreme being or high god
iwi	people; sometimes used as a synonym for tribe
karakia	ritual incantation; invocation; prayer
kaitiaki	guardian spirit, appears in bird or animal form
kehua	ghost
mana	supernatural power; status; prestige
marae	open space in front of a meeting-house
mata	face
matakite	second sight (when used of a person means seer, or diviner)
mauri	life principle of anything
ngaro	lost; hidden
noa	ordinary; common; free from *tapu* restrictions
po	night; darkness; realm of the dead
Papatuanuku	Earth Mother; primeval parent (abbreviated as Papa)
rangatira	chief of a sub-tribe; aristocracy
Ranginui	Sky Father; primeval parent
Rarohenga	the 'below'; the underworld; realm of departed spirits
Rongo	god of agriculture; the moon
rongo	peace
Tane	god of forests
Tangaroa	god of the seas
tangi	to weep
tangihanga	rituals of death; funerary rites
taniwha	mythical monsters; sometimes applied to important persons
tapu	prohibited; sacred
taonga	chattels; when used with plural article *nga taonga* refers to historical ornaments and weapons having *mana*
tipuna	ancestors
Tawhirimatea	a god of winds and hurricanes
tohunga	an expert in any art or craft; especially applied to specialists of the sacred
taura	applied to second order of specialists in the sacred
Tumatauenga	god of war
wairua	spirit (soul); spirits (supernatural powers)
whakanoa	to make ordinary; purificatory rites
whakairo	carved, as in *whare whakairo* (carved house)
whare	house
whenua	land
Whiro	god of evil

Case-study 8: Madagascar

Alan Rogers

Although Madagascar is close to Africa, the Malagasy people are chiefly Asiatic, and speak a Malayo-Polynesian language. Malagasy has no word for religion. 'Ancestral customs' rule every aspect of life. These customs have been slightly influenced by Arab and European cultures, but still rule the lives of more than half the population, and affect deeply the Christian and Muslim minorities. Malagasy religion has no scriptures or creeds, and has few religious stories.

Honoured by ox-skulls

In the centre of Madagascar the

In parts of Madagascar, the ancestors are honoured by being dug up periodically and danced round the family estate.

twelve hills of Imerina, associated with former kings, are highly honoured. So too are the tombs of the Vazimba, half-mythical former inhabitants. Everywhere tombs of the ancestors are important. In some parts these are prominent stone buildings, in others hidden deep in the forest, and in others burial-grounds or caves marked by elaborate carved poles and the skulls of oxen killed to honour the dead. There are many upright stone pillars, usually to record an ancestor. Trees, rocks, springs, rivers and other natural features may form the centre of a cult, but the tomb of nobles are particularly important. In some tribes special cult-houses containing sacred objects set the pattern for all the houses constructed. Many villages have sacred poles at their centre, where rituals are performed.

Talismans

All sacred places have a kind of spiritual power—*hasina*. But spiritual power is present in many man-made objects. These range from charms and amulets, which protect the wearer from

evil, to the famous talismans or fetishes (*sampy*). In former times warriors went into battle with these. They graced the accession of sovereigns, and gave advice through their human guardians. Few, if any, talismans were in human form; to call them 'idols' is misleading. They might be pieces of cloth tied to a spear, or bundles of polished wood decked with silver ornaments. The chief royal talismans were burned in 1869, but their memory is still venerated and their spiritual power continues.

Some animals convey spiritual power also, especially the crocodile, which is honoured in places by songs and occasional banquets. Cats and owls convey omens, and to some people pigs are unclean—perhaps as a result of Arab influence. No pig was allowed in the same village as a talisman. Spiritual power is a force that can be tapped in human need; but it also needs to be protected from contamination. To fail to do this is to break a taboo (*fady*)—a dangerous fault.

Dancing mania

Various sacred people act as guardians of shrines, tell the future by casting seeds on the ground, offer cures from sickness brought on by witchcraft, cast horoscopes, or guide other people through sacred rituals. Prominent men have a domestic holy man to guide all their actions. In some localities groups of people open themselves to spirit-possession (*tromba*) by smoking hemp or by other rituals. An individual may be possessed and foretell the future, using strange voices and unusual dialects. In times of national upheaval, whole bands of Malagasy have joined in a dancing mania, and broken normal taboos. Every human is valuable for his soul ('the soul makes the man' says the proverb). Above all men, all spirits and all ancestors is the fragrant

Lord Creator, Andriamanitra Zanahary—remote but good.

Bone-turning

Until the coming of European influence in the nineteenth century, an adjusted form of the Arab calendar was used. Days were marked for certain actions, or barred to others. Children born on certain days had such evil fortunes that they were killed in infancy. The New Year, at the end of the dry season, was marked by the monarch's ritual bath. The water, possessing spiritual power from the royal body, was sprinkled to bring fertility to crops, animals and people. The blood of sacrificed victims was smeared over doors, and quarrels were made up. Now there is no monarch, but the ideas and some of the customs live on. Everywhere funerals are great occasions, and the dead are regularly honoured by sacrifices and rituals. In Imerina the bones of the dead are dug up, danced round the family estate, and are thought to get pleasure from their annual outing. In return the people get protection for another year. This ceremony is called bone-turning (*famadihana*).

Rituals of family life

Important steps in life are marked by rituals. At birth, after consulting a soothsayer, the child's name is given. The after-birth is carefully disposed of. The mother purifies herself by jumping over a holy fire. All boys are circumcised at a few years old; otherwise they are not really people. Circumcision feasts are family affairs, accompanied by feasting, drinking and ribald songs. At the onset of the first menstruation girls assume the adult dress; betrothal and marriage quickly follow. Child-bearing is woman's chief function. Rituals underline this, such as climbing sacred hills, consulting a witch, or securing fragments of shroud and rotten flesh at the annual bone-turning. After fun-erals the whole family bathes and hair is shaved. Long periods of mourning follow: signs are special dress and unbraided hair.

Rum for the gods

Sacrifices are offered to the ancestors at any crisis, and holy places are honoured in the same way. The greatest sacrifice is oxen, but on lesser occasions chickens, rice, honey, rum, sugar-cane, or even sweets are enough. The prudent traveller drops small coins in rivers, hangs a scrap of cloth on each holy tree, and pours a mouthful of rum on the standing stones.

The old ordeal by poison (*tangena*) has died out, but poison is still a frequent weapon. Friends bind themselves by mingling their blood in the ceremony of *fati-dra*. In any perplexity—perhaps after breaking a taboo, or after a nightmare—people go to the local soothsayer, who prescribes a ritual to remove the threat.

'Morality' is taught by proverbs. Hundreds of these are learned, loved and used. They guide every action in life. Innovation is rash. Conforming to set patterns brings security and peace of mind. *Aza manaram-po hoatra ny kary an-efitra*—'Don't follow your own fancies: that's how cats behave in the wild.'

These model birds represent the spirits of the ancestors. They are taken to the graves to witness the annual 'bone-turning' ceremony.

Case-study 9: African Religions

Newell Booth

By far the largest number of people in southern and central Africa speak 'Bantu' languages. The present Bantu-speaking peoples have developed through migrations and mixings of groups over the centuries, and have adapted to a number of environments, from rain forest to desert. We concentrate here on the Baluba of southern Zaire, who are in some ways typical—also mentioning other Bantu-speaking groups including the Ndembu, the Sotho-Tswana, the Zulu, the Shona and the Kikuyu.

There are other language-groups in the area such as Khoisan and Nilotic; when we use the term 'African' we include these as well as the Bantu-speaking people.

Listen to the elders

African religion is traditional; 'handed down', usually orally, from one generation to the next. A child accepts the word of the elders as final. There is no other authority. If the elders cannot be trusted, nothing can be trusted.

It is true that what is heard from the elders is what they have received from *their* elders, and so on back. But it is also true that the tradition has been 'filtered' as it passes through several generations. The story of Nkongolo, Mbidi Kiluwe and Kalala Ilunga (see *The Luba Epic*) is told differently by various sub-groups of the Baluba, although it is the same basic story.

So we cannot say that because people today are not believing or doing exactly the same things as their ancestors 100 years ago, tradition has come to an end. If a visitor recorded a belief of 100 years ago, and a present-day African discovers that it is not now being taught by the elders, he cannot say that they have 'departed from tradition', for tradition is what the elders are handing on.

Some customs described here are no longer carried out, or have almost disappeared. This does not necessarily mean that the traditional religion is dying out, but it is undoubtedly changing.

Telling the same story

A community is made up of those who remember and share the same tradition. The Baluba are those who tell each other the story of Nkongolo, Mbidi Kiluwe and Kalala Ilunga.

In African religion community is of the highest value. The individual exists only in the community. To be cut off from the community is worse than death. But in Africa there are as many religions as there are communities.

Becoming human

African religion focusses on human beings rather than natural phenomena or supernatural beings. It aims to enhance human values in the community.

In the Bantu languages the word for 'human being' is *muntu* (or a similar word). The plural is

This article considers tribes in the southern half of Africa.

Shrines to the gods may be simple wayside altars at which offerings are made.

bantu, from which we get the language-family name.

Birth is only the beginning of becoming *muntu*. The new-born child must first have a name, frequently an ancestral or 'spirit' name. Often it has to be decided what ancestor has 'returned' in the child, so that the child can have the right name. If a child dies before he receives this name, he was not really human at all but some sort of spirit pretending to be human.

People who are 'different' may be seen as threats to the community and therefore treated differently. Albinos, deformed people, children whose teeth came in the wrong order, and twins are all different. Most Africans consider twins to be 'special'. In some areas, one or both twins used to be destroyed for the good of the community. In other places, they were treated with special reverence; sometimes they were believed to be close to the gods. Among the Baluba, they were linked with incest and thus with the time which ended with Nkongolo.

Marking maleness
One of the most important events in the process of 'becoming human' is initiation. Among the Baluba, the male initiation ceremony is known as *mukanda*, and usually takes place at the beginning of the dry season, in May. The first stage is separation, especially from their mothers and the whole female world. This separation includes circumcision, which makes clear the maleness of the boys. Next the boys spend several months at camps away from the village, where they undergo trials and are instructed in traditional beliefs and practices. Finally, they return to the village as men prepared to take a full part in communal life. This change parallels the change in the life of the whole people that took place when Kalala Ilunga replaced Nkongolo.

Similar initiations are carried out by many groups. Others have simpler ceremonies, without circumcision. The initiation of girls is usually on an individual basis, at or just before the first menstrual period. Among some groups it is quite complex, and may even be more important than male initiation.

Marriage and the community
Initiation is the gateway to full involvement in the community. The marriage of an uninitiated person would be considered an outrage. Once initiation takes place, however, marriage normally follows.

Not to marry is practically unheard of, except for seriously abnormal people. It is a community more than an individual matter; we might say that families marry, not individuals. This does not mean that the individual has no choice, but certainly his preference comes second to the good of the community. Since the purpose of marriage is to have children, any marriage which does not produce children is a failure and is usually ended.

To have children is really the most important responsibility of life. To be childless is to have failed the community, including the ancestors. A person without children cannot be an 'ancestor' and does not participate in the continuity of communal life.

The lizard and the chameleon
Life ends in death. To Africans, this is inevitable, yet in a sense unnatural. Many Africans believe that God originally intended human beings to live for ever, but due to some misunderstanding, accident or failure, death came on the scene. A common story is that God sent to mankind a message of life, but trusted it to a slow-moving animal, such as a chameleon. Later he sent a message of death, but trusted this to a swiftly-moving animal such as a

lizard who, of course, arrived before the chameleon. Although God originally intended life, death cannot be escaped.

Death certainly is not welcomed. Yet there is a sense in which death makes possible the fulfilment of life. By death a person becomes an 'ancestor' living in the realm of the dead, usually believed to be underground or on the other side of our world, a land which is a mirror image of our own. Not all the dead become ancestors; only those who have children, who die in an appropriate way, and who are correctly buried. The spirits of the childless dead, of those who died of certain kinds of diseases and accidents, or far from home, and of witches, may become wandering, dissatisfied spirits who pester or harm the living in various ways.

Life continues
The kindly dead do not stay in the underworld; they continue to have dealings with their living descendants. The grave is one place where contact is made with offerings of food and drink. There may also be 'spirit houses' or shrines, frequently just outside the homes of the living, where ancestors are contacted. Snakes and other animals, especially if seen near a grave, may embody the dead. Most important, the dead may be 'reborn' into the living world.

Birth and death are complementary events. Humans move between the realms of the living and the dead. But what is 'reborn' is not the whole personality of the deceased. One who has been 'reborn' is still seen as existing in the underworld, approachable at his grave or shrine, and perhaps as appearing in an animal. A person may even be reborn in more than one descendant at a time! The dead are very much 'alive', a belief expressed in various ways.

What's in a name?

In a sense, it is the 'name' which is reborn. For Africans, the name is more than a label. It represents the basic nature of a person. So to have the name of an ancestor is to be that ancestor, inheriting something of his nature, qualities and status.

The relationship between ancestors and their descendants forms part of the 'tradition'. The ancestors 'hand down' not only myths, rituals and other information, but also their names and their being itself. All that is 'real' comes from the ancestors.

The king is dead

Most ancestors are related only to specific families. But there are also 'communal ancestors', usually linked with the founding of the present community. Among the Baluba these are called the 'superior beings' (*bavidye*). They are associated with both natural objects and heroic figures of the past. The Luba Epic suggests that originally they were nature spirits, which at a certain point entered into human beings. For example, Nkongolo is both the rainbow and an ancient chief.

The 'superior beings' continue to have a close relationship with

The Luba Epic

Newell Booth

A group of people with reddish skins known as the Kalanga, once lived in what is now the south-central part of Zaire. They worshipped spirits living in trees, rocks and water. But many of them were dissatisfied; they wanted the spirit powers to be more closely linked with human life. One spirit was persuaded to come from the large rock where he lived and possess a man called Mujibu, who became the first Kilumbu, one through whom the spirit could speak to the people.

The making of a tyrant

Up to this time there had been no centralized government. A young man named Nkongolo watched black ants fighting and defeating white ants. He asked his father how they did this, and his father replied, 'By organizing in bands and showing no mercy.' Nkongolo decided to follow their example. He organized a band of warriors who showed no mercy on their enemies, and soon became ruler of a large area.

Nkongolo was a tyrant, hated by his people, and suspicious of everyone except his family. He lived with his mother and sisters; possibly he was married to a sister. But Nkongolo was worried about Mujibu's prophecy that a stranger from the east would soon appear to set up a royal line in the area.

The dark stranger

One day, two of Nokongolo's sisters were collecting fish from traps along the shore of a nearby lake, when they met a hunter. He was very black, unlike the reddish local people, and obviously an aristocrat. They hurried home to tell their brother, who immediately concluded that this was the stranger from the east. He sent out warriors to capture or kill the stranger, but they could not find him.

Later Nkongolo's sisters returned and found the hunter. Nkongolo now permitted the hunter, who was called Mbidi Kiluwe, to marry his sisters. But he was still suspicious; Mbidi Kiluwe had odd habits, such as eating alone and insisting that his food be cooked on a special fire. Mujibu confirmed the view that he was the stranger from the east.

Nkongolo began to plot to get rid of Mbidi Kiluwe, who accordingly prepared to escape. His wives were now pregnant, and he gave them special arrows which only he used, saying, 'If your children are boys, and need my help, they can identify themselves with these arrows.' Then he left for his own kingdom in the east.

The dance of death

One of Mbidi Kiluwe's wives gave birth to a son, Ilunga, who grew up to be a great warrior and helped his uncle Nkongolo extend his kingdom. He was so successful that he received the title 'Conqueror' (Kalala). Nkongolo became jealous and began to plot his death. He arranged for Kalala Ilunga to lead a victory dance, secretly digging a pit in the middle of the dance area, filling it with spears with their points up, and covering it over.

When the dance began, Kalala Ilunga headed for the pit, but the drummer warned him by drumming that something was wrong. Soon Kalala Ilunga understood, threw his spear through the pit-covering, ran home to get his father's arrows, and escaped to the east. Nkongolo failed to catch him. He became fearful and hid in a cave with his sisters, who betrayed him to Kalala Ilunga on his return. Nkongolo was beheaded, and the following morning a red ant-hill had sprung up where his head had fallen.

Kalala Ilunga became king and Nkongolo, who had been resented in life as a tyrant, in death became the guardian spirit of the kingdom. 'Nkongolo' is also the Balubas word for rainbow. It is said that two large snakes, living in different lakes, sometimes rise and meet in the sky, forming the rainbow. So Nkongolo is an ancient king, a guardian spirit, and also a nature spirit. The Baluba people sometimes call themselves the 'children of Nkongolo'. But they consider Mbidi Kiluwe, the 'stranger from the east' to be the founder of the royal line which provides them with a living authority.

Spirits are responsible for many forms of evil, including sickness. To exorcise the evil, ritual dances are performed.

the kings or chiefs, who are both political rulers and religious figures. Kings and chiefs stand for the wholeness of the community, and link it with the heroic past. Sometimes it is more important for them to be in touch with the spirit world than to control the living. A ruler cannot be deformed, ill or in any way weak, because he represents the community. In some areas it was the custom to kill a ruler who was ill for more than a few days.

The house of incest
The installation of a ruler frequently involved re-enacting events of the heroic age. Among the Baluba, the new ruler was supposed to commit incest with a close female relative and then come out of the 'house of incest' to dance the victory dance of Kalala Ilunga. In this way he linked himself with the chaotic, powerful past, associated with Nkongolo, when incest occurred and brought its power into orderly society, associated with Kalala Ilunga.

Not all southern or central African groups have had centralized political systems. A village may

be the highest unit, and rule may be by consensus of elders rather than by a chief. Even where there was a chief or king, he was usually not an absolute authority but stood for the consensus of the community, which included the ancestors.

Upside-down people
We have seen that African religion involves a 'web' of past as well as present relationships. Sometimes, however, this web comes 'undone'. For instance, the dissatisfied dead are a threat to the living. There are also living persons who work against the community: witches or sorcerers.

Sometimes a distinction is drawn between people who are by nature or inheritance antisocial, and even unconscious of what they are doing (witches), and those who choose to harm others (sorcerers). Both tend to do the same kind of things, destructive to the community. A witch or sorcerer is basically an 'upside-down' person. Sometimes he is actually believed to travel upside-down. He may also be 'white', whereas normal people are 'black'. He relates to animals, especially owls and hyenas, but destroys people. Normal people improve the community; a witch or sorcerer tears it down.

Death is unnatural
Individual deaths are usually blamed on a particular person. Death is seldom believed to be 'natural', except perhaps in a few cases of extreme old age. Certain kinds of death, for example from smallpox or from being struck by lightning, may be credited directly to God. Most death and disease is due to a witch or sorcerer, or to a dissatisfied spirit. It is possible that a basically kind ancestor may cause trouble, to warn the community that offerings are being neglected or standards of behaviour broken.

The basket of fortune
When disease, death or other evil occurs, the cause must be discovered through divination. There are two kinds of divination. One uses various objects to get an answer. For example, 'Ngombu', among neighbours of the Baluba such as the Ndembu, involves using a basket of objects referring to various human situations. The basket is shaken, and interpretation is based on the objects which appear at the top and how they relate to each other.

Another example would be the 'Hakata', used by the Shona people. Four pieces of wood or bone, standing for old man, young man, young woman and old woman, are marked 'up' and 'down'. The diviner throws these, and interprets on the basis of how each piece lands. Spirits are believed to be giving messages through the objects.

Secondly, spirits speak directly through persons, whom they 'possess', using their voices to speak. An example is the *kilumbu* of the Baluba, who is possessed by one of the *bavidye*. A *kilumbu* speaks especially about community matters, although he may also deal with individual problems, such as disease and childlessness.

A slightly different form is the oracle. Here a spirit dwelling in a particular spot, often a cave or a body of water, makes its will known through a medium, who is not actually 'possessed', in the sense that his or her personality is replaced by that of the spirit.

Medicine

Once the cause of a disease has been discovered, steps must be taken to produce a cure and to prevent future occurrence. Among many Bantu-speaking groups substances or actions that restore health are called *bwanga*. Africans are quite aware of the physical causes of certain problems and take practical action to deal with these. A splint would be put on a broken limb. But this is really a form of first aid, which fails to deal with the basic problems of human relationships, revealed by divination. For healing, the 'web' of tradition and community which has somehow been disturbed must be restored.

The person who uses *bwanga*

to make such repairs is the 'medicine man' or 'doctor' (*nganga*), often wrongly called 'witch-doctor'. He is not a witch, who destroys relationships, but the opposite, one who repairs or protects relationships. Of course, he may use some of the same methods or powers as a witch, but he uses them positively. It is true that, using such powers, he may be tempted to use them selfishly against the community. But a *nganga* is no more a witch than a policeman is a criminal because he sometimes uses the same weapons as a criminal, and may be tempted to misuse them and become a criminal.

Many African groups have 'secret societies', with healing activities. Among the Baluba such are sometimes called *bwanga*. Members of the societies frequently perform dances which, by providing entertainment, promote harmony in the community and so keep evil away. In this way recreation, healing, politics

and religion are all closely tied together in the traditional community.

The Supreme Being

Most African societies believe in a number of spirits, but also in one supreme power, responsible for creating the world. The Baluba believe in the 'superior beings' (*bavidye*); they also believe in the 'Supreme Being', *Vidye Mukulu* (*mukulu* means 'great' or 'old'). He is different from the *bavidye* who may serve him and share his being, but do not exist on the same level.

Similar beliefs appear to exist throughout southern and central Africa. Other names are used for 'God', such as Nzambe along the western coast, Leza in the south-centre, Mwari among the Shona,

In many tribes, certain people become members of a 'secret society', in order to perform special roles such as healing. These girls are about to be initiated into a secret society in Sierra Leone.

Modimo among the Sotho-Tswana, Tixo among the Zulu and neighbouring groups, Mulungu along the east coast, Ngai among both Bantu and Nilotic-speaking groups in Kenya, and Jok among several Nilotic-speaking groups. Some of these names may also mean 'spirit'; others are linked with the sky and what comes from it.

The traditional religion of most of the peoples of southern and central Africa includes belief in a Being who is in some sense the creator and ultimate power of the universe, standing behind a variety of lesser spirits. In many societies there has been little or no direct worship of this Being. He is too great, too powerful and too different from people to need or want worship of sacrifice. Or, it may be that he is too overwhelmingly present. In any case, it is unnecessary, and perhaps unwise, to call yourself to his attention. Certain groups, however, appeal to him in emergencies such as drought or epidemic, which threaten the whole community, and in a few he may receive regular worship. This seems to be more common among the Khoisan and Nilotic peoples than among the speakers of Bantu languages.

The Supreme Being holds together the 'web of relationship' between man and his environment. He is the ultimate source of the lesser spirits' power and of the power of human beings, living and dead.

Case-study 10: The Zulu

Axel-Ivar Berglund

Recent studies on African traditional beliefs have shown quite convincingly that African ideas and religious convictions are not primitive in an evolutionistic sense. Nor are they 'backward' and without sense. Quite the contrary! Thoughts and beliefs, expressed in rituals and in life-attitudes, make sense and are fully logical, if they are seen from the angle of those who live these thought-patterns.

Zulu, who live on the east coast of South Africa and belong to the Nguni family of Bantu-speaking people, are a good illustration of how an African traditional religion can adapt and accommodate itself to new ideas and symbols.

The Lord-of-the-Sky

Early literature on Zulu religious ideas, dating back some 100 years, seems to indicate that Zulu of that time hardly entertained thoughts of a god in the sky. The preoccupation was with the shades.

Due chiefly to the presence of, and challenge by, Christian missions there has developed among traditional Zulu an idea of the Lord-of-the-Sky, 'iNkosi yezulu'.

He is believed to be the eternal one; from him flows power and might. The Lord-of-the-Sky is the source of both good and evil. He is both kind and generous, but also erratic and unpredictable. In times of crisis such as drought or childlessness, Zulus turn to him; but he also sends lightning that will strike 'the one he wants to be his slave up there in heaven'. He will cause barrenness 'because the woman has irritated him, sometimes by talking too much, sometimes because the Lord-of-the-Sky is fretful'.

The chameleon is linked with the Lord-of-the-Sky. It, too, is unpredictable. It continually changes colour! It has five legs (the tail is said to be a leg because it coils around branches), and has eyes that look in different directions at the same time! 'How could such a thing as a chameleon be created? There can be no sympathy with the one that made such a creature as this.'

Although the Lord-of-the-Sky can be approached, he must be avoided lest you become insane. Only on special occasions should he be approached, and only after long preparation. Certain well-known hills in Zululand are recognized as his. On these no cattle graze and people rarely ascend them.

'Only when we plead for rain will we go up this mountain. First there must be fasting and much prayer. When everybody i ready and the set day arrives, we gather at the foot of the hill. Everybody is quiet. We climb with awe, looking down and walking humbly. Then prayer is offered by the rain-doctor. We kneel or lie down when he speaks to the Lord-of-the-Sky. When he has finished we return, without speaking. We do not talk, for the one in whose presence we are is fearful.'

The brooding shades

In the lives of the Zulu people the shades play an all-important role. But in times of crisis the shades brood over their descendants 'as a hen broods over her chickens'. The chief occasions are childbirth, puberty, marriage, death and burial. Diviners are constantly brooded over by the shades, but because they 'eat the right medicines, they do not become mad. All other people would have gone mad long ago, if they had been in the same situation'.

When a hen broods over her eggs, the chickens eventually hatch. Likewise the brooding of the shades heralds the emergence of a different person.

'It is like this. There is the bride. She is one kind of person. At marriage, when the shades brood, she becomes another person. She is now the wife. When they brood again, she changes from the childless to the mother of a child.'

A world reversed

Zulu diviners claim they see things upside-down. Shades are believed to be pale-coloured; in the world of the shades, dark stands for light and light for dark Shades are said to like gall 'because gall to them is sweet as honey'. Men work during daytime, the shades are active at night. The right hand is left, and the left is right in the world of the shades. So diviners, servants of the shades, often use the left hand when divining. Up stands

for down and down for up!

These reversals and opposites make sense in the context of a flat earth viewpoint (and the global concept is, after all, relatively recent, even in Europe).

If Zululanders believe we live on top of a pancake-like world, it follows that those who live on the other side are opposite. On the top, men walk with their heads upward and feet downward; in the underworld they move upside-down.

When it is night on top it is day-time underneath! Hence people were buried at night, not to avoid the grave-site being known to thieves and evil-minded people, but so that the deceased can reach the land of the dead 'at a time when he can see in this new country'.

A diviner uses divination bones and other objects, which he throws on to a special mat in front of him.

Christianity and the Primal Religions

Harold Turner

Surprisingly, primal religion—the religion that seems farthest from Christianity and has been most despised—is in fact closer than the rest. Christianity has expanded most, not into the areas of the great culture religions of Asia, or into Islam, but among the peoples of the primal religions, starting in the Mediterranean.

The public religions of Greece, Rome and the ancient Near East were basically primal, although linked with sophisticated cultures. The religions of North Africa and Europe were also primal, like those of Oceania and black Africa south of the Sahara, and of aboriginal North and South America, whose peoples have largely been brought inside the Christian fold. Christianity has advanced most in Asia, too, where primal religions predominated—in the Philippines, in Korea with its shamanistic religions, and among the tribal hill-people of south-east Asia, Taiwan and India, and the people of Indonesia who are not Muslim.

An easy knock-down?

Some scholars explain this response as due to primal religions' fragility, primitiveness or inadequacy as compared with the great Asian religions; Christianity can deal only with religions that are an easy knock-down! This fails to take account of the deep religiousness of many primal religions. Frequently they are remarkably good at adapting to modern conditions, for example the Mwari cult of the Shona in Zimbabwe. Others have persisted through over four centuries of Western pressure and Christian penetration, for example the Hopi and other American Indian religions.

Primal religions seem to be closer to Christianity in form and structure than the major Asian religions. Often, when Christian missionaries first arrive, people say: 'This is what we have been waiting for.' A vast range of new religious movements has arisen out of a mixing of primal religions and Christianity in all continents. There is no interaction on this scale between primal religions and the other universal religions.

We are not alone

Some of the basic emphases in primal religions are also found in Christianity. These include a closeness to nature and love of the land; a profound awareness of human weakness and of the need of a greater power for successful living. There is a deep conviction that we are not alone in the universe, but that there is a spirit world from which all blessing and help come; and that while the spirits are active in the physical world, there is another world beyond death where life is purified and transformed. Not all primal religions have all these features, but many do, and clearly have much in common with Christianity.

On the other hand, there are basic differences between primal world-views and those of the Bible:
● A number of gods;
● No revelation through history;
● Efficacy of sacrifice and ritual;
● Mixing of religion and magic;
● Gods and men belong to one cosmic system and depend on each other.

By contrast, Christians worship one God with a firm moral character, who freely created the universe out of nothing, and is not tied to it, and who has acted once for all to save all peoples.

Nevertheless, primal religion often survives in syncretist folk Christianity.

Case-study 11:
North American Indians

J. W. E. Newbery

Contrary to popular belief, primal religions are today reviving in many parts of the world. The superior attitude, which spread European civilization over the globe, spurred on by Western Christianity and materialism, has been discredited in the twentieth century. Native faith-ways—scorned, forbidden, almost destroyed—reached their lowest point at the end of the nineteenth century. Their flame was extinguished.

But today the disregard for the earth, for community, for spirituality, have brought the whole human enterprise into jeopardy. Arising like the phoenix from the ashes, tribal peoples are gathering again in their ceremonial circles, remembering discarded teachings, renewing the ancient ways. As they do so, perhaps they are laying the foundations for what they themselves are calling 'the fourth world', and a hope for a new beginning on the earth.

Life is one

Wisdom, for such people, is found in the past, in the long experience of the race, in tradition. A very frequent expression in their ceremonies is, 'it is said...' The teaching of the ancients is meant. The teacher is the Elder. He is closest to those things of the past that are important. For tribal people, life is one. The sacred is very real—and specially real in some times and places. But the sacred is not divided off from times and places called secular. All life is sacred. All things are 'indwelt' to some degree. The whole range of life is open to spirit.

● The tribal peoples of North America proclaim the One Great Spirit. Their thought and action is governed by the circle, which they see as basic in nature: the shape of moon and sun, the wheeling stars above them, the rotating seasons, the actions of birds and animals. 'Everything tries to be round.' This form is evident in everything they do—in myth, ceremony, art and community organization.

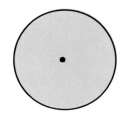

Essential to the circle is its *centre*. From that point it is created. This is the symbol of the Great Spirit. It is reflected in all the dances around the fire, drum or pole, and in ceremonies such as the sacred pipe.

● **Two realities.** Tribal people also reflect upon the two-ness of life and nature. North American natives symbolize this by a divided circle, as in the Plains shields and many forms of art and craft.

Nature presents itself in pairs: dark and light, cold and hot, male and female, good and bad and so on. These are not contradictory but complementary. They are depicted in native North American shields as mirroring each other. This two-ness is also expressed in the myths, such as that of the two sons of Mother Earth; in the totems of the west coast such as Sisutl of the Kwakiutl, the two-headed serpent which punishes and protects; in the Thunderbird, threatening and caring; or in ceremonies such as the forked pole of the Sundance.

But the *two* are always seen as aspects of the one: the circle. They are different, but they appear to us in balance, in *harmony*, the over-riding virtue. We find contentment not by conflict, but by coming to terms.

An example of this is the native Arctic dweller, the Inuit. The intruding white man complains about a harsh, cruel environment, and insists when he goes north on taking with him all manner of technologies to beat the climate. The Inuit, on the other hand, lives face to face with nature and, when untouched by the intruder, is happy. He has found harmony with his surroundings, and treats the ice and snow as friends, not enemies.

● **Three-fold action.** Give and take is, for Amerindians, the basis of all healthy relationships. It can be symbolized as a triangle on a circle.

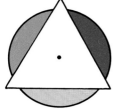

Primal people search for the support that will make their ventures succeed. This help is obtained in the *ceremonies*, whose action is three-sided. For example, a Mohawk community is threatened by drought. The corn withers in the fields. Help lies with the Thunderbeings; the rain must be sought by their aid. The thing to do is the rain dance. The community gathers in the fields. The drum and shaker sound. The dance begins. Prayer is sung. Water is sprinkled. The rains come.

The same give and take, between human need, heavenly power and particular action is found in all ceremonies for healing, guidance, power.

● **The four powers.** Native people in North America, as elsewhere, tended to see the structure of the world, and of the powers that control it, as four-sided. The symbol they used for this is a circle, with four points on the circumference.

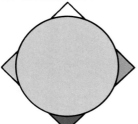

Lame Deer, a present-day Sioux, explains: 'Four is the number that is most sacred (*wakan*). Four stands for the four

quarters of the earth . . . the four winds . . . seasons . . . colours . . . four things of which the universe is made (earth, air, water, fire). There are four virtues which a man should possess . . . We Sioux do everything by fours . . .'

Into this structure of fours is gathered and classified all life's variety. It is made one (the circle) through the 'great law of sacrifice', in which each part depends upon and contributes to all the others. 'One dies that another may live.' The 'wheel' is the pattern of all ceremonies, because it symbolizes the variety of life in the wholeness of life.

This concept of unity in variety and variety within unity is basic to the goal of harmony and balance in life, seen by primal people as the foundation of all health, peace and well-being in the world.

● **The seven 'Grandfathers'.** A 'mystery of sevens' lies at the root of ancient wisdom and is found among ancient cultures in all parts of the world. We find this same feeling about seven among the primal people of North America. We hear of the seven sacred rites of the Sioux, the seven prophecies (or fires) of the Ojibwa Midewiwin and the seven stopping-places in their ages-long migration westward. We hear of cycles of seven years and seven-times-seven years; we hear of the seven Grandfathers.

The seven Grandfathers are found in Ojibwa mythology. They are symbolized in the teaching staff hung in the centre of the ceremonial circle. The staff

is made up of three straight sticks bound together at their centres. These sticks have six points standing for the four directions, plus the 'above' power (sky) and the 'below' power (earth). There is a seventh, at the crossing-point. It is the 'here' place of power, the *self*, the power within. This is not to say that *I* am the centre of all, but that all the powers are available to me, are flowing through me and I can be a power with them. They come to me in visions and dreams, and in teachings and ceremonies working through me.

● **The quartered circle.** Finally, there is the simple quartered circle, the symbol of wholeness.

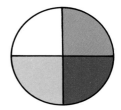

When taking part in the ceremonies, as the sweet grass is burned, the water drunk, the pipe smoked, one hears from each worshipper the words 'All my relations'. All are *related* to each and each to all. The participant is conscious that the whole universe is around him, sharing in his need and his prayer.

Case-study 12: The Andes

Leslie Hoggarth

The Tukano Indians live in the forests of Colombia.

The Andean Highlands stretch almost the whole length of the west coast of South America, from Colombia to the south of Chile. They form the longest mountain chain on any continent, with some forty-five snow peaks towering above 20,000 feet/6,080 metres.

In the mountains and valleys live many tribes, each with its own language and culture, religious beliefs and practices. The high mountainous regions are very different from the lower eastern slopes, where the rivers flow down to the Amazon forests. Physical conditions greatly affect the pattern of life and religion. But some basic concepts are common to all: beliefs about gods, spirits, the natural world, sacred places and objects possessing supernatural power and influencing every aspect of life.

Native people are concentrated in the mountain regions of Ecuador, Peru and Bolivia. Inca civilization flourished up to the time of the Spanish Conquest in 1533. It is still the homeland of some 10 million Indians. The main group are the Quechuas, but there are also about 1 million Aymara Indians, living at 12,000 feet/3,648 metres, on the 'altiplano' stretching for hundreds of miles between the main mountain ranges of southern Peru and Bolivia. The languages of the two groups differ, but there are many similarities in their life and religion.

Sacrificed to the spirits

The people of the Andes are mainly farmers, cultivating the land in the valleys and herding their sheep, llamas and alpacas as high as 14,000 feet/4,256 metres. They struggle fiercely against the harsh elements. In order to assure security and well-being, the people seek to live in harmony with their natural surroundings. Solemn rites and

An Indian shaman *from Peru.*

keep up good relations with them.

Struck by lightning

August marks the beginning of the agricultural cycle. At this time Pachamama is spoken of as 'being alive'. She is ready to receive the seed; therefore the ceremonies must be performed to ensure a good harvest. Token portions of coca, food and drink are 'served' and an offering containing the foetus of a llama or some other animal, coca leaves, animal fat, and other items is burned in a special place. A prayer will be offered, such as—'Pachamama, this is your due, that I serve you in August at the beginning of the year. You are the one who nourishes me, receive this offering. You feed me like a mother from her breast, or as a bird feeds its young. Receive this kindly, and defend me from all harm. Remove sorrow and illness far from me, and may I live well through another year.'

Similar prayers, burnt offerings, and in some places blood sacrifices, are made in animal fertility ceremonies.

In times of sickness people will consult the *paqo* (medicine man and medium) to discover the cause of the trouble. There are different types of *paqo*; some work by divination, such as reading the signs in the coca leaves—others contact the spirits direct. A genuine *paqo* is one who has been struck by lightning and survived, and is therefore considered to have been chosen as priest.

ceremonies are performed throughout the year to ensure good crops, animal fertility and freedom from illness and disaster. These ceremonies involve a complex ritual of prayers, offerings, drink-offerings and even animal sacrifices offered to the spirits of the region.

The mountain people see the Earth Mother, Pachamama, as the provider and sustainer of life. In the high, snow-capped peaks live the Apus. These are the 'lords' who control everything in the area. The spirits of the lower hills are known as Aukis and are not as powerful as the Apus. All the Apus and Aukis are named after the mountain or hill where they live. They are the chief gods in the Indian world. But thunder, hail, rain, wind, fire, springs, rivers and special rocks and stones are all very important. They are all alive, and possess life-power, and have to be recognized with token offerings.

The Apus, Aukis and Pachamama exercise their power in the growing of crops, making animals fertile and looking after the community. They can become hungry, angry, neglected or offended, and people must take care to give them their due and to

Part Four
Living Religions of the East

The Eternal Teaching: Hinduism

Raymond Hammer

The religious tradition we call 'Hinduism' is the product of 5,000 years of development. The name, however, dates only from about AD 1200, the time when the invading Muslims wished to distinguish the faith of the people of India from their own.

'Hindu' is the Persian word for 'Indian'. Indians themselves, however, prefer to speak of the eternal teaching or law (*sanatana dharma*), indicating the 'givenness' or revelatory character of the beliefs to which they are committed.

No founder, no creed

Hinduism has no founder and no prophet. It has no particular ecclesiastical or institutional structure, nor set creed. The emphasis is on the way of living rather than on a way of thought. Radhakrishnan, a former president of India, once remarked: 'Hinduism is more a culture than a creed.'

Not everyone who is born a Hindu is a practising Hindu. But it is claimed that 'they are Hindus because they were born as Hindus'. The origin of the name suggests that the common ingredient in Hinduism is the Indian origin of its adherents. (In fact, one writer somewhat cynically asserts that the only unifying features in Hinduism are the Indian character of the faith and the universal reverence for the cow!)

Mother India

The Hindu religion is closely inter-twined with tradition about the land of India, its social system and its history. The Indian subcontinent has clear geographical demarcations. Triangular in shape, it is bounded on two sides by the ocean and to the north by the impenetrable Himalayan range of mountains. The actual shape of the land recalls for Indians the figure of a mother and speaks to them of 'Mother India'.

A large part of the country is a rich, fertile plain. This is what makes the mountains, and the rivers which flow from them, so significant. In the north it is the rivers, in the south the monsoon rains, which make plentiful harvests possible throughout the year.

The whole of nature is seen as vibrant with life—trees, rocks and waterfalls provide a focus for the sacred, becoming shrines at which worshippers discover meaning in life. The mountains and forests often speak to the Indians of the powers that confront human endeavour and so become pointers to the struggle between divine and demonic powers.

Although the yogis go on pilgrimage to desolate regions in search of 'Reality', it is primarily the rivers which are seen as the source of support and spiritual life.

Sacred river

The sacred River Ganges not only provides water for the land; the water is itself the symbol of life without end. Hundreds of thousands flock to its banks daily to perform their ritual ablutions in its waters and sip from its life-giving stream. Once every twelve years as many as 10 million people share in ritual bathing at the great Kumbh Mela festival at Allahabad, where the waters of the Ganges and Jumna combine. Varanasi (on the Ganges) is the most sacred city—*the* place for a Hindu to die. Then, after cremation, the ashes can be cast upon the waters of the sacred river and life continues!

A rich variety

The population of India is far from homogeneous. Each district has its own language and customs as well as its own religious ideas and practices. The vast majority of the people are agricultural and, despite large populous cities, most live in small villages, of which there are almost 700,000. This factor contributes to the tremendous local variety within the larger regions.

The oldest continuous culture is to be found in the four southern states, where the languages are classified as 'Dravidian'. The north, as a result of the Aryan invasion which took place in the middle of the second millennium BC, possesses a group of related languages, in which Hindi is dominant. The north-eastern states are dominated by Bengal which was late in receiving Aryan influence.

About 400 million people in the Indian subcontinent may be regarded as Hindus. And wherever Indians

Varanasi (Benares) is the most holy city in India. Millions of pilgrims visit it each year, to bathe in the sacred Ganges.

Hindus cremate their dead. Scattering the ashes together with sacred marigold flowers onto the River Ganges ensures the soul's continued life.

have gone, they have taken with them their culture and religious ideas and practices.

One faith or many?

Hinduism embraces a wide diversity of religious belief.

● The vast majority of Hindus believe in God in some way or other, but there are some who do not.

● Some Hindus believe that a respect for all living creatures demands that they be vegetarians; others will sacrifice animals at the temple and joyfully share in a roast by the river-side.

● Some Hindus worship Shiva; others Vishnu or his incarnations (*avatars*), most notably Krishna or Rama; others again are worshippers of the goddesses.

● The inhabitants of one village do not share in the precise focus of worship which will unite the villagers in another place.

● The individual Hindu may reverence one god, a few, or many, or none at all!

● He may also believe in one god *and* in several gods as manifestations of him.

● He may express the ultimate in personal or impersonal terms.

It has been suggested that Hinduism is 'a federation of cults and customs, a collage of ideas and spiritual aspirations'. So, is it possible to speak of 'Hinduism' in the singular, or are there many 'Hinduisms'?

Under one umbrella

For Hinduism, as for other religious traditions, the name is an umbrella term which does not demand a total homogeneity. (To draw a parallel: the ritual of an African independent Christian church will be far removed from a Coptic or Armenian liturgy, and yet all come under the name 'Christian'.) But if Hinduism embraces a 'family of religious beliefs', we still need to find something which can be called the 'ethos' of Indian religion.

The flow of life

One concept which is found everywhere within Hinduism today is the idea of reincarnation or transmigration. Whereas Christianity thinks in terms of the importance of decision-making within one life, and sees salvation in terms of the individual (though not neglecting the group or the whole), the Hindu thinks of the flow of life through many existences. This lies behind the notion of *samsara* which expresses this flow from birth to death and then on to rebirth, and so on. As a result the limited span of history is lengthened to billions upon billions of years.

Linked with the notion of *samsara* is the concept of *karma*. *Karma* literally means 'work' or 'action', but also indicates the *consequences* of actions within one existence which flow into the next existence and influence its character—and so the chain goes on. Hindu hope, therefore, is for release (*moksha*) from this chain or cycle.

The other great unifying feature is the attitude of Hinduism to society (see 'Roots').

Roots: The Development of Hindu Religion

Raymond Hammer

The roots of Hinduism (as we now meet it) go back thousands of years. So what do we know about the earliest forms of religion in the Indian subcontinent?

Temple-citadels

The earliest evidence we have comes from excavations that have taken place since 1922 in the Punjab and the Indus Valley. A homogeneous urban culture was established in the third millennium BC, and two cities have been excavated: Harappa, the prehistoric capital of the Punjab on the banks of the River Ravi, and Mohenjo-daro, 400 miles/645 kilometres away in Sindh, on the banks of the Indus.

It is evident that the rivers were vital for their inhabitants, irrigating the broad, fertile plains with their flood-waters. Ritual purity was most important to these early people and the ancient temples incorporated ceremonial ablutions (as they still do today). Ritual bathing was not confined simply to the baths at the sanctuary. People also bathed in the rivers which provided the livelihood for their community, and so could be thought of as 'rivers of life' and therefore sacred.

The finds at the temple-citadels suggest that there was a unity of the political and the religious. There may be parallels with the sacral kingship in ancient Babylon, where the ruler was seen as a 'son' of the divinity—in both cases a mother-goddess, the symbol of creativity and the ongoing flow of life. There are many figurines of the goddess, signifying the origin of life (a pregnant figure) or the nurture and continuance of life (figures which emphasize the breasts). All the indications are of an early matriarchal society as the background to the host of goddesses in India today. Each village seems to have its own goddess, venerated as the giver of life and fertility. They may also be seen as embodiments of the female principle, called *Shakti* in developing Hinduism.

There are figures of a male god, too, with horns and three faces (seemingly the original of the triad, *Trimurti*, later expressed by the three deities Brahma, Vishnu and Shiva). He is shown in the position of a yogi (one who practises yoga, the way of self-discipline) in a state of contemplation. He is also seen surrounded by animals, which suggests that he is the original form of the great god Shiva, who is often spoken of as 'Lord of the Beasts'. The fertility symbols, the *lingam* and *yoni* (representing the male and female sexual organs), both still present in popular forms of Hinduism, have also been found.

It would appear, therefore, that this ancient Indus Valley civilization shows traits which are still a powerful force in Indian religion.

The Aryan faith

In the middle of the second millennium BC the Aryan (literally 'noble') peoples invaded India, bringing their language and traditions and profoundly influencing, although in no way ousting, the older religions, ideas and practices. Their language developed within India into what we call Sanskrit—a parallel of Greek, Latin and other Indo-European languages. It appears that their religion, too, had close affinities with that of Homer's Greece. At any rate, the Aryan pantheon recalls the gods of *The Iliad* and *The Odyssey*—fundamentally manifestations of nature.

Whereas the older Indus Valley religion seems to have included yoga, renunciation and purification rites—all of which continue to mark the 'holy men' of India—the Aryans appear to have been much more world-affirming. They were originally nomads (coming perhaps from the Baltic regions). They appreciated the 'openness' of nature—trees, fields, sky and so on. Like Homer's Greeks, they made their sacrifices to gods who represented the forces of nature. Animal sacrifice was very much a feature of their practices. Whereas rivers provided the meeting-place for the pre-Aryan worshippers, the Aryans gathered around fire and performed their ceremonies there. They would cast grain, butter and spice into the flames.

Unfortunately there have been no archaeological finds from the early period of Aryan settlement, but we do possess a literature (written down probably about 800 BC, but reflecting an oral poetical tradition from centuries before). The Vedic texts (*Vid* expresses 'knowledge') enshrine the main evidence for the original Aryan faith.

Songs of knowledge: the Rig Veda

The *Rig Veda* ('songs of knowledge') are the oldest. Many of these religious hymns may have been composed when the Vedic peoples were still in central Asia. But most of them probably date from a time after the settlement in India. In later times they were considered to be a revelation from Brahman (the ultimate source of all being) in the form of words, received by the inspired sages (*rishis*). The sages, it was held, had been granted the ability to apprehend the knowledge which was eternal (hence the title *sanatana*—'eternal'—*dharma*) and divine. The religious tradition later distinguished between what was revealed (*shruti*) and what was remembered (*smriti*) and so possessed not direct, but only a secondary, inspiration.

The gods

The *Rig Veda* is made up of more than 1,000 hymns. They are usually addressed to a single god, and several dozen different gods feature in them. The most popular is Indra, who is portrayed as a warrior who overcomes the powers of evil and brings the world into being. The god Agni is the personification of the sacrificial fire (Latin *ignis*) and so links earth and heaven, carrying the gifts which the priests pour into the flames into the presence of the gods.

'May that Agni who is to be extolled by ancient and modern seers, conduct the gods here.'

The divine parents, Heaven and Earth, symbolize the expanses of nature. Their marriage indicates the indissoluble link between two worlds, the celestial and the terrestrial. Varuna (Greek Uranus) is the chief of the gods, because ceremonial rite (*rita*) and law (*dharma*) are administered and regulated by him. The cosmic order is within his control and he ensures that there is no transgression, cosmic or human.

The *Veda* distinguishes between the World Soul (*purusha*)

Hinduism Outside India

Raymond Hammer

From the seventh century AD Hindu culture and religion exercised a widespread influence throughout south-east Asia, taking in the modern-day countries of Burma, Thailand, Kampuchea, Laos and Vietnam as well as many of the islands of Indonesia. (For 1,000 years, even then, there had been contact with Sri Lanka, formerly Ceylon, and during the time of Ashoka who was ruler in the third century BC, Buddhist ideas had been introduced.) Generally speaking, this influence persisted for about eight centuries and is dominant on the island of Bali to the present day.

In most countries, however—and this is also true of Bali—the Hindu culture incorporates a great deal of popular, indigenous, pre-Hindu religion. The Angkor Wat structures in Kampuchea reflect interest in Brahminic religious rites, the worship of Vishnu and Shiva, as well as pronounced ideas of kingship. A stylized religious art marks most of the countries, and in Thailand and Kampuchea the sculptures bear witness to the popularity of the *Ramayana* cycle of stories.

Since Hinduism, in some form or other, is the religion of most Indians, we would expect to find Hindus wherever Indians are to be found. The dispersion takes in Europe (especially, of course, the United Kingdom), the Americas and Pacific areas as far as Fiji. Until recently, there were also a considerable number of Indians in eastern and southern Africa.

Although it has been largely through Buddhism that Indian thought (and especially religious ideas) has had its impact on the West, Indian *swamis* and gurus have had a considerable following and Hare Krishna groups are to be found in both Europe and America.

Many in the West also look to yoga. Just as Buddhism had its Eightfold Path, so royal yoga (Raja Yoga) had its eight stages—mainly physical disciplines directed to the goal of deep, concentrated meditation. This involved self-control (to which the name yoga points), observance, posture, control of breath, restraint of the senses, control of the thought-processes and contemplation.

Although many in the West regard yoga simply as a discipline which strengthens the body and provides relaxation and a quiet mind, in the context of Hinduism it is the means by which a person strives for salvation. This is achieved when the dualism of self and Brahman is overcome and all selfhood is lost in the streams of being. Movements such as Transcendental Meditation (TM) look to this goal with yoga.

and substance (*prakriti*). The former is seen as the cosmic sacrifice, which ensues in life and order. There can be no life without sacrifice, we are told, and the divisions of the World Soul are seen as the basis of the human social order. The mouth is the priestly order (the Brahmins), the arms are the rulers (Rajanya, later known as the Kshatriya), the thighs are the land-owners, merchants and bankers (*vaishya*) and the feet are the workers, artisans and serfs (*shudra*). (It is likely that the *shudras* represented the subject-peoples who came from the indigenous population and were subordinated to the conquering Aryans.)

Power for the priests

The priority of the priestly class is linked with the crucial position given to sacrifice and the magical use of incantations. The priests alone could bring the people into touch with the cosmic powers and guarantee the continuation of life. This priestly ascendancy was not accepted without question, as the ruling class seem to have held the leadership for much of the time. It was only the elaboration of rite and ceremonial which increased the power of the priests. The more complicated the forms of worship, the more essential it was to have the expert!

But the *Veda* also reflects a growing speculation which was to lead to the *Upanishads* (the *Vedanta*, the end of the *Veda*) with which the revealed word was to terminate. In the early creation myth Indra was seen as the personal agent in creation, bringing existence out of non-existence. In later speculation the 'One God', described in personal terms, gives way to 'That One'— the impersonal force of creation.

There is also a questioning note:

'Who knows it for certain; who can proclaim it here; namely, out of what it was born and from what creation proceeded ... whether he made it or whether he

has not? ... he alone knows, or, perhaps, even he does not know.'

In this passage we have the basis for the future philosophizing which was happier to describe the ultimate or transcendent in negative rather than in positive terms and which was to accept a basic relativism in all attempts to describe the absolute.

Classes and castes

From the four class groupings of the poem on creation, the idea grew that some hierarchic structure in society is a part of the divine intention for the natural order. The classes (*varnas*—colours) were later to proliferate into

The god Shiva is the destroyer. This Nepalese carving shows him killing an evil demon.

a large number of birth-groups (*jutis*), which differentiated families much more according to work done in the community.

Although some aspects of the caste system have been outlawed by the Indian government in recent times, the system continues as an integral part of Indian society. Questions of marriage and eating are all linked with the class caste groupings. The first three classes are cut off from the fourth by being 'twice-born', or 'the initiated'. They

The Ramayana *is an epic poem which tells the story of Rama, the sixth incarnation of Vishnu. He was a great hero, dedicated to ridding the earth of evil-doers.*

dominated the sacrificial system. It was at this point that the movements of Jainism and Buddhism (see relevant articles) emerged within Hinduism. At the same time the *Upanishads* provided a redirection of the Vedantic tradition, being accepted as 'revelation'. These formed an indispensable ingredient in the new synthesis which was to emerge and be called 'Hinduism'.

The Jains

Both Mahavira (?599–527 BC), the figure behind Jainism, and the Buddha (about 563–483 BC), the founder of Buddhism, belonged to small republican city-states that had emerged amongst the Aryan tribal units. They came from 'noble' families of the ruling class which had once held the leadership in society.

The Jains believe that Mahavira was the twenty-fourth 'Ford-maker' in the current era of cosmic decline. (The cyclical view of history was unquestioningly accepted.) He, like the Buddha after him, had wandered in search of 'release' or 'salvation' from the age of thirty. He found it when he was forty-two, when he became a completed soul (*kevalin*) and conqueror (*jina*). (The name 'Jain' is derived from *jina*.) He died at Pava (near Patna in Bihar) after teaching for thirty years.

Mahavira was much more of a rationalist than the Brahmanists. He rejected revelation and based his religious scheme on logic and experience. He accepted the somewhat pessimistic view of the human situation and was concerned for release. As he saw the situation, the human soul was enmeshed in matter and needed to regain its pristine purity and thereby achieve immortality. It can only gain liberation as it loses its accumulation of actions and their consequences. Each soul is seen as an entity in its own right. Jainism in this way affirms a plurality of beings as against one

wear the sacred thread as an indication of superior status. In addition, birth-groups differentiate between the 'pure' and the 'impure', indicating both the importance of ritual purity and the impurity that accrues from mixing with another group.

It is likely that the *shudras* were first despised by the invading Aryans and regarded as belonging to an inferior colour (*varna*), being dark instead of light-skinned as they were. The idea of the

cycle of rebirth later indicated that the *shudras* could hope for salvation only in a future life, as they were not yet among 'the initiated'.

The priests were gaining a stranglehold on society through class differentials. But this was not to go unchallenged.

Revolt in the temple!

By about 600 BC the ascendancy of the priest in society was commonly accepted in northern India. The priestly ritual of sacrifice and its appropriate *mantra* (verbal utterance) as set out in the manuals of the priestly class

Men and Movements
Raymond Hammer

Over the past 200 years Western culture and the fundamental beliefs of Christianity have had a profound impact upon Hinduism. For quite a time it was customary for the more educated Indian to identify himself with the religion of the foreign occupier of his country. Hindu belief and practice continued unchanged in the villages, but in the cities the more affluent tended to undervalue Indian culture and literature and to disassociate themselves from popular religious practice.

Rammohan Roy
Rammohan Roy (1772–1833) has been called 'the father of modern India' because of his attempt to reform Hinduism, whilst reaffirming Hindu values. He claimed that all that was of value in Christian ethics was already present in his own Hindu heritage. He came from a Brahmin family and showed himself a remarkable student from his early years. He not only studied Hindu and Buddhist texts in Sanskrit, but mastered Persian, Arabic, Greek and mathematics. He organized the Brahmo Samaj (a society for the worshippers of God) and, as the ideals of the society, selected those passages in the classical Hindu scriptures which came closest to an ethical monotheism.

Although he was not unsympathetic to Christianity and was deeply moved by the person of Jesus, he rejected what he termed the 'doctrinal shell', welcoming only what he felt to be its 'humanitarian message'. As a result of his influence, the study of the *Vedas* and *Upanishads* was popularized and he laid the basis for the Hinduism of the Indian intelligentsia.

Sri Ramakrishna
Another significant figure in Hindu renascence was Sri Ramakrishna (1836–86) who came from a Brahmin family in Bengal. From an early age he experienced religious ecstasy and was particularly involved in the Kali cult. In his mystical trances he sought for communion with the 'Divine Mother' and, from the age of twenty, he was the chief priest of the Kali temple in his neighbourhood. Later, however, he came under the influence of Vedantic philosophy and so came to approach salvation by combining the paths of devotion and knowledge. He held that there was a universal truth present in all religions and saw God present in a variety of manifestations—as the Divine Mother, as Sita, as Rama, as Krishna, as Muhammad and as Jesus Christ. He was accordingly ready to accommodate himself to the dress, food or prayer patterns of other religions when he associated with their adherents. He had great influence among the Westernized middle class in Calcutta, and his deep piety and patent sincerity led them, in turn, to value their Hindu origins.

'I am a child of God,' he asserted; 'the son of the King of Kings; who can bind me? . . . I am not bound, I am free.'

The Ramakrishna Mission was organized in 1897, after his death, to carry on both his missionary and his social and educational work. It was reorganized in 1909, when its educational, charitable and missionary activity was separated from the monastic side (identified with the *ashrams*—open monasteries or retreat houses). The mission stresses the universal character of Hinduism (thus facilitating missionary work amongst Westerners) and adapts to the needs of a society in transition.

Vivekananda
The growing influence of the Ramakrishna movement and its international appeal were largely due to Vivekananda (1863–1902). Named Narenda Nath Datta, he had planned to study law in England, but was 'converted' by Ramakrishna. After twelve years of ascetic discipline he became famous as a religious teacher (*swami*), the apostle who carried Ramakrishna's teaching to the world. He was responsible for the stress on social work and religious education, and his fiery speeches aroused a new idealism among the young elite of India, so that they devoted themselves to uplifting the millions of poor and starving in India.

At the World Congress of Faiths in Chicago in 1893, he 'sold' to the world the greatness of the Hindu tradition. Not only were Indians given a pride in their own culture but, for the first time, Westerners who were disillusioned with Western society and had rejected the Christianity of the West turned to India for religious values and a new spirituality. (Madame Blavatsky's Theosophical Society was one group influenced by Vivekananda.)

His fundamental message was that each person was potentially divine and so should work to unleash the unlimited power within and also enable others to do the same. The mingling of theistic and monistic language which marks much Hindu thought is present in his teaching, although 'panentheism' (i.e. everything is within God) might better describe his standpoint.

'He is in everything; he is everything. Every man and woman is the palpable, blissful, living God. Who says God is unknown? Who says he is to be searched after? We have found God eternally. We have been living in him eternally.'

Vivekananda was ready to accept caste, regarding it as part of the natural order, but he rejected the notion of privilege derived from caste differentiation. Instead, he advocated equal chances for all.

Rabindranath Tagore
A contemporary of Vivekananda was Rabindranath Tagore (1861–1941) who gained the Nobel Prize for Literature in 1913 and whose poems were quoted by the elite of British Edwardian society in their drawing-room parties. He reflected the continuing influence of the Brahmo Samaj, giving it artistic expression. Nehru once

said that 'Tagore was primarily the man of thought', as contrasted with Mohandas Karamchand Gandhi (1869–1948) whom he spoke of as the man 'of concentrated and ceaseless activity'.

Gandhi

Gandhi had been influenced by Vivekananda and once observed: 'My life is my message.' For him truth was God, and non-violence (*ahimsa*) was the way to achieve the realization of God. His life was devoted to winning independence for India and raising the country's status. His Hinduism was all-embracing. Although he respected the Vedantic tradition and had a particular affection for the *Bhagavad Gita*, he claimed that his version of Hinduism included 'all that I know to be best in Islam, Christianity, Buddhism and Zoroastrianism'.

On the other hand, his teaching cannot be understood apart from the three basic Hindu concepts of *dharma* (duty), the *karmayoga* (the discipline of action) and *moksha* (spiritual deliverance). He interpreted the *Bhagavad Gita* as selfless action (*anashakti*), seeing Arjuna as the one who has to be calm and yet generous in the midst of suffering. Non-violence is not to be thought of in terms of passivity—it is the way of action. (There is some parallel here with the fact that Christians see in the suffering of Christ God's supreme action—the liberation of mankind from sin and death. It is not without significance that the cross of Christ had a fascination for Gandhi and that his favourite hymn was 'When I survey

the wondrous cross'.

Gandhi rejected the caste system. He regarded it as an accretion to Hinduism. He was particularly concerned for the untouchables or outcaste groups, demanding that, far from being rejected by society, they should be seen as the privileged children of God (*Harijans*). In his retreat-house (*ashram*) he demanded of his followers the same vows which he had taken upon himself: the pursuit of truth, non-violence seen as love in action, abstinence from sexual activity (his own stance from 1906) and poverty.

Aurobindo Ghose

Another influential figure in recent times was Aurobindo Ghose (1870–1950). He also displayed Western influence in his thought, emphasizing cross-cultural fertilization between East and West. The son of an English-educated Bengali doctor, he studied at Cambridge, but then turned to Indian culture and politics. Like Gandhi he was influenced by Ramakrishna and Vivekananda and interpreted the Vedantic tradition through their eyes. When in prison for his political activities, he claimed to hear the voice of Vivekananda, guiding him in the practice of yoga. Although he saw all men as incarnations of God, evolving in their consciousness, he saw India's national revival as the first step in spreading 'the universal truth of Hinduism' throughout the world.

'That which we call the Hindu religion is really the eternal religion, because it is the universal religion which embraces all others.'

It is not without reason,

therefore, that some have caricatured the Hindu approach as being: 'All religions are equal, but Hinduism is a bit more equal than the rest!'

CHARISMATIC LEADERS

In addition to these reformers, a large number of charismatic leaders have been responsible for the emergence of a number of popular sects. These have been influential both within India and in Hinduism outside India. Most come within the *bhakti* tradition, although in some cases there is an attempt to fuse *bhakti* with the Vedantic understanding of Hinduism.

Swami Narayan

One example is a Gujurati called Ghanshyama (1781–1830). As leader of the Satsang sect, he was known as Swami Sahajananda and Narayana. The last name stressed his claim to be divine. A vigorous preacher and masterly organizer, he won a large following. He had a hypnotic influence on his followers, whom he prepared to face persecution and suffering. He was the 'Guru Nanak' of the Gujuratis: as the Punjabis had become Sikhs, so large numbers of the Gujuratis joined the Swami Narayan sect. They saw in the Swami authority in teaching and the focal point of their devotion. The Swami Narayan sect exercised a strong influence upon Indians in East Africa and from there it entered Britain.

Sai Baba

Another movement, largely among the Gujuratis, is that

associated with Sai Baba (died 1918). It is *bhakti* in character, but strangely enough, Sai Baba is held to have been an *avatar* of Shiva. His successor, Sathya Sai Baba (born 1926), is held to be an *avatar* of Shiva and Shakti. He has attracted a huge following. As immigrants have brought the movement to the West, there has been stress on the fact that there is only one human race and so, fundamentally, only one caste. It is sometimes affirmed that the Sai Baba movement is no new religion, nor a particular form of Hinduism, but a spiritual path that any religionist may follow, because it is held to bring fulfilment to all.

'My life is my message.'

Gandhi

ultimate reality (monism) which was the most significant affirmation of the *Upanishads*.

Though the existence of superhuman beings is not explicitly denied, the approach of Jainism is fundamentally atheistic, rejecting both the concept of creation and all thought of the operation of providence in the world. The path to knowledge is the important thing, and the Jain analysis of right conduct. (See the article on Jainism.) First of the five virtues was non-violence (*ahimsa*), or what Albert Schweitzer called 'reverence for life'. This was adopted by Buddhism and, in modern times, has been the fundamental element in Hinduism, as Mahatma Gandhi interpreted it. The other virtues in Jainism are speaking the truth, honesty, chastity and a non-attachment to worldly things.

The Buddha

If we can sift history from legend, the Buddha, Siddharta (his personal name) Gautama (his family name) rejected the sacrificial cults and the caste system, and taught a new way to release and salvation, which he described in terms of a 'quenching' (*nirvana*). What needed quenching was the desire which kept a person prisoner to the cycle of rebirth by reason of his actions. If desire was the reason for the anguish and suffering which marked the human lot, it was clear that the desire had to be set aside before release was attained and *nirvana* reached.

Like a doctor, he not only analysed the symptoms of the human malaise, but also prescribed a cure. Here he pointed to a 'middle way' which came out of his own experience. For he had found that neither a sensual life in the world nor the extreme asceticism of the hermits had satisfied him. His teaching set forth the Noble Eightfold Path to *nirvana* (see further the articles on Buddhism).

The Buddha's message was perpetuated through the community of his disciples and Buddhism spread rapidly—to the south of India and from there to Sri Lanka and Burma. Schools of Buddhism grew up and from the first century BC Mahayana ('the great vehicle') emerged.

Mahayana Buddhism made some accommodation to Hindu thought and there was interaction with it. The Buddha was thought of as the incarnation of the ultimate Buddha for this age (i.e. an historical manifestation) and the *dharma* came to be virtually identified with Brahman in the sense of an absolute and eternal law within the universe. Nagarjuna, the great Buddhist thinker, introduced the notion of accommodated teaching, which allowed for a multiplicity of religious approaches, because none, as such, was grasping at the reality. The 'Buddha nature' was within all and needed to be expressed, but the truth was to be apprehended intuitively and not through sense-experience.

The Upanishads

Although Jain and Buddhist ideas had a great influence on the development of Hinduism, later Hindu teachers regarded them as unorthodox. By contrast, there was another form of semi-secret teaching which was circulated by teachers who were within the Vedic heritage, but reshaped the Hinduism of the future. This teaching came to be known as the *Upanishads* (*upa* = near, *ni* = down, *shad* = sit), because those who received it sat down beside their teachers!

These teachers were not involved in pleading with the gods or ritual sacrifice. They were more concerned to discover the ground of the universe, the Reality (Brahman) which was prior to all other existence. At the same time they were concerned to explore the nature of human consciousness. They came to the

---

'Arjuna, of this be sure: None who pays me worship of loyalty and love is ever lost. For whosoever makes me his haven, base-born though he may be, Yes, women too, and artisans, even serfs— Theirs it is to tread the highest Way ...'

Bhagavad Gita IX.31,32

'If men thought of God as much as they think of the world, who would not attain liberation (*nirvana*)?'

Maitri Upanishad 6.24

'At the heart of this phenomenal world, within all its changing forms, dwells the unchanging Lord. So, go beyond the changing, and, enjoying the inner, cease to take for yourself what to others are riches.'

The first verse of the *Isha Upanishad*

'The Self is all-knowing, it is all-understanding, and to it belongs all glory. It is pure consciousness, dwelling in the heart of all, in the divine citadel of Brahma. There is no space it does not fill.'

From the *Mindaha Upanishad*

'Thou art the Eternal among eternals, the consciousness within all minds, the Unity in diversity, the end of all desiring. Understanding and experience of Thee dissolve all limitations.'

From the *Shivatashvatara Upanishad*

The large Hindu temples are breathtaking buildings. This gatetower or gopuram *leads into the temple of Minakshi at Madura. Minakshi is a consort of the god Shiva.*

conclusion that what was basic to the individual self (*atman*) was none other than the Reality which undergirded the cosmos.

Like the Jains and the Buddhists they were concerned to overcome the fundamental sense of anxiety and frustration which marks human existence. They also recognized the sense of flux and impermanence in life. But they looked for the essence of permanence not only outside man, but also within. Their way to salvation was that of knowledge or spiritual insight.

Like the manuals of the priests, each *Upanishad* is attached to one of the four Vedic hymn-collections. They are speculative treatises which draw upon parable to communicate their view of reality. Every book on Hindu religion quotes the story of Svetaketu in the *Chandoya Upanishad*. He is asked to split off the fruit from the banyan tree and then continue to subdivide it until he can see nothing at all. His father reminds him that nothing comes from nothing and that even within the infinitesi-

mally small there is still present the power which pervades the whole universe and is the basis of all existence.

'Have faith!' he is told. 'That is the spirit-breath (Brahman) which lies at the root of all existence, and that is what you are too, Svetaketu!' 'That is what you are' expresses the unity of the human self (or soul) with the ultimate Reality. He is told, too, to see the impossibility of extracting salt from water in a saline solution. It penetrates the whole. In the same way, he is assured that the reality within the human self (*atman*) is Reality itself (Brahman).

Radhakrishnan has stressed the subjective and the objective sides in the *Upanishads*. Svetasvatara (one of the speakers), he says, 'saw the truth owing to *his power of contemplation* and the *grace of God.*' It follows, therefore, that the truths are to be verified not only by logical reason but also by personal experience.

Although the *Upanishads* are speaking of the ultimate there is a great deal of personalized language which could later be brought into devotion (*bhakti*). We are told that 'Brahman dwells within all and outside all— unborn, pure, greater than the greatest, without breath, without mind' and yet Brahman is 'ever present in the hearts of all—the refuge of all and their supreme goal'. 'In Brahman exists all that moves and breathes.' Brahman is seen as 'the adorable one'. To 'know' Brahman is to find one's being within Brahman.

Age of the epics

The period from 300 BC to AD 300 was crucial for the emergence of what we may call classical Hinduism. Although Buddhism and Jainism reached their widest growth within India during this time, it was also the period when Vedantic 'orthodoxy' was developing. *Sutras* were written. These were for the most part collections of aphorisms which sought to highlight the teaching of the *Vedas* and *Upanishads*.

But, even more significantly for the future of popular religion, this was the time when *bhakti* (devotion to one of the gods) entered religion, so that what was already part and parcel of religion at the grass roots received approval. There was also a wider synthesis of Aryan and non-Aryan elements in the tradition. The divinities of the *Vedas* were either replaced by the older gods or identified with them. For example, Rudra, the powerful one in the Vedic hymns, was identified with Shiva, the 'dancing god' whose figurines are among the finds in the Indus Valley excavations.

Legend and story

This was also the time for writing up stories of the past. What had originated and been circulating as local legends came to be regarded as the best statement of the Indian view of the world. Although there may be some historical allusions to events long past, the epics point rather to the perennial struggle between good and evil, cosmos and chaos in human affairs. They provide the assurance that order will prevail and that there is a way through the morass of doubt and puzzlement.

The basic thesis of both the *Ramayana* (which has 24,000 couplets) and the *Mahabharata* (90,000 couplets) is that history is divided into cycles. At the beginning, righteousness and order (*dharma*) marks the world. But then, through four ages, standards deteriorate until the gods decide to destroy the world and fashion it afresh. The poems indicate the need to discover meaning and purpose, even during the period of disorder.

The loving husband and faithful wife: Ramayana

The *Ramayana* is placed within the second age, when order,

though under attack, is still largely intact. It is the story of intrigue in which Rama is ousted from the throne and his faithful wife Sita abducted and taken off to Sri Lanka. The monkey-god, Hanuman, the symbol of loyal service and ingenuity, assists in the rescue of Sita by establishing a monkey-bridge from the mainland of India to Sri Lanka. Rama is the personification of righteousness and is looked upon as one of the ten incarnations (*avatars*) of Vishnu. The notion grew up that the gods send one *avatar* for each age. (This same notion of a series of ages or aeons and the appearance of a saviour-figure in each age is also present in Buddhist thought.)

In popular Hinduism the Rama story is not only heard from earliest childhood, but becomes the basis for everyday life. Rama will be invoked at the start of any undertaking and thanked on its successful completion. His exploits become an example to

follow and an encouragement to upright behaviour. His name will be used to console the aged and chanted by the assembled mourners, as the bodies of the dead are taken away for cremation.

Sita, too, becomes the model of the faithful wife who is so identified with her husband that, at one time, she would even ascend his funeral pyre and be cremated with him. Sita is praised for the virtues of piety, loyalty and unassuming courtesy.

'Song of the Lord': Bhagavad Gita

The *Mahabharata* story is set towards the end of the third age. And the civil war of which it tells ushers in the fourth age, the era of final disintegration and un-

It has been said that the one unifying theme in the diversity of Hinduism is the honour paid to cows. Why they are considered sacred is not known. But they are permitted to go anywhere and eat anything.

This modern carving shows the age-old Hindu theme of the 'wheel of life'. The doctrine of samsara *teaches that after death the soul moves to a new body.*

righteousness. Two sets of cousins claim to be the rightful rulers. The five Pandora brothers prevail in the end, but only after a bitter and lengthy conflict.

The reaction of the five brothers is crucial to the story. The eldest, Yudhishthira, finds war distasteful and wishes to opt out of the conflict. He looks in the direction of ascetic meditation. Attention finally rests on the third brother, Arjuna, who shares his brother's distaste for war, but shows great ability as a general.

The high point of the lengthy epic is the section entitled *Bhagavad Gita* ('Song of the Lord'), where Arjuna is hesitating about entering the battle against his kith and kin. He is engaged in dialogue with his charioteer, who is none other than Krishna, the eighth incarnation of Vishnu.

The *Bhagavad Gita* has some-times been called 'the bible of Hinduism' because of its popular appeal. There have been more commentaries written on it than on any other Indian writing. The story tells how Arjuna is finally persuaded by Krishna to issue the order for battle against the Kuru family. Krishna argues that death does not destroy the soul and that a man must fulfil his duty in accordance with his class. To perform one's duty does not involve guilt, if it is done in a spirit of detachment. Krishna points out that knowledge, work and devotion are all paths to salvation. Through devotion to himself (in whom the impersonal Brahman becomes a personal, loving god), Arjuna can be freed from his doubts and attachments. The *Gita* stresses that salvation is available to all: class distinctions are not a barrier but a way of securing salvation.

The Krishna cycle

There is a further cycle of stories about Krishna, which are widely circulated. The most important is the *Bhagavata Purana*. The stories begin with him as a prince of the tribe of the Yadavas, and there are miraculous stories of his birth and infancy. In devotional art-forms he is often portrayed as a plump baby full of vitality.

During his youth he fled from his wicked cousin Kamsa and dwelt among the cowherds of Vrindaban. The stories tell of his skill as a flute-player and the pranks he played upon the wives and daughters of the cowherds, outdoing Don Juan in his ways of seduction. The suggestion is that he is father, friend and elder brother to his worshippers—but also lover and husband. The sexual imagery of union with Krishna is symbolic of the intimacy of the worshipper with God, which is a feature of the *bhakti* emphasis in Hinduism. The Krishna stories are not intended to be taken literally as something to emulate!

The sacred cow

The fact that Krishna is commonly portrayed as the cowherd is also significant, for it brings Krishna-worship into the context of the ancient cult of the mother-goddess. The cow is the living symbol of Mother Earth and of the bounty she bestows upon mankind. Feeding the cow is in itself an act of worship. Even the cow's urine is seen as sacred, being used, for example, in purification rites by those who have broken caste taboo. (Although some Hindus eat meat, the majority are vegetarian, for reverence for the cow is also a symbol of reverence for all animals.)

Approaches to Truth:
The Great Interpreters

Raymond Hammer

The Vedic tradition ended with the *Upanishads* and the emergence of the notion of the identity of the individual self (*atman*) with the absolute (Brahman). The next step was to see the identity of every individual with every other individual and so to postulate that there is only one reality. This understanding of existence is called monism. It is the basis of Vedantic philosophy and it became the main philosophical tradition within Hinduism, though with a great variety of interpretation.

This variety was partly due to the attempt to systematize Hindu thought—done first during the period of the epics, when Hinduism in its classical form was emerging. A number of *sutras* (collections of aphorisms) emerged, but they were often too brief to be intelligible and so a commentary was needed. The production of commentaries led on the one hand to a tradition of interpretation, and on the other to several variants in interpretation. The *Brahma Sutra* (belonging to the sixth century AD) sought to sum up the teaching and so came to be known as the *Vedanta Sutra*.

Parallel with *Vedanta* was a school which gave pride of place to scripture. It stressed those portions of the *Veda* which spoke

of appeasing the gods and accumulating merit to acquire heavenly joy. There was also reasoning (*shankhya*) which stressed the two entities of spirit and matter. Matter is without feeling, but spirit acts upon it and brings about evolution within matter. It is also seen as responsible for human experience and misery. The yogic philosophy followed *shankhya*, but had a place for Ishvara as the supreme, omniscient, ever-existing teacher.

Much of the philosophical development had parallels with the earlier schools of Buddhist thought, but there was one fundamental difference. Buddhism rejected the notion of a continuing self and saw everything as subject to flux. But all Hindu thought presupposes the permanence of the self (the *atman*).

The three great interpreters of *Vedanta* were Shankara (about AD 788–820), Ramanuja (died AD 1137) and Madhva (about AD 1197–1276).

Shankara

Shankara wrote commentaries on the *Brahma Sutra* and the *Bhagavad Gita*, and also produced spiritual treatises and hymns (for he was a worshipper of Shiva). He was responsible for a revival of Hindu thought, over and against Buddhism, although

he owes a debt to the Buddhist concept that nothing has substance, all being void. The mystic appreciates this and so is set free from a world which is mere illusion. Nothing can be said about reality; what is needed is mystical insight. He therefore postulated two levels of truth. At the lower level of appreciation of the truth, everything is provisional and transitory. But much of life is lived at this level.

For Shankara the world is seen as illusion (*maya*). Even the idea of each of us as a separate self is also regarded as illusory. The truth, however, is that there is only one being—the 'Brahman *atman* reality', which involves not simply my *atman*, but that of others as well. He sought to establish a link with the *Vedas*, where God is seen as the wielder of *maya*. But this, in turn, raises the question of whether God is himself an illusion and the creator of an illusory world. It is here that Shankara accepts being itself as his ultimate. The world may seem to be vividly real but, from the standpoint of the higher level of truth, it is then seen to be illusory.

Ramanuja

Ramanuja came from a background with a strong tendency

towards *bhakti*.

The *bhakti* movement had been seen as a threat to Brahmin orthodoxy, based on the *Veda*, but Ramanuja sought to create a bridge between the two, to bring *bhakti* within the classical Hindu tradition. He began by accepting the authority of the *Vedas* and the inspiration of the *Bhagavad Gita* and wrote commentaries on both the *Brahma Sutra* and the *Gita*. He saw the cosmos as God's body, but, just as the self transcends the body, so God transcends the material mani-festation. The world functions in dependence on the purposes of God. So *karma*, too, has to be understood as the expression of God's will.

Ramanuja interpreted the 'thou art that' in the *Upanishads* as meaning not that the individual self is identical with God, but that God is the reality within the self. So he rejects Shankara's threat to the religion of worship and devotion and his assumption that salvation comes from within. Salvation, deliverance, for Ramanuja is a gift from above.

Madhva

Madhva was influenced by the Jain belief in the difference between souls and non-living matter. He therefore stresses particularity and plurality. He postulates the existence within God of attributes that no other being could possess. In the same way, each individual is different from every other, and no sequences of *karma* can ever be the same. This means that each soul must have something within itself which somehow or other determines its destiny.

The Hindu Gods

The gods of the Vedic period

AGNI
The life-force of nature. The god of fire and sacrifice.

INDRA
The sky-god and god of war.

VARUNA
The upholder of the cosmic order, with power to punish and reward.

The later gods

BRAHMA—THE CREATOR
The lord of all creatures. He is above and beyond worship, and there are hardly any temples dedicated to him.

VISHNU—THE PRESERVER
The controller of human fate. He draws near to mankind in ten incarnations (*avatars*). He is generally kindly.

SHIVA—THE DESTROYER
The source of both good and evil. The destroyer of life and also the one who re-creates new life.

SARASVATI
Consort of Brahma. The goddess of knowledge, learning and truth.

LAKSHMI
Wife of Vishnu. The goddess of fortune and beauty.

KALI/DURGA
Consort of Shiva. The 'great mother'. She is the symbol of judgement and death.

The ten avatars of Vishnu

1. MATSYA
The fish. He appeared at the time of the great flood, to warn mankind.

2. KURMA
The tortoise. He rescued treasures from the flood.

3. VARAHA
The boar. He raised the earth from the flood.

4. NARA-SIMHA
The man-lion. He defeated evil demons.

5. VAMANA
The dwarf. He defeated evil demons.

6. PARUSHA-RAMA
'Rama with an axe'. He destroyed the members of the Kshatriya warrior-caste who threatened to dominate the world.

7. RAMA-CHANDRA
The hero of the *Ramayana* epic. He was a noble hero who combatted the evil in the world. He is the epitome of virtue.

8. KRISHNA
As well as being an *avatar* of Vishnu, Krishna is a god in his own right, the most popular of all the gods. He is also the hero of many myths, depicted as a lover, a warrior and a king.

9. BUDDHA
'The enlightened one'. The ninth *avatar* is Gautama the Buddha, founder of Buddhism.

10. KALKI
The tenth *avatar* is yet to come.

Concepts of Hinduism

Raymond Hammer

In the *Veda* the ultimate or absolute is Brahman, defying all atempt at definition.

The Absolute

Brahman is neutral and impersonal—the origin, the cause and the basis of all existence. In it are to be found:

- pure being (*sat*);
- pure intelligence (*cit*);
- pure delight (*ananda*).

Brahman is the unknowable one. But the only way he can be considered is in terms of a personal deity. So it was natural for the Indians to see the several attributes or functions of divinity manifested in a multiplicity of forms. In the Vedic hymns god is not fully seen in human terms. The gods are the manifestations of nature or cosmic forces. The divine names may be countless, but they are all understood as expressions of Brahman. For, although it may have limitless forms, it is still regarded as one in essence.

So Hinduism is not troubled by the fact that each village may have its own divinity or divinities. The multiplicity is not seen as polytheism, since Brahman is One. The gods are simply ways of approaching the ultimate.

The phallic lingam *pillar is the symbol of the creative god Shiva.*

The Vedic gods

Indra is the god most frequently invoked in the *Veda* and many stories are told of his deeds of prowess. With his thunderbolt he was able to suppress the dragon that sought to stem the flow of the waters. He appears as conqueror of the sun, releasing from the sun's grasp the imprisoned dawns. He is depicted astride an elephant, bejewelled and with a kingly turban or tiara, thunderbolt in hand. Like the other divinities, he has his female partner, **Indrani** or **Saci**.

Agni is the god of fire and sacrifice—the one who unites earth, heaven and the atmosphere in between. He is seen as the life-force within nature. The *Rig Veda* hails him as the one who 'restores life to all beings'. 'The all is reborn through you!'

Chief of the Vedic gods is **Varuna** who is the preserver of the cosmic order. He is described as clothed in a golden mantle and is often associated with **Mitra** (the Mithra of Persian religion—the deity in Mithraism).

There are, of course, a number of other gods and goddesses—symbolizing the sun, the moon and the stars—as well as **Dyaus-pitr**, the 'heaven father' (Jupiter in Roman religion and Zeus in Greek religion), **Vayu**, the wind, and **Prajapati**, the father of the gods (*devas*) and the demons (*asuras*) and lord of all creatures.

The Vedic pantheon, however, gave place to another hierarchy of divinities, which reflect the non-Aryan elements in the religion. At the head of the other array of divine forms stands a divine triad (*Trimurti*) who share the activities of **Ishvara**, the one supreme god who symbolizes Brahman:

● The power to create belongs to **Brahma**.
● Preservation is in the power of **Vishnu**.
● **Shiva** is the great destroyer.

Their three-fold activity corresponds to the rhythm of the world. This is seen first as emerging from Brahman; next as reaching its full embodiment; then as being reabsorbed either into Brahman or into the period which precedes the next age. Creation, like history, is understood in cyclical terms. There is no true beginning or end. The beginning is an end and the end a new beginning.

Brahma

Despite his function as creator, Brahma remains fairly abstract. His function is to bring multiplicity into being in place of a primal unity. His female counterpart is **Sarasvati**, the energy that comes from him. She is identified with the Word on the one hand, the goddess of the sacred rivers; on the other, the symbol of knowledge and of 'the waters of truth'.

Brahma is often portrayed with four faces, embracing the four points of the compass, and with four arms, in which he holds the four *Vedas*. At times he is depicted as riding on a swan; at other times he sits upon a lotus—a symbol of the fact that he comes from himself and is not begotten.

Vishnu

Vishnu, as the great preserver, is thought to be in charge of human

This image of Shiva, the destroyer, is uncovered once a year, when a ritual sacrifice of bullocks is made to him.

fate. He is usually portrayed in symbolic form. He may be reclining or asleep on the ocean, which stands for chaos—the thousand-headed serpent. He may preside over the heavenly court. Or, as a symbol of the sun, he may appear mounted upon the heavenly eagle (Garuda), traversing the heights of heaven. The cult of Vishnu is very popular. He is the symbol of divine love—sometimes in company with **Lakshmi**, his female counterpart—

the symbol of beauty and good fortune; but more often drawing near in grace to mankind through his ten 'descents' or incarnations. Many of these incarnations are thought to be partial. The significance of **Krishna** (by far the most popular of the manifestations of Vishnu) is that in him the being of Vishnu is held to be totally present. There is a similar approach to Rama on the part of his worshippers. They would see in him, too, all the fullness of the being of Vishnu.

Shiva

The third of the *Trimurti* is Shiva. He is the deity in whom all opposites meet and become resolved in a fundamental unity. Although the phallus (lingam) is his symbol and he is naturally identified with the masculine role in fertility and procreation, he is often portrayed as perpetually chaste. (In most of the temples dedicated to Shiva there is the statue of a bull, the symbol of virility.)

He is the destroyer of life and yet also its recreator; the terrible one, and yet the epitome of mildness. In him there is both ceaseless activity and eternal rest. In him there is sexual differentiation and yet he is also the symbol of unity which transcends all division. He is the source of both good and evil.

In artistic representations from the twelfth century AD onwards he is often portrayed as the king of the dancers—the embodiment of cosmic energy. The sculptures show both the unfolding of the universe and its ultimate destruction. The dance speaks of rhythm at the heart of all existence—whether in the cosmos or in the individual consciousness, the will or the emotions, where knowledge and illusion (maya) are in conflict. He is also shown with many hands, one pair to express the balance between life and death, another indicating the clash between good and evil, and so on.

Both Vishnu and Shiva are the focus of cults in which the worshipper seeks for unity with the god. In the Shaivite form (which looks to Shiva) it is identity with the source of movement (life itself) which is the goal. But the sense of creatureliness is not lost. The strength of Shiva worship in south India from the twelfth century AD and also in Bihar and Bengal (areas where the Aryan influence was late) reflects the rejection of the Brahminic Aryan forms of worship—animal sacrifice, prayers for the dead and other rites.

In one popular story Shiva is the one who averted a catastrophe, when the waters of the River Ganges flowed down upon the earth. Knotting his hair, he received the waters upon his head, so that they flowed harmlessly away. But he is also the master of the yogis (the disciplined ascetics) and, in this capacity, he is portrayed as half-naked, smeared with ashes, with skulls around his waist and a necklace of intertwining serpents.

Kali

Shiva, like the other gods, has his female partner to whom his powers are delegated, but the different names probably reflect the varying qualities of the 'Great Mother', who is present in Indian thought from the earliest times. Most significant is Durga or Kali who, in her strength and dominance, reflects the matriarchal approach of the older, pre-Aryan culture. This is probably the background to Shaktism, where the divine being is thought of in female terms and the female is the dynamic and the male the more passive manifestation. There is a contrast between the inner self-sufficiency of Shiva and the creative-destructive power of Durga-Kali.

Kali is portrayed in paradoxical terms. On the one side, there is the ferocious aspect, expressing judgement and death—with the figure of Kali wearing a garland of skulls and a skirt of severed hands. On the other side, her serenity is indicated by her portrayal as the night of rest and peace between the cycles of world-creation. Even in her most fearful aspect, Kali is understood as granting peace to her followers by overcoming their fears. She can therefore be the object of an intense and passionate devotion. Although Shiva is sometimes considered to be the supreme deity—far removed from time and creation—it is Kali who touches him and brings him into the world of time and touch as the creator and animator of all.

The act of destruction can be interpreted as the abolishing of ignorance, in order that the soul may come to knowledge, or the removal of all dross and impurity, so that the heart becomes pure and god-like.

These portrayals are never meant to be representational. Hindu art, unlike Greek art where the divinities are portrayed simply as humans, indicates that the divinities are far more than humans. Power is expressed by a multiplicity of arms, and divine wisdom (as in the case of Shiva) by a third eye in the middle of the forehead. Even animal characteristics are pointers to special qualities possessed by the god. Ganesha is always portrayed with an elephant's head and a single tusk. The portrayal speaks of the strength of the one who protects through life. The monkey form of Hanuman is the pointer to dexterity and intelligence.

Bhakti and the concept of grace

Bhakti, the devotion to a particular god, which became such a strong element in popular religion, was perhaps a reaction to the severity and rigour of yoga. The yogis had sought to suppress desire, love and feeling in general. How, then, were the worshippers' emotional needs to be met? By bringing together bhakti, knowledge (jnana) and karma, the Bhagavad Gita suggests that it is not simply the expression of the emotional; it is always associated with the intellectual and practical side of human living. Nevertheless, at the popular level, the intellectual or rational element is often lacking, and it is the ecstasy and rapture of a loving relationship which come to the fore.

Between the seventh and tenth centuries AD a number of Tamil writers (Tamil is one of the four Dravidian languages in south India) expressed their religious

feelings and experience with tremendous warmth and fervency. And in the *Bhagavata Purana* (which was written about AD 900), the source of many of the Krishna stories, there is even more passion. One writer has said that, in this work: 'Bhakti is a surging emotion, which chokes the speech, makes the tears flow and the hair thrill with pleasurable excitement and often leads to hysterical laughing and weeping by turns, to sudden fainting fits and to long trances of unconsciousness.'

In the eleventh century Ramanuja brought *bhakti* within the classical, developed Hindu tradition. For him it was more a type of intellectual meditation accompanied by love, but lacking the rapture and ecstasy which continue to be present at the popular level. He pointed to the significant link with the *avatara* doctrine in the Vaishnavite form of *bhakti*, when he asserted that God becomes incarnate simply out of compassion, 'to give light to the whole world with his indefectible and perfect glory and to fill out all things with his loveliness'. The Vaishnavite usually dresses in orange or white with a rosary in his hand. He paints red or white vertical lines on his forehead or red, black or white spots between his eyebrows.

In the fifteenth century AD the Chaitanya sect of the Krishna *bhakti* movement was established in Bengal. This sect lies behind the Hare Krishna movement, seen in the West, where music and dance mark the worship of Krishna and ecstatic trance is a means of achieving unity with the

A Hindu holy man meditating.

Hindus living in Jinja in Uganda hold an annual nine-day festival in honour of Kali. A sacred fire is kept burning by feeding it with ghee, a concentrate of butter.

The red mark on an Indian woman's forehead usually signifies that she is a Hindu, but practices vary from area to area.

deity. In the West, because of the stress on history in the Christian tradition, adherents of the movement tend to accept the myths attached to Krishna as historically true and they give unquestioning adherence to every utterance of Chaitanya.

If it is a person's duty to commit himself in loving devotion to God, it follows that the attainment of *moksha* (release) is made possible by God. Does this mean that it is 'grace alone', or is human effort also involved? Something like the debate about grace which emerged in Christian theology is present in the Hindu debate.

Two theories of the operation of grace were put forward: the 'kitten' and the 'monkey' approach. A she-cat seizes the kitten and carries it where she wills. This involves a total passivity on the part of the kitten and there were those who stated that God's grace operates in the same way. All is effected by God, and man does nothing to achieve *moksha*. By contrast, the baby monkey clings to its mother. The mother monkey is responsible for the baby monkey's continuance of life and movement, yet there is not total passivity. Most Hindu teachers within the *bhakti* tradition took this standpoint. We cling to God, and God effects our salvation.

The path to salvation

For the Hindu, the great goal is *moksha*. The word speaks of 're-lease'—deliverance, emancipation and liberty. On the negative side, it points to 'being loosed from' or 'rid of' something felt to be undesirable—i.e. the cycle of rebirth and attachment to the material world. On the positive side, it indicates an expanded outlook, a sense of calm and security, the notion of attainment (reaching a goal) or the power to be and to do. More often than not, this goal of salvation is described in negative terms—the

negating of evil, grief and decay.

The way of knowledge
The idea of *moksha* was not always present in Indian religion. It is likely that, as the cycle of rebirth (*samsara*) became the fundamental presupposition (about the seventh century BC), indicating an unending round of existences which were influenced by the deeds each individual performed (*karma*), the desire for release emerged.

The desire for freedom was not political, but spiritual, and the Upanishadic tradition stressed release from the bonds of ignorance. It was ignorance which tied a person to the round of birth-death-rebirth which was expressed by *samsara*. Release would be attained as knowledge replaced ignorance—when reality was properly understood and the transient or illusory rejected.

This was, basically, the way of knowledge (*jnana-marga*) towards *moksha*. It would involve yoga and the ascetic practices associated with it. It was thought

The term 'sadhu' applies to any Indian 'holy man'. Some are ascetic hermits, others are popular wonder-workers. Devotees of Vishnu mark their foreheads with three vertical lines of ash. Devotees of Shiva have three horizontal lines.

Karma and Dharma: Hindu Ethics

Raymond Hammer

In classical Hinduism actions (*karma*) and duty (*dharma*) were the dominant concepts. *Karma*, as the accumulation of good and bad acts, would influence a person's destiny, but there was no one way to acquire good *karma*. Early in the *Veda* there had been the notion of an overriding moral law (*rita*) of which Mitra and Varuna were the guardians. Man had to recognize a divine imperative, and prayer and sacrifice were necessary to maintain a right relationship between the divine and the human. Sin, however, could be either moral or ritual.

All relative
The moral law expressed the basis of the social order, controlled by the manuals of the priests and enforced by the rulers. But responsible action was increasingly within the framework of one's class. That is why *dharma* came to be not an absolute duty, but one related to a person's status and so to the class/caste complex. The *Bhagavad Gita* considers it wrong to try to fulfil someone else's *dharma*. It is better to do your own *dharma* badly than that of another well! The action as such does not modify *karma*. It is action appropriate to the person and to the time of life. The epics stress a child's duty to parents, the love and attachment that parents must show to children, the mutual respect to be displayed in marriage, and the love and harmony

belonging to other relationships.
For those living in the world, ethical pursuits— the pursuit of wealth (i.e. engagement in a livelihood), the enjoyment of pleasure or ritual piety— were all relative. The only absolute ethic was related to the release of the individual from the cycle of rebirth. This was what the ascetic concentrated on. For him the duty of 'seeking for salvation' was paramount. He had to maintain a basic morality, refraining from killing, stealing, sexual impurity, lying or the consumption of intoxicants. Unless he observed these prohibitions he could not attain the basic purity required to take him further on the path to *moksha*.

Source book
The *Laws of Manu*, a metrical work of 2,685 verses dealing with religion, law, custom and politics, is the most often quoted 'source book' of Hindu ethics. Its date is uncertain, but it belongs perhaps to the first century BC or first century AD and its author is well versed in the Vedic literature. It is concerned primarily with duty, whether the general *dharma* incumbent upon all or the particular *dharma* arising from caste or relationship. The *Laws* are concerned to bolster up conventional thought at a time when it was being threatened. They accept the class structure in terms of a common endeavour for a common good. Each has

to perform the function for which his nature best suits him. Right and wrong are determined in four ways: through the authoritative scriptures, through the other inspired writings, through good conduct and through conscience.

The four orders
Four separate orders are considered—the student, the householder, the hermit and the ascetic— and, each has an appropriate duty to perform. For example, the student has to study the *Vedas*. There is an initiation ceremony for the three upper classes, appropriate to each grouping, and rules of personal purification, of sacrifices and the morning and evening devotions to be followed are duly taught by a teacher (the guru or *rishi*). The student, we are told, gains the nether world by honouring his mother, the middle sphere by honouring his father, but the world of Brahman (the absolute) if he obeys his teacher!
It is important not to seek to discharge the *dharma* of another grouping, because this involves forfeiting membership in one's own. Ethics and ritual acts are, of course, intermingled and it is the priest's *dharma* to go through no fewer than twelve sacramental rites from his foetal period to marriage.
In modern times, there is more stress on progress than on cycles of time. Universal values such as truthfulness, kindness and love are stressed and the need to alleviate suffering. Present-day Hindus will speak, too, of the common good as a goal to be attained.

that the control of breath would allow the self to escape from the body by closing the artery from the heart to the forehead—the path by which the self was understood to move to its home in the heart. The special knowledge is attained through meditation, accompanied by yogic discipline and the repetition of the mysterious *mantra* 'Om', which represented the ultimate in all its fullness (some would say 'the triad of gods seen in their fundamental unity as Brahman, the absolute'). The repetition of the phrase would both assert and effect the unity of the worshipper with the ultimate—and this would be *moksha*. But the unity need not be identity. It is sometimes seen as the condition of a gnat in a fig or a fish in water—neither total identity nor complete disassociation.

The later songs in the *Rig Veda* saw man groping in darkness, but becoming conscious of the unfathomable mystery at the very centre of being. Nevertheless, bit by bit, he becomes assured of reality and light in the world around him, and so reaches out for *moksha*.
'From the unreal lead me to the real!
From darkness lead me to light!
From death lead me to immortality!'
But this release will also be from life as it is now experienced. The way, therefore, will be by the suppression of a craving. As the Buddha put it, the craving is itself what links a person to the cycle of rebirth. Even the rapturous assurance of release must be purified of the element of desire which may cause us to accept a fantasy for the reality.

The *Bhagavad Gita* sees *moksha* as involving liberation from evil, from the body, from lusts and anger, from decay and death, from *karma* and from *maya*. In other words, *moksha* speaks of release from bondage, however conceived. The rapture is to be experienced at the level of

Members of the International Society for Krishna Consciousness have been a familiar sight on the streets of Western cities for the past decade.

emotion, for *moksha* involves a sense of security and assurance.

The way of action

But there is also the way of action (*karma-marga*). This path to release recognizes that we live our lives in the world, where there is work to be done and there are obligations to be met. Our status in society involves duty. We are not to opt out of the ethical demands of which we are conscious. The *Bhagavad Gita* indicates that it is 'not by refraining from action' that 'man attains freedom from action'. It is not by mere renunciation that he 'attains supreme perfection'. 'Action,' we are told, 'is greater than inaction' and so there is the command to 'perform your task in life'.

The way of devotion

Faith comes in with the way of devotion or love (*bhakti-marga*). It is in commitment to God that we accept the leap from the tem-

Indra is the god of war.

Krishna was a playful and often mischievous incarnation of Vishnu.

Ganesh, the elephant-god, is very popular as god of wisdom and good fortune.

poral to the eternal, the realm of limitation to the boundlessness of what is ultimate and absolute. This path accepts the truth that the absolute confronts us in personal form—so there can be human response to divine grace. In place of an impersonal Brahman, God is seen as approachable, evoking within humanity a spirit of adoring faith.

The *Bhagavad Gita* speaks of Arjuna seeing in Krishna countless visions of wonder, as Krishna asserts that 'only by *bhakti* can men see me and know me and come to me'. For the followers of this way—and this is the path to

which most Indians instinctively lean—salvation is not the result of human striving, but is seen as a gift from God. Obviously, very few frame for themselves an articulated theology or religious philosophy. It is a faith expressed in life and not as dogma.

But *bhakti* also demands acts of worship. Apart from ritual acts and ceremonies, there are the hymns of praise to be sung and the statues to be venerated and adored. It is not 'idol-worship' as such. The idol becomes the focus through which God (who cannot be represented in any image) is worshipped.

Hindu Worship and the Festivals

Raymond Hammer

In Aryan times, worship took place in the open air, often concentrated on the sacred fire. Temple worship, as such, probably comes from the early Indus Valley practices. Early temples were made of wood and so have not survived. Later ones were patterned on the royal court. As the gods were thought to dwell in the mountains, many temples were built in the style of a mountain home. There was a tower and walls, with the symbol of the divinity in the centre, surrounded by the many symbols of the spirit world.

In the temple

The needs of the gods would be met by the worshippers who had to prepare themselves through purification rites to draw near to their god. For example, in Vaishnavite morning worship there were sixteen operations, including washing the feet, rinsing the mouth, bathing, dressing, perfuming and feeding. During these there was hymn-singing, bells were rung, incense burnt and ritual music was played. Then the worshippers would come to perform their *puja*, first paying respect to the god and

In the River Ganges at Varanasi this woman is offering up the sacred water to the rising sun.

The Festivals of Hinduism

DIVALI/NEW YEAR
A festival of lights, when presents are given. Lakshmi, the goddess of good fortune, visits every house which is lit by a lamp.

HOLI
A joyful spring festival dedicated to Krishna. Originally a fertility ceremony. It is celebrated with street dancing, processions and bonfires.

January March May July September November

February April June August October December

DASARA
Ten days of celebration in honour of Kali. There are processions, dances and presents are given.

Local festivals
There are many festivals specific to certain areas or towns. Some of these are held in honour of the great gods such as Shiva and Sarasvati. Others are the annual festivals of local gods.
　Religious pilgrimages often take place at specific times of the year, accompanied by festivities.

At many Hindu festivals, worshippers go into ecstatic trances and then inflict wounds on themselves with no signs of any permanent damage.

making their requests, and then sharing in the divine banquet—water and *prasada* (the technical name for food first offered to the deity and then shared out among the worshippers). Usually the chief statue in the temple would receive food and refreshment during the day and be put to bed at night!

The statue is the symbol of the divine presence and the house in which it dwells. Ramakrishna expressed this by saying: 'We shall believe in the Divine Presence infilling the Images of the Deity.' For the more sophisticated worshipper, each part of the temple has a spiritual or symbolic meaning. The central shrine is the heart of the worshipper; the tower indicates the flight of the spirit to heaven. Each and every god stands for a particular function or attribute of the supreme.

A priest might add to the worship by reading the *Vedas* to the assembled worshippers, just as he might read to a group standing in shallow water in the Ganges at Varanasi after their ritual bathing. But any 'twice-born' Hindu (from the first three classes) may perform the reading of the prayers and *mantras*. The worshipper in the temple makes a gift of flowers or money and goes round the shrine, always keeping it to his right shoulder. Worship in the temple is never fully congregational. It is largely individual. That is why rites in the home are as significant as those in the temple.

At home

Duties in the home vary according to class, those of the Brahmin priestly caste being most arduous. Many set a room aside for *puja*—with a shrine, containing an image of the favourite deity or (in poorer homes) pictures of deities. Some have a *mandala*, a symbolic representation (usually a picture) of the universe. Fire and water are used for purification, and there are food-offerings, incense, flowers and coloured powders (for ornamentation).

'Twice-born' Hindus perform their rites three times a day. They wear the sacred thread (over the left shoulder and hanging to the right hip)—cotton for the Brahmin (priest), hemp for the Kshatriya (ruler) and wool for the *vaishya* (landowners/merchants). In addition, each has a caste mark on his forehead, and sometimes on his arms and other parts of the body.

In the early morning, worship starts with the uttering of the *mantra* 'Om', a humming to the sounds of the letters A,U,M. Then the worshipper repeats the name of his god, calls to mind the sages (*rishis*) and identifies himself with Brahman. He binds up the tuft of hair on his head and repeats the *Gayatri mantra* from the *Rig Veda*:

'We meditate on the adorable glory of the radiant sun; may he inspire our intelligence.'

He worships bare to the waist and barefoot, sitting cross-legged on the ground, with eyes looking at the tip of his nose and his face towards the rising of the sun. He then sips water, repeats the name of the god and sprinkles water around the seat. He touches six parts of the body—an indication of God within, repeats his prayers, meditates and repeats the words of the *Gayatri*. Water is offered to the images, verses from the *Veda* repeated and worship ends with a final water-offering and obeisance. Evening devotions are similar, but shorter. Midday worship may include consulting a teacher (guru). As they perform *puja*, priests, householders and ascetics (*sadhus*) incorporate special postures, gestures and utterances.

Festivals

Festivals are largely linked with the seasonal changes. But they also incorporate the myths of the *Ramayana* and of Krishna's activities.

Holi is the most popular festival of all. It is a spring festival associated with Krishna, and caste and taboo are set aside. In this festival there is a strong emphasis on pleasure.

Divali is the autumn festival (a festival of lights) linked with Kali (Shiva's female counterpart) and Lakshmi (Vishnu's counterpart). Pilgrimages are linked with the story-cycles. And centres such as Vrindaban (a focus for the Krishna cult), Varanasi and Allahabad welcome hundreds of thousands of pilgrims.

Escape from Life?

Raymond Hammer

How far is Hinduism concerned with everyday life and how far is 'escape' from life fundamental to the tradition? Life is broken into a number of orders.
● First there is the life of the student.
● Then there is the life of the householder.
● Then there is life far removed from the ordinary demands of family, community or society.

Hinduism is associated not simply with the bustling festival, but also with the wandering *sadhu* (holy man) or the almost-naked ascetic who, in yogic posture, seems entirely unconscious of physical constraints. For most of his married life Mahatma Gandhi had no sexual relationship with his wife. There are many illustrations of apparent world-denial, even though Gandhi, for instance, was at the same time fighting for political freedom and to improve the status of the outcaste groupings, demanding that they should be treated with consideration and granted their dignity.

If the world of everyday existence is illusion and if the fruit of past deeds in a previous existence determines the character of the present one, does this mean a denial of freedom? Does it remove any incentive to make life better in the present?

Unrest in the soul

There is a sense in which Indian thinking springs from an unrest in the soul rather than from intellectual curiosity, and this is what leads to a negation of the world. Philosophy, in a Hindu context, can never be an academic game, isolated from life and speculative in character. Knowledge must, therefore, be transformed into 'vision', an understanding of reality.

Whereas Western thought (in its non-religious form) sees man as 'the measure of all things' and so veers in an individualistic direction, the Hindu regards mankind as part of a cosmic whole and this involves respect for life in all its manifestations. Life 'apart' (an individualist approach) is seen as the disintegration of life. Hence the demand for a strict discipline (yoga) and meditation, so that the individual may re-integrate into the whole.

The rejection of individualism can lead to the rejection of activism. And there is often an element of passivity in Indian life, although the element of freedom would still be claimed and a charge of fatalism rejected. As a result, scientific knowledge and material progress have not traditionally been the goals of Indian endeavour.

Paradox

None the less, there is a certain paradox. Asceticism goes along with the acquiring of wealth and property (*artha*) which belongs to the duty of the householder, and the experience of pleasure (*kama*). Strict religious discipline is coupled with an extreme sensuousness and the wild abandon of cults which cast aside all inhibitions and restraints. Sculptures of the gods often show these elements.

It is likely that the two poles of 'attachment' (or affirmation) and 'aloofness' (or denial) ultimately express a unity. The extremes meet in the notion of the divinity and his female counterpart. Passivity must be wedded to creativity; weakness to strength; the negative to the positive. Only in this way can 'order' embrace 'freedom'. But it is ultimately release from the prison of meaninglessness that is sought. One Indian writer has put it that the Hindu's entire way of life and thought is determined by the 'yearnings of the soul rather than by the quest of the mind or the needs of the body'.

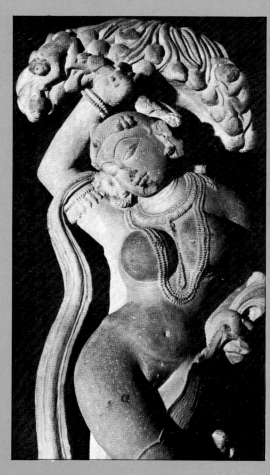

This tree-goddess is a typical example of Hindu carving.

Religion of the Gurus: The Sikh Faith

Douglas Davies

The Sikh religion originated in the area of Pakistan and north-west India called the Punjab, meaning 'land of the five rivers', at the end of the fifteenth century. At this time both Hinduism and Islam were present in the area, and a number of people were asking themselves whether a formal and ritual way of life would bring them near to God. The Sikh religion offered an alternative way of life.

The movement started as a small group of disciples gathered around the Guru Nanak (1469–1539) to seek the presence of God. Over the years it grew under the leadership of Nanak's nine successors. Beginning as a close fellowship of devotees whose goal was a sense of union with God, the Sikhs increased in number. They also developed a strong military power, until they became a distinct community.

Because the growth of Punjabi identity was closely related to the rise of the Sikh idea of life, the Sikh religion can be called an ethnic religion. As in Judaism and much of Hinduism, membership of the community and of the religion go hand in hand. This is what makes their faith so important to Sikhs who live outside the Punjab, for it provides them with a strong sense of identity.

God the true Guru

At the heart of Sikh religion lies the idea of the guru.

● God is the true Guru: his divine and creative word (*shabad*) came to mankind in a distinctive way through ten historical figures, each of whom was called a guru.

● The Sikh community, continuing the faith of the tenth guru, is itself called the guru.

● And the sacred scriptures are said to be a guru (the *Guru Granth Sahib*).

God is one, the ultimate and eternal Guru (*Satguru*), who provides enlightenment and understanding for the disciple who sets his heart on finding and serving him. In his transcendent state he is beyond description. But if he were no more than that, man would be unable to find and to understand him. Man would find it impossible to relate to a God without any attributes, so God manifests himself in and through certain phenomena which are known to man. Man's religious life is directed towards this more immediate and available form of God. But when Sikhs say that God, as they can experience him, possesses these characteristics, they do not mean to say that he has ever appeared or been born on the earth like the *avatars* or divine manifestations of the Hindu tradition. Rather, he has created the world, which enables man to understand something of his power and will. More than this, his grace enables sincere devotees to experience him through worship and meditation.

In its origin the Sikh religion possesses a strong mystical and devotional basis. For the early disciples who gathered around Nanak, the goal of life was to devote themselves to dwelling upon the name of God; to sing and lodge within their hearts the hymns composed by their leader. Nanak enabled his followers to gain access to the true Guru by providing a fellowship of believers who could devote themselves to the hymns. The hymns were the means by which their hearts could reach out towards God, and also by which God could move within their hearts.

Because Nanak provided such a vital focal point for early devotees, he came to be called a guru—in the Hindu tradition of holy men who are guides to those who seek the truth, whose very presence seems to instruct the beginner, and whose direction is necessary for spiritual progress. Nanak is never considered to be a special manifestation of God, the ultimate and true Guru.

Sikhs meditate on the divine Name.

The ten gurus

One distinctive feature of Sikhism as a guru religion is that Nanak and his nine successors are seen as making up a definite historical phase of individual or living gurus. They are said to share the same truth, to have possessed the same distinctive insight into God, and even to have held a basic common identity. The Sikhs say that the ten gurus are like candles which have been lit from each other.

The orthodox Sikh gurus	
Nanak	1469–1539
Angad	1504–1552
Amar Das	1479–1574
Ram Das	1534–1581
Arjan	1563–1606
Har Govind	1595–1644
Har Rai	1630–1661
Har Krishan	1656–1664
Tegh Bahadur	1621–1675
Gobind Singh	1666–1708

Most of them served as the guru and leader of Sikhs only in later life. Each

was chosen for the task by his predecessor on the basis of his spiritual insight and worthiness.

During the period of the first five gurus, most of the Sikh doctrines were developed. The community emerged as a devotional group of religious seekers. This group had much in common with the north Indian tradition of the mystics, who sought a union with God through devotion and love. Many people see the Sikh religion as possessing two basic features, one being this mystical aspect, the other more aggressive, military and world-affirming. This first major period of Sikh history—from about AD 1500 when Nanak's active ministry began until roughly 1600 when the Muslim Empire passed from Akbar, the friend of the Sikhs, to his evil successor Jehangir—was not devoid of worldly and political interest. Each of the early gurus contributed something which would become important later, when open conflict broke out between Muslims and Sikhs.

● Nanak taught that 'there is no Hindu, there is no Muslim'. This came to serve as the basis for a separate Sikh identity. What was chiefly a religious idea for Nanak later became the justification for a distinctive political and military community.

● Angad had a liking for physical fitness. He organized games among his followers. These activities were not aimed at military training, but when such training became necessary, they were seen to have prepared the way for it.

● Amar Das established the *langar* or communal eating facilities served by a common kitchen. This was paid for by Sikhs associated with a particular temple. The aim was to encourage Sikhs of all castes to eat together without the caste prejudice which characterizes much of the ordinary Indian way of life. It strengthened brotherhood and helped the underprivileged. Non-Sikhs, too, were welcome.

This great ideal of the Sikh gurus was a reaction against the Hindu caste system and involved their rejection of orthodox priesthoods such as the Brahmins. During the later period of Sikh history, when they were facing fierce aggression from the Muslims, it was relatively easy for caste divisions to be submerged in the defence of the Sikh community. Contemporary Sikhism, however, still possesses internal divisions of caste. Although the Sikh ideal speaks of the casteless brotherhood of fellow-seekers after God, in practice this ideal has not been completely achieved.

● Arjan, the fifth guru, serves as a turning-point in Sikh history. After him, there was a marked increase in political strife between Sikhs and Muslims. He built the renowned Hari Mandir, the Golden Temple at Amritsar, which became the centre of Sikh religious and national life. It was the focal point of Sikh identity and expressed many of the basic Sikh hopes and beliefs.

The war with Islam

In 1606 Guru Arjan was killed while in Muslim custody. Opinion is divided as to the justice of what happened, but the Sikhs see the death as a martyrdom. Under Arjan's leadership the Sikhs had begun to stand against Muslim aggression. This made the guru a rallying point for others in the Punjab, and soon many members of the Jat farming caste had aligned themselves with him. A switch of emphasis from a peaceful spreading of the faith to an assertion of the right to defend that faith took place among the Sikhs, now grown greater in numbers and strength. Islamic pressure forced Arjan's successor, Har Govind, into retreat, and after his death in 1644 Guru Har Rai took up the leadership and lived in the mountainous area of east Punjab. His son and successor in office, Har Krishan, could not escape the attention of Emperor Aurangzeb quite so easily, and died under house arrest at Delhi.

Tegh Bahadur had been named as the next guru but, like Har Rai, he was more of a devotional man than a soldier. It was only after Aurangzeb began to destroy temples and oppress Sikh groups in the Punjab that he was summoned from Bengal, where

1. The home of the Sikh
faith is the agricultural
Punjab area of north
India. 2. Some Sikhs still
wear the full military-style
uniform. 3, 4. The Golden
Temple at Amritsar.
5. Sikhs have pictures of
the Gurus, especially
Nanak, in their homes.
6. Inside a Sikh temple in
New Zealand.

he had been living with his family, to rally the Sikhs against the enemy. As a result he was taken to Delhi, where he died as a martyr. His son Gobind Singh, then only nine years old, took up the leadership. As it turned out, over the next thirty or so years he became a renowned warrior.

Gobind Singh led the Sikhs against the Islamic powers with considerable success. He welded together an active community with a profound sense of its calling to preserve its religious tradition intact. After a first victory at Bhangani in 1686, a twenty-year period of conflict ended in defeat. Defeat in the immediate battle, though, began a period of success for Sikh religion, because Guru Gobind Singh brought about a radical difference in the way the community viewed itself.

The people and the book

According to the orthodox Sikh interpretation of what took place at the very end of the seventeenth century, the living guru transferred his authority in 1699 to the community itself on the one hand, and (in 1708) to the collection of the sacred scriptures on the other. A change in the idea of guruship was taking place. At the centre of the religion, instead of a living individual directing men in their spiritual quest and guiding them in worldly affairs, there is a community (the *Guru Panth*) and a book (the *Guru Granth*).

The tradition tells how the *Panth* (the path or way followed by the seekers; a term used to describe the community itself) was formed by Gobind Singh. He challenged his followers, who had gathered together at his request, to come forward as human sacrifices. This was a test of their faithfulness. After some thought, five men volunteered their lives to the guru. He did not, in fact, kill them but dressed them in a new form of uniform and presented them to the gathered assembly as his five beloved ones. These represented the new community of the pure ones, the *Khalsa*. (This is another name for the *Guru Panth*. It indicates the moral dedication of those who wish to follow the teaching of the historical

gurus.) This new community was to be powerful and strong in the defence of the faith and in establishing a strictly moral society. The names of *Singh* (Lion) and *Kaur* (Princess), given to the male and female members of the new community, were to express the change of status which the Sikhs were to undergo in the world, replacing names which indicated caste, and giving women a more equal standing with men.

When boys and girls are about fourteen, they may be initiated into full membership of the *Khalsa*. This ritual is often called baptism. But that is only a loose description of what actually happens. This act of 'taking *amrit*' involves present-day Sikhs in what they believe took place on that first initiation day.

Five respected members of the community represent the beloved ones of Guru Gobind Singh. After singing certain prayers and preparing a solution of sugar in water, they initiate the candidates by sprinkling the solution on their heads and eyes. They are also instructed in the basic rules of *Khalsa* membership, of loyalty and moral conduct. Their hair must be left uncut. They must avoid adultery and tobacco. And they must reject meat killed in the Muslim way.

The holy scriptures

At the heart of this ritual, as of all Sikh rites, is the holy book. The ceremony begins with a reading from it, and many of the prayers and songs are related to it. The *Guru Granth* contains the spiritual poetry of the historical gurus. It is largely the product of Guru Arjan's labour, though Guru Gobind Singh produced the final edition in which he included the work of the gurus after Arjan. This compilation is called the *Adi Granth*, or the original and first book of scriptures. Guru Gobind Singh's own hymns and poetry were not included. But the collection made by a disciple after his death is called the *Dasam Granth*—the collection of the tenth guru.

When Guru Gobind Singh invested the book with his own authority in 1708, he changed the whole structure of the Sikh religion, provid-

'There exists but one God, who is called the True, the Creator, free from fear and hate, immortal, not begotten, self-existent, great and compassionate. The True was at the beginning, the True was at the distant part. The True is at the present, O Nanak, the True will be also in the future.'

The beginning of Guru Nanak's hymn, from the *Adi Granth*. It is recited by Sikhs each morning as an expression of faith.

ing a solid, permanent focus of attention for Sikh congregations. Indian religion had always emphasized in practical ways the human need for a spiritual focus and a visible basis for worship. Temples, centres of pilgrimage, holy rivers and holy men had long been the foundation of Indian spirituality.

Although Guru Nanak himself argued that all such outward forms of religion were useless unless the heart was right with God through loving meditation, the vast majority of later Sikhs needed outward objects as a stimulus to devotion. So when Guru Gobind Singh established the book as a source of divine truth and as a vehicle of spiritual insight, it soon acquired great status. It is now always the central feature of every Sikh ritual and endeavour. Sikhs bow down before it, as Hindus before their images. When babies are brought to the temple, a random reading from the *Granth* will be used as a basis for choosing their names. Marriage centres on the book. The bride follows her groom around it four times, while songs of duty and obligation are sung. Death involves special readings from the book for seven- or ten-day periods. And continuous reading over two days accompanies certain festivals.

The Sikh temple or *gurdwara* (the guru's door) is, essentially, a place where the book is located and where

The Golden Temple

The Golden Temple can serve as a symbol of the Sikh religion, and a visual aid to our understanding of its spiritual meaning, and of how the past has influenced the present. For Sikhs this temple is the court of the Lord (*Darbar Sahib*). In its precincts are to be found peace and the possibility of access to God. The Hindi and Punjabi hymns of the early gurus, together with those of other non-Sikh mystics, were collected together in the *Gurmukhi* (mouth of the guru) script and first installed here by Arjan in 1604. Later editions of this volume, which include the devotional poetry of the later gurus, constitute the focal point of devotion and meditation. The hymns are sung from morning to night at the temple, and a constant stream of visitors and pilgrims comes to listen to the words which confer a blessing on their believing hearers.

The whole temple site consists of an outer paved area with shaded cloisters surrounding the large pool or tank from which Amritsar ('pool of nectar') takes its name. At the centre of the pool lies the beautiful Golden Temple itself, in which the sacred book is placed early in the morning. This temple has served as the basis for many interpretations of the religious life. It is, for example, like a lotus plant growing from the murky water of life, yet producing a beautiful flower of devotion and good works, teaching man to reach above the evil of the world which would choke his higher desires. The outer courtyard possesses four entrances, unlike the single doorways of Muslim and Hindu shrines, This expresses the universality of Sikh truth, which is open to all.

Another gold-topped building stands in the outer area, facing the long walkway to the inner holy place. This is the Akal Takht, a political and community centre where important pronouncements are made concerning the life of Sikhs. Built by the sixth guru, it indicates the rise of political and social awareness among Sikhs, as they sought to establish a code of conduct for themselves and a way of organizing their relations with other groups. Here in the temple area religion and politics are clearly distinguished. There are, in fact, four other major Takhts (or thrones) and many other important temples, but Amritsar provides a clear demonstration of the great unity of social and religious life which has emerged in Sikh culture.

The Golden Temple at Amritsar was built by Arjan, the fifth Guru of Sikhism, at the end of the sixteenth century.

the congregation of Sikhs may gather around it. Book plus congregation equals guru. The *Guru Granth* and the *Guru Panth* add up to the presence of the guru in the world today. An obvious consequence of this development has been the greatly increased responsibility for the faith which falls on the shoulders of each member. There are no priests; anyone can conduct the worship, though some are specially trained to read and expound the *Granth*. This has made the Sikhs particularly aware of themselves as a special group, for they are a much more congregational religion than any other in India (apart from Islam), and one in which religious and community identity correspond closely.

Despite this strong communal aspect, Sikh religious teaching is itself intensely personal. We can see this by looking at the doctrines expressed in the *Guru Granth*. One word of caution is needed here: Sikh thoughts about God and men should not be forced into overly rigid doctrinal systems. Sikh doctrines have emerged more as an attempt to express human experience of God in the course of religious living and searching, than as an exercise in academic theology.

What the Sikhs believe

As man begins to become aware of God, he is prompted to see his own life in a different way. The individual seeker realizes that he is tangled up in his own self-seeking pride, ignorance and selfishness, with a consuming passion for the world and its pleasures. It is as though people are blinded to the true nature of life by the hypnotic allure of material goods. The whole world seems to be a sea in which they are drowning with little hope of escape. Even some religious people appear to follow their rituals and creeds in a similar spirit of ignorance.

The love of God

The only hope for sinful men lies in

At Sikh gurdwaras volunteers prepare meals for the 'free kitchen' where visitors are fed.

the fact that the true Guru, God himself, is merciful. He will grant to the true seeker a sense of his presence which lifts and transports man from this life of evil and bondage. He should join a company of other seekers and there sing the hymns of those who have already found knowledge of God. As he dwells upon the name of God, by repeating sacred verses with sincerity and love, so the divine Lord will embrace him and give him a deep inner awareness of his nature. Then the disciple will feel at one with his master.

The language of love, often a bride's longing for her husband, is typical of the Sikh pattern of devotion and spirituality—a mysticism of love. Although God is essentially beyond description, he appears as one who is merciful, eternal, all-powerful. His will determines all that takes place, whether good or evil. He is present everywhere, in the worm as in the elephant.

True spiritual pilgrimage, which takes place in the heart and will—not by travelling to sacred sites—is a shift of emphasis from the self to God. The Sikh expressions are *manmukh* and *gurmukh*, where *man* (pronounced *mun* as in sun) indicates the entire personality of an individual, both heart and mind, and *gur* represents God. The way of salvation is therefore by regarding God, and not the self, as the centre.

Pride and selfishness

The world and its people are under a delusion—the power of *maya*—which prevents clear thought and understanding. Ultimately God is also responsible for that. But Sikhs do not focus on this as a theological problem of evil. People respond to the world in its negative aspect because they are under the power of *haumain*, the self-centred pride of men and women. Only as the power of *haumain* is destroyed by praising the name of the Lord are people set free to serve him. But without the help of the true Guru egotism is not destroyed, nor its disease removed. Salvation is a love-union with God, and that results from a devotional relationship of worship between the

disciple and God. Until that union (*sahaj*) takes place, individuals must live many times by being reincarnated. This process of transmigration of the soul ends only when a person finds the true Guru. Only a few seek him truly, and of these only a few find him.

Love and a longing to serve well up in the hearts of those who find the true Guru. Service is important in the Sikh religion. It is applied to many tasks, both menial and exalted, performed by members of the *Khalsa*. Sweeping out the *gurdwara*, cooking the food to be eaten there, representing the Sikh community to the non-Sikh world—all such acts count as service.

The style and content of the *Guru Granth* is poetical and highly metaphorical. It resembles the biblical Psalms. It is not a systematic explanation of beliefs. Its power lies in catching the mind and stimulating the heart to love God.

'The man who is lost in selfishness is drowned without water, his mind is like a frog and his vice like mud. Yet the Lord is the ocean and the disciple a little fish; once this is realized then a union becomes possible, and that is like metal being welded to metal, like water mixing with water. This union is achieved by the word of the true Guru. Man's heart is penetrated by the Guru's word, it is imperishable and has the power to create and to destroy. Once it comes it is as though a lotus flower blossoms in the heart; it serves as a ship whereby we may cross the evil ocean of existence. The one who is asleep is awakened, and he who was aflame with fever is cooled. Once this experience comes no one will assert that he has deserved it. It is as though the disciple has no purity of his own, but the Lord seizes his arm and washes him. Then the body ceases to be a puppet of *maya* and is free to serve the true Guru.'

Sikhs have many ways of interpreting their scriptures, but the goal of all explanation is to aid man in his search for union with God. In many respects it is a very practical religion which prefers saints to scholars, or at least wishes scholars to be saints. This has led to some interesting reactions when Sikhs have sought to make their beliefs intelligible as a world religion in the twentieth century. For the wishes of scholars are not always those of pious men, nor of the ordinary members of a religious movement.

Identity and community

The twentieth century has witnessed a rapid spread of Sikhs outside the Punjab. In the early part of the century and shortly after the Second World War, many single men and married men without their wives made their way to America, Britain, Canada and parts of South and East Africa. Many of these Sikhs abandoned the wearing of the turban, long hair and beards in an attempt to be accepted by the communities into which they moved to look for employment. Very few Sikh temples existed then but, since weekly attendance at a *gurdwara* was not an established custom in the Punjab, the fact that few attended worship did not mean any abandonment of the Sikh religion.

Sikhs in the West

The late 1960s saw a significant change in Sikh groups in the West, for this was the period when wives and families came to join their husbands and sons. It was a time when Sikh homes ceased to be mere dormitories where the men slept between shift-work, and so Sikhs became far more socially visible. There were now many women, and large numbers of Sikh children attending school. Many buildings were converted into Sikh temples in the larger industrial towns, and these served as social centres as well as places of worship. They helped the newly-arrived Punjabi women to adjust to the new world in which they found themselves.

In 1969 the Sikh Missionary Society was founded in Britain and the Sikh Research Centre in Canada, with similar movements in America.

Sikhs were becoming more aware of their community identity. They sought to produce literature which taught Sikh children about the history of the Sikh religion, as well as encouraging the teaching of the Punjabi language. The aim was to bind the Sikhs together and to enable them to gain recognition as a distinctive community. This growth in self-awareness expressed the idea that being a member of a Punjabi community could not be separated from the idea of being a Sikh.

Traditional practices

Some Sikhs now began to let their beards and hair grow again, and wore

A Sikh wedding in the Punjab. Marriage is both a social and a spiritual union.

their turbans. *Khalsa* Sikhs are supposed to be distinguished by the five symbols, often referred to as the five *k*s because their Punjabi names begin with that letter. These are:

● *kesh*, or uncut hair;
● *kangha*, or comb used to keep the hair clean;
● *kara*, or metal bangle;
● *kaccha*, or special knee-length underwear;
● *kirpan*, or dagger.

Sometimes the children of Sikhs with cut hair have returned to the more traditional pattern, showing the changed relationship between the early immigrant generations and those born in their adopted country and more sure of their social standing.

Though there have been many changes in these settlements of Sikhs, some of the traditional Punjabi practices have continued, especially that of arranged marriages. In these, the families of young men and women decide on marriage partners on their behalf; they may or may not be given the chance to add their own opinion. Some youngsters prefer this decision to be taken for them, but others would rather have a love-match of their own choice. Caste is one of the most important factors in arranging marriages, despite the teachings of the historical gurus. In some towns one major caste-group meets in one *gurdwara* while other groups meet in theirs. The Jat groups are often distinguished from the Ramgarhias and Bhatras, divisions which can be traced back to occupational differences in the Punjab.

The Sikh religion is not a missionary religion in the sense that it tries to win members from outside. It is an ethnic religion which seeks to maintain the community intact. Some splinter groups in America have converted Americans to the faith, just as in the Punjab there are a few movements which believe that there is still a need for living gurus today, and which do in fact possess them. But, generally speaking, the Sikh religion is focussed on the community, and on that ethical life which brings honour to the *Khalsa*. For that is the fellowship of true believers in which alone access to God may be found. The Sikh religion does not deny the existence of truth in other faiths, but its main concern is that its members strive to be devoted to God.

Respect For All Life: Jainism

Myrtle Langley

For a religion of only 3 million people, almost all of whom live in India, Jainism has wielded an influence out of all proportion to its size and distribution. This influence has been felt most keenly in the modern world through Mahatma Gandhi. Although not himself a Jain, he grew up among Jains and embraced their most distinctive doctrine—non-violence to living things, *ahimsa*. But the influence of Jainism has also been felt in the Jain contribution to India's banking and commercial life.

As Buddhists are followers of the Buddha (the enlightened one), so Jains are followers of the *Jina* (the conqueror), a title applied to Vardhamana, last of the great Jain teachers. It is applied also to those men and women who, having conquered their passions and emotions, have achieved liberation and attained perfection. And so the very name Jainism indicates the predominantly ethical character of this religion.

The birth of Jainism

The period from the seventh to the fifth centuries BC was a turning-point in the intellectual and spiritual development of the whole world: it produced, among others, the early Greek philosophers, the great Hebrew prophets, Confucius in China and probably Zoroaster in Persia.

For north India, the sixth century BC was a time of particular social, political and intellectual ferment. The older and more familiar tribal structure of society was disintegrating. In its place were appearing a few great regional kingdoms and a number of smaller tribal groupings known, for want of a better word, as republics. These kept some of the characteristics of tribal structure but had little political power, being dependent on the largest of the kingdoms. In this transition period, when the old social order was passing away and a new one had not yet taken shape, many people felt themselves adrift, socially and morally. Religious confusion also arose as divergent streams of religious thought and practice came into contact and conflict. It was probably from this conflict that the so-called heterodox teachers associated with Buddhism, Jainism and the Ajivikas sect emerged. They, in turn, probably owed their origin to the Shramanas, the ancient religious teachers distinguished from the Brahmins by their doctrine of salvation through atheism and asceticism. They were considered heterodox because they refused to accept the authority of the *Vedas*, the authoritative Hindu texts, and rejected the institutions of caste and sacrifice.

Mahavira the Path-Maker

Vardhamana, known to his followers as Mahavira (the Great Hero), was an elder contemporary of the Buddha. Although the legends surrounding his life are less attractive than those surrounding the Buddha's, being even more formalized and unreliable, he was undoubtedly a historical person. Under the name of Nigantha Nataputta, he is often mentioned in the Buddhist scriptures as one of the Buddha's chief opponents.

The second son of Siddhartha, a Kshatriya chieftain, Mahavira was born around 540 BC at Kundagrama, near modern Patna in Bihar, and died in 468 BC (according to scholarly opinion; tradition says 599–527 BC). On both sides of the family he belonged to the ruling warrior classes which were a powerful force at the time. Educated as a prince, according to one tradition Mahavira remained a bachelor for life; according to another he married a princess who bore him a daughter. Either way, at the age of twenty-eight, on the death of his parents, he renounced his family life to become a beggar and ascetic, seeking liberation from the dreary round of birth, death and rebirth.

At first he followed the ascetic practices of a group founded some 250 years earlier by a certain Parsva. Parsva is known as the twenty-third and Mahavira as the twenty-fourth of the *Tirthankaras*, the 'Ford-makers', 'Path-makers' or great teachers of Jainism, who guide their followers across the river of transmigration. For over twelve years Mahavira wandered from place to place, living a life of the greatest austerity and engaging in disputation. At first he wore only a single loincloth, but after thirteen months he discarded even that encumbrance and for the rest of his life went about naked.

The enlightenment

In the thirteenth year, when aged about forty, and at the end of a long fast, he achieved liberation and full enlightenment. In the language of his followers he had become a conqueror (*jina*). He had attained a state of full, clear and unimpeded knowledge and intuition known as *kevala*, becoming a perfected soul (*kevalin*). And by attaining this omniscience, Mahavira had released himself from the forces (*karma*) which had bound him to the wheel of rebirth.

Mahavira was then acclaimed a leader of an Order (a *Tirthankara*), and for the remaining thirty years of his life he propagated his beliefs and organized his community of followers. He called himself the successor of a series of legendary *Tirthankaras* who had proclaimed Jain beliefs through countless ages. And although his claims may not be wholly true, there is little doubt that the tradition from which Jainism derives goes back beyond Mahavira, Parsva and even Nemi (alleged cousin of Krishna of the Mahabharata war) to the farthest recesses of Indian prehistory. He died, of voluntary self-starvation, at Pava, a village not far from his birthplace, and a great centre of Jain pilgrimage to this day. Thus he entered *nirvana*, his 'final rest'.

The rise of Jainism

Mahavira drew his followers mainly from the Kshatriya aristocracy and organized them into a regular community with lay and monastic members of both sexes. There is good reason to believe that before they joined him some of these followers believed that all possessions, including clothing, should be abandoned,

A Jain home shrine.

The general plan of a Jain temple is of a portal and colonnades, a closed hall or open courtyard, and an inner shrine for the images. The principal image, of the *Tirthankara* to whom the temple is dedicated, is flanked by two attendants and by smaller images of the twenty-four *Tirthankaras*. In Digambara temples, the image sits naked with eyes downcast. In Svetambara temples it sits clothed with a loincloth, has protruding eyeballs and is often adorned with jewels and flowers.

Every Jain temple also has a 'saint-wheel' (*siddha cakra*). Its basic form is that of a stylized flat lotus with four petals attached to a circle in the centre. Placed in the petals and in the circle are representations of the Five Great Beings in meditative posture (seated with crossed legs). Often the principles of right knowledge, right faith and right conduct are incorporated too. The diagram is invoked for the destruction of sin and for the common good to prevail.

in the pursuit of passionless detachment, while others stopped short of making nudity a requirement. It was this difference, and later disagreement about the contents of the canon of the scriptures, which were to distinguish the two major sects of Jainism. No fundamental doctrinal differences emerged, even in later centuries.

The two sects

For two centuries, Mahavira's followers remained a small community. Then there was a big increase in Jain numbers as the founder of the great Mauryan dynasty, the Magadhan Emperor Chandragupta (about 321–297 BC), abdicated his throne and joined the order. History here confirms tradition, at least to some extent. However, towards the end of Chandragupta's reign, a serious famine led to the exodus of a large number of Jain monks from the Ganga Valley in north India south to the Deccan. There, in the state of Mysore, they established great centres of the faith.

Then, so tradition has it, when Bhadrabahu, the leader of the emigrants and eleventh elder of the community, returned to Bihar after an absence of twelve years he found that in the confusion and hardship of famine the northern monks, under Sthulabhadra, had abandoned the ancient ways laid down by Mahavira and had taken to wearing white robes.

Thus arose the two sects of Jainism, the Digambaras (the 'sky-clad' or 'space-clad') and the Svetambaras (the 'white-clad'). The schism became fixed in the first century AD and persists to this day.

The scriptures

Similarly, according to tradition, a sacred literature had been passed down orally through the generations, from Mahavira. But Bhadrabahu was the last person to know it perfectly. On his death at the beginning of the third century BC, the canon was reconstructed as far as possible in

The pessimism of Jainism is nowhere better illustrated than in the famous parable of the man in the well, said to have been told by a Jain monk to a prince in order to persuade him of the evils of the world.

'There was once a man who, oppressed by his poverty, left home and set out for another country. But after a few days he lost his way and found himself wandering in a dense forest. There, he met a mad elephant which charged him with upraised trunk. Immediately he turned to flee there appeared before him a terrible demoness with a sharp sword in her hand. In fear and trembling he looked about him in all directions for a way of escape until he saw a great tree and ran towards it. But he could not climb its smooth bole, and afraid of death, flung himself into an old well nearby. As he fell he managed to catch hold of a clump of reeds growing from the wall, and clung to them desperately. For below him he could see a mass of writhing snakes, enraged at the sound of his falling, and at the very bottom, identifiable from the hiss of its breath, a mighty black python with its mouth wide open to receive him. And even as he realized that his life could last only as long as the reeds held fast, he looked up and saw two mice, one black and one white, gnawing at the roots. Meanwhile, the elephant, enraged at not catching its victim, charged the tree and dislodged a honeycomb. It fell upon the man clinging so precariously. But even as the bees angrily stung his body, by chance a drop of honey fell on his brow, rolled down his face and reached his lips, to bring a moment's sweetness. And he longed for yet more drops and so forgot the perils of his existence.

'Now hear its interpretation. The man is the soul, his wandering in the forest is existence. The wild elephant is death, the demoness old age. The tree is salvation, where there is no fear of death, but which no sensual man can attain. The well is human life, the snakes are passions, and the python hell. The clump of reeds is man's allotted span, the black and white mice the dark and light halves of the month. The bees are diseases and troubles, while the drops of honey are but trivial pleasures. How can a wise man want them, in the midst of such peril and hardship?'

twelve sections (*Angas*) which replaced the fourteen former texts *Purvas*). Although accepted by the Svetambaras, this canon was rejected by the Digambaras, who held that the old one was hopelessly lost. Eighty-four works are recognized as belonging to the Svetambara canon, inally fixed in the fifth century AD. Among them are forty-one Sutras, a number of unclassified works, twelve commentaries and one great commentary. All were written in the Ardha–Magadhi language.

Rise and fall

In subsequent centuries Jainism spread from east to west across India. From time to time it enjoyed the patronage of kings and princes, under whose auspices it produced some of the most magnificent temple architecture in the world. But with the rise of Hindu devotional theism *bhakti*), particularly to Shiva and Vishnu, in the Middle Ages, it went into relative decline. It became concentrated in two regions, where it remains to this day: Gujarat and Rajasthan where the Svetambaras prevail, and the Deccan, or modern Mysore, where the Digambaras have their headquarters. But, unlike Buddhism, Jainism continued in the land of its birth. This was probably due largely to its emphasis on the lay as well as on the monastic calling. In times of persecution it had the resources of an influential and wealthy lay following to fall back on.

One final aspect of Jain history remains to be mentioned: the rise of the 'dwellers in halls' (*Sthanakavasi*) branch of the Svetambaras in AD 1653. Parallel with the Protestant Reformation in Europe, and probably owing to Muslim influence, reformers arose to condemn all forms of idolatry and temple worship as inconsistent with the teachings of Mahavira. Fundamental doctrines, however, remained unaffected by his further schism.

Jain beliefs

Mahavira and other unorthodox teachers of his age were primarily interested in seeking liberation from the wheel of rebirth.

The universe

Jain philosophy differs in important respects from the systems of Buddhism and Hinduism. Jainism upholds the existence of an infinite number of animate and inanimate substances—*jivas* or souls, and *ajivas* or non-souls, representing the mind/matter dichotomy—each of which possesses an infinite number of individual characteristics of its own. Moreover, all substances exist independently of our perceptions or awareness of them. Thus Jain philosophy is realist.

But because the number of souls inhabiting the universe is infinite, most of them will be compelled to transmigrate eternally in *samsara*, the world of birth, death and rebirth. And this world is itself subject to a process of growth and decline. It is part of a universe which, without beginning and without end, passes through an infinite number of cosmic cycles, each divided into phases of

Carving from the marble temple on Mt Abu.

ascent and descent during which civilization rises and falls. At present we are in the fifth period of a phase of descent.

The apparent fatalism and determinism of the system is opposed by Jain philosophers by means of the distinctive theory of 'many-sidedness' (*anekantavada*). This relates the truth of any proposition to the point of view from which it is made. The rise and fall of civilizations is rigidly determined from the universal point of view, but from the individual viewpoint a man is free to work out his own salvation. Only the liberated soul knows the full and absolute truth. A popular illustration of this is the parable of the six blind men and the elephant. Each, having grasped a part of the great beast, was asked what it was like. One said a wall, another a rope, another a snake, another a fan, and so on. Only the soul in *nirvana* has complete and perfect knowledge.

The soul

The soul's essential character is consciousness and knowing. In its original state, the soul knows everything: nothing is hidden from it, it commands the knowledge of existence in all its various aspects, and at all times, past, present and future. In its present state in this world, ensconced in a material body, the soul's knowledge is made imperfect and incomplete by the limitations matter places on it.

The soul is graded into five levels according to which form it takes in its earthly existence.

● At the lowest level are the souls possessing only one sense—touch; these include the elements themselves, earth, water, air and fire, and the vast vegetable kingdom.

● At the second level are the souls possessing two senses: touch and taste—including worms and shell creatures.

● At the third level are the souls possessing three senses: those of touch, taste and smell—including ants, bugs and moths.

● At the fourth level are the souls possessing four senses: touch, taste, smell and sight; these include, for example, wasps, locusts and butterflies.

● At the fifth and highest level are the souls possessing all five senses—touch, taste, smell, sight and hearing. These include four types of creatures: infernal beings, the higher animals, humans, and heavenly beings.

The soul's journey from one level of consciousness to another, and from one grade to another, up or down the scale, depends on the inexorable law of *karma*.

Karma and rebirth

Like all Indian religions, Jainism upholds the universal law of *karma*. According to this law, every action—thought, word or deed—produces an effect, which in turn serves as the cause of another action, and so on. This chain of cause and effect is known as 'karmic bondage' or simply *karma*. And because Jainism, as we have seen, subscribes also to the doctrine of transmigration and rebirth, it follows that the state of the soul at any given time is due to the *karma* accumulated over countless ages.

However, the Jain doctrine of *karma* is distinctive. Whereas Hindus view *karma* purely as a law of nature, Jains believe *karma* to consist of fine and subtle particles of matter which adhere to the soul, as clay to a pot. Yet, by effort, discipline and knowledge, man can control *karma*. Selfish, careless and cruel actions lead to the accumulation of heavy *karma* which weighs the soul down. But the *karma* accruing from good deeds is dissipated almost immediately and has no serious effects. Moreover, suffering willingly undertaken has the effect of dispersing the *karma* already accumulated, so helping to lighten the soul.

To achieve salvation (*moksha*) man must therefore free his soul from matter. Thus freed, its natural lightness will float it to the top of the universe to dwell there for ever in all-knowing bliss. The souls of heroes like Mahavira virtually achieve salvation in this life. It is only residual *karma* which binds them to the earth, but when that is exhausted through fasting and penance, they rise immediately above the highest heavens of the gods to the eternal rest of *nirvana*.

Jainism is not fatalistic, but it *is* atheistic. There is no world-soul, no supreme being, no creator and sustainer of the universe, no one beyond himself (except the *Tirthankaras* as guides and examples) to aid man in his endeavours.

Similarly, for all the subtlety and sophistication with which its doctrine of *karma* and rebirth has been elaborated, Jainism is in practice profoundly pessimistic. The world is a place of utter misery and sorrow, in no way compensated for by life's few moments of happiness.

The way of salvation

Because of the infinite number of souls in the universe and the length of the cycle of rebirth, it happens only rarely that a soul obtains human birth. Therefore, man should use every opportunity to pursue the way of salvation by acquiring the Three Jewels:
● Right knowledge;
● Right faith;
● Right conduct.
Right knowledge comes through knowing the Jain creed, right faith through believing in it and right conduct through following it. The first two are worthless without the last, and so Jain monks and nuns, laymen and laywomen take vows of right conduct, the most important and all-embracing of which is non-violence.

Non-violence

To injure living beings, even unwittingly, is to engender the most harmful of karmic effects. To injure with deliberate intent has the gravest of consequences. And since the whole universe throbs with life, this means in practice that a Jain's diet and livelihood are severely restricted. Even the Jain layman must be a strict vegetarian. He may not be a farmer, for when ploughing the soil he might injure animals and plants, not to speak of the earth itself. He may not ply certain crafts, for the metal on the blacksmith's anvil and the wood on the carpenter's bench suffer excruciating pain as they are worked. Instead, he will follow the safe professions of trading and money-lending and most likely become a wealthy merchant or prosperous banker.

The everyday life of a Jain

Jains go through special ceremonies at birth, marriage and death as do members of most religions. But there is a difference. The rites through which the Jain passes are Hindu rather than Jain. And it is often Hindu priests or officiants who perform them.

The life of a layman

Full salvation is not possible for the layman unless, as the end approaches, he takes the vow of old age, containing the promise to die by voluntary self-starvation. And, according to the Digambaras, it is never possible for a woman unless she is first of all reborn as a man.

Jainism recognizes four sources of *karma*:
● Attachment to things of this life, such as food, clothing, lodging, women and jewels;
● Giving rein to anger, pride, deceit and greed;
● Uniting the body, mind and speech to worldly things;
● False belief.
Karma can be controlled by renouncing all activity. Jainism also recognizes eight kinds of *karma*, three tenses of *karma* and fourteen steps to liberation from *karma*. Between steps one and four a person acquires knowledge and faith, but only on the fifth step does he realize the importance of conduct and thus become able to take the twelve vows which mark the layman's religious life.

First in the series of twelve vows are the five 'limited vows':
● Non-violence to souls with more than one sense.
● Truthfulness.
● Non-stealing.
● Chastity.
● Non-attachment or the limitation of possessions and worldly goods.
Next in the series are the three

The Parsvanath temple in Calcutta reflects the wealth of the Jain community.

'assistant vows' which help a person to keep the first five:
● Restriction of travel (so curtailing sin by restricting the area in which it can be committed).
● Restriction on the use of certain things, so discouraging lying, covetousness, stealing and so on.
● Discouragement of carelessness in speaking ill of others, taking life, keeping weapons and having an evil influence.

The remaining four vows in the series are intended to encourage the laity in the performance of their religious duties:
● To spend at least forty-eight minutes every day in unbroken meditation (*samayika*), thinking evil of no one, being at peace with the world and contemplating the heights which may be reached by the soul, and if possible to repeat this exercise three times, morning, afternoon and evening.
● To set aside at least one particular day to be more serious about the vows of travel restriction and meditation.
● To live as a monk for a temporary period of twenty-four hours, touching no food, drink, ornaments, scents or weapons and remaining celibate while using only three cloths by day and two by night—thus forging a link between the lay and monastic communities (called *posadha*).
● To support the ascetic community by giving its members any of the

fourteen articles which they may accept without blame, such as food, water, clothing, pots, blankets, towels, beds, tables and other furniture.

Jains believe that to keep the twelve vows brings great physical and moral advantage. The body becomes fit and healthy and the soul is freed from love and enmity.

The layman wanting to reach a higher stage in the upward path towards liberation must undertake to keep a further eleven promises:
● To worship the true *deva* (i.e. a *Tirthankara*), reverence a true guru (teacher), and believe in the true doctrine (*dharma*, i.e. Jainism), while avoiding the seven bad deeds of gambling, eating meat, wine-bibbing, adultery, hunting, thieving and debauchery.
● To keep the twelve vows, facing death by voluntary self-starvation in complete peace.
● To engage in meditation at least three times a day.
● To live the life of a monk temporarily at least six times a month.
● To avoid uncooked vegetables.
● To refrain from eating between sunset and sunrise and from drinking water before daylight, in case an insect is accidentally eaten.
● To keep away from his own wife and never to scent his body so as to seduce her.
● Never to begin anything that might entangle him in worldly pursuits which might lead to destruction of life.
● To be a novice for his remaining days.
● To eat only left-overs.
● To wear the dress of an ascetic, live apart in a religious building or in the forest, and live according to the rules laid down in the scriptures for ascetics.

By the time he has taken the last of these eleven promises, the layman is virtually an ascetic.

As the layman endeavours to reach this exalted state, he will strive to develop the twenty-one qualities which distinguish the Jain 'gentleman'. He will always be 'serious in demeanour; clean as regards both his clothes and his person; good-tempered; striving after popularity; merciful; afraid of sinning; straightforward; wise; modest; kind; moderate; gentle; careful in speech; sociable; cautious; studious; reverent both to old age and old customs; humble; grateful; benevolent; and, finally, attentive to business'.

The life of an ascetic

The life of an ascetic begins with initiation. First he gives away his clothing and jewels to relatives, and dons the dress of an ascetic (*sadhu*), three upper garments and two lower ones which vary in colour according to sect. Next, he has his hair removed. From now on he is a homeless wanderer and must remain possessionless except for his robes, a few pieces of cloth with which to strain insects from his daily drink of water, a cloth mask with which to cover his mouth for fear of hurting the air, a few wooden jugs or gourds, and a brush or whisk with which to sweep insects from the path before him.

The five great vows taken by the Jain ascetic are stricter versions of the first five taken by the layman:

● Non-violence—not to kill any living thing, whether five-, four-, three-, two-sensed or immovable (one-sensed), even through carelessness.

● Truthfulness—to speak only of what is pleasant, wholesome and true.

● Non-stealing—not to take what is not given.

● Chastity—to have no dealings with gods, human beings or animals of the opposite sex.

● To renounce love for any thing or person, which means ending all likes and dislikes with regard to sounds, colours or smells as well as people—in other words, to be indifferent to anything mediated through the senses.

As there exists an ideal for the Jain layman, so too there exists the picture of a perfect monk. It has been said that the true ascetic should possess twenty-seven qualities, for he must keep the five vows, never eat at night, protect all living things, control his five senses, renounce greed, practise forgiveness, possess high

ideals, and inspect everything he uses to make sure that no insect life is injured. He must also be self-denying and carefully keep the three rules for controlling mind, speech and body, he must endure hardships in the twenty-two ways, and bear suffering till death.

Ways of worship

Jainism's rejection of God does not entail rejection of prayer and worship, more precisely termed contemplation. But of all beings, including the gods and the saints, only liberated souls or *Tirthankaras* made perfect are worshipped. Even they are not appealed to for help or mercy; they serve more as an inspiration to those still struggling for freedom and perfection.

That is the theory. The practice is very different. Many of the Jain laity pray to Hindu gods for help, many Jain temples house images of Hindu deities, and many Jain festivals incorporate Hindu customs.

Temples and domestic shrines

One of the glories of Jainism is its heritage of magnificent temple architecture. Two of its outstanding developments are the temple-cities, some of which have hundreds of shrines from many different periods, and the fretted ceilings and ornamented pillars with their delicately carved figures and flowers in marble, perhaps the finest of their kind in the world. The numerous modern temples in the towns and cities are smaller and undistinguished.

Jain homes incorporate domestic shrines. According to scriptural instruction they are supposed to be made of wood, and some with elaborately carved doors and door-frames have survived.

Prayer

Jain temples are filled with images of the *Tirthankaras*: 'Contemplating the form of the passionless Lord in a Jaina temple, the mind becomes filled automatically with a sentiment of renunciation... The mind is purified by the contemplation and worship of the *Tirthankaras*.'

The great statues of south India best convey the Jain ideal. This is a description of the sixty-foot-high stone replica of the hero Gomatesvara at Sravana Belgola:

'[He rises] huge, stony and naked. So rigid is his stance, so austere his stillness, that creepers are growing up his legs. On his lips is an expression of total impassivity. His nudity of course symbolizes possessionlessness. It is a sign of indifference to the good things of this world. It is not even a matter of laying up treasures in heaven. The Jain saint should be indifferent even to those. Any sort of treasure binds us to this world, and even the heavenly world should be transcended. Karma which weighs us down, like weights which depress balloons, must be got rid of, destroyed. This is a supremely hard task. The saint is the culmination of a struggle which has continued over many, many lives. He gazes, unseeing, over the dry south Indian landscape, a spiritual Gulliver among dark-skinned Lilliputians. Every twelve years, the Jain faithful have a great festival in which innumerable pots of milk and curds and sandal paste are poured over the head of the stone hero.

The faith celebrates those who have through heroism and insight gained liberation and thus shown the path to others.'

Ninian Smart

Every day devout Jains rise before dawn and, with rosary of 108 beads in hand, invoke the Five Great Beings, bowing, with folded hands to east, north, west and south.

As a Jain worshipper approaches the temple, he leaves his shoes and socks outside. At the porch he puts a saffron mark on his brow and repeats the *Nissahi* (which enables him to put aside all sin and care). Inside, he comes to the shrine and bids for the right to wash the principal *Tirthankara* image. Removing the jewels and old flowers, he washes it with water, milk and five nectars. When it has dried, he then rubs it over and marks it with liquid saffron in fourteen places, from head to toe. Meanwhile, verses are sung in its praise, incense and lamps waved at the threshold and an offering of rice placed on a table before the door. Finally, the worshipper performs spiritual worship, prostrating himself three times before the image, recalling the virtues of the *Tirthankara*, singing his praises, walking backwards to the door as he repeats the *Avassahi* (which allows him to engage in worldly pursuits again), and with hands together bowing out.

Festivals

The most important festival of Jainism is held at Pajjusana, the solemn season which closes the Jain year. For eight days or longer, during the wet monsoon period, usually in August, devout Jains fast and attend special services. All householders are urged to live a monk's life for at least twenty-four hours, living in a monastery, meditating and fasting. On the closing day of the festival, every Jain abstains from food and water. At the close of the temple gathering, he performs an act of penitence in which he asks forgiveness of his neighbours for any inadvertent offence and determines to carry no grudge or quarrel over into the next year.

The second most important festival is Divali, the great Hindu festival in honour of Lakshmi, goddess of wealth, which Jains have adapted in honour of Mahavira's liberation.

Jains also observe fasts at full moon, and great excitement is found in going on pilgrimages to Jain holy places.

Jainism is a religion of austerities. Its goal—passionless detachment—is reached only through the most severe and disciplined of life-styles, culminating ideally in death by voluntary self-starvation. And the aim is to achieve it solely by self-effort, without the help of God or gods.

Yet self-imposed austerities often benefit others. And Jains have long been active in promoting public welfare. They are known especially for their endowment of schools, also of hospitals—for both people and animals.

Courage and Faith:
The Parsis

John Hinnells

The word 'Parsi' denotes the 'Persians' or people who left Persia (Iran) at the end of the ninth century AD to seek a new land of religious freedom. They were believers in the ancient Zoroastrian religion, and left Persia rather than forsake their religion, in the face of fierce Islamic persecution. The story of their voyage to India is recounted in the Tale of Sanjan, the *Qissa-i Sanjan*, written in 1600.

Acting on the advice of an astrologer-priest, a group of Zoroastrians left their home in northern Persia, journeyed across the country and set sail to Div, on the coast of present-day Pakistan. There they settled for nearly twenty years, before they moved on again at the advice of an astrologer-priest. When they were at sea, a storm blew up threatening their lives. They prayed to God to rescue them and vowed that if he answered their prayers they would build a great Fire Temple as an act of thanksgiving.

Their prayers were answered and they landed at Sanjan on the north-west coast of India in AD 936. They approached the local prince for permission to settle. This he gave on certain conditions—that they speak in the local language (Gujarati); that they should observe local wedding customs; and that the men should not carry arms. To assure him of their peaceful intentions, the Parsis presented sixteen statements (*shlokas*) regarding their faith and practice. In these they stressed those features of their faith which resembled Hinduism and the social customs which would offend no one. The ruler also gave the Parsis land on which they could build their temple.

The story shows that Parsis believe their journey to India to be part of the divine plan—written in the stars. They landed where they did as an answer to prayer; they have been required to make only minimal adaptations to their way of life in India, and there is a degree of harmony between their religion and that of their Hindu hosts. These beliefs are true of Parsis both then, in the seventeenth century, and now.

Under Hindu rule the Parsis lived a quiet, secure and settled life. In AD 1297 Muslim armies invaded Gujarat, an invasion they followed up in 1465 to secure their hold on the region. Parsis feared there would be a return to the persecution they had suffered in Persia, so they fought alongside the Hindus, but to no avail. Although there have been instances of Muslim oppression on the Parsis (and others), conditions were never as bad as those in Persia.

British rule

The arrival of European and particularly British traders in the seventeenth century was the event which most drastically affected Parsi fortunes. The British developed the islands of Bombay as a new commer-

A Parsi boy is given a sacred shirt and a sacred thread at the naujote *ceremony. Following this initiation rite, Parsi children – both boys and girls – are eligible to take part fully in the religious life of the community.*

cation than any other community in proportion to their numbers.

As a result, they occupied a correspondingly high proportion of official posts. They were very influential in the early phases of the Indian National Congress, the party which led the campaign for independence and which has ruled India practically ever since. In west Indian politics they were an extremely powerful voice. Further, the only three Indians ever to be elected to the House of Commons at Westminster were all Parsis. The fact that they were elected by the English voters to represent London constituencies, not India, shows how educated and Westernized these Parsis had become. What was true of these three individuals was true of many in Bombay also. Parsis ran and owned much of India's commerce, such as banks, the textile industry and the trade with the East.

Modern trends

In the twentieth century, Parsi wealth and influence has declined as other communities have taken their share of the wealth. But still the Parsis remain a highly respected, largely middle-class, well-educated community. The numbers have begun to decline since the Second World War, largely owing to a falling birth rate. Something like 70 per cent of India's Parsi population (now about 92,000) live in the one city, Bombay, so they are hit especially hard by its typical inner-city problems.

Such tremendous social changes have inevitably influenced Parsi religion. Naturally their Western education has resulted in a Western religious influence. A number of Parsis have studied abroad, some have studied their own religion at Western universities. Most have studied under Protestant scholars and this has affected their reform movements. They have called for the use of the vernacular instead of the sacred language of Avestan in prayers, and a higher Western education for trainee Parsi priests. Some even denied that revelation was a valid religious concept, because of the educational principle that a truth per-

cial base. To do this they needed to attract immigrants to these almost uninhabited islands and so offered attractive conditions. In particular they offered freedom of religion and justice for all, which appealed particularly to minority groups such as the Parsis. As early settlers in Bombay, the Parsis played a leading part in developing it as the leading port of western India and as India's commercial capital. What is more, they obtained a substantial proportion of the wealth that flowed to the island in the nineteenth century. By 1850 it was estimated that Parsis owned half the island.

After 1857, when the government of India passed from the East India Company to the crown and parliament in London, Indians needed new resources to influence official policy. Local influence and wealth were insufficient; a Western education was essential in order to argue with the British in London. Parsis rose to positions of considerable power in these changed conditions, because more Parsis received a Western edu-

ceived and learned for oneself is better understood than a truth imposed from above. Other, more secular, Parsis called for the complete Europeanization of the community.

Theosophy and the Parsis

Such extremes naturally provoked a backlash among the orthodox. The form which this took was an unexpected one, for it involved Theosophy, a religious movement started in the West which called on Indian religions not to be misled by 'the materialist West' into abandoning their ancient practices. This message inspired many Parsis who, without necessarily becoming members of the Theosophical Society, accepted a number of Theosophical teachings.

Then, early in the twentieth century, a specifically Parsi form of Theosophy was begun by Behramshah Shroff (1857–1927). He claimed that he had been taken to an unknown hideout in the Persian mountains by a wandering group of secret Zoroastrians. There, hidden in caves, he claimed, were ancient treasures and teachings from Zoroastrian Persia. The religion revealed to Shroff contains many Theosophical teachings. For thirty years after his return Shroff remained silent, but spent the last twenty years of his life preaching. There is no way of estimating the followers of his teaching called the path of knowledge, *Ilm-i Kshnoom*), because they have not formed a clear, distinct sect. They are probably relatively few, though they are very vocal among the Parsis.

The great majority of Parsis follow neither the Westernized nor the Theosophical approach. They practise quietly, and unquestioningly, the faith of their forefathers. They know little of the official or historic theologies of their religion. What they do know are its basic ideals and values. Above all, they live out their faith in their daily lives.

Joining God's army

The rite of initiation (*naujote*) is traditionally carried out at the age of puberty, though nowadays there is a tendency for it to take place at about nine years of age. It is never per-

formed on infants because the whole idea of the rite is that the initiate of his or her own free-will chooses to be made a member of God's army. Until a child is old enough to know the difference between right and wrong, Zoroastrians do not believe it can sin.

Naujote is not a sacrament conferring saving grace, but rather an initiation into the responsibilities of the religion. The actual rite involves the first public donning of the badges of the religion, the sacred shirt and cord. The shirt is white, a symbol of the purity of the religion, and made of cotton. It is worn at all times next to the skin. The cord is made of lamb's wool; it is untied and retied at least five times each day to the accompaniment of traditional prayers. As the worshipper rejects the devil he flicks the ends contemptuously; as he mentions God he bows his head in reverence; as he ties the knots he makes a vow to be good in thought, word and deed. These simple acts and prayers can be performed anywhere and must be said five times a day.

Death ceremonies

Death ceremonies in most religions are the ones that change least with the passage of time. Because death, to Zoroastrians, is the temporary victory of evil, it is a place where demons are present. The purpose of the funeral rites is to limit the spread of that evil. The corpse is removed as soon as possible to a place apart. It is washed and dressed in clean but old clothes—old because wastefulness is considered a sin. The funeral should take place the same day as death if possible.

After prayers, and when the mourners have taken their last look at the deceased, the bearers then carry the corpse into a *dakhma* or, as the British called them, a 'Tower of Silence'. These are round structures with high walls to prevent people seeing or getting in. There are a few steps for the corpse-bearers to enter. The tower is open to the sky and there the corpse is stripped, so that the vultures and crows may devour the flesh. It is reckoned that it takes a vulture thirty minutes to devour a

Parsis honour fire as the symbol of Ahura Mazda. The fire is kept in a fire temple, attended by a priest.

Parsis dispose of their dead in secluded buildings known as Towers of Silence.

corpse, during which time the relatives pray in a nearby building. When they return home they wash and observe certain ceremonies for three days while the soul awaits its judgement. On the third day it is usual for those who can to announce the gift of money to a charitable cause in memory of the deceased, a better memorial in Parsi belief than erecting a gravestone. The sun-bleached bones are later cast into a pit.

The initial Western reaction to this rite of exposure is one of horror, a reaction stirred up from time to time by inaccurate newspaper reports. This is a mistaken impression. In theory these places should be on a hill-top apart from all life, so that the

corruption of death will not affect the living. But those in cities such as Bombay and Surat have an air of natural peace and calm about them. Parsis expose bodies in this way because they believe the earth and the waters are the sacred creation of God. They must not, therefore, be polluted with death, the work of evil. Fire, too, is a sacred creation so that cremation is equally wrong. God, they believe, created the vulture for the very purpose of devouring corpses. Parsis argue that it is a far more natural form of disposal than any other, and find Christian graveyards horribly morbid!

Fire temples

Fire has been the focus of Zoroastrian rites and devotions from earliest times. The nomads used the household fire as the centre of their rites, having the sky as their dome, not a man-made temple. Temples were first introduced into Zoroastrianism by the Achaemenid monarch Artaxerxes II (404–359 BC), probably in imitation of Babylonian practice. He also introduced the cult of statues, but this was too radical a break with tradition for it to succeed. Instead of man-made statues, Zoroastrians placed the divinely created 'icon' of fire at the centre of their holy buildings. Temple worship was, then, a late entry into the religion. One can be a good Zoroastrian and never go to a temple, though in practice many do so because they find spiritual help there.

There is no set time or day for temple worship, nor any fixed ritual to perform. For the layman it involves essentially a personal pilgrimage. Before entering the temple he washes and then offers prayers, so that he is clean physically and spiritually. The prayer room itself is very simple. Against one wall there is the sanctuary, marked off by ceiling-high walls, with a door for the priest to enter and windows for the faithful to see through. The sacred fire is kept burning in a large vessel, sometimes as much as 6 feet/2 metres high. The ordinary layman approaches the door of the sanctuary, touches the ground with his forehead, leaves an offering of wood for the fire, and takes a pinch of ash from a ladle left by the priest. He then stands to offer his prayers in private. There is no congregational worship; prayer is offered by each person directly to God.

Fire temples have an enormously powerful sense of the holy. The prayer room is bare of all decoration, so that attention is focussed exclusively on the fire, the living image of God, 'the pure flame of the fire symbolizing him who is himself eternal light', as a Parsi has said. No artificial lights must shine, lest they dim the glory of God's own creation. The priests are expected to undertake many important 'higher' ceremonies on behalf of the layman, but for the ordinary Zoroastrian his duty is primarily the life of good thoughts, words and deeds; the daily prayers and the inspiration of a personal pilgrimage to the temple.

Beauty and simplicity

It is the simplicity of the requirements and the beauty of its ideals, as well as the courage of its followers, which have kept alive the oldest of the world's prophetic religions for some 3,500 years. These have sustained it not only in the face of Muslim persecution, but also in other lands. For the Parsis have dispersed to different parts of the globe, wherever trade took them. There are now Parsi communities in Pakistan (Karachi), East Africa (though the political policies there have forced Parsis, along with other Indians, to leave), Britain (mainly in London), Canada (Toronto, Montreal and British Columbia) and the USA (mainly in New York, Washington and California). The faithful few (approximately 17,000) in present-day Iran, who have survived over 1,000 years of persecution, are now a tolerated religious group. So although the number of followers remains small—perhaps 200,000—Zoroastrianism is still a living religion.

The Enlightened One: Buddhism

Wulf Metz

There is today, in contrast to the last century, hardly any doubt that the 'historical' Buddha, founder of Buddhism, actually lived. His life is greatly interwoven with legend, and rather than a detailed biography, tradition offers an idealized portrait of what all good Buddhists should strive to become. Nevertheless, certain facts about his life can be established fairly clearly.

Siddharta Gautama, later known as Buddha, was born in about 560 BC in a village called Lumbini, near the modern border between India and Nepal. His father, Shuddhodanna, reigned as the rajah of a small principality in the area. As is common with the founder of a religion, all sorts of legends have grown up around the child's birth. In accordance with the idea of rebirth, these even include details of his previous existences! The story is told, for instance, that during his last but one incarnation, the Buddha looked down from the 'Tushita heaven', the 'seat of contented gods', to find the right time, place and parents for his reincarnation. He chose the period of history when human life could last up to 100 years—neither too long nor too short for his teaching to be grasped. As a place he chose northern India, regarded as the central land. And for his mother he took the virtuous Maya, wife of Shuddhodanna, who had shown her purity and excellence during previous existences in 100,000 ages of the world.

One night Maya, who had made a vow of chastity, dreamed that a white elephant entered her womb. Ten months later in the grove of Lumbini, on the day of the full moon in May, she bore her child. The earth trembled and supernatural beings were present at the birth; and Maya died seven days later, for she who has borne a Buddha may never serve any other purpose afterwards.

The name chosen for the boy by his parents, Siddharta, meant 'he who has reached his goal'. Later, as was the custom in noble Indian families, he chose a second name, Gautama, after a famous Hindu teacher from whom he was descended. Buddha, the name by which he came to be known, is actually a title of honour meaning 'the awakened one' or 'the enlightened one'. This title became attached to his name in much the same way that the title 'Christ' became attached to the name of Jesus.

The young prince was brought up by his mother's sister Mahapatjapati, in the greatest luxury and splendour. It had once been prophesied to his father that the boy would become either a great ruler or a homeless wanderer; in order to protect him from the second and ensure the first, Shuddhodanna sheltered his son from all outside influences. He was educated in the arts and sciences and encouraged to do physical exercises;

as he later admitted, according to the Buddhist scriptures:

'I was spoiled, very spoiled. I anointed myself only with Benares sandalwood and dressed only in Benares cloth. Day and night a white sunshade was held over me. I had a palace for the winter, one for the summer and one for the rainy season. In the four months of the rainy season I did not leave the palace at all, and was surrounded by female musicians.'

The prince married a girl called Gopa or Yashodara. He also had a harem of beautiful dancers. Yet he called his only son Rahula which means 'chain', for in the midst of all this luxury he felt as if he were in chains. Life gave him no satisfaction, and so he decided to leave and become homeless.

The great awakening

Before he left his home for good, Siddharta made three journeys on which he was faced with life's realities in a way which he had never known before. He saw the suffering of the world in three forms: a frail old man, an invalid racked with pain, and a funeral procession with weeping mourners. When he asked in amazement what all this meant, the answer was given that this was merely the common fate of all mankind. Deeply troubled, he returned to his palace.

Gautama The Buddha in His Setting

Richard Drummond

Siddharta Gautama, who came to be called the Buddha ('enlightened one') and was the founder of the Buddhist religion, was born about 560 BC, and died at the age of eighty. He lived in north-eastern India, at a time when that area was one of the world's great centres of intellectual and spiritual activity.

Gautama's birth occurred at the end of a long period of development of the Hindu religious tradition. A thousand years before, the Aryan tribes had first entered India from the north-west, and their military and political power, religious practices and other customs had increasingly come to dominate the entire subcontinent. The religious literature of the Vedas had long been composed, and most of the Upanishads were in existence by this time. Within this long tradition Buddhism came as a kind of reform movement, which was only partly accepted, and was eventually more or less expelled. Since the end of the first millennium AD, Buddhism has seen its greatest flowering outside its native land.

Gautama was born the son of the rajah of Kapilavastu, and brought up as a prince. He married at an early age, and had a son. At the age of twenty-nine, however, he was driven by an inner compulsion to leave this outwardly splendid existence for the homeless life of a holy man. His decision was evidently the result of a long-felt aspiration to higher things. It was also in keeping with the more inward religious orientation of the Upanishads, and the emergence within India of the homeless life as a proper method for earnest seekers after spiritual truth and reality.

Gautama took instruction from religious teachers, but apparently most of the first six or seven years after he left home were spent in religious exercises on his own. These exercises became increasingly severe and ascetic; for example, he fasted to the extent that the hair fell off his limbs. The key turning-point prior to his enlightenment was his realization of the spiritual and moral futility of extreme asceticism, and his adoption of the quieter methods of meditation and faith. This was the specific context of his enlightenment, the religious experience which was decisive for his entire later life.

The Buddha began to teach shortly after his experience of the enlightenment and soon won disciples who followed him into the homeless life and missionary service. His teaching, as that of his disciples, was also aimed at ordinary men and women who did not expect to enter the monastic life. The way of life of the inner group may be characterized as meditative, mendicant and missionary. They were in effect a missionary order, and the sense of universal mission which the Buddha evidently held had no parallel in the previous religious history of India. Travelling with his disciples throughout the Ganges river basin, he devoted the rest of his life to proclaiming the liberating truth of dharma and nirvana.

Siddharta Gautama spent many years of extreme asceticism, almost starving himself to death. But it was not until he renounced this way that he achieved enlightenment.

On his fourth journey he met a monk, contented and joyful, travelling around with a begging bowl. This journey was decisive; it showed him that all life's pleasures and attractions are vain and worthless. What he now longed for was true knowledge.

So Siddharta left his home and family, stealing away in the night while his wife and child were asleep. He began to search for knowledge in the traditional Hindu way, striving through constant yoga exercises to unite his self (*atman*) with the origin and meaning of the world (*brahman*). But this method, under the guidance of two Brahminic teachers or gurus, did not satisfy him, or appear to lead to true knowledge.

He continued on his travels until he settled at Uruvela in northern India, where he lived in extreme self-denial and discipline with five followers for six years. All this achieved was to ruin his physical health; he realized that this was not the way to set people free from the cycle of death and rebirth. External treatments were no use; what was needed was an insight into the essence of reality, and a radical change of the basic attitude of greed for life.

Despairing of finding a way out, he suddenly remembered how he had succeeded in his first meditation, at home under an apple-tree. Abandoning his strict life-style (to the horror of his friends who left him in disgust), he resolved to direct all his energies to achieving holiness by meditation.

Immersed in contemplation under a fig-tree, which came to be called 'the tree of enlightenment' or *bodhi*-tree (often shortened to *bo*-tree) he finally reached the highest knowledge, and became the Buddha. His enlightenment had three stages. In his first night of meditation he saw his previous lives pass before him. In the second night he saw with a supernatural insight the cycle of birth, death and rebirth and recognized the law that governs it. In the third night the four holy truths were revealed to him: the knowledge of suffering, the source of suffering, the removal of suffering and the way to the removal of suffering.

The reluctant teacher

Now that he was the Buddha, the 'enlightened one', Siddharta Gautama was in a state of complete redemption and could have entered *nirvana*, the Buddhist heaven, at once. Legend has it that the demon Mara, who had earlier tried to deflect him from his search for truth, now tempted him to do just that. There was no point, the demon said, in teaching the common folk what he had discovered; they were not mature enough for it, and would rather hang on to the enticements and vanities of the world.

Buddha himself had doubts about whether mankind was ready for his teaching. But the god Brahma Sahampati appeared and asked him to pass it on, if only for the sake of a few people. So he decided to set the 'wheel of teaching' in motion, and preached his first famous sermon at Benares. His five former companions were present and became his first disciples.

Buddha had soon gathered around him a group of followers, convinced as much by the serene calm and unshakeable authority of his manner as by the content of his teaching. Discarding the Hindu caste system, he included in his *sangha* or community of monks both Brahmins, the highest caste, and merchants. Among them were members of his own family, including his son Rahula and his cousin Ananda. The order grew quickly; when there were sixty of them, Gautama sent them out to spread the new teaching.

Only women were excluded at first from the order; Gautama felt they were dangerous because they kept the cycle of rebirth in motion, and thus embodied the greed for life. Eventually his stepmother and cousin persuaded him to admit them; but he remained sceptical about this. He maintained that if women had not been admitted, his teachings would have lasted 1,000 years, but that now they would only last 500. History shows us that this pessimistic prophecy was not fulfilled.

A reclining Buddha at the Shwe Dagon pagoda in Rangoon.

A worshipper at the feet
of Aukana Buddha in Sri
Lanka. Images of the
Buddha are often very
large: it was believed that
the Buddha's 'glorious
body' was eighteen feet/
six metres high.

After his enlightenment, Gautama travelled about India for about forty-four years, living as a beggar-monk and teaching. In the rainy season from mid-June to mid-October he and his companions would stay in parks in the towns, where halls (*viharas*) had been built in the Buddha's honour. At the age of eighty, he was taken ill during a meal and died in the town of Kushinagara. Colourful legends describe his ecstatic entry into *nirvana*, and report that a terrible earthquake shook the land when his body was burned. The Buddhist scriptures record his parting speeches to his favourite disciple Ananda:

'Do not cry, Ananda. Have I not been telling you for a long time that it is in the nature of all things, however close or dear they may be to us, that we must part with them and leave them? . . . The wise man sees that all created things, formed from care and suffering, disappear again, but the truth will endure. Why should I keep this fleshly body when the noble truth will last? . . . You have acted well, Ananda. Make every effort, and soon you too will be free of the great evils, of sensuality, selfishness, illusions, uncertainty.'

What Buddha taught

Buddhist thinking does not centre around the veneration of one person, human or divine. Buddha is not a god, nor a god-sent mediator; he cannot act as a saviour or redeemer for others.

Far more important than the person of Buddha is the idea of teaching (*dharma*). According to the Buddhist understanding this is something timeless, not linked to history or subject to change. In line with Indian tradition, the teaching revealed by Buddha was passed on first of all by word of mouth, having been carefully memorized; only much later was it written down.

Knowledge and awakening

After his awakening it was believed that Gautama had passed from an unredeemed state to a state of re-

Buddha—Just a Good Hindu?

Wulf Metz

It is widely recognized that Siddharta Gautama, who was to become the Buddha, came out of the religious world of Hinduism. According to at least one scholar, an understanding of this background is vital to understanding his thought. Buddha, by this interpretation, was a reformer with a similar relationship to Hinduism as that which Luther had to Roman Catholicism. Just as Luther struggled with the problem of how sins can be forgiven, Gautama struggled with the question of how to be freed from the misery of endless rebirths.

It is not enough, however, to say that Buddha merely wanted to re-establish Hinduism in its original form. He was genuinely a founder of a new religion. His teaching does indeed share some central ideas with the traditional Indian religion—above all the doctrine of reincarnation and the law of *karma*. Hinduism and Buddhism can fairly be grouped together as the religions of the eternal world law. Where they differ significantly is in the idea of an individual soul (*atman*) which must be united with the source of the world (*brahman*). This Buddha absolutely rejects.

There is a belief in India that Buddha is the ninth incarnation or *avatar* of the Hindu god Vishnu. In spite of this, it must be recognized that he made a decisive break from Hinduism, most of all in not taking over the Hindu holy writings. He also abandoned the caste system and denied the existence of God in the sense of a higher being.

Of course, as Buddhism developed, many elements entered which were diametrically opposed to the original intentions of Gautama. In many of these the Hindu heritage can again be detected.

The Buddhist Lands

Wulf Metz

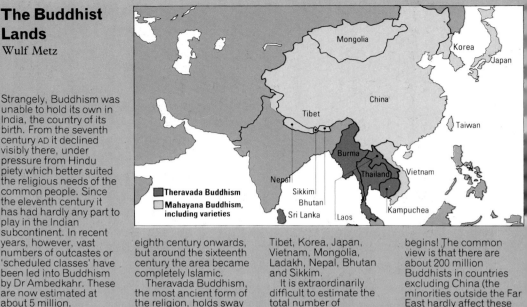

Theravada Buddhism

Mahayana Buddhism, including varieties

Strangely, Buddhism was unable to hold its own in India, the country of its birth. From the seventh century AD it declined visibly there, under pressure from Hindu piety which better suited the religious needs of the common people. Since the eleventh century it has had hardly any part to play in the Indian subcontinent. In recent years, however, vast numbers of outcastes or 'scheduled classes' have been led into Buddhism by Dr Ambedkahr. These are now estimated at about 5 million.

In other regions where it found a foothold at first, Buddhism was later driven out by Islam. Excavations and ancient monuments witness to a blossoming of Buddhism in central Asia, especially East Turkestan, which came to an abrupt end in the ninth century. In the Indonesian islands Buddhism increased in importance from the eighth century onwards, but around the sixteenth century the area became completely Islamic.

Theravada Buddhism, the most ancient form of the religion, holds sway to this day—partly even as a 'state religion'—in Sri Lanka (formerly Ceylon) and in the countries beyond India: Burma, Thailand, Kampuchea and Laos. In other regions of the Far East, Buddhism appears in the form of the more widespread and less strict Mahayana school, or in other variations. This is the case in China,

Tibet, Korea, Japan, Vietnam, Mongolia, Ladakh, Nepal, Bhutan and Sikkim.

It is extraordinarily difficult to estimate the total number of Buddhists in the world. Religious conditions in China, Tibet and Mongolia in particular, but also in Japan, are unclear. One reason for this is that from time immemorial Buddhism has entered into the most varied alliances with other religions. It is not always easy to identify where Buddhism stops and Taoism or Shintoism

begins! The common view is that there are about 200 million Buddhists in countries excluding China (the minorities outside the Far East hardly affect these figures at all). Some people guess the 'unknown quantity' within China to be twice as high as this. So the total world membership of the Buddhist religion may be as high as 600 million people.

demption. Enlightenment and salvation are thus closely linked in a way which is typical of Buddhism. This link makes it clear that the 'knowledge' Gautama received is something very different from the intellectual understanding which Westerners generally mean when they use the word knowledge. In Buddhist terms it is essentially a special religious knowledge, a knowledge which goes far beyond the limits of reason and the intellect.

But where did Buddha's knowledge come from? The story of his experiences shows quite clearly that it did not come from any outside influence such as study, or holy writings, or a revelation from a god. The

guidance of others can certainly direct a person towards the goal of enlightenment, but no one can relieve him of the effort required to achieve it.

At the same time we cannot definitely say that Gautama brought about his own salvation. Therefore some researchers talk of an unknown quantity which defies explanation. It can neither be introduced at will nor attributed to any divine being.

Because of this, Buddhism has sometimes been described as an 'atheistic religion'. Miracles have little importance, and Buddha himself is merely a human being who has awoken from the darkness of error to live in freedom from selfishness,

1. Inside the Marble Temple in Bangkok.
2. Buddhist boys often spend several months in a monastery as part of their education. 3. The Shwe Dagon pagoda in Rangoon is said to contain the hairs of Gautama and the clothes of previous Buddhas.
4. Monks cleaning a statue of the Buddha in Vientiane, Laos.

'I have run through the course of many births looking for the maker of this dwelling and finding him not; painful is birth again and again. Now you are seen, O builder of the house, you will not build the house again. All your rafters are broken, your ridge-pole is destroyed, the mind, set on the attainment of *nirvana*, has attained the extinction of desires.'

Gautama, on receiving the light of illumination; *Dhammapuda* 153–4

Technically, a Buddha is anyone who has reached enlightenment. At Wat Po in Bangkok there are 394 gilded images of Buddhas.

greed and ignorance. He therefore stands far above the rest of humanity, at a spiritual level which even gives him magical powers.

While the Buddha himself is unique in history, other human beings are also called to Buddhahood, though according to the oldest teaching only a few will reach this goal. By looking to the Buddha they are to strive for true knowledge and become Buddhas themselves.

The fatal law

During the second night of Buddha's awakening, he understood the law governing the endless cycle of birth, death and rebirth. The term *dharma*, used earlier to describe the teaching of Buddhism, is also used of this law.

According to Buddha, every part of the universe—not only human beings—is subject to change and decay. Everything that is created must perish. Moreover, neither people nor the world are units complete in themselves and separated from other units. They are composed of many individual elements which are in a constant state of flux, always dissolving and combining with one another in new ways.

These components do not re-arrange themselves at random. They are regulated by strict laws. In the case of human beings, the crucial factor is the law of *karma*, originally a Hindu idea. *Karma*, meaning roughly 'action' or 'works', is the quality which shows itself in the thoughts, words and deeds of an individual. It determines the nature of the individual's rebirth: good works automatically bring about a good rebirth, bad works a bad one. So each rebirth is conditioned by the *karma* of the previous life. This is the moral order of the world, from which no one can escape.

Dharma—in the sense of law—means not only this moral law but also the physical laws ruling the universe; indeed it also denotes the individual parts which make it up. Examples of these *dharmas* are the four elements of earth, water, fire and air; the colours and sounds; organic life; the senses, emotions, impulses of the will, the power of reasoning, consciousness, ignorance; fame, beauty, riches, true and false

The Buddha's Teaching
Richard Drummond

Karma
The law of *karma*, or cause and effect, operates in both moral and physical dimensions of human life. Man is in bondage to this cycle of the results of good and evil actions.

Reincarnation
Through reincarnation or rebirth all human beings reap good or evil consequences of their actions. The quality of their deeds of body, their speech and thought in previous lives determines the circumstances of their rebirth.

Liberation from karma
By a proper understanding of the human situation—imprisonment in the process of *karma*—and by obedience to the right conditions, it is possible to transcend the human situation. This means, not abolishing *karma*, but liberation from its inner grip and a reorientation of life. A new process is begun by which so-called 'good *karma*' may be created and its good effects experienced in oneself and others.

The Four Noble Truths
The Buddha's experience has been summed up in the Four Noble Truths.
● The first is that the universal human experience of suffering, mental and emotional as well as physical, is the effect of past *karma*.
● The second is the perception that the cause of such suffering is craving or grasping for the wrong things, or for the right things in the wrong way. The basic human problem is a misplaced sense of values, assigning to things or persons in the world a value that they cannot sustain. Nothing in the material world is worthy of ultimate reverence, or can be depended upon in any ultimate sense.
● The third is that it is possible for suffering to cease. Gautama proclaimed that the universal human dilemma can be solved.
● The fourth is also the Noble Eightfold Path, the way to the solution.

The Noble Eightfold Path
● Right knowledge
● Right attitude
● Right speech
● Right action
● Right living (or occupation)
● Right effort
● Right mindfulness
● Right composure
The eight items of the path may be classified under three headings:
● the first two under the heading of wisdom or understanding;
● the next three under ethical conduct;
● the last three under mental discipline.

Nirvana
The goal of life is *nirvana*. This is not annihilation of the self (a Buddhist heresy). On the contrary, *nirvana* is a transformed mode of human consciousness, also an independent reality with a dynamism of its own. It is radically other than the material world: the eternal realm, the utterly dependable, the true refuge.

Dharma
Dharma is the way to the goal of *nirvana*, the 'quasi-personal' dynamism that gives inner power and quality to life.
  The Buddha spoke of *dharma* as lovely and taught that the essence of the religious life 'consists in friendship, in association, in intimacy with what is lovely'. Friendship with the lovely is the prior condition for both the beginning and the sustained practice of the Noble Eightfold Path.

teachings; sexuality, sleep, hunger, illness; growing, ageing and dying.

It is impossible to classify these *dharmas* in any systematic way. The main point is that the physical world and everything in it results from the working together of these separate components. So while it seems that the human being is an independent unit, this is only an illusion. The person is actually a flowing stream of *dharmas*, which continually changes and which after death rearranges itself to form a new individual.

Thus the teaching of Buddha does not recognize the Hindu idea of the self (*atman*) which remains constant through the cycle of rebirths. It is fair to ask whether the one who has died and the one who has been reborn on the basis of his *karma* are not in fact two different beings. In one sense this is true, for there is no immortal 'soul' to link the two. Yet at the same time, the new incarnation is inseparably bound to a particular preceding life by the *karma* it inherits, and which it will now express.

All is suffering
In his third night of meditation under the *bo*-tree, Gautama discovered the Four Noble Truths. These are the core of Buddhist philosophy.
● The first truth is the knowledge of suffering. This states that all individual existence is miserable and painful. In the Buddha's own words as

The Buddhism of South Korea has been influenced by Chinese and Japanese developments.

Buddhist boys often spend a few months in a monastery as part of their education.

by means of the Noble Eightfold Path, which formed Gautama's basic teaching on Buddhist life-style.

Eight signposts to freedom

The Eightfold Path is as follows:
● *Right knowledge* or understanding. This of course means a recognition of the Four Noble Truths.
● *Right attitude* or thought indicates a mental attitude of goodwill, peaceableness, keeping far from oneself all sensual desire, hate and malice.
● *Right speech* Lying, useless chatter and gossip are outlawed; instead speech must be wise, truthful and directed towards reconciliation.
● *Right action* embraces all moral behaviour. Murder, stealing and adultery are especially prohibited.
● *Right occupation* means that one's way of earning a living must not be harmful to others.
● *Right effort* Evil impulses must be prevented and good ones fostered, so that the individual can develop noble thoughts, words and deeds.
● *Right mindfulness* or awareness means careful consideration, not giving in to the dictates of desire in thought, speech, action and emotion.
● *Right composure* is achieved by intense concentration, which frees the holy man from all that holds him back in his quest.

Essentially the Eightfold Path is concerned with three things: with morality (right speech, right action, right occupation); with spiritual discipline (right effort, right mindfulness, right composure); and with insight (right knowledge, right attitude). It is worth noting how far this is from any strictness or severity. It is a middle way, avoiding both the extreme of self-mortification or asceticism, and the extreme of sensuality, of giving oneself up to every impulse. This middle way cannot be called a compromise; it offers a demanding life-style that is both practical and balanced.

Nirvana: where desire ends

We have seen that according to the idea of *dharma*, the unity of the human personality is an illusion. The reality is a constantly changing arrangement of the different elements

reported in early writings: 'Birth is suffering, ageing is suffering, illness is suffering, worry, misery, pain, distress and despair are suffering; not attaining what one desires is suffering.'
● The second truth concerns the origin of suffering. Suffering and indeed all existence (since they are the same) has its source in desire and ignorance: 'But what, O monks, is the noble truth of the origin of suffering? It is that desire (*tanha*) which results in rebirth, that desire bound up with longing and greed, which indulges itself now here, now there; the desire of the senses, the desire to be, the desire to destroy oneself.'
● The third truth deals with the destruction of suffering. Suffering must be totally extinguished; there is to be no remainder. The central aim of Buddhism is to give eternal release from suffering. This means being freed from the endless cycle of rebirth (*samsara*) and entering the blessed state of *nirvana*.
● The fourth truth indicates the way to this removal of suffering. This is

which make up the world. Belief in the self is rejected; 'I' and 'my' are concepts bearing no relation to truth.

The man who perceives this truth will therefore no longer cling to an imaginary 'I'. Indeed, it is precisely this false attitude to life which is the main cause of suffering. The Western mind finds it hard to grasp this doctrine of the non-self (*an-atman*); nevertheless it has been described as the most important contribution of Buddhism to the field of religious thinking.

Inextricably bound up with the idea of *an-atman* is that of *nirvana*. The word is derived from a verb meaning 'to waft away', and it indicates the goal of all religious effort in Buddhism. *Nirvana* is commonly described as 'nothingness', but this is totally inappropriate. The *Tripitaka*, an early Buddhist scripture, describes it thus:

'Nirvana is the area where there is no earth, water, fire and air; it is not the region of infinite space, nor that of infinite consciousness; it is not the region of nothing at all, nor the border between distinguishing and not distinguishing; not this world nor the other world; where there is neither sun nor moon. I will not call it coming and going, nor standing still, nor fading away nor beginning. It is without foundation, without continuation and without stopping. It is the end of suffering.'

From Memory to Writing

Wulf Metz

After the death of Gautama it became necessary to establish his teaching clearly and gather it in a coherent form. So a few months later a council was held in Rajagha, and its conclusions were reviewed 100 years later at the second Buddhist council in Vesali. The crucial meeting however was the third synod, which met in Pataliputta in 253 BC, nearly 200 years after Gautama's death, under the patronage of Emperor Asoka. A thousand monks were occupied for nine months in checking, completing and finally classifying the traditions that had been passed down. At this stage the material was still in spoken form; it was not until the first century BC, on the island of Ceylon, that the first Buddhist scriptures were written down.

This basic collection of writings, or canon, is called the Pali canon,

after the language in which it is written. It forms the main body of teaching for the conservative Theravada Buddhists; other groups have additional writings. More commonly, the Pali canon is called the *Tripitaka* or 'triple basket' because it is in three parts which were originally written on palm leaves and preserved in baskets.

The first part is called *Vinaya-Pitaka*, the 'basket of order'. As well as material about the life of Buddha and the origin of the monastic community, it contains the rules of discipline for monks.

The second part is known as the *Sutta-Pitaka*. *Sutta* is the Pali form of the Sanskrit *sutra* meaning 'guide-line' or 'instruction book'. It deals with the teaching of the Buddha and the monks, and also contains 547 legends and stories from previous existences of the Buddha.

The last part is the

Abhidhamma-Pitaka, the 'basket of higher teaching'. Its seven books, probably originating from the third to the first century BC, are written in a dry, academic style, intended for specialists and not for the common people.

In addition to the Pali canon, there are many other important Buddhist writings in Pali, Sanskrit, Chinese and other Asian languages. Of these the most prominent are the *Questions of King Milinda*, written in the first century AD; the dogmatic work *The Way to Purity*, written by Buddhaghosa in the fifth century; and the 'Summary of the meaning of higher teaching' (*Abhidhammattha-sangaha*), which dates back to Anuruddha in the eleventh century.

Mahayana Buddhists also recognize many more texts as authoritative than do the more traditionalist Theravada Buddhists. Among these are the 'Description of the Paradise of Sukhavati' (*Sukhavativyuha*); the 'Lotus of the Good Law' (*Sadharmapundarika*), particularly used by the Tendai sect of Japan; the

'Revelation of the teaching in Lanka' (*Lankavatara*); and above all the 'Guide to Perfect Wisdom' (*Prajnaparamita-Sutra*), a comprehensive explanation of the state of being a Buddha.

Some of these writings are geared to practical piety; others are more philosophically oriented. Whole schools of thought gathered around the various manuals or *sutras*, and then wrote their own teaching books (*shastras*), to give a thorough grounding in Buddhism and a further interpretation of it.

As you will notice, it can only be defined by negatives!

Interestingly, *nirvana* is understood as a *dharma*. It is the only one out of the 170 known to Buddhism that is unchanging and independent (all the others depend on each other) because it is not created by the power of impulse or desire.

Nirvana can be experienced before death by means of meditation. This is however not a full experience of *nirvana*, since there are still some *dharmas* at work.

Two versions of truth

The Four Noble Truths and the Eightfold Path are the heart of Buddhist teaching. Immediately after Gautama's death, however, there were arguments in the community of monks about the correct interpretation of other aspects of his teaching. Soon two groups, opposed to each other, stood out above all others. These were the strict and conservative Theravadins, and the more liberal Mahasanghikas, the 'members of the great community'.

Theravada means 'teaching of the ancients', and the Theravadins pride themselves on keeping to Gautama's original teaching as found in the earliest Buddhist writings. The group has acquired the nickname Hinayana, meaning 'small vehicle', which they dislike and find irreverent. It derives from a scripture of their rival group in which the world likened to a burning house. To escape it, the inhabitants call for a cart to which an animal is harnessed. But there is only room in the cart for the few true believers, not for the rest of humanity.

Theravada Buddhism emphasizes the individual's efforts towards salvation and recognizes no divine help in this. It rejects all rituals and images, even frowning on statues of the Buddha; it is, of course, pointless to pray to Buddha since he has been swallowed up in *nirvana*.

This severe and spiritualized teaching is indeed in line with the teaching of Buddha himself and his early followers, for according to them it is almost impossible to become a Buddha, and even to be a holy man

(*arhat*) requires relentless effort. It goes without saying however that such strictness cannot easily satisfy the needs of the masses. Even in the countries where it does hold sway, it has been adapted for the man in the street by the inclusion of spirit and demon worship and the presence in the temples of statues of gods and other spiritual beings.

The Mahasanghikas chose for their school of thought the name Mahayana, meaning 'great vehicle'. According to them, salvation is not intended for a few people of particular moral excellence but for all mankind. Above all, Mahayana Buddhism is a humane and magnanimous religion which makes many con-

A Buddhist priest in Vietnam.

A Buddhist monk in Sri Lanka.

Bodhisattva postpones his goal of becoming a Buddha in order first to save as many others as possible. By a solemn vow he promises to help everyone, even in the reincarnations which lie ahead of him. To this end he gathers others into his own being—an idea which is not difficult when you do not believe in the reality of the individual self. The apparent difference between yourself and others can be put aside in meditation.

The sacrificial love of the Bodhisattva can be so great that he completely denies himself the promised entry into *nirvana*, so that he can continue indefinitely to work for the good of others. Thus the Bodhisattva is undeniably more than a teacher; he has become a kind of saviour or redeemer. One can expect help from him not only in the search for salvation but also in everyday life. He is the helper of the needy in every situation.

Theravada does not regard Siddharta Gautama as the only Buddha nor did he himself. Early texts mention six forerunners and one Buddha Maitreya, still to come. The later Theravadins list as many as twenty-eight Buddhas, though of these Gautama is certainly the most important.

Mahayana doctrine in this area is quite different. Here the number of Buddhas is said to be as many as the grains of sand. It must be stressed that these are ultimately all united in the absolute being or Dharmakaya. If the Dharmakaya is seen as personal, then it can be identified with the original Buddha or Adibuddha who has been enlightened from all eternity.

The Adibuddha has sent out from himself five 'meditation Buddhas' or Dhyanibuddhas: Amitabha, 'the one of immeasurable brilliance'; Vairocana, 'the radiant one'; Akshobya 'the unshakeable'; Rathnasambhava 'the one born of precious stones'; and Amoghasiddhi, 'the one of unfailing strength'.

Dhyanibodhisattvas are derived from the Dhyanibuddhas, and both can become physical beings and appear on earth. Siddharta himself is understood to be a projection of the

cessions to popular piety.

As well as accepting the basic writings of the Theravada school, Mahayana uses numerous other texts, some of which are even preferred to the older ones because they develop the Buddha's teaching and modernize it. While in Theravada Buddhism only the monk (*bhikshu*) can achieve salvation—and for this reason in the Theravada countries everyone attempts to spend at least part of his life in a monastery—in the 'great vehicle' everyone can be saved.

A particular feature of Mahayana teaching is its doctrine of the Bodhisattva—one who is destined for enlightenment, or Buddhahood. According to this doctrine, the

One Goal, Many Paths

Wulf Metz

Very early in its history Buddhism divided into two main movements: Theravada Buddhism, the strict and narrow teaching of the ancients, and Mahayana Buddhism, more liberal and open to a wider range of ideas. Later in the history of the religion, as it spread further afield, many other varieties of Buddhism grew up:

Vajrayana Buddhism

Vajrayana Buddhism is the first of these. 'Vajra' originally meant the thunderbolt of the god Indra; later it came to mean a special substance which is imagined to be bright, transparent and as indestructible as a diamond. So Vajrayana is usually translated as 'the diamond vehicle'.

This strange and impenetrable Buddhist movement originated in the middle of the first century AD in India, and from there it spread to Nepal, Tibet, China and Japan. Because of its mysterious character it is very hard to define. It could be described as a version of Mahayana Buddhism that has become overlaid with occult, magical and mystical elements. In the background can be seen the very ancient Indian philosophy of Tantrism, which has influenced both Buddhism and Hinduism.

The result is a religion which in some ways resembles the early Christian heresy of Gnosticism, though this comparison should not

be pushed too far. Certainly it is very far removed from both Theravada and Mahayana Buddhism.

Vajrayana seeks to pass beyond the appearances of things into an emptiness through which the individual is identified with the absolute. To achieve this, quite specific techniques are used:

● The *mantra* is a magic saying which is recited over and over again. Its power is believed to go out to the furthest limit of the universe. It is also possible to write the *mantra* on paper and place it in a 'prayer wheel' which sends out the magic power of the phrase when it is set in motion. The best-known *mantra* is 'Om mani padme hum', used particularly in Tibet. 'Mani padme' means 'jewel in the lotus' while 'om' and 'hum' are sounds believed to have special supernatural power.

● *Mudra*, or physical gesture, is just as important as the *mantra*. Vajrayana has a wealth of special movements, especially of the hands, that express the fact that the whole being is striving to be united with the divine. Especially in Tibet, Vajrayana has also acquired a strong erotic element, known as Shaktism, after the Indian idea of Shakti who is an eternal feminine power. Through directly orgiastic worship the worshipper is joined to the universal feminine and so realizes

the ultimate unity of all things. It need hardly be said that this addition to Buddhism is despised by other stricter movements.

● The *mandala*, meaning 'meditation circle', is a round or many-sided diagram which represents particular cosmic and spiritual relationships. Contemplation of the *mandala* and concentration on the powers that emanate from it lead to an experience of the divine.

As with all religions of this nature, it is necessary in Vajrayana to be instructed by a guru and to commit oneself to constant, devoted religious practice.

Lamaism

Lamaism is the dominant Tibetan form of Buddhism, practised by Tibetan monks both in their own country and in the lands surrounding it. Originally 'lama' was a word for a high-ranking spiritual teacher, but later it came to be used of every monk.

Lamaism's beginnings date from the seventh century AD, when King Srong-btsan-sgam-po introduced Buddhism (in the form of Vajrayana) to Tibet. At first there was strong resistance from the followers of the traditional Bon religion, which involved a ritual calling on gods and demons by magician-priests. However, towards the end of the century, the Indian missionary Padmasambhava managed to create a blend of the two religions in his monastery, and soon further orders were founded.

After the eleventh century Lamaism went into a decline, largely through the neglect of the law of celibacy and the

resulting nepotism and power politics. It was renewed by the reformer Tsong-kha-pa in the fourteenth century, and the leadership succession after this derived from his two favourite pupils. One of these was supposed to be an incarnation of the Bodhisattva Avalokiteshvara, while the other was a reincarnation of the Buddha Amitabha. From these two there evolved a dual system of leadership; firstly the Dalai Lama or 'lama great as the ocean' who has worldly rule, and secondly the Panchen Lama or 'jewel of the scholars' who is the spiritual head. When a reigning lama dies, messengers are sent throughout the country to find a child who is a reincarnation of the dead lama. This system of the 'transformed body' is known as *chubilghan*.

In 1959 the fourteenth Dalai Lama escaped to India after the Chinese communists invaded his country. After this, Buddhism lost almost all of its influence in Tibet, though liberalization in China may lead to a limited revival of religious life.

Zen Buddhism

Zen Buddhism, of great importance in Japan, originated in China under the name of Ch'an, the Chinese for meditation.

Buddhism first entered China in the first century AD, but it encountered quite strong opposition, particularly from the practical philosophy of Confucianism. In the year 526 Bodhidharma, the twenty-eighth leader of an Indian meditation sect, came to China and founded the first Ch'an school. The Ch'an movement grew and became more and more a separate entity from its parent, Mahayana Buddhism. The most important landmark after this was the transplantation of Bodhidharma's views to Japan in the twelfth century.

Central to both Chinese Ch'an and Japanese Zen is the practice of meditation according to strict rules. This was particularly prized by the Samurai warriors as a path to self-discipline. A principal means of reaching enlightenment (*satori*) is by meditation sitting in the lotus position (cross-legged, with each foot on the opposite thigh).

In addition to sitting meditation (*zazen*), the riddle (*koan*) is of great importance. These questions which have no answer serve the purpose of radically altering the Zen student's way of thinking, to help him towards *satori*. The following examples are typical *koans*:

'If you meet someone in the street who has reached the truth you may neither walk past him in silence, nor speaking. How then should you meet him?'

'When you clap both your hands together a sound results. Now listen to the sound of *one* hand clapping!'

Through these *koans* thinking is pushed to the limit of the absurd. It is useless to seek rational answers to them; the tension they produce must be borne to the utmost. Both *zazen* and *koans* must be used under the direction of a Zen master, who controls and disciplines the student.

The two branches of Zen, the Rinzai and Soto schools, differ as to whether *satori* is a sudden and spontaneous experience or whether it can develop gradually. Common to both movements, however, is a clear opposition to intellectualism and the supremacy of reason. Concern with 'teaching' is rejected. Zen is entirely intuitive.

Zen Buddhism leaves clearly observable marks on the society that practises it, especially as it often attracts prominent individuals who may even take its philosophy into the political realm. Physical expressions of the Zen spirit are visible in such exercises as the tea ceremony, judo, the 'ikebana' art of flower arranging, landscape painting, handwriting, archery and fencing. These practices are much more than mere techniques; they have a great religious significance.

Japanese sects

Japanese sects, formed by the combination of Buddhist ideas with those of the traditional Shintoism, are numerous and varied. Since the introduction of Buddhism to Japan by Shotoktaishi in 621, history records a wide range of religious expressions, drawing partly on the influence from China, and partly on the traditional Japanese culture.

● The Tendai sect goes back to a Chinese model and was founded in 805. It concentrates on encouraging everyone to take the path to becoming a Buddha.

● The Shingon sect, founded in 807, is very mystically inclined and stresses meditation (*shingon* is the Japanese translation of the Sanskrit *mantra*).

● The Amida sects are very far from traditional Buddhism. The twelfth-century monk Genku or Honen founded the Jodo sect which believes that only through the Buddha Amida (Japanese for the Sanskrit Amitabha) can a person be redeemed and enter the 'pure land'. Salvation cannot be gained by one's own efforts, only by calling on Amida in prayer. Influenced by Genku, Shinran Shonin founded the Shin sect, which emphasized even more the uselessness of human effort towards salvation. He dismissed the difference between monks and lay people as unimportant, rejected celibacy by getting married, and made great contributions to the equality of women.

● Nichiren, a monk of the thirteenth century, founded another sect which was later named after him. His version of Buddhism stresses the importance of the historical Buddha as an embodiment of the eternal Buddha. Enlightenment consists in recognizing that man, the world and Buddha are in the final analysis all one.

● Soka Gakkai, the 'value-creating society', is a lay movement which emerged at the turn of the century after freedom of religion was introduced in Japan in 1899. Like Nichiren from which it derives, it is intolerant of other movements and lays great stress on duty and morality. A special emphasis is placed on the creation of a 'contented society'. Soka Gakkai now has about 20 million members.

Amitabha-Buddha.

While Theravada Buddhism can describe *nirvana* only by negatives, Mahayana introduces a very concrete idea of it. The best-known description is in the story of Amitabha. As a monk he took an oath that he would become a Buddha if as a result of this a paradise could be formed in which all who had prayed to him in their lifetime could live happily after death. The resulting land of Sukhavati or 'paradise of the west' is a place where all hindrances to full salvation are removed, so that the way to *nirvana* is clear. This preliminary stage to *nirvana* has increasingly become an end in itself, where the blessed live in ecstasy after their death.

Mahayana Buddhism allows much more scope for special cults and ritual than the Theravadins do. Although following a cult (for instance, the worship of a particular Buddha) is valued less highly than following the teaching, it is accepted as a route to holiness for those who are weaker in the faith.

Buddhism today

If Buddhism has undergone many changes and developments in its early history, the same is just as true of it today. In several countries of

The Main Streams of Buddhism

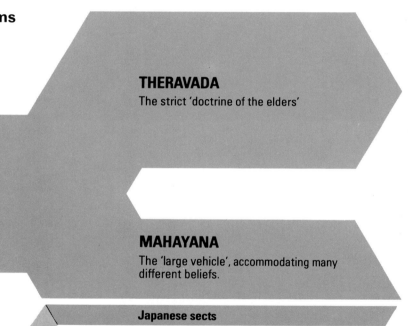

GAUTAMA THE BUDDHA

THERAVADA
The strict 'doctrine of the elders'

MAHAYANA
The 'large vehicle', accommodating many different beliefs.

Japanese sects

Ch'an/Zen

Vajrayana/Lamaism/Tibetan Buddhism

Shinto

Chinese meditative practice

Tantrism, occult, Tibetan Bon

Tibetan Buddhists honour the maternal White Tara. She is considered to be a Bodhisattva—a perfected being who has not entered nirvana, choosing instead to help human beings on earth.

Avalokiteshvera is one of the greatest Bodhisattvas, 'the regarder of the cries of the earth'. He is the patron of Tibet.

south-east Asia, particularly Burma and Sri Lanka, attempts have been made to combine Buddhism with Marxism. At the end of the 1940s the then Prime Minister of Burma, U Nu, introduced and sought to propagate his 'social Buddhism'. In his opinion it was private property, above all the ownership of land and its unjust distribution, that hindered people from leading a leisured life, free from worry and completely directed towards religious goals. The seeker of *nirvana* must not be plagued with the fight for survival nor agitated by the greed for riches; both of these are obstacles in the way of meditation.

This combination was easier to make since the traditional Marxist critique of religion was not really aimed at Buddhism. The formation of a Buddhist-based anti-capitalism was influenced by experiences from the colonial days; moreover, Marxism appeared to be a suitable vehicle for a contemporary interpretation of the Buddhist religion, since after all it promised to reduce the suffering in

the world. Even if Buddhist teaching originally meant something quite different by 'freedom from suffering', the idea still offered a useful way of combining the two philosophies.

In Sri Lanka, as a reaction against the capitalism of the former colonial rulers, Solomon Bandaranaike, and after his assassination his wife, revived the old ideal of a 'Buddhist welfare state' and incorporated socialism into the range of Buddhist teaching.

Of course such moves were also heavily criticized. Communism, after all, makes its own demands and is not content merely to be a support to Buddhism. The dangers of the alliance soon became visible not only in south-east Asia but also in China.

Despite the practical similarities, the two are really very different in their basic attitudes. Buddhism, unlike Marxism, has a goal which is not confined to the visible world. Political and social matters essentially play a minor part or none at all.

The Western Buddhists

The growth of Buddhism in the West owes much to the work of the Theosophical Society, founded in New York in 1875. In America the next important development was the great wave of immigration from China and Japan at the end of the nineteenth century. Temples, meditation schools and monasteries grew up; because of the origin of the immigrants, it was overwhelmingly Mahayana Buddhism which gained a foothold. Today, most of the schools and movements are united in the Buddhist Church of America, in which strong influences from American culture and Christian forms are to be seen.

In Europe, Buddhism was first widely known through the philosopher Arthur Schopenhauer, who influenced many scholars and artists including the composer Wagner. Edwin Arnold, who wrote *The Light of Asia* (1879), popularized the religion, and the Buddhist Society of England was formed at the beginning of the twentieth century.

It should not be forgotten that Buddhism is not by its nature an

organized religion. Its real influence cannot therefore be measured by the number of its members. There is also what might be called an unofficial or anonymous Buddhism, which can be seen through the wealth of literature related to the subject. Eastern-inspired courses on meditation are on offer in almost every small town. Young people, weary of their own culture, reach out for 'Eastern wisdom' and create for themselves a hotch-potch of religious ideas which normally ends up having very little in common with actual Buddhism. Yet even in this climate of home-grown religiosity, elements of the Buddha's teaching and of the Buddhist way of life break through.

The Appeal of Buddhism in the West
Wulf Metz

Few of those in the Christian world attracted to Eastern spirituality actually become members of the Buddhist religion. It offers, however, an opportunity to set up one's own world-view or private religion. People often turn to books on the subject after a trip to the Far East, or perhaps a museum visit.

It is always the same few aspects of the religion that attract Westerners:
● They have the impression that Buddhism is tolerant, at least more tolerant than Christianity. There may be a body of teaching but it does not dominate or preach to people. Isn't this the ideal world-view for the modern sceptic or doubter? It offers the chance to be an atheist without having to dispense with religion.
● People also admire the justice of the Buddhist system, according to which a man reaps what

he sows. The good man will receive his reward and the evil man his just deserts. Isn't that more natural than the Christian teaching of grace?
● The high quality of Buddhist ethics is held up for praise. Who would quarrel with the splendid character of the Four Noble Truths and the Noble Eightfold Path? The history of Christianity is stained with blood, which can certainly not be said of Buddhism. Which religion then is to be preferred?
● Among many other Buddhist viewpoints which are singled out for admiration, the idea of nirvana is prominent. The idea that the final goal of man is to be eliminated: isn't this a highly contemporary idea, and more natural than the Christian hope of resurrection?

Buddhism today presents a challenge the Christian must take seriously. How then might these points by answered from a

Christian viewpoint?
● The breadth and tolerance of Buddhism cannot be denied. It is doubtful, however, whether this really gives a faith credibility. It must be a matter of truth, not personal preference.
● The Buddhist system may be just, but it is without mercy or grace. Buddhism is a religion of self-redemption. According to Christian teaching, however, man is not in a position to save himself. We can look to God alone for our salvation. So Christians speak not only of God's justice, but above all of his grace and mercy.
● Of course the Christian will want to show respect for Buddhist morality. But the fact that Christian works of love are imperfect and incomplete should not be blamed on the Christian religion, but on man's sin which keeps him in debt to God and his neighbour. It is true that Christian morality lives on forgiveness; but it is precisely here that its value lies. The Christian will also be ashamed of the sinfulness of Christian people. But at least Christianity is realistic about sin and evil. We can live good

lives only when given new life by Jesus Christ: otherwise we are powerless to do what we ought to do, and totally unable to escape the cycle of sin and death.
● For the Christian who accepts the world as God's creation, life is not identical with suffering. Suffering is one result of humanity's estrangement from God. God however does not reject his creature: he wants to give him life in all its fullness, and this is the meaning of salvation. God does not want a human being— whom he has created in his own image—to sink into oblivion. The idea of nirvana seems pessimistic in contrast to the good news of forgiveness and new life in Jesus Christ.

Buddhism and Christianity differ completely, not only in their beliefs about man and the world, but in their view of God. On this subject Siddharta remains for ever silent.

Cao Dai and Hoa Hao

Barbara Boal

In the late nineteenth and early twentieth centuries Vietnamese nationalism was firmly, sometimes harshly, repressed by the French. The intellectuals who traditionally led nationalist movements began in the 1920s to profit financially from the situation and to enjoy privileged status like the French. Organizations therefore arose under new forms of nationalist leadership, seeking to end French domination and to establish a republic. Some of them followed communist principles, but three were under the religious leadership of monks and priests: the Cao Dai, the Hoa Hao and, less important, the Binh Xuyen. All three feared and hated things foreign. They were products of local education and aimed not only at expelling foreigners but also establishing local rule by religious leaders—something quite new to the Vietnamese pattern of rule by the privileged.

Political melting-pot

During the next decade the Communist Party of Indo-China (CPI) began to gain sympathy abroad. At this point the three religious movements began armed opposition to the French colonial troops. Their own men were well-trained local recruits. The Cao Dai held the Mekong Delta, the Hoa Hao the border of Kampuchea and the Binh Xuyen the Saigon area.

From 1941 until the end of the Second World War, Japanese military commanders directed the French colonial forces for the Vichy government in France. For a brief period in 1941 the combined French and Japanese all but defeated the local troops, but for the remainder of the war the latter again gained strength. After the final defeat of the Japanese, America, in the grip of its anti-colonial convictions, aided the communist-controlled Viet Minh, and independence was declared on 2 September 1945.

Because American and European interests in Vietnam were at variance with each other, a decade of confused political, cultural and religious action and reaction resulted. It led finally to the Geneva Accord of 1954 and the partition of North and South Vietnam. The communist Viet Minh held the North while the South was under the nationalist government of Ngo Dinh Diem. Close on 1 million refugees from North to South added to the confusion. The French, as part of their opposition to Diem, had supplied arms to the Cao Dai, Hoa Hao and Binh Xuyen, but by 1956, with American aid, Diem had smashed the military strength of the three sects. Their followers, numbering about a quarter of the total population, were resentful but remained active in a less military context.

Out of the maze of political aims, cultural diffusion and varied religious beliefs that form the background to twentieth-century Vietnam, four principal religious groups have emerged to play a significant part in more recent years. These are the Buddhists, the Roman Catholic Church, the Cao Dai and the Hoa Hao.

The Cao Dai

The Cao Dai sect arose from a séance communication received by Ngo Van Chieu, an administrator for the French in Cochin China, in 1919. In 1926 it was formally organized by a wealthy compatriot, Le Van Trung. Its name means 'Supreme Palace' or 'High Altar'.

Strikingly syncretistic, Cao Dai is also known as 'The Third Amnesty' of God. The first 'amnesty' has Moses and Jesus Christ as its principal figures; the second has Buddha and Lao Tse. Cao Dai is the third and highest because it requires no human representatives; God communicates directly through trance to certain devotees. It follows the pattern of the Roman Catholic Church, with its own pope dwelling in a village outside Tah Ninh city near Saigon, where an ornate cathedral was built in 1937 at the foot of a high mountain.

In addition to Catholicism and Buddhism, it combines Confucianism, Taoism and traditional cults of spirits and ancestors. Amongst a host of additional figures revered in its pantheon are Victor Hugo, Sun Yat Sen, Joan of Arc, Louis Pasteur and Jean Decoux, the French admiral of the Second World War who administered Vietnam for the Japanese. Its breadth thus appeals to the integrated view of peasant peoples; they have become its followers in entire village communities. The wealthy Le Van Trung had, like the Buddha, renounced the luxurious life; but for the villagers, to whom poverty is nothing new, it is the magical elements that prove attractive.

Cao Dai revived traditional Buddhist rules regarding vegetarianism, attitudes towards animals and rules for social behaviour. Female celebrants are permitted, and matrilineal descent is newly important. Its initially rapid expansion led to struggles for leadership. Despite splitting into several sects, Cao Dai has continued to grow and its numbers are thought to be over 2 million.

The Hoa Hao

This neo-Buddhist sect was started by Huynh Phu So in the village of Hoa Hao in Vietnam near the Kampuchean border. Born in 1919, he was the son of a leading Roman Catholic peasant in the local community. He received religious training as a young man in the hope of improving poor health. In 1939 he experienced a violent nervous spasm from which he emerged not only cured but with great power to preach and teach a new religion.

By claiming to be the incarnation of several past heroes, he set this religion on a supposedly ancient foundation which also indicated a political role for himself and his followers. He combined a revised form of Buddhist rituals with a teaching that no intermediary nor holy place is necessary for direct prayer to the Almighty.

There are four main precepts in his sect's teaching:

● honouring one's parents;
● love of one's country;
● respect for his interpretation of Buddhism;
● love towards one's fellow-men.

Not in temples, but in teaching-centres spread over former South Vietnam, his teachings were communicated in forms attractive to the peasant population. These sometimes had nationalistic overtones and strangely predicted the coming of Americans two decades ahead of their arrival. Viewed in the 1940s as a 'living Buddha', his reputation rapidly drew followers to the sect. The French, however, saw him as a centre of political unrest and detained him in a psychiatric hospital, then later under house arrest. This enhanced his reputation and from his home he taught continuous groups of pilgrims. A few days before a French plan to exile him to Laos could be put into action, his followers, aided by Japanese secret police, removed him to Saigon. There he was kept out of French hands.

Later it became obvious that the various nationalist movements, including Cao Dai and Hoa Hao, would each be seeking their own supremacy in the power struggle. By the late 1960s increasingly disillusioned nationalist urban intellectuals joined the Hoa peasants' religious movement, though it remained fundamentally of rural appeal.

By the time Huynh Phu So was murdered by communists in April 1947, sub-sects had arisen which were far more active and united within themselves than were the sub-sects in the Cao Dai. They utterly rejected the bribery and betrayal that discredited some Cao Dai leaders—who also suffered disunity and decline after the death of their pope in 1959. The vigorous teaching activities of Hoa Hao continued to appeal to the large rural population in the Mekong Delta and the sect has remained a powerful force in southern Vietnam.

Sages and Immortals: Chinese Religions

John Berthrong

Chinese religion is unique. This is partly due to the fact that, alone among the great religions of mankind, Chinese religion first developed in isolation, without the influence of the other great world religions. Confucianism and Taoism, two of the three faiths of China, developed their distinctive forms before there was any significant contact with the rest of the world. For this reason, Chinese religion has taken a form which often seems quite unlike any other. For example, neither Confucianism nor Taoism is like Judaism, Christianity or Islam—monotheistic religions with God at the centre. Confucianism, especially, became a religion without any great speculation on the nature and function of God. For this reason it was often not even considered to be a religion. However, it is clear that Confucianism *is* a religion and that it was the dominant tradition of pre-modern China.

The Shang

The earliest forms of Chinese religion are not clear. We know hardly anything definite about the religion of the great Shang dynasty (1751–1050? BC), the first historical dynasty. But although we know little of the detail, we are certain that religion played a very important part in the life of the Shang. In fact, the Shang lived in a world of spirits and powers who directly influenced the lives of the living—their success or failure—and who required sacrifice and appeasement.

The Shang sought to fathom the wishes of these spirits through a complicated system of divination. We still have the records of these divinations, the famous 'oracle bones'. The diviner, at the request of the king, would put the question to the spirit, and record the question and its answer on the carapace of a turtle or the shoulder-blade of an ox. The Shang were concerned to know the will of the spirits for just about everything they did.

Although the nature of Shang religion is clouded in mystery, a certain continuity remains between the

This 'oracle bone', over 3,000 years old, records questions the king asked of the spirits, and answers received by the king's diviner.

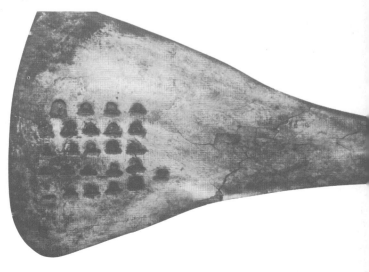

Shang and later Chinese religion. There is a persistent belief in the balance of nature, an idea which was later explicitly defined as the famous concepts of Yin and Yang: the forces of dark and light, of soft and hard, of female and male. Another important idea which continues throughout the history of Chinese religion is a constant concern for the well-being of the people. This idea of the well-being of the people later became the concept of *t'ien-ming* or the Will of Heaven.

Therefore, even if much of Shang religion is lost to us, it is clear that the Shang were distinctively Chinese and that their religion formed the basis for the development of Chinese religion, just as their political, social and material culture provided the seeds of the ongoing Chinese civilization.

Sense of concern

Prior to the rise of Confucianism, certain elements of the Shang and Chou religion took more definite shape. This is not surprising, since all great civilizations make certain choices about religion which give them their historical distinctiveness.

If there is one idea, one characteristic which informs the entire history of the development of Chinese religion, it is a 'consciousness of concern'. Even in the western Chou and eastern Chou one finds the persistent claim that high Heaven itself has concern for the well-being of the people. In fact, Heaven is said to hear and see, as the people hear and see, and hence to have a most active concern for them.

This sense that concern is the basis of the cosmos makes Chinese religion different from such religions as Judaism, Christianity or Islam, where a sense of awe or dread of a supreme power informs religious consciousness. This is why Chinese religion has always had such a close connection with the ethical thought of the people. A sense of concern and participation pervades the Chinese understanding of mankind's relationship to the transcendent and with other people.

Philosophy or religion?

In Chinese terms, what then are Confucianism and Taoism? Are they philosophies or religions? Do they have any kind of mystical traditions which seek to aid the faithful to achieve the perfected aims of a religious life?

There is a common Chinese distinction which is helpful in answering this question—the distinction between the terms *chia* (schools of thought, philosophy) and *chiao* (teaching, religion). The former refers more to the great thinkers and their teachings, and the 'great traditions'. The latter refers to the religious and, by extension, to the unique ways in which the great traditions have been appropriated by the people at grass-roots level. A distinction between the great intellectual traditions and the cultic and devotional side of religious life has been made in all the Chinese traditions, Confucianism, Taoism and also Buddhism, after its introduction into China in the second century AD.

The Chinese traditions have never felt the need to contrast *chia* and *chiao* in a hostile fashion. In a very characteristic way, they are said to represent two different parts of one continuum. They are different yet related. In traditional China, each of the great religions operated on both levels: there were great Confucian, Taoist and Buddhist philosophers, as well as masters of the various religious arts of meditation, liturgy and ritual.

Confucianism

The Latinized name, Confucianism, is a Western invention which has come down from the seventeenth-century Jesuit missionaries. Interestingly enough, these early Western missionaries clearly saw the religious nature of Confucianism, even if they did not agree with its traditions and rituals.

The Chinese term for Confucianism, *Ju* (scholars, literati—with the special meaning of Confucian from the T'ang dynasty), points to its broader character as intellectual culture. It is usually regarded as philos-

The Worship of Ancestors

Chua Wee Hian

Ancestral worship was first introduced to China at the beginning of the Chou dynasty (1122–325 BC). It was Confucius (551–479 BC) who popularized this practice by his teaching on filial piety, decreeing that parents and elders are to be honoured and respected while they are alive. This sense of reverence continues after their deaths.

The Chinese believe that at death the soul of the deceased ancestor resides in three places. One part goes to heaven, the second remains in the grave to receive sacrifices and the third is localized in the ancestral tablet or shrine.

The soul has to be assisted as it journeys to heaven. Hence, at Chinese funerals, elaborate rituals are meticulously carried out to ensure that the soul is amply provided for on its course. With the help of a Taoist priest, members of the family chant prayers, offer sacrifices of food and burn paper money— and in some cases even paper cars, planes and servants—so that there will be no lack of provisions. Evil spirits who oppose the deceased are propitiated by appropriate sacrifices and by loud wailings.

The siting of the grave is very important. A geomancer, in Chinese *feng shui sien sheng*, is consulted to determine the ideal location. The tomb must be maintained, and occasional offerings are made to the part of the soul that resides in it. The heirs continue to visit it, especially during the spring festival (*ts'ing meng*).

Within 100 days of the burial a memorial service is held in the home of the oldest male heir. The ancestral tablet is dedicated by a Buddhist or Taoist priest; this now normally contains a photograph of the deceased with his name, rank and status in life. Joss-sticks are burned and placed on the tablet, and on certain feast days food offerings are included. Newly-married couples in the family have to bow before this tablet. Its presence strengthens family solidarity, and it also offers protection and blessing to all in the family.

Chinese Christians have sometimes been accused of not honouring their ancestors by not becoming involved in ancestral worship rites. Their firm but gracious reply is that they will always respect and honour their elders while they are alive. Many are prepared to be the first in cleaning family tombs, and some Christians have even set up halls of remembrance for their forebears. Non-Christian relatives and friends may be invited to special memorial services where Christ is proclaimed as victor over the grave.

'While they (the parents) are alive, serve them according to the ritual (*li*): when they die bury them according to the ritual; and sacrifice to them according to the ritual.'

Confucius, *Analects* 2:5

Since the Chinese pay great reverence to ancestors, funerals are very important. At this Chinese funeral in Bangkok, the proceedings are watched over by effigies of Confucius.

Many Chinese homes, offices and factories have their own Buddhist or Taoist shrines.

A modern image of Confucius at the Tiger Balm Gardens in Singapore.

southern Sung (1126–1279 AD), explicitly states that the sage, having realized true integrity (*ch'eng*), becomes one with Heaven and Earth. Confucian moral metaphysics reaches over into the religious quest for unity with the ground of being.

None the less, Confucianism gives primary emphasis to the ethical meaning of human relationships, finding and grounding the moral in the divine transcendence. The perfect example of this is Confucius himself. He is best remembered as a great teacher. The basis of his teaching was the concept of humanity (*jen*). Just as compassion is the greatest Buddhist virtue, and love the Christian, *jen* is the ultimate goal of conduct and self-transformation for the Confucian. And whereas most of Confucius' teachings stress the ethical dimension of humanity, he made it clear that it was Heaven itself which protected him and gave him his message: 'Heaven is the author of the virtue that is in me.'

The Way of Heaven

Confucius stands as a prophet, giving an ethical teaching grounded in religious consciousness. Mencius (371–289? BC) projects the image of a teacher of mysticism. He proclaims an inner doctrine, alluding to the presence within the heart of something greater than itself.

'All things are present in me. When I reflect upon myself in all sincerity, my joy is boundless.'

What was an implicitly religious message in Confucius, becomes explicit in Mencius. For example, Confucius is said not to have discussed relationship, human nature and the Way of Heaven. Yet Mencius made his whole system of thought revolve around these two concepts. He attempted to show how the very essence of the Way of Heaven, the divine power of the cosmos, became human nature. He felt that if this human nature could be correctly cultivated and nurtured, even the common person could become a sage.

The Confucian classics (there are thirteen of them) prefer to discuss the work of spiritual cultivation in terms

ophy (*chia*), although such terms as *Ju-chiao*, *K'ung-chiao* (K'ung being Confucius' family name), or *Li-chiao* (Li referring to Confucian rituals) are also used. All of these terms refer to those elements of worship, ritual and sacrifice which are religious teachings, which is, of course, what *chiao* itself refers to.

Moral philosophy

Confucianism is best known for its moral philosophy, represented by Confucius (551–479 BC), Mencius (371–289? BC) and Hsün-tzu (fl. 298–238 BC). It is clearly grounded in religion—the inherited religion of the Lord-on-high, or Heaven. Even the great rationalist Hsün-tzu sees society founded on the penetrating insight of the sagely mind. And though Confucianism is less known for its mysticism, the *Book of Mencius* as well as other works cannot be fully understood except in the light of mysticism.

The *Chung-yung*, one of the 'Four Books' which became the basis for Confucian self-cultivation in the

of emotional harmony and psychic equilibrium—a harmony of due proportions, rather than the absence of passions. The 'Doctrine of the Mean' (*Chung-yung*), one of the 'Four Books', distinguishes between the two states of fundamental mind, the 'pre-stirred' state (before the rise of emotions), and the 'post-stirred' state (after contact with the things and events of the world). The meaning, best expressed by the concept of true integrity (*ch'eng*), lies in the harmony of emotions which have arisen, but resembles the equilibrium of the 'pre-stirred' state.

The *Chung-yung*, as we have seen before, claims that this harmony puts a person in touch with the cosmic processes of life and creativity. 'If they can assist in the transformation and nourishing process of Heaven and Earth, they can thus form a trinity with Heaven and Earth.'

Practical conduct

The third of the founding fathers of Confucianism, Hsün-tzu, is best remembered for his doctrine of ritual action (*li*). If Confucius begins Confucianism with the dramatic, almost prophetic, demand that we live a life of *jen* or perfect humanity, and Mencius expands upon the concept of *jen* to show that this is a life of heightened inter-subjectivity and intuition into the boundless joy of the enlightened sage, Hsün-tzu provides the practical side of Confucian religion.

It is his genius to demonstrate the power of correct ritual action needed to transform the human heart, which is prone to err, into the mind of a sage. In doing so, Hsün-tzu provides a model for daily life which supports the religious and ethical intuitions of Confucius and Mencius. Without a life of ritual—a liturgy of daily life ennobled by humility and graced by beautiful conduct—the supreme insights of religious geniuses such as Confucius and Mencius would be impossible to maintain.

In the course of time, the meaning of the word 'Heaven' becomes ambiguous, shifting from the early reference to a supreme deity (the *Analects* of Confucius), to a vacillation between that and moral force (Mencius), to the universe itself (Hsün-tzu).

Neo-Confucianism

Confucian mysticism, especially in its second great phase, Neo-Confucianism, leans more and more in the direction of pantheism. This is borne out by the later philosopher, Chang Tsai (1020–77). It is here that Confucian religion and mysticism show the imprint of Taoist—and Buddhist—influences. Yet Chang Tsai still shows a profoundly Confucian bent to his mystical vision of the unity of the world, by expressing this as one of a perfected family. In this vision, all the world becomes related to him as his own family. The note of inter-subjective concern sounded by Confucius and Mencius is reaffirmed.

Two ways

The first great flowering of Confucianism produced such diverse thinkers as Mencius and Hsün-tzu. Neo-Confucianism gives us Chu Hsi (1130–1200) and Wang Yang-ming (1472–1529). Both started from a desire to reform the Confucianism of their day, and then sought to give practical guidance for the perfection of the mind. Their schools, respectively, were called 'the teaching of principle' ((*li-hsüeh*) and 'the teaching of mind' (*hsin-hsüeh*). In actual fact, both were primarily concerned with the task of achieving sagehood. The great debate between them

This procession is part of a Chinese festival in Taiwan. The god of the local temple is carried through the streets.

centred on how to achieve this.

Chu Hsi believed we must go through a long and arduous process of self-cultivation and ethical activity in order to reach *jen*. He stressed the method of 'the examination of things' (*ko-wu*), as the best means to achieve this end. But this was more than a scientific interest in the material matters of the cosmos. It was to be an examination of all the various ethical and spiritual states of the mind, an attempt to know the self, in order to perfect the original nature, which he held to be good.

Chu Hsi expressed his spiritual goal in this way:

'The mind of Heaven and Earth, which gives birth to all things, is humanity (*jen*). Man, in being endowed with matter-energy receives this mind of Heaven and Earth, and thereby his life. Hence tender-heartedness and humanity are part of the very essence of his life.'

Wang Yang-ming agreed on the goal of sagehood, but rejected Chu Hsi's gradualist method. For Wang, only the 'enlightenment experience' of the absolute unity of our minds with the mind of the Tao would suffice to achieve sagehood. All other methods, including Chu Hsi's attempt at gradual self-cultivation, were a waste of time if they did not provoke this realization of the enlightenment experience. After Wang himself had had such an experience he wrote:

'My own nature is, of course, sufficient for me to attain sagehood. And I have been mistaken in searching for principle in external things and affairs.'

Life models

The great Neo-Confucians gave Confucianism a new lease of life. They provided a whole new explanation of the Confucian vision which could compete philosophically with Taoism and Buddhism. But, even more, they provided a practical set of life-models for the earnest seeker of sagehood. Although Chu Hsi consulted gradualism and Wang Yang-ming immediate experience, both sought that moment when the mind of man, precarious in its tendencies to good

and evil, would be transformed into the Mind of Heaven, the state of perfected excellence.

Taoism

The great Taoist religion is, in many ways, the opposite of Confucianism. Confucianism seeks to perfect men and women within the world, a goal of the secular as sacred. Taoism prefers to turn away from society to the contemplation of nature, seeking fulfilment in the spontaneous and 'trans-ethical'. The *Tao*, a metaphysical absolute, appears to have been a philosophical transformation of the earlier personal God. The way it teaches leads to a union with itself—a way of passive acceptance and mystical contemplation. Such is the teaching of the great Taoist thinkers, of Lao-tzu and Chuang-tzu. Little is known about their lives, if indeed they ever existed. This is perhaps fitting for men who had allegedly chosen a life of obscurity and taught a way of silence.

Taoism is not just passive contemplation. The texts of Lao-tzu and Chuang-tzu (also the name of the book, *Chuang-tzu*) served a later generation of religious-minded thinkers anxious to transcend the limited conditions of human existence. Their ambition was to 'steal the secret of Heaven and Earth', to wrench from it the mystery of life itself, in order to fulfil their desire for immortality.

The goal of the Confucian was to become a sage, a servant of society. The goal of the Taoist was to become an immortal (a *hsien*). They revived the belief in personal deities, practising a ritual of prayer and appeasement. They fostered the art of alchemy—the external alchemy, which 'internalized' the golden pill of immortality—and sought it through yoga and meditation. They also saw sexual hygiene as another means of prolonging human life.

This new Taoism has been called 'Taoist religion', to distinguish it from the classical philosophy of Lao-tzu and Chuang-tzu and its acceptance of both life and death. This Taoist religion developed its own mystical tradition, embellished with

'The Tao that can be expressed is not the eternal Tao;
The name that can be defined is not the unchanging name.
Non-existence is called the antecedent of heaven and earth;
Existence is the mother of all things.'

The opening lines of Lao-tzu's *Tao Te Ching*

stories of marvellous drugs and wonder-working immortals, of levitations and bodily ascensions to heaven. Basing itself on the early texts—the *Lao-tzu*, *Chuang-tzu*, *Huai-nan-tzu*, and *Lieh-tzu*—the Taoist religionists created long-lasting religious institutions.

Some of these groups still exist today, and can trace their roots back to the Taoist movements at the end of the second century AD. With their esoteric and exoteric teachings, their lines of orthodox teachers, their social organizations, they more closely resemble the other great religious traditions of mankind. But their persistent Chinese style comes through: they seek unity with the *Tao* which cannot be named.

Quest for freedom

How can Taoism be distinguished from its great sister religion, Confucianism? One major goal of all the various schools and sects of Taoism was the quest for freedom. For some it was a freedom from the political and social constraints of the emerging Confucian state. For others it was the even more profound search for immortality. And for others it was the search for oneness with the *Tao* itself. This *Tao* was the sum total of all things which are and which change, for change itself was a very important part of the Taoist view of reality. As the *Chuang-tzu* tells us, the *Tao* is 'complete, all-embracing, the whole: these are different names for the same reality denoting the One'.

This One, this totality of the *Tao*, worked as a liberating concept for the Taoists. Within the ceaseless flux of the *Tao* they found the power to live life in a spontaneous fashion. Probably the most famous statement of the freedom of the Taoist immortal is that of Lao-tzu where he says, 'The ways of men are conditioned by those of Heaven, the ways of Heaven by those of the *Tao*, and the *Tao* came into being by itself.' The *Tao* is therefore the principle of the universe and is also a pattern for human behaviour, often called 'uncontrived action' (*wu-wei*).

'All things alter and change,
Never a moment ceasing,
Revolving, whirling, and rolling away,
Driven far off and returning onward,
Like the mutations of cicada,
Profound, subtle, and illimitable,
Who can finish describing it?'

'The Owl', Chia Yi (200–168 BC)

The Taoist imagination was totally unfettered by the confines of Confucian etiquette or sensibility. They provided the magic garden of the Chinese people. Some took this magic very seriously. Some found that this too was just another illusion of the changing *Tao*. For example, at the end of a report of a magical spirit journey attributed to King My of the Chou dynasty, the magician who has been his guide for the trip explains:

'Your majesty feels at home with the permanent, is suspicious of the sudden and temporary. But can one always measure how far and how fast a scene may later turn into something else?'

Or, as the next story in the *Lieh-tzu* puts it:

'The breath of all that lives, the appearance of all that has shape, is illusion.'

But unlike many of the great religions of India and the East, the Taoists never felt that the *Tao* could be called a conscious god.

'How can the Creator have a conscious mind? It spontaneously takes place but seems mysterious. The breath and matter collect together, coagulate and become shape: constant with transformation it continues on without ever ceasing.'

Life rolls on

Throughout its whole history, the diverse masters of Taoism have sought, in various ways, to become part of this 'self-so-ness' of reality. Life rolls on by itself in an unbroken wave of creative spontaneity. Neither the Confucian Heaven, nor the rule of earthly kings and emperors, nor the folly of demons or goblins can defy it.

'Being of themselves as they are
Silently brings them about,
Gives them serenity,
gives them peace,
Escorts them as they go and
welcomes them as they come.'

The true immortal lives to learn a life
in tune with the *Tao*.

In all Taoist religion there is a
poetic touch, a realization that life is a
beautiful, and frightening, panorama
of transformations. No religion has
been more successful at invoking the
sense of wonder which these transformations cause to human beings.
Set within their mountain retreats
and their lake pavilions, the Taoists
have truly been the poets of nature.
The great T'ao Ch'ien (365–427 AD)
expresses this sense of wonder tinged
with serene resignation and hope.

'Just surrender to the cycle of
things,
Give yourself to the waves of the
Great Change,
Neither happy nor yet afraid,
And when it is time to go, then
simply go,
Without any unnecessary fuss.'

Today this sense of poetic beauty and
desire to achieve oneness with the
Tao still informs the Taoist religion.
Because of the great revolutionary
changes in China, it is hard to tell just
how Taoism will develop there in the
future. However, the Taoist Association is again functioning, and
Taoism has been recognized as an
important part of China's great cultural history. This means that there is
probably a future for the Taoist religion very like its past. Taoism has
always been at odds with the government. Yet it survives as long as
Chinese culture itself exists.

Cross-fertilization

The great Chinese religions have
always influenced each other's development. In early China great
debates and arguments went on
between the Taoists and Confucians.
But the arguments helped both sides
develop their own distinctive attitudes.

The picture becomes even more
complicated with the introduction of

*A distinctively Chinese
Buddhist temple in
Taiwan.*

*Chinese communities
throughout the world
have their own places of
worship. This Taoist
temple is in Penang.*

Buddhist shrines in China take the distinctive form of pagodas.

And on the practical level, they learned a great deal about meditation, which they called 'quiet-sitting', from the Buddhists.

'The three are one'

The great heyday of cross-fertilization of religions in China came in the Ming dynasty (1369–1644). At this period many great religious thinkers, such as Lin Chao-en (1517–98), sought to effect a harmonization of the three great religions of China. Their cry was that the three religions are one.

Lin sought to combine the best features of Taoist and Buddhist meditation with a Confucian sense of shared concern for fellow creatures in a uniquely Chinese synthesis. This kind of syncretistic religious life is still present in China today. And, in fact, it would not be far wrong to say that most religious Chinese are in fact a mixture of all three great religions. The syncretists had such a great effect that no one thinks it odd to be a Buddhist, Taoist and Confucian at the same time.

Finally there is the element of Western culture in modern China's intellectual development. Along with the development and cross-fertilization of their indigenous traditions, the Chinese have been rapidly coming to terms with the West and its great missionary religion, Christianity. Christians, like the Taoists, are again active in present-day China, even if as a tiny minority. The Chinese are assimilating a new cultural perspective, just as they did in the case of Buddhism almost 1,800 years ago. Religious and secular Western influence will no doubt have just as great an impact on China— witness the tremendous transformative power of Maoist thought, based in part on Marxist concepts—as did Buddhism. The future of Chinese religion will therefore certainly be as interesting as her past, and probably just as complex. It is impossible to say what will survive from the past. But we can be absolutely certain that what will emerge will be distinctively Chinese at all levels.

Buddhism into China. Both Taoism and Confucianism borrowed a great deal from the new Indian religion. The Taoists reformed their religious structures, founded monasteries and wrote a huge canon of sacred texts in imitation of Buddhist models.

The great Neo-Confucian revival in the eleventh and twelfth centuries BC would also be unthinkable without the stimulus and challenge of Buddhist philosophy. Although the Confucians did not borrow nearly as much as the Taoists from the Buddhists, they were certainly stimulated to work out their own mature philosophic response to Buddhist thought.

A Tapestry of Traditions:
Japanese Religions

Michael Pye

Religion in Japan is a rich tapestry of diverse traditions with a history of nearly 2,000 years. Many Japanese people display some kind of allegiance to more than one religion; a person will usually be expected to have a Shinto wedding and a Buddhist funeral, though Buddhist and secular weddings are also possible. With this may go a personal or family interest in a particular Buddhist denomination or practice, or membership of one of the various new religions which attract almost a third of the population.

These different forms of religion have separate organizations, buildings, festivals, sacred writings, ministers or priests and so on. However, it should always be remembered that the paths of these religions have touched at many points in Japanese history, and that they still meet in the lives of many Japanese people. For this reason it is possible to speak both of 'Japanese religions' and of 'Japanese religion'—especially as the Japanese language itself does not usually distinguish between the singular and the plural.

Land and religion

The general pattern of Japanese religion is in some ways a reflection of the country's geographical position and character. Japan has received a great deal from the Asian continent, but almost entirely from or via Korea and China. The major imported religions are therefore Buddhism, mainly in its Mahayana form, and Confucianism. The influence of Taoism, incidentally, has been largely indirect, bearing partly on divination practices and partly on the style of Zen Buddhism. It was in reaction to the powerful Buddhist and Confucian systems, with their scholarly prestige and political influence, that Japan's native Shinto faith first became clearly organized and defined. Indeed, the impact of Chinese and then of Western culture, and Japan's responses to these, provide the overall cultural perspective in which Japanese religion can be understood.

The fact that the country consists mainly of four great islands, spread over a vast distance from north to south, has also had its effect. The most famous historic Shinto shrines and Buddhist temples are found in the southern part of the main island, Honshu. Extremely ancient Shinto shrines which are still of national importance are located at Ise, where the sun-goddess Amaterasu is revered and where a new prime minister usually 'reports' on the formation of his cabinet, and at Izumo, where all the gods or *kami* of Japan are said to return once a year. Between these two sites are the former capitals, Nara and Kyoto, which themselves boast not only some well-known Shinto shrines such as the Kasuga

Worshippers at a Shinto shrine purify themselves, then approach the shrine and ring a bell or knock to attract the attention of the kami.

Shrine at Nara, but also many fine Buddhist temples and images. The thirteenth-century sectarian development of Buddhism is reflected in the temple buildings and images at Kamakura, also on the main island of Honshu, but further east near modern Tokyo.

The smaller island of Shikoku, which together with Honshu cradles the scenic Inland Sea, has never been of the slightest political importance and so lacks major religious monuments. But it does have a famous pilgrimage route which takes in no fewer than eighty-eight Buddhist temples. Today these are frequently visited by coach-parties of tourists, an example of the intimate link be-

tween holiday travel and religion in Japan today. Other pilgrimage routes are found in other parts of the country, the most famous being the thirty-three places in western Honshu where the Bodhisattva Kannon-sama is revered.

The island of Hokkaido in the north was largely undeveloped until the nineteenth century, when young Tokyoites were sent out in a pioneering spirit to cope with its less favourable climate. The main city, Sapporo, was a centre of Protestant missionary effort at that time, although its people today practise the more usual forms of Japanese religion.

Kyushu, the southernmost major

sland, claims some of the oldest
known historical sites in Japan, because of its proximity to Korea. Its
importance as a maritime trading
approach from the west meant that it
became the main base for Roman
Catholic missions in the sixteenth
century, and also the scene of martyrdoms, especially at Nagasaki; Roman
Catholic Christianity was suppressed
partly because it was espoused by
feudal lords in Kyushu who showed
separatist tendencies. In a similar
way, Kyushu was also the geographical base for the Shinto-inspired
reassertion of imperial power in the
mid-nineteenth century, when the
central military government in Edo
(now Tokyo) came to the end of its
two and a half centuries of undisturbed rule.

Mountain-top shrines

The mountainous terrain of the country has also had a major effect on the
forms of Japanese religious life.
Many mountains have shrines at their
summit, and not a few attract pilgrim
groups who seek purification and
heightened spiritual powers. The
most famous is of course Mount Fuji
itself, which is a quasi-religious
symbol for the whole nation.

Buddhists had already used mountains in China as isolated retreats
from the world and this practice was
carried over to Japan. The most
famous example was Mount Koya,
one of the leading headquarters of
Shingon Buddhism (see below). The
mountain cult encouraged one of the
most fascinating syncretistic movements in the history of religion, the
Shugendo movement, which linked
Buddhism and Shinto. This movement used ascetic exercises aiming
at enlightenment in a quest for
shamanic magical powers, performing spiritualist healing and fire-walk-
ing rites. Though it flourished in
historical times, it has by no means
died out today and indeed has had
considerable influence on the formation of new religions.

Shinto

Shinto is the name given to a wide
conglomeration of religious practices
with roots in prehistoric Japan. Little
is known about Japanese religion
before the emergence of a unified
state in the Yamato period (fourth to
seventh centuries AD), but in its simplest forms it was broadly animist,
believing that a supernatural living
force resided in natural objects such
as mountains, trees and animals.

The oldest literary works in Japan
were composed on a basis of the
combined myths and legends of the
various clans which had been forged
into political unity. The oldest of
these official works is the *Kojiki* (AD
712), but this was soon replaced by
the *Nihongi* (AD 720) also known as
the *Nihonshoki*. These two works
retain to this day an honoured position in the minds of most Japanese
people and are considered especially
important by the advocates of Shinto.
On the other hand, they are not
recited or even studied by ordinary
believers.

From the Yamato period onwards,
the imperial household took a central
position within Shinto. Its ancestry
was traced back through legendary
emperors and empresses as far as
Ninigi, believed to have been the
grandson of the sun-goddess Amaterasu. For this reason, Ise Shrine has
always had a close connection with
the imperial household. From 1868
onwards, when the monarchy was
restored to a central position in
Japanese politics under Emperor
Meiji, up until the end of the Pacific

*Japanese homes often
have their own small
shrines.*

War in 1945, the Shinto religion was focused sharply on Ise Shrine and the emperor cult. After the war, the emperor's semi-divine status was officially denied and Shinto was disestablished. Since then, religious teaching has no longer been given in state-run schools and the observance of Shinto practices has become a voluntary matter. Nevertheless the imperial family still enjoys very high esteem among the people, and leading Shinto shrines remain important symbols of Japanese nationhood.

Shinto shrines

Shinto today is based fundamentally on each individual shrine. Although most shrines large enough to have an organizing staff are affiliated to the Association of Shinto Shrines, most of the people who visit a shrine or take part in a festival are hardly aware of this. Each shrine has some individual reason for its existence, whether it be a natural phenomenon such as a mountain, a historical event of importance to the local community, or an act of personal devotion or political patronage. There is an endless variety.

For example, the ancient shrine at Kashima, near the Pacific coast of Honshu, is patronized particularly by those devoted to the martial arts, such as swordsmanship and *kendo*. At the same time it has various sub-shrines within its grounds. One of these celebrates a spring of fresh water tumbling out of the side of a hill and has its symbolic gate planted in the pool at the foot. Another is a fenced enclosure surrounding a mighty stone, of which only the rounded top is visible sticking up through the sand. This stone is supposed to hold down beneath the earth the giant catfish which is believed to be responsible for earthquakes. The god or *kami* of a shrine may be the natural object itself, it may be one of the divinities mentioned in the *Kojiki* or the *Nihongi*, or it may be a legendary or historical person. In shrines where a specific object is kept in the inner sanctuary it is usually not known what the object is, for nobody ever sees it.

Shinto shrines have certain common features which are almost always to be seen. The first of these which the visitor will notice is the large symbolic gate consisting of two uprights and two crossbars, marking the entrance to the shrine. These gates (*torii*) sometimes stand quite far off at the bottom of a busy street with shops and stalls catering for visitors; there may be two or more, or even a long line of them, leading to the shrine itself. Inside the precinct there is a large trough of clean water, usually sheltered with a roof and provided with clean wooden ladles. Here the worshipper rinses face and hands in a simple act of purification.

The main shrine buildings, of which there are several traditional architectural types, consist of a worship hall (*haiden*) and a main hall (*honden*) standing behind. The main hall is usually smaller and is not entered, being the physical location of the *kami* itself. The worship hall is entered from time to time by small groups for petitionary prayer. Individual visitors to the shrine simply stand outside before the worship hall, toss a coin into the offerings box, pull on a dangling rope with a bell or clanger at the top, clap their hands twice, bow briefly in prayer, clap their hands again and leave. The sound of the clanger and of the hand-clap are intended to alert the *kami* to the believer's presence. The front of the worship hall is often decorated with a thick rope (*shimenawa*) and folded white paper strips, which are regularly used to designate a sacred area or sacred object. Sometimes these are simply strung around a rock or a tree, indicating that these too are considered as shrines for the *kami* of the rock or the tree.

There are three main types of shrine. First, there are those of purely local significance, housing the *kami* of the locality (*ujigami*). Second, there are shrines of a particular recurrent type, such as the Inari Shrines, which are visited with a view to winning business success. These may be found in any part of the country. Third, there are shrines of great national and semi-political importance such as the Ise and Izumo Shrines mentioned earlier. Another shrine of national importance is the Meiji Shrine in Tokyo, honouring the former Emperor Meiji, which is visited by about 3 million people at New Year alone. Yet another is the Yasukuni Shrine, also in Tokyo, commemorating the souls of Japan's war dead. Since the end of the Pacific War, the status of Ise Shrine and of Yasukuni Shrine has been a matter of some controversy, because critics fear a revival of Shinto-led nationalism if relations with political leaders or with the imperial household become too close or too formal.

Other types of shrine that recur throughout the country include the Hachimangu Shrines, dedicated to the *kami* of war and martial prowess; the Toshogu Shrines, sacred to the memory of the dictator-general Ieyasu (died 1616) and reflecting the colourful pomp of his mausoleum at Nikko; and the Tenmangu Shrines where a loyal but wrongfully banished aristocrat is revered and believers pray for success in literature and study.

Shinto practices

Much of Shinto practice is an individual matter, as when a person simply visits a shrine to make his or her own request—before a journey, before an examination, before some new enterprise, or perhaps because they just happen to be passing that way. In such cases the form of wor-

The way into Shinto shrines is marked by gate-like torii. There is sometimes just one of these; sometimes there is a whole colonnade.

ship is as described earlier. Family occasions also involve visits to the shrine. It is common, though not universal, to take a new-born baby there so that prayers may be said for its health. Shinto priests officiate at the majority of Japanese weddings, though these usually take place in a purpose-built hall run on business lines with reception rooms and other facilities.

Shrines are visited by particularly large numbers at New Year, especially on 1 January but also on 2 and 3 January. Some people go just after midnight on 31 December, while others go at dawn. Some visitors to mountain shrines make a point of observing the rising sun and bathing their faces in its first rays. At the New Year visit there is a brisk sale of feathered wooden arrows (to drive off evil), protective charms and stiff paper strips bearing the name and seal of the shrine (*fuda*). These are taken home and kept on the *kami* shelf if there is one, or just in a high place, for the coming year. Last year's accessories are taken back to

the shrine at the New Year visit and burned on a bonfire or handed in to be burned later by shrine staff.

Another personal charm sold in great numbers at this time of year is the papier-maché *daruma* doll, originally a representation of the Zen Buddhist master Daruma (or Bodhidharma). Though Buddhist in origin, these dolls are on sale at the entrances to many shrines and are also brought back to shrines for burning. Some Buddhist temples share in the New Year practices by encouraging a first visit on a specified day in January, selling various kinds of talisman and offering prayers for safety in the home, traffic safety, prosperity in business and avoidance of bad luck.

Festivals

Perhaps the most important feature of Shinto practice is the festival (*matsuri*), since this forms the main occasion on which a particular shrine takes on meaning for all its worshippers at once. A Shinto festival usually includes a procession or a fair with stalls and side-shows, and so it easily draws large numbers of people, many returning to visit relatives at the same time. The more spectacular festivals bring in visitors and sightseers as well, thus being good for trade; for festivals which achieve national fame, special trains may be laid on and accommodation booked for months in advance. One shrine may hold several festivals in a year, but among these just one or two may be of special importance, particularly at spring or autumn.

Festivals famous throughout Japan for their huge floats hauled along in procession are the Gion Festival in Kyoto, the Takayama Festival in the Hida region and the Chichibu Festival in the mountains north-west of Tokyo. In the last of these the vehicles, representing various parts of the town of Chichibu, are illuminated by lanterns and drawn through the town at night as the *kami* from the town shrine is brought to meet the *kami* of the nearest large mountain. In many cases, the floats or the standards and banners are taken through the town by groups of young men wearing

A female priest at the Shinto shrine in Meiji.

The bronze Daibutsu statue at Kamakura is a statue of Amida Buddha, who is worshipped in Japan.

clothes representative of their part of the town. Sometimes they wear only a loincloth because of the strenuousness of the work, especially if they have to wade through water. Almost always they are fortified by plenty of rice wine (*sake*) which is particularly associated with Shinto and often offered at shrines in neatly wrapped bottles or large casks. Sometimes the processions recall a historical event such as a battle, in which case period costumes are worn.

Very often, the focal point of a procession is a portable shrine (*mikoshi*) which is taken from the main shrine to various points in the locality, symbolizing a journey made by the *kami*. Not all of those taking part in a procession enter the worship hall of the main shrine on arrival. Usually it is representatives only who go inside with the priests to present offerings such as evergreen branches of the *sakaki* tree, and to offer prayers for the safety and prosperity of the neighbourhood.

Japanese Buddhism

The history of Japanese Buddhism can be traced back to the early sixth century AD when images and *sutras* (Buddhist scriptures) were sent from Korea. The first major act of patronage took place when Prince Shotoku, regent from AD 593–622, established Buddhism as a national religion, linking it to Confucian ideals of morality and statecraft. A stream of eminent monks brought more knowledge of the new religion from Korea and China, and the early traditions at the capital of Nara were superseded in AD 805 by a much bigger Buddhist establishment on Mount Hiei, overlooking the new capital of Kyoto. This new Buddhist centre drew its inspiration from the Chinese T'ien T'ai school, which came to be known in Japan as Tendai Buddhism. This in turn was rapidly affected by the doctrines and practices of an esoteric form of Buddhism, not unlike that of Tibet. Almost immediately a rival headquarters for this type of Buddhism was set up on the then almost inaccessible Mount Koya, some distance to the south of Kyoto. This

school, Shingon Buddhism, was established by the famous monk Kukai (744–835), posthumously known as Kobo Daishi and revered as a great saint.

The Tendai and Shingon sects were rapidly supplemented by others, partly drawing on special trends in Chinese Buddhism and partly resulting from Japanese innovation. The first main development was the growth in the practice of chanting the name of Amitabha Buddha, who, according to the *sutras*, had vowed to take all living beings with him into a heavenly paradise called the 'pure land' from where they would surely attain *nirvana*. The formula chanted, called the *nembutsu*, runs in Japanese 'Namu Amida Butsu' ('Hail Amida Buddha'), though in practice the last syllable is omitted. Chanting the *nembutsu* was believed by many to have magical powers, bringing health and warding off disasters. However, according to the influential teachers Honen (1133–1212) and Shinran (1173–1262), it was symbolic of simple and sincere faith in the 'other power' (*tariki*) of the Buddha Amitabha to bring about salvation. Associated with these two teachers are the Pure Land sect (Jodoshu) and the True Pure Land sect (Jodo Shinshu) respectively.

Before long there came a new emphasis on the *Lotus Sutra* inspired by Nichiren (1222–82). The *Lotus Sutra* had already been of great importance in Tendai Buddhism, but Nichiren gave it a new centrality, and his interpretative writings provided the basis for a number of sects. Among these are counted some of the most influential lay Buddhist movements of modern times. Nichirenite sects share in common the recitation of the simple formula 'Nam(u) Myoho Renge Kyo' ('Hail Wonderful *Dharma Lotus Sutra*').

In the meantime, the Japanese Zen masters Eisai (1141–1215) and Dogen (1200–53) had been establishing their schools of practice aimed at the direct achievement of enlightenment (*satori*). Consequently two more sects were formed, the Rinzai sect and the Soto sect, becoming the two most important Zen sects in Japan. The Rinzai sect encourages active mental training by means of well-known riddles (*koan*) such as 'What is the sound of one hand clapping?' The Soto sect prefers to concentrate on seated meditation (*zazen*) during which the practitioner is identified with the enlightenment position and with the nature of the Buddha himself.

Within each of these various types of Buddhism there are many more sub-sects, each based on some local initiative and giving emphasis to a particular practice or teaching, or simply asserting the independence of a vigorous and popular temple. A recent Japanese handbook lists no fewer than seventeen Shingon sects, nine Tendai sects, nine Nichirenite sects, sixteen Zen sects, ten True Pure Land sects and four Pure Land sects. A dictionary of Buddhist sects in Japan lists many more.

In their various ways these sects all express significant themes in the tradition of Mahayana Buddhism which spread from India across east Asia.

While some people have a clear allegiance to one or other sect, especially in the case of the *nembutsu* sects or the Nichirenite sects, there are many features of popular devotion which cut across sectarian distinctions. Two of the most widely revered saviour figures are the Bodhisattvas Jizo-sama and Kannon-sama. Jizo-sama is believed to care especially for children or for infants who have died during childbirth or pregnancy. Kannon-sama (*Avalokitesvara* in Sanskrit) offers many kinds of protection and solace and is found in many places, not least in the precincts of Soto Zen temples.

Buddhism in the home

In the home many families are reminded of Buddhism by the presence of a domestic Buddhist altar (*butsudan*). This usually contains a central Buddhist image or other symbol, tablets commemorating ancestors, a booklet with portions of Buddhist scriptures, a place for lighting incense, and various other accessories. As a morning devotion a small offer-

Zen Buddhist sand-gardens are used as an aid to meditation.

ing of food may be placed on the altar, a passage recited from a *sutra* and a stick of incense lit. Individual sects introduce many variations.

Buddhism is also particularly influential as the religion of funerals and cemeteries. Again the different sects make slightly different provisions, though cremation and a stone memorial are universal. Thin wooden posts placed by visitors at a tombstone bear texts written in heavy black ink which reflect the distinctive faith of the temple in question. Cemeteries are visited particularly at *higan*, which occurs twice a year at the spring and autumn equinoxes. The other main commemoration of the dead is in midsummer at *o-bon*, which is marked by outdoor fires and dancing.

Buddhist festivals

To some extent Japanese Buddhism borrows the characteristic Shinto concept of festival (*matsuri*). In early April, for example, some Buddhist temples celebrate a flower festival which centres on the commemoration of the Buddha's birthday on 8 April. At this time a small standing statue of the infant Buddha is placed in a framework decorated with flowers, and worshippers anoint it with liquid from a bowl beneath.

Another well-known festival, climaxing at a Buddhist temple in Tokyo, is that of the forty-seven masterless Samurai (*ronin*). These forty-seven have been applauded for centuries because they avenged the unjustly forced suicide of their master and then committed suicide themselves. This is one of the classic cases of premeditated ritual suicide (*harakiri*), carried out in connection with a feat inspired by loyalty. The theme is worked out in the well-known traditional drama *Chushingu-ra*, regularly shown at the time of the festival in December. The festival itself consists of a procession re-enacting the arrival of the forty-seven Samurai at the temple to report the completion of their deed of vengeance. Following this, crowds of people light incense at their tombs.

Buddhism is linked to Japanese

Exuberant festivals are an important feature both of popular Shinto and Japan's New Religions.

culture at many points: through the traditional way of the Samurai, generally known as *bushido*, through the austere *no* drama with its many Buddhist themes, through the tea ceremony which is intended to communicate simplicity and naturalness, through calligraphy and painting, and so on. The most lively aspect of Japanese Buddhism however remains the popular faith directed towards the various Buddhas, Bodhisattvas and saints of the Mahayana Buddhist tradition.

The flowering of new religions

Innovation is an accepted feature of Japanese religious life. Many Shinto shrines are the result of some fresh religious experience or message from a medium, long since incorporated into the general pattern of Shinto. In some more recent cases such initiatives have led to the growth of separate religious bodies. One of the best known of these is the Religion of the Divine Wisdom (Tenrikyo), founded in the early nineteenth century by a lady named Miki Nakayama. This religion began with revelations and healings, but instead of merging into the wider pattern of Shinto it formulated its own independent sacred writings, constructed its own sacred city named Tenri, and shaped its own forms of worship including a special dance.

Another well-known example is the popularly-named Dancing Religion (Odoru Shukyo) which also has the longer formal name of Tensho Kotai Jingu Kyo, incorporating alternative names for the goddess Amaterasu and Ise Shrine. The foundress, named Sayo Kitamura, believed that a *kami* was speaking through her abdomen, and these revelations are the basis of the religion's teaching. She also initiated a form of ecstatic dance which encourages believers to experience a state of non-self (*muga*). It may be noted that this is one of the 'three marks' of Buddhist teaching. The religion known as the Teaching of the Great Source (Oomotokyo) is also a major independent religious group having a Shinto background combined with belief in a new revelation of its own.

Other new religions have moved further afield from the traditional faiths of Japan. The House of Growth (Seicho no Ie) claims to overcome disease and suffering through its new teachings propounded by Masaharu Taniguchi, a former Oomotokyo member. He has a modern headquarters in Tokyo with symbols expressing the unity of all religions and a good supply of literature for sale. The Church of World Messianity (Sekai Kyuseikyo) is also loosely derived from Oomotokyo. The leader, Mokichi Okada, preached freedom from disease and from poverty, and his following grew rapidly after the Pacific War. The movement now boasts a fine art gallery. Another body with the name of PL Kyodan sees the whole of life as art, and religion as a means of realizing this vision in the member's experience. The 'PL' in the name of this group stands for the English words 'Perfect Liberty'. There are many different explanations for the appearance of new religions, but at least it is clear that they provide a kind of barometer of the needs and aspirations of much of Japan's population.

New Buddhist movements

Japanese Buddhism also gives plenty of scope for innovation since the proliferation of sects and independent temple organizations is accepted as a normal feature of religious life. It is hardly surprising that several of Japan's new religions are in fact recently-developed forms of Buddhism. The most influential are those based in some way or other on the *Lotus Sutra*, for together they claim about a fifth of the population as adherents. Of these, the Reiyukai began as a movement caring for untended tombs and stressing the virtues of gratitude and loyalty towards ancestors. Today it boasts a huge central hall in Tokyo.

Several groups split off from the Reiyukai, however, in a series of organizational and doctrinal disputes. Of these the largest is the Rissho Kosei-kai. This movement was strongly influenced in its beginnings by the religious messages of Mrs Myoko Naganuma, whose house is still tenderly cared for today long after her death. The dominant figure, however, is the founding president, Nikkyo Niwano, who emphasized the exposition of the *Lotus Sutra* as the doctrinal basis of the movement. It is notable that this is a lay movement which is entirely independent of any previously-existing monastic sect. It also has an impressive complex of buildings in Tokyo. As far as practices are concerned, the main emphasis is on a form of group counselling in which the individual's problems are analysed in Buddhist terms, though of course the *Lotus Sutra* is recited and studied as well.

Also based on the *Lotus Sutra*, but with different doctrinal tendencies, is the lay movement commonly known as the Soka Gakkai. This is linked with a monastic sect named Nichiren Shoshu, claiming a direct tradition back to Nichiren himself, and the full name is therefore Nichiren Shoshu Soka Gakkai. The members support one of Japan's larger political parties, the Komeito (Clean Government Party) which was founded under the stimulation of Soka Gakkai leaders, although remaining legally distinct.

The future of Japanese faiths

The new religions draw in many ways on the wider religious culture of Japan. This is formed mainly by traditional Shinto and Buddhism, but is also influenced by Confucian ideas and values, and to a lesser extent by a rather Western-looking Christianity. Historically, Confucianism has provided the main moral backing for Shinto, emphasizing family duty and loyalty and extending these concepts to school, industry and state. Though Confucianism has no organization of any note, many religious bodies in Japan stress such values as loyalty or sincerity (*makoto*), gratitude, correctness of behaviour and brightness of attitude.

Modern Christian missions have had little impact numerically or even ideologically, but they have had some unintentional influence on other Japanese religious bodies. A number of Buddhist sects now run Sunday schools, for example, and some of the new religions use books looking remarkably like Christian Bibles and prayer-books, but with different contents. Christianity itself has a total membership of less than 1 per cent of the population, probably because it is strongly identified as belonging to the Western world. The Christian churches in Japan have only the most tenuous links with the general religious culture of the country.

Secular Japan?

In spite of the startling success of several of the newer religious movements, it would be quite wrong to think that Buddhism and Shinto have lost support in recent times. In some ways, particularly in politics and education, Japan has become remarkably secularized, and there is much ignorance about the deeper teachings of the religions. At the same time, most Japanese people are involved in various kinds of religious behaviour at certain times of the year and at the appropriate points in their lives.

They also share many deeply-held, if simplistic, assumptions which draw strength from and reinforce the traditional religions. This is partly made possible by a naturalistic acceptance of the yearly routine of the calendar, which unites a wide range of religious events in a general awareness of seasonal change. It is also made possible by their pragmatic acceptance of many kinds of minor religious practices as social obligations. This general state of affairs will probably continue for a long time to come.

Unity and Peace: The Baha'i Faith

Werner Schilling

The Baha'i religion sees itself as a revelation addressed by God to the whole of mankind. It developed from the teachings of two religious visionaries in nineteenth-century Persia.

The first of these was one Mirza Ali Muhammed (1820–50), who called himself the Bab, meaning 'The Gate', and believed himself to be the latest in a long line of spiritual leaders. He attracted relatively few followers—though they were strong enough to stage armed uprisings against the government—and was executed by the Persian authorities for alleged complicity in an attempt to assassinate the Shah.

The second, who was far more influential, was Mirza Husain Ali (1817–92), a follower of the Bab who called himself Baha'u'llah, meaning 'Glory of God'. In 1863 he declared himself to be the manifestation of God foretold by the Bab, sent to redeem the world at the end of the age and to interpret God's will for a new era. He sent many proclamations of this to kings and other contemporary heads of state, an activity which brought him frequent persecution, imprisonment and exile. He lived at various times in Constantinople, Adrianople and Acre in Palestine.

His group of followers, small at first, continued to grow after his death, until today the movement can claim to be represented in over 70,000 centres in different parts of the world. The main strength is in south-west Asia, but there are also centres in Europe, Africa, North and South America and south-east Asia. Actual statistics of followers are hardly possible to arrive at, but some very high estimates should be treated with caution.

Cycles of history

Baha'i teaching is syncretistic, derived from many religions. Running through it all is the idea that the history of mankind goes in cycles. One of these began roughly 6,000 years ago with Adam, first of its prophets. His successors were Moses, Krishna, Buddha, Zarathushtra, Christ and Muhammad. The latest and most important of these is Baha'u'llah himself—with others yet to come. The Baha'is believe that these earlier religions contained his teaching in embryonic form.

The teaching of Baha'u'llah

Baha'u'llah saw himself as the fulfilment of the promises in all religions of a coming world-renewer or messiah. He was to teach the true 'religion of God', fill the world with justice and rescue it from its lost state and from the disintegration of moral values in modern civilization. In the eyes of his followers he is a kind of divine healer, relieving the sufferings of humanity and uniting mankind. In modern times, when not only philosophers but even theologians can talk

Haifa in Israel is the administrative centre of Baha'i. The Shrine of the Bab contains the body of Mirza Ali Muhammed, the forerunner of Baha'u'llah.

f God being 'dead', Baha'u'llah roclaims that the transcendent God alive and has spoken anew to nankind. Baha'u'llah came to clear way the errors and misunderstandngs of former religions and to shape better culture in truth and ghteousness; to lead mankind to nity, and to bring about the 'kingom of God' awaited by all religions.

However, no abrupt end of this age r intervention by God is predicted. nstead, according to Baha'i teachgs, there will be an inner change in an and in society. It is through this at the world will come from ruin to harmony again.

Justice is not done to the Baha'i eligion if it is simply dismissed as a inor sect. It claims to be a wholly ndependent revealed religion. hough derived from Islam, it is not terely a sect built up from elements f another religion. On 10 May 1925 n Islamic court in the town of Baba id down that the Baha'is had roken away from Islam; the same eclaration was made by the Grand lufti of Egypt on 11 March 1939.

Neither do the Baha'is see themselves as a religion constructed artificially from other faiths, such as Christianity or the Indian religions. The Baha'i faith claims to be one of the great universal religions of the world.

The voice of God
All the writings of Baha'u'llah are considered sacred, but they are not to be observed to the letter. He authorized his eldest son, 'Abd ul-Baha, to be the interpreter of his writings; he alone carries any weight as an interpreter. He in turn nominated an 'authorized interpreter' at his death. This was his grandson Shoghi Effendi who died in 1957. His expositions, however, and those of Baha'i writers today, no longer count as sacred literature; they interpret the 'voice of God' for the present situation.

Mankind made one
Crucial for an understanding of the Baha'i religion is its belief in a divine plan for the world which was made known to the Baha'is. Yet its ethic is

not confined to the Baha'is, but open to all. World peace is striven for, as well as the settling of all social problems and the achievement of racial equality. The teaching of the Baha'is is especially concerned with the problems of the individual in the community, and Baha'is seek to work hand in hand with science. Unity is to be brought to mankind by God's universal dispensation as revealed to Baha'u'llah. This is to be brought into effect by a universal executive and legislative body, a universal language, a single currency and a uniform judicial and police system. The carrying out of Baha'u'llah's instructions is to be achieved by means of religious services through which there is spiritual preparation for these social tasks. Man is required to adopt a new attitude to his role as a partner in the family and the whole social structure.

Persecution of the Baha'is

Werner Schilling

From the start of their history the Baha'is in the Middle East have been persecuted and subjected to violent attacks as apostates from Islam, particularly in Iran. They became the object of official oppression by the government. The last Shah (Mohammed Reza Shah), in particular, made them second-class citizens by continual victimization.

The first systematic persecution was as early as 1921–22, when the Baha'i Centre in Sangsar was taken over and demolished. Baha'is were deprived of civil rights. Baha'i civil servants lost their pensions. In 1925 a law was passed by the Shah making all Baha'i marriages invalid. Children already born were declared illegitimate. Married couples were not even allowed to share a hotel bedroom. In 1932 the Baha'i schools in Tehran were closed down.

But the Baha'is refused to be defeated. In 1939 a renewed, particularly vicious press campaign was launched against them. A large number who had become officers were dismissed from the army and forced to pay back the cost of their education. After Mohammed Reza Shah had come to power in 1941, his centralized administration began an even more effective period of oppression. From 1951 onwards, the Baha'is were suspected of collaboration with the communists. The Baha'i House in Shiraz was occupied by troops, desecrated and destroyed. Even Baha'i cemeteries were violated.

The protests of Baha'is in other countries were of no avail. Discrimination against this minority was kept up constantly. During the 70s the Shah's secret police organized a systematic anti-Baha'i movement. The Baha'is were deprived of all rights and accused of being worthless citizens. Their human rights were not even considered.

Khomeini's seizure of power brought no relief to the Baha'is in Iran; indeed, a number have been put to death. The Fada'iyan-i-Islam, one of the most powerful associations in present-day Iran, was founded about twenty years ago specifically to harass the Baha'is. The same is true of the organization Tablighat-i-Islami (Society for the Propagation of Islam). No birth certificates are issued to new-born Baha'i babies because their fathers are Baha'is and the Baha'i religion is not among the recognized minority religions. In Iran, however, there are no papers other than the birth certificate by which a person can prove his identity.

Baha'u'llah's own words speak directly to such a situation.

'Nations and tribes of the world, who are always at war, turn your face towards unity and let the brightness of its light shine upon you.'

Baha'u'llah

'You are the fruit of one tree and the leaves of one branch.'

Part Five
People of a Book

Chosen People: Judaism

David Harley

'The Lord ... said to
Abram ...
"I will make you into a
great nation
and I will bless you;
I will make your name
great,
and you will be a
blessing.
I will bless those who
bless you,
and whoever curses
you I will curse;
and all peoples on
earth
will be blessed
through you."'

God chooses a people:
Genesis 12:1–3

Judaism is the oldest of the world's three great monotheistic religions and is the parent both of Christianity and Islam. At the heart of Judaism is the belief that there is only one God, who is the creator and ruler of the whole world. He is transcendent and eternal. He sees everything and knows everything. He has revealed his Law (*Torah*) to the Jewish people and chosen them to be a light or example to all mankind.

The people

The choice of the Jewish people by God began when their ancestor Abraham migrated from Ur of the Chaldees to Canaan. According to the biblical narrative, God appeared to Abraham and said, 'Go from your country ... to the land that I will show you. And I will make of you a great nation, and I will bless you ... and by you shall all the families of the earth be blessed.'

Several centuries later, in the account of the exodus of the people of Israel from Egypt, God is recorded as saying to the Israelites, 'You shall be my own possession among all nations. You shall be a kingdom of priests and a holy nation.'

Both these passages imply that the Jewish people were called to a special relationship with God and a special role towards their fellow men. To be the chosen people was a great privilege but it was also a great responsibility. They were to be a 'kingdom of priests' who served the only true God and they were to be a 'holy nation' who reflected the character of that God in their personal, social and national life.

Today there are about 13 million Jews in the world: 6 million in the USA, 3 million in Israel and the rest scattered throughout the world, many in Russia and Eastern Europe. Their customs, liturgy, way of life, even their pronunciation of Hebrew may vary considerably, but they are one people, united by their common ancestors, the patriarchs Abraham, Isaac and Jacob.

The land

God promised to Abraham not only to make him and his descendants a great nation but also to give them the land of Canaan 'for an everlasting possession'. This land (later known as Palestine, or Israel) has always had a prominent place in the thinking of Jewish people. Even during periods of exile their thoughts have constantly turned towards it and the holy city of Jerusalem. Centuries of persecution by Christians led Jews to realize that the only way to avoid suffering as a religious minority was to live again in their own land. Such aspirations led to the birth of Zionism and ultimately to the founding of the State of Israel.

The Law

Judaism has no formal creed but the

A thirteen-year-old
Jewish boy preparing for
his Bar Mitzvah
ceremony, when he will
become a full member of
the Jewish community.
He is practising reading
his portion of the
scriptures.

The Ten Commandments:
Exodus 20:1–17

**'And God spoke all
these words:
"I am the Lord your
God, who brought you
out of Egypt, out of the
land of slavery.
"You shall have no
other gods before me.
"You shall not make
for yourself an idol in
the form of anything in
heaven above or on the
earth beneath or in the
waters below. You
shall not bow down to
them or worship them;
for I, the Lord your
God, am a jealous God,
punishing the children
for the sin of the
fathers to the third and
fourth generation of
those who hate me, but
showing love to
thousands who love
me and keep my
commandments.
"You shall not misuse
the name of the Lord
your God, for the Lord
will not hold anyone
guiltless who misuses
his name.
"Remember the
Sabbath day by
keeping it holy. Six
days you shall labour
and do all your work,
but the seventh day is
a Sabbath to the Lord
your God. On it you
shall not do any work,
neither you, nor your
son or daughter, nor
your manservant or
maidservant, nor your
animals, nor the alien
within your gates. For
in six days the Lord
made the heavens and
the earth, the sea, and
all that is in them, but**

essence of the faith is found in the *Shema*, the name given to three passages of the Bible that are read every morning and evening by the devout Jew. (*Shema* is the Hebrew word for 'hear'. The *Shema* begins, 'Hear, O Israel, the Lord our God, the Lord is one, and you shall love the Lord your God with all your heart, and with all your soul, and with all your might. And these words which I command you shall be upon your heart.' The pious Jew seeks to love God with his whole being and that love is expressed in practical obedience to the law of God in everyday life. Hence 'the Law' is of paramount importance to the Jew.

This Law is found in the first five books of the Bible (the Pentateuch or *Torah*) which record the revelation of God to Moses on Mt Sinai 3,000 years ago. It contains 613 commandments covering every area of daily life from civil law to personal hygiene and diet. These instructions, summed up most succinctly in the Ten Commandments, have proved the foundation of many of the subsequent great legal codes of the world. Although many Jews no longer rigidly adhere to all the laws of the *Torah*, orthodox Jews observe them to the finest detail. They take delight in obeying the will of God and find in these practices a meaning and significance which is not apparent to the casual observer. Some have sought to

he rested on the seventh day. Therefore the Lord blessed the Sabbath day and made it holy.
"Honour your father and your mother, so that you may live long in the land the Lord your God is giving you.
"You shall not murder.
"You shall not commit adultery.
"You shall not steal.
"You shall not give false testimony against your neighbour.
"You shall not covet your neighbour's house. You shall not covet your neighbour's wife, or his manservant or maidservant, his ox or donkey, or anything that belongs to your neighbour.'

'Hear, O Israel: The Lord our God, the Lord is one. Love the Lord your God with all your heart and with all your soul and with all your strength. These commandments that I give you today are to be upon your hearts. Impress them on your children. Talk about them when you sit at home and when you walk along the road, when you lie down and when you get up. Tie them as symbols on your hands and bind them on your foreheads. Write them on the door-frames of your houses and on your gates.'

The 'Shema':
Deuteronomy 6:4–9

adapt the regulations of the *Torah* to life in the twentieth century. Others are selective in what they choose to observe. By and large it is left to each man's conscience as to how far he carries out the commandments of the *Torah*.

The synagogue

Most Jews belong to a synagogue, though this by no means implies that they attend every week. Synagogue (a Greek word meaning 'a place of meeting') is a translation of the Hebrew *Bet Hakeneset*. The origin of the synagogue is uncertain but it may date from the time when the Jews were exiles in Babylon, after the fall of Jerusalem in 586 BC. After the return from exile they began to set up synagogues or religious teaching houses to study the *Torah*. There were many synagogues in the temple area in Jerusalem and, after the destruction of the temple in AD 70, the synagogue assumed a role of vital importance in the preservation and development of Judaism.

The most prominent feature of a synagogue is the 'ark' or cupboard set against the eastern wall and facing towards Jerusalem. The ark contains the scrolls of the Law, written in Hebrew on parchment. These are covered in velvet, silk or brocade and carry ornaments of bells, a crown and a 'breastplate' of precious metal. Immediately in front of the ark is a lamp that is kept burning perpetually. In the centre of the synagogue is a platform or pulpit from which the service is conducted and the Law is read. The service follows the order set out in the *Siddur*, the Hebrew prayer-book. Worshippers usually cover their heads in the synagogue as a sign of reverence. In orthodox synagogues men and women sit separately.

Every Saturday during the morning service the ark is ceremonially opened and the scroll of the Law is lifted high and carried in procession around the synagogue. Several portions of the scroll are read in Hebrew using ancient Jewish modes. Members of the congregation are called up to recite the traditional blessing before and after each reading. When

the reading is complete, the scroll is again carried round the synagogue before being returned to the ark. Members of the congregation may touch the scroll with the fringes of their prayer-shawl (Hebrew *tallit*) and then kiss the fringes as an act of devotion and reverence to the word of God.

The service is led by a cantor (*chazzan*) rather than by a rabbi. The duties of a rabbi are to instruct the congregation in the faith and to make decisions concerning Jewish legal questions. He is entitled to be called 'rabbi' only after reaching a high standard of studies in Jewish Law.

The festivals

New Year

The Jewish religious year includes a number of festivals and days of fasting. The first of these is New Year's Day (*Rosh Hashanah*, 'head of the year') and it occurs in September or October. This festival speaks both of God's creation of the world and of his judgement of the world. The Hebrew prayer-book states, 'This is the day that the world was called into existence. This day He causeth all creatures to stand in judgement.' A ram's horn (*shophar*) is blown in the synagogue to remind people to return to God, and the next ten days are set aside for self-examination and repentance. It is customary to eat apple dipped in honey and to wish others 'a good and sweet year'.

Atonement

The Day of Atonement (*Yom Kippur*) is considered the holiest day in the Jewish religious year. It comes as the conclusion to the period of penitence that began on New Year's Day. The day is characterized by prayer, fasting and the public confession of sin. Traditionally this was the day when the high priest made sacrifice for the sins of the people of Israel and entered the 'holy of holies' in the temple (earlier, in the tabernacle). Today there is no temple and no sacrifice is offered, but atonement is sought through repentance. The devout worshipper fasts for twenty-four hours, spends all day in the

The Festivals of Judaism

ROSH HASHANAH/ NEW YEAR/ TRUMPETS
A time of reckoning with God.

YOM KIPPUR/THE DAY OF ATONEMENT
The most holy day in the Jewish year.

SUKKOT/ TABERNACLES
A joyful harvest festival, giving thanks for God's goodness, and his care for the Hebrews on their forty-year journey from Egypt to the land of Israel.

SIMCHAT TORAH/ REJOICING IN THE LAW
Joyful celebration, giving thanks for the Law—the first five books of the Hebrew Bible.

HANUKKAH/LIGHTS
An eight-day festival which commemorates the re-dedication of the temple in Jerusalem after Judas Maccabeus had expelled the occupying Syrians in 164 BC.

PURIM
A joyful celebration which commemorates the events of the book of Esther when the Jews in Persia were saved from massacre.

PESACH/PASSOVER
A joyful family festival which celebrates the deliverance of the Hebrews from slavery in Egypt.

FIRSTFRUITS
The week-long Passover festival ends with a spring harvest-festival.

PENTECOST/ SHAVUOT
Another harvest festival, celebrated seven weeks after Passover. It also commemorates the giving of the Law to Moses.

THE NINTH OF AV
A day of mourning and fasting, commemorating the destruction of the temple in AD 70.

Chart months: Nisan, Sivan, Av, Tishri, Kislev, Shevat, Iyar, Tamuz, Ellul, Cheshvan, Teveth, Adar

---

synagogue and wears a white robe as a symbol of purity and of the grave. At the conclusion of this day he will consider himself to have been spiritually reborn.

Tabernacles
Five days after the Day of Atonement comes the Feast of Tabernacles (*Sukkot*) which lasts for a week. This is one of the three harvest festivals in the Jewish year (the others are Passover and Pentecost), and as such it has served as the model for Christian harvest celebrations. During the festival Jewish people remember how God provided all their needs when they wandered for forty years in the wilderness. They build temporary shelters or 'tabernacles' of branches in their gardens or next to their synagogues. They eat their meals in them and may even sleep in them— though this may depend on the climate, as they are left open to the sky.

Celebrating the Law
After the Feast of Tabernacles comes the 'Rejoicing of the Law' (*Simchat Torah*). During the course of a year the whole of the Law, the first five books of the Bible, is read in the synagogue. On this festival day the reading is completed with the last portion of Deuteronomy and begun again with the first verses of Genesis. The service is characterized by great joy and the scrolls of the Law are

carried in procession around the synagogue with singing and dancing.

Festival of Lights

At about the time that Christians celebrate Christmas, Jews celebrate *Hanukkah*, the Festival of Lights. This commemorates the victory of Judas Maccabeus over the Syrians, and the rededication of the temple in Jerusalem in 164 BC. The festival lasts eight days and many Jewish families light an eight-branched candlestick or *menorah*. (It actually has nine candles; the additional one, called 'the servant', is used to light the others.) One candle is lit on each day of the festival until on the eighth day all are alight.

Purim

In February or March comes Purim, the festival which recalls the story of Esther. Purim means 'lots' and refers to the lots cast by Haman to choose the day on which to destroy all the Jews in the Persian Empire. In th[e] synagogue the book of Esther is rea[d] and, whenever the name of Hama[n] occurs, the boys present make a nois[e] with rattles or stamp their feet. In th[e] home Purim is a time for parties, often in fancy dress, and for eatin[g] special pastries called *Hamantaschen*[.]

Passover

Best-known of all Jewish festivals i[s] Passover (*Pesach*). It coincides mor[e] or less with Christian Easter an[d] recalls the deliverance of the peopl[e] of Israel from their slavery in Egyp[t.] A special meal or *seder* (meanin[g] 'order') is held in the home. Tra[-] ditional dishes are eaten, songs ar[e] sung and the story of the deliveranc[e] from Egypt is recounted. Th[e] youngest child asks the question[:] 'Why is this night different fro[m] other nights?' and that is the father'[s] cue to relate the events of the biblica[l] book of Exodus, as they are set out i[n] the special order of service or *Hag*[-]

The fertile Jordan valley runs from Galilee in the north of Israel to the Dead Sea.

adah. (*Haggadah* means 'showing forth' or 'telling the story'.) Traditionally a place at the table is left vacant and a glass of wine is set aside for the prophet Elijah who is expected to come as the herald of the Messianic Age.

On the eve of Passover a thorough search is made in each Jewish home to ensure that no leaven (yeast) has been left anywhere. In the place of ordinary bread, flat, unleavened bread (*matzah*) is eaten. The *matzah* serves as a reminder of the 'bread of affliction' which the Jewish slaves ate in Egypt, and hence the festival is also known as the Feast of Unleavened Bread.

Pentecost

A period of seven weeks of mourning follows Passover. This is associated with the failure of the Jewish revolt against Rome in the second century AD and the loss of many Jewish scholars at about the same time through plague. The Festival of Pentecost (from the Greek word meaning 'fiftieth') or Weeks (*Shavuot*) is celebrated fifty days after the second day of Passover and commemorates the giving of the Law by God to Moses on Mt Sinai. In the synagogue service the Ten Commandments are read and some Jews sit up all night meditating on God's Law. Pentecost is also the 'Feast of the First Fruits'. The synagogue is decorated with flowers and plants, and dairy foods are eaten.

A day of mourning

On *Tishah B'Av* (the ninth day of the Jewish month Av—roughly July/August), the Jewish people remember the destruction of the temple in AD 70 by the Romans. Some also link the same date with the destruction of the first temple by Nebuchadnezzar in 586 BC. It is a day of mourning and fasting, and all ornaments are removed from the synagogue.

The Covenant

Robert Banks

At the heart of the Jewish religion lies the existence of a covenant between God and his people. The term 'covenant' signifies an agreement made between two parties and must be distinguished from related ideas such as 'testament' and 'contract'. Unlike a testament, a covenant involves a personal response on the side of the second party to make it effective. Unlike a contract, however, it is not a mutually negotiated affair but is offered unilaterally by one side to the other.

The covenants we are concerned with are between God and man. But investigation of purely civil treaties from the adjacent Hittite culture of the fourteenth and fifteenth centuries BC has provided interesting insights. These treaties between king and people always included, amongst other things, three elements:
● a historical prologue describing the deeds of the maker of the treaty;
● a list of obligations binding the lesser of the two parties;
● a list of punishments and rewards.
The Jewish covenants generally reproduce this pattern. They are grounded in certain divinely-ordered events; they contain a set of stipulations; and they are concluded with a list of 'woes and blessings'.

God's chosen people

The first covenant referred to in the Jewish scriptures is that between God and Noah (Genesis 9:8–17). The basis for this lies in God's preservation of Noah and his family during the flood. Through Noah, a promise is made to mankind and the animal world that this disaster will never be repeated. The promise has its sign, the rainbow, which is to act as a reminder, both to God and to all living creatures, of this undertaking.

The covenant with Noah provides the basis on which the later, more specialized commitment to Israel follows. To begin with there is the covenant between God and the great patriarch of Israel, Abraham. God first promises to make Abraham the ancestor of a great nation (Genesis 12) and to give him and his descendants the land of Israel (Genesis 13). The covenant itself (Genesis 15 and 17) begins with a historical introduction, stating that God is the one who brought Abraham out from Ur of the Chaldees. It then outlines obligations about living righteously and justly, which are elaborated in later books. Circumcision becomes the sign of this covenant.

Over 600 years later, this covenant is reaffirmed and extended at Mt Sinai, with all the people who have come out of Egypt (Exodus 19–20). This covenant recalls God's historical deliverance of them from Egypt and his promise that Israel will be his special possession among all nations. There is a series of obligations in the form of the Ten Commandments, and the people's acceptance of their responsibilities is also indicated.

This covenant, therefore, is again an expression of both God's grace and his demand. Even his instructions are as much a gift as an obligation, for they show Israel how they may appropriately respond to his choice of them. And since God later maintains his side of the covenant, even when certain elements within Israel fail to obey, the fact that the covenant is based on God's grace remains transparent.

These things are nowhere clearer than in the Old Testament book of Deuteronomy. Deuteronomy is the record of Moses' farewell addresses to Israel, on the eve of their entry into the promised land. Deuteronomy 5 recounts the Sinai covenant; Deuteronomy 7 refers to the covenant with the patriarchs of Israel; and Deuteronomy 29 is a renewal of the covenant with the whole people. Throughout the book, insistence on God's continued gracious maintenance of the covenant, despite Israel's failure to fulfil its conditions, is a prominent theme.

In the later historical books a still more specialized covenant is recorded—that with David and his descendants and, associated with this, with the Levitical priesthood (1 Chronicles 17:7; 28:4). Here again there are the standard elements:
● the prologue reminds David that it was God who turned him from being a shepherd into a victorious king;
● the outlining of conditions indicates that God's blessing is not automatically guaranteed (1 Chronicles 22:11);
● the promise tells of God's commitment to establish David's descendants upon the throne for ever.

A renewed covenant

So presumptuously did the people take the covenant on which their nation was based, that the great prophets (except Hosea and Jeremiah) rarely referred to the Sinai agreement. It was only after the exile had shattered Israel's presumption that the later prophets were less reticent about the covenant (Zechariah 9:11; Malachi 2:4). The later historical writings also speak of significant covenant renewals (Ezra 9; Nehemiah 9).

Most significant in a number of these writings is the promise of a new covenant to replace the broken one for which Israel had been punished (see, for example, Jeremiah 31; Ezekiel 16). The decisive difference between the two is that the new covenant will have its obligations inscribed on the wills of the people rather than existing merely as external obligations which the people must seek to observe. When this happens, Israel will receive back all that they have lost and more.

In the post-biblical writings, further changes in the understanding of the covenant take place. The idea of a new covenant either drops away altogether, or becomes simply a reiteration of the old one (Baruch 2:30).

In the apocryphal writings the word for covenant refers, much more frequently than before, just to the obligations within it. This pushes the Law into a more prominent position and the covenant into more of a contract. Meanwhile the covenant with the Fathers comes to be regarded as an irrevocable one, leading to the use of the term for the Jewish nation itself (Judith 9:13).

The apocalyptic writings preserve the same emphasis and the term for covenant is used more often than previously also for its sign, circumcision (Jubilees 15:13–14). The Law is now said to precede the covenant, moving into a position of greater prominence (Ecclesiasticus 24:6; 44:19).

The Qumran and rabbinic writings maintain this perspective. The former do take up the idea of the new covenant made with its community, but this is basically just a reaffirmation of the old covenant. The rabbinic writings occasionally suggest that God's covenant with Israel rests upon their obedience rather than his free choice.

A modern sculpture of the seven-branched candlestick which stood in the temple.

Story of a Nation

Geoffrey Cowling

A religion continually develops over ages of time. Whatever historical point we look at, religion always has links with the past. Rabbinic Judaism sees itself today as a direct development from the time of Moses, the giver of the *Torah*, over 3,000 years ago.

To understand the developing beliefs and practices, we need to know something of the social and political events which affected the Jewish communities. We also need to observe the ideas of their neighbours, to see the influences of the cultures with which they came into contact. Greek thought, Christianity, Islam, medieval philosophy, charismatic movements—all have affected the intellectual activity and popular customs of Judaism.

The Exile and after: 539–333 BC

The story of Judaism begins in the late sixth century BC (or, in Jewish terms, BCE, 'Before the Christian Era'). In the years 539–333 BC, the Persian Empire was dominant. And it was in this period that Judaism consolidated as a religion based on the Bible.

In 586 BC, Jerusalem was destroyed by Nebuchadnezzar II and the people taken captive to Babylon.

In July 539 the army of Cyrus II ('the Great') of Persia, commanded by Gubaru, in turn captured Babylon. Cyrus thus gained nominal control of the whole Babylonian Empire. Fourteen years later Egypt was captured by Cyrus' successor. Cyrus permitted the Jews to return from exile and to rebuild their temple in Jerusalem.

In both Babylon and Egypt there were communities of people who still considered themselves Judeans. These communities consisted largely of mercenary soldiers or prisoners of war and their families. The Judeans were agents of the ruling power, and privileged for that reason. In Egypt this caused much resentment, and the Judeans remained separate, following the religion (which was *not* strictly biblical) and customs they brought with them. In Babylon, biblical religion appears to have been dominant among the Judeans, though we know very little about their life there.

As soon as Cyrus made it possible, the priests returned to Jerusalem and the city was established as a temple community, led by the priests. There was a strict separation between Judean (Jew) and non-Judean in Judah which, the Bible records, was enforced by Ezra and Nehemiah. This separation was marked by circumcision, observance of the Sabbath, the Sabbatical year, recognition of the Law (*Torah*) of Moses and obligations to the temple in Jerusalem. The rigorists also required that marriage arrangements should be made only between Judeans.

The temple and the synagogue

The Judeans believed that there must be only one temple. The temple was the only place where the Jewish religious sacrifices could be carried out. And this belief, enforced by Persian authority, had far-reaching consequences. When all Judeans lived in Judah, it was possible for them all to make the pilgrimage to Jerusalem. When Judeans lived abroad this was out of the question—though the Jews of the Dispersion made great efforts to visit Jerusalem in obedience to the *Torah*. The priestly regulations in the *Torah* became a dead letter, and a new form of religion had to emerge for the ordinary Jew. This form culminated in the setting up of 'synagogues', where prayer, singing, reading, discussion and teaching (but not sacrifice) took place.

In the temple at Jerusalem the old religion continued. And here

'I was glad when they
said to me,
"Let us go to the house
of the Lord!"
Our feet have been
standing
within your gates, O
Jerusalem!
Jerusalem, built as a
city
which is bound firmly
together,
to which the tribes go
up,
the tribes of the Lord,
as was decreed for
Israel,
to give thanks to the
name of the Lord.
There thrones for
judgment were set,
the thrones of the
house of David.
Pray for the peace of
Jerusalem!
"May they prosper

who love you!
Peace be within your
walls,
and security within
your towers!"
For my brethren and
companions' sake
I will say, "Peace be
within you!"
For the sake of the
house of the Lord our
God,
I will seek your good.'

Psalm 122

'By the rivers of
Babylon we sat and
wept
when we remembered
Zion.
There on the poplars
we hung our harps,
for there our captors
asked us for songs,
our tormentors
demanded songs of
joy;
they said, 'Sing us one
of the songs of Zion!'
How can we sing the
songs of the Lord
while in a foreign land?
If I forget you, O
Jerusalem,
may my right hand
forget its skill.
May my tongue cling
to the roof of my mouth
if I do not remember
you,
if I do not consider
Jerusalem
my highest joy.'

Psalm 137:1–6

the procedure was governed by written regulations, by a book. The book began to create its own ambience over and against—even in opposition to—the rituals of the priests.

Some time in this period the first scribes appear. Their home is the synagogue. Their job is to understand the *Torah* and to interpret its rules for the contemporary situation. They are also the bearers of tradition and of conduct. With hindsight, we can see how this 'guild of scholars' evolved into the rabbis of rabbinic Judaism. But at this time they were only one strand among many in Judaism.

The Hellenistic kingdoms: 333–63 BC

The victory of Alexander the Great at Issus in 333 BC began a new era, an era of much greater prosperity. Cities, founded on the Greek pattern, began to grow

rapidly in size. In Egypt, Alexandria became the leading city within a few years of its foundation. The Judean community there was substantial, and Greek, instead of Aramaic, became their language. Government by democratic rule by a small nucleus of citizens (who were, or considered themselves to be, Greek) brought new political ideas to the East. The Greek language rapidly spread. People even tried to look Greek.

After the death of Alexander, his empire broke up into smaller units. The principal kingdoms were Macedonia (Greece), Egypt (ruled by the Ptolemies), and the Seleucid kingdom. (Seleucid kings did not rule Phoenicia or Judea at the beginning.) In the third century BC, the Parthian Empire rose to power. The Seleucid kingdom was gradually reduced to the Syrian region only and Babylon came under Parthian control. The Jews in Babylon became somewhat cut off from

all other Jewish communities. Aramaic remained the language of Babylonia—so a barrier of speech was added to the barrier of politics.

These communities inevitably developed differently. But they were still united through having a common Bible, and also through their emphasis on Jerusalem, and the temple in particular. The priests were still undisputed leaders. The high priest was the glory of the city, powerful both politically and economically.

Tension and revolt

In 191–190 Antiochus III of Syria was defeated by the Romans, who were now turning their eyes toward the East. Prisoners of war from these battles were probably the founders of the Jewish community in Rome. Jews also settled in Antioch in Syria, and in Asia Minor (modern Turkey). The Romans

Moses

Geoffrey Cowling

Moses is central to rabbinic Judaism. In that tradition he is founder and Law-giver. He is the first and greatest of all the prophets. Through him came the instruction, the *Torah*, for all Israel, the Jewish people, and any laws are binding only if they are *halakat Moshe mi-Sinai*, 'a Mosaic rule of conduct from Sinai'. Not only is the written *Torah* the work of Moses, but the oral Law was also given to him on Sinai and passed down by word of mouth until written down in the *Mishnah*, *Tosefta* and *Baraithoth*, the collections of the traditions and the discussions of the rabbis which aim to determine what is the *halakhah* or rule of conduct.

Nothing outside the Bible adds anything of historical value to the picture of Moses. The Bible describes him as a man born in Egypt to exiled slaves belonging to the tribe of Levi. He was educated in the Egyptian court, met with God in the desert and became leader of the 'children of Israel'. Ten miraculous plagues enabled him to lead the people out of Egypt, further miracles protected them from Egyptian pursuit and sustained them in the desert. At Mt Sinai God revealed himself again to Moses, made a covenant with the people and laid down the pattern of their behaviour. Moses himself did not cross into Canaan, the land that God had promised to his people.

Today there is renewed debate about when Moses actually lived. Despite this uncertainty, a date round about the beginning of the Iron Age (1200 BC) is probably close.

Ezra

Geoffrey Cowling

In rabbinic Judaism, only Ezra can be compared with Moses. 'If Moses had not anticipated him, Ezra would have received the Torah' (*Tosefta Sanhedrin* 4:7). Authoritative traditions which are not traced back to Moses are traced back to Ezra.

The Bible appears to suggest that Ezra, a priest and scribe from Babylon, was an agent of the Persian government in establishing the *Torah* as the national law for Judeans in Judah and Syria. He was either a contemporary of Nehemiah's in the mid-fifth century BC, or lived a century later. His exact task and achievement are not at all clear, as he is not credited with exercising any political authority. He is credited with extreme views on purity of genealogy, asserting that all 'foreign' wives were to be divorced. Ezra is ignored in early apocryphal books like Ecclesiasticus and 1 Maccabees.

In rabbinic tradition Ezra is seen as the founder and first leader of the legendary 'Great Synagogue'. This body (which appears to be thought of as an early Sanhedrin) was supposed to have continued until the time of Simon the Just.

Ezra was important to other groups in Judaism apart from the rabbinic circles. In 2 Esdras, an apocryphal book probably written about AD 100 whose text is found only in Latin, Ezra finds the *Torah* burnt. Under divine inspiration he dictates ninety-four books—twenty-four of the Old Testament and seventy 'secret' books—no doubt including 2 Esdras.

'Ezra was a scholar with a thorough knowledge of the Law which the Lord, the God of Israel, had given to Moses. Because Ezra had the blessing of the Lord his God, the emperor gave him everything he asked for. In the seventh year of the reign of Artaxerxes, Ezra set out from Babylonia for Jerusalem with a group of Israelites which included priests, Levites, temple musicians, temple guards, and workmen. They left Babylonia on the first day of the first month, and with God's help they arrived in Jerusalem on the first day of the fifth month. Ezra had devoted his life to studying the Law of the Lord, to practising it, and to teaching all its laws and regulations to the people of Israel.'

Ezra 7:6–10

imposed tribute on Antiochus. This meant increased taxes. It seems that tension between rich and poor in Jerusalem and Judah became extreme at this time. This factor, added to political and cultural differences (those for and against the Greek way of life) made for an explosive situation.

The explosion came in the reign of Antiochus IV. When the Jews resisted his nominee for the high priesthood, he sent troops to sack Jerusalem. He established pagan practices in the temple and attacked the Jewish religion. Some Jews gave in. But those who loved the Law, especially the Hasidim ('The Pious') endured great suffering. Eventually there was full-scale revolt, led by the family of the Hasmoneans.

In 165 BC Judas Maccabeus won peace with the Syrians, marched into Jerusalem, and the desecrated temple was solemnly cleansed. (The victory is still celebrated today in the Festival of Lights or *Hanukkah*.)

The Maccabee family began a line of rulers—the Hasmonean dynasty. Ironically the Hasmoneans became typical Hellenistic despots. But they won a real measure of freedom for the Jewish realm before the Romans, under Pompey, annexed Judea in 63 BC.

Under the Roman Empire: 63 BC–AD 200

Judea was now a vassal of Rome. The current Hasmonean king was confirmed as the nation's leader and high priest, but the Romans would not recognize him as king. Successive Roman governors kept a firm hold on Judea.

In 40 BC, following a Parthian invasion of Syria and Judea, the Roman Senate gave Herod the title 'king of the Jews'. Although Herod's personal life was disastrous, the country prospered under his rule. Herod is remembered as a builder—of cities (Sebaste, Caesarea), of fortresses (Masada, Herodium), of palaces, theatres and amphitheatres, of the temple in Jerusalem and pagan temples abroad. Those who opposed Rome and the Greek way of life hated him.

During the Roman period the Jewish hope of a Messiah (a king of David's line, for some a priest-king) came to the fore. He would rescue his people from the Romans and restore the Judean state.

There were several revolts in Judea during the time of Herod and his successors, and many 'prophets' drew large followings. The most serious threat to the Jews came in the time of the Emperor Caligula (AD 37–41). He demanded that all his subjects worship him, and ordered a statue of himself (as Zeus) to be placed in the temple.

The temple is destroyed

Judea became more and more unsettled. Conflict between Greeks and Jews was constant in the coastal cities. Conflict between the Roman governors and the people increased. Finally in AD 66 the Jews rose in a general revolt against Rome. Initial success was followed by crushing defeat. Jerusalem was taken and the temple destroyed in AD 70.

The destruction of the temple was decisive for the future of Judaism. The temple and the high priesthood and the council (Sanhedrin) were finished. No longer could Jerusalem, as centre of pilgrimage, be the unifying force within Judaism. Jewish communities were now simply descent groups within larger communities. Although they remained distinct, they were inevitably affected by the culture of the city or nation in which they found themselves. Unless something took the place of the temple, the scattered com-

The world-wide distribution of Jews

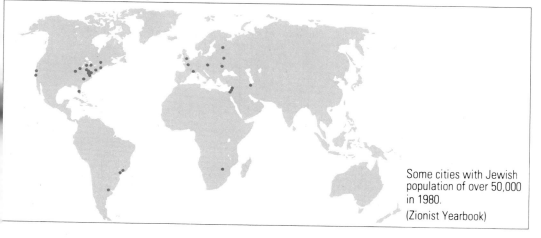

Some cities with Jewish population of over 50,000 in 1980.
(Zionist Yearbook)

munities would grow apart.

It was a seemingly insignificant event which provided the new direction for Judaism. Jochanan ben Zakkai founded a school at Jamnia. The Romans made no objection because this act had no political implications. At this school the mode of address 'rabbi' ('master') became a formal title. The teachers in the school were 'rabbis'. Jochanan may not have been a Pharisee, but his successor, Gamaliel (?grandson of Hillel) was. The ethos of the school was essentially Pharisaical: and this gave the tone to emerging rabbinic Judaism.

This school at Jamnia came to exercise the function of a council, and even to adopt the name 'Sanhedrin'. Jochanan fixed the calendar for the Jews abroad, once the prerogative of the high priest. Jews began to look to this council for advice and judgements. The extent of the influence of the council is impossible to determine. As happens so often, the writings which came from the council were even more influential than the council itself. The rabbis of this early period are known as *Tanna* (plural *Tannaim*: 'teachers'). Their earliest surviving works are the 'sayings' in the *Pirkay Avot* and the second-century commentaries, or the laws, written in Hebrew.

Most other varieties of Judaism died out gradually. Jewish Christianity survived into the second century AD, even though the rabbis tried hard to exclude Jewish Christians from the synagogues after about AD 90. In the Greek world Christians broke entirely with Judaism, all too often becoming anti-Jewish.

Persecution continues

Jewish revolts were widespread and they were brutally put down.

In AD 70 the Romans sacked Jerusalem, taking the temple treasures to Rome.

The Judean revolt of 132 may have been sparked off by the establishment of the new Roman city of Aelia Capitolina on the ruins of Jerusalem. (The Old City of present-day Jerusalem is the linear descendant of this Roman town.) This revolt was led by Simeon ben Koseba, who claimed to be the Messiah, and he was supported by the greatest rabbinic scholar of the day, Rabbi Akiba, then an old man. The attempt was hopeless. Though considerable casualties were inflicted on the Romans, this only made the final defeat more disastrous.

The governors of Palestine (the name the Romans now gave the country) were now Romans of a much higher rank. Aelia Capitolina was completed and Jews were forbidden to enter the city. Galilee now became a centre of Jewish life and various towns successively became the seat of the council.

Judaism was not banned, but since the circumcision of converts was forbidden, conversion was made difficult, if not impossible. Many Jews in Palestine still hoped for a Parthian invasion to free them from the Romans. Simeon II, son of Gamaliel II, became 'patriarch' of the Jews with—at least in theory—authority over the Jews of the Roman world. Simeon's son, Judah I ('the prince') appears to have exercised considerable political power. He appears to have been a considerable scholar, and in his time the *Mishnah* was codified and published.

The patriarchate declined in power after this, but rabbinic discussion continued in Palestine, Babylon and Rome.

In Babylon (from 223 BC a part of the Persian Empire), the recognized rulers of the Jews were the 'exilarchs' or princes of the captivity. They enjoyed a status perhaps higher even than that of Judah I and certainly much greater than that of their contemporaries in Galilee.

Israel and abroad: AD 200–640

Within the land of Israel the patriarch was almost always a descendant of Hillel. The patriarchate was abolished by the Romans in 429, but the council, the Sanhedrin, continued until 640.

The conversion of Constantine to Christianity in 313 was not auspicious for Jews. Although Judaism was never made illegal, it became very difficult to be a Jew. Many, perhaps most, Christian leaders, writers, monks and bishops hated the Jews.

In Egypt, the Jewish communities began to recover, though numbers were never the same as they had been in earlier centuries. Greek culture was on the wane, and with it Hellenistic Judaism. Relations between the Jews and the Persian authorities became less amicable from the fifth century onward. The Jews there were thus ready to welcome the Arab conquerors. Similarly, in Palestine, the harshness of the Byzantine rule caused the Jews to look for redemption abroad. They aided the invading Persian forces in 614, but in 617 uprisings among the Jerusalem Jews were subdued by military force. The Byzantine army re-entered Jerusalem and the Jews were once more expelled from the city.

The age of the Gaons: 634–1096

The Muslim conquests were spectacular. In 634 the Byzantine army was defeated. Syria and Palestine were conquered. Persia fell in 637. Egypt followed soon after. Spain was invaded in 711, and an independent Muslim state was set up there around 750. The armies reached France, but were driven back to the Pyrenees.

Within 100 years, many Jews came under Muslim rule. The general conditions of life for most improved considerably. The Jews shared in the great intellec-

tual ferment of the Arab world. Great advances were made in mathematics, astronomy, philosophy, chemistry and philology. Some Jews in the enlightened Spanish area rose to influential positions in the courts of the rulers. The tenth and eleventh centuries in Spain were especially a 'Golden Age' of literary achievement. The type of Judaism known as 'Sephardic' developed in Spain with its own synagogue rituals and its own Spanish-Jewish dialect, Ladino.

The rite of the other Jews in Europe, especially in Germany, is known as the 'Ashkenazi', with its own language—the German-Jewish dialect, Yiddish.

In Christian France the Jews were relatively well-treated in the

The home is the most important religious centre for a Jewish family. Each Friday evening, at the start of the Sabbath, the wife prepares the Sabbath lights before the meal together.

ninth century. But from then on, hatred of the Jews and riots became common. The crusading armies marched to 'The Holy Land', looting and slaughtering the Jews in particular as they went. The capture of Jerusalem, hailed throughout the Christian world as a great triumph, merely meant death to the Jews there—burnt in the synagogues. Life in Christian Europe became harsh for Jews.

The Jews saw these deaths as martyrdom, the ultimate form of witness, or 'sanctification of the Name' (*kiddush ha Shem*). Some committed suicide rather than renounce their faith. It became clear that the authorities, even when sympathetic, were helpless before the Christian mob. The rules of conduct (*halakhah*) stated plainly that while laws could be broken when life was at stake, there were times when death must be preferred, to avoid the guilt of idolatry, incest or murder, or to 'sanctify the Name'.

The influence of Babylon

In Babylon, the authority of the exilarch continued under the Muslims. At this time the authority and importance of the heads of the Babylonian academies (the Gaons) grew immensely. It was these men who ensured that the Babylonian *Talmud* was accepted throughout the world. A gaonate was established in Palestine in the ninth century which was recognized as authoritative by Jews in Spain, Egypt and Italy. Under the Gaons collections of Talmudic laws were made, synagogue poetry was written, prayer-books were drawn up, the text of the Bible was fixed and annotated. Most influential of all the work of the Gaons were their *Responsa*: questions on matters of practice were sent to the Gaon, these were debated in the academies and an answer was sent out in the name of the Gaon.

There were variants from rabbinic Judaism. In the eighth cen-

tury Anan ben David, and the Karaites of the tenth century, rejected the *Talmud* and all forms of oral law, taking their stand on the Bible only. The Karaites seemed likely to divide the Jewish world, but their movement soon became merely a sect. It still survives today (like the Samaritans), but in small numbers (perhaps 5,000 in the USSR, 7,000 in Israel and 1,000 or so in Egypt).

The Western teachers: 1096–1348

From the middle of the eleventh century scholars in the schools of the West became more significant than the Gaons. One French scholar is outstanding. Rabbi Solomon ben Isaac (known, from his initials, as Rashi) produced standard commentaries on the Bible and *Talmud*. His commentary on the Bible was used by Nicholas de Lyra, whom Luther often consulted, and his interpretations were frequently adopted in the translation of the Authorized King James Version of the Bible. Rashi's commentary and the additions of his successors are printed in the *Talmud* today.

Rabbi Moshe ben Maimon (see article on *Developments in Judaism*) in his *Mishneh Torah* presented a code containing all the *halakhah*, all the rules and laws that ever applied to Judaism. Other scholars applied themselves to this task after him: mostly Sephardim (after the expulsion from Spain).

Massacres in Europe

In this period Jewish communities continued to be founded in new areas and communities which had been decimated by massacres were re-established. Jews entered England in the eleventh century, but were expelled in 1290, not to return until after 1650. A new round of massacres began in the late thirteenth century. The Jewish com-

The God Who Speaks

Robert Banks

For the Jewish prophets, one of the most distinctive characteristics of their God, in comparison with the idols of the surrounding nations, was that he was the God who speaks. Moreover, in contrast to the pagan gods, he is the God who acts. In fact, these two belong inseparably together. It is precisely through his speaking or in fulfilment of his speaking, and as subsequently confirmed or interpreted by his teaching, that things happen.

This is already clear at the beginning of the biblical accounts. It is as a result of God's spoken command that the created order comes into being. And only as this is sustained by his words does it continue in existence. At the commencement of his historical purposes for Israel this same pattern is repeated. First, there is his spoken instruction to Abraham to leave the security of his homeland, then the promise made to him and his descendants. In the same way, the liberation of the Israelites from Egypt starts with God's confrontation with Moses at Horeb and finally takes place at his command. The preservation of the nation, in spite of its later defection from God, and the ultimate promise of a new covenant is also effected through his word.

Indeed, at every step of God's purpose for Israel, the sovereign power of God's word is present. Always it accomplishes what it says will happen. This word is frequently associated with, even at times described as, God's spirit or breath, and equated with his thoughts and purposes.

Prophets, priests and wise men

God spoke through people. And these fall into three main groups. Of first importance are the prophets, among whom Moses takes pride of place. The prophets proclaim and recall God's basic promises and commands to Israel, but their primary task is to deliver his contemporary word to the people, a word which sometimes includes predictions of what the future holds. They become so identified with their message that on occasions they address their audiences in first-person terms as if God himself were directly present.

One of the chief tasks of the priests within Israel was to teach what God had already revealed. They not only instructed people in what the covenant required of them but also recounted the history of God's promises and deeds which underlay these obligations. The application of past demands to present circumstances was also part of their work, with new legal decisions sometimes resulting. Occasionally they also received a direct word from the Lord.

The third group within Israel responsible for making known God's will comprised the wise men. Unlike the prophets and priests, they drew their instruction neither from God-given insight into his present purposes nor God-given deduction from his past manifestations. Their concern was with the understanding of God, man and the world drawn from human experience and observation. Indeed, their instructions and advice have a relatively timeless quality. They do not refer to God's historical covenant with Israel, or to the Mosaic Law. This does not mean that they are any less authoritative than their prophetic and priestly counterparts, for the covenant and the Law clearly provide the broader framework for their instruction.

Alongside prophet, priest and wise man, God also makes himself known through individual people's responses to their message, as, for example, in the Psalms.

The post-biblical writers continued to claim God's authority for their words. For example, the apocalyptic writings mention a prophetic concern for determining God's will in the present, though this is modified by their practice of casting such messages into the mouths of earlier figures and the fact that the chief emphasis is always upon future events. The apocryphal books display a less dynamic approach to God's law. The later wisdom literature, however, actually strengthens the authority of the wise man's instruction.

'In the beginning God created the heavens and the earth. Now the earth was formless and empty, darkness was over the surface of the deep, and the Spirit of God was hovering over the waters. And God said, 'Let there be light,' and there was light. God saw that the light was good, and he separated the light from the darkness. God called the light 'day' and the darkness he called 'night'. And there was evening, and there was morning— the first day.'

The opening words of the Bible: Genesis 1:1–5

munities in southern Italy were almost wiped out between 1290 and 1293 and many forced conversions were made. Jews were expelled from France in 1306 and further massacres occurred in 1348. The great achievements of Jews in medieval France came to an end. Jews were falsely accused of poisoning wells and causing the Black Death which killed off a third of the population of Europe in 1348. From Spain to Poland Jews were massacred.

At this time two ghastly lies were current: the so-called 'blood libel' and the 'libel of desecration of the host'. The blood libel, which claims that Jews are guilty of ritual murder, using the blood of Christian children during Passover is, alas, still perpetuated.

The Golden Age of Spain had come to an end in this period. In the twelfth century Christians tried to recapture Spain from the Muslims. In response, fanatical Muslim tribes, 'Almohades', from North Africa poured into Spain. These Muslims did not show the usual tolerance towards Jews and drove them northwards. Christian leaders welcomed these Jews at first, but their tolerance did not last long.

Jewish influence: 1348–1517

When massacres, the expulsions and the plague had ceased, the Jews were allowed to return to their cities. With other means of livelihood closed to them many Jews became moneylenders. Now the rulers needed their expertise; the new economy demanded their help.

In Christian Spain attacks on Jews reached a peak in 1391. Many Jews professed conversion, and were known by the insulting name of *Marranos* (swine). Jews left Spain in large numbers. In 1492 Jews were offered the choice of converting or leaving. Many converted, but thousands fled.

Wherever they went, in Europe and beyond, from Amsterdam to Safed in Galilee, the exiles had an enormous impact.

Europe in ferment: 1517–1700

In the sixteenth and seventeenth centuries, the Muslim Ottoman (Turkish) Empire was in the ascendancy. The Ottomans captured Palestine in 1515, Egypt in 1517, and expanded into Europe until they were halted in Vienna in 1683. During these centuries, the greatest number of Jews lived in countries of the Ottoman Empire, or else in Christian Poland—Lithuania.

Christian Europe was also in ferment. The Protestant Reformation on the whole favoured Jews, though Luther's personal attitude changed over the years from tolerance and defence to

For 2,500 years the focus of Judaism has been the study of the Law.

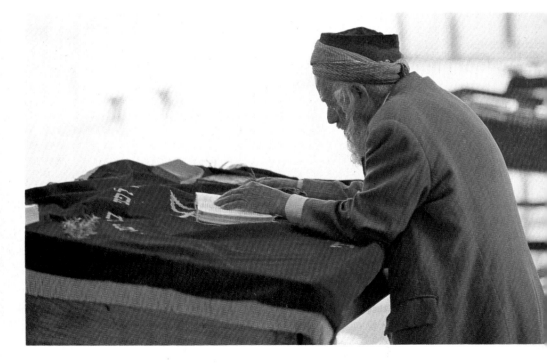

Torah and Mishnah

Robert Banks

The distinctive message of Judaism is that God reveals himself to his people. And the most common term for God's revelation and for the holy scriptures is *Torah*. *Torah* was also the most important term for the Law in the Jewish scriptures. The earliest codification of the leading interpretation of that Law took place in the *Mishnah*.

God's instruction

The primary meaning of the word *torah* is 'divine instruction' and its chief purpose was the practical guidance of God's people in their everyday life. This first came to clear expression in the instructions contained in the covenant at Sinai. These instructions have the character of a prophetic revelation of God's will rather than a legal code. They are grounded in the historic evidence of God; his choice of, and promises to, Abraham, and his freeing of Abraham's descendants and covenant with them. The instructions also have the character of a gift, as well as an obligation, for they reveal to the people how to respond to God's actions on their behalf. Yet they are also linked with the danger of judgement if disobedience occurs.

The instructions given at Sinai arose out of a definite historical situation and they were later reinterpreted (Deuteronomy 12), extended (Deuteronomy 0) and crystallized (Deuteronomy 6) in the face of new situations. They consist chiefly of a list of basic prohibitions which mark out the broad limits within which life is to be lived and a manageable number of more specific rulings which nevertheless leave large areas of life comparatively unregulated—personal and social relations, civil and political responsibilities, individual and family worship. But the Law does deal both with inner attitudes and with outward activities, for God desires to see the whole man and the whole of Israel's life conformed to his wishes.

The written Law

Writing down the Law began quite early in Israel's history, at the time of the exodus from Egypt, but a more comprehensive setting down of its contents took place later at the hands of the priests. Their writings display an increasing interest in extending the Law into new areas and emphasizing the ritual commandments, but the essentially non-legalistic and basically moral emphasis of the Law is always preserved.

The writings of the prophets continue to reveal the *Torah*. They continually appeal to Israel's historical beginnings but combine this with an insistent stress upon certain fundamental moral principles. They endorse the centrality of the Mosaic Law, but it is these underlying requirements such as

'righteousness' and 'justice' which really lie at the core of their message, and are indeed referred to as *torah* alongside the Mosaic Law.

The more general moral and prudential advice in the wisdom literature is also described as *torah*. There is no specific reference in these writings to the Mosaic Law, or to the covenant with Israel, but these undoubtedly form the base on which their instruction is built.

Torah is also used to describe the teaching of the priests, prophets and wise men. And this wide usage is a significant step on the way to its later application to the whole of scripture.

In the writings of the post-biblical period, *torah* is looked at differently. The apocryphal Jewish writings begin to talk about the Mosaic Law in more unhistorical terms. The apocalyptic books speak of it as an eternal affair which existed before God chose and made his covenant with Israel. In the wisdom literature of this period, the Mosaic Law is referred to more frequently, indeed 'Wisdom' is often bluntly equated with it. In all these writings, more stress is laid upon ritual regulations which are exclusive to the Jews. At the same time, Greek ethical ideals also begin to come in. In these two ways a more legalistic and/or humanistic note enters into Jewish thinking about the Law.

In the Dead Sea Scrolls the same characteristics can be seen but they still insist strongly on God's grace as the basis of the Law, on the need for inner as well as external obedience, and on broader ethical and social

responsibilities. The teaching of the Pharisees is similar, though within it there is a more noticeable stress upon human achievement and on the development of a more extensive oral law equal in authority with the written *Torah*. This development enabled the Pharisees to get to grips with contemporary needs in a more relevant way than other Jewish parties such as the conservative Sadducees.

Studying the Law

It was at about this time that all parts of the Jewish scriptures came to be known collectively as *Torah*—in recognition that all of it is filled with God's instructions for his people. But the Pentateuch still holds the pre-eminent place.

And at this time, too, the first collections of the oral *Torah* were made. This codification, the *Mishnah*, took in leading opinions of the scribes and rabbis on matters of law. It was drawn from four centuries of *Torah* interpretation and was characterized chiefly by teaching arising from one of the schools of Pharisaism, that of Hillel. The editor of the *Mishnah* was Rabbi Judah the Prince. The *Mishnah* has sixty-three tractates, grouped according to six main divisions: laws dealing with agriculture, statutory feasts, the place of women, property and legal affairs, the temple and its accoutrements, and uncleanness. In Jewish eyes, the Talmud ranks second only to the scriptures in authority. Its contents show how dominant the Law was in post-biblical Judaism, and its increasing legalism.

The Talmud is made up of the *Mishnah* and a commentary on it called the *Gemara*. This *Gemara* is a combination of discussions on the *Mishnah* ranging over the next five or six centuries. The standard edition of the Talmud today runs to nineteen volumes and contains both the *Mishnah* and *Gemara*, together with later and other Rabbinic commentaries on these works.

Clearly this was a most unwieldy source of day-to-day guidance—particularly because the Talmud was more a record of discussion than a series of rulings. So Rabbi Joseph Karo in the sixteenth century compiled a book entitled the *Shulhan Aruch* (a Laid Table) which set out in four fairly straightforward sections the basic guidelines for a Jew's day-to-day life.

For the Jew today, the Talmud is the scholarly work and the *Shulhan Aruch* the popular source of a Jewish lifestyle in accordance with God's will.

Jews living in Frankfurt were attacked by a mob in the summer of 1614—just one example of centuries of persecution.

abid anti-Jewish fulminations. Anti-Jewish riots continued to occur, but the authorities tended to protect the Jews, who were seen as useful. The massacres of 1648 and 1649 came as a severe blow to the Jews in the Ukraine and Poland. The Jewish writers claim that all those 'who could not flee were slain and were martyred with unnaturally cruel and bitter deaths'.

Looking more closely we see that these massacres were more than just a matter of ignorant peasant superstition. The Jewish leaders were seen to be on the side of the Polish overlords of the Ukraine, both economically and politically. It is the tragedy of history that Jews have often had the skills most appreciated by a ruling class. They have also often been forced into such occupations as money-lending, and therefore greatly resented by the lower classes.

In Italy severe penalties were inflicted on the Jews. In the Ottoman Empire conditions were generally better, but they were subject to the arbitrary and capricious actions of the rulers.

The hope of a Messiah
In the late seventeenth century a number of messianic movements arose. No doubt these were partly a product of the insecurity of Jewish life. The most important was centred on Shabbetai Levi (1628–1716), and his prophet, Nathan of Gaza. They found acceptance and a following throughout the world.

Nathan behaved very much as latter-day John the Baptist. He called for deep repentance, with severe ascetic practices and morfication of the body. Fasting, bathing in freezing water and constant prayer were called for and practised.

Shabbetai was imprisoned in Gallipoli in 1665–66, and in 1666 he yielded to threats and converted to Islam. Jews were devastated: 'The paradox of a traitorous Messiah is far greater than an executed Messiah', wrote Gershom Scholem. The Shabbeteans who continued to exist were viewed with deep suspicion and inevitably the general result was a great disillusionment with Messianism.

A pointer to the new times coming was Baruch Spinoza (1632–77). A great philosopher, he ceased to be a Jew without becoming a Christian—or a member of any other religion.

Enlightenment and persecution: 1700 to the present day
From the beginning of the seventeenth century, Jews gradually began to move outwards from Poland and the Ottoman Empire into the new cities of the West. There was a growing realization of the value of Jewish commercial activity and Jews began to be associated with the most developed social and economic systems. In the nineteenth century, for example, large numbers of Jews migrated to America.

Those who opposed all religion, or all revealed religion, still found Judaism a convenient target, but generally there was a growing tolerance. In the nineteenth century 'equal rights' were eventually obtained, though often with very great difficulty.

The possibility of emancipation was based on the separation of church and state. Judaism was regarded as a religion only. The Jew in England, say, or in Germany, was to be a loyal English or German citizen, differing only in religion.

The Jewish enlightenment
At the same time, there were important new directions in Judaism. The so-called Jewish enlightenment, the *haskalah*, was a humanist movement. The founder, Moses Mendelssohn (1729–86) was a practising Jew, though many of his followers were not. Mendelssohn advocated the separation of church and state, so that religious bodies should not be able to compel, only persuade. He emphasized the universal principles of religion within Judaism, and encouraged the use of German by translating the *Torah* into German. After his death the members of this movement, now led by Leopold Zunz (1794–1886), began to be more radical. They rejected the *Talmud* and traditional ideas—even the idea of revelation. Modern Jewish studies began.

The dark counterpoint to increasing tolerance was modern anti-semitism, based on spurious pseudo-biology and a belief in the 'soul' of a people. A sharp contrast was drawn between the 'Semite' nature (in practice only Jews) and the 'Aryan' or 'Slavonic' nature. The strong anti-semitic movements began in Germany and France in the 1880s.

The direct consequence of all this in 1939–40 was the 'elimination' of 6 million breathing human beings merely because they were Jewish. European Jewry almost ceased to exist. One third of all the Jews in the world were killed. The blow this dealt to security, sanity and faith is incalculable. The Holocaust, and the sorry role played by most governments and Christian leaders, is a central fact in all relations between Jews and non-Jews today.

Branches of Judaism

Marvin Wilson

The majority of Jews throughout the world today are descendants either of the Ashkenazim or the Sephardim. The Ashkenazim came from central Europe, notably Germany ('Ashkenaz' means Germany) and France, and later moved to Poland and Russia. Ashkenazic Jews developed Yiddish (medieval German) as their language. Around it they produced a rich culture in art, music and literature.

Sephardic Jews ('Sepharad' means Spain) created the language of Ladino (a vulgar Spanish). Before being driven from Spain in the Inquisition of 1492, the Sephardim became closely involved with the Muslim world. This enabled them to develop a unique intellectual culture. The wide difference in cultural background between the Ashkenazim and Sephardim is especially evident in Israel today where each supports its own chief rabbi.

Clearly the Jews are not a race. And Judaism is not an unchanging institution. Due to intermarriage, conversion, and dispersion among the nations, there has been a 'branching out' over the centuries. Wide cultural differences between Jews have resulted. The gap between the black Falasha Jews in Ethiopia and the Indian Jews in Mexico, for instance, is immense.

In addition to these cultural groupings, several religious branches can be distinguished within Judaism today. Modern Judaism is rooted [in] rabbinic (Talmudic) Judaism, an[d] both evolved from biblical Judaism.

Orthodox Judaism— submission to the Law

Orthodox Judaism regards itself the only true Judaism. During th[e] first half of the nineteenth century [it] developed into a well-defined mov[e]ment. It sought to preserve tr[a]ditional (classical) Judaism again[st] the emerging Reform movement [in] East Europe.

Orthodox Jews are characterize[d] by a '*Torah*-true' approach to li[fe]. They teach that God personally an[d] decisively revealed himself in givi[ng] the Law at Sinai. The words of *Tor[ah]* are therefore divine and hence ful[ly] authoritative. They are the chang[e]less revelation of God's eternal wil[l].

Every aspect of the orthodox Jew['s] life is to be governed by the com[m]mandments (*mitzvot*). Daily the Je[w] is to study *Torah* and conform his li[fe] obediently to its propositions an[d] rituals, including the strict rules [of] Sabbath observance, dietary laws an[d] prayer three times a day. In shor[t] Orthodox Judaism is '*mitzvahce[n]*tric'.

The East European Jew at the sta[rt] of the nineteenth century lived in [a] close-knit community known as [a] *shtetl*. In this stockaded culture [he] was shut off from the secular worl[d]. Toward the end of the century, how[w]ever, a new orthodoxy slowly beg[an]

The annual Passover meal celebrates God's deliverance of the Hebrew people from slavery in Egypt.

o emerge. As large numbers of Jews started to emigrate to the United States, orthodox leaders like Rabbi Samson Hirsch encouraged Jews to involve themselves in the contemporary culture of the Western world, pursue secular university education and develop philosophical minds. Today, most orthodox Jews believe that adjustment to the modern world is essential so long as it does not conflict with the teachings of *Torah*.

Orthodox Jews maintain a high regard for the rabbi as teacher and interpreter of the Law. They place a strong emphasis upon education, particularly day schools where traditional learning can be acquired. Most orthodox Jews are Zionistic and support the State of Israel. Many hope for a personal Messiah, an ideal man who will one day fully redeem Israel.

Of all the branches of Judaism, Orthodox Judaism places the greatest demands on its adherents.

Reform Judaism—response to change

Reform Judaism had its beginnings in Germany. The Enlightenment of the eighteenth century had stressed reason and progress. The Emancipation in the following century opened the Jewish people to new freedoms, to equal rights as citizens, and to new opportunities to explore secular society.

The mood of the day was geared to change and growth, scientific inquiry and critical evaluation, and Jews quickly began to adapt to this new age. To stem this tide away from Jewishness, certain changes occurred within European Judaism. Abraham Geiger (1810–74) was one of the powerful forces in this movement.

Influenced by the spirit of the age, Geiger and others taught that scientific man could no longer accept the revelation of *Torah* as factual and binding. Hence changes in ritual law and worship were encouraged. Dietary laws were abandoned. Prayers were translated from Hebrew into the vernacular. Synagogue worship changed: the organ was introduced; services were shortened; the 'family pew' replaced segregation of sexes. Some even began to worship on Sunday rather than the Sabbath.

In the USA, dynamic leadership in the Reform movement was provided by Isaac Wise. After founding an organization of Reform congregations, in 1875 Wise established Hebrew Union College, the main seminary in the USA today for training Reform rabbis.

Reform Judaism represents the most progressive branch of modern Judaism. Liberal (Reform) Judaism is still evolving, since revelation is thought to be a continuing process. It seeks to keep current with each new generation by using reason and experience to establish the relevance or truth of a proposition. This means that the ethical teachings of the prophets are emphasized rather than the ritual Law. Reform thus provides an approach to religion which is highly individualized and non-authoritarian. A law is observed not because God said so, but because it is meaningful to modern religious experience.

Today the Reform movement remains dynamic and innovative. It has been aggressive in the area of dialogue between faiths. In the 1970s Hebrew Union College began to ordain women rabbis.

Conservative Judaism—the preservation of the people

Many European Jews were uncomfortable with the radical changes introduced by Reform Judaism. Con-

Theodore (Binyamin Ze'ev) Herzl (1860–1904)

Geoffrey Cowling

Herzl may be credited with the creation of political Zionism. He sought to secure the settlement of Jews in Palestine by political means, to win a homeland by negotiating with governments.

Herzl spent the first eighteen years of his life in Budapest. His parents then moved to Vienna, where he studied law at the university. After graduation he practised law for a short time. Then in 1884 he began writing full-time. He was a newspaper correspondent in France from October 1891 to July 1895. There he experienced the startling growth of anti-semitism which culminated in the infamous 'Dreyfus Case'. Herzl, who had once thought that assimilation—loss of peculiarly Jewish identity—was the answer to the problems of the Jews, changed his mind. He now decided they must have a state of their own. They would not be tolerated in any other country.

This conviction led him to write Der Judenstaat (The Jewish State). Through this he came into contact with other Zionist movements. Not all Zionists were in favour of his methods, but many gave him and his ideas their support. Particularly influential were the Hovevei Zion ('Friends of Zion', members of the Hibbat Zion movement), especially those in Eastern Europe. Herzl disagreed with their attempts to buy land in Palestine, and establish small settlements. He described this as 'infiltration'.

He tried to negotiate with the Turkish authorities to establish a Jewish state with some degree of autonomy, but part of the Turkish Empire. He also explored other possibilities—the establishment of a Jewish state in Argentina or Uganda. His support especially for the latter brought him into conflict with other members of the Zionist council, even though he declared that this was not a negation of their ultimate aim—return to Israel.

Herzl's proposal to form a united Zionist council was accepted and he chaired the first Zionist Congress in Basle in 1897. He died shortly after his efforts in April 1904 to maintain the unity of the movement.

Herzl's vision may be seen as a secularizing of Judaism's messianism. His aim was the recreation of the (biblical) state of Israel, but by political not supernatural means. There was no room for a Messiah. He kept the idea of the 'people of Israel', but without commitment to rabbinic or any other orthodox form of Judaism. The 'people' were seen as a nation without a country. Herzl was a product of the Jewish enlightenment. He accepted the nationalist movement of his time, but sought, unlike his contemporaries, to reconcile this with the continued distinctiveness of the Jews.

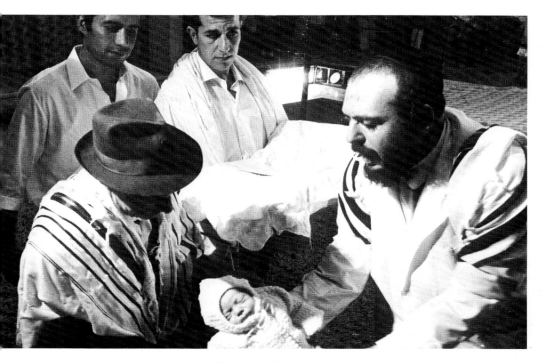

Other branches

servatism arose as a new movement at the end of the nineteenth century. It sought to emphasize the positive historical elements of the Jewish tradition.

In the USA, Solomon Schechter (1850–1915) became a leading figure as president of the newly-founded Jewish Theological Seminary. He stressed the need for commitment to tradition, but with adjustment if necessary. Schechter urged that preservation of the Jewish people was the way to achieve both tradition and change. Correspondingly, Conservativism has maintained a strong emphasis on the people of Israel and modern Zionism.

Lay people have considerable influence, particularly in instituting change. Some congregations, for instance, permit the use of an organ; others reject it. Some stress keeping dietary laws; others do not.

Other branches

The Hasidim are the ultra-orthodox wing of Judaism. Living in isolation from the Gentile world, these Jews maintain a strict commitment to the Law in every phase of life. They are characterized by their distinctive style of dress (including black coats and ear locks) and their joyful form of worship (song and dance). The movement was founded in Europe by Israel Baal Shem Tov (1700–60). The Hasidim have many sects around the world, each led by its own *rebbe*. In the United States, the sects of the Lubavitch and Satmar are especially influential.

The youngest branch of Judaism is known as Reconstructionism. It was founded by Mordecai Kaplan (born 1881) who stressed Judaism as an evolving religious civilization. It gives equal importance to religion, ethics and culture.

Eight days after birth Jewish boys are circumcised by a doctor or a rabbi.

Developments in Judaism

Geoffrey Cowling

Hellenistic Judaism

When Judeans abroad adopted Greek as their mother tongue, a change in outlook inevitably followed. The Greek language was the medium by which Greek ideas, attitudes and ways of reasoning were passed on. These ideas were not necessarily terribly profound. The riches of classical Greek culture had been diluted, mixed and to a degree cheapened. But it was still a powerful, exciting and stimulating experience. People who could read Greek—especially those living in Alexandria—might have had a chance to read the great philosophers in the original.

But it seems that the Greek-speaking Jews were not drawn away from their customs as much as some feared they would be. They still regularly visited Jerusalem to celebrate the festivals in the temple, for example.

The home of Hellenistic (Greek-speaking) Judaism was the Roman Empire, and there were also branches in Palestine.

At the age of thirteen, a Jewish boy becomes 'Bar Mitzvah', 'son of the commandment', entering into full legal and religious membership of the community. This multiple Bar Mitzvah ceremony is being held at the Western 'Wailing' Wall in Jerusalem.

The most important effect of Greek thought was the conscious use of logical rules of thinking. Instead of relying on personal charisma in their teaching, the rabbis drew up rules to prescribe what methods of biblical interpretation would be accepted as valid. As well as drawing from Greek ideas, Hellenistic Jews attempted to influence Greek thought in return. But it seems that they largely failed; non-Jewish writers of the period show great ignorance of Judaism.

Philo of Alexandria sought to explain the Bible from the point of view of Greek philosophy. Philo himself was a preacher and commentator rather than a profound philosopher. He explained the great events of Israel's history as allegories of eternal truths and adopted the Stoic idea of Reason (*Logos*), which he called a 'second God', an intermediary between God and the world.

Many Jewish works, such as the *Book of Wisdom*, were written with an eye to convincing Greek readers. Their critique of Greek ideas never went very far—the greatest gulf they saw between the Jewish and the Greek world was the worship of idols—and as propaganda they were useless.

Community life

The life of the ordinary Jew in Greek-speaking areas was centred on the synagogue. Both worship and practical matters of community life were conducted there. Strangers were lodged, the poor helped, discipline enforced, public gatherings held and children taught in the synagogue. The authority was in the hands of the 'ruler of the synagogue'.

Associated with the synagogue was the 'house of study'. Here the Bible was studied and there was a library for scholars.

The synagogue was the first Jewish centre of worship which had no rite of sacrifice. Worship consisted of prayer, singing and reading of scripture. Visiting preachers might give a sermon, but the resident scholars probably did not.

The Talmuds

The *Talmud* is a vast collection of writings which contains the teaching of the rabbis. Its basis is the collection of rabbinic teachings made by Judah the Prince (the *Mishnah*). But the *Gemara*, the collection of discussions of the *Mishnah*, forms the larger part of the *Talmud*.

In fact there are two *Talmuds*, the Palestinian and the Babylonian. The former is a record of the discussion in the rabbinic schools of Galilee, especially

A Jew at a week-day morning service, wearing the prayer-shawl and phylactery–a box containing portions of the Law.

Tiberias, during the fourth century AD. The latter records the views of Babylonian schools and was not completed until the seventh or eighth century.

Both *Talmuds* have much in common—they represent parallel attacks on the same questions. Further, interchange of personnel was common, and the two *Talmuds* often quote from each other. But they differ somewhat in conclusions and interpretations.

A sea of knowledge

The bulk of the *Talmud* consists of an exhaustive discussion of the *Mishnah*. The opinions of various rabbis are quoted, with summaries of their evidence and arguments. The arguments take the biblical texts as authoritative, but

exactly *which* texts are applicable to any particular question is often open to debate. Considerable ingenuity is expended. The quality of argument may be keen and incisive on real philosophical and ethical questions. But at other times it is apparently mere cleverness.

The rabbis call on all sorts of evidence in their arguments, and it is the record of this which gives the *Talmuds* their massive encyclopedic character. Within them are found allusions to the whole store of the rabbis' knowledge—from popular sayings, folk-tales, legends, anecdotes, puns and dreams, to the scientific knowledge of the day. To the outsider this looks like the jumbled contents of a filing cabinet, a looseleaf encyclopedia with no index. It is virtually inaccessible to all but those who have memorized it.

The traditional way of mastering the *Talmud* is by continuous reading with help of commen-

taries, arguing about it and putting forward interpretations until it becomes familiar territory. The traditional Western aids, indexes and concordances, have only recently begun to be used. Today there is still a breach between the traditional scholar with his deep acquaintance and the modern scholar with critical insight but not the knowledge.

We have to be very careful about taking any opinion in the *Talmud* as 'the teaching of Judaism'. The *Talmud* records all authoritative minority views and therefore it is necessary to discover *who* said what, how authoritative it was, whether it was accepted by the later authorities and what later commentaries said about it!

It took centuries for all the communities even to know about, let alone accept, the *Talmuds*. The Babylonian *Talmud* gained much dominance, since Judaism flourished strongly in the Muslim Empire, in which Babylonian Judaism was dominant. The Palestinian *Talmud* was most influential in Italy and in Egypt, places which had close links with Palestine.

Jewish philosophy

Oddly enough, it was thanks to the Arab Empire that Jewish philosophy blossomed in the ninth to twelfth centuries. The Arab Empire gathered the wealth of thought of past civilizations, translating into Arabic the learning of Greece, Persia and even China and India. Much of their most original work in philosophy, science, mathematics and medicine was done by Jewish scholars. And many of these were concerned with religious philosophy.

One of the greatest Jewish philosophers—Saadiah Gaon (882–942)—was concerned with the problem of 'faith and knowledge', discussing proofs of God's existence.

The most influential philosophers after Saadiah lived in Spain. Until the eleventh century the greatest influence on them was Neo-Platonism. This philosophy considers that God is separated from the world by a descending series of 'emanations'. The Jewish philosophers had an impact beyond Judaism. The work of Solomon ibn Gabirol was translated into Latin and made a profound impression on Christian thought. His influence can also be seen in the Jewish mystical tradition known as the Kabbalah. Judah Ha Levi of Toledo (1085–1140) wrote a fictional dialogue between a Jewish scholar and the king of the Khazars (a Turkish tribe converted to Judaism). He showed how philosophy could prove the existence of God, but revelation was then necessary to know more of him.

Tackling atheism

In the eleventh century there was a shift in philosophical thought: Aristotle became more important than Plato. Aristotle's science seemed to leave no room for religion, and Jewish scholars set about tackling the problem of whether his philosophy could be reconciled with biblical religion.

Ibn Daud (active around 1180) was the first, but the greatest thinker of this time was Rabbi Moshe ben Maimon (1135–1204, known as Maimonides in English). Exiled from Spain to Egypt, he brought the thought of Spain to the East. His great philosophical work was *The Guide for the Perplexed*. As the title suggests, he was concerned with the difficulties Aristotle's philosophy gave to the believer. In contrast to many Jewish scholars, Maimonides saw 'right belief' as of great importance. He met great criticism for this at the time. Maimonides drew up thirteen 'roots' of Judaism, the Thirteen Principles of the Faith:

● Belief in the existence of a creator and of providence
● Belief in his unity
● Belief in his incorporeality
● Belief in his eternity
● Belief that worship is due to him alone
● Belief in the words of the prophets
● Belief that Moses was the greatest of all the prophets
● Belief in the revelation of the *Torah* to Moses at Sinai
● Belief in the unchangeable nature of the revealed Law
● Belief that God is omniscient
● Belief in retribution in this world and in the hereafter
● Belief in the coming of the Messiah
● Belief in the resurrection of the dead.

A century later, the Christian philosopher, Thomas Aquinas, also tackled the problem of Aristotle's philosophy. He was deeply indebted to Maimonides, frequently quoting him as 'Rabbi Moyse'.

The Jewish philosophers were not concerned with the concept of 'the chosen people'. It does not appear in Maimonides' thirteen roots (except perhaps to some degree in the idea of the Messiah). They were much more concerned with universal truths. This may partly explain why, when Spanish Jews were persecuted in the fifteenth century, many of the philosophers yielded and converted, while the ordinary people (with more to lose) resisted to the death. This led to a suspicion of philosophy.

Jewish mysticism

Mysticism forms an important strand of Judaism. It is the belief in some kind of direct 'vision' of divine things, a way to experience things and events otherwise

Judaism has a mystical tradition known as Kabbalism. Amongst other things it considers that numbers and letters have an inherent creative power.

than through our ordinary senses. Mysticism may deal with the same ideas as philosophy, but it claims to rely not on argument or thought but on mystical experience.

The Kabbalah, a Jewish mystical tradition, developed in Spain. It brought together many earlier traditions, such as ideas from the *Talmud* and the 'Book of Creation' (*Sefer Yetsirot*), which emphasized the mystical meaning of the letters in the Hebrew alphabet and the philosophy of Neo-Platonism. Direct from Neo-Platonism came the idea of how God related to the world. In the Kabbalah, God was known as the 'limitless' (*En Sof*). From him came the ten aspects of God (*Sefirot*), ways in which he is manifested or made known. They are 'emanations' of God, intermediate between the *En Sof* and the world.

The most important work of Kabbalah is the *Zohar*. It was attributed to Rabbi Simeon bar Yohai (second century AD), but in reality was written in thirteenth-century Spain. The final editor/author was probably Rabbi Moses de Leon. This is a book of extreme historical importance. It is the *Talmud* of Jewish mysticism. After the Jews were expelled from Spain it became known to the West, producing the school of 'Christian Cabbalists', and still attracts those interested in the occult today.

The study of *Torah* is still central in Kabbalah, but the aim is to find hidden, secret meanings. The *Zohar* expounds the *Torah* by literal, allegorical and expository techniques and, most important, by mystical insights. Astrology is bound up in the *Zohar* as well: each day is under the influence of one of the ten *Sefirot*.

After the expulsion from Spain, Safed in Galilee became the centre of Jewish mysticism.

Here Rabbi Isaac Luria (1544–72) gave a new twist to the Kabbalah. His work, which, like the *Zohar*, made much of erotic imagery, had great influence on later movements such as Hasidism. In Luria's view, when the *En Sof* created the universe he withdrew from it. The *Sefirot* are vessels which contain the 'divine light'. But the last six *Sefirot* could not contain the light, and shattered. Some of them sank, trapping sparks of the divine light within them. This is the origin of evil; and redemption will come when these sparks are returned to their source.

Hasidism

Hasidism arose in Poland in the eighteenth century. From the start it was a popular movement. It gave hope and interest and excitement to people who were frightened, deprived and confined. The Shabbetai movement had led to disillusionment, and the 'worship through study' of rabbinism offered them no consolation. But Hasidism was a movement with emphasis on emotion and devotion. It may be paralleled with many similar movements of the time, such as the rise of Methodism in England.

The key figure in this movement was Israel Baal Shem Tov (about 1700–60). He was a dynamic, charismatic figure, widely known as a miracle worker. Baal Shem Tov means 'master of the NAME', which reflects the belief in his powers. His teaching contained much from the Kabbalah, especially the *Zohar*. Many legends are told about him, and much popular belief, indeed superstition, was caught up into the movement. But the essence was a passionate devotion to God, expressed in ecstatic prayer, singing and dancing. From the outside, Hasidic life may seem a miserable, deprived, narrow existence, but within it is sustained by the Hasidic 'joy'—a genuine religious 'high'. In fact, from its early days asceticism was played down.

Unlike rabbis, the leaders of the Hasidic groups were more gurus than scholars. The leader, the *rebbe* or *zaddik*, is a man who is able to live the life of devotion and thus act as intermediary between his followers and God. The leader's word is absolute: his followers leave their families to be with him, they even contend to get a share of the food he has touched. Various leaders have created the different branches of Hasidism today.

Women played a much more prominent role in the beginnings of the movement than they do today. Generally, Hasidism is a man's world. Women are responsible for the survival of the community but they are definitely neglected, deprived and largely ignored.

Opposition

The Hasidic movement met strong opposition from the establishment of the Jewish communities. There was something of a class struggle, as the *rebbes* replaced the rich and learned. Excommunication was used as a weapon against them by their opponents. One of the most hostile, certainly the most influential, was the 'Gaon of Vilna', Elijah ben Solomon (1720–97). The emphases of Hasidism were anathema to his ascetically-oriented intellectualism. In his time the excommunicated were even betrayed to the hostile authorities.

It was Shneur Zalman (1745–1813), the philosopher of Hasidism, who drew the movement back to being accepted. Under his influence Hasidism, or at least his branch of it, was reconciled to Talmudic study.

The Influence of Judaism

Marvin Wilson

It is in the area of religion and ethics that Judaism has made its greatest impact upon modern civilization. What Greece brought to the world in the realm of philosophy and aesthetics, what Rome bequeathed in politics and law, Israel contributed in its understanding of the one invisible God and the revelation of his will for mankind.

Leo Tolstoy wrote concerning the Jew: 'he who has been for so long the guardian of prophecy, and who transmitted it to the rest of the world—such a nation cannot be destroyed. The Jew is everlasting as is eternity itself.'

The vocabulary of Judaism—the words of the Hebrew Bible—has itself had considerable impact on world thought. Both literature and conversation in the Western world are punctuated today by expressions such as 'lick the dust', 'apple of the eye', 'flesh of my flesh', 'put out the fleece', 'a still small voice', 'scapegoat', 'holier than thou', 'pride goes before a fall' and 'can a leopard change his spots?' All of these phrases come straight from the pages of the Bible.

Branches from the trunk

The ancient trunk of Judaism has produced two branches, Christianity and Islam, which in turn have experienced unparalleled growth over the whole earth.

Christianity has received from Judaism its basic understanding of God, his nature, his Law, his dealings with men and the standards he expects between man and man.

Many of the terms of Christianity—such words as amen, hallelujah, Satan, Sabbath, Messiah, paradise, cherub, and jubilee—have been adopted directly from the Hebrew Bible, even if they have subtly changed meaning.

The synagogue of Judaism gave birth to the Christian church as a place of assembly for the reading of scripture, prayer and worship. The sermon, the use of incense, the singing of psalms, the practice of baptism and the celebration of the Lord's Supper (Holy Eucharist), the organization of the church, the methods of biblical interpretation—each finds its root in Judaism.

The life and teaching of Jesus as recorded in the Gospels is likewise best understood in the light of his thorough Jewishness. For example, the Lord's Prayer (Matthew 6) is thoroughly Jewish, reflected in ancient Jewish prayers such as the *kaddish* and the 'Eighteen Benedictions'.

Through the influence of Muhammad its founder, Islam, the other daughter religion of Judaism, also preserves many teachings derived from the Hebrew Bible. In the Qur'an the names of Abraham, Moses and other biblical characters frequently appear. Muhammad eventually broke from Judaism when he failed to convince the Jews of his day that he was 'the Seal of the Prophets'.

Many of the laws of Islam are derived directly from, or adapted from, Judaism. Its strict monotheism, its opposition to idolatry, the practice of facing a holy city (Mecca) in daily prayer, regular fasting, the avoidance of pork and the observance of a weekly holy day all reflect the influence of Judaism upon Islam.

The wholeness of life

The distinctive theological and ethical values of Judaism have made an impact not only on the religious world, but on the political and social spheres as well.

The first distinctive value is the Jewish understanding of history. History is no aimless seasonal cycle. Rather it is unique. Events are invested with moral purpose and directed according to a divine plan. Thus the Jew is urged to remember history. Time has meaning for the future as well. History is a developing process, moving toward a glorious goal as depicted in the Hebrew prophets. So Judaism anticipates that final day of redemption when a perfected society will proclaim the God of Israel to be King of all the earth.

From the time of Moses, Judaism has also reflected a passion for maintaining justice and righteousness. Belief in the brotherhood of all peoples has resulted in displaying acts of charity, compassion and kindness. Acts of inhumanity and exploitation are a disgrace to a God of justice. Indeed, in Judaism, the obligation to 'love your neighbour as yourself' has extended not only to the poor, the widow and the orphan, but even to the animal world.

Reverence and holiness for all of life is another distinctive value of Judaism. Life is sacred, for man is created in the image of God. Man's task is to hallow every area of life—even mundane and commonplace activities can be imbued with divine meaning. The key to Jewish survival has been through following the way of holiness, a separateness from the corrupting pagan influences of the secular world. Unlike the upper classes of ancient Greece, Jews never viewed physical labour with disdain. Rather, the dedicated work of human hands could bring glory to the creator. In contrast to other religions which have sought to flee the pains of this material world for the heavenly joys of a spiritual world above, Judaism has persisted in focussing almost exclusively upon this present world of flesh and blood. Hence the laws of Judaism cover such areas of daily life as eating, sex and working the land. These commandments reflect the need to sanctify the wholeness of present human experience.

The one ideal that over the centuries Judaism has prized perhaps more than any other is that of freedom. It has been said that since the time of the escape from slavery in Egypt, the exodus, freedom has spoken with a Hebrew accent. Many of the political principles and civil liberties basic to Western democracy were originally based on the Hebrew scriptures. The historian, William Lecky, observed that 'Hebraic mortar cemented the foundations of American democracy'.

But to the Jew, freedom means far more than religious or political independence. It is a mandate for the individual to shape his own destiny and that of society. It is an affirmation that, no matter how bleak the surroundings and the future appear, progress is possible. There is an unquenchable hope that this world can be changed, and the prophetic dream of peace can be realized.

'If I am not for myself, who will be for me? If I am only for myself, what am I? If not now, when?'

Rabbi Hillel, *Mishnah*

'Why does this workman ascend the highest scaffolding and risk his life, if you do not pay him his wages as soon as they are due?'

The Talmud

'It is forbidden to destroy fruit-bearing trees but whoever breaks vessels, tears clothes, demolishes a building, stops up a fountain or wastes food, in a destructive way, offends against the law of "thou shalt not destroy".'

Maimonides

'If you wish it, it is not a dream—to live as a free people in your own land.'

Theodore Herzl

Life in a Jewish Family

David Harley

Birth and Bar-Mitzvah

According to orthodox Jewish law, a Jew is one born of a Jewish mother, although it is possible to become a Jew by conversion. On the eighth day after his birth, a Jewish boy will be circumcised. This may be either a medical operation performed by a doctor or a religious rite performed by a *mohel*, a trained and registered circumciser. When he is circumcised, the boy receives the Hebrew name which will be used at his *Bar-Mitzvah*, his wedding and on his gravestone.

During his early years his mother is responsible for his religious education. As soon as he can speak, he is taught the words of the *Shema* (see *Chosen People: Judaism*). At about the age of five he is sent to a synagogue religion class which is held after school hours on weekdays and also on Sunday mornings. One of the main activities of the religion class is to learn Hebrew and study the sacred books. For a girl it is particularly important to learn how to keep a Jewish home.

At the age of thirteen a boy becomes *Bar-Mitzvah* (son of the commandment); on the Sabbath after his birthday he reads from the scroll of the *Torah* during the synagogue service for the first time. After the service there is usually a party for family and friends. From this point on he is regarded as a responsible person. He is expected to fulfil all the duties of a Jew and may count as one of the ten adult men who are required to make a quorum for public prayer (*minyan*).

A Jewish girl automatically comes of age at twelve and is considered to be *Bat-Mitzvah* (daughter of the commandment). It is the custom of some synagogues to hold a ceremony to mark the occasion.

Prayer

A devout Jewish man prays three times a day—morning, afternoon and evening, either in his home or in the synagogue. When he prays he covers his head with an ordinary hat or a skull-cap (*yarmelka* or *kippah*). In the morning he wears a prayer-shawl (*tallit*) which has tassels or fringes at the four corners in obedience to the command found in the *Torah*. On weekdays he may also put on phylacteries (*tephillin*). These are black leather boxes containing four passages of scripture: Exodus 13:1–10 and 11–16; Deuteronomy 6:4–9 and 11:13–21. They are strapped to the forehead and left upper arm.

When he goes out, the orthodox Jew may continue to cover his head as a mark of reverence towards God in whose presence all life is lived. By the front door he passes the *mezuzah*, which is another reminder of his religious obligation to God. The *mezuzah* consists of a tiny scroll of parchment on which are written in Hebrew the opening paragraphs of the *Shema*: Deuteronomy 6:4–9 and 11:13–21. The scroll is housed in a wooden or metal container and fixed to the upper part of the right-hand doorpost of the front door. A similar *mezuzah* is fixed to the doorpost of every other living-room in the house.

Kosher food

It is the duty of a Jewish housewife to safeguard the religious purity of the home, and one of her many responsibilities is to make sure that the food eaten there is *kosher* (fit or clean according to Jewish dietary laws).

Meat and dairy products must not be served at the same meal. If meat is eaten, there can be no butter on bread or milk in coffee. To avoid any possibility of mixing meat with milk the traditional Jewish housewife uses two sets of dishes, one of which is only used for meat, the other only for milk foods. In addition she may use two sinks for washing-up and two sets of tea-towels. In Jewish hotels there are two separate kitchens.

Only certain kinds of meat may be eaten in a Jewish home. These are listed in Leviticus 11 and Deuteronomy 14. Lamb, beef and chicken are among those permitted, pork and shellfish among those that are not. The animals must be slaughtered by a trained and ordained *shochet*. He follows carefully prescribed regulations which cause the blood to drain quickly from the body and ensure the minimum of pain. After the animal is properly slaughtered, the meat must be soaked in cold water and salted to remove all the blood that remains.

Jewish people vary a great deal in the degree of their observance of these dietary laws. Some do not observe them at all. Some abstain from food that is expressly forbidden but are not so particular about the details of keeping a *kosher* kitchen. However, orthodox Jews will follow these regulations meticulously as an act of religious obedience, whereby the taking of food is sanctified and the family table becomes an altar.

Before each meal a traditional blessing is recited, and though this may vary according to the food that is being eaten, the most common words are, 'Blessed art thou O Lord our God, King of the universe, who brings forth bread from the earth.'

The Sabbath

The Sabbath is considered to be the most important of all the Jewish religious festivals. It commemorates both the creation of the world and the deliverance of the people of Israel from Egypt. It has played a significant role in the preservation of Judaism. It is a day with a special atmosphere of joy and peace, and as such is thought of as a foretaste of the age to come.

The beginning of the Sabbath, sunset on Friday evening, is marked by the lighting and blessing of the Sabbath candles by the mother. The father attends synagogue with his sons, and on his return blesses his children and praises his wife with the words of Proverbs chapter 31. The family then enjoys a Sabbath meal together, which begins with the blessing of bread and wine. The bread is a special plaited loaf called *challah*. Usually two loaves are used, in memory of the double portion of manna that fell in the wilderness on the day before the Sabbath.

No work is permitted on the Sabbath and the orthodox Jew has to be employed in an occupation which allows him to be home before sunset on every Friday throughout the year. This often means that he will be self-employed or work in a Jewish firm.

No fires may be lit on the Sabbath, though a fire which was lit before the Sabbath may be left alight. Some employ a *shabbos goy*, a non-Jew, to perform types of work not permitted to the Jew on the Sabbath. Others install time-delay switches.

No long journeys may be undertaken on the Sabbath, though those on board ship do not have to get off. An orthodox Jew will live within easy walking distance of his synagogue since he must not drive his car on the Sabbath or use public transport.

These restrictions, far from being a burden, are seen by the religious Jew as a means of releasing him from the

Orthodox Jews in Jerusalem

ardours of the daily round. It is a day
when he can rest completely from his
ordinary work and be spiritually
renewed.

At the close of the Sabbath, the
family again gathers for a brief ceremony. Blessings are recited over a
cup of wine and a box of sweet spices.
The spices speak of the fragrance of
the Sabbath day, which, it is hoped,
will be carried over into the new
week.

Marriage and divorce

In Judaism marriage is considered
to be a holy covenant. Before the
ceremony the bridegroom signs the
marriage document (*ketubbah*) in
which he pledges himself to his
bride. During the service the couple
stand under an embroidered canopy
supported by four poles, which
represents their future home. The
ceremony ends with the breaking of a
glass under the bridegroom's foot.
This symbolic act is thought by some
to represent the idea that even times
of great joy need to be balanced by
moments of serious reflection. Others
see it as a reminder of the destruction
of the temple of Jerusalem, a theme
which constantly reappears in
Hebrew prayers.

In the event of the breakdown of a
marriage, the local community tries
in every way possible to reconcile
husband and wife. If this is not
possible, a *get* or bill of divorce may
be issued by the Jewish religious
court. This document, written in
Aramaic and signed by two witnesses, is handed by the husband to the
wife. It frees her from all her marital
obligations to him. In most countries
a civil divorce is required first, and
then the issuing of a *get* serves as a
religious ratification of the divorce.

Death and resurrection

The last words uttered by the religious Jew when he is dying—or said
on his behalf if he is too weak—are
the words of the *Shema* which he first
learned as a child: 'Hear, O Israel,
the Lord our God is one Lord . . .' At
the moment of death those present
make a small tear in their clothes as a
mark of grief. The funeral service,
which is characterized by simplicity
even among wealthy families, is arranged as soon as possible and preferably within twenty-four hours of
death. No prayers for the dead are
offered but *kaddish*, a prayer of praise
to God, is recited in their memory. It
is the particular responsibility of a
son to say *kaddish* on behalf of a
deceased parent.

After the funeral the close relatives
return home for a week of private
mourning. This period is known as
shivah or the seven days, during
which those who have been bereaved
sit on low stools or even on the floor.
On the anniversary of the parent's
death, the children light a memorial
candle and recite the *kaddish* at the
end of the synagogue service.

The doctrine of the resurrection is
not found in the *Torah* and it is
considered by some as a foreign
import from Christianity. However,
the idea of life after death can be
traced back within Judaism at least
2,000 years, and it is expressed in
the Thirteen Principles of the Faith
(see *Developments in Judaism—
Maimonides*) in the words, 'I believe
with perfect faith that there will be a
resurrection of the dead at a time
when it shall please the Creator'. Yet
it remains true that Judaism is concerned primarily with this life rather
than the next and with obeying the
Law of God in the present rather than
speculating about the future.

The Way of the Prophet

Montgomery Watt

Islam began in Mecca about AD 610. The dominant religion of Arabia at this time was a form of the old Semitic religion, with shrines of various gods and goddesses in many places. There also appears to have been a widespread belief in a high god or supreme god, Allah. The other gods were sometimes regarded as angels, and could be asked to intercede with the supreme god on behalf of the worshippers.

Most of the Arabs were members of nomadic tribes and believed more in human excellence than in any divine power. They believed that what happened to them was determined by Fate or Time, which they thought of not as a being to be worshipped, but simply as 'the course of events'. Some tribes or parts of tribes had become Christian and there were Jewish communities in Medina and elsewhere in western Arabia. Thus, certain Jewish and Christian ideas were familiar to many Arabs.

Messages from God

Islam began not among nomads but among city-dwellers engaged in far-flung commercial enterprises. Towards the end of the sixth century the merchants of Mecca gained monopoly of trade between the Indian Ocean and the Mediterranean, which passed up the west coast of Arabia by camel caravan. Mecca had a sanctuary, the Ka'ba, which was an ancient pilgrimage centre, and the surrounding district was sacred. All this facilitated the growth of trade, but the wealth which poured into Mecca led to social tensions, especially among the younger men.

Muhammad (see special article) was born in Mecca around the year 570. It was in about AD 610 that he came to believe that he was receiving messages from God which he was to convey to his fellow Meccans. These messages or revelations were later collected and form the Qur'an. They asserted that God was *One* (Allah) and that he was both merciful and all-powerful, controlling the course of events. On the Last Day he would judge men according to their acts and assign them to heaven or hell. Part of the conduct which he expected of men was a generous use of wealth. In the revelations, Muhammad himself was spoken of sometimes as merely a warner telling of God's punishment for sinners, sometimes as a prophet or messenger of God. Muhammad sincerely believed that these revelations were not his own composition, but were the actual speech of God conveyed to him by an angel. This is still the belief of Muslims.

Muhammad gained a number of followers, who met frequently with him and joined him in worship of God. But his messages were not all well received. The Meccan merchants were roused to vigorous opposition by the criticisms of their

'He is Allah, besides whom there is no other god. He is the Sovereign Lord, the Holy One, the Giver of Peace, the Keeper of Faith; the Guardian, the Mighty One, the All-powerful, the Most High! Exalted be He above their idols! He is Allah, the Creator, the Originator, the Modeller. His are the gracious names. All that is in heaven and earth gives glory to Him. He is the Mighty, the Wise One.'

The Qur'an, sura 59:23–4 tr, N. J. Dawood

The Merciful;
the Compassionate,
the Forgiver,
the Forgiving;
the Clement,
the Generous,
the Affectionate,
the Kind ...

Some of the Ninety-Nine Names of God

Muslims at prayer in Brunei. Islam is the religion of much of southeast Asia.

A painting showing the four archangels bringing a message to Muhammad. Muhammad's face is blanked out, since the Qur'an forbids the representation of any living creature.

opponents, who were often their own relatives. Eventually it became impossible for him to carry on his religious activity in Mecca, and in 622, preceded by about seventy men and their families, he emigrated to Medina. This emigration, the *Hijra*, became the event which marked the beginning of the Islamic era.

Medina was a fertile oasis, but the inhabitants were divided into two hostile groups. Most of them accepted Muhammad as prophet and agreed that they and the emigrants from Mecca would form a single community or federation. Perhaps they were the more ready to accept Muhammad because they had heard from the local Jewish clans that a messiah was expected. They were also hopeful that he would help them to overcome their divisions.

It was at Medina that the religion of Islam took shape. The main ritual forms, modelled on Muhammad's example, were: worship (or prayer), almsgiving, fasting (for the whole month of Ramadan), and the pilgrimage to Mecca (including ceremonies at neighbouring sites). At Medina the messages revealed to Muhammad included legal regulations for matters where Arab custom was unsatisfactory, such as the inheritance of wealth and the avoidance of incest.

The Jewish clans in Medina were associated with Muhammad's federation as allies of Arab member clans, but nearly all the Jews refused to accept him as prophet. They mocked parts of the Qur'an and sometimes actively opposed the Muslims. Muhammad expelled two Jewish clans from Medina and had the men of a third executed. Until after the conquest of Mecca he had few contacts with Christians.

At first, Muhammad had no special political powers at Medina beyond being head of the emigrants from Mecca. After a year or two, however, all his followers there (now called Muslims) became involved in hostilities with the pagan Meccans. By 630 Muhammad was strong enough to take Mecca. He treated his enemies generously and won most of them over to become Muslims. Many

practices implied in the Qur'an. The merchants spoke of the old pagan gods but the Qur'an came to emphasize that there is only one God—that 'there is no deity but God'. As opposition grew, the Qur'anic messages began to speak of former prophets who had met with opposition, and of the way in which God had preserved them and their followers and brought disaster on their opponents. Among the stories were those of Noah and the Flood, Lot and the destruction of Sodom, and Moses escaping from Pharaoh.

To Medina

Muhammad's followers were now persecuted in various ways by his

tribes all over Arabia also joined his federation and became Muslims. Because of his successes his authority as head of state was unquestioned.

The first caliphs

'He who honours Muhammad must know that he is dead. But he who honours the God of Muhammad must know that he is living and immortal.' Muhammad died in 632, and with these words his first successor, Abu Bakr, encouraged the Muslim community and pointed them to the task ahead.

On his death, Muhammad left both a religion and a state. At first the state had the form of a federation of tribes or clans, but as it expanded it became more organized. The head of state was known as the 'caliph' (*khalifa*)—the 'successor' or 'deputy' of Muhammad. Raiding their neighbours had been a normal occupation of the nomadic Arab tribes, and Muhammad and the first caliphs realized that they could not keep peace within the federation unless they found some outlet for the ener-

gies of the tribesmen. They therefore organized raiding expeditions (*razzias*) in the direction of Syria and Iraq. The aim of these was to obtain booty, including domestic animals.

The first raids from Medina were very successful. There was in fact a power vacuum in the region, because the two great powers of the day, the Byzantine and Persian Empires, had been almost constantly at war for half a century and were now exhausted. In a few decisive battles the Muslims overcame such opposition as the empires presented. Instead of returning to Medina after each campaign, they established forward base camps so that they could go further afield in the following expedition. Following this strategy, they had occupied Egypt, Syria and Iraq within twelve years of Muhammad's death, and were advancing westwards into Libya and eastwards into what is now Iran.

The Byzantine and Persian governors of the provinces fled, and the Muslims made treaties with the local inhabitants, giving them the status of 'protected minorities'. These groups

The Muslim world

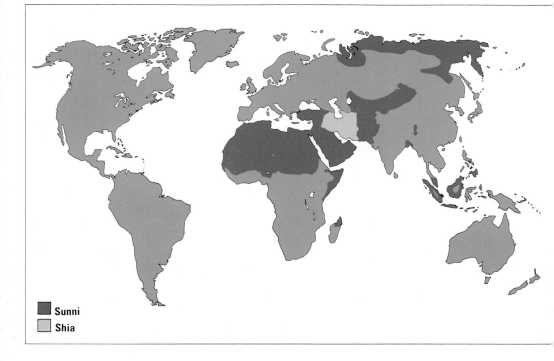

Sunni
Shia

Muhammad

Lothar Schmalfuss

Muhammad's life is surrounded by legends. They paint a picture of a sort of wonder-working super-human, whose special calling by God was clearly evident to all. The historical facts, however, reveal quite simply a man—a caravan leader who had grown up in bitter poverty, a father who lost most of his children, a moderately successful business man. Above all, a man who perceived in everything that God is in close control, that God is the beginning and end of this world and that he holds in his hands the life of every human being.

Muhammad was born in Mecca, about AD 570. Mecca was a prosperous trading and religious centre of the Arab world. Early in life Muhammad lost his parents. He experienced the misery of being an orphan, but he also learned what it meant to be surrounded by a community wider than immediate family. First he was looked after by his grandfather and then by an uncle. At the age of twenty-five he led the caravans of a business woman, Khadija, so successfully that she offered him her hand in marriage. He was now rich and became a respected and influential citizen of Mecca. He seemed to have reached his goal.

But Muhammad was not satisfied by material security. Early on he had shown a love of solitude. Questions oppressed him. Restlessness drove him round in circles, and before long he came to a severe crisis point in his life. Increasingly he withdrew from business and family and sought the loneliness of the desert. It was there that the event occurred which was to change his life and to affect the history of the world.

The night of destiny

His first biographer, Muhammad Ibn Ishaq, recorded the events of that night. Muhammad was spending time alone on the Hira mountain.

'I was lying asleep,' he reports in his own words, 'when an angel came to me with a piece of material and said: "Read this!" I replied: "I cannot read!" Then he pressed the material against me so hard that I thought I would die. Then he let me go and said again: "Read!" The angel repeated his command once more. Nervously, I replied: "What am I to read?" The angel said:

"Read in the name of your Lord.
He who created and made man from an embryo.
Read, for your Lord is merciful like no one on earth.
He who instructed man by the pen,
He taught him what he did not know."

'I awoke from my sleep,' Muhammad went on, 'and it was as if these words were written in my heart. I came out of the cave and stood on the mountain-side. Then I heard a voice calling to me from heaven: "Muhammad, you are God's messenger and I am Gabriel." I lifted my eyes up and saw him on the skyline. I did not move. When I tried to look away I could still see him.'

The prophet of God

From then on, Muhammad was sure that he had been called to be the prophet of the one God. He returned to Mecca and on the street corners preached about the resurrection of the dead and God's judgement.

'God will judge you according to your works,' he called to the town traders, and he challenged them to submit their lives to God and to practise love towards the poor and imprisoned, to slaves and foreigners. His language had something gripping about it. But many of the citizens of Mecca thought he was possessed, or a dangerous revolutionary. They recognized at once that he was directing his preaching against the polytheism of the town. But this was the focus of the pilgrimages which were their most important source of income. Feeling threatened, the traders' opposition grew. They became increasingly aggressive, forcing Muhammad and his small group of followers to live in a ghetto. When his wife died and, soon afterwards, the uncle who had protected him, Muhammad left Mecca.

Just as Abraham left his ancestral land to form the Jewish nation, so Muhammad left the town of his father and family behind him and went to Medina. AD 622, the year of this journey, or Hijra, is the year which marks the start of the Islamic calendar. From then on Islam was no longer just a religion but also a distinct political power. In Medina the community of believers became a state, with Muhammad as its religious and political head, and the social and religious practices of Islam were developed.

Muhammad expected that the Jewish inhabitants of the town would recognize him as God's prophet, but he was disappointed. So he drove out and destroyed the Jewish clans. Enlisting the help of nomadic Arab tribes, Muhammad began armed raids on Mecca, and in 630 he took the town with ease. Surrounded by jubilant followers he rode on a camel straight to the centre of pilgrimage, the Ka'ba. Mecca was quickly cleared of all images and symbols of pagan belief. Then Muhammad raised himself on the saddle and formally announced the end of idolatry and the start of the new age of the one God. There was no resistance, and the victors pronounced no judgement on their former opponents. Mecca remained the focal point and the place of pilgrimage of the new state of God.

Two years later, Muhammad again led the train of pilgrims to the Ka'ba. In front of all the people he declared the last message of God:

'Today I have completed my religion for you and I have fulfilled the extent of my favour towards you. It is my will that Islam be your religion. I have completed my mission. I have left you the Book of Allah and clear commandments. If you keep them you will never go wrong.'

The same year, Muhammad died.

ordered their own internal affairs, but paid tribute or tax to the Muslim governor. The status of protected minority was open only to 'people of the book'—communities who believed in one God and possessed a written scripture, i.e. Jews, Christians and Zoroastrians.

The explosion of Islam

Apart from some periods of civil strife among Muslims, the expansion continued for a century. Westwards the Muslims occupied North Africa to the Atlantic, crossed into Spain, and for a few years held the region round Narbonne in southern France. In the famous battle of Tours in 732 a Muslim raiding expedition was defeated by a French army, but this did not loosen the Muslim hold on Spain. Northwards they raided as far as Constantinople (modern Istanbul), but failed to occupy any of Asia Minor (Turkey). Eastwards, after occupying the whole of Persia and Afghanistan, they penetrated into central Asia and crossed the line of the River Indus in modern Pakistan.

The entrance to a mosque in Damascus. Before prayer, Muslims take off their shoes and wash their feet.

Until 750 this vast area remained a single state ruled by the caliphs of the Umayyad dynasty.

Most of the inhabitants of these regions were not immediately converted to Islam but became protected minorities. The military expeditions, though dignified with the title of 'holy war' (jihad), were raids for booty and not to make converts. The idea that opponents were given the choice of 'Islam or the sword' is false, except in the case of pagan Arab tribes. The protected minorities were on the whole well treated, since Muslim rulers felt it to be a point of honour that their 'protection' should be effective. Members of these minorities, however, saw themselves as second-class citizens, and there was a steady trickle of converts to Islam over the centuries. It is in this way that Islam has become the dominant religion in lands which were the original home of Christianity. In the seventh century though, Zoroastrianism—the official religion of the Persian Empire—was in decline, and conversion from it to Islam was quite rapid and extensive.

Consolidation

In 750 the Umayyad dynasty of caliphs, based in Damascus, ended. For the next 500 years, the 'Abbasid dynasty ruled from Baghdad. They never took over control of Islamic Spain, however. They also gradually lost control of other outlying provinces. A local governor with a powerful army would insist on being succeeded by a person of his choice, maintaining only weak links with the caliph. In 945 the 'Abbasid caliph was even forced to delegate supreme political and military authority over Baghdad and the central provinces. But there continued to be 'Abbasid caliphs in Baghdad, though without political power, until the destructive Mongol invasion in 1258.

Whereas the Umayyad period was one of growth and adaptation for Islam and the Arabs, the first century or two of 'Abbasid rule was marked by consolidation. All the cultural forms needed for the life of a great empire flourished. A central place was given to the development and

A Muslim reading the Qur'an inside the beautifully-decorated Blue Mosque in Istanbul.

elaboration of Islamic law, the Shari'a, which formed the basis of social structure. The Shari'a was derived in part from rules in the Qur'an, but to a greater extent from the example of Muhammad. His example was known from the collections of *Hadith* (sometimes translated 'traditions')—stories about his deeds and sayings. This study of law or jurisprudence became the core of Islamic higher education.

Subordinate scholarly disciplines were concerned with the text of the Qur'an, the interpretation of the Qur'an, grammar, lexicology and theological doctrine. There were also the 'foreign sciences'—Greek philosophy, medicine, mathematics and natural science. Many Greek books were translated into Arabic and considerable advances were made in the sciences, in literature, in the arts and in the skills of government and administration.

To the east

After 750, military expansion slowed down, and almost the only advance was that into India. Here the climax of Islamic power was under the Mogul emperors from 1556 until 1707, when most of the subcontinent was subject to them. Hindus were treated as 'people of the book' because their philosophers (though not most ordinary Hindus) were monotheists. Though there were group conversions to Islam, most of the population remained Hindu.

Islamic rule also spread by peaceful methods. Muslim traders with camel caravans took it into the West African steppe, and sea traders carried it to the East African coast. From India it spread, mainly through trade, to Malaysia, Indonesia and the Philippines; and from central Asia it moved into eastern China.

Local people were impressed by the confidence and high culture of the Muslim traders, allowed them to marry local women, and often after a time decided themselves to become Muslims. Converts often kept many of their old customs, and did not immediately observe the Shari'a fully. But over the centuries they moved closer to standard Islam, and at the same time the number of Muslims kept increasing.

The one area where Islam contracted was Spain. Christian military pressure gradually whittled away the area under Muslim control, and in 1492 the last sultan of Granada had to surrender. Muslims continued in Spain for a time, but were executed or driven out by the Inquisition.

The impact of Europe

A new era in the history of Islam began about 1500. The Portuguese sailor Vasco da Gama, having rounded the Cape of Good Hope and disrupted the Muslim trade on the East African coast, reached India in 1498. This was the beginning of the impact of Europe on the eastern part of the Islamic world. In the west the Ottomans had restored the caliphate which had lapsed in 1258, conquered much of south-eastern Europe and the southern coast of the Mediterranean during the fifteenth and sixteenth centuries, and were then in military and diplomatic contact with European states, as well as having commercial dealings. The full force of the European impact, however, was not felt until after the Industrial Revolution. Napoleon's invasion of Egypt in 1798 is a significant date.

The impact of Europe on the Islamic world (as on Asia and Africa generally) was many-sided: economic, political, intellectual and religious. It began with ocean-borne trade but went on to political interference and finally colonization. As European technology developed in the nineteenth century, the richer Muslims wanted to share in the comforts and conveniences, and independent rulers wanted their countries to have railways and other forms of communication, plumbing, electricity for lighting, telephones, and so forth. Military hardware was high on the list, and then it became necessary to train men to use it. Colonial powers also introduced Western-type education to train men for minor administrative posts. After 1800 the Christian churches sent missionaries to most parts of the world, but in Islamic lands they made few converts and their chief contribution was to the development of education and medical care.

By the early twentieth century, intelligent Muslims were aware of their situation. Movements for political independence grew and were eventually successful. Some industry was developed, based on Western technology. Most Muslim countries adopted an essentially Western educational system, because the religious leaders were not prepared to adapt the traditional Islamic education they controlled. The discovery of vast quantities of oil in the Middle East was at first exploited by Westerners, but later, when taken over by Muslim governments, became a weapon in world politics. Until the end of the Second World War, Muslim countries were united in their struggle to be free of colonialism. Since then, however, splits between 'progressive' and 'conservative' groups have become increasingly apparent.

The Qur'an
Christy Wilson

The Qur'an is the sacred book of the Muslims. It is seen as a perfect revelation from God, a faithful reproduction of an original engraved on a tablet in heaven which has existed from all eternity. Copies of the Qur'an are therefore venerated very highly and are only touched and read by Muslims after ceremonial cleansing. Volumes are usually carefully wrapped in silk or an ornate cloth and placed in an elevated position, such as above a door in a home. Many Muslims memorize in Arabic the whole book—which is almost as long as the Christian New Testament. Those who have done this earn the title of *Hafiz*. And Muslims all over the world quote the short first chapter of the Qur'an in Arabic over and over again in the five daily prayers.

A collection of writings
The word Qur'an comes from the Arabic verb 'to recite', *qara'a*. This bears out the fact that most of the book is in the form of the words of Allah which Muhammad was commanded to proclaim. After the first chapter, the Qur'an consists of 114 chapters (*suras*). These are arranged according to length, the longest near the beginning, the shortest at the end. They are not organized chronologically or even by subject. Rather they are a composite collection of verses written at various periods of Muhammad's life.

All the *suras* start with the words, 'In the name of God, the Merciful, the Compassionate' (except number nine which may originally have been joined to eight). Each of the 114 chapters has a name derived from a prominent or recurring word in the particular chapter: *The Opening* (1), *The Cow* (2), *Jonah* (10), *Joseph* (12), *Abraham* (14), *Mary* (19), *Angels* (35), *Muhammad* (47), *Divorce* (65), *Noah* (71), *Earthquake* (99), *Swift Horses* (100), *Elephant* (105), *Infidels* (109) and *Men* (114).

The *suras* are divided into verses (*ayat*). The word *ayat* also carries the meaning of 'a miracle'. When Muhammad was asked for an authenticating wonder to prove his prophetic role, he simply referred to the Qur'an and its verses: they were his miracle. With its rhymed Arabic prose, the Muslims' holy book certainly has great literary beauty and a special attraction in the original.

The Qur'an does not follow a chronological arrangement, but from internal evidence many of its sections can be placed either in Muhammad's time at Mecca before the emigration of AD 622, or in his time at Medina afterwards. The Medina passages reflect the change in role from being a prophet or preacher to becoming a military leader.

The Qur'an contains several different sorts of writing. Muhammad records experiences of earlier prophets, mostly from the Old Testament, who were often models of his own experiences. There are also frequent proclamations of imminent judgement and of sensuous enticements in heaven and vivid descriptions of the sufferings of the dammed in hell. A strict monotheism is taught throughout. Legislative sections for the Muslim community as well as laws governing family relations and inheritances are also included. There are a few historical references: in the thirtieth *sura* the war between the Greeks and the Persians (which probably took place around AD 614) is mentioned.

Proclaimed piecemeal
In the earlier parts of the Qur'an, Muhammad expressed friendship towards Jews and especially Christians as 'people of the book'. Furthermore, the Qur'an acknowledges much Jewish and Christian writing—the Pentateuch (*taurat*), the Psalms of David (*zabur*) and the Gospel (*injil*) of Jesus—as being revelations from God. But later, when the Jewish and Christian people would not accept him as a prophet, the attitude of the Qur'an towards them changes. In order to account for differences between the Jewish faith and the Qur'an, Muhammad charged the Jews with corrupting their scriptures: 'They have perverted the words.' The same charge was made against the Christians.

The angel Gabriel is the one who is credited with revealing the Qur'an to Muhammad. Parts were proclaimed by him piecemeal even though Muhammad claimed that the whole Qur'an existed complete in heaven. *Sura* 25:32 states: 'The unbelievers say, why was the Qur'an not sent down to him as a whole? We wished to strengthen thy heart thereby and we arranged it thus.'

According to Islamic tradition, the Qur'an was originally written on palm leaves, on shoulder-blade bones of camels and on stones. Following Muhammad's death in AD 632, tradition states that the first caliph, Abu Bakr, ordered Muhammad's former secretary, Zaid, to collect and arrange the writings. This was done in co-operation with others and finally an authorized revision of the text was established by Caliph 'Uthman. Other versions in existence were ordered to be destroyed. Thus, although Islam has many sects, all Muslims do use the same Qur'an going back to this original version. (Many groups claim to have other authentic sayings of Muhammad left out of the Qur'an which are called the traditions or *hadith*.)

There are alterations and abrogations within the Qur'an itself. For example, Muhammad originally ordered his followers to pray towards Jerusalem (*sura* 2:150), but when the Jewish people refused to follow him, he changed the direction of prayer to Mecca (*sura* 2:125). Such alterations are explained by *sura* 2:106, 'If we abrogate a verse or consign it to oblivion, we offer something better than it or something of equal value.'

Even though none of the Bible was translated into Arabic until after Muhammad's time, he did have access to Jewish and Christian oral traditions (though this is

A thirteenth-century manuscript of the Qur'an.

disputed by Muslims). For example, one of his wives was a Jewess and another was a nominal Christian from Ethiopia. Having to depend on oral traditions and being acquainted with heterodox forms of Christianity accounts for the fact that Muhammad in the Qur'an misunderstood the Christian teaching concerning the Trinity. In *sura* 5:77 he writes 'They misbelieve who say, "Verily God is the third of three."' He goes on to say 'Oh Jesus, son of Mary, hast thou said unto mankind: "Take me and my mother as two gods beside God"?'. Muhammad thought that Christians worshipped a trinity of a holy family which included God the Father, Mary the Mother and Jesus the Son. For this reason the Qur'an attacks the sonship of Christ stating that 'God neither begets nor is begotten'.

Another misunderstanding which seems to have come from the influence of Jewish or heterodox Christian teaching was a denial of the crucifixion of Christ. The Qur'an in *sura* 4:156 states 'They slew him not and they crucified him not, that they had only his likeness . . . They really did not slay him.' The Qur'an, however, also teaches that Jesus was born of a virgin, worked miracles, was the Messiah, lived a sinless life, went up alive into heaven and is coming again before the end of the world.

'Praise be to God, the Lord of the worlds! The compassionate, the merciful! King of the day of judgement! Thee only do we worship, and to Thee do we cry for help. Guide Thou us on the straight path, The path of those to whom Thou hast been gracious— With whom Thou art not angry, and who go not astray.'

The most common prayer among Muslims; the words of *sura* 1 of *The Qur'an*

'By the star when it setteth, Your compatriot erreth not, nor is he led astray, Neither speaketh he from mere impulse. The Qur'an is no other than a revelation revealed to him: One terrible in power taught it him. Endued with wisdom.'

The words of Muhammad, *The Qur'an, sura 53*

The Worship of Islam

David Kerr

The Qur'an sees men and women as religious beings. 'I created ... humankind only that they might worship me,' the Muslim hears God say in the Qur'an. Each individual is an *'abd* of God, a term which conveys the twin meanings of 'worshipper' and 'servant' in a single word. And this description applies to all aspects of human life, all of which is lived under the command of God. There is no distinction between worship and the wholeness of human life.

Submission to God

Islam understands itself fundamentally as being 'natural religion', in that *every* created thing exists in dependence upon God, in obedience to his creative and sustaining power and with the purpose of expressing adoration to God. For the human, this should lead to a conscious commitment to a life of thankful and praise-giving obedience to God. The word *muslim* means one who lives his life according to God's will. *Islam* means 'submission to God'.

Worship (*'ibada*) and the activities of the work-a-day world (*mu'amallat*) are joint expressions of the character of *'abd*. The mosque cannot be separated from the market-place, nor politics from praise.

As far as worship is concerned, the Qur'an sees body and spirit as inseparably combined in the wholeness of human worship. Islam has no term for 'spirituality'; for its religious devotion seeks to preserve an equilibrium between the 'outward' and the 'inward' in worship. The believer's external acts of worship depend on his internal intention, and the Qur'an is concerned that both should be 'for the pleasure of God'. So while the holy law provides a code of practice as a framework for Muslim worship, the worship depends on the inner dynamic of thankful and praise-giving obedience, the discipline of the soul to 'remember God always'.

The confession of faith

The Islamic code of conduct is founded upon the bedrock of the testimony of faith, the *shahada*. This is the first pillar of Islam. When spoken in Arabic and with sincere intention, it is a commitment to obey God and follow the prophet.

'I bear witness that there is no god but God; I bear witness that Muhammad is the Apostle of God.'

These are the first words breathed into a child's ear at birth and the last which a Muslim would utter with his dying breath—the lantern for life and the hope for the mercy of God in the life hereafter. They point to the one God who has spoken finally through the Qur'an; and they point to Muhammad, 'the Seal of the Prophets', sent to all mankind to transmit and interpret the Qur'an. The words of the *shahada* summon Muslims to worship throughout the world, and their meaning is the heart of prayer and meditation.

Praying together

The Qur'an identifies a human being as 'worshipper'. It also places the individual worshipper, male or female, in the context of a worshipping community.

'Hold fast, all of you, to the rope of God, and do not separate ... and may there spring from you a community who invite to goodness, enjoin right conduct and forbid indecency; such are they who are successful.'

The Shari'a codifies and co-ordinates the practice of a worshipping community. Worship is a communal act as well as one of individual commitment. To affirm the unity of God (*tawhid*) is necessarily to affirm the unity of the created order and of mankind in right worship.

This community orientation of Islamic worship is symbolized and demonstrated in the ritual of *salat*, the liturgical form of prayer, which it is the duty of all Muslims to observe at fixed hours. Prayer is the second pillar of Islam. There are five prayer times, each preceded by obligatory ritual washing—dawn, midday, mid-afternoon, sunset and night—and they serve to remind Muslims in a regular and disciplined manner of their status before God as 'worshipful servants'. From the moment of the muezzin's call and the preliminary washings *salat* is a communal act.

An expression of this is the common direction (towards the Ka'ba in Mecca) in which all Muslims turn in prayer. Around the globe all are united in direction and in intention within a human circle of worshippers. At a signal from the prayer leader, the *imam*, men and women assemble separately in rows, at the mosque or in the home or place of work, taking care that each person is close to the next. Carefully following the lead of the *imam*, they pray as a single body, quietly reciting words of prayer from the Qur'an. At the same time they bow their bodies in a series of ritual movements until, from an initial standing position, all are upon their knees with foreheads touching the floor—the whole congregation enacting as a single body its submission before the majesty of God and asking for his guidance and mercy. Each of the five sets of prayers includes the repetition of *Allahu akbar* ('God is greatest') and of the first *sura* of the Qur'an, itself a prayer. At the end of the prayer each person passes the Arabic words of peace to neighbours on right and left: *as-salamu alaikum*, 'peace be upon you'. Private prayers often follow the public service.

The twofold fruit of giving

'O you who believe, perform the *salat* and give the *zakat*.' Prayer is linked closely with almsgiving, the third pillar of Islam, often described by modern Muslims as the pillar of social action. Externally *zakat* is the duty of sharing one's wealth with the poor, the needy, the debtor, the prisoner, the wayfarer—all who are less fortunate than oneself but equally part of the worshipping community and equally precious to God. The Qur'an is less concerned with the quantity, and more with the quality of giving. When it is offered 'in search of God's pleasure and for the strengthening of their own souls, it is as the likeness of a garden on a hill; the rainstorm smites it and it brings forth its fruit twofold'. The inward attitude is all-important; discretion is preferred to ostentation, and reproach on the part of the giver makes the action worthless.

The Shari'a is meticulous in determining the amounts of alms which should be given on different categories of possessions, but contemporary practice simplifies the matter to an annual rate of 2½ per cent of one's cash balance. But Muslim devotional literature reflects equally the inwardness of *zakat* as 'purification' of the soul. It is a mercy to the giver as much as to the recipient. It is a means to atone for sins which are motivated by human self-centredness, or by irresponsible stewardship of possessions.

The most-loved duty of worship

Special alms are given on the two main religious festivals of the Islamic calendar, the first of which, *'Id al-Fitr* or *Bairam*, marks the end of Ramadan, the holy month of fasting. Fasting (*sawm*) is the fourth pillar of Muslim worship, and involves a total abstinence from food and drink through the daylight hours of the entire month, from early dawn to sunset.

In some ways this is the most obviously communal of the duties of Islamic worship. The physical discipline means that social behaviour of the whole community has to change for the duration of the month; the pace of life slows down and there is time for reflection. It is a period when social relationships are reaffirmed, reconciliations encouraged, and the solidarity of the community is expressed. Mosque attendance swells, particularly on the Night of Power (*laylat al-qadr*) towards the end of the month, when Muslims commemorate the descent of the

Every adult Muslim is encouraged to make the pilgrimage to Mecca once in his lifetime, preferably in the great month of pilgrimage.

Qur'an from heaven and the beginning of Muhammad's ministry.

The fundamental intention of fasting is thanksgiving. Inwardly the fast is thought of as a disciplining of the soul to wait patiently upon God who guides and provides. This inward aspect is of great importance. Muhammad is reported to have said that of all the duties of worship, *sawm* is the most loved by God since it is seen only by him.

To Mecca

The fifth of the fundamental duties of Islamic worship, to be fulfilled once in a lifetime if at all possible, is the *Hajj*, the pilgrimage to Mecca and its vicinity. Here are the most holy of holy places for Muslims, full of 'memorials' of God's guidance in times past. There are associations with Muhammad who began his life and ministry in the city, and also with his prophetic precursor Abraham who, according to the Qur'an, built the Ka'ba, helped by his son Ishmael, as a sign of their submission to God, with the prayer that God would show them 'our ways of worship'.

A visit to Mecca has religious significance for Muslims at any time of the year. But with the twelfth month of the calendar, *dhu alhijja*, the season of the *Hajj* or Great Pilgrimage arrives. (At any other time it is a Little Pilgrimage.) Pilgrims flock to Mecca, each wearing the simple pilgrimage garb of white cloth denoting the state of ritual purification. They congregate in the Great Mosque and the first rite of pilgrimage is performed—the circumambulation around the Ka'ba. This is followed by running seven times between two small hills, recalling the plight of Hagar and her son Ishmael who, in Islamic, Jewish and Christian

Preparation for prayer outside the mosque at Qum in Iran. The Muslims of Iran are Shi'ites, the smaller division of Islam.

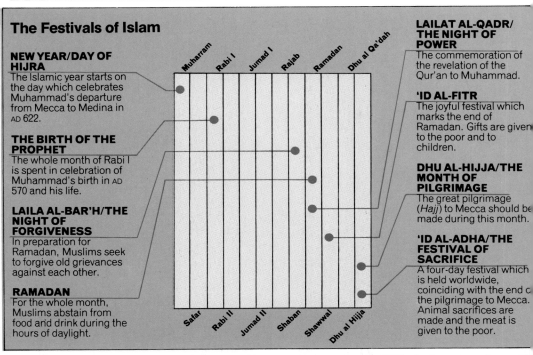

The Festivals of Islam

NEW YEAR/DAY OF HIJRA
The Islamic year starts on the day which celebrates Muhammad's departure from Mecca to Medina in AD 622.

THE BIRTH OF THE PROPHET
The whole month of Rabi I is spent in celebration of Muhammad's birth in AD 570 and his life.

LAILA AL-BAR'H/THE NIGHT OF FORGIVENESS
In preparation for Ramadan, Muslims seek to forgive old grievances against each other.

RAMADAN
For the whole month, Muslims abstain from food and drink during the hours of daylight.

Months across top: Muharram, Rabi I, Jumad I, Rajab, Ramadan, Dhu al Qa'dah

Months across bottom: Safar, Rabi II, Jumad II, Shaban, Shawwal, Dhu al Hijja

LAILAT AL-QADR/THE NIGHT OF POWER
The commemoration of the revelation of the Qur'an to Muhammad.

'ID AL-FITR
The joyful festival which marks the end of Ramadan. Gifts are given to the poor and to children.

DHU AL-HIJJA/THE MONTH OF PILGRIMAGE
The great pilgrimage (*Hajj*) to Mecca should be made during this month.

'ID AL-ADHA/THE FESTIVAL OF SACRIFICE
A four-day festival which is held worldwide, coinciding with the end of the pilgrimage to Mecca. Animal sacrifices are made and the meat is given to the poor.

---

tradition, were saved from certain death by a spring of water which God caused to break through the desert sands. This well is named in the Islamic tradition as *zamzam*, and from it the pilgrims may draw holy water before journeying a few miles out of Mecca to Mount Arafat where the *Hajj* comes to its climax. Here the pilgrims observe the rite of 'standing' from midday to sunset in meditation before God. Then they begin the return

Mecca was the birthplace of the prophet Muhammad. It is the centre of Muslim pilgrimage, towards which Muslims turn to pray. The focal point of the city is the cube-like shrine, the Ka'ba, which contains the sacred Black Stone.

journey to Mecca, stopping overnight at Mazdalifa where each pilgrim gathers pebbles. The following day these are thrown ritually against three stone pillars in the neighbouring village of Mina, recalling the moments in Abraham's life when he resisted Satan's temptations to disobey God. God had commanded him to prepare his son (Ishmael) for sacrifice as a test of his obedience (*islam*). The Qur'an tells how the child was ransomed 'with a tremendous victim', and in joyful recollection of this act of divine mercy the pilgrims offer the ritual sacrifice of sheep or camels, the meaning of which is clearly stated in the Qur'an: 'their flesh and blood reach not to God, but your devotion reaches him'.

With the intention of magnifying God and remembering him 'with a more lively remembrance', Muslims throughout the world join with the pilgrims in Mina for the Feast of the Slaughter, which brings the *Hajj* to an end. Muslims remember their corporate identity and responsibility as a worshipping community created by Muhammad. Muhammad believed that this festival was the fulfilment of the Muslim community for which Abraham is said to have prayed before the Ka'ba: 'Our Lord make us submissive to thee, and of our seed a community submissive to thee, and show us our ways of worship, and turn towards us. Lo! thou, only thou art the Relenting, the Merciful (Qur'an 2:128).

The Law of Islam

Norman Anderson

Down the centuries the traditional education of a Muslim has rested on twin pillars. Theology taught him what he should believe, and the sacred law prescribed how he should behave. And in practice the law has been the senior partner, for Islam has always been far more explicit about the quality of life God has ordained for his creatures than about the nature of the Creator himself. Although the role of Islamic law has changed considerably in recent years, it can still be described as 'the epitome of Islamic thought, the most typical manifestation of the Islamic way of life, the core and kernel of Islam itself'.

The Path of God's commandments

The sacred law of Islam is called the Shari'a—a word which originally meant 'the way to a watering-place', but came to be used of the path of God's commandments. It is regarded by Muslims as firmly based on divine revelation, derived from four main sources:

● the Qur'an—which, they believe, has existed eternally in Arabic in heaven, and was revealed piecemeal to Muhammad by the angel Gabriel as occasion demanded.

● the sunna—or practice of the

Prophet, as enshrined in countless traditions of what he said, did or permitted.

● the ijma—or consensus of the Muslim community or of its leading scholars.

● qiyas—analogical deductions from the first three sources.

Orientalists have, however, shown that the raw material of the Shari'a was actually provided by pre-Islamic customary law and the administrative practices of early Islam—systematized and Islamicized by scholar-jurists in the light of those Islamic norms which had come to be accepted. They also insist that, for a number of decades, the law was wide open to foreign influences current in the conquered territories or ingrained in the minds of converts to Islam.

The Shari'a has often been classified under five categories:

● what God has commanded

● what God has recommended but not made strictly obligatory

● what God has left legally indifferent

● what God has deprecated but not actually prohibited

● what God has expressly forbidden.

As such its scope is much wider than any Western concept of law, for it covers every aspect of life. Obviously a great deal of it could never be enforced by any

human court, and must be left to the bar of eternity. But in theory the Shari'a was a divinely revealed blueprint to which every Muslim, from caliph to slave, must attempt to approximate.

In theory, man-made regulations were only appropriate in those matters which God had left 'legally indifferent'. In practice, though, from a very early date even the official courts allowed a number of 'devices' which eased the inconvenience of some of the Shari'a's precepts.

Muslim rulers, moreover, found its standards of proof too exacting for the maintenance of public order. Muslim merchants found its prohibitions too restrictive for the life of the markets. And local communities of Muslims found its rigid prescripts too alien to their age-old customs. So less rigid courts soon appeared beside the official qadis' courts. But the fact remains that, until little more than a century ago, the Shari'a remained the basic (and residual) law—to which lip service, at least, was almost always paid—through the length and breadth of the Muslim world.

Interpreting the law

But the Shari'a was not a system of law which was either codified or uniform. For although it is regarded as firmly based on divine revelation, it has been developed and elaborated by generations of legal scholars.

The scholars interpreted the relevant verses in the Qur'an and those traditions which they accepted as authentic. They also drew from these sources a plethora of analogical deductions. At first, moreover, any adequately qualified jurist had the right of *ijtihad*—going back to the original sources to derive a rule of law to cover any problem that arose.

At a very early date, however, the Muslim community became divided between the Sunni, or 'orthodox', majority and the Shi'a and Khariji minorities. These two minorities proceeded to split into further exclusive sub-sects, and the Sunni majority divided into a number of different schools or 'rites'. As these schools and sects crystallized, the right of independent deduction was progressively replaced by the duty to accept the authority of the great jurists of the past (*taqlid*). Today even the most learned Sunni jurists are normally considered to be under this authority. The Ithna 'Ashari sub-sect of the Shi'a (which is still the dominant sect in Iran, for example) still recognizes *mujtahids* who may exercise *ijtihad* in certain circumstances. It is only among the Isma'ili Shi'is that their *imam*—or, in some cases, his representative, the Da'i Mutlaq—can give a wholly authoritative ruling.

Civil law

Since about the middle of the nineteenth century, the position of Islamic law has changed radically throughout the greater part of the Muslim world. First in the Ottoman Empire, next in what was then 'British India', and subsequently elsewhere, the impact of modern life has loosened the sway of the Shari'a in two major ways.

The first change is plain for all to see. In many spheres of life the Shari'a has been displaced by new codes of law, largely derived from the Western world. In the Ottoman Empire, in the 1850s and 1860s, for example, the Commercial Code, the Penal Code, the Code of Commercial Procedure and the Code of Maritime Commerce were all based on French models. But when the Ottoman reformers came to the law of obligations (contract, tort, etc.), they debated whether again to turn to European law or to compile a comparable code derived from Islamic sources.

Eventually the latter view prevailed. So the resultant code (commonly known as the Majalla, completed in 1876) was compiled from the rulings of a selection of Sunni jurists—although all these opinions had received some form of recognition from the Hanafi school. The Majalla was thus of immense jurisprudential significance. For the first time in history, a code of law based firmly on principles derived from the Shari'a was enacted by the authority of the state. And for the first time, again, a compilation was made of provisions of heterogeneous origin selected on the broad principle of their suitability to modern life, rather than their established precedent in one particular school. Moreover, all these new codes were administered in secular courts by personnel trained in modern law schools. It was only the family law which continued to be applied in the age-old way in the Shari'a courts, uncodified and unreformed.

The second change was less obvious but equally important. In 1915 the intolerable lot of Muslim wives under the dominant Hanafi rules virtually compelled the sultan to intervene even in matters of family law. So he issued two imperial decrees permitting wives to request a judicial dissolution of marriage in certain circumstances sanctified by one or other of the Sunnic schools. Once this dyke had been opened the tide came in very fast indeed. In 1917 the Ottoman Law of Family Rights was promulgated based on an extended application of these principles.

In one Muslim country after another, much the same happened. In 'British India' the new secular codes were, of course, based on the Common Law of England rather than the Civil Law of France. Here both secular

Islamic law, the Shari'a, deals with family life and religious requirements as well as matters of civil concern.

Muslim children are taught the Qur'an in daily lessons. This class is taking place in Senegal.

law and the uncodified family law of different religious communities were administered by the same courts. In Turkey, by contrast, the Shari'a was abolished and European codes (only slightly adapted) were adopted in its place.

In Saudi Arabia, on the other hand, the Shari'a remains dominant—though even there statutory regulations have begun to proliferate. Most Muslim countries, however, now have largely secular codes in all except family law—which must, they insist, remain distinctively Islamic. And even this has been codified—in whole or in part—in a way which makes it more suitable for modern life. In countries such as Somalia and the People's Democratic Republic of Yemen the presence of Marxist influence in such codes is sometimes plain to see.

Thus the present picture is very different from that of the past. Whereas the once-dominant Shari'a is now, for the most part, confined to family law, the current tendency is to produce civil codes which incorporate principles derived from Islamic law alongside those of an alien origin. A few countries have, even more recently, begun to reintroduce some of the Islamic criminal sanctions—a clear evidence of a resurgence of Islamic fundamentalism. In most Muslim countries, moreover, the law—whatever its origin—has been codified by legislative enactments. Thus the authority of the law, once implicit and transcendent, is now, in most countries, constitutional, resting on the will of the people as expressed by their executive or legislature.

A Day in the Life of a Muslim Family

Anthony Harrop

A slight wind sweeps across the flat countryside. There is still no sign of dawn on the eastern horizon. Her family still asleep, Latifa Begum crosses to the tube-well in the yard. She pumps the handle until the clear cold water rises. Neighbours are stirring now. She calls to her eldest child, daughter Safina, 'Tell the boys to get up immediately. Their teacher will soon be here.'

The pale line on the horizon is now a band of mauve shading into yellow. Suddenly, from the newly-installed loudspeaker on the minaret of the mosque 100 yards away, the call to the morning prayer (*fazur*) resounds: 'Wake up, wake up, prayer is better than sleep.'

Prayer

Latifa's husband, Abdul Khaliq, comes out of the house, donning his prayer-cap as he heads for the mosque. As he reaches the gate, his distant relative Abdur Rahman arrives. Rahman is a student, half-way through his ten-year training to become a Muslim religious teacher, a *maulvi*. In order to help him financially during his studies, the family have appointed him to give religious instruction to the children. He leads their prayers each morning.

As they hear his voice the boys run out and together the three of them perform the ceremonial ablutions. Then, with their prayer-mats laid out on the verandah, in careful alignment towards Mecca, they recite the prayer following the example of their teacher. Latifa Begum and Safina, after their own ablutions, also recite the prayer, but separately inside the house, away from the gaze of any outsider, as befits women in Islam.

The prayer finished, Safina joins her brothers for the instruction. Seated on a rush mat on the cement verandah, they recite in unison as Abdur Rahman leads them in a section of the holy Qur'an. The boys are still sleepy and they make many mistakes. But Safina has a good memory and Rahman only has to correct her pronunciation of the classical Arabic. Again and again the section is repeated. After almost an hour, all three children can recite it word-perfect.

Meanwhile, their mother has been preparing breakfast—some rice left over from the previous evening's meal, chapatis, biscuits, a cup of tea for the adults and cow's milk for the children. The teacher stays for the meal, and husband Khaliq comes in.

Part of the community

Khaliq has been delayed at the mosque after the morning prayer. He and the leading religious teacher were talking about payment of the *zakat*, the annual religious tax. The month of fasting (Ramadan) commences in a few weeks' time, and Khaliq's household has been assessed for 200kg of rice, half to be paid

The Muslim community is called to prayer by the muezzin, *who then leads them in prayer.*

during the fast to the mosque authorities for distribution to the poorer members of the village community. As one of the wealthier men of the village, Khaliq's payment of the tax will be a significant contribution to community well-being.

Across the compound from Khaliq's family lives his widowed mother. That afternoon, when the midday sun has lost some of its heat, Khaliq, his mother and Latifa Begum discuss the arrangements for the fast and the payment of the tax:

'Everyone will need a new set of clothes for the festival at the end of the fast. That means fitting out the whole family. And we should also give something to Abdur Rahman,' they decide.

Khaliq's mother wants to invite her two married daughters for '*Id-al-Fitr* ('the Little Festival'). Their husbands will come, too, but will probably only stay a few days. Still, that will almost double the number who must be fed, and the relatives should also receive presents.

'Can we think of any other relative we should give to?'

'Yes, there's my dead cousin's second wife's children,' says Khaliq. 'The boy has a place in a *madrassa* as a charity student, but the family is too poor even to buy him a new suit of clothes.'

'That too is our responsibility,' insists the older lady. 'In addition to our responsibility to our own family, we must pay half the tax during the fast, to help the poorer people in the village to have a better festival'.

'But can we afford it at this time, with so many relatives coming to stay? And in three months' time we shall need a good animal for the sacrifice at the Great Festival.'

'No, we must pay our share of the tax during the fast, even if that means we only have a goat, not a calf to sacrifice.'

The afternoon glides into evening. Dusk breezes dissolve the day's heat to a freshening coolness. Two hours after sunset the day ends as it began, with the late evening prayer (*isha*) echoing around the groves of bamboo and palm, over the thatched houses and out into the still countryside.

Science, Art and Culture in Islam

Lothar Schmalfuss

Islam has produced not only successful army leaders and statesmen but also equally talented poets and musicians, architects and builders. But above all there were the Muslim philosophers and naturalists, whose achievements between the ninth and fourteenth centuries laid the foundations of modern science on which our civilization was built.

For Muslims to start to study the world, they needed a 'supernatural' incentive. Allah was looked on as the Unapproachable, the Impenetrable, so Islam had taught that his creation was similarly unapproachable. It was Mahmun, caliph of Baghdad from 813–833, who supplied that incentive. In a dream, Mahmun saw the ghost of Aristotle, who convinced him that there is no contradiction between religion and reason. Thus freed from all his scruples, Mahmun ordered a 'house of wisdom' to be built. In the library all available books in the world were to be collected.

The works of Greek, Persian and Indian writers were brought together and translated into Arabic, and the knowledge obtained was examined, remodelled and developed. So the starting-point and basis of Islamic knowledge was the Greek conviction that behind the visible chaos of the world there is a fundamental order, ruled by general laws and accessible to human reason. Thus scientific effort pursued primarily philosophical goals, the discovery of the 'basic laws' of the world.

Muslim doctors built on the experience and knowledge of ancient Persia. They discovered the principle of the circulation of the blood, evolved treatment methods for smallpox and practised painless operations under anaesthetics. Their learning, known as the *Avicenna* (after Ibn Sina, the great philosopher and physician) was used as an important textbook in the universities of Europe until the seventeenth century.

In mathematics, Islamic academics learnt from India. From there they adopted the decimal system and also the use of the zero. They called this *sifr*, the empty one. Leonardo de Pisa, who had studied with the Arabs, translated this foreign concept as 'cephirum' and it then developed via 'zefiro' to 'zero'. It was the Arabs also who developed the subject of algebra, using symbols to represent unknown quantities.

Early on, the Arabs had used the stars as guides in the desert. When they became familiar with the work of Ptolemy in the eighth century, they also began to investigate the sky scientifically. Star names and astronomical terms such as zenith, nadir and azimuth are an enduring witness to this work. Scholars also collected their geographical knowledge in atlases and travel guides which recorded the main roads of all known countries, as well as the names and positions of the large towns and their distances one from another. They also calculated the circumference and diameter of the earth.

A worldwide influence

At the height of their culture the knowledge of the Muslims extended to all areas. The fascination they inspired in Europe was enormous. Wherever the West met the East, the West started to learn. In Sicily the court of Friedrich II became a centre of Arabian philosophy and science. In the Levant the Crusader knights became familiar with the Eastern way of life. Above all, this contact took place in Islamic Spain. As early as the tenth century towns were thriving. Cordoba had over 500,000 inhabitants with 700 mosques, 300 public baths and seventy libraries. Its streets and squares were paved and brightly lit at night. Everything which made life pleasant was offered for sale: marzipan, soap and perfume, coffee, damsons and sugar, mattresses, caps and jackets, oranges, asparagus. Their influence spread right through Europe. Travelling singers from Andalusia brought their songs and also Arabic instruments—lute and guitar, trumpet horn and flute. Through Muslim philosophers such as Averroes (Ibn Rushd) and Avicenna (Ibn Sina), Aristotle was rediscovered in the West.

A mosque in Java. Islam is the religion of much of south-east Asia.

In the fine arts, calligraphy, ceramics and architecture, Islam absorbed influences into itself. It took the cultural inheritance of the peoples it conquered and transformed them, creating an all-embracing culture of a unique type. Islamic architecture can be seen in Cordoba, Granada, Marrakesh and Cairo, in Istanbul and Damascus, Agra and Delhi. All reflect the form and style of the country they are in, as well as the Islamic influence which unites them. The 'Islamic' style has a

particular sensitivity for the de orative, and strives to turn t natural appearance of things in the abstract.

The Qur'an teaches that a object and its image are magical united. This was probably t reason why representational a was prohibited.

With the sack of Baghdad t the Mongol invaders in 1258 a the general decline of the Islam world, the development of ar culture and science in Islam w halted.

The architecture of the Alhambra in Granada dates from the thirteenth century when much of Spain was a Muslim country.

The glory of Islamic art can be seen in mosques throughout the world.

The Unity and Variety in Islam

David Kerr

Islam has two basic groups—the Sunni and Shi'a. Their origins can be traced back to a question which faced the first generation of Muslims: how was Muhammad, 'the Seal of the Prophets', to be succeeded as leader of the Muslim community? For Muslims, this question was always a religious as well as a political one.

Sunnis—the community consensus

The answer of the Sunnis, who constitute the Muslim majority of approximately 90 per cent, can be summarized as follows. No one could succeed Muhammad in his nature and quality as prophet, for the Qur'an finalized and perfected the revelation of divine guidance and declared Muhammad to be 'the Seal of the Prophets'. Muhammad's successor could therefore be no more than the guardian of the prophetic legacy. He would be a caliph (*khalifa*) with subordinate authority as leader of the believers, having responsibility for the administration of community affairs in obedience to the Qur'an and prophetic precedent. By the process of consensus (*ijma*) the community would select its caliph from amongst the male membership of the Quraish tribe to which Muhammad belonged.

Following Muhammad's death in AD 632, caliphal succession passed from Abu Bakr (632–634) to 'Umar (634–644) to 'Uthman (644–656) and to 'Ali (656–661). These, 'the four rightly-guided caliphs' are deemed to have lived so close to the Prophet that their example, together with Muhammad's, is taken to comprise the authoritative *sunna*, or custom, for all later generations of Muslims to follow.

The Sunnis gradually developed a comprehensive system of community law, the Shari'a. This provided cohesion within the community while allowing for variance between four orthodox law schools, the Malikis, Hanafis Shafi'is and Hanbalis. The principle of *ijma* remained central. Notionally *ijma* is the consensus of the whole community, though in practice it is that of the legal scholars.

After the 'rightly-guided caliphs' the caliphate became a dynastic institution, regarded as the guardian of the Shari'a. But in 1924 it was abolished. The

The vigorously missionary Ahmaddiya sect, founded in India in the early part of this century, is considered heretical by other Muslims. Ahmad announced himself as the awaited saviour of Islam, Christianity and Hinduism.

jma of contemporary Sunni Islam seems to be that if the Shari'a is observed by the national governments of Muslim states, there is no need for the transnational office of caliph to be restored.

Shi'a—authority and leadership

For Shi'a Muslims the principle figure of religious authority is the *imam*. Muhammad, 'the Seal of the Prophets', completed 'the cycle of prophethood' and with it the possibility of further divine revelation. But Shi'a Muslims believe that he instituted 'the cycle of initiation' for the continuing guidance of the community, by appointing as his successor an *imam*. The *imam* was invested with the qualities of inspired and infallible interpretation of the Qur'an. Accordingly, the Shi'a speak of themselves as 'people of appointment and identification'.

The first *imam* was 'Ali. As cousin, adopted son and later son-in-law of Muhammad (by marriage to Fatima), he was not just a member of Muhammad's tribe but also of 'the people of his house'. This intimate family relationship is significant: the Shi'a believe that 'Ali inherited Muhammad's *wilaya*. He was infallible in his interpretation of the Qur'an and leadership of the community. And he passed these qualities on to the sons of his marriage with Fatima, Hasan and Husayn, and they to their descendants in the line of *imams*. The Shi'a believe that 'the cycle of *wilaya*' will continue until the end of human history when, on the Last Day, mankind will be resurrected and judged for the afterlife.

The majority of Shi'a, known as Imamis (most of whom live in Iran), believe that the cycle will be completed with the messianic return to the twelfth *imam*, often referred to as the '*imam* of the period'. He is said to have been withdrawn into 'occulation' since the third century of Islam. His guidance is still accessible through 'agents' or 'doctors of the law' (*mujtahidun*) of whom the most senior in Iran are the *ayatollahs*. It is they who have the right to interpret the Shari'a and to make religious rulings.

The history of the Imamis has seen two important offshoots. The Saidis, mostly found in Yemen today, do not limit the number of *imams* to twelve and interpret their function in a manner similar to the Sunni caliph. The Isma'ilis, meanwhile, have developed highly esoteric doctrines surrounding the *imam*. They have two major groups, the Nizaris, who look to the Aga Khan as their *imam*, and the Musta'lis (more commonly known as the Bohora Muslims) who believe in a hidden *imam*

The Main Streams of Islam

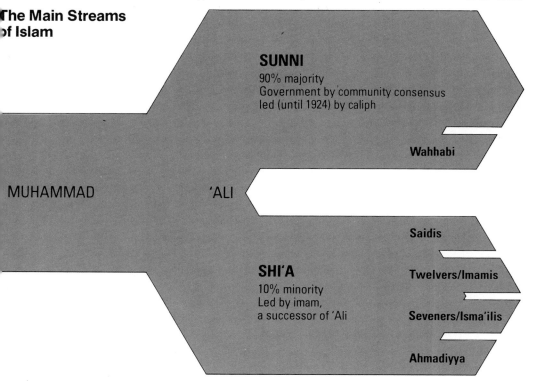

MUHAMMAD — 'ALI

SUNNI
90% majority
Government by community consensus
led (until 1924) by caliph

Wahhabi

SHI'A
10% minority
Led by imam,
a successor of 'Ali

Saidis

Twelvers/Imamis

Seveners/Isma'ilis

Ahmadiyya

who is not descended from Hasan and Husayn.

The two dimensions

Sunni and Shi'a Islam reflect the diversity of the Muslim response to divine revelation. Sunni Islam tends to be more concerned to create and preserve structures of society within which the community may fulfil its God-given responsibilities.

Shi'a Islam began in the martyrdoms of 'Ali and his son Husayn, and has always been conscious of suffering and alienation in the human condition. It searches for answers in a more esoteric interpretation of the Qur'an and Shari'a. But there is obviously no hard and fast distinction. Sunni Islam is also con-

In Shi'ite Islam, religious leaders, mullahs, mujtahids and ayatollahs, define the social and religious law of the community.

cerned with the inner life and Shi'a with the outer. Moreover, the important mystical tradition of Sufism has seen a confluence of Shi'a and Sunni consciousness.

The Future of Islam

Norman Anderson

The initial expansion of Islam in the Middle East, North Africa and Western Europe was achieved by military conquest. Much the same was also true, at a later date, in central Asia, the Indian peninsula and Eastern Europe. In Africa south of the Sahara, Malaysia and Indonesia, on the other hand, Islam spread chiefly by peaceful means—trade, settlement and penetration. But what pattern of expansion or contraction is likely to be seen in the future?

Further expansion by force of arms seems only a remote possibility, except in a few limited areas. But there can be no doubt whatever that a new spirit of self-confidence vis-a-vis the Western world is clearly apparent in the Middle East today—largely based, politically, on the vast reserves of oil in the Gulf area, and the wealth, influence and power which these represent. Throughout Europe and North America, moreover, there are growing numbers of Muslims who are increasingly concerned to preserve their identity and protect their traditions, and Islam is actively competing with Christianity and Marxism for the soul of Africa. But the claim that Islam is attracting significant numbers of converts all over the world has been much exaggerated. To surmise what may happen in the future, however, we can only look at the trends which are apparent already in the Muslim world. There are a number of pointers.

Increasing secularization?

In many countries where Muslims represent a minority of the population, the current tendency is for governments to put forward uniform national laws which replace the religious laws of the Muslim community. In Kenya, Tanzania, Uganda and Ghana—and even Indonesia, where Muslims not only constitute the majority, but the largest Muslim population in the world—tentative steps in this direction have been taken. In India, however, the large Muslim minority has so far resisted the tendency. Among basically Muslim countries, Turkey officially secularized its law many years ago, and more recently Tunisia, Somalia, the People's Democratic Republic of Yemen (and, until their revolutions, Iran and Pakistan) have introduced certain radical innovations.

So the attitude of some Muslims today represents a distinct retreat from the traditional Islamic position. Ultimately this would reduce Islam to a purely personal matter between an individual and his God, rather than a religion which moulds, and is partially enforced by, society. Yet to erase the social influence of Islam would take many years, very severe repression (as experienced already by many previously solidly Muslim areas of the USSR), or the expulsive influence of a new religion or ideology. On the secular level, probably only communism could achieve this: since a Muslim disillusioned with his religion would find it comparatively easy to switch from one monolithic ideology to another, which may appear to him as more effective.

Radical revolution?

Diametrically opposite, there is the possibility of a fanatical resurgence of Islamic fundamentalism—as seen recently in Iran, Libya and Pakistan. It seems distinctly doubtful, however, whether any future movements of this sort will be able, in the long term, to resist the insidious pressures of modernity and materialism which would assail them from outside.

The middle way?

On the whole, it seems most likely that Islam will neither

In Iran, Muslim self-awareness has been expressed in revolution.

wither away nor return to its primitive past. Rather, it will continue to evolve, adapting itself to its contemporary environment.

If it is to develop in this way, there are certain hurdles to be cleared. The doctrine of holy war (*jihad*), for example, calls Muslims to wage war in all suitable circumstances in order to bring the non-Muslim world under the dominance of Islam. But to join the United Nations Organization with any integrity, Muslim countries must, of necessity, repudi-

ate this classical doctrine—at least tacitly.

Islamic law prescribes the death penalty for a Muslim who 'apostasizes' from Islam. It prescribes stoning for illicit sex relations for any Muslim who has ever enjoyed a valid marriage, amputation of the hand for theft and flogging for certain other offences. For several reasons—including international relations, the Universal Declaration of Human Rights and other international conventions—some of these practices would come under severe criticism today. Similarly, though the Qur'an prohibits 'usury', most Muslim countries now take the view that this does not preclude the receipt of fixed rates of interest on bank deposits or from stocks and shares—although much thought is currently being given to this subject.

From a purely human point of view, it seems probable that Islam will continue to follow the somewhat chequered pattern which at present prevents the many and various countries of the Muslim world from achieving any stable unity. They realize that it is only on such a basis that they can ever exercise a really effective influence; and they can, and do, unite to meet particular threats or needs. But the factors which separate them—economic, political, sectarian, tribal and personal—are so acute that fissures soon appear in any united front.

So it seems likely that the three tendencies—growing secularization, sporadic revivals and evolving adaptations—will continue to co-exist or alternate in the Muslim world.

Christianity and Islam

Contacts and relations between Islam and Christianity have been almost uniformly unhappy. Muhammad himself seems to have been acquainted with only a very distorted presentation of Christian faith and teaching. The initial (and spectacular) Muslim conquests were, moreover, greatly facilitated by sad divisions and bitter disputes between rival Christian churches; and in the succeeding years, large numbers of nominal Christians came to adopt the religion of their new rulers—doing nothing to help mutual understanding. The antagonism was certainly not helped by the long centuries of virtual isolation which followed, broken only by the tragic episode of the Crusades.

During the last two centuries Christian outreach to Muslims has been renewed. But the impact on the Muslim world has been small in most areas. In part this is because Muslim misconceptions of the Christian faith have proved remarkably resistant. In part it is because the work of Christian missions has all too often been associated with the political and economic imperialism of the West and with the love-hate reaction of most Muslims to European patterns of life and thought. It has also been hindered at times by cultural insensitivity, by an unnecessarily negative attitude to indigenous family and community customs and by a positive proclamation of the Christian Gospel which has failed to convince because of its lack of theological content, sympathetic presentation or experimental authentication.

Part Six

Religion: or the Fulfilment of Religion?

Jesus

Richard France

Christianity is founded on the worship of Jesus Christ ('Jesus the Messiah') as Son of God, the unique self-revelation of God to man. At the same time it remembers this same Jesus as a real historical figure, a man of insignificant social standing who during his life was unknown outside the obscure corner of the Roman Empire where he lived and died.

Looking for liberation

Born just before the death of Herod the Great, king of Judea, in 4 BC, Jesus lived for a little over thirty years, scarcely travelling outside Palestine throughout his life.

The Jews were a subject people, living either under local princes appointed by the Roman emperor, or under the direct rule of Rome itself. A priestly party, the Sadducees, accepted Roman rule, to which they owed their influence. The Pharisees, who later became the dominant party, were mostly less concerned with politics, and concentrated on the study and application of the Old Testament Law. Some stricter Jews, Essenes, opted out of Jewish society and set up isolated communities—such as *Qumran*—where they could devote themselves to preserving their religious purity. But there were many Jews who resented Roman rule, and from time to time revolts broke out, leading eventually to the disastrous 'Jewish War' of AD 66–73.

The Jews had long hoped for 'the day of the Lord', when God would act to save his people. There were several different hopes of a 'Messiah', a saviour, whom God would send, and such hopes ran high at the time of Jesus. Some saw the Messiah in more spiritual terms, as a priestly or prophetic figure, but in popular expectation he was to be a political liberator, and there were occasional 'messianic' movements centred on popular leaders. Galilee was known as fertile ground for such movements.

Jesus was born at Bethlehem in Judea, but was brought up in Galilee, and most of his public activity was in that region. Judean Jews regarded Galilee as an uncultured, half-pagan area: Jesus' distinct 'northern accent' would have been conspicuous in Jerusalem.

His family was respectable, if not affluent: he was a 'carpenter', or general builder, an important figure in village life. But Nazareth was an obscure village, and Jesus' background was remote from urban culture.

The birth and early life of Jesus

Despite its provincial obscurity, Jesus' family had an honourable pedigree. So his birth took place in King David's town of Bethlehem. Owing to the overcrowding of the town for the Roman census, however, the circumstances were not very regal; his birth in a stable, visited by

The Christian faith depends from beginning to end on Jesus Christ, who was born in Israel around the year 4 BC.

shepherds from the neighbourhood, has become one of the best-known stories in the world.

But, along with the very down-to-earth circumstances of his birth, the Christian Gospels record the fact that it was far from ordinary. Angels proclaimed him the promised saviour, and his parents maintained that he was not conceived by human intercourse, but by the power of God. This bringing together of earthly poverty and obscurity with a miraculous birth is typical of the Gospels' portrait of Jesus, as truly human but also uniquely the Son of God.

Virtually nothing is known of Jesus' life from his infancy until about the age of thirty. He clearly received a sound education in the Old Testament scriptures, presumably in the local synagogue school. However, his upbringing was not in academic studies, but in the practical work of the carpenter.

The event which launched Jesus on his public ministry was the mission of his relative, John 'the Baptist', down in Judea. John called Israel to return to God, and baptized those who responded in the River Jordan. He attracted a large following, and Jesus joined him, was baptized, and himself began preaching. When John was put in prison, Jesus moved back to Galilee, and continued to preach in public.

Healing and preaching

The Gospels summarize Jesus' activity as 'preaching, teaching and healing', and that is how he would have appeared to his contemporaries during the three years or so of his public ministry.

He and his closest followers deliberately adopted a wandering and dependent style of life. They had no permanent home, but moved around as a group, accepting gifts and hospitality when offered. Jesus spoke frequently of the danger of becoming preoccupied with possessions, and called his followers instead to an almost reckless generosity.

As a preacher he drew large crowds, who followed him constantly. He taught with a vivid simplicity and an authority which contrasted sharply with other Jewish religious teachers. We shall consider the content of his preaching later.

Jesus was clearly well-known as a healer from the beginning of his public activity. The Gospels record his curing of many different types of illness and deformity, usually by a simple word and a touch, sometimes by a word alone. There is no elaborate ritual, nor any search for patients, rather a power which responded to physical need as he met it. He is also recorded as an exorcist, driving out demons by a word of command. It was apparently as much for his healing power as for his teaching that he was sought out by the Galilean crowds.

Most of Jesus' recorded miracles are healings, but a number of incidents are recorded where he displayed a supernatural control over nature. Again these were in response to actual needs, not mere arbitrary displays of power, as when he multiplied a little food to feed a hungry crowd, or calmed a dangerous storm on the lake by a command. The

The heart of the Christian message is that Jesus rose from the dead, having conquered sin and death. The picture shows a first-century rock-cut tomb, like the one in which Jesus was buried.

Gospels present him as one who did not go out of his way to gain a reputation as a miracle-worker, but whose personal authority extended beyond his words to a practical control over nature which inevitably made a deep impression on those around him.

Like many other Jewish teachers, Jesus quickly gathered a group of committed followers, known as his 'disciples'. He demanded of them an absolute commitment to the ideals he preached, and to himself personally, and a total dependence on God to supply all their needs. They acted as his spokesmen, going out on preaching and healing missions of their own. An inner group of twelve disciples were his constant companions.

An increasing amount of time was spent in teaching his disciples privately, preparing them to continue his mission. He told them that he would soon be killed, and expected them to be the focus of the new community created by his work. He taught them to see themselves as distinct from other men, and to make it their aim to win others to be his disciples.

Opposition

While Jesus was, at least at first, popular with the ordinary people of Galilee, he very quickly aroused the opposition of the leaders. His attitude was in many respects unconventional, and he posed a threat to the Jewish religious establishment.

He refused to recognize the barriers which divided men from one another in society. His habit of mixing with the ostracized classes, and even of eating with them, earned him the name of 'friend of tax-collectors and sinners'. Women held an unconventionally high place in his following, and not all of them were very respectable. He seemed to delight in reversing accepted standards, with his slogan: 'The first shall be last, and the last first.'

He did not share the general Jewish disdain for Samaritans—a despised minority of mixed blood. He even made a Samaritan the hero of one of his most famous stories, at the expense of respectable Jewish clerics. Although he seldom travelled outside Jewish territory, he welcomed the faith of a non-Jewish soldier and a Syrian woman, and declared that non-Jews, the Gentiles, would even displace Jews in the kingdom of God. As for economic barriers, Jesus deliberately gave up a secure livelihood, and made no secret of his contempt for affluence. It is no wonder that the establishment found him uncomfortable.

On religious questions he was equally radical. He clashed with the religious authorities because of his free attitude to the observance of the Sabbath, the day of rest, and his declaration that ritual purification mattered less than purity of heart. His bold reinterpretation of the Old Testament Law moved consistently away from an external keeping of rules to a deeper and more demanding ethic. He declared the will of God with a sovereign assurance which cut through centuries of evolving tradition, and set him on a collision course with the scribes and Pharisees whose heartless legalism he denounced.

Nor could he please the Sadducees, the priestly rulers. He taught that the Jewish nation was ripe for God's judgement, and predicted even the destruction of the temple on which their national religion was centred. In a symbolic gesture he 'purified' the temple by violently expelling the traders whose presence the priests encouraged. Moreover his enthusiastic popular following threatened to upset the delicate balance of their co-operation with Rome.

All this, we may be sure, did not diminish Jesus' popularity with the ordinary people, who soon came to see him as the expected deliverer, and even on one occasion tried to force him to be their king in rebellion against Rome. But Jesus made it clear that his idea of salvation was not a political one. So gradually his popular following dwindled, as those who wanted a military Messiah became disillusioned. Even one of his twelve closest disciples betrayed him in the end, and none of them under-

'"I'm ready to accept Jesus as a great moral teacher, but I don't accept his claim to be God." That is the one thing we must not say. A man who was merely a man and said the sort of things Jesus said would not be a great moral teacher. He would either be a lunatic—on a level with the man who says he is a poached egg—or else he would be the Devil of Hell. You must make your choice. Either this man was, and is, the Son of God; or else a madman or something worse. You can shut him up for a fool, you can spit at him and kill him as a demon, or you can fall at his feet and call him Lord and God. But let us not come with any patronizing nonsense about his being a great human teacher. He has not left that open to us. He did not intend to.'

C. S. Lewis, *Mere Christianity*

'For God loved the world so much that he gave his only Son, so that everyone who believes in him may not die but have eternal life.'

The New Testament
Gospel of John, 3:16

'The Father and I are one.'

John 10:30

stood his real purpose until after his death.

Death and resurrection

The opposition to Jesus came to its climax at the Passover festival in Jerusalem. Jesus rode into the city in a deliberately 'messianic' gesture—though on a peaceable donkey, not a war-horse—and was enthusiastically welcomed by the crowds, who probably expected him now to declare himself their national leader. Instead, he carried out his demonstration against the temple regime, and engaged in a series of increasingly bitter exchanges with the religious authorities; but he showed no sign of acting against Rome.

Eventually he was arrested by the Jewish leaders with the help of Judas, his disillusioned disciple, and was tried according to Jewish law on a charge of blasphemy, because he claimed to be the Messiah and the Son of God. A death sentence was passed, but a Roman conviction was required to make it effective. This was secured by a charge of sedition, pressed upon the Roman governor by the religious leaders with a show of popular support. So, ironically, the Jesus who had forfeited his popular following by his refusal to take up arms against Rome was executed by Rome as a political rebel, 'the king of the Jews'.

He was executed by crucifixion, the barbaric method reserved by Rome for slaves and rebels. Some highly-placed followers obtained his body and buried it in a nearby tomb. The cross has rightly become the symbol of Christianity. In that death, with all its cruelty and injustice, is the focus of salvation, and Jesus had already taught his disciples to see it that way, little as they had yet understood him. But the cross alone could have no such significance. It was the sequel that gave it meaning.

Two days later his disciples found the tomb was empty. Their failure to understand this is not surprising—there was much about Jesus they had not understood. But the meaning of it was brought home to them by a series of encounters with Jesus himself, alive and real, though no longer bound by the limitations of time and space (he could appear and disappear suddenly, even inside a closed room).

For a few weeks they met him in a variety of situations, sometimes one or two alone, more often in a larger group. He explained to them again the meaning of his life and death, and the mission he had entrusted to them. Then he left them, and they began to preach to the world that Jesus, triumphant even over death, was Lord and Saviour. It was the resurrection of Jesus which formed the focus of the earliest Christian preaching; it was the risen Lord whom they worshipped.

What Jesus taught

The Gospels sum up Jesus' preaching in Galilee in the challenge: 'The time has come; the kingdom of God is near. Repent and believe the good news!' This summary is a convenient framework for setting out some of the main points of his message.

● **'The time has come'** The Old Testament pointed forward to God's great work of judgement and salvation, when all Israel's hopes and the promises of God would be fulfilled. Jesus saw his mission as this time of fulfilment. In other words, however little he shared popular ideas of a political deliverer, he saw himself as the Messiah, come to save God's people. He called himself the Son of man, echoing a figure in the Old Testament book of Daniel who represented the ultimate deliverance and triumph of the true people of God.

● **'The kingdom of God is near'** The kingdom of God (more accurately the 'reign of God'; it is an activity not a place or a community) is central in Jesus' teaching. It means that God is in control, that his will is done. So he called men to enter God's kingdom, to accept his sovereignty and to live as his subjects. He taught them to look forward to the day when this kingship of God, already inaugurated by Jesus ('Yours is the kingdom') would find its fulfilment when all men acknowledged God as king ('Your kingdom come'), when Jesus himself would return in glory, and share the universal and everlasting dominion of his Father.

● **'Repent'** Jesus' call was issued primarily to his own people, Israel. He called them to return to their true loyalty to God. He warned them of God's judgement if they refused. There was an urgency in his appeal, and as it was increasingly rejected he spoke of God calling others to be his people instead. Finally, after his resurrection, he sent his disciples to call all nations into the kingdom of God. God's demands are absolute, and disobedience or disloyalty would not be overlooked.

● **'Believe the good news'** Now was the time for deliverance. Jesus preached this not in a political sense, but in terms of the restoration of a true relationship with God. Those who repented would find forgiveness and a new life. And as Jesus predicted his own suffering and death, he saw this as the means of restoration; he was the servant of God whom Isaiah had foretold, 'by whose wounds we are healed'. So he came 'to give his life as a ransom for many', to institute 'the new covenant in my blood', a new people of God redeemed from sin as Israel had been redeemed from slavery in Egypt to be God's special people.

This was the focus of Jesus' teaching, the call to repentance, to membership of a new people of God, forgiven and restored through his atoning death. His famous ethical teaching takes second place, for it is

Christianity is a world faith, for people of 'every nation and language'. This young church group is in Java.

'I am the bread of life. He who comes to me will never be hungry.

'I am the light of the world. Whoever follows me will have the light of life and will never walk in darkness.

'I am the gate for the sheep ... Whoever comes in by me will be saved.

'I am the good shepherd, who is willing to die for the sheep.

'I am the resurrection and the life. Whoever believes in me will live, even though he dies; and whoever lives and believes in me will never die.

'I am the way, the truth and the life; no one goes to the Father except by me.

'I am the vine, and you are the branches. Whoever remains in me, and I in him, will bear much fruit; for you can do nothing without me.'

Jesus' great statements about himself, from John's Gospel

primarily an ethic for disciples, for those who have thus entered the kingdom of God.

For them life is new. It is focussed on God, their king, but also their Father, for Jesus taught his disciples to depend on God with a childlike trust. Their relations with one another were to be those of members of the same family, inspired by an unselfish, uncalculating love. In this new community many of the world's standards would be reversed, and a concern for material security and advancement would be swallowed up in an overriding longing to see God's kingdom established. It is an other-worldly ethic which has profound this-worldly implications. Jesus expected his disciples to be clearly different, the 'light of the world', showing the world what life was meant to be like. They were to be like God their Father.

Who was Jesus?

He was hailed as a prophet, a man sent by God. In his preaching, teaching and healing he matched up to that role, and as such he is one of a long and noble sequence of men of God before and since. But Christians believe, and his own life and teaching suggest, that he was much more than that.

In his appeal to Israel there was a clear note of finality. This was not just another prophetic warning, but God's last call. Its rejection would spell the end of Israel as God's special people; its acceptance would create a new people of God in whom all God's purposes would reach their climax.

The criterion was not only the response to Jesus' message, but the response to Jesus himself. He called for faith in and loyalty to himself, and presented himself as the final arbiter of men's destiny. He not only proclaimed forgiveness and salvation: by his own life and suffering and death he achieved it. He is the messenger, but he is also the heart of the message. He calls men to God, but he is also himself the way to God.

During Jesus' earthly life his disciples only dimly understood all this, though they understood enough to make them tenaciously loyal to him. But after his resurrection they quickly came to speak of him as more than just a man, and to worship him as they worshipped his Father. And even during his earthly teaching Jesus had prepared the way for this by speaking of himself as the Son of God in a unique sense, and of God as his Father in an exclusive relationship quite different from the sense in which his disciples could use the term. 'All things have been committed to me by my Father. No one knows the Son except the Father, and no one knows the Father except the Son and those to whom the Son chooses to reveal him.'

The worship of Jesus the man as the Son of God did not have its origin in some fanciful piety long after his death, but in the impression he made on his disciples during the three years of his ministry. His resurrection deepened that impression and confirmed it. Without in the least doubting his real humanity, they realized that they had been walking with God.

Community of a Common Life

Chua Wee Hian

For many, the church is a building where Christians gather for worship. Others think of it as an institution where rites such as baptisms, weddings and funerals are conducted. The constant appeals in Western Europe for funds to preserve ancient cathedrals and churches give the impression of the church as a crumbling structure.

But basically the church is *people*. In the New Testament, the Greek word translated 'church' meant 'a called-out gathering'. The church is the people of God called out to know, love and serve the living God. The New Testament uses different pictures to describe it. Portrayed as 'the body of Christ', it is a growing organism with Christ as its head. Pictured as 'the bride of Christ', its members are vitally related to him. To them, Christ entrusts the sacred deposit of biblical revelation—hence the church is 'the pillar and bulwark of truth'.

Although the church has been summoned into existence by God himself, it is made up of ordinary human beings. As such they have their imperfections and limitations. Their perspectives and actions are coloured by the spirit of their generation.

Roots

The church traces its origins to the life, ministry and mission of its founder, Jesus Christ. Through his apostles, he was going to build an indestructible community. Those who confessed their faith in him as the promised Messiah, the 'Son of the living God', were to be the first 'living stones' of God's house. They, and successive generations of Christ's followers, were to be his witnesses. Central to their testimony was the death of Jesus for man's sins. His resurrection confirmed his uniqueness as the world's true Saviour. Men and women were summoned to repent of their sins, to trust him and serve him in the fellowship of his new community—the church.

After an initial period of preaching to Jews only, the early church took the commands of Jesus to witness 'to the ends of the earth' and 'to make disciples of all nations' very seriously. In spite of opposition, the early messengers of the faith, notably the apostle Paul, spread the gospel or good news of Jesus to a spiritually and socially needy world. Those who believed were baptized and incorporated into local churches. By the end of the third century the Christian faith had taken root throughout the Roman Empire.

The majority of believers were drawn initially from the lower classes. The good news of God's love to all people through Jesus Christ appealed to them. Churches as communities that transcended barriers of sex, race and social status welcomed converts in thousands. The political and intellectual elite treated

'Offer yourselves as a living sacrifice to God, dedicated to his service and pleasing to him. This is the true worship that you should offer. Do not conform yourselves to the standards of this world, but let God transform you inwardly by a complete change of your mind. Then you will be able to know the will of God—what is good and is pleasing to him and is perfect.'

Paul's words in his letter to the Romans, 12:1–2

'Whoever comes to me cannot be my disciple unless he loves me more than he loves his father and his mother, his wife and his children, his brothers and his sisters, and himself as well. Whoever does not carry his own cross and come after me cannot be my disciple.'

Jesus' words to those who wanted to follow him; Luke 14:26–27

Christianity with disdain. Sometimes when calamities occurred, Christians were the scapegoats; they experienced repression and persecution. But the martyrs' blood became the fertile seed-bed for the church to grow.

Turning-point

The crowning of Constantine as emperor in AD 313 marked a turning-point in church history. Not only did he profess conversion, he elevated Christianity almost to the position of a state religion. He saw in this faith a unifying force for his divided empire. He gave his patronage to the church's Council of Nicaea.

Constantine's recognition of the church proved a mixed blessing. Many were baptized and joined the church as membership became a stepping-stone for favourable positions in civil and military structures. By the early fifth century, no one could be a soldier unless he was a Christian!

Such questions of faith and practice had to be hammered out as the church grew. From its inception, the church's faith was subject to attack by pagan philosophers and to distortion by some of its adherents. The apologists of the second and third centuries argued for the rationality and validity of Christian revelation. Some—for instance, the Alexandrian school headed by apologists such as Clement and Origen—used Greek philosophical language to refute their critics. This led to unwarranted theological speculation. By contrast, Tertullian in the second century declared that there was no common ground between 'Athens and Jerusalem'. The biblical revelation was unique.

It was during periods of relative political calm that the church was forced to define its beliefs in precise theological terms. The nature of Christ as truly God and truly man was publicly debated. Prestigious councils such as those of Nicaea (325), Constantinople (381), Ephesus (431) and Chalcedon (451) formulated and affirmed the great creeds. In the Nicene Creed, Christians confess their belief in 'one, holy, catholic and apostolic church'. These four adjectives reflect the theological identity of the church. They also serve as criteria to evaluate the faithfulness and effectiveness of churches in fulfilling their role and status as God's people.

Unity

'The church is one, because it is the body of Christ—of that there can only be one.' But in what way is the church, with all its diversity of denominations and church traditions, one?

Some churchmen maintain that there should be no separate organizations, and that Christians should strive for visible unity. In the ecumenical climate of this century, the World Council of Churches was established in 1948 to foster dialogue amongst different churches and to advocate union either locally or nationally—and some progress has been made, especially in India and Pakistan.

Other Christians assert that the unity of the church envisaged by Jesus Christ and the apostles is a spiritual union. The unity of believers matches the union between the Father and the Son. Unity is produced by the Holy Spirit and is there amongst those who truly belong to Christ's body. Hence they are exhorted 'to maintain the unity of the Spirit in the bond of peace'.

As the church grew after the time of Constantine, unity was interpreted mainly in terms of adhering to a church tradition under one pope or patriarch. In the fourth and fifth centuries, theological battles were fought amongst the bishops of Rome, Constantinople and, to a lesser extent, Alexandria for primacy. Western Christianity as defined by the Church of Rome sought to impose its structure, liturgy and government on other traditions. Unity was basically maintained through the hierarchy of bishops and the clergy.

The Protestant reformers in the fifteenth and sixteenth centuries, with their rediscovery of personal faith and so the 'priesthood of all believers', opened the door for a greater freedom of liturgy and government. Following the theology of Augustine (354–430), they distinguished between the true church, to which believers of all times belong, and visible churches which have in their membership true and false followers of Christ. But in stressing spiritual unity, Protestant congregations opened the way for divisions based on minor doctrinal interpretations and personalities. Today Protestant Christianity is fragmented organizationally into many different churches, groups and movements, even though the divisions are transcended by the spiritual unity of a common life in Christ.

Holiness

The church is said to be 'holy' in the creed because holiness is the hallmark of God's people. No fewer than 100 passages in eighteen different New Testament writings describe Christians as 'saints': not stained-glass window figures, but those who are separated from sin and set apart for God. The Holy Spirit resides within them, and therefore their lifestyles and behaviour express likeness to a holy God.

Some Christians, particularly those from the second to the fifth centuries, equated sanctity with escape from the contamination of the world. Hundreds of Christians lived alone or in small groups, spending their time in meditation and solitude.

'Love is patient and kind; it is not jealous or conceited or proud; love is not ill-mannered or selfish or irritable; love does not keep a record of wrongs; love is not happy with evil, but is happy with the truth. Love never gives up; and its faith, hope, and patience never fail ... It is love, then, that you should strive for.'

Paul's first letter to the Corinthians, 13:4–7; 14:1

'You have made us for yourself, and our hearts are restless till they find their rest in you.'

Augustine

A monk from the ancient Ethiopian Orthodox Church.

Asceticism became a virtue. Even the celebrated Bible translator Jerome (345–420) denigrated marriage, exalted celibacy and lived as a recluse in Bethlehem.

Not all monks were recluses, however. Monastic communities combined service in their neighbourhood with the disciplined life of their particular orders. In medieval times, monks and priests from the orders were instrumental in establishing educational and medical centres.

Most Christians, however, have seen their concern for holiness as something to be lived out in the world, acting as 'salt' and 'light' within it, as Jesus himself expressed it. Personal piety motivated some to committed social action. A concern for holiness led social reformers such as William Wilberforce (1759–1833) and Anthony Ashley Cooper, seventh earl of Shaftesbury (1801–1885) to fight to abolish the slave-trade and overcome the appalling living conditions brought about by the Industrial Revolution.

A monk from Mt Athos in Greece upholds the centuries-old traditions of the Orthodox church.

A worldwide church

When Christians profess belief in the 'catholic' church, they subscribe to the universality or worldwide nature of the church. Membership in the church transcends racial, social and cultural backgrounds. Members are Christ's witnesses and ambassadors, urging men and women to be reconciled to God through Christ.

When churches faithfully discharge their evangelistic responsibilities in their neighbourhoods and beyond, they multiply and grow. The early churches, starting with the church at Antioch in Syria, were missionary congregations. Whether they sent small apostolic bands of messengers or encouraged their members to share their faith through their natural network of relationships, missionary activity was their constant concern.

The Celtic monastic communities established churches in the British Isles long before Augustine reached Canterbury in 597. In the seventh century, Boniface, the great English missionary-pioneer, won vast areas of Germany to the Christian faith. Christian merchants from Syria and Persia brought the Nestorian form of Christianity to China in the same century.

There is inevitably a creative tension when spiritually-minded church members embark on any missionary venture. These normally attract to their cause dedicated workers and generous lay supporters. Their vitality can create tension with church leaders who are preoccupied with the housekeeping problems of their ecclesiastical structures.

The missionary forces of the Roman Catholic Church were spearheaded by the monastic orders: the Franciscans (founded 1209), Dominicans (1216) and the Jesuits (1540). Hundreds of missionaries accompanied Portuguese and Spanish merchants and soldiers on their expeditions to colonize new lands for the Iberian kingdoms and the pope. Others went as far as India, Japan and China.

Towards the end of the eighteenth century, there was an upsurge of missionary activity on the part of

A packed church in Zaire.

Protestant churches. The Church Missionary Society, an important missionary arm of the Church of England, was founded in 1799, but its first pioneer workers were Germans. The Moravian Church in Germany had already sent out its own missionaries to Asia and Latin America. William Carey (1761–1834) and Henry Martyn (1781–1812) stirred the imagination of many when they translated the Bible into the main Indian languages. Their sacrificial labours challenged many to serve as missionaries.

The nineteenth century saw thousands of Protestant missionaries from Europe and North America proclaiming the gospel, establishing churches, schools and hospitals in Asia, Africa and Latin America.

Apostolicity

The Roman Catholic Church defines 'apostolicity' in terms of a continuing line of descent from the apostles to the modern-day church through the consecration of its bishops. In contrast, the Protestant reformers interpreted apostolicity in terms of *doctrinal* succession. Christ had entrusted certain revealed truths, embodied in the New Testament scriptures, to his apostles. The church is apostolic in nature in so far as its members continue in the apostles' doctrine and teaching.

The attempts to place ecclesiastical traditions or human reason on a par with or even above biblical revelation have caused deep divisions amongst Christians. The battle for the church to be apostolic in its doctrine is a constant one.

Resilience

At various periods of its history, the church has been threatened with extinction. The early church survived the onslaught of persecution in the first centuries. The Muslim invaders in the seventh and eighth centuries overthrew a vast church structure in North Africa and Turkey. Corruption and decay crept into the leadership of churches. Churches sometimes projected the image of an establishment that protected the interests of the rich and powerful.

But even in times of spiritual decline there has been revival and renewal. Eighteenth-century Britain experienced great spiritual awakenings through the preaching of the Wesleys and George Whitefield. New life flowed into the churches, but the Church of England was unprepared to cope with the masses of new converts. The Methodist Church emerged in order to incorporate many of them.

The church had to contend with the sharp attacks of humanistic philosophies in the nineteenth century; theological liberalism undermined biblical authority. From 1917 onwards vast areas of the world were

'When men cease to believe in God, they will not believe in nothing, they will believe in anything.'

G. K. Chesterton

overrun by communism. Its atheistic bias and all-demanding ideology forced Christians either to make a firm stand or to compromise. But the Christian communities in the Soviet Union, Eastern Europe and China continued to flourish in spite of restrictions and opposition.

Today, although there is decline in the West, there is church growth in many lands. In Africa in 1900 the Christian population was estimated at 9 million; today there are around 150 million Christians. African independent churches flourish, with distinctive forms of worship and witness.

In many parts of Latin America, the Christian church is growing more rapidly than the population. Some Pentecostal churches in Chile and Brazil have a membership of several thousand active members per congregation. In the USA, church membership remains at 70 per cent of the population and American missionaries constitute around 60 per cent of today's Protestant missionary task force.

In some parts of Asia, home of the world's great faiths, the church is also growing rapidly. The late '60s provided the stage for a remarkable popular movement in Indonesia. Just after the failure of the communist coup in 1965 and the subsequent vengeance of Muslims, there was a deep vacuum in the lives of many Indonesians. Then, as local Christians and missionaries shared their faith with Muslim community leaders, whole towns and villages embraced the Christian faith.

Membership of the church in South Korea is increasing at the rate of 10 per cent per year. Korean Christians give sacrificially to support missionaries working in other lands. Amongst the 30 million Chinese outside mainland China, there has also been a widespread turning to God. Students around the world have been exceptionally responsive to the gospel.

Traditionally, missionaries are classified as those who are from the West. Today there is a steady growth of a new missionary task force. Between 6,000 and 7,000 missionaries from Asia, Brazil and Africa are engaged in spreading the Christian faith and establishing or strengthening churches in lands other than their own. A new era of partnership is demonstrating the reality of people *from* all nations proclaiming the good news of Jesus Christ *to* all nations.

Christian Beliefs

Howard Marshall

The Christian faith is directly descended from the religion of the Jews. At the time of Jesus this had the following characteristics, as taught in the sacred book of the Jews, the Old Testament:

● Belief in the existence of one God, the Creator and Lord of the universe who is sovereign over all.

● Belief in the fact that man is made in the image of God, but has rebelled against his Creator and stands in danger of judgement.

● Belief that God, who is the righteous judge, is also gracious and merciful. He has provided a way for man to be set free from judgement by the penitent offering of sacrifices.

● Belief that God revealed himself to the nation of Israel and called them to be his people.

● Belief that God would some day establish his rule in a sinful world, setting his people free from their enemies, and appointing his chosen agent, the Messiah, to rule over them for ever.

● The practice of a moral life under the guidance of the Law given in the Old Testament; the maintenance of a religious ritual based on the temple and involving the offering of sacrifice.

The significance of Jesus

These beliefs were decisively affected by the coming of Jesus, his resurrection from the dead, and the gift of the Spirit of God received by his followers. There remained a basic similarity with the Jewish religion but there were some fundamental changes.

The most important of these changes was due to the Christian understanding of Jesus. From a very early date, the Christians began to realize that the Jewish hope of God's chosen agent coming to set up his rule had been fulfilled in Jesus. He was the Messiah whom the Jews awaited. It is the rejection of this by Jews that constitutes the decisive difference between them and Christians. For Christians the coming of Jesus means that God's future plan, announced in the Old Testament, has already begun to happen. God's rule is being established in a new way.

But the way in which it has happened is different from what the Jews had come to expect. They thought that God's rule would be achieved by the military overthrow of their enemies and would lead to their own establishment as the dominant nation. But Jesus attacked not the external enemies of the Jews but the sinfulness of their hearts. The rule of God advances by the conversion of individuals to a new way of life, and the way of violent revolution is firmly rejected.

The death of Jesus

God's action in Jesus was also seen as including sacrifice. The death of Jesus was understood as a means

An African Christian is baptized in the sea, in public declaration of his faith in Christ.

Baptism pictures a person's identification with Christ's death and resurrection. Some churches baptize only adult believers, others baptize children born into Christian families.

of cancelling sin, provided by God himself and displaying his love for sinners. Man's sinfulness must inevitably bring separation from God, or death. But Jesus died this death himself. A variety of pictures—drawn from the slave market, the law court, the temple, and personal relationships—are used to express the fundamental belief that the death of Jesus is the means of reconciling God and man and freeing man from the fear of judgement.

The effect of this understanding was to bring to an end the system of animal sacrifices. They were understood as pictures pointing forward to the spiritual sacrifice of Jesus and now made obsolete by the offering of the perfect sacrifice. Christian worship was no longer a matter of offerings in a temple. Rather it was the expression of gratitude to God for *his* provision of a sacrifice.

At the same time the coming of Jesus was seen as bringing to an end the ritual Law of the Jews which regulated the temple worship and a host of other matters. The ethical principles which lay behind the Law, seen especially in the Ten Commandments, were not abolished, but the detailed ritual and other observances were no longer needed.

In practice, the Jews had come to regard the observance of the Law in minute detail as the means of gaining and maintaining a good relationship with God and obtaining his favour. It was Paul who insisted that God's favour could not be gained by keeping the Law: all have sinned and come short of God's glory. So man's

proper relationship with God can only be that of faith, the grateful and obedient trust which comes to God on the basis of what *he* has done, in contrast to the approach of works which insists that *man* must do something to merit God's favour.

Though Christian worship abandoned the temple, it was deeply influenced by the synagogue, the Jewish meeting-house in which the teaching of the Law was central. But the rejection of the Law as the means of salvation led to a shift in the understanding of the Old Testament. Interest turned more to its prophetic character as a book which looked forward to the coming of Jesus, and it was studied more and more for what it taught about him. At the same time, other writings were increasingly placed alongside it as equally inspired and authoritative scriptures. The writings of the infant church, the letters written by its leaders and the accounts of the ministry of Jesus that we know as the Gospels, were seen as a corpus of scriptures alongside the Old Testament. The whole collection became the Bible of the Christian church.

The recognition that observance of the Jewish Law was no longer binding on Christians together with the simple fact that almost from the beginning non-Jews, the Gentiles, were attracted by the message, led quickly to the development of a community composed of both Jews and non-Jews. Despite initial uncertainties it was recognized that non-Jews did not need to adopt the practices of the Jewish Law, especially circumcision and the observance of Jewish holy days, in order to become Christians. Christianity, which might have remained a Jewish sect, was thus poised to become a world faith, open to all mankind on the basis of belief in Jesus.

The characteristic rites of the new faith, which roughly parallel the Jewish rite of circumcision and the festival of the Passover (which celebrated the deliverance of the people of Israel from slavery in Egypt), were baptism and the Lord's Supper. Baptism was a ritual washing with water which signified cleansing from sin, the reception of God's Spirit, and the dedication of the candidate to God and his entry into the new people of God. The Lord's Supper, or Eucharist ('thanksgiving'), was a token meal of bread and wine—elements used by Jesus at his Last Supper before his death to point to his self-sacrifice and the shedding of his blood to open up a new covenant or agreement between God and his people.

The resurrection of Jesus

Alongside the death of Jesus, his resurrection was the crucial event for the beliefs of Christianity. Christians saw it as God's vindication of Jesus after he had been rejected by the Jewish leaders and put to death. It was the confirmation of his claims to be God's agent, and above all it demonstrated that he was triumphant over the power of sin and death. The resurrection was seen as the decisive stage in the ascent of Jesus to share the throne of God in heaven (to use the picture-language of the New Testament). This belief had several important consequences.

First, it confirmed the Christian belief that God would act again in history through the return of Jesus at the end of the world. The exaltation of Jesus meant that he was the agent appointed by God to carry out final judgement and to bring in God's eternal reign in peace and justice.

● Second, it led to the conviction that Jesus was to be seen as divine. Already in his lifetime he had displayed a unique consciousness that he was God's Son and that God was his Father. After the resurrection, Christians recognized increasingly that all the functions of God were exercised through Jesus and that he shared in the rule of God. He was to be regarded as the Son of God, who had 'come down' into the world in human form and then 'ascended' to be with God. The consequences of this belief were shattering. Jews and others who believed that there was one God could not accept the Christian claim. Christians for their part had to revise their ideas about God and recognize that, though God is one, alongside the Father there was also the Son; they were each divine in nature, yet in such a way that the Son could be regarded as dependent on the Father. The earthly Jesus was the Son of God made flesh, 'incarnate', become a human being.

● Third, now that Jesus has been exalted to heaven he remains active and living in the same way as the Father is the living God. Sharing the status of the Father, Jesus is now the Lord, so that the relation of the Christian to him is not simply one of belief and trust but also of obedience and commitment. To be a Christian is to make the confession 'Jesus Christ is Lord', a confession that he is both my Lord whom I obey and also the one to whom the whole universe

Radical Christian groups in Russia meet together in homes or out of doors.

'I believe in God the Father Almighty, Maker of heaven and earth: And in Jesus Christ his only Son our Lord, Who was conceived by the Holy Ghost, Born of the Virgin Mary, Suffered under Pontius Pilate, Was crucified, dead, and buried, He descended into hell; The third day he rose again from the dead, He ascended into heaven, And sitteth on the right hand of God the Father Almighty; From thence he shall come to judge the quick and the dead. I believe in the Holy Ghost; The holy Catholic Church; The Communion of Saints; The Forgiveness of Sins; The Resurrection of the body, And the life everlasting.'

The Apostles' creed, from *The Book of Common Prayer*

will one day bow the knee.

Such faith and obedience is part of a spiritual relationship between the Christian and Jesus. The Christian can be said to be united with Jesus, a whole variety of metaphors from the language of personal relationships being used to express the reality of this link. The new life which the Christian begins when he believes in Jesus is the reproduction of the life of Jesus in him. He dies to his old way of life and rises again to a new God-centred and divinely-inspired life, in the same way as Jesus died and rose again by the power of God. The Christian community is a vast organism or body through which the spiritual life of Christ flows.

The gift of the Holy Spirit and the birth of the church

After the resurrection came the third decisive event which determined the character of Christianity. The Jews already believed in the communication of God's power and guidance to particular individuals, especially the prophets, by the activity of the divine Spirit. The birthday of the church is reckoned from the day of Pentecost when all the believers in Jesus became conscious of the gift of the Spirit given to each one personally. So universal is the gift that a Christian can be defined as a person who has received the gift of the Spirit. The initial experience can be spoken of as a second, spiritual birth, bringing the new life of Jesus to the believer. The Spirit works in the Christian community by giving different abilities to different individuals to enable them to lead and help the church as a whole. He also acts in the life of each Christian to foster the qualities of love and freedom from sin which were seen in Jesus himself.

Thus the Spirit can be seen as the personal agent of God in the lives of individuals and the Christian community. This meant a further development in the understanding of God. The Spirit was recognized as being divine in the same way as the Father and the Son, so that the Christian concept of God had to recognize a fundamental 'three-ness'

or 'Trinity' in the nature of God as one being who exists in three persons. Thus the understanding of God as Trinity, which in this form is peculiar to Christianity and sharply differentiates it from other religions in the same Judaic tradition (Judaism and Islam), sums up the distinctive and vital elements in Christian faith.

Christian belief takes the holiness and judgement of a righteous God seriously. This is seen in the character of the Christian message which includes the warning that all people are sinners who have rebelled against God and therefore face judgement. It is only against this background that the Christian message makes sense as 'gospel', as good news that the same God is merciful and longs for the salvation of all mankind; he has provided the way of forgiveness and life in Jesus. Thus the gospel faces mankind with the alternatives of judgement or life.

Variety and error

The Christian message has naturally been subject to fresh thinking and reformulation down the ages as theologians have tried to express the biblical teaching in ways that are philosophically acceptable and logically coherent. It is not surprising that there have been differences in understanding in different times and places, and that some expressions of Christianity have veered away from the biblical witness.

Thus the doctrines of the Trinity and the incarnation have caused particular difficulty. Since the nature of God, who is infinite, lies beyond the scope of our finite understanding, attempts to explain his nature can lead to dangerous misunderstandings and one-sided statements. This has led to a variety of attempts to simplify the doctrine of God, by restricting full divinity to the Father or by regarding the three persons simply as three different aspects of one God. Theologians have found it hard to believe that Jesus is the eternal Son of God, and some have regarded him as a separate, subordinate being. The tendency in modern times has been to deny that God could truly be

united with man in one person, and to say that Jesus was a good man who possessed the divine Spirit to an unusual degree, or that true humanity is the same thing as divinity. Another tendency has been to regard the Spirit as less than a full person.

The Christian understanding of the work of Jesus has also been the cause of difficulty. Some Christians have denied that any sort of action is necessary to enable God to forgive sins and have seen in the death of Jesus nothing more than a demonstration of supreme love. Others have carried the idea of sacrifice over into Christian worship and seen the Lord's Supper as some kind of repetition of Christ's sacrifice on the cross.

At times there have been tendencies to legalism; the need for doing good works in order to merit salvation has been taught. The church has on occasions claimed an authority almost equal to that of God, and developed a hierarchy or set of graded authorities surrounded by pomp and prestige. At other times the doctrine of God as judge has been watered down and replaced by a belief that God will ultimately save all men, no matter how they behaved in this life.

While, therefore, the main thrust of Christian teaching, especially as expressed in the New Testament, is clear, the existence of the various denominations, and of different groups within them, demonstrates that there has been considerable variety and even error in the expression of the faith. Christians need to be prepared continually to go back to the Bible and to test their beliefs and their practice by its teaching. Jesus himself—the Christ of the Bible and of experience—is after all far greater than any human formulation of dogma or teaching about him.

By sharing bread and wine, Christians commemorate and celebrate the death and resurrection of Jesus.

Branches of the Church

Michael Sadgrove

Two historic movements were the primary cause of the various branches of Christianity which exist today. The first was the so-called 'Great Schism' between East and West, usually dated at 1054, although the debate between Greek and Latin Christianity had begun centuries before this. The second was the sixteenth-century disruption generally known as the Reformation whose legacy was Protestantism.

The Eastern Orthodox churches The separation of the Eastern churches from Western Christendom was largely a rejection of the claim of the bishop of Rome to supreme authority. There was also disagreement over the clause added to the Nicene Creed by the Western church in which the Spirit is said to proceed from the Son as well as from the Father, a doctrine rejected by the Orthodox to this day. The best-known members of the Orthodox communion are the Greek and Russian churches, but there are several others, belonging mainly to Eastern Europe and the eastern Mediterranean (reflecting to some extent the Byzantine Empire in which the cultural roots of Orthodoxy belong). Authority in the church belongs not to any individual, but to the Ecumenical Council, whose function is to interpret the 'holy tradition', and administer discipline. Each national church has its own Patriarch; the Patriarch of Constantinople is 'first among equals'.

The Roman Catholic Church The largest single Christian grouping, Roman Catholics, are those who acknowledge the primacy and authority of the pope, the bishop of Rome. As Christ's repre-sentative on earth (the 'Vicar of Christ'), the pope stands at the head of a hierarchy of bishops and priests, amongst whom the cardinals have the responsibility of electing the pope. When said to

be speaking with full authority (*ex cathedra*) and defining matters of faith or morals, the pope's utterances are regarded as infallible and binding upon all Catholics, although the Second Vatican Council of 1962–65 resulted in greater attention being paid to the authority of the bishops corporately, as an episcopal college. At the centre of Roman Catholicism is the Mass (the communion service), along with six other sacraments: baptism, confirmation, penance (or reconciliation), ordination, marriage and the anointing of the sick ('extreme unction').

The Anglican Church The Anglican 'communion' is a worldwide family of churches in fellowship with the Archbishop of Canterbury, whose status amongst the heads of other Anglican churches is 'first among equals'. The parent Church of England itself is seen by many Anglicans as having roots in Celtic Christianity which flourished in Britain long before Augustine of Canterbury brought Christianity from Rome. Despite the break with Rome at the Reformation, Anglicanism retained a Catholic type of ministry and a liturgy heavily indebted to her Catholic past, but rejecting the doctrines of the papacy and the Mass as sacrifice, together with the concept of priesthood which this implied.

The Lutheran Church, embodying the teaching of the German reformer Martin Luther, represents the chief Protestant presence in Germany and Scandinavia, whence it has found adherents across the world. Only in

some countries did the Lutherans retain bishops. The normal form of government is by an assembly (synod) presided over by a general superintendent. Like Anglicanism, Lutheranism adopted a largely conservative attitude towards liturgy, although the preaching of the sermon has always been central.

The Presbyterian churches, in contrast to Lutheranism, followed the principles of John Calvin as exemplified in Geneva at the time of the Reformation, but like the Lutherans stressed the authority of the Bible as greater than that of the church. Church government is in the hands of presbyteries and synods, or courts of ministers and lay elders belonging to a particular region. Like other Reformed churches, Presbyterians have a simple approach to worship, in which the reading and preaching of Scripture, extempore prayers and the singing of psalms and hymns are basic.

Congregationalism stresses the independ-ence of the local church. Independency was largely the result of separatists within English Puritanism making their stand against any involvement with the national church. In common with other 'free churches' such as Baptists and Brethren, they stress the fact that membership is made up of believers, not society at large. The United Reformed Church is a merger of Congregation-alists and Presbyterians.

The Baptist churches, now to be found across the world, reject the baptism of infants,

The Main Streams of Christianity

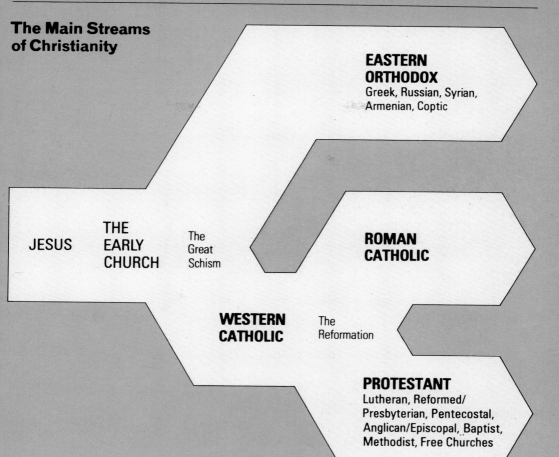

EASTERN ORTHODOX
Greek, Russian, Syrian, Armenian, Coptic

JESUS **THE EARLY CHURCH** The Great Schism

ROMAN CATHOLIC

WESTERN CATHOLIC The Reformation

PROTESTANT
Lutheran, Reformed/ Presbyterian, Pentecostal, Anglican/Episcopal, Baptist, Methodist, Free Churches

claiming that baptism was given as a sign of an adult's declaration of faith. Baptist churches are essentially independent. Like the other Reformed churches they stress the importance of Scripture.

The Methodist churches owe their origin to the revitalizing movements ('evangelical revivals') of the eighteenth century, and to the evangelistic activity of John Wesley. Although Wesley himself remained an Anglican, Methodist converts were not absorbed into the established church. Churches (or 'societies') are organized into circuits and districts. Government is by a conference of ministers and representatives of church members. The styles of worship include both the highly sacramental and less formal.

Pentecostal churches emphasize the role of the Holy Spirit. The churches are fast-growing, particularly in South America. Services are often characterized by speaking in tongues and prophecy.

The Salvation Army was started in the nineteenth century to bring the gospel and social action to the poor, especially in inner-city areas. Members reject the sacraments.

The Quakers, or Society of Friends, meet for mainly silent worship and inner guidance, and also stress social action. They reject the sacraments and definitions of the faith.

Christian Brethren are independent groups without hierarchy stressing the different ministries of every member, especially in the distinctive communion service; they also stress the primacy of the Bible, and are active in missionary work.

The World Council of Churches was constituted in 1948 as a fellowship of churches united in their loyalty to Jesus Christ 'as God and Saviour'. All the major denominations described above are member churches, with the exception of the Roman Catholic Church, the Christian Brethren and most Pentecostals. The Council exists not so much to sponsor unity schemes as to enable the churches to debate matters of common concern, and where possible, to speak and act as one. It has been particularly active in the fields of social involvement and education, and in taking up the cause of oppressed peoples in Third World countries. Assemblies of the Council meet every seven years.

In remote Australian communities the local church serves the needs of the people, as in this country town in Tasmania.

The 'church' is strictly not a building but a gathering of people. But the word is also used of the places where Christians gather for worship, prayer and learning.

The Claim to be Unique

Christopher Lamb

The Christian claim is that Christ is unique: Christianity is not. Christianity can be classified under all the normal headings of a study of human society and religion. It has a long and complex history, leading exponents, a massive literature, distinctive rituals and characteristic social forms. All these can be paralleled by the communities of other world faiths, especially Judaism and Islam, and scholars have compared the 'truth-claims'—for example, the finality of the Qur'an—which are made in the different religious traditions.

This study of comparative religion has alarmed some Christians because in it the features of different religions have been placed side by side and their essential similarity examined. When this process moves from the externals to the inner core of religious faith, Christians often feel their faith is being 'relativized', reduced to the common level of human experience.

Christianity and religion

I believe Christians need fear this kind of study as little as a loving married couple fear the sociologist who tells them they belong to the same sub-group of society and have been culturally conditioned in the same way, and that is why they are happy. They know there is more to it than that! And Christians know that they belong to the human race and that God's creative power has made them one with all other human beings in the way that their minds and bodies and their social natures work. Therefore it is foolish to resist the idea that, as historians and sociologists look at it, Christianity is one more of the religions of the world. But history and sociology is not the whole story, though it may be told as if it is.

For many who live in the North Atlantic region, however, Christianity is still identified with the culture which has dominated world history in recent centuries by its technological and industrial skills. As this region enters a period of relative decline, Christianity, associated with the past, is thought to be in decline too. So the general impression left by comparative religion seems to be confirmed by observation of present trends. Christianity is relative to other religions, and relative to the success and prosperity of the culture which has adopted it.

Strictly speaking this is undeniable, but it states only part of the truth. The fact is that Christians began as a socially deprived and frequently persecuted group, and for much of their history European Christians belonged to a culture which was backward in comparison with the Muslim community. Moreover, Christianity may be in institutional decline in Europe, but it is certainly not so in Africa, Latin America or east Asia. The resilience

'Give glory to your Son, so that the Son may give glory to you. For you gave him authority over all mankind, so that he might give eternal life to all those you gave him. And eternal life means knowing you, the only true God, and knowing Jesus Christ, whom you sent. I have shown your glory on earth; I have finished the work you gave me to do. Father, give me glory in your presence now, the same glory I had with you before the world was made.'

Jesus' prayer, John 17: 1–5

of Christianity under the harsh conditions of the Soviet Union and Maoist China is also highly significant.

When the student of religion searches for explanations of the past and present vitality of the Christian faith he cannot find the secret in any one culture or any particular stage of economic and cultural development, for that vitality has existed in every kind of human situation. What has always sustained Christians has been the conviction that they have a personal relationship with a unique Saviour who is both God and man.

Christianity and culture

Today Christians in the West have to come to terms with more than the *studies* of religion which have gone on for more than a century in European and American universities. They must adjust to the living presence of people of other faiths as fellow-citizens. Islam is now the second most numerous faith-community in Western Europe, far outstripping Judaism. Western countries have substantial populations of all the principal world faiths, as well as adherents of the cults and new religious movements. Since many of these new citizens are from Asian backgrounds, they encounter prejudice and discrimination because of their skin-colour and way of life. Christians and others have attempted to fight these evils by affirming the value of Asian cultures, and resisting the view that the Western way of life is intrinsically better than any other. Many now accept that only a minimum of adjustment should be required from the newcomers to Western society, and that justice and common sense both point to the basic equality of all cultures.

It is clear that religion and culture are inextricably entwined, and many will go on to assert that the basic equality of all cultures means the radical equality of all religions. Even some who are serious about their own Christian identity will say, 'We have our way to God and they have theirs. Ours is true/works for us, and theirs is true/works for them.' Such attitudes strike most of our Western contemporaries as tolerant, balanced and true to the complex social situations of our time. Often one senses an underlying feeling of guilt about the imperialist exploitation of the past, and the devaluation of Asian cultures which went with it. A new tolerance of faiths is often reckoned to be part of the reparation due to the East from the West.

It is important to notice that Christians with much longer experience of life in multi-faith societies do not often share these attitudes. Christians in the Middle East have maintained their discipleship for centuries without admitting any such fundamental identity between Islam and Christianity. If they had adopted such an idea they would have had no reason to reject Islam for themselves, but they preferred to accept an inferior position in society and occasional persecution rather than put the two faiths on the same level.

A bishop from Sri Lanka noted in 1979 that British Christians were unwilling 'to make critical evaluation of the experience and truth-claims' of other religions, and warned them that this stemmed in part from 'the general loss of self-confidence among many people in the Western world in a post-imperial era. Bishop Wickremesinghe went on to describe how people of different faiths—Buddhist, Hindu, Muslim and Christian—lived and worked together in the same national culture of Sri Lanka, trying to establish justice, peace and prosperity, yet never losing sight of the fact that their respective understandings of the truth were in the end irreconcilable. He talked of what will surely be the experience of many Western nations in the future, how other religions 'are always present before us as alternative explanations of the mysteries of life and death, and especially of suffering. In our region comparative religion is not confined to university faculties or small groups with an interest in this subject. It is a facet of our normal experience and within which we have to make concrete options in the traumatic situations we face as we go through life.'

Christianity and other faiths

Western Christians do not have the same opportunities as Sri Lankans. Nevertheless there are many opportunities to meet people of other faiths, and to study their beliefs at firsthand. It is vital that Christians do not come to easy conclusions about other faiths without some such study of them. Because the claims of the different religions conflict, it is extremely tempting to compare the best of your own faith with the worst of another. Sometimes those who insist that there are positive features in other faiths are thought to be disloyal to their own. There is no doubt that Christian history is full of 'religious tribalism'. Because people were unwilling to believe anything good about other faiths all sorts of inaccuracies and distortions became accepted as fact. Europeans still suffer from the caricature of Islam popularized in the Middle Ages, and Jews have been grossly and consistently libelled by Christians, even by respected church leaders and theologians. This has been one of the principal causes of the centuries-old persecution of the Jews.

Of course Christians have not been alone in misrepresenting other faiths. Muslims have made their own misrepresentations of Christianity, but with the growth of modern communications this 'bearing of false witness' is both unnecessary and dangerous. It mattered less what a Hindu believed about a Christian or a Buddhist about a Jew if they were never likely to meet. But today they will and do. God is not honoured by lies, and the Christian faith is not defended by defaming other faiths. Such defamation is in any case likely to be self-defeating, since uncommitted people who take the trouble to investigate what lies behind the propaganda will feel that it is Christianity which is exposed as false.

But a Christian may happily set aside self-serving descriptions of other faiths and still feel that his study of other faiths must come to a stop somewhere. Even the specialist in his technical vocation of study

In many parts of the world, Christians have seen the need to be involved in education as part of their total contribution to the community.

cannot adequately examine all the possible alternatives to the Christian faith. No religion can be properly understood without a real knowledge of its scriptures in their original language. Is he then to attempt the mastery of Hebrew, Arabic, Sanskrit and Pali, as well as New Testament Greek? It is a lifetime's work to plumb the depths of even one other faith. It is true that there are many scholars to help us, and Christians have actually made much deeper studies of other faiths than, for the most part, scholars of other faiths have made of Christianity. But can a Christian say nothing about his faith and other faiths with confidence unless he can make a claim to be some kind of expert?

To put the same question more sharply: can we be sure that in making Christ central to our lives rather than one of his rivals we are not making a great mistake? Or is that very form of the question evidence of our theological vulgarity, and the Christian faith is really only *our* path to God, neither better nor worse than many others?

This second position is very widely held, but it is well to be clear what is involved in it. If the Christian path is only one of many, and perhaps not even the best, then it is arrogant to suppose that others may benefit from my religious experience, when that experience is so limited and partial. Evangelism then becomes impossible, and mission must be limited to service, for proclamation would be 'theological imperialism'. The church then is to be limited to biological growth alone. Moreover, *all* the missionary activity of the past must be called in question, including the missionary activity which created the churches of Europe and the ancient churches of the Middle East. In short, the very basis of the church is destroyed, for our existence as Christians is little more than a historical accident and rests on an illusion—the illusion that there was a message to take to the ends of the earth.

If this is the consequence of the conventional view, how can we be

The Christian world (approximate present-day distribution)

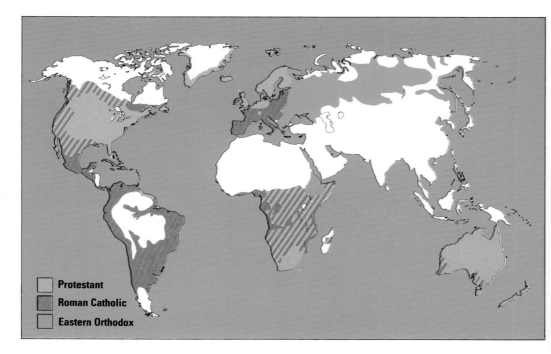

Protestant

Roman Catholic

Eastern Orthodox

sure it is mistaken? The whole question hinges of course on the person of Jesus Christ. For the Christians of the New Testament Jesus Christ is uniquely definitive of the authority and love of God. Jesus himself claimed to be 'the way, and the truth, and the life; no one comes to the Father, but by me'. And shortly after his death and rising again, the first disciples were saying to the Jewish leadership about Jesus: 'There is salvation in no one else, for there is no other name under heaven given among men by which we must be saved.' And the missionary Paul was later to write to a church in Asia Minor that 'He is the image of the invisible God ... he exists before

everything, and all things are held together in him.' Jesus is the true centre of human history and the person in whom God has revealed himself with complete authority.

Such is the consistent witness of the New Testament, but how can such a claim be proved? The evidence of the life and death and resurrection of Jesus, and the testimony of his followers over centuries can be set out for inquirers, and evangelists and writers are constantly doing it. But if it were possible to *prove* that Jesus was finally authoritative for men, appointed by God, it could only be done by citing another authority more final than Jesus himself, and the proof would collapse. The most

Young Christians from East Malaysia lead the singing in their open-air church.

Christian doctors in Korea pray together for God's help before an operation.

'Before the world was created, the Word already existed; he was with God, and he was the same as God. From the very beginning the Word was with God. Through him God made all things; not one thing in all creation was made without him. The Word was the source of life, and this life brought life to mankind. The light shines in the darkness, and the darkness has never put it out.'

The opening words of John's Gospel, speaking of Jesus

elegant logic and compelling arguments in favour of Jesus are no more than requests to listen to him and look at him. His life and teaching are self-authenticating—they are their own authority, because only in this way can they be ultimately binding on us.

The uniqueness of Christ

This means that when a Christian sets out to consider the nature of other religious traditions, he does so on the basis of God's self-revelation in Jesus Christ. Jesus is the perfect expression of God's nature in human terms, and in Jesus God has reversed his previous judgement of condemnation on the human race. The Christian finds both his identity and his total security in belonging to God through Jesus, and the community of Jesus. His personal shortcomings and inadequacies, though still a source of pain and grief to him, are not allowed to rob him of his sense of being favoured by God, and he knows the privilege of being used by

God in his plan for the whole of mankind. He prays continually for the special quality of joyous affection which marked the life of Jesus and hopes to pass after this life into his presence.

He looks for echoes and reflections of the Spirit of Jesus everywhere, including the communities of other faiths, and is delighted when he finds them, not trying to belittle them but being glad that 'God has not left himself without witnesses', as the apostle Paul put it when speaking to a pagan audience. For acknowledging the supreme authority of Jesus means a committed mind but not a closed mind. Commitment to Jesus is commitment to a total availability to every human being. Jesus' openness to every kind of person was notorious to his religious critics, who were frequently scandalized by the company he kept. His parables reflected the basic human goodness to be found in the Samaritan, theologically at odds with Judaism. He said about a pagan soldier who took him at his word, 'I tell you this: nowhere, even in Israel, have I found such faith.' Christians need not fear that commitment to Jesus means that they will not be open to others, for his own example precludes that.

At the same time a Christian cannot be loyal to Jesus and also consider the possibility of other fundamental loyalties for himself. He cannot remain a Christian and have an open mind about the final authority of Jesus. If he does it means that he really takes his own judgement as the final authority, usually on some philosophical principle. Of course I have to be responsible in the end for all my judgements, but that is not the same as saying that I am capable of pronouncing my judgement on Jesus. Once I have found where the final word of God is expressed, I can only submit to it. I cannot sit in religious or philosophical judgement on it. I can only respond with my whole being, which is why love, the expression of the whole person, is at the root of Christianity. And human beings are only able to respond in love to God because of the love he has shown them in Christ.

Religion under judgement

Jesus continually sought this whole-hearted response to God, for which another word is 'faith'. 'When the Son of Man comes, will he find faith on earth?' he asked. His complaint against the religion of his day was that it was not whole-hearted but hypocritical. At times it was even manipulative and cynical. Here Jesus passes judgement not just on the religion of his own day but on all established religion, including Christianity in its historic and contemporary forms. Jesus' harshest words are reserved for the Pharisees and the scribes, the religious and theological leaders of Judaism—not because he wanted to destroy the Jewish faith (other rabbis made similar attacks) but because the very best of human religion is inwardly corrupt. Human frustration and evil are not brought about by external things, and cannot be dealt with just by external means: for it is 'out of the heart', said Jesus, that come 'evil thoughts, murder, adultery, fornication, theft, false witness, slander. These are what defile a man; but to eat with unwashed hands does not defile a man.' Religious prescriptions do not reach the heart of the matter, so at the heart of Christianity lies the knowledge that religion is not free from the desperate wickedness of man, for Jesus was condemned and crucified by the *religious* authorities, acting in concert with pagan politicians.

Beyond religion

Christianity in all its historic forms is not unique. It shares in the sinful character of all human activity, and is most at risk when it tries to deny that character. But it carries the message of the uniqueness of Jesus Christ, of his final authority for men and women, and his final solution to the helplessness of a world fit only for the scrap-heap. For Jesus came, not with a new 'religion', a new code or a new philosophy, but to meet human bankruptcy and rottenness with its pain and separation from God and to absorb it into himself by his total obedience to God—to the point of an agonizing and humiliating death. He came also to initiate a new order, a completely new start for the human race, a new creation which began with his own resurrection from death. Men and women are invited to abandon their own futile attempts to reach and please God and simply to put their trust in Jesus, who alone truly knows him. They are invited to become part of the community of those who live by that faith and share the life of Jesus while they wait for the new age in which all will acknowledge him.

So Christians say 'yes' to Christianity as the vehicle of Jesus, but 'no' to it when it betrays that message, as it often has. Christians say both 'yes' and 'no' to other faiths too. Yes, when insights from them fill out and underline and tell in a new vocabulary the glory of God as Jesus has shown him to be. But no, when as so often in human thought and action, the image of God in man is defaced because man has turned his face away from God to bow down to ideas and idols of his own invention, or when the glory of God in Jesus is set aside and controverted. If Christianity is unique, it is only because Christ is. If it ceases to witness to him, it ceases to have any value for the human race.

'Whoever believes in the Son of God has this testimony in his own heart; but whoever does not believe God, has made him out to be a liar, because he has not believed what God has said about his Son. The Testimony is this: God has given us eternal life, and this life has its source in his Son. Whoever has the Son has this life; whoever does not have the Son of God does not have life.'

John's first letter, 5:10–12

'Come to me, all of you who are tired from carrying heavy loads, and I will give you rest. Take my yoke and put it on you, and learn from me, because I am gentle and humble in spirit; and you will find rest.'

Matthew 11:28–29

The Bible

Richard France

The word 'Bible' comes from the Greek *Biblia* meaning simply 'The Books'. The plural is significant: the Bible is a collection of books written over a period of more than 1,000 years, in widely-differing cultural and historical situations, and in a rich variety of styles and language.

Yet this collection has come to be regarded by Christians as a single unit, 'The Bible', as its books have been recognized as standing apart from other books.

The Old Testament

There are two unequal parts to the Bible. The first and by far the larger, called by Christians 'the Old Testament', is simply the Hebrew (and Aramaic) scriptures of Judaism. They present the history and religious thought of the people of God up to the time when Jesus came as the Jews' Messiah.

Christians have always regarded themselves as the legitimate heirs to the religion of ancient Israel, and so accept the books of the Hebrew Bible as fully 'canonical', or part of Scripture. Without them, the specifically Christian scriptures could hardly be understood.

A number of later Jewish works (in Greek) are included in Roman Catholic editions of the Old Testament, sometimes distinguished as 'deutero-canonical', of lesser importance than the Hebrew scriptures. Protestant Bibles do not include these works, which Judaism did not accept as canonical, in the Old Testament; but they are sometimes printed after the Old Testament as a separate section, known as 'The Apocrypha'. Protestant Christians may read them for their interest and profit but do not accept them as Scripture.

The New Testament

The specifically Christian books of the Bible, known as 'the New Testament', comprise twenty-seven writings by Christians of the first century AD, mostly quite short. While most of the writers were of Jewish origin, the books are in Greek which was the common language of the Roman Empire.

They consist firstly of four 'Gospels' setting out from different points of view the life and teaching of Jesus together with the 'Acts of the Apostles' which is a continuation of the Gospel of Luke to tell the story of the first thirty years of the Christian church. There are then thirteen letters by Paul, the great missionary leader, to churches and individuals; eight other letters by early Christian leaders; and the 'Revelation of John' a visionary work cast in the mould of Jewish apocalyptic literature.

The New Testament writings, while produced within a relatively short period compared with the many centuries of the writing of the Old Testament, are mixed in style and content; even the literary quality of

Beautiful stained glass has been used as a 'visual aid', teaching the stories of the Bible to those who cannot read.

The Festivals of Christianity

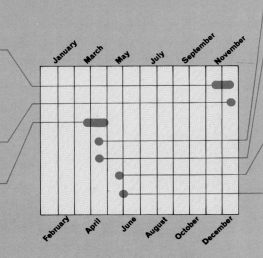

ADVENT
The Christian year begins with a period of preparation for Christmas. It is also the time when Christians particularly look forward to Jesus' second coming.

CHRISTMAS
The joyful celebration of Jesus' birth.

LENT
A forty-day period of preparation for Easter. It corresponds to the 40 days Jesus spent fasting in the wilderness before beginning his public ministry.

GOOD FRIDAY
The solemn memorial of Jesus' death by crucifixion.

EASTER
The greatest Christian festival, celebrating the resurrection of Jesus. The date of Easter (and therefore of Lent, Good Friday, Ascension and Pentecost) changes each year.

ASCENSION DAY
The celebration of Jesus' ascension to heaven 40 days after Easter.

PENTECOST/ WHITSUN
The celebration of the day when God sent his Holy Spirit to the apostles, 10 days after Jesus' ascension. This marks the birth of the church.

the Greek varies widely. The different interests and personalities of the writers are clear on even a quite superficial reading.

The inspiration of the Bible

Yet Christians have regarded these varied writings of both the Old and New Testaments as a unity, often called the 'Word of God'.

They have spoken of the Bible as 'inspired', meaning by this not merely that it is great literature or that it brings spiritual enlightenment, but that it comes from God.

It is not that its authors were merely passive channels for a divine revelation independent of their own thoughts; the stamp of the writers' personalities on their books is clear. But the classic Christian belief is that what they wrote in their own language, and in their own historical setting, was directed by God so that

Christians read in the Bible of the life and teaching of Jesus, and the principles by which people should live.

the result was no less his word than theirs.

So while the biblical books must be interpreted with proper attention to their background and literary form, what they declare is, Christians believe, God's word to men.

This is why the Bible, for all its variety, is treated by Christians as a unity, progressively revealing not only God's acts, but his mind and will.

The authority of the Bible

In theory, therefore, all Christians accept the Bible as authoritative, both in guiding their actions and in forming their beliefs.

In practice, however, Christians have differed on this. The Protestant Reformation aimed to restore the Bible to a place of authority above the pronouncements of the leaders of the church and the traditions which had grown up. Within Protestant Christianity, the Enlightenment of the eighteenth century led to a new confidence in human reason as the ultimate guide to truth, and the Bible was treated only as a record of human religious development, not as a divine revelation.

Today, while evangelical Christianity accepts the Bible as its supreme authority, more liberal Protestantism increasingly questions its importance. In Roman Catholicism since the Second Vatican Council there has been a remarkable resurgence of interest in the Bible.

Any recognizably Christian faith must be based on the Bible. That is why Bible translation is a major concern of the Christian churches. Teams of translators are at work all over the world, making the Bible available in the mother tongues of even quite small ethnic groups. Today the whole Bible is available in some 250 languages, and the New Testament in 450 more, while translation is in progress in a further 850.

These Peruvian Indians are leaders of their local churches. They are also involved in translating the Bible into their own language.

Christian Worship

Colin Buchanan

All institutions live by their rituals, and religious institutions are no exception. The Old Testament is, from one standpoint, the history of the religious life—including the 'cultic', or worshipping, life—of the people of God. Its pages record the beginnings of Christian worship.

It is recorded in the book of Acts that the infant church began a rhythm of church life which in outline is what would be called 'worship' today. (Indeed, a modern pattern for a Communion service might well have the same elements.) The believers gathered for the apostles' teaching, for prayer, fellowship and the 'breaking of bread'.

The Lord's Supper, Communion or Eucharist, was the distinctive event of Christian worship. Jesus himself commanded it and there is reason to think that the church observed it as a weekly (sometimes a daily) event from

the outset. Originally, the commemoration of Jesus, especially his death and resurrection which the 'sacramental' bread and wine signified, was held within the context of a larger meal, called an *agape* or love-feast. But for various reasons this context fell away in the first 150 years after the resurrection, and a ritual meal of solely bread and wine remained.

The New Testament also describes what has been called the Christian 'initiation rite', baptism. This was certainly a means for the new convert to enter the life of the church. But in sharp distinction to contemporary mystery religions, it was open and simple. Baptism was a public 'washing', identifying the believer and his household with the death and rising again of Jesus. Today the churches which are 'Baptist' in conviction hold that this should take place on confession of personal faith. Others baptize children who are 'confirmed' in their faith later, when they themselves come to have a personal belief.

There is other evidence in the New Testament of early church practice. Psalms and hymns were sung. To express corporate solidarity with missionaries, elders or deacons serving the church, there was 'laying on of hands' at their commissioning. The sick were anointed and prayer made for their recovery. Money was collected for other, poorer churches. The 'ministry' of the church was divided amongst those who had the 'gifts of God's Spirit' for both practical and spiritual leadership.

There seems to have been no such concept as 'having a service'. The 'business' part of church life, such as organizing for the care of widows or the relief of famine, was all bound up with the 'worship' part of praying and singing and teaching.

Established patterns

In the post-apostolic years, patterns gradually settled down, and a clear structure of leadership emerged, in which the bishop would normally preside over the worship of the local church. Bishops wrote down for themselves the great thanksgiving prayer they uttered over the bread and wine of communion, and these 'eucharistic prayers' began to be used regularly and over wide areas, as others copied them.

As congregations grew, they sometimes overflowed from the homes in which they originally met. Groups started (even in times of persecution) to put up special buildings for worship. They produced an ever more detailed pattern of the church's year—not only keeping the 'week' of creation (though making the first day of the week

The Orthodox Churches, such as the Armenian Church, emphasize the importance of ritual in their worship of God.

One of the leaders of the protestant Reformation in the sixteenth century was Martin Luther. He preached the message of 'salvation by faith alone' in language which the ordinary people could understand.

holy in place of the seventh), but also keeping annual commemorations: first of all the Passover (when Jesus had died and risen), then Pentecost (when the Spirit had come), and finally Christmas (celebrating Christ's birth) and the 'death day' of the various martyrs.

The Peace of Constantine in AD 313 gave a new boost to church building, and the assimilation of church and state which followed not only encouraged the use of pagan festivals for Christian commemorations (as happened with Christmas), but also started to shape church organization on the lines of the official civic structures. Whole communities were baptized, and the Western concept of 'Christen-

dom' was born. Later, the natural conservatism of the followers of any institution which has rituals ensured that Latin remained in use rather than the language of everyday speech, that fourth-century garments remained in use by those who led the worship (even though fashions changed for other uses) and that church building attracted the energies of architects and builders whilst other civic buildings were neglected.

In many ways the Eastern Orthodox churches have remained closer than any other to the spirit of the fourth and fifth centuries. Generations of a minority position have built in a great regard for the tradition and its conservation. The East has never had a Reformation or even a Vatican II!

In the Middle Ages in the Western church the role of the clergy became much more dominant. Celibacy added to the mystique of the clergy. They alone took an active part in worship. The concept of their special—indeed miraculous—power to transform the bread and wine into the body and blood of Christ gave them the functions of priesthood. The part of ordinary believers was to attend Mass and to adore the presence of Christ. The people could not understand the Latin used for the Bible readings and prayers. Neither did they receive communion, except at Easter, and then (from the late thirteenth century onwards) only the bread.

Reform

The Reformation, which took a stand against these abuses, was essentially a movement of 'the Word'. It involved the return to God's Word written in the Bible, and also a swing in ritual away from drama, colour and movement to a word-centredness, emphasizing intelligibility and an understanding of doctrine. The reformers themselves often tried hard to bring the celebration of

communion into the centre of church life, but the longstanding habits of their congregations defeated them. Weekly worship in most Protestant churches focussed on the sermon. In the Lutheran churches there was a growth of hymn-singing to accompany services of the word and of prayers. The Church of England adopted a sober Prayer Book routine, in which the daily round of Bible readings, psalms and prayers took on more importance than preaching.

The Reformation also gave birth to more distinctive traditions. The Anabaptists, for example, included those who not only rejected infant baptism but also gave voice to their emotions in worship, expressing personal piety in prayer in gatherings 'led by the Spirit'. And in the seventeenth century the Quakers originally quite literally 'quaked' before God in worship.

A big change started to affect the whole of English-speaking Protestantism in the eighteenth century. The Evangelical Revival which gave birth to Methodism was characterized by enthusiastic hymn-singing. The hymns were objective in their rich doctrinal content but also expressed emotions towards God. In this revival old metrical psalters were swept aside, and the hymns of Watts and the Wesleys, Cowper and Toplady, started to take their place. Also the Lord's Supper was more frequently celebrated.

Hymns apart, Protestantism has tended to be like Roman Catholicism in that its worship is usually dominated by the man 'up front', and in its solemnity: for the man-in-the-pew religion is not only passive, but also serious. But in the twentieth century, a 'liturgical movement' among both Catholics and Protestants has striven for just those ends which seem so often to have been missed—active participation by the whole congregation, understandable services, and a genuine building up of the fellowship of

the body of Christ.

In the Church of Rome this led in time to the Second Vatican Council's reforms of the liturgy, including the admission of local languages into worship, after 1,600 years of Latin. The spill-over from this movement into Protestantism along with other shifts of conviction has led to a new emphasis on the corporate-ness of the sacrament, and on lay participation. Many denomina-tions have gained a new sense that worship might be more than a sermon with some formal pre-liminaries.

Twentieth century

However, there have always been more radical movements. This century, for instance, has seen the rise of the Pentecostal denominations. These are 'Spirit-directed' rather than 'word-directed', and the characteristic expression in worship has in-volved a full release of feelings, a free use of body movement and an openness to contributions (not always, but quite often, 'tongues', 'interpretation of tongues' and 'prophecies') from all the worshippers. A parallel movement in the last two decades has been the 'charismatic' move-ment, which has found a strong home in the 'mainline' Protestant denominations and the Church of Rome.

Today Christianity is once again in a 'missionary' situation in the West, as Christendom fades into secularism. But the various Western forms of Christ-ian worship are not now confined to the West. Young churches flourish in Asia and Africa and

Over the past few years many Christians throughout the world have discovered a new joy and spontaneity in their worship and response to God.

elsewhere. They often tend in worship to be as traditionalist as the Western churches from which they sprang, but the free-dom does not exist for them to be culturally relevant to their own contexts. The worship of a truly missionary church loses its re-spectability, takes on a new edge of realism and, above all, streng-thens, unites and equips believ-ers for their daily life and witness in an alien world. Where worship does not build up the body of Christ, the church perishes. The churches of the Western world are slowly awaking to this chal-lenge.

The Christian Life

Michael Sadgrove

The Christian life is the whole life lived before God as he has revealed himself in Jesus Christ. What makes it distinctively Christian is that it is a response to the 'good news', the gospel: that in Christ, men and women enjoy a new quality of life, open to a new dimension of existence and new possibilities of action. As the apostle Paul expressed it in the New Testament: 'I appeal to you, therefore, brethren, by the mercies of God, to present your bodies as a living sacrifice, holy and acceptable to God, which is your spiritual worship.' The word 'therefore' was the link between the gospel he had been describing and the Christian life. It is to be a life of grateful response to what God has done in Jesus Christ.

Christian living

What is it that shapes Christian character and life? Three themes arising out of the New Testament are of particular importance.

● **The kingdom** The 'kingdom' in the first three Gospels means the coming reign of God, and Jesus' preaching of the kingdom is the announcement that this new age has broken in upon our world. With the kingdom comes the summons to accept the rule of God: 'Repent and believe the gospel.' So the Christian life is what marks out the person who belongs to the kingdom, whose values have become the values of a subject claimed by a monarch. In all his praying, behaving and living, the Christian is a kingdom-man, living on the frontier between the old world and the new.

● **Justification** At the heart of the gospel expounded by Paul in the New Testament letters lies the doctrine of justification by faith—being made right with God through trusting in him. In Christ, men and women are freely accepted by God. Their sin is forgiven. They are offered new life in the Spirit as sons and heirs. Reconciliation with God is the unearned and unearnable gift of God. It is offered on the basis of the fact that Jesus Christ died our death, and rose again from death. It is received by faith. The Christian life is therefore a life of freedom, lived in the joyful awareness of an unafraid relationship with God. And it is therefore also a life of glad self-surrender in love to the God who first loved us.

● **The incarnation** 'The Word became a human being and ... lived among us' is the starting-point of John's Gospel. God has joined himself in Christ to the stuff of the created world and of our own humanity. The Christian life is deeply concerned with what is material, what is human, for it is here that God has met us in his Son. So, on the one hand, Christian life is world-affirming, unashamedly enjoying the goodness of created things. But, on the other, it takes seriously the sufferings and struggles of a world gone wrong, of human beings yearning for wholeness. For to this human condition of suffering and alienation God came in Jesus Christ.

Christian religion

If the word 'religion' means the response of human beings to God, then Christianity is profoundly religious. But because the gospel calls for a total response from man, Christian religion can never be a hermetically-sealed 'spiritual' affair untouched by the demands of human life in the world God has made. Those 'belonging to the Way', as the first Christians were known, were identified by a radically new life-style that included both a Godward dimension of prayer and worship, and a manward dimension of a common life and care for the poor.

So Christian prayer on the one hand and Christian character and conduct on the other are the inseparable parts of Christian religion. For the 'whole duty of man' is to deepen our relationship with God through the spiritual life, and so to grow into mature Christian attitudes and conduct. In the words of the Shorter Catechism, man's chief end is 'to glorify God and to enjoy him for ever'.

Christian prayer

Prayer is possible because God is accessible through Christ. In him, Christians believe, God may be known, loved and adored. And if this is where Christian prayer begins, it must continue with thanksgiving, penitence (asking forgiveness for sin) and supplication (requests to God):

● **thanksgiving**, because in Christ God has revealed his good-will to man;

● **penitence**, because in Christ God has forgiven and forgives;

● **supplication**, because in Christ God has declared a purpose for history and for humanity.

Prayer in the New Testament

The cry 'Abba!', the familiar Aramaic word for 'Father', is eloquent testimony to the way in which early Christians prayed. Jesus taught his disciples to pray to God as Father. The Lord's Prayer, given twice in the New Testament as the pattern, beginning with the words 'Our Father', has been used as a prayer throughout the centuries by Christians of all traditions. It is basically about the kingdom. The seven petitions that follow all ask in various ways that the blessings of the new age may come upon those who have become members of the kingdom of God. The prayer is nothing if not concrete. It lifts up before God the raw material of human life: material need, failure in relationships with both God and man, the experience of suffering and trial. It is the new age that puts

In the Eastern Church, icons— beautiful paintings of the holy family and the saints—are used as an aid to contemplation and worship.

human experience in its proper perspective.

The spiritual life

How has spirituality developed since New Testament days? There is, of course, a rich heritage of devotion and spiritual life expressed in an infinite variety of ways. But three distinctive approaches can be identified, associated with a Catholic, Orthodox and Protestant outlook.

**'Jesus said:
"When you pray, say this:
'Father: May your holy name be honoured; may your Kingdom come.
Give us day by day the food we need.
Forgive us our sins, for we forgive everyone who does us wrong.
And do not bring us to hard testing.'"'**

The Lord's Prayer, Luke 11:2–4

Catholic spirituality

Catholic spirituality is fundamentally 'sacramental'. Because God became man in Christ, the material world is seen as a vehicle for the spiritual. Grace does not destroy nature, but perfects it. And so the 'journey' of the Christian life begins at baptism, with the Eucharist as nourishment, and sacramental confession the means by which the soul is kept on the way that leads to the vision of God. And because the church, with its rites and institutions, is a divine society, the journey is a splendid one, transfigured by the glory of Christ at every stage.

Orthodox spirituality

The Orthodox churches of the East are also deeply rooted in a sacramental understanding of grace. But their distinctiveness lies in their use of icons. An icon is a representation of Christ, the Virgin Mary or one of the saints. But it is more than a mere picture. It is a kind of 'open window' between earth and heaven. The worshipper sees the icon as a proclamation of God's salvation, the material of the object conveying God's grace just as the flesh and blood of Christ had done. But if it 'images' the incarnation, then the icon is also a primary focus for the worshipper's prayers, offered not *to* it but *through* it to the God who is beyond, and yet within it.

Protestant spirituality

What sacraments and icons are to Catholic and Orthodox spirituality, the Bible is to Protestantism. The reading of the scriptures, in the conviction that in them the word of God is to be found, was basic to the prayer of the Protestant reformers. With this went an assurance that the believer had free access to God through Christ, uninhibited by the structures of sacraments and priests erected (as the reformers saw it) by the medieval church. A distinctive mark of early Protestantism was the new value placed on the individual—a consequence of the claim that the individual, justified by faith, mattered to God. The word-orientated 'feel' of traditional Protestantism contrasts sharply with the numinous ethos of symbol and rite that belongs to Catholic spirituality.

Prayer today

Christians today are concerned with relating prayer to life at a number of points. The impact of secularism has led radical theologians to look for more meaningful ways of talking about God and praying in the 'secular city'. Prayer is seen not as withdrawal from the world but as involvement in it. 'Liberation theologians' would go further: the search for political and social goals provides a spirituality of liberation in which prayer is 'made flesh' in the struggle against oppressive economic systems and political regimes.

A parallel development has been to react against the secular and to seek inspiration (often

Following Jesus' example, Christians have always been involved in helping the poor and needy. In 1980, Mother Teresa was awarded the Nobel Peace Prize for her self-sacrificial work in the slums of Calcutta.

'Happy are those who know they are spiritually poor; the Kingdom of heaven belongs to them! Happy are those who mourn; God will comfort them! Happy are those who are humble; they will receive what God has promised! Happy are those whose greatest desire is to do what God requires; God will satisfy them fully! Happy are those who are merciful to others; God will be merciful to them! Happy are the pure in heart; they will see God! Happy are those who work for peace; God will call them his children! Happy are those who are persecuted because they do what God requires; the Kingdom of heaven belongs to them! Happy are you when people insult you and persecute you and tell all kinds of evil lies against you because you are my followers. Be happy and glad, for a great reward is kept for you in heaven. This is how the prophets who lived before you were persecuted.'

The Beatitudes from Jesus' *Sermon on the Mount*

mystical) in other faiths. At the same time within mainstream Christianity, both Catholic and Protestant, the contribution of the 'charismatic' movement has been to encourage the renewal of a spontaneous life of prayer, joyfully liberated from the shackles of formality and convention.

Christian life-style

God's will for human beings is that they should be 'whole': complete in every aspect, whether as individuals, in the intimate relationships of family and community, or in the wider social, national and international context. In Christ, people can become, and indeed are already becoming, what God intended them to be.

Words such as behaviour, conduct, morals, ethics, suggest sticking to rules. A great deal of Christian thinking on morals has looked suspiciously like moralism: the 'oughts' and the 'musts' of duty goading wilful humans into joyless and reluctant obedience. But the Christian life is not something imposed from outside, but something that arises freely and spontaneously from within as the gospel takes root. So Christian behaviour means not only what a Christian does or does not do; it also means how a Christian thinks, and what kinds of values and attitudes he holds as his response to Jesus Christ.

Ethics in the New Testament

How did the early church understand the challenge of the gospel to live 'Christianly'?

● **The Jewish background** Christianity inherited from its Jewish roots the Law of Moses. The Law (with its summary in the Ten Commandments) stood at the centre of Jewish life. God's laws were to be the pattern of a Jew's responsibility towards God and his neighbour. The Law of the Old Testament was not given as a strait-jacket. It was given to guide man's response to a God who had already loved him, and invited him into a relationship of love called the covenant. And so, when Jesus says that all the Law and the prophets hang on the great commandments to love God with all your being, and your neighbour as yourself, he is spelling out what was already there. As the apostle Paul puts it: 'love is the fulfilling of the law.' For Jew and Christian alike, love is the basis of all true response to God.

● **The Sermon on the Mount** Jesus' teaching known as the 'Sermon on the Mount' is the manifesto of the kingdom breaking in with Jesus. The blessings of this new age are for those whom men naturally despise: the poor, the meek, the oppressed. The values of the kingdom, with the seemingly impossible summons to perfection, deal a death-blow to the easier standards of conventional morality. The ethics of the new age call men to live in the light of tomorrow and the coming of God.

● **Paul** If justification by faith is the charter of a Christian's freedom, is he not free to do exactly as he likes? 'Shall we sin, that grace may abound?' No, there is a difference between liberty and licence. Christian liberty is God's gift in an accepting relationship of love. Like all accepting relationships, God's acceptance of a person changes him. It enables him to respond by loving God back—something of which he was not capable before. And so, in a marvellous paradox, God's service is 'perfect freedom'. We can love God *and* do as we want (as Augustine recommended) because what we want as Christians has become precisely what God wants of us: trust, obedience and unconditional love.

Making moral choices

Human life demands that we make moral choices all the time. What is it that determines what is 'right' or 'wrong' in a particular situation? Some may say that a certain course of action is 'natural', or that it leads to the outcome of the greatest good, or that it does not go against the dictates of conscience. All these options have been canvassed by Christians at various times (for example, the concept of natural law invoked by medieval theologians).

But the Christian life is a response to God in Christ, so the overriding criterion for Christian thinking and conduct will be bound up with the gospel and its claims upon us. What was the way of Jesus?

As we have seen, Jesus reasserted the moral values of the Old Testament scriptures. In discussing marriage, he went back to the basic principles of creation, God's intention for man and woman to become 'one flesh'. The principles of creation and law—how God intended man to live—are basic to moral choices. For they are also the most loving way: and in the New Testament they are interpreted in a spirit of Christian love, a spirit of total self-giving. This is not a matter of feeling: what feels loving may not always be in another person's best interests.

In an increasingly pagan society, Christians are having to reaffirm basic moral attitudes on personal and social issues. They can not only point to the right way, they can also point to Jesus as the one who makes it possible to live the right way.

Competing Ideologies Today

It could be said that in the twentieth century popular religion is not religion at all, but the new faiths of existentialism and communism, which together have adherents in so much of the world.

So this book would not be complete without mention, at least, of these ideologies which, though not religions in the strict sense, often have the same place in people's lives as major religions had in the past.

EXISTENTIALISM
Anthony Thiselton

The term 'existentialism' is often used to denote a general attitude towards life and thought. But strictly speaking, there is no single philosophy of existentialism; only a group of highly individual thinkers whom others have labelled 'existentialist'. Some of the features which recur in these thinkers are as follows:
● The priority of the practical over the theoretical.
● The priority of the concrete and personal over the general and abstract.
● The importance of involvement, as against detachment, in the quest for understanding.

Those who attack existentialism would also want to add the following:
● Its pessimism about the possibility of reaching any comprehensive and coherent view of reality.
● Its tendency towards an individualism in which each is free to do his own thing. Truth, it is argued, has been reduced to a matter of what is true 'for me'.

The father-figure of existentialism was **Søren Kierkegaard** (1813–55), whose writings, however, did not become widely known until the early part of this century. After a personal crisis in his life, Kierkegaard came to feel that he had been living on the basis of values derived from his father at second hand, and that he

must seek his own more authentic values through firsthand experience and personal decision. In the course of long personal struggles, he came to believe that God was calling him to show in his life and personal commitment what true Christianity meant, in contrast both to armchair philosophy and to nominal Christianity. Christian faith, he believed, was a matter of practical obedience, not theoretical thought. On the positive side, Kierkegaard saw that Christianity was not an 'ism', but a personal commitment. But on the negative side, his devaluing of the Christian community led to an individualistic account of faith which no doubt contributed to his own experiences of deep doubt and anguish.

Martin Heidegger (1889–1976) argued that even the seemingly 'general' questions of philosophy can be asked only concretely from the standpoint of where the thinker already is. He can philosophize only from within his own horizons. To this extent, he can never completely escape the problems imposed by his own finitude and relativity. The Western tradition of philosophy, Heidegger argued, has tended to depersonalize man by ignoring the way in which he is part of his own personal 'world', in which what matters is what matters to him.

Without Kierkegaard's anchorage in Christian faith, this outlook can lead to an increasingly one-sided surrender to relativism and individualism. We find this already anticipated before Heidegger in **Friedrich Nietzsche** (1844–1900) and subsequently developed

in **Jean-Paul Sartre** (1905–80) and **Albert Camus** (1913–60). In atheistic versions of existentialism, life is seen as having no rational or universal meaning other than what seems to be authentic for a given individual. The individual must reject society's attempt to impose on him second-hand 'roles' of someone else's making.

In spite of these points of tension between existentialism and Christianity, there are also affinities. These include the priority of the personal over the impersonal emphasized especially by **Gabriel Marcel**; the recognition of the full implications of human finitude as meaning that I am 'placed' already within 'my' horizons; the importance of personal experiences such as anxiety and guilt in leading to appropriation of truth; and the limitations of mere theorizing over against active decision and practical commitment.

COMMUNISM
Robert Banks

Karl Marx (1818–83) combined and transcended three major streams of thought:
● German philosophical views, especially as filtered through Feuerbach's materialist critique, emphasized the need for human autonomy, a rational society and scientific progress. Marx's debt to them extended as well to his dynamic understanding of history and ideas about human alienation.
● French political theory

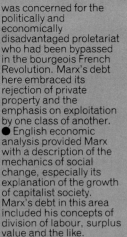

was concerned for the politically and economically disadvantaged proletariat who had been bypassed in the bourgeois French Revolution. Marx's debt here embraced its rejection of private property and the emphasis on exploitation by one class of another.

● English economic analysis provided Marx with a description of the mechanics of social change, especially its explanation of the growth of capitalist society. Marx's debt in this area included his concepts of division of labour, surplus value and the like.

All these were fused by Marx into a world-view that was genuinely new. Everything stems from matter, though matter itself is a dynamic phenomenon, giving birth to consciousness, thought, creativity, etc. Man is essentially a social creature who is capable of creating his own destiny. The emergence of primitive technology, however, and its formation of different classes, divided men from each other and locked them into particular social frameworks. All of these gave rise to specific legal, political, moral, religious and cultural systems which were ultimately reflections of the socio-economic base. Each type of society contained contradictions which sowed the seeds of its own destruction. So, from a state of primitive communism there followed classical slave society (or in the East its more despotic Oriental counterpart), feudal society and now capitalist

Jesus described the people of his day as 'sheep without a shepherd'.

society. Out of the inevitable demise of the latter, revolutionary proletarian activity would usher in socialist society. This would be marked by the dismantling of the state and the voluntary rejection of religion, for it would involve the full and free co-operation and contentment of all men.

Revolutionary Marxism?

Since Marx, the world-view he elaborated has undergone a number of modifications at the hands of later Marxist thinkers. His English compatriot **Engels** pushed it in a more scientifically mechanistic and less historically dynamic direction. So too did the Germans **Bernstein** and **Kautsky**, who also tempered Marx's political analysis in a more social-democratic direction. **Lenin**, on the other hand, replaced its view of inevitable capitalist collapse and mass proletarian ascendancy with one justifying a premature seizure of power by a vanguard party representing proletarian interests. His exiled former colleague— **Trotsky**—advocated a continuous revolution rather than simply the unfolding of a critical revolutionary situation.

In China, **Mao Tse-Tung** bypassed the small proletarian class in favour of the larger peasant class to initiate the revolution, thereby omitting what Marx saw as the necessary capitalist preparation for socialist society. Meanwhile, the failure of structural changes behind the Iron Curtain to solve fundamental human problems encouraged some Marxist philosophers to integrate existentialist or more humanistic elements into their outlook; others developed a more complex understanding of the relation between economic and other structures in the dynamics of social change.

Influential modifications of Marx were undertaken by the leaders of the Frankfurt School of Social Research. These sought to introduce a genuine psychological dimension into his social and political thought and argued that the transition from industrial to technological society rendered much of Marx's outlook irrelevant. The New Left in the '60s, on the other hand, ignored the more rigorous aspects of Marx's social and economic analysis in favour of expressions of moral outrage and belief in a purely political situation. This involved a highly romantic and utopian notion of the preconditions and consequences of revolution.

Russia and the Eastern bloc

Among European countries, Russia seemed least suited to Marx as a prospect for socialism. This was due to its absorption of elements of despotic Oriental society and its rudimentary development of a capitalist base. Modifying Marx's analysis, Lenin first sought to explain the increasingly dynamic success of capitalism in the West by arguing that the success was simply a postponement of its decay arising from exploitation of the colonies of the great powers. He also worked out the organizational theory, principles and tactics of a revolutionary (though from Marx's point of view premature) seizure of power.

The evolution of Russian communism under Stalin moved even further away from Marxist foundations in a totalitarian direction, though all the basic foundations had been laid by Lenin himself. The dominance of the single leader, the entrenchment of the party, the strengthening of government, the creation of a secret police force, the direct oppression of religious and racial minorities, all showed how powerful were pre-revolutionary Czarist/Oriental attitudes as well as post-revolutionary totalitarian tendencies. The less tyrannical mood under Khrushchev's, and later Brezhnev's, more low-profile, less overtly oppressive, regimes have partially but not radically modified this.

None of the East European communist governments came to power in the same manner as the Bolsheviks in 1917. All owed their existence to Russian interference in their post-war domestic affairs. Even the Yugoslav communist victory pre-eminently sprang out of a war of liberation against the Nazis, not a purely political seizure of power. In differing degrees, particular national institutions, religion and culture in these countries have prevented them from fully imitating the Russian model. (The role of Catholicism in Poland is a case in point.) Yugoslavia represents a more moderate approach with its greater freedom of religion, involvement of workers in industrial decision-making and political independence from Moscow. The tension between national aspirations and Russian domination has occasionally, though never successfully, disrupted the internal stability of these countries, as in Hungary in 1956 and Czechoslovakia in 1968.

China: Maoism

According to Marx, Oriental societies exhibited a different social and political structure from their Western counterparts. They were by nature essentially static societies rather than dynamic and self-transforming. No disaffected class strong enough to bring about the disintegration of this closed, despotic system existed. And their partial colonization by the West, certainly in the case of China, was insufficient to stimulate them even in a bourgeois-democratic, let alone proletarian-socialist, direction.

For all the Marxist rhetoric, generally quite unsophisticated and at times decidedly vulgar in character, the changes indicated by the communist victory in 1949 were of an essentially different kind. A return to the despotism that pre-dated the 1911 bourgeois Nationalist Revolution under Sun Yat Sen has taken place, though one pushed in a more totalitarian direction. This was centred on Mao Tse-Tung and his ever-changing circle of colleagues. Given the less inherently democratic character of Chinese, as distinct from Russian, society, the extension of ideological as well as bureaucratic control over the population has been more complete. The Cultural Revolution that began in 1966 was an extreme demonstration of the ideological dimension in this process at work. The present leadership seems likely to modify the development of Chinese communism in certain, probably major, respects.

The Third World
The strategy for the establishment of communism in Third World countries has been more the Yugoslav or Chinese than the Russian one. That is, it has generally come about as the result of a war of liberation. In some cases this has occurred in the aftermath of a nationalist war against an occupying power, such as in North Korea against the Japanese. In others, for

example Cuba, it followed a civil war. In Vietnam, a combination of the two was involved. Sometimes, as in Ethiopia, direct Russian assistance was involved in the creation of a communist government. Alternatively, the move in a communist direction has only gradually emerged after liberation occurred: as in the People's Republic of Zaire, and increasingly Angola, though Cuba was the first instance of this. The one example of a popularly-elected Communist government was Allende's in Chile, which was soon sabotaged by internal and external interference.

The strong patriotic aspirations involved in most of these revolutions make it difficult to separate out the specifically communist from the indigenous nationalist elements. Most are developing strong centralized governments engaged in fairly extensive political scrutiny of their subjects. But the basic reason is probably the need to control the means of production as fully as possible so that modernization can take place as quickly as possible. This suggests paradoxically that, more than its anti-capitalist political content, Marxism provides the most

attractive ideological framework by which underdeveloped nations, particularly those antagonistic to former Western masters, can effectively industrialize themselves. Certainly their relations with the communist superpowers have been extremely pragmatic.

A Fusion of Religion: Syncretism

John Allan

'Syncretism' is the name given to any attempt to combine many diverse religious elements into a new system of faith and belief. As this has been a fairly common human impulse down the centuries, the history of syncretism is long and confusing.

In the West, it goes back at least as far as the pre-Christian mystery cults of ancient Rome. The Romans were quite willing to tolerate the existence of private *superstitiones* alongside the official *religio* ordained by the state, and these cults drew from an international background of theological ideas—the cult of Isis from Egypt, Mithras from Persia, Cybele from Asia Minor, to name but three. These

mysteries eventually died out, thanks to a policy of brutal suppression, after the adoption of Christianity as the state religion in AD 392. But the earlier religious cosmopolitanism of Rome (in which, for instance, Augustus highly commended his grandson for visiting the temple in Jerusalem while staying in Palestine) had provided a seed-bed for all sorts of syncretistic schemes—Neo-Platonism, Gnosticism, Hermeticism (incorporating the alchemical and astrological systems of Egypt)—which survived in many guises in different movements, and often penetrated the church itself. For example, Synesius (370–413), who was bishop of Ptolemais

in North Africa, not only wrote Gnostic hymns, but also compiled a commentary on an alchemical treatise and dedicated it to the high priest of the cult of Serapis in Alexandria.

Resistance groups
Throughout the Middle Ages, syncretism flourished mainly amongst popular resistance groups who opposed the theological supremacy of Rome. In the thirteenth century, for instance, the Cathars or Albigensians emerged in the Languedoc area of France, teaching a form of Gnosticism, while at the same time the heresy of the 'Free Spirit' revived Neo-Platonist ideas in the north of Europe. The key to both movements may have been contact with the Arabs; the ideas which Christendom had condemned had passed from the Roman Empire into the keeping of the Arab races, who were now reintroducing them into European life.

At the Renaissance,

Europe experienced an explosion of interest in new ideas, and this often included the old lore of the previously banned movements. The human mind had been liberated from the boundaries set by the censor of the medieval Catholic church, and scholars such as John Dee and Simon Forman saw absolutely no conflict between magical pursuits and Christian orthodoxy. A further source of ideas was added to the syncretistic mix: scholars began to investigate the Jewish Kabbalah, itself a weird mixture of Judaism and magical ideas from many sources. Some daring thinkers went too far (Giordano Bruno's Hermetic ideas led to his death at the stake) but a tradition of speculative thought was established which later led to the foundation of the secret societies and occult groups we know today.

Secret societies
This process began in the eighteenth century, when

the Freemasons (a survival of the medieval craft guilds) were joined and transformed by a number of amateur occultists who suspected that Masonry might be 'the remains of the mysteries of the ancients'. The idea that a secret society of magical wisdom might exist somewhere had been common since 1614, when the 'Rosicrucian Brotherhood' had announced its existence in a manifesto published at Cassel. The likelihood is that the manifesto was a hoax and that no such group had ever formed, but nonetheless the possibility was raised in European minds. Masonry was one of many secret societies in eighteenth-century Europe. Druidism was another variety which grew in popularity in England, and again the fascination was syncretistic—Pythagoras, the Kabbalah, and the Chaldean Magi were claimed to have taught similarly.

Eastern thought

In the late nineteenth century, a growing fascination with Eastern thought in the West led to the flourishing of the Vedantist groups from India and the establishing of religious cults of Western origin with Eastern world-views. In Christian Science, for instance, Mary Baker Eddy taught that pain is an imaginary experience, that God is a 'Principle' rather than a person, that sin, death and evil are unreal. These teachings are markedly Hindu rather than Christian. In Theosophy, Mme Helena Blavatsky claimed to be rediscovering the ancient wisdom (*theosophia*) which lay at the heart of every religion: 'except the

initiates, no one has understood the mystic writing'. But the importance to her thinking of the doctrines of *karma* and reincarnation, together with her claim to be guided by a shadowy brotherhood of 'Masters' usually located in Tibet, shows clearly where the roots of her theology lay.

At the same time, an occult revival centred on Paris led to the foundation of magical and Rosicrucian groups, and the odd claims of a young Persian nobleman named Baha'u'llah brought Islamic syncretism into the West. Baha'u'llah believed himself to be the legendary Twelfth Imam of Islam, due to appear to guide the faithful to a new experience of God, as well as the 'other Comforter' whose coming was promised by Jesus. Thus his teachings—now known as the Baha'i faith—could unite world religions in one, and bring about an era of world peace. Baha'u'llah himself died a young man in 1893, but his impressive and persuasive son 'Abd ul-Baha had remarkable success in spreading the faith in Western high society circles.

This century, the West has seen a remarkable explosion of syncretist groups since the 1960s. The reason for this is probably the search for some kind of spirituality to replace the drug experiences of the psychedelic era. LSD and mescaline had been touted by Timothy Leary and other high priests of the chemical revolution as 'the religion of the twentieth century . . . turn on, tune in, drop out'. But the obvious dangers of drug-taking eventually led to disaffection, which by

1968 allowed a whole variety of Eastern groups to exploit the spiritual gap ex-addicts were experiencing.

'Drugs can't give you eternal peace, but I can,' proclaimed the Divine Light Mission's Guru Maharaj Ji. It is not without significance that both the 'Divine Light' experience and the 'Hare Krishna' experience had already been described (with no religious trappings) in a popular book of the time entitled *Thirty Ways to Get High Without Taking Drugs*.

Doctrinal mix

Most of the Eastern groups were vaguely syncretist: Jesus Christ featured alongside a variety of Hindu figures in the Divine Light Mission's Exhibition of Forty-Two World Saviours. But a Korean-based group, most prominent in the seventies, was the most outspoken in its syncretism. The Unification Church founded by Sun Myung Moon combined Christian ideas and terminology with Taoist notions of God and the complementarity of creation. As its name suggests, the Church sees as its aim the unification of all world religions under a coming messiah, who may well be Sun Myung Moon in person. Some limited attention is paid to Buddhist and Islamic ideas in the group's sacred work, *Divine Principle*, but these traditions add little to the Unification doctrinal mix.

The Unification attempt to combine a foreign religion—Christianity— with more familiar ancestral concepts probably arose out of a desire to forge a new, patriotic faith with Korea as its centre. This has

frequently been a factor in the rise of new syncretist groups. The Rastafarians, for example, with their strange mixture of Christianity and African nationalism, and the Black Muslims, a cross between revivalist Christianity and Islamic theology, have provided an outlet for oppressed people which has allowed them a sense of purpose and of self-respect.

Two more recent trends deserve note. There has been a rise in the popularity of personal therapy or counselling treatments, with names such as Scientology, est, esalen and Exegesis, which rarely admit to being religious, but which all involve the adoption of syncretistic views about the nature of life and the universe. Scientology, for instance (which *does* admit to being a religion, but more often describes itself as 'the modern science of mental health'), combines a course of therapy using a crude lie-detector with a series of ultimately Buddhist teachings: that we are not our bodies but are actually an immortal being called a 'Thetan'; that the Thetan was involved in the creation of the universe and is possessed of theoretically unlimited powers; that we progress through a series of incarnations; that salvation involves personal enlightenment which must be achieved by individual effort unaided by any deity.

Age of Aquarius

Second, the astrological belief that we are now entering the 'Age of Aquarius'—an age in human history when man's consciousness will be expanded and new spiritual powers will be

discovered—has led to the proliferation of a whole variety of self-styled 'New Age' groups, with interest in yoga, pyramid power, holistic health, UFO contacts, ley lines and geodetic forces, traditional magic and paraphysical research. These groups will often work together and see themselves as complementary rather than competing. Their basic theology tends to be Eastern but eclectic. Bhagwan Rajneesh, for instance, founder of the Kalptaru Meditation Centres, claims to have built his popularity upon the fact that he follows no one teacher or method, but draws from all. Beshara, another New Age group, claim that 'the man of wisdom, whatever may happen, will never allow himself to be caught up in any one definite form or belief because he is wise unto himself'.

It has been claimed that we are living in the age of the sub-cult, in which people are more likely to look for truth in the small group rather than in the large organized religious system. If this is a correct analysis, the prospects for new syncretisms must be fairer at this moment in history than they have been for a very long time.

Australia, like many secularized countries, has seen a decline in institutional Christianity, though there is a new interest in less formal expressions of faith. But world-wide, Christianity in general is stronger today than ever before.

The Future of Christianity

Robert Linder

Futurology is a tricky business, especially when it deals with religion. Even so, theologians, sociologists, economists, political scientists and occasionally historians attempt to divine the future. Some insight into it can be derived by looking at Christian history, the present world situation and current issues which will affect the future of the faith. From this, perhaps some indication of what Christianity will be like fifty years from now can be gained.

What was the position of Christianity fifty years ago, in say 1930? It was at about that time that the cliché was first invoked that the

Christians are concerned to show love for people, whether their needs are physical or spiritual. Medical work has been a key feature of Christian activity in the needy parts of the world.

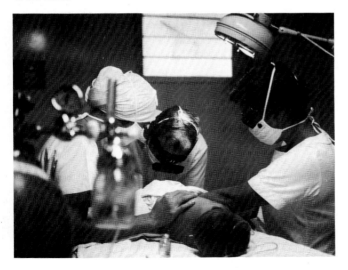

Western world had entered a 'post-Christian' era. During the next two decades, it appeared to many that this was only too true. Christianity in the USA was in the last stages of the debilitating fundamentalist-modernist controversy. Theological liberalism and religious apathy seemed to have permanently taken over in Europe. Christianity in the non-Western world appeared discredited by its former ties with colonialism. Secular humanism seemed to be the dominant intellectual force in the West, and education was accepted as the panacea for contemporary ills.

Thus, when the Great Depression struck in 1929, most people turned to government and science rather than religion for aid and comfort. At the same time, totalitarian fascism and communism were on the march in Europe and Asia. Many intellectuals in all parts of the world—Marxist and non-Marxist—predicted that it would be only a matter of time before Christianity disappeared altogether.

However, this was not the case. Now, fifty years later, professing Christians are more numerous than ever before in history and their presence seems to be increasingly important with each passing year, even in communist nations. In the 1980s, Christianity has nearly 1,000 million adherents on every continent—clearly out-distancing its nearest rival, Islam, which claims some 585 million followers.

The doom boom

However, though Christianity was growing numerically in the period 1930–80, it was also losing ground in terms of its percentage of total world population and of the population of most developed countries. For example, it decreased from 23.9 per cent of the world population in 1978 to 23.0 per cent in 1979, while the percentage of people affiliated to none of the five major religious systems increased from 40.9 to 42.7 per cent.

Also, the socio-political context of the world has deteriorated significantly since 1930. Incredible as it seems, in the short space of fifty years the world has gone from a major economic depression through a global war to a series of intense localized conflicts, to a period of unbelievable Western affluence, to the precipice of Western collapse and another world war. Not since the Reformation era has an apocalyptic mood been so evident and pervasive in the Western world as it is today. This 'boom in doom' is apparent almost everywhere, in the West as well as in other parts of the world—from the pulpits to the news-stands to the halls of higher learning.

Can or will Christianity help the world meet the threat of economic upheaval and its companion, world hunger? For instance, will Christians play a leading role in the reallocation of wealth necessary in order to feed the world and distribute resources equitably?

The massive problems of politics and economics are compounded by the fact that freedom is in retreat around the globe. Even in the Western democracies, government has become dangerously centralized; in the totalitarian countries it is lord and master. Personal freedom and individual responsibility have been replaced in many lands by personal welfare and corporate responsibility. Technological surveillance and espionage to control people is all too common, even in democratic countries.

How will Christianity respond to these totalitarian trends? In particular, how will the Christians of America respond to increasing fascist tendencies in their country? Can and will Christians in the USA do anything to head off a home-grown brand of American fascism or will they go the way of many believers in Nazi Germany in the 1930s? If America does go fascist in the near future, what will this mean for the cause of human freedom everywhere and for the worldwide missionary enterprise?

Facing issues

Another complicating factor related to economic chaos and the drift toward political totalitarianism has been the great surge of racial movement and unrest. People are leaving

There are flourishing churches in China today, despite the years of official repression.

and will continue to leave their native lands in increasing numbers as modern technology makes it both possible and desirable to do so in the wake of continuing social turmoil. As the different races and cultures rub against each other in great numbers in more and more parts of the world, tension will continue to mount. The movement of large numbers of refugees will be a major factor in world political unrest for years to come. Christianity too will have to cope with the increasingly difficult and interrelated issues of national boundaries, nationalism and population pressures. Christianity could provide a shared world-view which would serve as the 'glue' of multi-ethnic, multi-cultural, multi-linguistic nations.

Some of the recent literature on the subject of civilization's disintegration frankly acknowledges some of these momentous problems but embraces long-range optimism in which computer technology saves the day. Yet in America the polls show that not only have the masses lost faith in traditional political leadership, but people have grown sceptical about the ability of science and technology to solve their problems. In fact, scientific and technological advances have in some cases gone beyond mere problem-solving and begun to dabble with the essence of life itself. Christians will have to speak out on the human manipulation of birth, for example, (especially the growing practice of abortion), the manipulation of behaviour and the manipulation of death.

Can Christianity in fact contribute to the emergence of a new consensus of commonly-held values that will make a difference in terms of the future survival of humanity? For many have wondered, not just if there is a future for religion, but a future of any kind for the human race. Perhaps the bitterest irony is that amidst the general malaise of modern society and the fading confidence of people in their governments, the only major point at which most governments exercise any kind of leadership is in the area of national defence—or what others call the arms race. While millions of people starve in one part of the world, billions of dollars are spent on nuclear weapons and conventional arms in another. Most alarming, the military build-up and the possibility of a nuclear holocaust have become so familiar to many people that they now seem to dismiss them as threats to human existence. Can Christians act as peacemakers today? Or will Christians subordinate their faith to other considerations such as their country or economic ideology—and join in the killing?

The intellectual foundation for this worldwide political, economic and social drift is a generation cut off from its roots, isolated from its past and from its future, pathologically preoccupied with self. The threat of atomic disaster, ecological problems and the shrinking of resources all tend to concentrate the attention on the present. There is little serious historical and theological thinking being done about the future.

The world also faces the threat of spreading totalitarianism. The most dangerous challenge may come in embattled America where right-wing political forces have experienced a dramatic growth in the 1970s and where fear of the communist menace is still widespread. Elsewhere, totalitarian communist governments have fastened themselves on country after country following the Second World War—China, Cuba, North Korea, Vietnam, Angola and others—and authoritarian regimes of various stripes mark the political landscape of the newly-emerging nations of Africa, Asia and the Middle East. Christians, already suffering under the Marxist regimes of Eastern Europe, have the potential to reverse or head off such developments in many parts of the world if they take a vigorous stand for human rights. Otherwise, Christianity will become once again largely an underground religion throughout much of the world.

Religious revival

The final element which must be considered amongst the 'signs of the times' is the current religious awak-

Christians demonstrate their love of God in loving service to their fellow-men. Pictured right is a recent expedition attempting to bring medical aid by new means to Nepal.

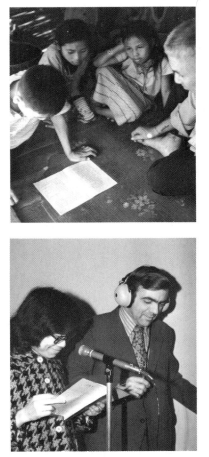

Jesus' last instruction to his disciples was to spread the 'good news' to all the world. Christians today take up this challenge in many ways, such as by using radio.

Middle Ages) or the dawning of a new day of national vigour (e.g. the Wesleyan revival in Britain).

Ironically, while the West experiences economic and political difficulties and Christianity in Western countries struggles to define its social responsibilities, the Christian religion is also experiencing unprecedented growth in many areas where previously it has not been strong. Based on past experiences and present circumstances, it appears that those nations which hold the most promise in the future in terms of Christian growth are Australia (long overdue and currently ripe for great revival), Brazil (where both Catholics and Protestants are enjoying a new spiritual vigour), the Indian subcontinent (where evangelicals appear poised for a new religious offensive), Indonesia (where the Pentecostal movement shows much promise) and Nigeria (the pearl of Africa in terms of both spiritual and economic potential). There are many others. Moreover, the faith will continue to be outgoing and relatively healthy in such places as Poland, Romania, South Korea and the USSR. All of this points to a shift in the centre of spiritual gravity in Christendom away from the USA and Western Europe to the emerging nations during the next fifty years. Thus, the year 2030 could well see countries such as Brazil and Nigeria supplying large numbers of Christian missionaries for work in the USA, Europe and the Muslim world.

The three Christian groups which should continue to expand most dramatically in the coming fifty years are the Roman Catholics, the Baptists and the Pentecostals—mostly because they are most certain about what they are declaring and have the greatest ideological cohesiveness in their proclamation of the gospel. Catholics have begun to experience a period of renewed vigour under the leadership of Pope John Paul II. Baptist work is now present in nearly every nation, and reports of significant gains continue to come not only from the USA but also from the Soviet Union, Romania, India, Burma, Brazil, Nigeria and Zaire.

ening around the world. Although this religious revival extends beyond the Christian religion, it is most intense and significant in terms of the spread of the gospel of Christ. In America, there has been a resurgence of evangelical (conservative biblical) Christianity similar to that which occurred during the nineteenth-century revival known as the second Great Awakening. There have been reports of significant Christian growth in Eastern Europe, Africa south of the Sahara, India, Indonesia and Korea as well as widespread charismatic renewal in Latin America. Historically-speaking, large-scale religious renewal portends the collapse of a civilization (e.g. Rome, the

Many observers feel that the Pentecostal-charismatic movement is the wave of the future, especially in the Third World. Certainly, it has become a potent force in many Latin American countries as well as in some parts of North America, Europe and Asia. In all three groups a decided evangelical thrust can be detected in their current resurgence. A common biblical base, a common commitment to Christ and common external foes could lead them into a much closer relationship by the year 2030.

In the context of these likely developments which will affect the course of Christianity in the next half-century, and in contrast to the destructive forces emerging among the peoples of the world, the Christian religion will continue to have a global impact in at least three ways.

● The faith is being planted more widely today than it (or any other religion) has ever been. This is true of nearly every part of the world with perhaps the exception of the Muslim countries; though here too new opportunities to replant the Christian faith in Islamic lands may occur in the next fifty years, thanks to the increased contact between the West and the predominantly Muslim areas.

● Christianity is more deeply rooted among more peoples than it or any religion has ever been. This does not mean that nominalism or theological liberalism are dead. However, it does mean that today there is in most of the world more serious commitment to Christ on the part of Christians than at any other time in history. This is true in both North America and Europe where the faith has been present for hundreds of years, and it is true for the former colonial areas where fresh, dynamic, indigenous leadership has emerged to replace that previously provided by Western missionaries. Nearly every nation of the world has now formulated statements of the faith in its own language and setting, thus proving once again the universality of the Christian message.

● Christianity in both the Western

There is an explosion in the number of Christians in South America, particularly among the huge student population.

and the non-Western worlds has developed fresh movements and techniques to meet the challenges of the day. An example of this is the 'electronic church' which has emerged to capture a portion of the TV airwaves for the Christian gospel. Evangelical academies, worker-priests and 'liberation theology' are also examples of the remarkable ability of the Christian religion to formulate new strategies to meet the challenge of an ever-needy world.

A new dynamic force

What will Christianity be like in 2030? It will continue to be the most vital spiritual force in the world. It will be the chief custodian of civilization as nations come and go. Moreover, just as the monasticism of the Middle Ages created communities which preserved a commitment to the full Christian life in the midst of a decadent world, so a new monasticism—this time more truly communal by its inclusion of the family—once again will preserve a commitment to the full Christian life in the midst of a decadent world.

Further, Christianity will provide the world with a link to its past, just as it has done since the collapse of Roman civilization. It will survive whatever difficulties engulf the world in the next fifty years and, if history is a faithful guide, will emerge stronger than ever in any new order. It will give larger numbers of people a wholesome connection with their past and a hopeful outlook for the future.

Finally, the Christian faith will continue to give millions of people a sense of balance, stability and purpose in the midst of an increasingly difficult and dangerous world. In addition to the innovations which will be introduced in order to meet new challenges, Christianity will continue to preserve those timeless values so necessary to civilization and life itself: love, peace, faith, sacrifice, discipline, responsibility and recognition of the dignity of all human beings. Long after the demise of the latest gimmicks and fads, Christian believers all over the world will be found listening to the simple preaching of the gospel and enjoying fellowship together and with God.

Part Seven

Rapid Fact-finder

Angela Tilby
John-David Yule

A

'ABBASID DYNASTY (AD 750–1055) The second great Islamic dynasty which ruled from Baghdad. Under the 'Abbasids the empire enjoyed a period of increased prosperity and trade. Libraries and centres of learning were established throughout the Islamic world. Baghdad fell to the Seljuk Turks in 1055.

'ABDUH, Muhammad (AD 1849–1905) Leader of an Egyptian Islamic reform movement who taught at the orthodox academy of Al-Azhar. He tried to balance the authority of the 'ULAMA' with modern knowledge, believing that faith and reason were complementary.

ABHIDHAMMA PITAKA
THERAVADA Buddhist scripture on techniques of mind-training. The aim is to eliminate the idea of the self. It is the key work of Buddhist psychology.

ABRAHAM, ISAAC AND JACOB
The three PATRIARCHS who are continually remembered in the Jewish liturgy as the original recipients of God's promise and blessing. According to tradition they are buried in the tomb of the patriarchs in the cave of Mach-pelah in the modern town of Hebron.

ABSOLUTE, THE Term for GOD or the divine often preferred by those who conceive of God predominantly in abstract or impersonal terms.

ABU BAKR MUHAMMAD'S father-in-law and traditionally his earliest convert. He was elected CALIPH after the Prophet's death and ruled for two years, fighting tribes who were trying to break away from the Islamic community. He began the compilation of the QUR'AN.

ADAE Ancestral customs held among the Ashanti and other peoples of Ghana. It refers particularly to the special rites which are held twice every forty-three days and require abstinence from work.

ADI GRANTH Sacred book of Sikhism. It is regarded as the eternal GURU for the SIKH community. It is the central focus of the Sikh home and of the GURDWARA

ADONAI See YHWH

ADONIS Greek god of vegetation whose rites included women mourning at his death and rejoicing at his resurrection. His MYTH describes him as a beautiful youth from Cyprus who was loved by APHRODITE but killed by a boar while hunting. His name is the Semitic *adon* ('lord') and he has features in common with TAMMUZ.

ADVAITA ('Non-twoness') The monist (see MONISM) doctrine of

SHANKARA that all reality is fundamentally one and divine.

AESIR The race of the gods in Norse mythology. It may derive from a root meaning 'wind'.

AFRICAN INDEPENDENT CHURCHES African churches which have arisen in the past 100 years and offer a synthesis of CHRISTIANITY with traditional PRIMAL RELIGIONS. Many have prophetic or charismatic founders and emphasize spiritual healing and communication with ancestors. Some have been a focus of nationalistic aspirations.

AFTERLIFE Any form of conscious existence after the death of the body.

AGAPE Greek word for 'love' which has come to express the Christian understanding of God's love which does not depend on any worthiness or attractiveness of the object of his love. Christians are taught to demonstrate this love to each other in the Christian FELLOWSHIP, and to others. Also, a EUCHARIST meal.

AGE OF AQUARIUS The approaching period of some 2000 years when, because of the precession of the equinoxes, the intersection of the ecliptic with the celestial equator will lie in the constellation Aquarius. This will mark the end of the present Age of Pisces. According to some NEW AGE RELIGIONS, the Aquarian Age will be marked by the decline of institutional and authoritative religion and an increase of self-awareness and spiritual knowledge.

AGNI Indian fire god of Vedic times (see VEDAS). As sacrificial fire, Agni mediates between gods and men and is especially concerned with order and ritual.

AGONES Greek public festivals of sport or drama held in honour of the gods. Most famous were the Olympic Games, dedicated to Olympian god ZEUS.

AHIMSA Indian virtue of non-violence. It usually applies to abstention from harming any living creature and hence to vegetarianism. The doctrine was developed in JAINISM, BUDDHISM and some HINDU sects. In Jain belief violence carries severe penalties of KARMA. MAHATAMA GANDHI applied the idea to the political struggles of the oppressed in his practice of non-violent non-cooperation.

AHKIN High priest of the MAYA who was one of a college of eight or twelve. They were guardians of the arts of writing; they kept the complex Mayan calendar and were experts on cures, SACRIFICE and prescribed methods of DIVINATION.

AHMADIYYA SECT Offshoot of ISLAM founded in India by Mirza Ghulam Ahmad (died 1908) who is believed to be the MESSIAH MAHDI. The sect denies the authority of the 'ULAMA', IJMA' and JIHAD. It is a missionary sect and has gained converts in Asia and Africa.

AHMAD KAHN, Sayyid (born AD 1817) Indian MUSLIM modernist. He believed that scientific advance was compatible with ISLAM and that CHRISTIANITY and Islam had much in common. He taught for some years in England before founding the Anglo-Oriental College at Aligarh.

AH PUCH God of death of the MAYA. Under the title 'lord of seven hells' he is portrayed as a human skeleton. He is accompanied by a dog and a groaning bird.

AHRIMAN See ANGRA MAINYU.

AHURA MAZDA/OHRMAZD ('Wise Lord') ZOROASTER'S name for God. His attributes are comparable to those of VARUNA, the Vedic sky god. He demands ethical and ritual purity and he judges the souls of men after death. His symbol is sacred fire.

AKHENATEN Name adopted by Amenophis IV, king of Egypt 1353–1335 BC, in honour of Aten ('the sun disc') whose cult he promoted to the exclusion of all others in a short-lived reform of Egyptian religion. He built a magnificent new capital at el-Amarna.

AKIBA, Rabbi (AD 50–135) Jewish teacher who developed the MISHNAH method of repetitive transmission of teachings. He began the work of systematizing the available interpretations of TORAH, laying the foundations for the work of JUDAH HA NASI. He was also famous for his use of MIDRASH, investing every detail of the Hebrew texts with significance.

ALA/ALE/ANA The earth goddess worshipped by the Ibo people of Ghana. She preserves the fertility of the land and the family. The dead are said to rest in her womb. She is also the guardian of morality: laws and oaths are made in her name.

AL-ASH'ARI (died AD 935) MUSLIM theologian and philosopher who laid the foundations of orthodoxy. He argued that the QUR'AN was eternal, in opposition to a school that claimed eternity belonged only to God. At the same time he claimed that the actual words, recited and written by man, were not eternal.

ALBIGENSIANS The CATHARS of southern France who flourished in the late twelfth and early thirteenth centuries. Their theology was a DUALISM that has been compared with that of the MANICHAEANS although they were probably unconnected. They saw CHRIST as an ANGEL whose teachings had been corrupted by the Catholic clergy. Their most rigorous adherents, the 'perfects', abstained from marriage and avoided animal products.

ALCHEMY Mystical science of chemical manipulation which seeks to change base metals into gold, find the universal cure for illness and discover the secret of immortality. Its study passed from Hellenistic Egypt through the Arabs to medieval Europe. It is also important in TAOISM.

AL-DIN AFGHANI, Jamal (AD 1839–97) Indian MUSLIM philosopher who tried to strengthen the influence of ISLAM as a social and moral movement. He believed that the best practical expression of Islam was democratic government. He worked also for unity in the Muslim world.

AL-GHAZALI (AD 1058–1111) Orthodox MUSLIM legal expert who renounced his post and became a Sufi (see SUFISM). He attacked the incursions of Greek thought into ISLAM and defended the teaching of the QUR'AN. He also defended the Sufi experience of God but denied the possibility of human deification.

AL-HALLAJ (died AD 922) Sufi MYSTIC who was crucified because of his confession 'I am the real' which was taken as a claim to divinity. He considered JESUS OF NAZARETH as the supreme example of human deification and at this death forgave his enemies in imitation of the passion of Jesus.

'ALI Cousin and son-in-law of MUHAMMAD who was elected fourth CALIPH in AD 656. War broke out between 'Ali and the governor of Syria who claimed that 'Ali had plotted 'UTHMAN's death. In AD 661 'Ali was murdered and his son Hasan renounced any claim to the caliphate.

ALLAH The supreme God proclaimed by MUHAMMAD. Allah is one; there are no gods beside him. He is undivided pure spirit, the creator and sustainer of all that is, known to man in the revelation of his holy will in the QUR'AN.

ALLFATHER In early Norse mythology, the oldest of all the gods and the creator god, probably at first a sky god. His attributes were taken over first by TYR and then by ODIN who retained the title Allfather.

ALMSGIVING The giving of free gifts, usually of money, to the poor. In ISLAM it is obligatory (see ZAKAT). In THERAVADA Buddhism the lay community is linked to the SANGHA by their provision of food for the MONKS which is collected on a daily almsround.

AL-RAHMAN AND AL-RAHMIN ('The merciful' and 'the mercy-giver') See BEAUTIFUL NAMES OF GOD.

AMATERASU Japanese sun goddess, the principal deity in SHINTO. She represents the power of light, growth and fertility and her symbol is a mirror. The EMPERORS of Japan claimed descent from her.

AMESHA SPENTAS/ AMAHRASPANDS 'Bounteous immortals' in ZOROASTRIANISM who surround AHURA MAZDA and are also his characteristic attributes. In later Zoroastrianism they are created spirits like ANGELS who help him in his fight with evil.

AMIDA Japanese form of AMITABHA.

AMIDAH ('Standing') The principal Jewish daily prayer, also known as the Eighteen Benedictions, recited standing. Today it actually comprises nineteen benedictions, including prayers for the restoration of ISRAEL and for peace.

AMITABHA ('Infinite light') Celestial BUDDHA worshipped in China and Japan (where his name is Amida). He is believed to live in a 'pure land' in the far west where those faithful to him go after death (see JODO SHINSHU; NEMBUTSA; PURE LAND BUDDHISM).

AMMA Supreme HIGH GOD among the Dogon people of Upper Volta in West Africa. He made the sun and moon out of clay and then united with the earth, producing people. Unusually for a high god, he is worshipped in temples and has his own priesthood.

AMON-RE State god of the Egyptian New Kingdom (sixteenth to eleventh centuries BC). He is a fusion of the sun god, Re, and a Theban god, Amun.

ANA See ALA.

ANALECTS One of the four books of the so-called Confucian canon. It contains the essence of CONFUCIOUS' teaching and was probably compiled about seventy years after his death.

ANANDA One of the most prominent members of the BUDDHA'S SANGHA. Traditionally he was the Buddha's cousin and many of the sayings are addressed to him, including the words of comfort shortly before the Buddha's death. He helped to fix the canon of Buddhist SCRIPTURE.

ANATTA Buddhist term indicating that there is ultimately no 'soul' (see SOUL (1)). All beings are merely a series of mental and physical states. Anatta is one of the three MARKS OF EXISTENCE.

ANCESTOR SPIRITS Spirits of the dead in PRIMAL RELIGIONS. They are sometimes thought of as living in a shadowy UNDERWORLD, sometimes in a place of happiness such as the Happy Hunting Ground of North American Indians. They are revered by the living who believe they can appear to them in DREAMS and warn them of danger.

ANCESTOR VENERATION The practice in PRIMAL RELIGIONS of making offerings to the spirits of the dead and expecting to communicate with them through DREAMS.

ANDRIAMANITRA ('The fragrant lord') The HIGH GOD worshipped in the PRIMAL RELIGION of Madagascar.

ANGELS Spiritual beings who in JUDAISM and CHRISTIANITY act as the messengers of GOD. They have two primary functions: to worship God and to support and encourage human beings. In ISLAM the Archangel GABRIEL is associated with the giving of the QUR'AN.

ANGLICAN CHURCHES Worldwide grouping of churches which recognize the primacy among equals of the Archbishop of Canterbury. They include both catholic and reformed elements and retain BISHOPS.

ANGRA MAINYU/AHRIMAN The chief spirit who is opposed to AHURA MAZDA in Zoroastrian belief. He works continually for evil in the service of the *druj* ('lie'). Later he came to be considered the leader of a vast hierarchy of evil spirits.

ANICCA Buddhist term for the impermanence and changeability which marks all existence.

ANIMISM A term formerly used to describe pre-literary religions. It was dropped because its meaning 'spirit-ism' was felt to be misleading. (See PRIMAL RELIGIONS; TYLOR, EDWARD BURNETT.)

ANTHROPOSOPHY Spiritual system invented by Rudolf STEINER. It stresses the threefold nature of man as physical, etheric and astral body and proposes a programme for spiritual education which includes techniques of MEDITATION.

ANU The sky god of ancient Sumerian religion and HIGH GOD of the Sumerian pantheon. He had little to do with human affairs and delegated his authority to ENLIL. From about 2000 BC he was called King of Gods and Father. His consort was ISHTAR.

ANU/DANU Celtic goddess of the earth and of plenty, and mother of all the Irish gods. The Christian St Anne has attracted some of her legends.

ANUBIS Jackal-headed god of ancient Egypt who conducted souls to judgement and weighed them in the great balance. Known as 'the embalmer', he watched over mummification and was the guardian of tombs and cemeteries.

ANUTU HIGH GOD of the universe worshipped by the Jabem and Bakava people of Papua New Guinea. He was believed to sit on the horizon where the sky meets the sea and hold the sky in his hands. LUTHERAN CHURCH Christians of the area use the name Anutu for God.

APHRODITE Greek goddess of love and patroness of beauty and sexual attractiveness. Her cult was imported from the Near East. The Greeks thought of her as vain and cruel but the Romans identified her with VENUS and honoured her as the mother of Aeneas, ancestor of the Romans. In Cyprus she was worshipped as the MOTHER GODDESS.

API Scythian name for the earth goddess.

APOCALYPTIC Genre of writing in CHRISTIANITY and JUDAISM, concerned with hidden truths, pointing to the ultimate triumph of faith and the judgement of nations. Daniel and Revelation are examples in the BIBLE.

APOCRYPHA Historical and wisdom writings found in the Greek version of the Hebrew scriptures but excluded from the canon of the HEBREW BIBLE fixed at the Synod of Jamnia around AD 100. The Roman Catholic Church accepts its authority, though Eastern Orthodox and Protestant Churches distinguish it from inspired SCRIPTURE.

APOCRYPHAL NEW TESTAMENT Early CHRISTIAN writings in the form of gospels, acts or epistles not included in the Christian canon of SCRIPTURE. Some express heretical teachings.

APOLLO A major god of both Greeks and Romans, though Greek in origin. He is sometimes seen as the sun and is the patron of the arts (especially music), of prophecy, of divination and of medicine. He was the inspiration of the DELPHIC ORACLE.

APOSTLE (1) 'One who is sent', name for the twelve original followers of JESUS OF NAZARETH, also PAUL. The 'apostolic age' is a time of great authority for the Christian CHURCH. (2) Title of MUHAMMAD.

AQUINAS, Thomas (AD 1225–74) Dominican theologian and philosopher whose teachings form the basis of official Roman Catholic theology. He taught a fundamental distinction between faith and reason, asserting that God's existence can be proved, but that the doctrines of the TRINITY and the INCARNATION are revealed and must be accepted on faith.

ARABIC Semitic language related to HEBREW. The language of the QUR'AN and hence of most MUSLIM legislation, theology and prayer. As ISLAM spread to non-Arab peoples, the Arabic language affected the development of their languages and there are African languages, such as Swahili and Hausa, which are a mixture of Arabic and a local dialect.

ARAHAT ('One who is worthy') THERAVADA Buddhist term for one who gains ENLIGHTENMENT by following the discipline of the SANGHA.

ARCHETYPES Term invented by C.G. JUNG to describe the concepts held in common by different people at different items and in different places. He believed that the concept of GOD was the archetype of the self and that it was the object of each individual to discover it.

ARES The Greek god of war, possibly imported from Thrace.

ARIANISM Fourth-century Christian CHERESY of Arius who denied the divinity of CHRIST, claiming that the Son of God was created and not eternal. It was condemned at the Council of Nicaea in AD 325 but flourished until the Council of Constantinople in AD 381.

ARISTOTLE (384–322 BC) Greek philosopher and scientist who taught on every branch of knowledge valued in his time. His work is characterized by acute observation, close reasoning and orderly exposition. His work was rediscovered in the Middle Ages and laid the basis for the theology of THOMAS AQUINAS and for the HUMANISM of the Renaissance.

ARK (1) Israelite religious artefact, probably in the form of a portable miniature temple, which was carried into battle as evidence of the presence of God (see YHWH). In Solomon's TEMPLE the ark lived in the Holy of Holies. (2) A cupboard in the wall of a SYNAGOGUE that faces JERUSALEM, where the handwritten parchment scrolls of TORAH are kept.

ARTEMIS Greek goddess and patroness of virginity, hunting, archery and wild animals. She was also the protector of the newly-born and the bringer of death to women. At Ephesus in Asia Minor, she was worshipped as the MOTHER GODDESS. (See also DIANA.)

ARTHUR Legendary hero of Celtic Britain who may have originated as a Romano-British chieftain. His legends were gradually worked into a coherent Christian framework in which he became the medieval ideal of a Christian king.

ARYAN Word describing the Caucasian people who invaded India around 2000 BC and who gradually imposed their language and culture upon the earlier inhabitants. Related

peoples settled in Iran and Mesopotamia.

ASCETICISM Austere practices designed to lead to the control of the body and the senses. These may include FASTING and MEDITATION, the renunciation of possessions and the pursuit of solitude.

ASGARD The home of the gods in Norse religion. It is a mountainous region rising out of MIDGARD and separated from it by a rainbow bridge.

ASHKENAZIM One of the two main cultural groups in JUDAISM which emerged in the Middle Ages. Their tradition is from Palestinian Jewry and they live in central, northern and eastern Europe. They developed Yiddish as their language, which is a mixture of Hebrew, Slav and German.

ASHRAM In Indian religion, a hermitage or monastery. It has come to denote a communal house for devotees of a GURU. It functions as a centre for building up the commitment of believers and for transmitting the guru's message.

ASHUR Chief god of ancient Assyria. He was a war god and his consort was ISHTAR.

ASHVAGHOSHA Buddhist writer and poet of the first century AD who traditionally lived in north-west India at a royal court. He wrote a verse poem telling the life of the BUDDHA up to the time of his ENLIGHTENMENT.

ASCLEPIOS Greek god of healing whose cult was located at Epidauros. He was struck dead by ZEUS for bringing the dead to life. Snakes were sacred to him and he was thought to be incarnate in their shape (see SACRED SNAKES). His cult was introduced to Rome in the third century BC.

ASOKA (270–232 BC) Indian king who inherited an empire in northern India. He renounced Brahminical statecraft which required him to pursue a policy of imperialist expansion and became a Buddhist lay follower. He had edicts of Buddhist statecraft inscribed on rocks and pillars throughout the country. His example and influence spread BUDDHISM throughout India and beyond.

ASSASSINS Members of a Muslim ISMA'ILI sect which flourished from the eleventh to the thirteenth centuries AD. They were thought to intoxicate themselves with hashish (hence their name) and then go out and murder their enemies.

ASTRAL PLANE The intermediate world, according to THEOSOPHY and SPIRITUALISM, to which the human consciousness passes at death. Some psychics and visionaries are able to project themselves there at will.

ASTROLOGY The study of the influence of the stars on the character and destiny of human beings. The locations of the planets in the field of the zodiac at the time of the subject's birth are the key data considered in the astrologer's analysis.

ATARGATIS Syrian name for the MOTHER GODDESS. She was particularly revered by the Roman Emperor Nero.

ATATURK, Kemal (AD 1881–1938) Founder and first president of the secular Turkish state. He abolished the Islamic law and the caliphate (see CALIPH) and introduced a programme of westernization, including Roman script.

ATHANASIUS (AD 296–373) Bishop of Alexandria who strongly resisted the teachings of ARIANISM and developed the Christian doctrines of the INCARNATION and the TRINITY.

ATHENA One of the great Greek goddesses of Mount OLYMPUS who sprang fully armed from the head of her father, ZEUS. She is the patroness of war, of the city of Athens and of many crafts and skills. She is usually portrayed in full armour, with an owl on her shoulder and the Gorgon's head painted on her shield.

ATMAN SANSKRIT word meaning 'soul' or 'self'. The UPANISHADS teach that atman is identical to BRAHMAN, i.e. the soul is one with the divine.

ATONEMENT (1) Ritual act which restores harmony between man and the divine, when it has been broken by sin or impurity. (2) In CHRISTIANITY, reconciliation between God and man required because of the absolute holiness of God and the

sinfulness of man. As man is incapable of achieving atonement, it is a work of God's GRACE, through the death of Jesus Christ for man's sin.

ATONEMENT, DAY OF See YOM KIPPUR.

ATTIS Vegetation god with a spring festival of death and resurrection which originated in Phrygia. He was worshipped as the consort of CYBELE. In one version of the myth he castrates himself, thus becoming the first of Cybele's eunuch priests.

ATUA Any god or spiritual power in Maori religion.

AUGUR In Roman religion, a member of the college of augurs, whose task was to give prophetic advice through the interpretation of omens. Taking the *auspices*, their principal method, involved observing the flight of birds.

AUGUSTINE (AD 354–430) BISHOP of Hippo in North Africa who was converted to CHRISTIANITY from the teaching of the MANICHAEANS. He stressed the absolute GRACE of God in man's SALVATION and the depravity of man through ORIGINAL SIN.

AUGUSTUS Title of the first Roman emperor, formerly known as Octavian, who ruled 31 BC–AD 14. He pacified and unified the empire, thus facilitating the later spread of CHRISTIANITY. After his death he was declared a god and worshipped throughout the empire.

AVALOKITESHVARA ('Regarder of the cries of the earth') Celestial BUDDHA worshipped by Tibetans and in Korea, Japan and China. The DALAI LAMA is believed to be a reincarnation of him. This Buddha is known under male and female forms and is depicted with a thousand arms, symbolizing endless labour for the welfare of mankind. (See also CHENRESI.)

AVALON Celtic island of immortality replete with miraculous apple trees. Here the hero ARTHUR was taken to recover from his mortal wounds.

AVATAR ('One who descends') In popular Hinduism, Lord VISHNU appears on earth at intervals to assert

ancient values and destroy illusion. The main tradition refers to ten descents, nine of which have already happened. The mythical KRISHNA is the most famous avatar. Some modern cults claim to worship a living avatar.

AVERROES See IBN RUSHD.

AVESTA The SCRIPTURES of ZOROASTRIANISM. It includes the *Gathas*, a series of poems reminiscent of the hymns of the VEDAS which may go back to ZOROASTER himself. They may have been used as a liturgy to ward off ANGRA MAINYU and his evil spirits.

AYATOLLAH ('Sign of God') Iranian term for a great MUJTAHID who has authority in the SHI'A Muslim community.

AZTEC NEW FIRE CEREMONY Ritual which took place at the end of every Aztec cycle of fifty-two years. It was performed at night on a volcanic hill visible from many parts of the valley of Mexico. When the constellation *Pleiades* reached the middle of the sky, the priests signalled that the world would continue for another cycle of fifty-two years. A human victim was sacrificed and a new fire was kindled in his chest cavity.

AZTECS American Indians whose empire in central Mexico flourished from the late twelfth century AD until the coming of the conquistador Herman Cortes in 1519. Their religion centred around a sacred calendar (see TONALPOHUALLI) and featured human SACRIFICE in which the heart torn from a living victim was offered to the gods. (See also CHICOMECOATL; HUITZILOPOCHTLI; NEZAHUALCOYOTL; QUETZALCOATL; TEZCATLIPOCA; TLALOC; TLOQUE NAHUAQUE; XIPE TOTEC; XIUHTECUHTLI.)

B

BA The breath or life-giving force in ancient Egyptian belief. In a ritual ceremony the ba was breathed back into the mouth of a mummified corpse to guarantee the survival of the dead person.

BAAL Divinity of ancient Canaanite or Phoenician fertility religion. The name means 'lord'.

BAAL SHEM TOV (about AD 1700–60) Jewish MYSTIC who founded the movement of HASIDISM. His name means 'Good Master of the Name (of God)' and it is often shortened to BEShT. His original name was Israel ben Eliezer. At the age of thirty-six he developed powers of healing and prophecy. He taught a kind of mystical PANTHEISM. He was greatly loved and became the source of many Yiddish legends and miracle stories.

BABISM See BAHA'I.

BABYLONIAN EPIC OF CREATION/ENUMA ELISH The story of the god MARDUK's fight with the primordial ocean, Tiamat, who is presented as a sea monster. Marduk slit Tiamat in two and made heaven and earth out of the pieces. This MYTH was probably re-enacted every spring at an ENTHRONEMENT FESTIVAL.

BABYLONIAN FLOOD STORY A parallel to the story of the flood in the BIBLE going back to a Sumerian original but best known from the EPIC OF GILGAMESH. It tells the story of a wise king, Utnapishtim, who survived the flood caused by the god ENLIL by taking refuge in a huge boat with his wife and various animals. He was rewarded by Enlil by being transported to a land of immortality.

BAHA'I Offshoot of the Persian Babism movement. The Bab ('gate'; died AD 1850) taught that he had superseded MUHAMMAD and heralded a new faith. One of his disciples, known as Baha'u'llah (1817–1892) developed his teachings into a universalistic religion based on a new scripture, the *Kitab Akdas*. The largest Baha'i communities are in India, Africa and South America; that in the USA is also quite large.

BAIAME HIGH GOD and creator of the world in the belief of the Aboriginals of south-eastern Australia.

BALDER The son of ODIN and FRIGGA, the wisest and most beautiful of the Norse gods. He was killed by the wiles of LOKI but could not be restored to ASGARD because Loki refused to weep for him. His name means 'lord' and he may be connected with the Middle-Eastern dying and rising gods, ADONIS and TAMMUZ.

BAPTISM The SACRAMENT of entry into the Christian CHURCH. By washing in water in the name of the TRINITY, it symbolizes the person's identification with CHRIST's death and resurrection, in dying to sin and being raised to new life. In the case of infants, promises are made on behalf of the child for later CONFIRMATION.

BAPTIST CHURCHES Protestant churches emphasizing the BAPTISM of adult believers by total immersion.

BARK PAINTINGS Paintings scratched on tree bark by Australian Aboriginals, depicting mythical scenes and supernatural figures.

BAR MITZVAH ('Son of the commandment') Ceremony by which Jewish boys, at the age of thirteen, accept the positive commandments of JUDAISM and are counted as adult members of the community.

BARTH, Karl (AD 1886–1968) Swiss Calvinist theologian who reacted against liberalism in theology and declared theology's central theme to be the Word of God.

BAVIDYE In the Kiluba and related Bantu languages, a word meaning 'superior being'. It refers to spirits associated with the community. It also refers to the creator god, often with the addition of *mulubu*: 'old' or 'great'.

BEAUTIFUL NAMES OF GOD Ninety-nine names which characterize the will of ALLAH in ISLAM. Seventy are found in the QUR'AN; the rest are traditional. The most important are *Al-Rahman* and *Al-Rahmin*, 'the merciful' and 'the mercy-giver'.

BEING OF LIGHT A figure occasionally reported to have been seen by those resuscitated from a state of near death. The figure is sometimes identified as CHRIST or an ANGEL.

BELENOS ('Bright') Celtic deity of spring and healing who may have been associated with the sun. The festival BELTANE may reflect his name. He became identified with APOLLO.

BELTANE Celtic spring festival and origin of May Day. The name means 'shining fire' and it is likely that sacred fires were lit for the people to dance round, encouraging the growth of the summer sun.

BENARES/VARANASI/KASHI The most holy city of HINDUISM, situated on the banks of the GANGES. It is a centre for the worship of SHIVA and attracts one million pilgrims every year. The BUDDHA preached his first sermon here, traditionally in the deer park on the outskirts of the city.

BENEDICT (about AD 480–550) Monk and reformer who wrote a Rule of monastic life which has been followed by MONKS and NUNS of the Western church ever since.

BHAGAVAD GITA ('Song of the lord') A section of the MAHABHARATA in the form of a battlefield dialogue between the warrior prince Arjuna and KRISHNA, disguised as his charioteer. Arjuna is unwilling to fight his kinsmen but Krishna encourages him, teaching him that wisdom requires him to fulfil his proper role while at the same time renouncing the consequences of his actions.

BHAGAVAN Indian title meaning 'lord' or 'worshipful'. It is frequently used of VISHNU. It is also a title of honour used by devotees of holy men.

BHAGAVAN SHRI RAJNEESH Indian spiritual teacher and philosopher who founded his own ASHRAM at Pune (Poona) in India. His daily talks and reflections are transcribed and widely published in the West.

BHAJANA An Indian song or HYMN in praise of God usually sung communally at devotional gatherings and accompanied by musical instruments.

BHAKTI Love of, or devotion to God. It is one of the Hindu paths to union with God (see YOGA). It is expressed in popular religion in which the worshipper develops a sense of personal relationship to God, responding to him as though to a father, mother, friend, lover or child, and looking to him for grace.

BHIKSHU ('One who shares') A Buddhist MONK who teaches the DHAMMA and receives his daily food from the community in return.

BIBLE The book of CHRISTIANITY, comprising the Hebrew OLD TESTAMENT and the NEW TESTAMENT which, Christians believe, together form a unified message of God's SALVATION.

BISHOP The most senior order of ministry in the Christian CHURCH, with authority to ordain PRIESTS. Many REFORMED CHURCHES do not have bishops.

BLACK MUSLIMS American Negro movement founded in 1930. Its founder was declared a PROPHET of ALLAH, a claim rejected by orthodox MUSLIMS. The Black Muslims exclude white people from their temples and practise strict morality.

BLACK STONE Sacred object set in the wall of the Muslim KA'BA sanctuary in MECCA. Tradition asserts that it was received by the biblical Ishmael from the archangel GABRIEL. During the rites of pilgrimage (see HAJJ) the faithful try to kiss or touch the stone.

BLACK THEOLOGY A movement developed in the USA which uses the experience of being black in a white-dominated society as a source for theological reflection and Christian action.

BLAVATSKY, Helena Petrovna (AD 1831–91) Founder in 1875 of the Theosophical Society (see THEOSOPHY), who claimed to have received the 'ancient wisdom' after seven years in Tibet being taught by various MAHATMAS. She wrote books defending SPIRITUALISM and various OCCULT teachings.

BODH GAYA Place of the ENLIGHTENMENT of the BUDDHA. Traditionally, he sat for seven days under a peepal tree and then realized the truth of all existence. The tree that witnessed the enlightenment was called the Bodhi-tree. There are many versions of the story.

BODHI In various schools of BUDDHISM, 'awakening', or 'perfect wisdom', or 'supreme ENLIGHTENMENT'.

BODHIDHARMA Traditionally the first teacher of CH'AN Buddhism who moved from southern India to China in AD 520. He introduced the methods of sharp questioning and paradox found today in Japanese ZEN.

BODHISATTVA In MAHAYANA Buddhism a saint or semi-divine being who has voluntarily renounced NIRVANA in order to help others to salvation. In popular devotion bodhisattvas are worshipped as symbols of compassion.

BOG Slavic name for GOD.

BÖN Religion of Tibet before the coming of BUDDHISM. It was a form of nature worship presided over by a chief SHAMAN who communicated with the earth and sky. Though the adherents of Bön violently opposed the introduction of Buddhism, many of their practices were absorbed into the Buddhist system.

BONA DEA Roman fertility goddess whose worship was open only to women. Her rites were celebrated annually in an all-night ceremony presided over by the wife of the chief magistrate.

BOOK OF MORMON Sacred SCRIPTURE of MORMONISM which was revealed to Joseph SMITH. It describes a conflict between two branches of a family which had emigrated under divine guidance from JERUSALEM to America in 600 BC. The Mormons regard it as the completion of the Biblical revelation.

BOOK OF THE DEAD Name given to various collections of SPELLS, often illustrated, buried with the dead of ancient Egypt to assist their souls through the judgement. Commonly the soul is depicted as

weighed in a balance against *ma'at*, a conception of 'right order' (depicted as an ostrich feather), by the god ANUBIS while the scribe THOTH records the result and OSIRIS presides. (See also TIBETAN BOOK OF THE DEAD.)

BOOTHS/TABERNACLES/SUKKOT Week-long Autumn Jewish festival marking the end of the harvest. Branch- or straw-covered booths remind JEWS of God's protection during their forty-year journey through the wilderness.

BRAHMA The creator god in the Brahmanical period of Indian religion (see BRAHMANISM) whose authority was mocked by the BUDDHA.

BRAHMAN In HINDUISM, the divine, absolute reality. The word is the neuter form of BRAHMA, the creator god of early Hinduism, and originally referred to the holy power evoked through sacrifice.

BRAHMANISM The religion of India at the time of the UPANISHADS and during the early Buddhist period. It was a religion of RITUAL and SACRIFICE with emphasis on the supremacy of the Brahmin class (see CASTE SYSTEM) who held priestly authority over all aspects of life. The use of SANSKRIT was emphasized and there was marked hostility to non-Brahmanical teachings.

BRAHMA SAMAJ Monotheistic HINDU movement founded by RAMMOHUN ROY. It held services influenced by Christian church worship with hymns and theistic readings but failed to make an impact on the Hindu community.

BRAHMINS See CASTE SYSTEM.

BREVIARY Liturgical book containing instructions for the recitation of daily services as followed by the Christian clergy, MONKS and NUNS of the Western church, with the proper hymns, psalms and lessons for each service.

BRIGHID Celtic goddess of poetry, prophecy, learning and healing. The Romans associated her Gaulish equivalent with Minerva. She was absorbed into Irish Christianity as St

Brighid whose feast day coincides with a Celtic spring festival.

BUBER, Martin (AD 1878–1965) Austrian Jewish theologian whose religious roots were in HASIDISM. Although a Zionist, he was critical of the politics of ZIONISM and of Talmudic tradition (see TALMUD). He believed that the central task of JEWS was to build up God's kingdom on the basis of the Jewish belief in an essential dialogue between God and man. He has influenced Christian spirituality and social teaching.

BUDDHA ('The enlightened one') (1) Siddharta GAUTAMA a sage of the SHAKYA tribe who lived in India in the sixth century BC, the founder of BUDDHISM. There is little doubt that there was a historical figure at the source of Buddhism though some branches of MAHAYANA regard this as unimportant. (2) Any human being or celestial figure who has reached ENLIGHTENMENT.

BUDDHAGHOSA Buddhist writer of the fifth century AD who wrote many commentaries on the scriptures and one original work, *The Path of Purity*. The Burmese believe he was a native of Burma but other traditions hold that he was an Indian who worked in Ceylon (Sri Lanka).

BUDDHA IMAGE Representation of the BUDDHA used in all forms of BUDDHISM. The Buddha is most commonly portrayed in the LOTUS POSTURE, but there are also versions of him standing or lying on one side. The various postures and position of the hands symbolize the defeat of evil, the achieving of ENLIGHTENMENT, the preaching of the DHAMMA and the final NIRVANA. The images are psychological aids rather than objects of worship, though in MAHAYANA Buddhism they act as a focus for devotion.

BUDDHISM The great missionary religion which developed from the teaching of the BUDDHA and which spread from India into south-east Asia, later expanding into northern Asia, China and Japan. The two principal divisions are the THERAVADA (HINAYANA) and the MAHAYANA. Special features are found in TIBETAN BUDDHISM, also known as VAJRAYANA or Lamaism.

BUTSU-DAN A Japanese domestic altar to the BUDDHA which contains images or objects of worship and memorial tablets to ancestors. There may be lights, flowers and incense and it is the focus of daily prayer, chanting and the offering of food and drink.

BWANGA 'Medicine' or 'effective cure' in the Bantu languages. It refers particularly to the dynamism or potency for healing or destruction in magical rites and SPELLS.

C

CALIPH ('Deputy' or 'representative') Title of the leaders of the MUSLIM community after the death of MUHAMMAD. The first three caliphs ruled from MEDINA; the UMAYYADS from Damascus, and the 'ABBASIDS from Baghdad. From AD 1517 the caliph was based at Istanbul. Kemal ATATURK abolished the caliphate in 1923.

CALVIN, John (AD 1509–64) French theologian who organized the REFORMATION from Geneva. He emphasized justification by faith and the sole authority of the BIBLE and in particular that each person's eternal destiny was decided irrevocably by God and only those destined for salvation would come to faith.

CAO DAI Religious and political movement which started in southern Vietnam around 1920. It is sometimes called the 'Third Amnesty'. Firmly nationalistic, its teachings are a mixture of BUDDHISM and TAOISM.

CARDINAL Member of a college of ordained high officials in the ROMAN CATHOLIC Church who, since 1179, have elected the POPE. Cardinals are appointed by the pope.

CARGO CULTS Term used for new religious movements of Melanesia and New Guinea which imitate European ritual in the hope of thereby receiving European-type material wealth—'cargo'. They look

for the arrival of a MESSIAH who will banish illness and distribute the cargo among the people.

CASTE SYSTEM The division of a society into groups reflecting and defining the division of labour. In India, caste is traditionally seen as the creation of BRAHMA, each caste emerging symbolically from different parts of his body. There are four chief groups: Brahmins, priests, come from Brahma's mouth; Kshatriyas, warriors, come from Brahma's arms; Vaishyas, peasants, come from Brahma's thighs; Shudras, unskilled labourers come from Brahma's feet. Groups of no definite caste were regarded as UNTOUCHABLES and were banished from society.

CATECHISM (1) Instruction on Christian faith; for example, instruction in question and answer form given to those preparing for BAPTISM or CONFIRMATION. (2) A popular manual of Christian doctrine.

CATECHUMEN Candidate in training for Christian BAPTISM.

CATHARS Members of a medieval heretical Christian sect which flourished in Germany, France and Italy before their suppression in the thirteenth century. (See also ALBIGENSIANS.)

CATHOLICISM CHRISTIANITY as practiced by those who emphasize a continuous historical tradition of faith and practice from the time of the APOSTLES to the present day.

CELTS Population group occupying much of central and western Europe during the first millennium BC. They included the ancient Gauls and Britons. They worshipped the MOTHER GODDESS and various local and tribal deities. Evidence from skulls excavated in Celtic sacred places suggests that they practised human sacrifice. Their priests were the DRUIDS.

CERES Roman grain goddess who became identified with the Greek DEMETER.

CERNUNNOS ('The horned one') Celtic horned god associated with the earth and fertility, and protector of the animal kingdom. Usually portrayed sitting cross-legged, he is often accompanied by a stag, or a horned serpent or a bull.

CHAC Rain god of the MAYA. He is portrayed as an old man with a long nose and weeping eyes. He is in quadruple form and faces in all directions. Benevolent and a friend to man, his name was invoked at planting ceremonies.

CHAKRAS According to Tibetan and Indian thought, the six nerve centres of the body from which psychic energy flows. They are: between the eyebrows; at the throat; at the heart; at the navel; at the genitals, and at the base of the spine where KUNDALINI, the serpent-energy, lies coiled. The chakras are sometimes called 'lotus centres'.

CH'AN School of Chinese BUDDHISM formed in perhaps the seventh century AD from a blend of TAOISM and MAHAYANA teachings. The school stressed experience rather than learning and distrusted a too intellectual approach.

CHANG TAO LING (born AD 34) Chinese Taoist priest who established a religious order on Dragon Mountain in Kiangsi. He claimed to have had a vision of LAO-TZU and to have discovered the elixir of life. He ordained his followers who inherited his secret formula and practised various kinds of ALCHEMY.

CHANT Type of singing in which many syllables are sung on a single note or a repeated short musical phrase. Many religions use chanting in worship. Jews and Christians chant the PSALMS; Buddhists and others their own sacred SCRIPTURES. The repetitive nature of chanting can aid MEDITATION.

CHARISMATIC MOVEMENT Renewal movement in Catholic and Protestant Churches stressing the work and manifestation of the HOLY SPIRIT in the life of the church and of the individual believer.

CHASTITY Sexual continence, sometimes undertaken temporarily or permanently as a religious discipline. It is especially valued in CHRISTIANITY where sexual relations are only permissible within marriage.

CHELA In Indian religion, a disciple, student or follower of a GURU.

CHENRESI Form of the Tibetan name for AVALOKITESHVARA, the great BODHISATTVA who is patron of Tibet and is reincarnated in the DALAI LAMA.

CHI/CHINEKE ('Creator') Name for the supreme HIGH GOD among the Ibo people of Nigeria.

CHICOMECOATL AZTEC goddess of maize. Numerous images of her have been found, indicating her popularity. She wears a four-sided head-dress.

CHILAN Soothsayer or godman in the religion of the MAYA, instructed in his arts by the AHKINS. He was usually carried about on a litter and when called on to prophesy, he retired to a darkened room for several days before emerging to give his prophecy in an ecstatic state.

CHINGIS/GENGHIS KHAN (around AD 1167–1227) Mongol 'universal ruler' who succeeded in uniting the various tribes and embarked on a programme of conquest into China, Korea, Russia, the Ukraine and much of the rest of Eastern Europe. On his death he was elevated to divine status.

CHINVAT BRIDGE The bridge of judgement in the teaching of ZOROASTER. Good souls found it broad and easy to cross but wicked souls slipped off as it narrowed, and fell into a chasm of torment.

CHORTEN Tibetan Buddhist shrine, found by roadsides, in fields and at gateways. It is shaped as a pointed dome, often with a spire, crescent and disc at the top, and built on a square base. The construction represents the five elements and may contain RELICS or images or texts of sacred scripture.

CHRIST Greek word for MESSIAH. First applied to JESUS OF NAZARETH by his followers who believed him to fulfil the hopes of ISRAEL, it later became more a proper name of Jesus than a title.

CHRISTADELPHIANS Christian sect founded by John Thomas (AD

1805–71) in the USA, which claims to have returned to the beliefs and practices of the original DISCIPLES. They accept the BIBLE as infallible and are particularly interested in the fulfilment of prophecy. They reject the doctrines of the TRINITY and INCARNATION and have no ordained ministry.

CHRISTIAN Follower of JESUS OF NAZARETH, the CHRIST; a member of the Christian CHURCH.

CHRISTIANITY Missionary religion based on the teachings of JESUS OF NAZARETH, the CHRIST, and the significance of his life, death and RESURRECTION.

CHRISTIAN SCIENCE Unorthodox Christian sect founded in the USA by Mary Baker EDDY in 1866. It began with a small group gathered 'to re-instate primitive Christianity and its lost element of healing'. There are 3,000 Christian Science churches in fifty-seven countries.

CHRISTMAS The festival of the birth of CHRIST celebrated in Western Christendom on 25 December (which is not necessarily the date believed to be the actual date of his birth). The date suggests that it was intended to replace the Roman festival of the birth of SOL INVICTUS in the fourth century AD.

CHUANG TZU Chinese Taoist teacher who lived in the fourth and third centuries BC. He commended a way of life according to nature which disregarded the conventions of CONFUCIANISM. His writings stress spiritual discipline which should lead to MEDITATION on the formless TAO.

CHU HSI (AD 1130–1200) Chinese philosopher who expounded a system rather similar to that of PLATO. He believed that by quiet daily MEDITATION one could see through diversity to the supreme reality behind all phenomena.

CHURCH (1) The community of all CHRISTIANS, seen in the NEW TESTAMENT as the 'body of Christ', of which he is the head. (2) Building used for Christian WORSHIP. (3) A local group, organized section or 'denomination' of the church(1).

CIRCUMCISION The cutting off of the prepuce in males or the internal labia in females as a religious rite. It is widely practised in traditional African religion, either shortly after birth or at puberty. In JUDAISM boys are circumcised at eight days of age in commemoration of ABRAHAM'S covenant with God. Male converts to Judaism undergo this rite. Circumcision is also practised in ISLAM.

CONFIRMATION Christian rite involving the laying on of hands on those who have been baptized, with prayer for the gift of, or strengthening by, the HOLY SPIRIT. It is often the sign of becoming a communicant member of the CHURCH. In Orthodox Churches it is performed at BAPTISM. Roman Catholics are confirmed at about seven years of age. Other Churches which accept confirmation offer it at puberty or later.

CONFUCIANISM The system of social ethics taught by CONFUCIUS and given imperial recognition in China in the second century AD. Opinion is divided on whether or not Confucianism should be regarded as a religion. (See FIVE RELATIONSHIPS; LI.)

CONFUCIUS/K'UNG FU'TZU (551–479 BC) Chinese civil servant and administrator who became known as a teacher, opening his classes to everyone regardless of wealth or class. His teachings, especially the idea of LI, became the basis of a system of social ethics which greatly influenced Chinese society after his death.

CONGREGATIONALISTS See INDEPENDENTS.

'CONSCIOUSNESS ONLY' SCHOOL Group of Buddhist metaphysicians who argued, after NAGARJUNA, that the world is made up of perceptions emanating from an absolute store of consciousness.

CONSERVATIVE JUDAISM Movement which tries to stand midway between Orthodox and Progressive JUDAISM. It claims to accept the Talmudic tradition (see TALMUD) but to interpret the TORAH in the light of modern needs.

CONVERSION A moral or spiritual change of direction, or the adoption of religious beliefs not previously held.

COPTIC CHURCH The Church of Egypt, a more or less tolerated minority in Egypt since the coming of ISLAM in AD 642. The Church is 'monophysite', i.e. it rejects the teaching about the INCARNATION of CHRIST agreed at the ECUMENICAL COUNCIL of Chalcedon.

CORROBOREE Ceremony of the Australian Aboriginals comprising festive and warlike folk dances.

COUNCILS OF THE CHURCH See ECUMENICAL COUNCILS.

COUNTER-REFORMATION The revival and reform of the Roman Catholic Church as a reaction to the REFORMATION. Its reforms included those of the Council of Trent (AD 1562–63).

COVENANT A bargain or agreement. In JUDAISM the chief reference is to that made with MOSES at SINAI: GOD, having liberated his people from Egypt, promises them the land of ISRAEL and his blessing and protection as long as they keep the TORAH. This confirms the earlier covenants with ABRAHAM and with Noah. The term is also used of God's special relationship with the house of DAVID. With the defeat of the Kingdom of Judah in 586 BC, Jeremiah's prophecy of a new covenant written on the people's hearts came into its own. In the Christian NEW TESTAMENT the sacrificial death of JESUS OF NAZARETH marks the sealing of a new covenant between God and the new Israel, the Christian CHURCH, which completes and fulfills the old covenant.

CRANMER, Thomas (AD 1489–1556) Archbishop of Canterbury under Henry VIII who helped overthrow papal authority in England and created a new order of English worship in his Prayer Books of 1549 and 1552.

CREATION The act of GOD by which the universe came into being. Hence also refers to the universe itself. In JUDAISM, CHRISTIANITY and ISLAM creation is usually thought of as being *ex nihilo*, from out of nothing

that existed before. In HINDUISM it is believed that the universe has been outpoured from God and will contract into him at the end of the age.

CREATION MYTH A story which explains the divine origins of a particular people, a place or the whole world. In some PRIMAL RELIGIONS and ancient religions (see ENTHRONEMENT FESTIVAL) it is ritually re-enacted at the beginning of each year.

CREED Formal statement of religious belief. In CHRISTIANITY, the two creeds used most commonly today are the Apostles' Creed and the Nicene Creed.

CRUSADES The military expeditions undertaken by Christian armies from Europe from the eleventh to the fourteenth centuries intended to liberate the Holy Land from ISLAM.

CUZCO Capital of the INCA empire and site of the great temple of the SUN GOD. In tradition, Cuzco was founded by MANCO CAPAC, the first Inca, on the instructions of the sun god.

CYBELE Phrygian MOTHER GODDESS whose ecstatic rites included a bath in the blood of a sacrificial bull (see TAUROBOLIUM). Her consort was the youthful ATTIS. Her cult spread to Greece in the fifth century BC and to Rome in 204 BC, though here it was virtually banned until the late first century AD because of the scandal caused by her oriental eunuch priests.

CYNIC Follower of the eccentric Greek philosopher Diogenes (about 400–325 BC) who taught that man should seek the most natural and easy way of life, ignoring conventions. He was nicknamed *Kyon* ('dog') and the name stuck to the beggar philosophers who followed him.

D

DAGDA ('Good God') King of the Tuatha De Danann ('People of DANU'), a legendary Irish tribe. The god of wisdom and knowledge, he is patron of the DRUIDS and identified by his magic club and cauldron.

DAGOBA Name for a PAGODA, used in Sri Lanka (Ceylon). Dagobas are bell-shaped buildings and usually enclose a Buddhist RELIC.

DALAI LAMA Former religious and secular leader of Tibet, widely held to be the reincarnation of AVALOKITESHVARA. Since the Chinese takeover of Tibet the Dalai Lama has lived in India. He is still regarded as the spiritual leader of Tibetan Buddhists. (See also LAMA.)

DANU See ANU.

DARUMA Japanese name for BODHIDHARMA. It is also the name of a doll used by Japanese children which resembles Daruma.

DASTUR Parsi priest who is responsible for the rituals of the FIRE TEMPLES and wears a white turban. The priesthood is hereditary. (See PARSIS.)

DAVID King of the Israelite tribes around 1000–962 BC who united them and extended their territory. He stormed the city of the Jebusites and made it his capital, JERUSALEM. He was a musician and poet, to whom a number of psalms in the BIBLE are ascribed. The belief is common to JUDAISM and CHRISTIANITY that the MESSIAH would be a descendant of David.

DEACON Junior minister in the Christian CHURCH. The word means 'servant' and the deacon's functions originally included the distribution of alms to the poor.

DEAD SEA SCROLLS Sacred writings of a breakaway Jewish sect which were discovered in 1947 at Qumran on the western shore of the Dead Sea. The several scrolls and fragments include much of the HEBREW BIBLE as well as hymns, treatises and rules for the life of the sect. Many scholars identify the sect with the ESSENES.

DEISTS Followers of a movement for natural religion which flourished in seventeenth-century England. They rejected the idea of revelation and held that the Creator did not interfere in the workings of the universe.

DELPHI Greek shrine held to be at the centre or navel of the earth. It was dedicated to APOLLO who slew there a great dragon or python which protected the earlier shrine of the MOTHER GODDESS. There also Apollo established the DELPHIC ORACLE.

DELPHIC ORACLE Most authoritative source of prophecy and political advice in Ancient Greece. Run by the priests of APOLLO, its prophet was a woman, the *Pythia* ('pythoness'), who uttered her oracles in a state of induced frenzy. The message was then interpreted by the priests and delivered in a cryptic, often ambiguous, form.

DEMETER Greek goddess of fertility and growth. Worshipped throughout the Greek world, she was identified with the Egyptian ISIS, the Phrygian CYBELE, and the Roman CERES as the MOTHER GODDESS. Her MYTH concerns the abduction of her daughter Persephone by HADES; yearly, in autumn, the earth becomes barren while she searches for her child. She initiated her own MYSTERY RELIGION—the ELEUSINIAN MYSTERIES—at Eleusis near Athens.

DEMIURGE Term used in GNOSTICISM to describe the creator god, seen as willful, passionate and ignorant. His creation is a cosmic disaster which traps in material existence the divine sparks that emanate from the true God.

DERVISH Islamic MYSTIC belonging to one of the orders which induced ecstasy by movement, dance and the recitation of the names of God.

DEVADATTA Cousin of the BUDDHA and one of his earliest disciples. In some texts he is in conflict with the Buddha and leads a schismatic movement. He was condemned to a period in hell for his misdeeds.

DEVIL Term generally used to describe an evil spirit. In CHRISTIANITY the devil (Satan) is the personification of evil who is permitted to tempt and accuse human beings within the overall providence of God.

DHAMMA/DHARMA The teaching of the BUDDHA—his analysis of existence expressed in the FOUR NOBLE TRUTHS and his cure as outlined in the NOBLE EIGHTFOLD PATH. Dhamma is sometimes represented as an eight-spoked wheel. (See also DHARMA.)

DHAMMAPADA One of the best-known texts of the PALI CANON expounding the essence of THERAVADA Buddhist teachings. It encourages the Buddhist disciple to achieve his own salvation, relying on no external saviour or authority.

DHARMA In HINDUISM, cosmic order, the law of existence, right conduct. Also, in BUDDHISM, the teaching of the BUDDHA (see DHAMMA).

DIANA Italian goddess who was associated with wooded places, women, childbirth and the moon. She became identified with the Greek ARTEMIS. The centre of her cult was a grove on the shore of the volcanic Lake Nemi.

DIASPORA The Jewish people who lived scattered among the nations and were therefore in EXILE (2) from the land of ISRAEL. The dispersion of the JEWS came about partly as a result of war and exile, partly as a result of travel and trade.

DIETARY LAWS Rules about food and drink that are characteristic of a particular religion. Thus JUDAISM prohibits the simultaneous preparation or eating of milk and meat products, bans totally the eating of pork and shellfish and regulates the ritual slaughter of other animals for meat. ISLAM proscribes pork and alcohol. JAINISM bans all meat products.

DIEVS Sky god of the Latvian people. He is related to ZEUS and VARUNA.

DIGAMBARAS ('Sky-clad') Members of a major sect of JAINS who followed MAHAVIRA in believing in the virtue of total nudity. Numerous in the warm south of India, they tend to wear robes in public.

DIONYSUS Greek god of wine and of liberation, a dying and rising god identified with OSIRIS. His cult probably came from Thrace or Phrygia. He is associated with vegetation and fertility and appears surrounded by satyrs, nature spirits promoting fertility. He is followed by a host of maenads, frenzied women leading orgiastic rites. Dionysus punishes unbelief with terrible vengeance. In the late Hellenistic world (see HELLENISM) the cult of Dionysus became an important MYSTERY RELIGION.

DIS Roman name for the god of the underworld, the Greek HADES. The name derives from *dives* ('rich'), which translates Hades' euphemistic name, Pluto.

DISCIPLE Follower of a religious leader or teaching. In CHRISTIANITY it refers to the original followers of Jesus in the NEW TESTAMENT and is widened to include all Christian 'followers' throughout history.

DIVALI Festival of light celebrated by HINDUS and SIKHS. For Hindus it marks the return of RAMA from exile and his reunion with SITA as told in the MAHABHARATA. For Sikhs it is a commemoration of the release from prison of the sixth GURU and his return to the city of Amritsar.

DIVINATION The art of the DIVINER.

DIVINE KINGSHIP The belief that kings and queens are descended from the gods and rule with their authority. The ritual purity of the divine king guarantees the community's welfare. Notions of divine kingship are found in some PRIMAL RELIGIONS. (See also PHARAOH; INCA; ENTHRONEMENT FESTIVAL.)

DIVINE LIGHT MISSION Devotional cult of the Indian teacher Guru Maharaj Ji (born 1957) whose devotees in India, Europe and America regard him as a *Satguru*, a perfect teacher in succession to KRISHNA, BUDDHA, CHRIST, MUHAMMAD and others. Initiates receive 'the Knowledge' in a

ceremony which is an introduction to secret MEDITATION techniques.

DIVINER One who tells the future either by reading the signs of nature in the weather, stars or the flight of birds, or by the manipulation of objects such as sticks, stones, bones or playing cards (see AUGUR; HAURUSPEX; I CHING TAROT CARDS). He may also share the powers of a MEDIUM or SHAMAN.

DIVINITIES Name given to minor gods or spirits in PRIMAL RELIGIONS who rule over an area of the world or some human activity—e.g. storms, war, farming, marriage. Divinities are usually worshipped formally with special RITUALS and festivals.

DOCTRINE A religious teaching or belief which is taught and upheld within a particular religious community.

DONN ('The dark one') The Irish god of the dead who lives on Tech Duinn, a rocky island off the south-west coast of Ireland. A god of storms and shipwrecks, he is also the protector of cattle and flocks.

DRAVIDIAN Word describing the pre-ARYAN civilization based in the Indus valley. It was overturned by Aryan invaders around 2000 BC. Today Dravidian peoples inhabit southern India.

DREAMS One of the chief sources of revelation to the individual in PRIMAL RELIGIONS. Dreams may contain warnings or commands or promises of blessing.

DREAMTIME In Australian PRIMAL RELIGION, the mythical period in which, according to Aboriginal tradition, ancestral beings moved across the face of the earth forming its physical features. The dreamtime is recreated in art, painting, chanting, dancing and cult ceremonies.

DRUIDS The priestly caste of Celtic society. It is likely that they presided at sacrifices, made and enforced legal decisions and passed on the traditions of learning, magic, healing and ritual.

DUALISM The belief that reality has a fundamentally twofold nature. Opposed to MONISM it describes the belief that there is a radical

distinction between God and the created world. Alternatively it describes the belief that there are two fundamentally opposed principles, one of good, the other of evil. This moral dualism is the basis of ZOROASTRIANISM. Again it can describe the belief that the mind and the body are fundamentally different yet act in parallel.

DUKKHA Buddhist term for unsatisfactoriness or suffering. Birth, illness, decay, death and REBIRTH are symptoms of a restless and continuous 'coming-to-be' which marks all existence as dukkha.

DURGA ('The inaccessible') In HINDU tradition, the consort of SHIVA in one of her terrifying forms.

E

EASTER The festival of the RESURRECTION of CHRIST, the greatest and oldest festival of the Christian CHURCH. Its date is fixed according to the paschal full moon and varies from year to year.

EASTERN ORTHODOX CHURCHES Family of self-governing churches looking to the Ecumenical PATRIARCH, the Patriarch of Constantinople as a symbol of leadership. (See also GREAT SCHISM.)

ECUMENICAL COUNCILS Assemblies of Christian BISHOPS whose decisions were considered binding throughout the Christian church. These ended with the GREAT SCHISM though the Roman Catholic Church has continued to assemble councils into the twentieth century. The most important of the Ecumenical Councils were held at Nicaea (AD 325, condemning ARIANISM); Constantinople (AD 381); Ephesus (AD 431, condemning NESTORIANISM) and Chalcedon (AD 451, concerning the INCARNATION of CHRIST).

ECUMENICAL MOVEMENT Movement for the recovery of unity among the Christian Churches. It dates from the Edinburgh 'World Missionary Conference' of 1910 and today focusses in the WORLD COUNCIL OF CHURCHES.

EDDY, Mary Baker (AD 1821–1910) American spiritual teacher and founder of CHRISTIAN SCIENCE. She believed that orthodox CHRISTIANITY had repressed CHRIST'S teaching and practice of spiritual healing and that healing was not miraculous but a natural expression of the divine will. She founded the First Church of Christ Scientist in Boston in 1879; it remains the mother church of Christian Science. She wrote the authoritative work of the movement: *Science and Health (with Key to the Scriptures)* and founded the newspaper the *Christian Science Monitor*.

EL Great god and 'creator of creation' among the Canaanite and Phoenician peoples.

ELDER An officer of the Church in the PRESBYTERIAN and INDEPENDENT CHURCHES. Teaching elders also deal with pastoral care; ruling elders help in church government and administration.

ELECTION God's choice of ISRAEL to be his people as expressed in the COVENANT at Mount SINAI and manifested in the gift of the land of Israel. In JUDAISM the election of the Jews carries responsibility. They are to bear witness to the reality of God in the world by keeping the TORAH. In Christian theology, the concept is widened to include GENTILE converts to CHRISTIANITY who spiritually inherit the promises made to the PATRIARCHS and to MOSES.

ELEUSINIAN MYSTERIES MYSTERY RELIGION of DEMETER centred at Eleusis near Athens. The Greater Mysteries were held at the time of the autumn sowing and went on for nine days. The myth of Demeter was probably re-enacted and the climax may have been a revelation of a reaped ear of corn. But only initiates were admitted and the exact nature of the mysteries was kept a secret.

ELIEZER, Israel ben See BAAL SHEM TOV.

ELOHIM Plural form of the Canaanite word for a divinity (see DIVINITIES), usually translated 'God' and used as a name of God by the HEBREWS (see also EL). It is sometimes treated as a common-noun plural, 'gods' or 'angels'. (See also ANGELS.)

ELYSIUM Paradise of Greek religion. It was held to be either far away across the sea, or a section of the underworld ruled not by HADES, but by Kronos, one of the ancient Titan race.

EMPEROR, Japanese Since the reign of the legendary JIMMU TENNO, the emperors of Japan claimed divine descent from AMATERASU O MIKAMI. SHINTO thus became an expression of imperial power and nationalism. The divinity of the emperor was formally repudiated in 1945.

ENKI The water god of ancient Sumerian religion.

ENLIGHTENMENT In BUDDHISM, the realization of the truth of all existence which was achieved by the BUDDHA in his meditation at BODH GAYA. Enlightenment or final enlightenment also refers to the passing into NIRVANA of anyone who follows the Buddha's way and attains release from the cycle of birth and REBIRTH. (See also BODHI.)

ENLIL The wind god in ancient Sumerian belief. He persuaded the other gods to plan the destruction of mankind in a great flood. He rewarded the flood's only survivor with the gift of immortality.

EN SOF Name for God used in Jewish MYSTICISM, in particular in the KABBALAH, meaning 'the endless', the absolute infinite whose essence is unrevealed and unknowable.

ENTHRONEMENT FESTIVAL Ancient Near Eastern ritual which re-enacted the creation of the world and the elevation of the creator-deity above the other gods. The part of the god was played by the king who had a sacred status. The festival guaranteed the continuing order of nature and the welfare of the nation. (See also DIVINE KINGSHIP.)

EPIC OF GILGAMESH Babylonian poem dating from the

seventh century BC which includes much earlier material. It tells the story of Gilgamesh's vain quest for the secret of immortality and includes the BABYLONIAN FLOOD STORY.

EPICUREANISM Philosophical school founded by Epicurus (341–270 BC) and holding an atomic theory of the universe. It teaches that the gods are irrelevant to human life, the chief end of which is happiness. Fulfilment comes from the prudent and restrained cultivation of pleasure.

EPISTLE (1) Letter in the NEW TESTAMENT to a Christian community or individual usually from one of the APOSTLES. (2) Letter on doctrine or practice addressed to a Christian community in post-apostolic times.

EROS Greek god of love, Cupid to the Romans, the son of APHRODITE. In Greek literature his cruelty to his victims is emphasized, also his omnipotence. In the Christian era, 'cupids' became angelic beings symbolizing divine benevolence and compassion.

ESOTERIC Word meaning 'inner', suggesting something, (e.g. a knowledge or a teaching) that is available only for the specially initiated and secret from outsiders, and perhaps even from ordinary believers.

ESSENES Jewish group which withdrew to live a monastic life in the Dead Sea area during the Roman period. They were celibates and stressed the importance of ASCETICISM. They also performed exorcisms and rites of spiritual healing and adopted OCCULT practices.

EUCHARIST ('Thanksgiving') The central act of Christian worship, instituted by CHRIST on the night before his death. It involves sharing bread and wine which are sacramentally associated with the body and blood of Christ. (See SACRAMENT.)

EVANGELICALS CHRISTIANS of all denominations who emphasize the centrality of the BIBLE, justification by faith and the need for personal conversion. In Germany and Switzerland, the term refers to members of the Lutheran as opposed to the Calvinist churches.

EVANGELISM The preaching of the Christian GOSPEL to the unconverted.

EXILE (1) The period between 597 BC and around 538 BC when leading JEWS from the former Jewish kingdoms were held in captivity in Babylon. (2) The condition of Jewish life in the DIASPORA, away from the land of ISRAEL.

EXODUS The flight of the people of ISRAEL from Egypt under the leadership of MOSES.

EXORCISM Removal of sin or evil, particularly an evil spirit in possession of someone, by prayer or ritual action.

EZRA Scribe of the Babylonian EXILE who was sent with a royal warrant from the Persian king to reform religion in JERUSALEM. Traditionally he arrived in 458 BC and embarked on a programme to purify the Jewish faith and install TORAH as the central authority in Jewish life.

F

FADY Something which must not be done, something forbidden or TABOO in the religion of Madagascar.

FAITH Attitude of belief in, trust and commitment to a divine being or a religious teaching. It can also refer to the beliefs of a religion, 'the faith', which is passed on from teachers to believers.

FALL OF JERUSALEM The capture of JERUSALEM and the final destruction of the TEMPLE OF JERUSALEM by the Roman general Titus in AD 70 at the end of a revolt which broke out in AD 66.

FAMADIHANA Term for ANCESTOR VENERATION in the religion of Madagascar.

FASTING Total or partial abstinence from food, undertaken as a religious discipline. In PRIMAL RELIGIONS it is often a preparation for a ceremony of INITIATION. In JUDAISM and CHRISTIANITY it is a sign of mourning or repentance for SIN. It is also more generally used as a means of gaining clarity of vision and mystical insight.

FATI-DRA Madagascan ceremony for making blood-brothers.

FELLOWSHIP The common life of Christians marked by unity and mutual love, a creation of the HOLY SPIRIT.

FIELDS OF AARU Paradise of Egyptian mythology, the abode of souls who have passed safely through the judgement before OSIRIS. It is pictured as a place similar to Egypt with a great river and cultivated land.

FIRE SERMON One of the BUDDHA's most famous sermons, traditionally preached at Gaya to 1000 fire-worshipping ascetics, in which he explained that all that exists is burning with lust, anger and ignorance.

FIRE TEMPLES Parsi temples where the sacred fire of AHURA MAZDA is kept continually burning. The fire is kept in a censer on a stone slab hanging under the central dome of the temple. There are no images: the fire symbolizes the purity and goodness of Ahura Mazda. (See DASTUR; PARSIS.)

FIVE PILLARS OF ISLAM Five duties enjoined on every MUSLIM as his response to God. They are: recitation of the creed 'LA ILAHA ILLA ALLAH'; SALAT (ritual prayer); ZAKAT (almsgiving); SAUM (fasting in the month of RAMADAN); HAJJ (pilgrimage to MECCA).

FIVE PRECEPTS Ethical restraints for Buddhists, who are to refrain from: taking life; stealing; wrong sexual relations; wrong use of speech; drugs and intoxicants.

FIVE RELATIONSHIPS The codification and application of CONFUCIUS' teaching to the five basic relationships of human life. These are father and son; older brother and younger brother; husband and wife;

elder and younger; ruler and subject. The inferior should show proper deference, the superior proper benevolence. The stress is on reciprocity and Confucius believed that such correct behaviour would weld society in 'the way of heaven'.

FOUR NOBLE TRUTHS The BUDDHA's analysis of the problem of existence—a four-stage summary of his teaching: (1) all that exists is unsatisfactory; (2) the cause of unsatisfactoriness (DUKKHA) is desire (TANHA); (3) unsatisfactoriness ends when desire ends; (4) desire can be ended by practising the NOBLE EIGHTFOLD PATH.

FOUR RIGHTLY-GUIDED CALIPHS Orthodox ISLAM accepts ABU BAKR, 'UMAR, 'UTHMAN and 'ALI as legitimate successors to MUHAMMAD.

FOUR STAGES OF LIFE HINDU outline of man's ideal spiritual life. There are four stages: Student; the Hindu boy learns the scriptures in the house of his GURU and lives a life of chastity; Householder; he marries, has children and earns his living; Forest dweller; when his family are grown up he gradually begins to withdraw from everyday life; Sannyasi (SANSKRIT: 'one who renounces'); he cuts all earthly ties and seeks liberation, often as a wandering beggar.

FRANCIS OF ASSISI (AD 1182–1226) Founder of the Franciscan order who lived by a simple rule of life rejecting possessions, ministering to the sick and having a special concern for nature.

FREEMASONRY Originally a religious brotherhood of English masons founded in the twelfth century. In the sixteenth century it spread to the European mainland where in Roman Catholic countries it became associated with Deism (see DEISTS). In the UK and USA today it is a semi-secret society which retains certain mystical symbols and ceremonies. Members are committed to a belief in GOD as 'the great architect of the universe', symbolized by an eye.

FREY Norse god of beauty with power over rain and sunshine and the fertility of the earth. His name means 'lord'.

FREYJA Norse goddess and sister of FREY; her name means 'lady'. She is patroness of love and sorcery and drives a chariot pulled by cats. She possesses half the corpses of those who are slain in battle, the other half going to ODIN.

FRIENDS, RELIGIOUS SOCIETY OF See QUAKERS.

FRIGG Chief of the Norse goddesses and wife of ODIN; the goddess of love and fertility. She knows the fates of men but cannot avert destiny.

FUNDAMENTALISM The doctrine that the BIBLE is verbally inspired and therefore inerrant and infallible on all matters of doctrine and history; from *The Fundamentals*, published in 1909.

FURIES Female spirits of retributive justice in Greek mythology. They came from TARTARUS, the Greek HELL, and pursued their victims until these went mad. They upheld the moral order by ensuring that crime was punished. The Greeks called them by euphemistic names, the most common being 'the kindly ones'.

G

GABRIEL One of the archangels of Jewish tradition. In ISLAM Gabriel is associated with the 'faithful spirit' by whom the QUR'AN was revealed to MUHAMMAD. Gabriel also transported Muhammad from MECCA to JERUSALEM and from there to the throne of God in the NIGHT JOURNEY.

GANESHA Elephant-headed god much loved in popular HINDUISM, especially in western India. He is the god of good beginnings and is a symbol for luck and wealth in business and daily life.

GANGES The holy river of India whose waters are sacred for all HINDUS. It is thought to flow from the toe of VISHNU. Pilgrims wash away evil in its waters and the ashes of the dead are thrown into it.

GAUTAMA/GOTAMA Family name of the BUDDHA. Legend depicts him as a great prince born into a royal household. Modern scholars think that his father was probably the head of an aristocratic family living in the town of Kapilavastu.

GENGHIS KHAN See CHINGIS KHAN.

GENIUS (1) In occult religion, a guardian spirit or familiar. (2) In Roman religion, the spirit of a man, giving rise to his maleness. A LIBATION was poured to the genius of the reigning emperor at every banquet.

GENTILE Person who is not a JEW.

GHAT ('Holy place') In HINDU use, a word which can refer to a range of hills, a ritual bathing place or a cremation ground.

GHOST DANCE A dance which sprang out of a religious movement of the 1870s among the North American Indians. It was believed that the dance would lead to the resurrection of all dead Indians on an earth free of disease and death. The movement was destroyed at the Battle of Wounded Knee in 1890. (See also WOVOKA.)

GINNUNGAGAP In Norse mythology the yawning gulf out of which creation sprang. A region of chaos, half of it was freezing fog, the other half flaming heat. In the centre was a roaring cauldron which became the source of all waters.

GINZA The chief scripture of the MANDAEANS, relating the creation of the world and describing the fate of the soul after death.

GLOSSOLALIA Expression in unknown tongues by people in a heightened spiritual or emotional state. In the Christian church it is used to express worship to God and prophetic messages, in other religions to express a state of religious ecstasy.

GNOSTICISM Movement of ESOTERIC teachings rivalling, borrowing from and contradicting early CHRISTIANITY. Gnostic sects were based on MYTHS which described the creation of the world by a deluded DEMIURGE and taught a way of

salvation through *gnosis*, 'knowledge' of one's true divine self. Gnostics contrasted their 'knowledge' with faith, which they considered inferior.

GOBINDH SINGH, GURU (AD 1666–1708) The tenth GURU of the SIKH community. He militarized the Sikhs, requiring them to adopt a distinctive name and dress. He also shifted the focus of authority from the gurus to the sacred scripture, the ADI GRANTH.

GOD (Common noun) A being with divine power and attributes; a deity, a major DIVINITY.

GOD (Proper noun) The creator and sustainer of the universe; the absolute being on whom all that is depends.

GOOD FRIDAY The Friday before EASTER; in CHRISTIANITY, kept by the CHURCH as a holy day, sometimes including FASTING, penance and witness, in memory of the crucifixion of Jesus CHRIST.

GOSPEL (1) One of the four accounts of the 'good news' about JESUS in the NEW TESTAMENT. (2) The Christian message, proclamation, 'good news', referring especially to Jesus' teaching about the KINGDOM OF GOD and to the preaching of the CHURCH about Jesus. (3) The ritual reading of a set portion from the gospels (1) in the context of the EUCHARIST.

GOTAMA See GAUTAMA.

GRACE (1) Unmerited favour, especially in the divine salvation of the unworthy. An essential concept in CHRISTIANITY, where it is contrasted with merit; Christians believe that nobody receives SALVATION because they deserve it, but only by God's grace. (2) A prayer or blessing before a meal.

GRANDFATHER, THE Common name for the supreme GOD among North American Indians. The word is sometimes pluralized and identified with a sevenfold being as in certain other PRIMAL RELIGIONS.

GREAT HOUSE Cult among North American Indians, paticularly those from Delaware and the north-west coast. It centres on a rectangular hall built in alignment with the four points of the compass and which represents the universe. In the centre there is often a pillar with two faces which represents the creator. Ceremonial autumn dances and prayers in the hut mark the beginning of a new year and the start of a new world.

GREAT SCHISM The SCHISM declared in AD 1054 between the Eastern and Western churches resulting from disagreements over the POPE'S claim to supremacy, and the doctrine of the HOLY SPIRIT.

GREGORY OF NYSSA (around AD 330–395) Christian theologian who helped develop the doctrine of the TRINITY and expounded the BIBLE as a spiritual path leading to the perfect contemplation of God.

GROUND OF BEING Phrase used by German–US theologian Paul Tillich (AD 1886–1965) to describe GOD. It stresses the immanence of God as depth or ground rather than his transcendence as creator.

GURDJIEFF, George Ivanovich (AD 1873–1949) Spiritual teacher whose book *Meetings with Remarkable Men* relates his search for wisdom. He invented a system of non-identification with the ego which he believed led to the realization of man's true essence. He was influenced by SUFISM. In 1922 he founded an Institute for the Harmonious Development of Man which attracted a number of western intellectuals.

GURDWARA SIKH temple and meeting place, consisting of a worship area which houses the ADI GRANTH, and a cooking and eating area for the symbolic meal which ends Sikh worship.

GURU ('Teacher') A spiritual teacher or guide who, in Indian religion, awakens a disciple to a realization of his own divine nature. In SIKH religion it refers to the ten teachers, from Guru NANAK to Guru GOBINDH SINGH, who ruled the community.

H

HADAD Storm god of Assyria and Babylonia. In the BIBLE he appears as Rimmon, 'the thunderer'. His symbol was lightning and his sacred animal was the bull.

HADES (1) Greek god of the dead and ruler of the UNDERWORLD. He was connected with growth and vegetation and the production of wealth. Because it was considered unlucky to speak his name, he is often referred to as Pluto (the 'rich'). (2) Greek name for the underworld, the abode of the dead. In the Septuagint version of the HEBREW BIBLE it translates *sheol*. In Christian usage it sometimes is used for the interim abode of the departed as distinguished from HELL, the abode of the damned.

HADITH Traditions of MUHAMMAD'S words and actions which are not found in the QUR'AN but are a source of authority in Islamic lawmaking. There are many spurious Hadith; one of the major tasks of MUSLIM lawyers has been to categorize Hadith into likely degrees of authenticity.

HAGGADAH A moral or devotional teaching derived from the midrashic exposition of a HEBREW text (see MIDRASH). There are many of them in the TALMUD where they take the form of narrative tales, poems and metaphysical speculations.

HAJJ Pilgrimage to MECCA which is one of the FIVE PILLARS OF ISLAM and which MUSLIMS are obliged to make at least once in a lifetime. It is more meritorious if it takes place in the pilgrim month. On arrival at Mecca, pilgrims make seven circuits of the KA'BA and touch the BLACK STONE. The pilgrims continue to Mina and 'Arafat where sacrifices take place.

HALACH UINIC Ruler of the MAYA. His authority was absolute and he was regarded as a demigod.

HALAKHAH (From HEBREW verb 'to walk') A legal teaching based on the midrashic exposition of a Hebrew text (see MIDRASH).

HAMMURABI (Eighteenth century BC) Mesopotamian ruler who produced a law code laying down punishments for various transgressions and enunciating principles for the conduct of business and social life. The breaking of his code incurred the enmity of the Babylonian gods.

HANUKKAH ('Dedication') Eight-day Jewish festival marked by the lighting of ritual candles which celebrates the rededication of the TEMPLE OF JERUSALEM by JUDAS MACCABEUS in 164 BC.

HANUMAN Monkey-god of popular HINDUISM. In the RAMAYANA he led a monkey army against a host of demons. He can fly and cover huge distances at great speed.

HARA KIRI Vulgar Japanese expression meaning 'belly cutting' which is used for the Japanese traditional practice of ritual suicide among the warrior classes.

HASIDIM ('The pious') (1) The group of Jewish quietist ascetics who were the forerunners of the PHARISEES. (2) A group of medieval MYSTIVS who were particularly important for the development of JUDAISM in Germany. (3) Followers of BAAL SHEM TOV who taught a new kind of HASIDISM in the eighteenth century AD.

HASIDISM Jewish mystical movement with roots in the KABBALAH which arose in the eighteenth century in response to the teachings of BAAL SHEM TOV after a period of persecution by the Cossacks. It stressed the presence of God in everyday life and the value of prayer. Chanting and dancing were used as aids to ecstatic communion with God. The movement was popular and had a wide appeal among ordinary JEWS.

HASINA Madagascan term for spiritual power which is inherent in all living things and is focussed in particular objects and ceremonies. (See MANA.)

HAURUSPEX In Roman religion, a soothsayer who divined from observing the entrails of sacrificed animals. The original *hauruspices* were Etruscans.

HEAVEN The realm of God or of the gods; in CHRISTIANITY the dwelling place of God and the ultimate home of the saved, regarded both as a place and a state.

HEBREW (1) A member of the Semitic tribes which emerged as the people of ISRAEL. (2) The (Semitic) language of the ancient people of Israel, of the HEBREW BIBLE and of the modern state of Israel.

HEBREW BIBLE The Jewish SCRIPTURES which comprise the Books of the Law (see TORAH), the PROPHETS and the WRITINGS. According to tradition the canon was fixed at the Synod of Jabneh about AD 100.

HEIMDALL White god of Norse religion, the watchman of the gods and guardian of the rainbow bridge between ASGARD and MIDGARD. He is a fire god, born of the ice-cold sea and the founder of the different classes of men. He will summon the other gods to fight at RAGNARÖK.

HECATE An earth goddess who probably originated in Asia Minor. Connected with magic and death, she was sometimes known as the ARTEMIS of the cross-roads. She is shown with three faces, carrying torches and followed by baying hounds.

HEL In Norse myth, the queen of the dead. Also her kingdom, the UNDERWORLD, a region of cold, fog and murky gloom, inhabited by the ghosts of the dead. At the battle of RAGNARÖK, Hel will be opened and its hosts will fight on the side of LOKI. The entrance to Hel is guarded by a bloody-breasted dog.

HELL Realm where the wicked go after death. Religious teachings differ over whether this punishment is reformatory or eternal. In CHRISTIANITY, it is total separation from God.

HELLENISM The adoption of the Greek language, culture, philosophy and ideas, particularly around the Mediterranean, from the time of Alexander the Great (356–323 BC). It was the dominant cultural influence during the rise of CHRISTIANITY.

HERA Greek goddess, the wife of ZEUS and Queen of heaven. She was the protectress of women and marriage and is presented as a model of chastity. She was worshipped throughout the Greek world. Her special bird was a peacock, a symbol of pride.

HERESY The denial of a defined doctrine of the Christian faith. The word means 'chosen thing' and refers to the heretic's preference for his own opinion over the consensus of the CHURCH.

HERM Roadside monument erected in honour of HERMES. Originally they were simply piles of stones; later they were decorated with a phallus and a carved head. There were many *hermae* in Athens.

HERMES Greek messenger god and son of Zeus, protector of travellers, bringer of luck and god of thieves and merchants. He is usually portrayed as a young man in winged hat and sandals, carrying a staff twined with snakes.

HERMETICISM Mystical movement based on a collection of Egyptian scriptures from the first to third centuries AD. The writings drew on Greek and Eastern ideas, and were ascribed to Hermes Trismegistus ('thrice-great HERMES'), who is identified with the god THOTH.

HERZL, Theodore (AD 1860–1904) Leader of the Zionist movement (see ZIONISM). He argued that a national homeland for the JEWS was a necessity. He travelled widely raising support from Christian governments for the Zionist cause. He convened the first World Zionist Congress in 1897 which formulated a political programme for the return to Palestine.

HESIOD Greek poet, probably of the eighth century BC, whose *Theogony* sought to draw together the ancestries of the Greek gods, understanding creation in terms of procreation.

HIGH GOD A god who is acknowledged as the supreme being in PRIMAL RELIGIONS. He is regarded as a creator, sometimes of the universe. He is good and requires moral obedience from men. He is frequently regarded as remote from normal life and is associated with the sky, mountains or other high places.

He is not often worshipped but may be called upon in times of necessity or danger.

HIGH PRIEST Traditional head of the Jewish priesthood and organizer of TEMPLE worship. His function was to enter the Holy of Holies and offer sacrifice on the DAY OF ATONEMENT. It was a key political appointment under the Seleucids and Romans. Talmudic tradition criticizes the corruption of some who held the office, which ceased at the destruction of the Temple in AD 70.

HIJRA ('Going forth') The migration of MUHAMMAD, preceded by some of his followers, from MECCA to MEDINA in AD 622). This was the decisive event for the development of ISLAM for it was in Medina that Muhammad established himself as a religious and political leader and organized his followers as an Islamic community. The MUSLIM calendar counts years 'after Hijra'.

HILLEL Pharisaic Jewish teacher of the first century AD. He was known for his humane and lenient interpretations of TORAH, in contrast to his chief opponent, the stern and rigorous Shammai.

HINAYANA ('Small vehicle') Buddhist term used to indicate the doctrine of salvation for oneself alone in contrast to MAHAYANA. Most Buddhists of south-east Asia prefer the term THERAVADA to describe this school of BUDDHISM.

HINDU Word used by Arabs to describe people living beyond the Indus valley. Today it refers generally to people practising Indian religion who are neither Muslim, Sikh, Parsi nor Jain, and also to their religion, 'Hinduism'.

HINDUISM The religion of India. (See also BHAGAVAD GITA; BRAHMANISM; VEDANTA; VEDAS; UPANISHADS.)

HINENUIOTEPO Guardian of the UNDERWORLD (see RAROHENGA) in Maori religion.

HOA HAO Offshoot of the Vietnamese CAO DAI movement. It is Buddhist-based and has been strongly nationalistic.

HOLI HINDU spring festival which celebrates the love of KRISHNA and RADHA. It is marked by boisterous games which are reminders of Krishna's amorous pranks with the cow-girls as told in the MAHABHARATA.

HOLINESS The sacred power, strangeness and otherness of the divine. In the BIBLE and the QUR'AN the term has moral implications and refers to God's purity and righteousness as well as to that which invokes awe. In CHRISTIANITY, believers are called to reproduce God's holiness in their own lives with the help of the HOLY SPIRIT.

HOLOCAUST (From the Latin BIBLE'S word for 'whole burnt offering') The name given to Hitler's extermination of 6 million Jews in the Nazi death camps in Europe 1941–45. Mass destruction was envisaged as the 'final solution' to the 'problem' of the Jews. The memory of the Holocaust is the key to modern Jewish theology and made the founding of the state of Israel an event of profound significance.

HOLY COMMUNION Name widely used by Anglicans and some Protestants for the Christian EUCHARIST.

HOLY SPIRIT The third person of the Christian TRINITY. In the BIBLE the Holy Spirit is the instrument of divine action and is portrayed as fire or wind. In this sense the Spirit is acknowledged in JUDAISM and ISLAM. The divinity of the Holy Spirit was agreed at the Council of Constantinople in AD 381. He is the source of faith and new life in the believer and the church, giving 'spiritual gifts', guidance, holiness.

HOLY TEMPLE/HOLY PLACE/ HOLY OF HOLIES See TEMPLE OF JERUSALEM.

HOMER Author of the Greek epics the *Iliad* and the *Odyssey* which date from between the eight and tenth centuries BC. According to the historian Herodotus, Homer was the first to detail the characters and functions of the gods of Mount OLYMPUS.

HONEN (AD 1133–1212) Japanese teacher of PURE LAND BUDDHISM. He taught that repetition of the word NEMBUTSU is all that is necessary for salvation. He is said to have recited it 60,000 times a day.

HORUS Egyptian hawk-headed sky god, associated with the king. The son of ISIS, conceived on the dead OSIRIS, he defeated the evil SETH and assumed the earthly rule Seth had usurped from Osiris.

HSUN-TZU Chinese Confucian scholar of the third century BC who blended the philosophies of CONFUCIANISM and TAOISM. He believed in the correct observance of ceremonial which helped to improve man's evil nature. He was critical of superstition and reinterpreted popular religious practices in rationalistic terms.

HUACA Any of the multitude of DIVINITIES recognized by the INCAS; also, an Inca holy place, shrine or temple.

HUBBARD, Lafayette Ron (Born AD 1911) American science-fiction writer who founded SCIENTOLOGY. This is based on his theories of the mind as outlined in his book *Dianetics: the Modern Science of Mental Health* (1950).

HUBRIS ('Unbridled arrogance') In Greek drama the hubris of man in setting himself up against the gods was a continuous theme. Hubris attracted the anger of the gods and so led to tragedy.

HUIRACOCHA See VIRACOCHA.

HUITZILOPOCHTLI AZTEC god of war and the sun. His name means 'hummingbird wizard' and he was perpetually at war with darkness and night.

HUI YUAN See PURE LAND BUDDHISM.

HUMANISM Way of life based on the belief that what is good for human beings is the highest good.

HUS, Jan (AD 1374–1415) Bohemian reformer who, under the influence of WYCLIFFE'S writings denounced the worldliness of the clergy. When he was burnt at the stake he was declared a MARTYR and national hero in Prague. His thought influenced the REFORMATION.

HYMN A sacred song sung in the context of communal worship; a PSALM of communal praise. Hymns are particularly important in Christian and Sikh worship and in the gatherings of the Hindu BHAKTI cults (see BHAJANA).

I

IBN AL-'ARABI (AD 1165–1240) Spanish Sufi teacher and poet (see SUFISM). He taught that the world manifested God and that human beings were created because God desired to be known. MUHAMMAD was 'the seal of the prophets' and Ibn al-'Arabi regarded himself as 'the seal of the saints'. Dante was influenced by his speculations.

IBN RUSHD (AD 1126–98) MUSLIM philosopher, known in the west as Averroes, who was greatly influenced by PLATO and ARISTOTLE. He believed that the Greek heritage was compatible with ISLAM. His synthesis, however, seemed suspicious to the orthodox and he was banished and his books burnt.

I CHING/BOOK OF CHANGES One of the five classics of Chinese literature which was originally attributed to CONFUCIUS but is now thought to be much earlier. It gives instructions and interpretations for a form of DIVINATION using six sticks which can fall in sixty-four significant configurations.

ICON A likeness of a divine figure or SAINT painted on wood or inlaid in mosaic and used in public or private devotion.

'ID AL-ADHA The great festival of the MUSLIM year. It coincides with the offering of the pilgrim sacrifice at Mina near MECCA.

'ID AL-FITR The MUSLIM feast which ends the fasting month of RAMADAN. Greetings cards are exchanged, presents are given and sugary sweets are eaten.

IJMA The consensus of opinion of the MUSLIM community. It is an important principle of Islamic lawmaking.

IJTIHAD ('Enterprise') A way for the Islamic community to develop its law to deal with new situations. It is a ruling given by one MUSLIM teacher, rather than by general consensus (see IJMA). It is controversial whether Ijtihad is always valid or whether the completion of SHARI'A will render it unnecessary.

IMAM (1) Religious leader and teacher of a SUNNI Muslim community. He leads the ritual prayer of the congregation and is expected to be an interpreter of the QUR'AN. (2) The agent of divine illumination among Shi'ite Muslims (see SHI'A) who believe that every age will produce an Imam whose function is to make the truth of MUHAMMAD contemporary. Among the Shi'a belief in the Imams is an additional article to the usual FIVE PILLARS OF ISLAM.

IMMORTALS Various beings who live in the Realm of Great Purity, according to the teachings of TAOISM. Best known are the 'eight immortals' who are portrayed with a variety of individual characteristics and symbols and feature in Chinese art and drama.

INANNA The MOTHER GODDESS as worshipped in ancient Sumer.

INCA The divine king who ruled over the INCAS.

INCARNATION (1) The Christian doctrine that GOD became man in Jesus CHRIST, so possessing both human and divine natures. (2) A term sometimes used for the HINDU doctrine of the AVATAR.

INCAS Empire centred on CUZCO in modern Peru from around AD 1100 until the Spanish conquest (1532). From the late fourteenth century the empire expanded to include parts of modern Ecuador, Bolivia, Chile and Argentina. The first INCA, MANCO CAPAC, was created by and given absolute authority by the SUN GOD. (See also HUACA; INCAS; PACHACAMAC; PACHACUTEC; TIUHUANACO; VIRACOCHA; VIRGINS OF THE SUN.)

INCENSE Sweet-smelling smoke used in worship, made by burning certain aromatic substances.

INCREASE RITES RITUALS performed by Australian Aboriginals to ensure the continual supply of the particular food associated with the rite.

INDEPENDENCE, DAY OF Jewish festival of thanksgiving on the anniversary of the birth of the state of ISRAEL (4). The liturgy includes prayers for the victims of the HOLOCAUST.

INDEPENDENTS/ CONGREGATIONALISTS CHRISTIANS who uphold the authority and independence of each local church, claiming this system to be the earliest form of church order.

INDEX OF PROHIBITED BOOKS The official list of books which members of the Roman Catholic Church are forbidden to possess or read, first issued in 1557. The *Index* was abolished in 1966.

INDRA ARYAN god of war and storm. There are 200 HYMNS to him in the *Rig Veda* (see VEDAS). He faded from significance in later HINDUISM.

INDULGENCE The remission by the Church of a period of correction in PURGATORY. The sale of indulgences by unscrupulous 'pardoners' was one of the abuses which led to the REFORMATION.

INITIATION Ceremony marking coming of age, or entry into adult membership of a community. It is also used of the secret ceremonies surrounding membership of the MYSTERY RELIGIONS. (See also CONFIRMATION; NAUJOTE; SACRED THREAD CEREMONY.)

INQUISITION Papal office for identifying heretics, founded by POPE Gregory IX and staffed by Franciscans and Dominicans. Torture became an approved aid to interrogation in 1252.

INTERCESSION Prayer offered on behalf of others by a believer on earth or by a SAINT in HEAVEN. In CHRISTIANITY, supremely the work of CHRIST who intercedes for men before GOD.

INTERNATIONAL SOCIETY FOR KRISHNA CONSCIOUSNESS Modern Hindu BHAKTI cult which has been successful in Europe and America. Shaven, yellow-robed devotees chant the MANTRA '*Hare Krishna*' as a way of reaching ecstatic union with God.

INTI The SUN GOD of the INCAS.

IO Supreme being in Maori religion. However, as he has only been referred to since around 1850, he may be derived from Christian teaching.

IQBAL, Muhammad (AD 1876– 1938) Poet, philosopher and president of the MUSLIM LEAGUE. He believed that MUSLIMS needed to study European thought and then construct an authentic Islamic state based on a reformed faith. He is regarded as the spiritual founder of Pakistan.

ISAAC One of the three principal Jewish patriarchs (see ABRAHAM, ISAAC AND JACOB).

ISHTAR Babylonian goddess, mother and wife of TAMMUZ and associated with the fertility rites of death and resurrection. She is also the consort of the Sumerian high god ANU (1). In mythology she is responsible for the great flood which almost destroyed the earth (see BABYLONIAN FLOOD STORY). Worshipped in various forms all over the ancient near East, she was known as Astarte to the Phoenicians and as Ashtoreth to the Hebrews.

ISIS Great Egyptian goddess of motherhood and fertility. The sister and wife of OSIRIS, she restored him to life after he was murdered by SETH. Sometimes represented as cow-headed, she had a great temple at Philae.

ISIS CULT MYSTERY RELIGION based on the MYTH of ISIS and OSIRIS which became particularly popular in the Roman world from the first century AD. Its sacred drama and liturgy express the experience of salvation from sensuality which is open to initiates through the grace of the goddess.

ISLAM (Infinitive of the ARABIC verb 'to submit') Teachings derived from the QUR'AN which is the revelation to MUHAMMAD, a religion of submission to the will of God. (See also ALLAH; MECCA; MUSLIM.)

ISLAMIC SOCIALISM A broad movement which advocates the unity of Qur'anic teachings and socialism.

ISMA'ILIS A group of SHI'A Muslims who believe that the seventh IMAM (2) was the final Imam who has disappeared and will return on the last day (see also ASSASSINS; MAHDI; TWELVERS).

ISMAIL SAFAVI First Shah of Persia who raised an army against the SUNNI Muslim Ottomans, capturing Tabriz in AD 1500. His armies later conquered Iraq. He founded the Safavid dynasty which did not make peace with the OTTOMAN EMPIRE until 1639.

ISRAEL (1) Name given by GOD to JACOB the patriarch and hence to his descendents, the 'people of Israel'. (2) The land promised by God to Abram (ABRAHAM) in the early traditions of JUDAISM. (3) The Northern Kingdom of Israel which seceded from Solomon's kingdom in 922 BC and was destroyed by the Assyrians in 722 BC. (4) The modern state of Israel, founded in Palestine as a Jewish state in AD 1948.

ITZAMNA Chief of the gods of the MAYA. A sky god whose name means 'lizard', he is portrayed as an old man with a long nose. Patron of learning and medicine, he was the inventor of writing.

IXCHEL Moon goddess of the MAYA and consort of ITZAMNA, patroness of childbirth and weaving.

IZANAGI The sky god in SHINTO and the father of AMATERASU. With his consort Izanami he created the islands of Japan.

J

JACOB One of the three principal Jewish patriarchs (see ABRAHAM, ISAAC AND JACOB; ISRAEL (1)).

JADE EMPEROR The supreme divinity in TAOISM, who came into prominence about the tenth century AD. He presided over life and death and kept account of human actions.

JAHANNAM MUSLIM name for HELL which is frequently mentioned in the QUR'AN as a place of scorching fire and black smoke. Sometimes it is personified as a great monster appearing at the Day of Judgement.

JAIN ('One who has conquered') A follower of the religion known as JAINISM.

JAINISM Religion which emerged in India as a protest against BRAHMANISM. There are 2 million Jains in India today. In Jainism salvation is seen in terms of acquiring god-like omniscience. The asceticism of the Jains has continually influenced mainstream HINDUISM. (See also DIGAMBARAS; JIVA; MAHAVIRA; PARSVA; SVETAMBARAS; TIRTHANKARAS.)

JAMES, William (AD 1842–1910) American psychologist of religion who attempted an analysis and assessment of individual religious experience in his Gifford Lectures, *The Varieties of Religious Experience* (1902).

JANUS Roman god of beginnings whose name derives from *janua*, 'entrance' or 'gate'. He is portrayed with a two-faced head, facing both ways. In Julius Caesar's reform of the calendar, his month became the first of the year.

JAROVIT Slavic war god.

JEHOVAH See YHWH.

JEHOVAH'S WITNESSES Unorthodox Christian sect founded in 1884 by C.T. RUSSELL. It propagates its own version of the BIBLE which it regards as infallible, and stresses the imminent return of CHRIST. Members are pacifists and are forbidden to have blood

transfusions. There may be as many as 3 million Witnesses in 200 countries worldwide.

JEROME (about AD 342–420) Translator of the BIBLE into Latin (the 'Vulgate' version). He wrote many commentaries on the text.

JERUSALEM Fortified city captured by DAVID in the tenth century BC which became the capital and principal sanctuary for the people of ISRAEL. It has remained the focus of Jewish religious aspirations and ideals (see TEMPLE OF JERUSALEM). It is a holy city for CHRISTIANS because of its association with the passion, death and RESURRECTION of JESUS OF NAZARETH. For MUSLIMS it is the holiest city after MECCA. The MOSQUE of the Dome of the Rock stands over the site of Muhammad's NIGHT JOURNEY.

JESUS OF NAZARETH Teacher, prophet and worker of miracles in first century Palestine and founder of Christianity. He taught the coming of the KINGDOM OF GOD with forgiveness and new life for all who believed. His claims to be the promised MESSIAH (or CHRIST) roused opposition from the religious authorities and he was put to death by crucifixion. But after his death his followers claimed that he was risen from the dead and he was seen alive by many. CHRISTIANS, members of his CHURCH, await his promised SECOND COMING which will bring the fulfilment of the Kingdom of God.

JEW (1) A person who is regarded as a member of the Jewish race. According to Jewish religious law Jewishness is inherited through the female line. (2) A person who identifies with JUDAISM, the religion of the Jews.

JIHAD ('Striving') The means of promoting the message of ISLAM by force of arms. MUHAMMAD introduced the idea of a sacred struggle in his war with the Meccans. The QUR'AN understands Jihad as a natural outcome of the FIVE PILLARS OF ISLAM Jihad justified the expansion of Islam under the first four CALIPHS and has been invoked against enemies throughout Islamic history.

JIMMU TENNO Traditionally the first Japanese EMPEROR who began his reign in 660 BC. He was thought to be a great grandson of the sun goddess AMATERASU and was credited with the unification of Japan and the establishment of its government under the guidance of the gods (see KAMI).

JINJA The SHINTO sanctuary. They vary in size from roadside shrines to beautifully located halls surrounded by trees and entered through traditional arched gateways (see TORII). They include halls for ceremonial dances, offerings and prayer rooms.

JINN Spiritual creatures in Islamic belief who are made of smokeless flame. They are capable of belief and unbelief: the good ones are regarded as MUSLIMS.

JIVA A soul or 'life monad' according to JAIN belief. Jivas are infinite and omniscient but in this world KARMA weighs them down into a material existence. Jivas are liberated by acquiring omniscience and this makes them float up to the summit of the universe.

JOCHANAN BEN ZAKKAI Creator of the academic SANHEDRIN in Jamnia after the FALL OF JERUSALEM in AD 70. He led the work of Jewish reconstruction within the limits of Roman law and ensured, through the Sanhedrin, that the Jewish community were represented before the Roman authorities.

JODO Japanese name for PURE LAND BUDDHISM.

JODO SHINSHU ('True Pure Land Sect') A refinement of PURE LAND BUDDHISM founded by SHINRAN. It was characterized by the doctrine of salvation through faith alone and the abolition of the SANGHA.

JOK 'Spirit', 'divinity' or 'god' in several East African languages.

JUDAH HA NASI ('The Prince'; AD 135–217) Leader of the academic Jewish SANHEDRIN in Galilee. He was responsible for compiling the MISHNAH which helped the Jewish community in developing a source of ritual authority in religious teaching. At his death 'Glory departed from Israel'.

JUDAISM The religion that developed from the religion of ancient ISRAEL and has been practised ever since by the JEWS. It is an ethical MONOTHEISM based on the revelation of GOD to MOSES on Mt SINAI and his giving of the Law (see TORAH). (See also ASHKENAZIM; CONSERVATIVE JUDAISM; ORTHODOX JUDAISM; PROGRESSIVE JUDAISM; SEPHARDIM.)

JUDAS MACCABEUS (died 160 BC) Jewish revolutionary who opposed the Hellenizing Seleucid emperor Antiochus Epiphanes who had set up an image of Olympian ZEUS in the TEMPLE OF JERUSALEM. Under Judas sporadic guerrilla revolt became full-scale war. In 165 BC Antiochus was defeated and in the following year the temple was rededicated (see HANUKKAH). Though he achieved religious freedom, he failed to establish a free Jewish state.

JUDGEMENT The divine assessment of individuals and the settling of their destiny, a notion found in many religions. Christianity teaches that judgement is based on the individual's response to Christ.

JUMIS Latvian harvest god.

JUNG, Carl Gustav (AD 1875–1961) Swiss psychiatrist who invented the theory of ARCHETYPES. He investigated the significance of MYTHS, symbols and DREAMS, and found in them evidence for a 'collective unconscious' which was at the root of religion.

JUNO Roman goddess, counterpart of the Greek HERA and wife of JUPITER. She was the patroness of women, marriage, childbirth and family life.

JUPITER/JOVE Principal god of the Romans, identified with the Greek ZEUS. He controlled the weather, particularly lightning and rain and was worshipped throughout Italy as almost a national god.

K

KA The guardian spirit of each individual which, according to Egyptian belief, survived death and lived on in the next world, where it was re-united with BA.

KA'BA ('Cube') The sanctuary in MECCA to which all MUSLIMS turn in prayer. Set in its eastern corner is the BLACK STONE. A pre-Islamic holy place, all its religious images were removed in AD 630 by MUHAMMAD when he purified it to be the central sanctuary of ISLAM. The QUR'AN associates Abraham and Ishmael with the building of the Ka'ba.

KABBALAH Jewish mystical tradition which flourished in the teaching of two schools: the practical school based in Germany which concentrated on prayer and MEDITATION; the speculative school in Provence and Spain in the thirteenth and fourteenth centuries. The tradition originates in Talmudic speculation on the themes of the work of creation and the divine chariot mentioned in the biblical book of Ezekiel. The most famous Kabbalistic book is *Zohar* ('splendour'), a MIDRASH on the PENTATEUCH. (See MYSTICISM; TALMUD.)

KABIR (probably 1440–1518) Indian poet and hymn writer who influenced the development of early Sikhism. He attempted a synthesis of ISLAM and HINDUISM, rejecting the CASTE SYSTEM and CIRCUMCISION, but teaching the love of God, rebirth and liberation.

KAITIAKI Maori word for a guardian spirit.

KALI Consort of the HINDU god SHIVA, a black goddess who is portrayed with a necklace of human skulls and fangs dripping blood. She is both the goddess of destruction and the Great Mother, giver of life.

KALKI In HINDU tradition, the last AVATAR of VISHNU who will descend on a white horse, with a sword, to kill the wicked and bring the world to an end.

KALUNGA Bantu word for the realm of the dead, the sea, the UNDERWORLD. It is also the name of an earth deity.

KAMI Powers of nature which are venerated in SHINTO. They are beneficent spirits who help in the processes of fertility and growth. They were generated by the gods and the Japanese people are descended from them according to Shinto mythology.

KAMMA PALI word for Buddhist concept of KARMA.

KARAITES ('Readers of Scripture') Heretical Jewish school of the eighth century AD which denied the validity of the TALMUD and the oral tradition. They held to a literalist view of TORAH. By the tenth century they had spread throughout the Middle East and Spain. They refused to mix with other JEWS. Under attack by SAADYA BEN JOSEPH the movement gradually disintegrated.

KARAKIA Maori term for any sacred ritual. To be effective and to avoid misfortune it must be recited without error, addition or omission.

KARMA SANSKRIT word for work or action. In Indian belief every action has inevitable consequences which attach themselves to the doer, requiring reward or punishment. Karma is thus the moral law of cause and effect. It explains the inequalities of life as the consequences of actions in previous lives. The notion of karma probably developed among the DRAVIDIAN people of India. In MAHAYANA Buddhism the concept is transformed by the idea of the BODHISATTVA. Merit can be transferred by grace or faith, thus changing the person's karma.

KARO, Joseph (AD 1488–1575) Jewish legal teacher and MYSTIC. He produced the *Shulchan Aruch* (1565) which is one of the most important and cohesive authorities in JUDAISM and is considered to be in accord with the purest Talmudic tradition (see TALMUD). His work is characterized by a devotional tone unusual in legal works.

KASHRUT The code in JUDAISM according to which food is ritually clean or unclean. It refers particularly to meat, which must be slaughtered so as to ensure the minimum of pain and the draining off of blood.

KASHI See BENARES.

KEHUA Maori word for a ghostly being.

KHALSA Originally the militant community of SIKHS organized by Guru GOBINDH SINGH in AD 1699. Now it is the society of fully-committed adult members of the Sikh community. Traditional marks of membership are uncut hair, a comb worn in the hair, knee-length breeches, a sword and a steel bracelet.

KHANDHA See SKANDHA.

KHARIJITES MUSLIM party of seceders from 'ALI, the fourth CALIPH. They opposed the UMAYYAD DYNASTY, believing that the succession should be based on a democratic vote. They were puritans, strongly critical of the moral laxity which developed as Umayyad power increased. Their stance inspired later reforming movements. They still exist as a separate sect in North Africa.

KILIBOB See MANUP AND KILIBOB.

KINGDOM OF GOD The rule of God on earth. In JUDAISM God is king of the universe, the sole creator and ruler. The JEWS are his witnesses and their task is to work and pray for the fulfilment of his rule among all people. The kingdom will be brought by the MESSIAH and will include the restoration of ISRAEL. JESUS OF NAZARETH proclaimed the arrival of the kingdom in himself. Christians share in the kingdom now, and it will be completed and fulfilled at his SECOND COMING.

KITAB AKDAS Scripture of BAHA'I.

KOAN Technique used in RINZAI ZEN to bring about SATORI. It is a mind-bending question given by a teacher to a pupil to help him break through the prison of mental concepts and achieve direct awareness of reality.

KOJIKI SHINTO scripture which is the oldest book in the Japanese language, though it is written using Chinese characters. It contains MYTHS and legends about the creation, the founding of Japan and the ceremonies and customs of the Japanese people.

KOKO Spirits of dead ancestors in the popular cults of the Zuñi people of northern Mexico. The spirits are represented in ceremonial dances in which all participating males wear god-like masks.

KOL NIDRE See YOM KIPPUR.

KONKO-KYO ('The religion of Golden Light') One of the most successful of the Japanese NEW RELIGIONS. It is based on SHINTO but claims to be universal and monotheistic (see MONOTHEISM) and may have 500,000 followers.

KOOK, Abraham Isaac RABBI (AD 1868–1935) First Chief Rabbi of the Holy Land. He believed the Zionist movement to be essentially religious and that the restoration of ISRAEL was necessary for the redemption of the world. He influenced orthodox JEWS in favour of ZIONISM though he was also tolerant of secular Jews.

KORAN See QUR'AN.

KOTEL See WESTERN WALL.

KRISHNA The eighth incarnation of VISHNU according to HINDU tradition. His name means 'black'. Though of noble birth, he was brought up as a cowherd. Eventually he obtained his inheritance and ruled in justice. He was also a great lover: the MAHABHARATA describes his romances with the cow-girls which are seen as a type of God's love for the soul. He is also the main character in the BHAGAVAD GITA where he appears disguised as the charioteer of Prince Arjuna.

KRISHNA CONSCIOUSNESS See INTERNATIONAL SOCIETY FOR KRISHNA CONSCIOUSNESS.

KRISHNAMURTI, Jiddhu (born 1895) Indian spiritual teacher who was brought up by a leading Theosophist Mrs Annie Besant, who proclaimed him as a World Teacher. He renounced this role in 1929 and became a solitary traveller, teaching liberation from dogma and organized religion by the rejection of belief in the individual ego. (See also THEOSOPHY.)

KSHATRIYA See CASTE SYSTEM.

KUAN-YIN Chinese name for the great BODHISATTVA AVALOKITESH VARA, especially when thought of in female form.

KUKAI (AD 774–835) Japanese Buddhist teacher who tried to reconcile BUDDHISM with SHINTO (see RYOBU SHINTO). He is sometimes regarded as a manifestation of the Buddha VAIROCANA. Some believe he exists in a deep trance from which he is able to perform miracles and that he will return one day as a saviour.

KUNDALINI Energy that is coiled like a serpent at the base of the spine, according to TANTRISM. When awakened by YOGA it leaps up the spine to the brain giving an experience of union and liberation, re-enacting the sexual union of SHIVA and SHAKTI.

KWOTH Word for god or spirit among the Nuer people of East Africa.

L

LA ILAHA ILLA ALLAH The first four words of the MUSLIM confession of faith: 'There is no god but God', which continues 'and MUHAMMAD is his prophet'. To accept this creed is to be a Muslim. It is the first of the FIVE PILLARS OF ISLAM. Its words form part of the Call to Prayer which is broadcast from the MOSQUE five times a day in Muslim communities.

LAIMA Latvian goddess of fate.

LAITY (From Greek: *laos*, 'people') The non-ordained members of a religious community (see ORDINATION), or those with no specialist religious function.

LAKSHMI Lord VISHNU's consort. She appears in the *Rig Veda* (see VEDAS) as good fortune. In the RAMAYANA she rises out of the sea

holding a lotus. She is involved in Vishnu's descents to earth as an AVATAR. Some associate her with SITA and RADHA, the consorts of RAMA and KRISHNA.

LAMA Tibetan religious leader, a title formerly applied only to abbots, but later used of any monk. Lamas have been credited with magical powers which are said to be attained through years of arduous training. Their most common feat is telepathy, but they are also reported to be able to leave their bodies at will, cover huge distances at great speed and know the time and place of their own death. (See also BÖN; SHAMAN.)

LAMAISM See TIBETAN BUDDHISM.

LAO TSE/LAO-TZU Traditionally the author of the TAO TE CHING and a contemporary of CONFUCIUS. His name means 'old master' which could have applied to any wandering teacher.

LARES Roman agricultural spirits who were worshipped at cross-roads and in the home as household gods.

LATTER-DAY SAINTS, CHURCH OF JESUS CHRIST OF See MORMONISM; SMITH, JOSEPH.

LECTISTERNIUM A Roman feast in which food was offered to images of the gods which were placed on couches (*lecti*) like human guests.

LENT In CHRISTIANITY a forty-day period of FASTING and penitence before EASTER, originally a period of training and examination for those who were baptized at Easter.

LEY LINES Straight geological lines of spiritual force which some adherents of NEW AGE RELIGIONS believe were discovered and used in the NEOLITHIC PERIOD. Their existence is said to be demonstrated by the many alignments between religious sites, MEGALITHS and unusual topographical features. There is no archaeological or statistical support for this view.

LEZA A name for God as supreme being, found in many parts of East, Central and Southern Africa.

LI CONFUCIUS' concept of propriety or reverence which he believed

should direct all relationships between members of society. Correct application of li was a guarantee of social welfare and harmony.

LIBATION The RITUAL outpouring of drink as an offering to DIVINITIES or ANCESTOR SPIRITS.

LIBERATION THEOLOGY Originating in Latin America, associates SALVATION with the political liberation of oppressed peoples. It is marked by a stress on the challenges to social action contained in the BIBLE, especially the prophetic books and the NEW TESTAMENT, and the reality of the KINGDOM OF GOD as a coming event.

LIMBO According to Roman Catholic doctrine, the dwelling place of souls (e.g. of unbaptized children) excluded from HEAVEN but not subjected to HELL or PURGATORY.

LITURGY ('Public service') (1) Any regular prescribed service of the Christian Church. (2) The EUCHARIST, especially in ORTHODOXY.

LOA Gods or DIVINITIES who are the objects of worship in VOODOO religion.

LOKI The opponent of the AESIR in Norse mythology who is bent on their downfall and the overthrow of the world order. His name may mean 'light' and he is associated with destructive fire. For his part in the death of BALDER he is fettered to underground rocks and poisoned by serpents until the day of RAGNARÖK. His agonies cause earthquakes and volcanoes.

LOKI'S BROOD The children of LOKI who, in Norse mythology, are fathered on the giantess Angrboda. They are the great wolf, Fenriswulf; the world serpent, Jörmungandr, and the goddess HEL. The serpent was cast into the sea where it ringed the world holding its tail in its mouth. Hel was thrown into the UNDERWORLD where she rules over the dead. The wolf was fettered by the AESIR until the battle of RAGNARÖK when he was to swallow ODIN.

LORD'S SUPPER Name for the Christian EUCHARIST favoured by the Protestant reformers who saw the Eucharist primarily as a memorial of CHRIST's death.

LOTUS Type of water lily, a Buddhist symbol of ENLIGHTENMENT. The roots of the lotus are buried in the earth while the flower opens out above the water.

LOTUS POSTURE Style of sitting upright and cross-legged, used as a position for MEDITATION in Hindu and Buddhist practice.

LOTUS SUTRA MAHAYANA Buddhist scripture in the form of a sermon preached by the BUDDHA to a vast throng of gods, demons, rulers and cosmic powers. It contains the essence of Mahayana teachings on the eternity of the Buddha, the universal capacity for Buddhahood and the compassion and power of the BODHISATTVAS. It is especially revered in Japan and is the basic scripture of the NICHIREN Buddhist NEW RELIGIONS.

LUCRETIUS (about 100–55 BC) Roman poet and philosopher who expounded the materialist and rationalist doctrines of EPICUREANISM in his poem *De rerum natura* ('On the nature of things'). He accepted the existence of the traditional gods but located them far away from our world and believed that they had no interest in or influence over events on earth.

LUGH (Irish: 'the Shining One'; Welsh: Lleu) Most honoured of the Celtic gods, a war god, the patron of commerce and moneymaking and prototype of human beings. Skilful in all arts and crafts he is often portrayed as a youthful traveller. His Gaulish name is unknown but Julius Caesar compared him to the Roman MERCURY.

LUPERCALIA Roman festival, possibly in honour of Faunus, an Italian pastoral deity, held on 15 February. Goats or dogs were sacrificed and youths dressed in their skins ran round a course beating people. Originally this may have propitiated a wolf god.

LURIA, Isaac (1514–72) Jewish teacher from Spain who developed the Kabbalistic teachings of the *Zohar* (see KABBALAH). He believed in reincarnation and taught that the dispersion of the JEWS was providential and would lead to universal salvation. His teachings inspired devotional poetry and hymns.

LUTHER, Martin (1483–1546) Founder of the German REFORMATION. He held that only by faith in Jesus CHRIST could man be justified before God, not by any 'works' of religion. So the priesthood and the 'mediating' role of the church are unnecessary.

LUTHERAN CHURCHES Important churches in Scandinavia, other parts of Western Europe and the USA. They value theological study and emphasize the weekly sermon.

M

MACCABEES The family and supporters of JUDAS MACCABEUS. They were the forerunners of the ZEALOTS in fighting a holy war against alien rulers.

MADHVA (AD 1197–1280) Indian philosopher who founded a dualist school (see DUALISM) in opposition to the MONISM of SHANKARA. He was a devotee of VISHNU and believed that God was eternally distinct from the natural world. He may have been influenced by Christian teachings.

MAGI Priestly class of ancient Persia who at first opposed the spread of ZOROASTER's teachings. By the fourth century BC they had been drawn into the service of the new religion and stressed the ritual and magic elements of it.

MAGIC The manipulation of natural or supernatural forces by SPELLS and RITUALS for good or harmful ends.

MAHABHARATA One of the two great epics of the HINDU scriptures, compiled in the third or second century BC. Ascribed to the sage Vyasa, it tells of the war between two families, the Kauravas and the Pandus. The divine hero of the epic is the AVATAR KRISHNA.

MAHARAJ JI, GURU See DIVINE LIGHT MISSION.

MAHARISHI MAHESH YOGI See TRANSCENDENTAL MEDITATION.

MAHA SABA Semi-religious, semi-political Indian organization founded in 1920. On the right wing of HINDU politics it opposed partition after Indian independence. Members are aggressively nationalistic and resist attempts to modify the CASTE SYSTEM.

MAHATMA SANSKRIT title of great respect or veneration meaning 'great soul'.

MAHATMA GANDHI (AD 1869–1948) Leader of the Indian independence movement and the greatest spiritual and political figure of modern India. Disowning violence, he advocated political change through non-violent resistance. After independence he tried to reconcile the Hindu and Muslim communities. He also campaigned against the social exclusion of UNTOUCHABLES. He was assassinated by a Hindu fanatic.

MAHAVIRA Great JAIN teacher who traditionally lived 599–527 BC, though this is disputed. He abolished the distinctions of the CASTE SYSTEM and tried to spread his teaching among the Brahmins. He starved himself to death at the age of seventy-two, having spent his last years totally naked.

MAHAYANA ('Large vehicle') The form of BUDDHISM practised in Nepal, China, Tibet, Korea and Japan. Mahayana accepts more scriptures than THERAVADA and has developed various forms of popular devotion based on the doctrine of the BODHISATTVAS.

MAHDI 'The guided one' who according to SHI'A teaching will come at the end of the world. The Mahdi is identified with Muhammad al-Mahdi who disappeared in AD 880 and is believed to be hidden until his reappearance. There have been a number of false Mahdis in the Shi'a community.

MAHOMET See MUHAMMAD.

MAIMONIDES, Moses (AD 1135–1204) Jewish philosopher who lived in Spain and later Egypt and attempted a synthesis of Aristotelian and biblical teaching. He listed the THIRTEEN PRINCIPLES of belief which have been treated in Judaism as a creed and are found in the Jewish *Daily Prayer Book*.

MAITREYA The Buddha-to-be, or the next BUDDHA to appear on earth according to MAHAYANA teachings. He is at present a BODHISATTVA awaiting his last rebirth.

MANA Polynesian word for the invisible spiritual power which permeates all things. It has been adopted as a general term in the study of PRIMAL RELIGIONS. It is not necessarily a personal power, though it can be focussed in particular individuals, places and objects.

MANABUSCH ('Big rabbit') Hero of the Algonquin and other North American Indian tribes. He is thought to have restored the earth after a great flood and to have introduced handicrafts and medicine.

MANANNAN Irish sea god, equivalent to the Welsh Manwyddan. He rode on the waves, gave immortality to other gods and possessed magic armour and a magic sword. His symbol is three joined revolving legs, which remains the emblem of the Isle of Man.

MANAQAN TENGRI Mongol name for the god of wild game.

MANCO CAPAC The first INCA who traditionally was created by the SUN GOD on an island in Lake Titicaca. He was instructed to bring civilization to all Indian peoples. He was guided to found the city of CUZCO as his capital.

MANDAEANS Members of a Gnostic sect teaching redemption through a divine saviour who has lived on earth and defeated the powers of darkness. The sole surviving practitioners of GNOSTICISM, about 15,000 still live in Iraq and Iran.

MANDALA A visual aid in the form of a series of coloured concentric circles used in TIBETAN BUDDHISM. Segments of the circles portray different aspects of the BUDDHA'S compassion. Concentration on the mandala enables the disciple to see himself in relation to the Buddha's compassion and thus to achieve ENLIGHTENMENT.

MANES Spirits of the dead in Roman religion.

MANICHAEANS Followers of Mani (around AD 216–276), a Persian teacher whose strict ascetic system was designed to release the divine spark trapped in every person by the wiles of SATAN. Their teaching influenced AUGUSTINE.

MANITO Name used by the Algonquin Indians of North America to refer to spiritual powers. It can apply to all kinds of NATURE SPIRITS or DIVINITIES, friendly or unfriendly.

MANTRA A symbolic sound causing an internal vibration which helps to concentrate the mind and aids self-realization, e.g. the repeated syllable 'om', and in Tibetan Buddhism the phrase OM MANI PADME HUM. In HINDUISM the term originally referred to a few sacred verses from the VEDAS. It came to be thought that they possessed spiritual power, and that repetition of them was a help to liberation. A mantra is sometimes given by a spiritual teacher to a disciple as an INITIATION.

MANUP AND KILIBOB Two semi-divine brothers whose story of separation and reconciliation has played an important part in the PRIMAL RELIGIONS and new religious movements of the Madang area of Papua New Guinea.

MAPONOS Celtic divine youth, worshipped in Gaul and North Britain. The Gauls connected him with healing springs, the British with music. In Wales he is Mabon, son of the Divine Mother. Irish myth speaks of Mac ind Og, the son of DAGDA.

MARA In BUDDHISM, the evil one, temptation.

MARA Latvian goddess of fate.

MARDUK Babylonian deity who superseded the Sumerian god ENLIL. He was associated with the sun and with vegetation. He was addressed as Bel, the Supreme Lord.

MARKS OF EXISTENCE In the BUDDHA'S teaching all existence is marked by the three characteristics: DUKKHA; ANICCA; ANATTA.

MARRIAGE, SACRED A religious rite involving real or simulated sexual intercourse which represents the marriage of earth and sky in the fertilization of the soil and the growth of the crops.

MARS Roman war god, regarded second only to JUPITER. Soldiers sacrificed to him before and after battle. Originally he was probably a god of agriculture.

MARTYR ('Witness') Title originally applied to Christians who died rather than renounce their faith during times of persecution. Now a term applied to anyone who dies for a religious belief.

MARY, THE MOTHER OF JESUS Because of her role in the divine plan of salvation, Mary is honoured by all Christians and venerated by Roman Catholic and Eastern Orthodox Christians. The GOSPELS describe her as divinely chosen to be the mother of the Saviour. Roman Catholic churches have attributed an intercessory role to Mary, and developed other doctrines concerning her nature.

MASBUTA Baptismal rite of MANDAEANS.

MASIQTA MANDAEAN ceremony consisting of a sacramental meal held at death to assist the soul to salvation.

MASORETES A group of Jewish scholars from the Babylonian and Palestinian schools who in the ninth century AD supplied the text of the HEBREW BIBLE with vowel points and divided it up into sentences and paragraphs. They also tried to exclude copyists' errors and noted all the variant readings they found.

MASS Name for the Christian EUCHARIST derived from the words of dismissal. The standard ROMAN CATHOLIC term, it emphasizes the sacrificial aspect of the rite.

MATRONAE MOTHER GODDESSES worshipped in Celtic religion. They are often portrayed in groups of three, carrying babies or bushels of fruit or sheaves—clear evidence of their association with earthly and human fertility.

MATSURI Japanese name for a solemn celebration intended to invoke worship of the SHINTO gods and obedience to their moral will. They take place at stated intervals in Shinto sanctuaries.

MAWU Supreme HIGH GOD among a number of West African peoples. He is the creator of gods and the sender of souls into men.

MAX MÜLLER, Friedrich (AD 1823–1900) German philosopher of religion and philologist who taught that religion originated in the personification of the forces of nature. He edited the fifty-one-volume series of translations, *Sacred Books of the East*. He worked in England from 1846.

MAYA Illusion or deception in HINDU thought. Maya is concerned with the diverse phenomenal world perceived by the senses. It is the trick of maya to convince people that this is all that exists and thus blind them to the reality of BRAHMAN and the oneness of existence. (2) Legendary mother of the BUDDHA (1).

MAYA People of an ancient Middle American empire which spread from Yucatan to El Salvador. Mayan civilization was at its height around AD 300–900 and was finally broken up by the Spaniards in the sixteenth century. The Maya developed a complex calendar and a form of writing. Their gods were linked with nature symbols, the most important of which was a double-headed snake. (See also AHKIN; AH PUCH; CHAC; CHILAN; HALACH UINIC; ITZAMNA; IXCHEL; POPOL VUH; YUM KAAX.)

MECCA Holy city of ISLAM, in Saudi Arabia, the birthplace of MUHAMMAD and later the base for his MUSLIM state after its conquest in AD 630. Pilgrimage to Mecca, HAJJ, is one of the FIVE PILLARS OF ISLAM and all Muslims face Mecca to perform ritual prayer five times a day.

MEDICINE MAN See WITCHDOCTOR.

MEDINA Formerly Yathrib, city 169km north of MECCA, the political base for MUHAMMAD from AD 622 until his conquest of Mecca. Pilgrims from Medina were among the first to accept and spread Muhammad's message. The city contains the site of Muhammad's tomb.

MEDITATION Deep and continuous reflection, practised in many religions with a variety of aims, e.g. to attain self-realization or, in theistic religions, to attain union with the divine will. Many religions teach a correct posture, method of breathing and ordering of thoughts for meditation.

MEDIUM One who is possessed by the spirit of a dead person or a DIVINITY and, losing his individual identity, becomes the mouthpiece for the other's utterance.

MEGALITHS Large stone monuments dating from the late NEOLITHIC PERIOD. Their original function is uncertain but they mark burial mounds and temples and they may have served as a calendar of times and seasons.

MEHER BABA (AD 1894–1969) Indian spiritual leader, regarded by his followers as an AVATAR. From 1925 until his death he did not speak once.

MENCIUS (born 371 BC) Confucian teacher who expanded and developed CONFUCIUS' teachings. He believed that the universe followed a moral order and that knowledge of this order could be attained by MEDITATION.

MENDELSSOHN, Moses (1729–86) German Jewish rationalist philosopher who taught that the three central propositions of JUDAISM are: the existence of God; providence; the immortality of the soul. He believed these to be founded on pure reason and to be the basis of all religion. The revelation to the JEWS preserves the Jews as an ethnic entity. He translated the PENTATEUCH into German and encouraged Jews to become more involved in European culture.

MERCURY Roman god, identified with the Greek HERMES. He presided over trade.

MERIT In BUDDHISM the fruit of good actions which can be devoted to the welfare of other beings. The idea develops in MAHAYANA where it is believed that the BODHISATTVAS have acquired almost infinite supplies of merit which they can transfer to believers.

MERLIN Bard and magician in the romances of the CELTS, later the mentor of ARTHUR.

MESSIAH ('Anointed one') A HEBREW word referring to the person chosen by God to be king. After the end of the Israelite monarchy it came to refer to a figure who would restore ISRAEL, gathering the tribes together and ushering in the KINGDOM OF GOD. JUDAISM has known several false Messiahs (see ZEVI, SHABBETAI). Modern Jews are divided as to whether the Messiah is a symbolic or a representative figure and whether the founding of the Jewish state is in any way a prelude to his coming. In the Christian NEW TESTAMENT, JESUS OF NAZARETH is described by Messianic titles, e.g. Messiah, CHRIST, 'the King', 'the One who Comes'. The account of Jesus' entry into JERUSALEM is deliberately phrased in Messianic terms. Jesus himself was cautious about claiming to be Messiah, probably because of its political overtones.

METHODIST CHURCHES Churches deriving from those which joined the Methodist Conference, first established in 1784 by John WESLEY. They are now spread world-wide promoting EVANGELISM and social concern.

MEZUZAH ('Doorpost') Sign placed at the door of a Jewish house, comprising part of the SHEMA.

MIDDLE WAY The BUDDHA's description of his teaching as a mean between the extremes of sensuality and asceticism. It is designed to lead to NIRVANA.

MIDEWIWIN A society of scholars and holy men of the Ojibwa Indians of North America who are charged with the preservation of the traditions of their people.

MIDGARD The home of human beings according to Norse cosmology. Made from the body of the primeval giant, Ymir, it was defended by THOR from attack by giants. Midgard is the middle of the nine worlds; it is in the centre of GINNUNGAGAP and surrounded by sea.

MIDRASH A method of exposition of HEBREW texts designed to reveal the inner meaning of the TORAH. Great attention to detail was paid because the texts were believed to be of divine origin. The method was originally oral; the most important midrashim were recorded and written down.

MIHRAB Semi-circular recess in the wall of a MOSQUE which indicates the direction of the holy city MECCA, which is the direction for MUSLIM prayer.

MIKI NAKAYAMA (AD 1798–1887) Founder of the Japanese religion TENRIKYO. In 1838 she was possessed by a divine being who announced he was the Creator and true God and gave her a series of revelations. Miki Nakayama gave away all her money and practised spiritual healing. Her teachings attracted a wide following. Adherents believe she is still alive, in non-physical form, in the shrine built on the site of her home at the city of Tenri.

MIMI Shy and harmless NATURE SPIRITS of the mythology of northern Australia.

MIMIR In Norse mythology, the fount of wisdom who guards the well of knowledge at the root of YGGDRASIL. He is ODIN's mentor. In one version of his MYTH, Odin comes to drink from the well and has to sacrifice an eye to do so; in another Mimir's head is cut off and brought to Odin who preserves it as a talking head which gives him advice.

MINARET ('Place of light and fire') A tower attached to a MOSQUE from which the Call to Prayer is broadcast to the MUSLIM community.

MINDFULNESS Buddhist method of contemplative analysis. It has two uses: in MEDITATION, where it refers to the practice of observing the arising and passing away of different mental states until one arrives at detachment; in daily life, where it refers to a quality of carefulness in thought, speech and action which prevents the accumulation of bad KARMA.

MING Chinese emperor (first century AD) of the Han dynasty who, according to tradition, introduced Buddhist scriptures from north-west India. According to tradition he had a dream of a golden man, which he took to be a revelation of the BUDDHA.

MINISTER (1) A lay or ordained Christian who has been authorized to perform spiritual functions (ministries, literally 'service') in the CHURCH. (2) General title for any clergyman, especially those of Protestant denominations.

MINOAN RELIGION Religion of the Bronze Age civilization of Crete. The Minoans probably worshipped the MOTHER GODDESS and reverenced SACRED SNAKES and SACRED BULLS.

MIRACLE An event which appears to defy rational explanation and is attributed to divine intervention.

MISHNAH A compilation of Jewish oral teachings undertaken by Rabbi JUDAH HA NASI in around AD 200. It quickly became second in authority only to the HEBREW BIBLE and formed the basis of the TALMUD. The Mishnah helped Jewish teaching to survive in a period of persecution when the future of the SANHEDRIN was in doubt.

MISSAL Liturgical book containing all that is said or sung throughout the year at the celebration of the MASS. It also includes appropriate directions.

MISSION The outgoing of the Christian CHURCH to the unconverted with its GOSPEL message. It is held that all mankind needs to hear the news of SALVATION.

MISSIONARIES Those who propagate a religious faith among people of a different faith. BUDDHISM and CHRISTIANITY have been the most notable missionary religions.

MITHRAEUM Cave-like sanctuary housing a statue of MITHRA slaying the bull.

MITHRA Originally a god of the Indo-Iranians, he was worshipped in the Hindu VEDAS as Mitra and was an important figure in ZOROASTRIANISM, where he was particularly associated with ideas on judgement and the priesthood. To this day, the term for Zoroastrian FIRE TEMPLES is *dar-i Mihr*, 'courts of Mithra'. (See also MITHRAISM; SOL INVICTUS.)

MITHRAISM Religion of Mithra which flourished throughout the Roman Empire in the second to fourth centuries AD. It was found in almost all parts of the empire, but concentrated in Rome, the Rhine Valley and what is now Hungary and Rumania. Popular among soldiers, it stressed the ethical values of courage and endurance. It was not open to women.

MODERATOR MINISTER of the PRESBYTERIAN CHURCH appointed to constitute and preside over one of the courts that govern the life of the church.

MODIMO/MOLIMO/MORIMO Word for spirit or god in many Bantu languages.

MOHAMMED See MUHAMMAD.

MOIRAI ('Fates') Three goddesses of Greek mythology, described by HESIOD as children of ZEUS and by PLATO as daughters of Necessity. They were Lachesis, who predestines each human life; Clotho, who spins the thread of life, and Atropos, who cuts the thread at death.

MOKSHA SANSKRIT word meaning liberation from the cycle of birth, death and rebirth. Moksha is achieved when virtue, knowledge and love of God cancel out the weight of KARMA which require the self to be reborn.

MONISM the belief that there is only one basic reality in spite of the appearance and experience of diversity. It applies particularly to the beliefs of the HINDU philosopher SHANKARA (see also ADVAITA.)

MONK A member of a male religious community living under vows which usually include poverty, chastity and the wearing of a distinctive form of dress. Monastic orders are found in Christianity and Buddhism. The Buddhist monk is a member of a SANGHA and, additionally to the FIVE PRECEPTS, vows to eat only at set times, not to handle money, use a high bed, use scent or go to stage performances. (See also BENEDICT; BHIKSHU.)

MONOTHEISM The belief that there is one supreme GOD who contains all the attributes and characteristics of divinity.

MOON, Sun Myung (born 1920) Korean engineer, businessman and founder of the UNIFICATION CHURCH. He claims to have authoritative visions of Jesus. Members of the Unification Church accord him a high, if publicly ill-defined, status.

MOONIES Disciples of Sun Myung MOON and members of his UNIFICATION CHURCH.

MORAVIANS Protestant Christians continuing the simple ideals of an earlier group 'The Bohemian Brethren'. They distrust CREEDS and oppose political involvement. They have been active MISSIONARIES since they were founded in AD 1722.

MORMONISM Unorthodox Christian sect founded in AD 1830 in the USA on the basis of the visionary experiences of Joseph SMITH. Under its second leader Brigham Young (AD 1801–77), the Mormons journeyed to found Salt Lake City (1847) where they developed into a strong missionary community. Mormons accept the BIBLE and the BOOK OF MORMON and some other revealed writings. The Mormon Church, officially the 'Church of Jesus Christ of Latter-Day Saints', has over 3 million members, two-thirds of them in the USA.

MORONI See SMITH, JOSEPH.

MORRIGHAN Battle goddess, the nightmare, phantom queen of Celtic mythology. She appears in a trio with Badb, the Crow, and Nemain, frenzy. Together they haunt battlefields, changing shape but often in the form of crows, and foretell war and doom.

MOSES The father of JUDAISM who received the TORAH from God on Mt SINAI having led the people of ISRAEL out of captivity in Egypt. The first five books of the BIBLE are traditionally ascribed to him.

MOSLEM See MUSLIM.

MOSQUE MUSLIM place of public worship, consisting usually of an outer courtyard for ablutions and a large unfurnished inner area where Muslims kneel, sit or prostrate themselves in worship. There is usually one main congregational service in the mosque between noon and 3 p.m. on Fridays.

MOTHER GODDESS/GREAT MOTHER The personification of nature and the natural processes of fertility and growth connected with the earth. Worship of a mother goddess was universal in the Ancient Near East, Asia and Europe (see CYBELE, DEMETER, INANNA, ISHTAR, ISIS). Her worship continues in HINDUISM where the consorts of SHIVA

(DURGA, KALI, PARVATI) have some of her characteristics. There is some revival of interest in her worship among modern feminist groups and practitioners of WITCHCRAFT.

MO-TZU Chinese philosopher and critic of CONFUCIANISM who lived in the fifth century BC. He taught universal love which he believed was the will of heaven. He defended popular religious practices and denounced war and extravagance.

MUEZZIN Person who calls the MUSLIM faithful to prayer.

MUFTI A canon lawyer in ISLAM who gives formal legal advice on questions brought to him in accordance with the QUR'AN, the SUNNA and the law schools.

MUGHAL EMPIRE Indian MUSLIM empire founded by Babur in AD 1526. The third emperor was the liberal Akbar who established good relations with HINDUS. Later rulers succumbed to Islamic puritanism, and after the reign of Aurangzeb the empire declined.

MUHAMMAD (about AD 570–632) Prophet and apostle of ISLAM, the final messenger of God whose message, the QUR'AN sums up and completes the previous revelations to the Jews and Christians. Muhammad saw the expansion of ISLAM in terms of military conquest and political organization and he was outstandingly successful as a commander and ruler in MEDINA and later MECCA.

MUHARRAM Festival kept by Shi'ite MUSLIMS (see SHI'A) commemorating the murder of Al-Huseyn on the tenth day of the month Muharram. A passion play is performed depicting the martyrdom.

MUJTAHID MUSLIM teacher who gives a ruling, legal decision or deduction on the basis of his own learning or authority (see IJTIHAD). In SHI'A Islam, the Mujtahid have great authority.

MUKANDA Male initiation rite among the Kiluba and other Bantu peoples.

MUKISHI Spirit associated with the dead, a spirit of natural phenomena

(see DIVINITIES) or a guardian spirit among the Kiluba and other Bantu peoples.

MULLAH A Persian form of an ARABIC word which means a 'teacher' or 'scholar'—an exponent of the sacred law of ISLAM.

MULUNGU/MUNGU/ MURUNGU In a number of East African languages a name for God as the supreme being.

MUNGU See MULUNGU.

MURUNGU See MULUNGU.

MUSLIM 'One who submits' to the will of God, a follower of ISLAM.

MUSLIM BROTHERHOOD Egyptian puritanical organization founded in AD 1928 by Hasan al-Banna. The brotherhood was influential after World War II and worked against ZIONISM and westernization. It fell into disrepute because of terrorist activities and was dissolved in 1954.

MUSLIM LEAGUE Organization founded in AD 1906 to promote the interests and political aspirations of Indian Muslims. One of its presidents was Muhammad IQBAL.

MWARI The name for God among the Shona people of Zimbabwe and in other Bantu languages.

MYSTERY RELIGIONS Cults based on ancient MYTHS which flourished in Greece, in Rome and throughout the Roman Empire. Initiates went through a dramatic and secret ceremony in which they identified with the divinity at the centre of the myth and experienced salvation and the assurance of immortality.

MYSTIC One who seeks direct personal experience of the divine. He may use PRAYER, MEDITATION or various ascetic practices to concentrate his attention.

MYSTICISM The search for direct personal experience of the divine. There is a distinction between seeing mysticism as leading to identification with GOD (as is common in HINDUISM) and as leading to a union with God's love and will (as in Islam, JUDAISM and CHRISTIANITY).

MYTH A sacred story which originates and circulates within a particular community. Some, aetiological myths, explain puzzling physical phenomena or customs, institutions and practices whose origin in the community would otherwise be mysterious. (See also CREATION MYTH.)

N

NAGARJUNA (around AD 100–165) MAHAYANA Buddhist philosopher who taught that the truth of reality was void or emptiness.

NAMANDI Malignant NATURE SPIRITS of the mythology of northern Australia who are thought to attack lonely travellers and to be in constant conflict with the MIMI.

NAMU MYOHO RENGE KYO Formula coined by NICHIREN as the essential truth of the LOTUS SUTRA. It means 'Reverence to the wonderful truth of the *Lotus Sutra*' and it is used by a variety of sects based on Nichiren's Buddhist teachings.

NANAK, GURU (AD 1469–1539) Indian religious teacher and founder of the SIKH religion. He intended to reconcile HINDUS and MUSLIMS and travelled widely preaching a monotheistic faith (see MONOTHEISM) which was influenced by BHAKTI and SUFISM. He appointed a successor to continue his teachings.

NATIVE AMERICAN CHURCH Religious organization of North American Indians founded in 1870. It teaches a synthesis of native religion and Christianity. Its rituals include the ceremonial use of peyote, a spineless cactus containing the hallucinogenic substance mescaline.

NATURE SPIRITS Spirits of trees, hills, rivers, plants and animals which are acknowledged with prayers and offerings in most PRIMAL RELIGIONS.

NAUJOTE INITIATION ceremony of the PARSIS at which a child is invested

with a sacred shirt and thread, symbolic of 'new birth' to adulthood.

NEBO Babylonian god of writing who was the son of MARDUK. His symbol was the pen and his gift of writing gave him the power to prolong life and revive the dead. He resembled the Egyptian THOTH.

NEMBUTSU ('Hail to the BUDDHA AMIDA') The formula of faith taught by the Japanese Buddhist teacher HONEN.

NEMESIS Greek goddess who personified the retribution due to evil deeds. Her vengeance was regarded to be inevitable and exact.

NEMETON 'Sacred place' in Celtic religion, usually an enclosed woodland grove.

NEOLITHIC PERIOD The New Stone Age, from about 10,000 BC until the Early Bronze Age.

NEO-PLATONISM Religious and philosophical movement from the third to the sixth centuries AD. It used the teachings of PLATO as a basis for ascetic practices and mystical experience. Its principal architect was PLOTINUS.

NEPTUNE Italian water god who became associated with POSEIDON and acquired his mythology.

NESTORIANISM CHRISTIAN HERESY that claimed that two separate persons, human and divine, existed in the incarnate CHRIST (as opposed to the orthodox view that God and man are one person in Christ). Although condemned in AD 431 it continued to flourish in Persia. A few groups of Nestorians survive in the present day.

NEW AGE RELIGIONS Term for the various movements which emerged or revived in the mid-1960s, particularly on the West Coast of the USA. These movements were characterized by a sense that man was entering a new phase of religious awareness. Their teachings were often a blend of Eastern and Western MYSTICISM designed to expand individual awareness.

NEW RELIGIONS New sects which have arisen in Japan in the

twentieth century. Many are Buddhist in origin (see NICHIREN), others have SHINTO roots, others are a synthesis, sometimes with Christian elements. (See also KONKO-KYO; P.L. KYODAN; SOKA GAKKAI.)

NEW TESTAMENT The second division of the Christian BIBLE, comprising the GOSPELS, the Acts of the Apostles, the Revelation of John and various EPISTLES.

NEW YEAR, JEWISH See ROSH HASHANAH.

NEZAHUALCOYOTL (AD 1418–72) AZTEC ruler who worshipped TLOQUE NAHUAQUE as the single god from whom all other gods derived their power and being. He built a great temple to him and tried, unsuccessfully, to curb the practice of human SACRIFICE.

NGAI Name for God in several East African languages.

NGANGA Medicine man or healer among the Kiluba and other Bantu peoples; one who practises BWANGA.

NGEWO The supreme HIGH GOD of the Mende people of Sierra Leone. He has neither temples nor priesthood because he has distanced himself from the everyday world since people were becoming too familiar with him.

NIBBANA PALI word for NIRVANA.

NICHIREN (AD 1222–82) Japanese Buddhist reformer who taught that the LOTUS SUTRA contained the ultimate truth and that it could be compressed into a sacred formula: NAMU MYOHO RENGE KYO. He denounced all other forms of Buddhism. When the Mongols threatened Japan he preached a fiery nationalism, urging the nation to convert to true Buddhism. His teachings have provided the inspiration for some modern Buddhist sects (see NEW RELIGIONS).

NIGHT JOURNEY The journey of MUHAMMAD from the temple in MECCA to the TEMPLE OF JERUSALEM which is described in the QUR'AN. Tradition asserts that he travelled on a winged horse accompanied by GABRIEL. By the sacred rock of Abraham, Muhammad met

Abraham, Moses and Jesus. Then he ascended up a ladder of light into the presence of ALLAH. He returned bringing instructions for the faithful.

NIHONGI SHINTO scripture which contains the Japanese CREATION MYTH and legends of the gods. It was originally written in Chinese.

NINIGI The son of AMATERASU in SHINTO belief. At a time of chaos in heaven Amaterasu sent him down to rule the islands of Japan, making him the first Japanese EMPEROR.

NIRVANA/NIBBANA ('Going out', 'becoming cool') In BUDDHISM the state when DUKKHA ceases because the flames of desire are no longer fuelled. It is a state of unconditioned-ness and uncompounded-ness beyond any form of known or imagined existence.

NKULUKULU ('The old, old one') Zulu name for God.

NOBLE EIGHTFOLD PATH In BUDDHISM the way to extinguish desire by adopting: right views; right motives; right speech; right conduct; right means of livelihood; right effort; right mindfulness; right contemplation.

NORNS The Fates of Norse religion. Of giant origin, they are immensely powerful, controlling the destiny of men. They tend and water the trunk of YGGDRASIL. The names of the three norns mean Past, Present and Future. Their association with time makes them more powerful than the immortal gods of ASGARD, since even they are bound to predestined fate. (See also MOIRAI.)

NUADHA Celtic deity who may have originated as an Irish king who relinquished his sacred office yet was saved by LUGH. In Wales he is known as Nudd and he is probably also to be identified with Nodens who had a Romano-British temple in south-west England.

NUMEN In Roman religion, the divine power suffusing nature. From this concept Rudolf OTTO developed the idea that the root of religion was a sense of holy power. This he termed the 'numinous'.

NUN A member of a female religious community as found in CHRISTIANITY and BUDDHISM. Nuns live under vows usually including poverty, CHASTITY and the wearing of a distinctive form of dress. (See also BENEDICT.)

NUT The sky goddess of Egyptian mythology whose body is lined with stars. Every evening she swallows the sun and gives birth to it again each morning.

NYAMBE/ZAMBE/NZAMBI Name for the supreme god in a large area of tropical Africa. It may be linked to a Sudanese word meaning 'power'.

NYAME ('The shining one') Name for the supreme HIGH GOD among the peoples of Ghana in West Africa.

O

OBEAH Religious and magical practices of the West Indies which are usually of West African origin. (See also VOODOO.)

OBO Pile of rocks representing the spirits of the departed in the religions of central Asia.

OCCULT Teachings, arts and practices that are concerned with what is hidden and mysterious, as with WITCHCRAFT, ALCHEMY and DIVINITION.

ODIN Chief of the Norse gods, the ALLFATHER. Originally he was a wild wind god who led the spirits of the dead through the air. The Romans associated him with MERCURY. In later mythology, he visits the earth as The Wanderer. There are two myths of his search for wisdom: the first that he sacrificed an eye as the price for his drinking from the well of MIMIR; the second that he hanged himself upon YGGDRASIL. He is associated with the gallows and there is evidence that victims were hanged on trees in sacrifice to him. As Allfather, Odin watched over the nine worlds and was brought daily reports by two ravens.

Variants of his name include Woden (Anglo-Saxon) and Wotan (German).

OGUN God of iron and metalwork among the Yoruba people of Nigeria. Cyclists, lorry-drivers, soldiers and blacksmiths carry protective charms of Ogun.

OHRMAZD See AHURA MAZDA.

OLD CATHOLIC CHURCHES A group of national churches which have separated from Rome. Since 1932 they have been in communion with the Church of England.

OLD TESTAMENT The HEBREW BIBLE as the first division of the Christian BIBLE.

OLUDUMARE/OLURUN Name for the supreme HIGH GOD among the Yoruba people of Nigeria.

OLURUN See OLUDUMARE.

OLYMPUS, Mount The highest mountain in Greece (2,917m), held to be the home of the twelve greatest Greek gods under the leadership of ZEUS.

OM MANI PADME HUM ('The jewel in the LOTUS') Tibetan MANTRA, whose six syllables are held to correspond to the six worlds of Tibetan Buddhist teaching: *om*, 'gods'; *ma*, 'anti-gods'; *ni*, 'humans'; *pad*, 'animals'; *mi*, 'hungry ghosts'; *hum*, 'hell'. Each world is present as a state of the human mind. The mantra sums up the whole of human existence and is an indispensable aid to self-realization.

ORDINATION Rite in the Christian CHURCH by which men (and in some churches women) are authorized as MINISTERS of the Word of God and the SACRAMENTS. In BUDDHISM the term denotes entry into the SANGHA.

ORIGEN (around AD 184–254) Theologian who tried to present Biblical CHRISTIANITY using the ideas of HELLENISM. He believed that all creatures would eventually be saved, a view condemned as heretical in AD 553.

ORIGINAL SIN The sin of Adam, the first man, in eating from the forbidden tree in the Garden of Eden, expressing independence from God. In Christian teaching the inevitable consequence is seen as separation from God: man is 'fallen', a state inherited by all men and women and resulting in the need for SALVATION.

ORPHISM Religious movement which began in Thrace and flourished in the sixth century BC. It was based on MYTHS of DIONYSUS and Orpheus, who was the supreme minstrel of Greek mythology. It taught a way of liberation through ASCETICISM and held also a doctrine of REINCARNATION.

ORTHODOX JUDAISM Traditional JUDAISM which is Talmudic (see TALMUD) in belief and practice. It is the largest of the modern groupings and it is the form of religion accepted as authentic in Israel.

ORTHODOXY CHRISTIANITY as practised by the Eastern Churches after the GREAT SCHISM. Orthodox Christians are found mostly in Eastern Europe, the Balkan States and Russia.

OSIRIS Egyptian vegetation god, the force behind the cycle of growth and decay. Mythology tells how he had originally lived on earth as a king. He was murdered and later dismembered by his jealous brother SETH. His wife ISIS searched for the pieces of his body and restored him to life. As a symbol of death and resurrection, Osiris became associated with life after death and the judgement of individual souls.

OTTO, Rudolf (AD 1869–1937) German philosopher of religion and author of *The Idea of the Holy* (1917) in which he argued that religious experience sprang from the intuitive and non-rational faculties in man and was characterized by a sense of the 'numinous' (see NUMEN), by awe and dread and amazement.

OTTOMAN EMPIRE (AD 1453–1918) The empire of the Ottoman Turks who were converted to ISLAM. It stretched from the Middle East to the Balkans and at its height to the frontiers of Austria. The Ottomans supported SUNNI orthodoxy against heterodox DERVISH movements. The empire went into slow decline in the eighteenth century and its religious life stagnated.

P

PACHACAMAC Leader of the gods in the religion of the INCAS. A great shrine was built for him near the modern city of Lima, Peru.

PACHACUTEC The ninth INCA (ruled AD 1438–71). A great king, he enlarged the empire and rebuilt the capital CUZCO. He exalted VIRACOCHA as the supreme god of the Incas.

PAGAN Originally a word used by Christians to describe a person who had not adopted the Christian faith. Today it tends to refer to a person who is neither Christian, Jew nor Muslim, or to a person who is irreligious or who adheres to some modern revival of an ancient religion.

PAGANISM The religion and worship of those who are neither CHRISTIANS, JEWS nor MUSLIMS.

PAGODA A Buddhist building in south-east Asia built over Buddhist RELICS and often characterized by a series of superimposed spires. (See also DAGOBA.)

PALAEOLITHIC PERIOD The Old Stone Age, before 10,000 BC in Europe and the Middle East.

PALI Vernacular language of northern India in the BUDDHA'S time and hence the language of early BUDDHISM and the THERAVADA SCRIPTURES. It is related to SANSKRIT.

PALI CANON The basic Buddhist SCRIPTURES—the only scriptures valid among THERAVADA Buddhists. Traditionally the collection began soon after the BUDDHA'S death when his followers met to recite the TRIPITAKA, or 'three baskets' of his teaching. The precise wording of the canon was fixed at a council in the time of king ASOKA.

PAN Arcadian fertility god, patron of shepherds and herdsmen, usually portrayed with goat's horns and legs.

PANCHEN LAMA Title given to one of the leading abbots of TIBETAN BUDDHISM, whose authority paralleled that of the DALAI LAMA, though its emphasis was more on spiritual matters. The Panchen Lama

was believed to be a reincarnation of AMITABHA.

PANTHEISM The belief that all reality is in essence divine.

PAPA Sky god of the Scythians.

PAPATUANUKU See RANGINUI AND PAPATUANUKU.

PAROUSIA See SECOND COMING.

PARSIS/PARSEES Descendants of the ancient Zoroastrian Persians (see ZOROASTRIANISM) living in India, mostly near Bombay. They practise an ethical MONOTHEISM with a RITUAL life that expresses the purity of AHURA MAZDA. The 125,000 Parsis in the world today are divided into three groups, differing over the religious calendar.

PARSVA Legendary founder of JAINISM. Born a prince around 850 BC, he renounced his throne and became an ascetic, finally gaining omniscience. He is considered to be the twenty-second TIRTHANKARA.

PARVATI ('Mountaineer') Consort of SHIVA in HINDU mythology, like Shiva both beautiful and terrifying.

PASSOVER Seven-day Jewish spring festival marking the deliverance from Egypt (see EXODUS). Since Talmudic times (see TALMUD) the festival has begun with a service in the home where unleavened bread, wine and bitter herbs symbolize the joys and sorrows of the exodus. There is a meal and the evening concludes with psalms and hymns which look to God's final redemption of ISRAEL.

PATAGALIWABE HIGH GOD of the Huli people in southern Papua New Guinea. He is a guardian of social ethics who punishes wrong doers with sickness, war, injury or death.

PATRIARCH (1) 'Father-figure'; especially in family and community; in JUDAISM and CHRISTIANITY, refers to the founders of the faith such as ABRAHAM, ISAAC and JACOB. (2) Head of one of the EASTERN ORTHODOX CHURCHES. The Patriarch of Constantinople is a figurehead for Orthodox Christians.

PAUL APOSTLE of CHRISTIANITY who established new churches throughout Asia Minor and Macedonia. Originally a PHARISEE, he was converted by a vision of CHRIST on the road to Damascus. He wrote several New Testament EPISTLES. Tradition asserts that he was beheaded at Rome under Nero.

PEKWIN Chief religious leader among the Zuñi people of northern Mexico. His power comes from the Sun Father and his task is the observation of solstices. He directs the people in times of prayer and RITUAL to ensure the fertility of the land.

PENATES Spirits or gods who protected the Roman household and family and were guardians over the household stores.

PENTATEUCH See TORAH (1).

PENTECOST (1) Jewish harvest festival, fifty-two days after PASSOVER. (2) Christian festival marking the coming of the HOLY SPIRIT upon the APOSTLES fifty days after EASTER. The second most important Christian festival, it commemorates the beginning of the CHURCH.

PENTECOSTAL CHURCHES Churches which have formed from a renewal movement which started in the USA in AD 1906. They teach the experience of 'baptism in the HOLY SPIRIT' which shows itself in speaking in tongues (see GLOSSOLALIA) and other 'spiritual gifts'.

PERKONS/PERKUNAS Supreme god of ancient Russia, particularly associated with thunder and lightning.

PERKUNAS See PERKONS.

PETER APOSTLE and close follower of JESUS OF NAZARETH, from whom he received the name *Peter*: 'Rock'. He held a position of leadership among the early apostles. Tradition asserts that he was martyred in Rome.

PHARAOH In the BIBLE the title of the king of Egypt. The reigning king was identified with the god HORUS and was held to be responsible for the fertility of the land. On death the king became OSIRIS, his body being mummified and buried in a tomb which from the Third Dynasty to the end of the Middle Period might be a PYRAMID.

PHARISEES Jewish anti-nationalistic party that emerged in the time of the MACCABEES. They believed that God was universal and taught the individuality of the soul and the RESURRECTION. They prepared the way for the survival of JUDAISM after the FALL OF JERUSALEM in AD 70.

PHILO OF ALEXANDRIA (about 25 BC–AD 40) Jewish philosopher who tried to reconcile Greek philosophy with the Hebrew scriptures. His commentaries used allegorical devices to penetrate the meaning of scripture. He developed the Greek doctrine of the *Logos* or Word of God into the status of 'a second God'. His speculations were widely studied by the early Christian fathers.

PHILOSOPHY OF RELIGION The branch of philosophy which investigates religious experience, considering its origin, context and value.

PHYLACTERIES See TEPHILLIN.

PILGRIMAGE A journey to a holy place, undertaken as a commemoration of a past event, as a celebration or as an act of penance (see also HAJJ). The goal might be a natural feature such as a sacred river or mountain, or the location of a MIRACLE, revelation or THEOPHANY, or the tomb of a hero or SAINT.

PILGRIM FATHERS Puritan Christian group who left England for America in the *Mayflower* in AD 1620 and founded the colony of Plymouth, Massachusetts.

PLATO (around 427–347 BC) Greek philosopher and pupil of SOCRATES. He taught the theory of Forms or Ideas, which are eternal prototypes of the phenomena encountered in ordinary experience. Above all is the Form of the Good, which gives unity and value to all the forms. Plato also taught the immortality of the soul.

P.L. KYODAN ('Perfect Liberty Association') One of the NEW RELIGIONS of Japan, founded in 1926. It is based on SHINTO but accepts KARMA from BUDDHISM and teaches that the ancestors have an influence on the lives of believers. Its motto is 'life is art' and it sponsors games centres and golf clubs as well as shrines and temples.

PLOTINUS (around AD 205–269) Egyptian philosopher and author of NEO-PLATONISM whose speculations influenced early Christianity. He dealt with the relationship between the world and the soul and blended Platonic teaching with oriental mysticism. His teachings influenced AUGUSTINE.

POLITICAL THEOLOGY Christian movement since the 1960s which stresses the solidarity of theology with the political struggles of oppressed peoples. Its origins are in Latin America but it has many European exponents and has been adopted by the WORLD COUNCIL OF CHURCHES.

POLYTHEISM The belief in and worship of a variety of gods, who rule over various aspects of the world and life.

PONTIFEX High priest of Roman religion and member of a guild of priests whose president was the *pontifex maximus*. From the fifth century AD the title was applied to Christian BISHOPS, usually the POPE.

PONTIUS PILATE Roman procurator of the province of Judea AD 26–36 under whose authority JESUS OF NAZARETH was crucified. Tradition asserts that he killed himself but the COPTIC CHURCH reveres him as a Christian MARTYR.

POPE BISHOP of Rome, Vicar of CHRIST and head of the ROMAN CATHOLIC Church, regarded as the successor of PETER. Since the FIRST VATICAN COUNCIL his pronouncements on matters of faith and doctrine have been regarded as infallible.

POPOL VUH The sacred book of a large group of Mayan people. It contains mythology and traditions and dates of the kings of the MAYA down to approximately AD 1550.

PORSEVIT Five-headed Slavic god from the island of Rügen.

POSEIDON Greek god of the seas and waters, usually presented as a tall bearded figure carrying a trident. He is responsible for sea storms and earthquakes and is also 'Lord of Horses'.

PRAYER The offering of worship, requests, confessions, or other communication to God or gods, publicly or privately, with or without words; often a religious obligation.

PRAYER WHEELS Wheels and cylinders used by Buddhists in Tibet and northern India. They are inscribed with the MANTRA: 'OM MANI PADME HUM', the powerful effect of which is multiplied as the wheels turn.

PREHISTORIC RELIGION RELIGIONS dating from the period before the development of writing. In the Middle East this is the period approximately up to 3000 BC.

PRESBYTER ('Elder') Term for a Christian minister used in the NEW TESTAMENT interchangeably with BISHOP. Later it was held that the authority of the presbyter (from which comes 'PRIEST') derived from the bishop.

PRESBYTERIAN CHURCHES REFORMED CHURCHES whose teachings and order of worship reflect Calvinism. They are governed by a pyramid of elected, representative courts.

PRIEST (1) One authorized to perform priestly functions including mediation between God or gods and man, the offering of SACRIFICE and the performance of RITUAL in many religions. (2) A Christian minister, the term deriving from PRESBYTER.

PRIMAL RELIGIONS Religious systems of tribal groups having no literary tradition. They are characterized by a belief in various spiritual forces behind natural phenomena, a reverence for ancestors and a tight-knit social system which is sanctioned and held in being by the power of common MYTHS.

PROGRESSIVE JUDAISM Term covering the Liberal and Reform movements which emerged in JUDAISM in nineteenth-century Europe. Both movements are critical of the Talmudic fundamentalism of ORTHODOX JUDAISM and welcome

scientific research on the Bible. They also tend to use the vernacular in worship and interpret the dietary laws more liberally than do the Orthodox.

PROPAGANDA, SACRED CONGREGATION OF Roman Catholic body concerned with MISSION in non-Christian countries. It dates from the COUNTER-REFORMATION.

PROPHET One who speaks for or as a mouthpiece of God or a god. (1) The Old Testament prophets were social and religious reformers of ISRAEL (3) and Judah and of the people of God in EXILE. They proclaimed God's prospective judgement of Israel; they recalled the people to obedience to God, some offering a hope of a future vindication. (2) In ISLAM 'the Prophet' is MUHAMMAD who brings the word and judgement of God to final utterance. The authority of the Prophet is an article of the MUSLIM confession of faith.

PROPHETS, THE The second division of the HEBREW BIBLE, including the histories and the prophetic books.

PROTESTANTISM Christian faith and order as based on the principles of the REFORMATION. It emphasizes the sole authority of the BIBLE; justification by faith; the priesthood of all believers. Since the nineteenth century it has embraced liberal trends which have stressed the subjective side of religion.

PSALM A sacred song or poem. The Book of Psalms in the BIBLE provides the basis for much Jewish and Christian worship.

PTAH The chief god of Memphis in ancient Egypt, usually depicted bearded, in mummified shape and carrying three sceptres. He was a creator god, the patron of craftsmen. Merged with Sokar and OSIRIS, he came to have a role in the rituals ensuring the survival of the dead.

PUJA ('Reverence') Refers particularly to temple worship in HINDUISM and to the keeping of rites and ceremonies prescribed by the Brahmins (see CASTE SYSTEM).

PUNCHAU The SUN GOD of the INCAS.

PURANAS Devotional texts used in Indian BHAKTI cults of VISHNU.

PURE LAND BUDDHISM Buddhist sect founded by a Chinese monk, Hui Yuan (AD 334–416). It was characterized by faith in the BODHISATTVA AMITABHA who was the creator of a 'pure land' in the west. Through faith his devotees hoped to be transported there after death.

PURGATORY In ROMAN CATHOLIC teaching, the temporary state of punishment and purification for the dead before their admission to heaven. Its existence was denied by the Protestant reformers.

PURIM ('Lots') Joyful Jewish festival celebrating the story of Esther, wife of the Persian king Xerxes, who defeated the anti-Jewish plot of the king's steward, Haman.

PYRAMID Type of Egyptian royal tomb, usually tapering to the top from a square base, constructed between about 2630 and 1640 BC.

PYTHAGORAS (about 570–500 BC) Greek philosopher, musician and mathematician who taught that number was the basis of reality and that mathematics offered insight into the invisible world. He was influenced by ORPHISM and taught REINCARNATION and a strict vegetarianism.

Q

QIYAS ('Analogy') Principle of Islamic lawmaking by which the answer to a problem may be inferred from the answer to an analogous problem in the QUR'AN or the SUNNA.

QUAKERS Members of the Religious Society of Friends which derives from a puritan group which formed around George Fox in the 1650s. They have no SACRAMENTS and no ordained ministry. Instead authority derives from the 'inner light of the living Christ' in each believer.

QUESTIONS OF KING MILINDA A Buddhist scripture in the form of a discussion between the Greek king Menander and a BHIKSHU called Nagasena.

QUETZALCOATL Mythological figure in MAYA and AZTEC religion. He may have been a king of a pre-Aztec civilization. He is associated with the rediscovery of the complex Mayan calendar. His name derives from the sacred Quetzal bird. In mythology he is a god of the air who descended to earth and taught men the arts of civilization. He opposed the practice of human SACRIFICE. His activities aroused the wrath of another deity and he fled in a boat made of serpent skin and he is often symbolized by a feathered serpent. The name Quetzalcoatl was given to the high priests of Aztec religion.

QUR'AN In ISLAM, the Word of God—the book of God's revelation to MUHAMMAD which was received as a faithful copy of the eternal Qur'an inscribed in heaven. The first three CALIPHS collected the material which was given final form under 'UTHMAN. The Qur'an has a significance for MUSLIMS which can be compared to that of CHRIST for CHRISTIANS.

QURAYSH The tribe of MUHAMMAD, who opposed his attack on idolatry because they were the traditional custodians of the KA'BA. They were defeated in Muhammad's attack on MECCA in AD 630.

R

RABBI ('My master') Jewish religious teacher and interpreter of the TORAH. In modern JUDAISM he or she is a minister to the community, a preacher and a leader of SYNAGOGUE worship.

RABBINIC JUDAISM The religion of the medieval RABBIS who expanded the interpretation of the TALMUD and produced authoritative codes of laws, responses, views and judgements, mostly in the form of correspondence with particular communities.

RADHA Wife of a cowherd in the MAHABHARATA who left her husband to become KRISHNA's mistress. The love of Krishna and Radha is a frequent theme of BHAKTI devotion where it is seen as a type of the love between God and man. The frank eroticism of the stories of Radha is not welcomed by all Hindus.

RADHAKRISHNAN, Sarvepalli (AD 1888–1975) Indian philosopher who became vice-president and then president of India. He taught that there is a basic unity of all religions and that HINDUISM is a useful meeting ground because of its breadth and tolerance.

RADICAL THEOLOGY (1) American movement of the 1960s seeking to reconstruct CHRISTIANITY on the basis of atheism. Its two tenets were that God had 'died' in human experience but that it was still possible to be a follower of JESUS OF NAZARETH. (2) Term sometimes used for theology committed to left-wing politics (see POLITICAL THEOLOGY).

RAGNARÖK The doom of the Norse gods, the end of the world order. ODIN and the gods ride out with the dead heroes of VALHALLA against LOKI and the hosts of HEL. The great wolf (see LOKI'S BROOD) swallows Odin and the whole creation is dissolved in fire. Out of the chaos emerges a new heaven and a new earth. There are Christian influences in some accounts of Ragnarök.

RAROHENGA The place of departed spirits, the UNDERWORLD, in Maori religion. (See HINENUIOTEPO.)

RAHULA Son of GAUTAMA the BUDDHA, by his wife Yashodara.

RAJNEESH, Bhagavan Shri See BHAGAVAN SHRI RAJNEESH.

RAMA The seventh incarnation of VISHNU according to HINDU tradition. His exploits in love and war are described in the RAMAYANA. He is the epitome of righteousness and moral virtue.

RAMADAN Islamic lunar month in which MUSLIMS are obliged to fast from food and water between sunrise and sunset. The old and sick, pregnant women and nursing mothers are exempt, though they are expected, if possible, to make it up later.

RAMAKRISHNA (AD 1834–86) Hindu Brahmin (see CASTE SYSTEM) who taught that all religions are paths to the same goal. He laid the foundation of Hindu universalism. He was a devotee of KALI, though philosophically he adhered to the teaching of SHANKARA.

RAMAKRISHNA MISSION Indian religious order founded in 1897 by VIVEKANANDA. Its aims are to teach VEDANTA and to care for the sick and needy. It has dispensaries, libraries and welfare centres throughout India and has teaching branches in Europe and the USA.

RAMANUJA (died AD 1137) Indian philosopher who opposed SHANKARA's stress on the oneness of being and denied that the divine lord belonged to a lower order of reality. He believed God and the world were related like body and soul, inseparable but distinct. He was a devotee of VISHNU and believed in the validity of personal devotion to God.

RAMAYANA One of the two great epics of the HINDU scriptures, compiled in the second or first century BC. Ascribed to the sage Valmiki, it tells of the life of the AVATAR RAMA.

RAMMOHUN ROY (AD 1772–1833) HINDU reformer and founder of the BRAHMA SAMAJ in opposition to the idolatry of popular devotion. He believed the VEDAS taught MONOTHEISM, though he also used Christian and Muslim ideas.

RANGINUI and PAPATUANUKU The primeval parents in Maori religion. Ranginui was the sky and Papatuanuku the earth. Their seventy children led by TANE forced them apart and propped the sky up with poles.

RASTAFARIANISM Religious and political movement centred in the Caribbean. It is a cult of Ras Tafari, better known as Haile Selassie (AD 1892–1975), emperor of Ethiopia (1930–74). Rastafarians believe that all West Indians came from Ethiopia and will return there to liberation. They are distinguished by keeping their hair in 'dreadlocks' and by their use of cannabis in worship. They helped develop the *reggae* style of soul music, which they use to express their political and religious aspirations.

REBIRTH Buddhist modification of REINCARNATION in the light of the ANATTA teaching. As there is no SOUL (2), there is no reincarnation as such, but the karmic (see KARMA) residue of one's life and actions are reclothed in the attributes and qualities acquired in the previous life. After a while this karmic 'bundle' is reborn.

'RECITE . . .' The beginning of the passage in the QUR'AN which recounts the revelation of God to MUHAMMAD. The word means making vocal what has already been written.

REDEMPTION God's saving work of buying back or recovering what is his. In JUDAISM it refers to the restoration of ISRAEL; in CHRISTIANITY to the ransoming of sinners from the power of sin and death.

RED HATS Unreformed branch of TIBETAN BUDDHISM whose practices owe much to the former Tibetan religion of BÖN.

REFORMATION The movement within Western CHRISTIANITY between the fourteenth and the seventeenth centuries which led to the separation of the Protestant Churches from Rome. The main issue was the authority of the POPE but doctrinal issues such as the precise meaning of the EUCHARIST and the authority and accessibility of Scripture were also important.

REFORMED CHURCHES Churches which inherit the Calvinist tradition, including Presbyterians, Independents, Calvinistic Methodists and Congregationalists.

REINCARNATION The belief that individual souls survive death and are reborn to live again in a different body, thus passing through a series of lives. Held in pre-ARYAN India, the belief is associated with the doctrine of KARMA. Some traditions believe rebirth is possible only in human bodies; others envisage hellish or heavenly states, while others suggest a transmigration in which human souls are tied to animal or vegetable forms. Some Hindu apologists

explain the doctrine as a mythical way of speaking about the continuity of the human race.

REIYUKAI A NICHIREN Buddhist sect and one of the NEW RELIGIONS of Japan. Founded in 1925, it claims 3 million members.

RELICS Bones or remains of SAINTS, venerated and accredited with miraculous powers in many religions.

RELIGION (From Latin: *religare*, 'to bind, restrain') A system of belief and worship, held by a community who may express their religion through shared MYTHS, DOCTRINES, ethical teachings, RITUALS or the remembrance of special experiences.

RESURRECTION (1) The Christian belief that JESUS OF NAZARETH was raised from death by God the Father who thus vindicated him as MESSIAH and defeat of death and SIN. (2) The raising of all the dead for JUDGEMENT as taught in JUDAISM, CHRISTIANITY and ISLAM.

RIDA, Rashid (AD 1865–1935) Syrian author and editor of the SALAFIYA periodical *Al-Manat*. He led the Salafiya movement in Egypt and was critical of the secularism of Kemal ATATURK'S Turkish republic.

RINZAI ZEN School of ZEN which employs startling and sometimes violent techniques (e.g. KOAN) to induce SATORI.

RISHIS Great saints or holy men in Indian tradition, many of whom lived as recluses in the forest. The teaching written down in the VEDAS and UPANISHADS is attributed to them. Some are credited with supernatural powers.

RISSHOKO-SEIKAI An offshoot of the REIYUKAI movement which is spreading the teachings of NICHIREN Buddhism beyond the boundaries of Japan. The sect claims 1 million members.

RITES OF PASSAGE Religious ceremonies which mark the transition from one state of life to another. In many religions these transitional periods are felt to be dangerous and to require spiritual protection. Examples include birth rites,

INITIATION rites, marriage rites and funeral rites.

RITUAL Religious ceremonial performed according to a set pattern of words, movements and symbolic actions. Rituals may involve the dramatic re-enactment of ancient MYTHS featuring gods and heroes, performed to ensure the welfare of the community.

ROMA The personification of the city of Rome, worshipped by the Romans as a goddess.

ROMAN CATHOLIC Catholic CHRISTIAN who recognizes the authority of the POPE, the bishop of Rome.

RONGO Maori god of agriculture and peace.

ROSENSWEIG, Franz (AD 1886– 1929) Jewish interpreter of the relationship between JUDAISM and CHRISTIANITY. He believed that both faiths manifested one truth. JEWS were witnesses to the holiness of God and were called to live as a distinct community. Christians were to be missionaries, spreading the call of God to all people.

ROSH HASHANAH The Jewish New Year, celebrated as the anniversary of creation. The liturgy is penitential in tone and looks forward to the KINGDOM OF GOD and the MESSIAH. The blowing of the ram's horn proclaims God as king of the universe.

ROSICRUCIANISM Mystical system founded in seventeenth-century Germany and based on an account of a 'secret brotherhood founded 'to improve mankind by the discovery of the true philosophy'. Several societies came into being based on this originally fictitious 'Meritorious Order of the Rosy Cross' with its private language and magical alphabet. They applied themselves to studies such as ALCHEMY.

RSS/RAHTRIYA SWAYAMSEVAK SANGH ('National self-rule community') Right-wing Hindu political party founded in 1925. It has consistently opposed any separation of the Indian state from Hindu religion.

RTA The cosmic order as understood in the Hindu VEDAS. It is the principle of ethical and physical organization throughout the universe and is the work of the sky god VARUNA.

RUDRA ('The red one') Indian god of destruction in Vedic times (see VEDAS) who was thought to live in the mountains and work with healing herbs. He may be an early version of SHIVA.

RUGIEVIT Slavic god with seven faces from the island of Rügen.

RUMI, Jalal al-Din (Died AD 1273) Sufi MYSTIC and poet, author of the *Mathnavi* and founder of a DERVISH order. He was a nature mystic and often used love and wine as allegories of the experience of the divine.

RUSSELL, Charles Taze (AD 1852–1916) US Bible scholar who started a periodical called *Zion's Watchtower* after being influenced by speculation about the return of CHRIST. This grew into the JEHOVAH'S WITNESSES movement.

RUSSIAN ORTHODOX CHURCH The principal church of Russia since AD 988.

RYOBU SHINTO A Japanese synthesis of BUDDHISM and SHINTO which was evolved in the Heian period (AD 794–1185). The Shinto gods were identified with BODHISATTVAS and AMATERASU with the BUDDHA VAIROCANA. A Buddhist sanctuary was attached to Shinto shrines.

S

SAADYA BEN JOSEPH (AD 892–940) Head of the Jewish academy at Susa in Babylon. He defended the cause of Talmudic JUDAISM (see TALMUD) against the KARAITES and the doctrine of the oneness of God against the Christian TRINITY. He was the first Jewish systematic theologian and he believed in the unity and divine origin of both revelation and reason.

SABBATH Jewish day of worship and rest lasting from Friday sunset to Saturday sunset. The Sabbath is holy because it commemorates God's rest on the seventh day of creation and reminds JEWS of the deliverance from Egypt.

SACRAMENT 'An outward and visible sign of an inward and spiritual grace' (*Book of Common Prayer*). REFORMED CHURCHES count only BAPTISM and the EUCHARIST as sacraments, both being instituted by CHRIST. Roman Catholic and Orthodox Churches add CONFIRMATION, marriage, ORDINATION, penance and extreme unction (the anointing of the sick).

SACRED BEARS In PREHISTORIC RELIGION ritual veneration of the slain bear. It remains common, especially in Arctic and sub-Arctic regions. The Japanese Ainu tribe have bear rituals, as do the Lapps, Finns, Eskimos and North American Indians. Eskimo SHAMANS receive the Great Spirit disguised as a Polar bear. Bear worship is frequently associated with the recognition of the constellation *Ursa Major*; MYTHS concerning the constellation are found among the Greeks and other European and Asian peoples.

SACRED BIRDS Often a symbol of transformation. In Greek mythology ZEUS disguises himself as a swan in pursuit of amorous adventures. The CELTS revere the swan as a symbol of divine transformation and also recognize ravens as appearances of war goddesses (see MORRIGHAN). South and Central American Indians venerate the plumed quetzal (see also QUETZALCOATL). The mythical phoenix of Arabia symbolized the cycle of death and rebirth, the ancient Egyptians finding in the similar benu a manifestation of the god Re-Atum worshipped at Heliopolis. A bird often symbolizes the departing SOUL freed from the shackles of earthly life. In the BIBLE, the HOLY SPIRIT is described as being like a dove.

SACRED BULLS Symbols of power and strength. They were connected with the worship of the MOTHER GODDESS, especially in the MINOAN RELIGION of ancient Crete where they gave rise to the MYTH of the Minotaur, a bull-like monster who had to be placated with human sacrifices. The slaughter of a bull (see TAUROBOLIUM) was important in some forms of Roman religion.

SACRED SNAKES Frequently associated with the MOTHER GODDESS, especially in MINOAN RELIGION. Because they shed their skin they are symbols of immortality. They are also associated with wisdom and healing (see ASCLEPIOS). In Chinese religion dragons replace snakes as sacred animals. In Norse mythology a Great Serpent, son of the evil LOKI, surrounds the earth. In CHRISTIANITY the snake is a symbol of evil and deceit, especially connected with the biblical MYTH of the Garden of Eden.

SACRED THREAD CEREMONY INITIATION ceremony performed on upper-caste Hindu boys. A sacred thread is placed around the neck indicating that the boy is one of the twice-born and has entered the first-stage of life. (See also NAUJOTE.)

SACRED TREES Objects of religious significance since they connect the earth to the sky. In Celtic religion tree species were sacred to particular tribes: Irish literature speaks of a sacred ash, a yew and an oak, among others. The connection of DRUIDS with the oak is likely but unproved. (See also YGGDRASIL.)

SACRED WELLS Springs, rivers and natural wells often have religious significance, particularly in Celtic religion. Regarded as passages to the UNDERWORLD, votive offerings such as brooches, bracelets and even severed human heads were deposited there. The custom of throwing coins into water may reflect these ancient practices.

SACRIFICE The ritual offering of animal or vegetable life to establish communion between humans and a god or gods.

SADDUCEES Aristocratic Jewish party which emerged in the times of the MACCABEES. They rejected the oral law and late doctrines like the RESURRECTION. They were nationalists and collaborated with the Romans to ensure the survival of the Jewish state. The party collapsed after AD 70.

SAFAVID DYNASTY See ISMAIL SAFAVI.

SAI BABA (Born AD 1926) Spiritual teacher from Brindavan in south India who is regarded by his followers as an AVATAR. Probably the most popular and influential GURU in present-day India, he specializes in curing illness and materializing gifts for his disciples.

SAINT (1) Holy person or dead hero of faith who is venerated by believers on earth and held to be a channel of divine blessing. The Protestant reformers rejected the practice of devotion to saints. (2) In the NEW TESTAMENT and some Protestant Churches, a term for any believer.

SALAFIYA Puritan Islamic party which emerged in nineteenth-century Egypt. It accepted the authority only of the QUR'AN and the SUNNA and rejected the 'ULAMA'. In time it grew closer to the WAHHABI MOVEMENT. It published a journal *Al-Manat* which circulated in the Middle East. (See also RIDA, RASHID.)

SALAT Islamic ritual prayer which is carried out five times a day, facing MECCA and using ritual movements to accompany the words. Salat is one of the FIVE PILLARS OF ISLAM.

SALVATION (1) In the BIBLE, deliverance of God's people from their enemies, and especially from SIN and its consequences, death and HELL; hence also the whole process of forgiveness, new life and final glorification for the believer. (2) In eastern religions, release from the changing material world to identification with the ABSOLUTE.

SAMHAIN Celtic festival marking the beginning of winter, celebrated on 1 November with feasting and carousals. Regarded as a period outside the normal flow of time when the dead could freely return to communicate with the living, it was the subject of many MYTHS and legends, mainly concerning death.

SAMPY Madagascan term for a sacred cult object in which the power and particularity of the people is thought to reside (see TOTEMISM).

SAMSARA ('Stream of existence') Sanskrit word which refers to the cycle of birth and death followed by rebirth as applied both to individuals and to the universe itself.

SANCTUARY A place consecrated to a god, a holy place, a place of divine refuge and protection. Also, the holiest part of a sacred place or building. Historically, in some cultures, a holy place where pursued criminals or victims were guaranteed safety.

SANGHA Community of Buddhist MONKS which started with the BUDDHA's first disciples. The functions of the sangha are to promote through its own lifestyle the best conditions for attaining individual salvation and to teach the DHAMMA to mankind.

SANHEDRIN Jewish supreme council of seventy which organized religious life during the period of independence following the revolt of the MACCABEES. Under Herod the Great the Sanhedrin was divided: the SADDUCEES dealt with political matters; the PHARISEES concentrated on the interpretation of the TORAH. After the FALL OF JERUSALEM (AD 70) an academic Sanhedrin was organized in Jabneh to reorganize Jewish life.

SANNYASI ('One who renounces') The last of the Hindu FOUR STAGES OF LIFE.

SANSKRIT The language of the ARYAN peoples and of the HINDU scriptures. It is an Indo-European language related to Latin, Greek and Persian.

SARIPUTTA One of the BUDDHA's principal disciples, described as the 'Captain of the DHAMMA'.

SATAN In the BIBLE, the personification of evil and identified with the DEVIL.

SATANISM Worship of SATAN or experimentation with evil spirits, which may include the perversion of religious RITUALS, as in a black mass, WITCHCRAFT, or a variety of pseudo-religious and ecstatic practices.

SATGURU See DIVINE LIGHT MISSION.

SATORI ENLIGHTENMENT in ZEN Buddhism.

SATURNALIA Roman festival of Saturn, a mythical king of Rome and father of the god JUPITER, which began on 17 December. A time of banquets and present-giving, some of its characteristics were transferred to the festival of CHRISTMAS.

SAULE Latvian sun goddess.

SAUM See FIVE PILLARS OF ISLAM.

SCHISM A deliberate division or split between Christians which disrupts the unity of the CHURCH.

SCIENTOLOGY Religious philosophy based on the teaching of L. Ron HUBBARD. It teaches development through personality counselling and mind-training, the aim of which is the 'clearing' of the individual and the recognition of his immortal nature.

SCRIBES Officials who organized the religious life of the Jewish community after the EXILE of 586 BC. They regulated the observance of the SABBATH, communal prayer and fasting and were the interpreters of the Law. One of their tasks was to develop 'fences' around the TORAH to prevent its infringement.

SCRIPTURE Writings which are believed to be divinely inspired or especially authoritative within a particular religious community.

SECOND COMING/PAROUSIA The personal second coming of CHRIST which, Christians believe, will be a time of judgement and the inauguration of the KINGDOM OF GOD in its fulness.

SECT SHINTO Term applied to new religious movements and associations in Japan, especially before 1945 when, to be legal, NEW RELIGIONS had to conform to SHINTO patterns.

SEFIROT According to the teachings of Jewish Kabbalistic MYSTICISM (see KABBALAH), the potencies and attributes by which God acts and makes himself known.

SEPHARDIM One of the two main cultural groups in JUDAISM which emerged during the Middle Ages. Sephardic JEWS lived in Spain and Portugal and their traditions go back to Babylonian Jewry. They developed Ladino as their language.

SERAPIS State god of Ptolemaic Egypt whose worship spread throughout the Mediterranean. He took over many characteristics from the ancient Egyptian OSIRIS, but was also associated with the bull god Apis, in turn associated with PTAH. He was both a healing god and a ruler of the UNDERWORLD.

SETH The evil brother of OSIRIS in Egyptian mythology. He murdered his brother and seized his earthly rule until in turn defeated by HORUS. He became the god of war, storms, deserts and disorder.

SEVEN PRECEPTS OF THE SONS OF NOAH The obligations placed on all men and women, regardless of race or faith, according to Jewish teaching. They comprise abstinence from idolatry, blasphemy, incest, murder, theft and the eating of living flesh, and the implementation of justice.

SEVENTH DAY ADVENTISTS Christian sect which emerged from a number of nineteenth-century groups stressing the imminent return of CHRIST. They observe the Jewish SABBATH instead of Sunday. They accept the BIBLE as infallible and require a lifestyle of strict temperance.

SEVERED HEADS A recurring motif in Celtic art and legend. Carvings of human heads are common and niches containing skulls have been found in many Celtic sanctuaries and at the bottom of ancient wells. These probably reflect a tradition of human sacrifice. In legend, severed heads can often talk and distil wisdom.

SHAH WALI ALLAH (AD 1702–62) Indian Sufi writer and teacher (see SUFISM), who led a reform movement aimed at broadening ISLAM into a kind of universal HUMANISM.

SHAIVISM Worship of the Hindu god SHIVA. It is particularly strong in southern India and appeals to extreme ascetics. From Shaivite texts have come the strongest affirmations of MONOTHEISM within HINDUISM.

SHAKTI ('Energy', 'power') A feminine word, particularly associated with SHIVA and his consorts (see KALI; PARVATI; DURGA). In TANTRISM shakti is universal creativity and exists in man as a latent energy which is located at the base of his spine (see KUNDALINI). In tantric YOGA this energy is awakened to travel up the spine and unite with Shiva who is present as mind.

SHAKYAMUNI ('The wise man of the SHAKYAS') One of the names of the BUDDHA.

SHAKYAS Tribe to which the BUDDHA's family belonged. They occupied territory in the Himalayan foothills.

SHAMAN (1) An ecstatic priest-magician among the Tungu people of Siberia. (2) By extension, a similar figure in other PRIMAL RELIGIONS and ancient religions (see also CHILAN). The shaman induces a trance experience in which he is believed to leave his body and visit other worlds. This enables him to convey sacrifices to the gods, to escort the dead to their destination and to return with divine prophecies.

SHAMASH Babylonian sun god and lord of justice who rewards honesty and loyalty and brings retribution on the wicked. He is depicted as giving a ring and sceptre to the lawgiver HAMMURABI.

SHAMMAI See HILLEL.

SHANGO Storm god of the Yoruba people of Nigeria. His symbol is an axe and his sacred animal a ram. Reverence for Shango has travelled to the Caribbean, Haiti and South America where he has a place in VOODOO cults.

SHANKARA (AD 788–820) The best known exponent of classical HINDU philosophy. Developing the thought of the UPANISHADS he declared that only the eternal being is real; the diverse, phenomenal world is an illusion of MAYA. Even the notion of a personal God is part of maya. Liberation comes from realizing oneness with the ABSOLUTE, which is defined as Being, Consciousness and Bliss. (See also VEDANTA (2).)

SHARI'A ('The path') Body of law for the MUSLIM community which derives from the QUR'AN, the SUNNA and other sources, the legitimacy of which is debated in the different schools of law. Shari'a is regarded as divinely authoritative.

SHAVUOT See WEEKS.

SHAYK Sufi spritual teacher (see SUFISM), somewhat analogous to the Hindu GURU.

SHEKINAH The presence or manifestation of God as described in the TARGUMS and later Jewish writings. It came to refer to the indwelling of God in creation. In KABBALAH the Shekinah is exiled from the eternity of God, EN SOF, because of the SIN of man and will only be restored at the final REDEMPTION.

SHEMA The Jewish confession of faith, recited in the morning and evening service. 'Shema' is the opening word in HEBREW of the confession: 'Hear, O Israel, the Lord our God, the Lord is One . . .' Three passages from the TORAH confirm that there is one God and that Israel is chosen to witness to him.

SHI'A/SHI'ITES The minority group in ISLAM, comprising ten per cent of MUSLIMS. They reject the first three CALIPHS, believing 'ALI to be MUHAMMAD's true successor. They also hold that authority resides in the IMAMS(2) who are the infallible messengers of God in every age. The Shi'a live mostly in Iraq, Iran, Lebanon, Pakistan and India. The two main Shi'a divisions are the ISMA'ILIS and the TWELVERS.

SHINGON 'True Word' sect of Japanese Buddhism founded in the ninth century AD and characterized by a complex sacramental and magical ritual which may have been influenced by TANTRISM and by indigenous SHINTO practices.

SHINRAN (AD 1173–1263) Disciple of HONEN and founder of the Japanese Buddhist sect JODO SHINSHU.

SHINTO The indigenous nature religion of Japan which has provided a focus for nationalistic aspirations. (See also AMATERASU; EMPEROR, JAPANESE; IZANAGI; JIMMU TENNO; JINJA; KAMI; KOJIKI; MATSURI; NIHONGI; NINIGI.)

SHIRK ('Associating') In ISLAM the greatest SIN, that of ascribing equals to God. (See also TAUHID.)

SHIVA One of the great gods of HINDU devotion. He is a god of contrasts, presiding over creation and destruction, fertility and asceticism, good and evil. He is the original Lord of the Dance who dances out the creation of the universe. As god of ascetics he is portrayed as a great YOGI, smeared with ashes, holding the world in being through meditation. His symbol is a phallus-shaped pillar denoting procreation.

SHOTOKU, PRINCE Japanese ruler who introduced BUDDHISM as the state religion. During his reign (AD 593–621) he built a Buddhist academy and temple near the state capital at Nara.

SHUDRAS See CASTE SYSTEM.

SHULCHAN ARUCH See KARO, JOSEPH.

SIDDHARTA Personal name of GAUTAMA the BUDDHA.

SIKH ('Disciple') Follower of the Sikh religion which developed in the fifteenth century AD in North India as a synthesis of ISLAM and HINDUISM. (See also ADI GRANTH; GOBINDH SINGH; GURDWARA; KABIR; KHALSA; NANAK; SINGH.)

SIN (1) An action which breaks a divine law. (2) The state of rebellion against God which, in Christian teaching, has been man's state since the Fall of Adam and his expulsion from the Garden of Eden.

SIN Babylonian moon-god and guardian of the city of Ur. He usually appears riding on a winged bull. He is the father of the sun, SHAMASH, and god of vegetation.

SINAI, MOUNT Mountain in the south of the Sinai peninsula where, according to tradition, God revealed himself to MOSES and gave him the Ten Commandments.

SINGH Surname used by SIKHS. It means 'lion' and expresses the militant stance which Guru GOBINDH SINGH impressed upon the Sikh community.

SITA Consort of RAMA in Hindu tradition.

SKANDHA/KHANDHA Term referring to the five factors which compound human personality according to Buddhist teaching. They are form, sense perception, consciousness, intellectual power and discrimination. The relation between them is continuously changing in accordance with the action of KARMA.

SKILFUL MEANS Buddhist practice of compassion in sharing the DHAMMA with the unenlightened. Tradition describes the BUDDHA explaining the Dhamma at different levels to different people. In the LOTUS SUTRA tricks and deceptions are among the skilful means employed to lead the lost to salvation.

SMITH, Joseph (AD 1805–44) Founder of MORMONISM who claimed to be the recipient of a divine revelation to the former inhabitants of America in the form of golden plates inscribed in ancient languages. With the help of the ANGEL Moroni, he translated these and they became the basis of the BOOK OF MORMON. Ordained priest by the heavenly messenger, he founded the Church of Jesus Christ of Latter-Day Saints in 1830. He died at the hands of a mob.

SMITH, William Robertson (AD 1846–94) Scottish theologian and philosopher of religion who

developed the study of comparative religion with his own researches into the religion of Semitic peoples.

SOCRATES (469–399 BC) Greek philosopher and teacher and mentor of PLATO. He taught by a method of question and answer which sought to elicit a consistent and rational response and hence to arrive at a universally agreed truth. He was executed in Athens for corrupting the youth and introducing strange gods.

SÖDERBLOM, Nathan (AD 1866–1931) Swedish theologian and philosopher of religion who developed the study of comparative religion with his own researches into ZOROASTRIANISM.

SOKA GAKKAI 'Value-creating society' of lay members of the Japanese Buddhist sect NICHIREN. It was founded in 1930 in a wave of new cults. It is evangelistic, exclusive and highly organized. It runs its own political party and has schools and a university.

SOL INVICTUS ('Unconquered sun') A name for MITHRA. From the time of the emperor Aurelian (AD 270–275) until displaced by CHRISTIANITY, his was the official imperial cult of Rome.

SOMA The juice of the Indian *soma* plant which may have been fermented or had hallucinogenic properties. It was drunk by gods and men in the VEDAS and was regarded as a mediating god with power over all plants and as a conveyer of immortality.

SORCERER A practitioner of harmful MAGIC. In PRIMAL RELIGIONS sorcerers are sometimes believed to be able to kill others through magic.

SOTO ZEN School of ZEN Buddhism which teaches a gradual and gentle way to SATORI.

SOUL (1) The immortal element of an individual man or woman which survives the death of the body in most religious teachings. (2) A human being when regarded as a spiritual being.

SPELL A formula of words with or without accompanying RITUAL actions which is believed to have the power to manipulate natural or supernatural forces for good or evil ends. The exact form of the spell is often the secret possession of the SORCERER or tribal leader.

SPIRITUALISM Any religious system or practice which has the object of establishing communication with the dead. Most modern spiritualist churches derive from a movement which grew up in mid-nineteenth-century America. Spiritualists seek to communicate with the dead through such means as table-turning and automatic writing. All mainstream Christian churches denounce the practices of spiritualism.

SHRI AUROBINDO (AD 1872–1950) HINDU intellectual and nationalist who attempted a synthesis of Indian and Western thought based on the theory of evolution. He also developed Integral Yoga as a system of YOGA teachings acceptable to East and West.

STEINER, Rudolf (AD1861–1925) Founder of ANTHROPOSOPHY. He originally followed THEOSOPHY and ROSICRUCIANISM but he broke with these groups and developed his mystical ideas into an educational, ecological and medical programme for spiritual progress. He founded a number of highly successful schools which today cater for some 40,000 pupils.

STOICISM Philosophical school founded by Zeno of Citium (approximately 335–263 BC) and named after the porch or *stoa* where he taught in Athens. Stoics believed that the world order reflected the divine intelligence. Men could attain virtue—harmony with the universe—by learning self-sufficiency and behaving with courage and self-control.

STONEHENGE Megalithic monument (see MEGALITHS) on Salisbury Plain, England. It may have been a sanctuary for sun worship or regulated an agricultural and astrological calendar.

STUPA A mound built up to mark a Buddhist holy place or collection of relics. Many stupas in India date from the reign of king ASOKA.

SUBUD Spiritual teaching of the Javanese Muslim teacher Pak Subuh (born AD 1901). It emphasizes submission to the Life Force through a course of spiritual training designed to open up the individual to the reality of GOD and to mastery over the lower nature. The Subud training is open to members of all faiths.

SUFISM Islamic mystical movement originating in the eighth century AD as a reaction to the worldliness of the UMAYYAD DYNASTY. Sufis claimed direct experience of ALLAH through ascetic practices. The orthodox rejected them at first but today Sufi orders are accepted among SUNNIS and SHI'A. (See also ISLAM.)

SUKKOT See BOOTHS.

SUN DANCE Four-day ceremony which grew up among North American Plains Indians in the 1870s as a reaction against white attempts to break up the traditions and beliefs of the people. It was held in the summer inside an immense circular area. The ceremony was crushed by the US army and regulations were imposed against such PAGAN rituals.

SUN-GOD In the INCA religion, the creator of MANCO CAPAC, the first Inca and father to all the Inca rulers. His names include Inti and Punchau.

SUNNA ('Trodden path') The source of authority in Islamic lawmaking which is second only to the QUR'AN. It refers to the words and actions of MUHAMMAD and, in a lesser degree, to the words and actions of the first four CALIPHS.

SUNNI The majority group in ISLAM, comprising ninety per cent of MUSLIMS. They accept the authority of the FOUR RIGHTLY GUIDED CALIPHS and the developed process of law-making guided by the community's legal system. Sunni Muslims live in the Arab states, in North, West and East Africa and in India and Indonesia.

SUTTA PITAKA The most important collection of THERAVADA Buddhist SCRIPTURES. It consists of sermons of the BUDDHA including the DHAMMAPADA.

SUZUKI, Daisetz T. (AD 1870–1966) Japanese ZEN scholar who

played a major part in introducing Zen Buddhism to the western world. He was a member of the RINZAI sect and was sympathetic to CHRISTIANITY.

SVANTEVIT Slavic god with four heads, from the island of Rügen.

SVETAMBARAS ('White-clad') Members of a major JAIN sect who rejected the DIGAMBARAS' stress on the virtues of nudity. They are numerous in the north of India.

SWAMI General term for a HINDU holy man or member of a religious order.

SWEDENBORG, Emanuel (AD 1688–1772) Swedish scientist who became a MYSTIC and visionary. He taught a kind of pantheistic THEOSOPHY (see PANTHEISM) centred on Jesus Christ in whom he found a Trinity of Love, Wisdom and Energy. He founded the New Church.

SYNAGOGUE Jewish meeting place for worship and study. Synagogues grew out of the TORAH schools of the SCRIBES during the EXILE. After the destruction of the TEMPLE OF JERUSALEM (AD 70), synagogues became the centres of Jewish life. They are built to face JERUSALEM and contain an ARK(2) in which the scrolls of the law are displayed before a perpetual lamp. Worship in synagogues includes readings from the *Torah*, psalms, sermons and communal prayers.

SYNCRETISM The growing together of two or more religions making a new development in religion which contains some of the beliefs and practices of both.

T

TABERNACLES, FESTIVAL OF
See BOOTHS.

TABOO Polynesian word applied to an object, place or person which is prohibited because of its holy or dangerous character. It may include the sense of being 'marked off' and therefore separate from everyday usage.

T'AI CHI The 'absolutely transcendent' in Chinese philosophy. The working of T'ai chi in the production of the YIN AND YANG is represented by a circle divided into complementary pear-shaped light and dark halves.

TALLIT Jewish prayer shawl, fringed at the four corners and used during morning prayer and on YOM KIPPUR.

TALMUD The written interpretation and development of the HEBREW scriptures. It is based on the MISHNAH of JUDAH HA NASI with the addition of some excluded teachings and commentary recorded from the debates and controversies of the Schools of Babylon on Palestine. There are two versions: the Palestinian, compiled while the Jews were under duress from the Christian Church, and the Babylonian which is more detailed and complete.

TAMMUZ Babylonian/Syrian fertility deity. A young god who, in mythology, died and was resurrected after the pattern of the Egyptian OSIRIS.

TANE/TANENUIARANGI The creator of vegetation and vanquisher of darkness in Maori religion.

TANGAROA Maori god of fishes and the sea.

TANGENY Madagascan ceremony of giving poison to one accused of a crime to establish his guilt or innocence.

TANGIHANGA Maori word for a funeral gathering.

TANHA ('Craving') The main cause of suffering as analysed by the BUDDHA in the FOUR NOBLE TRUTHS.

TANTRISM Tibetan Buddhist practices which aim at direct experience of the enlightened self through symbols, visual images, repetition of sounds, prescribed movements, breath control and ritualized sexual intercourse.

TAO ('Way') In TAOISM, the underlying principle of reality.

TAOISM Chinese philosophy outlined in the TAO TE CHING. Its aim is to achieve harmony with all that is by pursuing inaction and effortlessness. Taoism gradually evolved an elaborate mythological system and incorporated notions of spirit possession, ALCHEMY and DIVINATION. (See also CHANG TAO LING; JADE EMPEROR; LAO-TZU.)

TAOISM Chinese philosophy outlined in the TAO TE CHING.

TAO TE CHING Chinese religious work compiled in the fourth century BC and ascribed to LAO-TZU, though it is probably the work of several writers. It describes the TAO as the underlying principle of reality which can only be attained to by passivity.

TARGUM An Aramaic translation of a HEBREW scripture reading. The translator was expected to make a free interpretation. Some of these have become famous in their own right and are used by pious JEWS alongside the appointed text.

TAROT CARDS Set of seventy-eight cards marked with various symbolic figures which are shuffled and dealt as a form of DIVINATION.

TARTARUS Probably an early name for the Greek god of the UNDERWORLD, replaced later by HADES. Tartarus came to signify a place below the realm of Hades where particularly wicked men and gods were sent to be punished. (Compare HELL.)

TATHAGATA ('One who has succeeded') Title of the BUDDHA found particularly in popular MAHAYANA texts.

TAT TVAM ASI ('Thou that art') Phrase from the UPANISHADS which expresses the claim that BRAHMAN, the divine power sustaining the universe, and ATMAN, the soul, are one.

TAUHID ('Asserting oneness') The essential MUSLIM doctrine of the unity of God. He is oneness in himself without parts or partners.

TAUROBOLIUM Rite in Roman religion where initiates entered a pit over which a bull was slaughtered; they washed themselves in and drank the blood. This gave them participation in the life and strength of the bull (see also SACRED BULLS). This ritual slaughter is often wrongly attributed to Mithraists. It featured in initiation into the cult of CYBELE and gave a guarantee of rebirth for twenty years.

TAWHIRIMATEA Maori god of winds and hurricanes.

TE AOMARAMA The world of light and reality in the Maori CREATION MYTH.

TEPHILLIN ('Phylacteries') Small boxes containing scriptural texts written on parchment. They are worn by JEWS on the head and arm during daily prayer.

TEMPLE Building designed for WORSHIP of God or gods, usually containing a SANCTUARY or holy place where SACRIFICE may be offered.

TEMPLE OF HEAVEN Great Chinese temple in Peking where the Chinese emperors received the mandate of heaven (see T'IEN) to rule over the Chinese people. It is still used for great state occasions.

TEMPLE OF JERUSALEM/ HOLY TEMPLE TEMPLE first built by Solomon on a site bequeathed by DAVID. It was divided into the Holy Place and the Holy of Holies where dwelt the presence of YHWH. This temple was destroyed in 586 BC. The second temple was dedicated in 515 BC. It was desecrated by the Hellenistic Seleucid king Antiochus Epiphanes but rededicated by JUDAS MACCABEUS. Rebuilding was begun under Herod the Great in 20 BC. The temple was virtually completed in AD 62 but destroyed by Titus in AD 70.

TENDAI Japanese Buddhist sect based on a former Chinese sect, *T'ien-t'ai*, and founded in the ninth century AD. Tendai was an attempt at a synthesis between MAHAYANA teachings which stressed MEDITATION and those that stressed devotion.

TENGRI The supreme god of the Mongols. It was also used as a collective name for gods.

TENRIKYO 'Religion of Heavenly Wisdom' founded in Japan by MIKI NAKAYAMA, and based at the city of Tenri near Nara at the site of the founder's home. This is believed to be the centre of the world and it is the place of divine homecoming for the sect's 2 million adherents.

TE PO Primeval chaos and darkness according to the Maori CREATION MYTH.

TETRAGRAMMATON See YHWH.

TEUTATES, ESUS and TARANIS Gaulish gods mentioned by the Roman writer Lucan (AD 39–65). They required to be appeased by bloody sacrifices. Teutates in particular may have been a god of war, healing and fertility and the guardian of his people.

TEZCATLIPOCA ('That which causes the Black Mirror to shine') AZTEC god of night and the north, a magician, symbolized by a jaguar. He was one of the most important of the Aztec gods.

THEISM The belief in one supreme GOD who is both TRANSCENDENT and involved in the workings of the universe.

THEOCRACY ('Divine government') Term describing a state which is constituted on the basis of divine law. It is an important concept in ISLAM where it is sometimes believed that the law of the land should be identical with the SHARI'A. The regime of CALVIN in Geneva was also theocratic.

THEOLOGY (1) A systematic formulation of belief made by or on behalf of a particular individual or CHURCH or other body of believers. (2) The critical study of RELIGION, particularly CHRISTIANITY, with regard to its origins, SCRIPTURES and other texts, DOCTRINES, ethics, history and practices.

THEOPHANY A divine appearance, revelation or manifestation, usually inducing awe and terror in those who witness it. Examples are the appearance of God to MOSES on Mt SINAI amidst thunder, lightning, smoke and trumpet blasts; the appearance of KRISHNA in his divine form 'like a thousand suns' as described in the BHAGAVAD GITA.

THEOSOPHY ('Divine wisdom') A term applied to various mystical movements but which refers particularly to the principles of the Theosophical Society founded by Madame BLAVATSKY in 1875. These comprise a blend of Hindu, Buddhist and Christian ideas, together with particular stress on REINCARNATION, immortality and the presence of GOD in all things. Theosophists also believe in a series of World Teachers who are incarnated to express the divine wisdom.

THERAVADA ('The doctrine of the elders') The form of BUDDHISM practised in Sri Lanka, Burma, Thailand, Kampuchea/Cambodia and Laos, which sticks firmly to the teachings of the VINAYA PITAKA and rejects the doctrine of the BODHISATTVAS.

THIRTEEN PRINCIPLES Articles of Jewish faith which were formulated by Moses MAIMONIDES in the twelfth century AD. They assert faith in God as creator, as formless unity, First and Last and only hearer of prayer. They also affirm the words of the PROPHETS, MOSES as the chief of the prophets, the unchanging nature of TORAH, the Creator's knowledge of men, the judgement, the coming of the MESSIAH and the RESURRECTION of the dead. The Thirteen Principles are found in the Jewish Prayer Book.

THOMAS, John See CHRISTADELPHIANS.

THOR Norse god of thunder and lightning. He is portrayed as wild and red-haired, wielding a great hammer. The son of Mother Earth, his wife Sif is a corn goddess. He is associated with agriculture and is the protector of MIDGARD against the giants.

THOTH Ibis-headed Egyptian god, patron of writing and counting, who recorded the weighing of souls in the judgement after death.

THREE BODY DOCTRINE MAHAYANA Buddhist teaching that the BUDDHA exists in three aspects. His human existence was his 'transformation body'. In his celestial existence he appears in his 'enjoyment body'. But the ultimate basis of his Buddhahood is his 'truth body' which unites all three bodies. This is identified with ultimate reality.

THREE REFUGES Brief dedication used by Buddhists and traditionally given by the BUDDHA himself: 'I take refuge in the Buddha; I take refuge in the DHAMMA; I take refuge in the SANGHA.'

THUNDERBIRD A totem (see TOTEMISM) found widely among North American Indians. It represents the eagle, the great bird of the eastern doorway of the world. It also represents thunder spirits who bring rain; the clap of his wings sounds the thunder and the flash of his eyes symbolizes lightning. The Thunderbird is frequently found at the top of Indian TOTEM POLES.

TIBETAN BOOK OF THE DEAD Book of instructions and preparations for death and the rites to be performed for the dying. In TIBETAN BUDDHISM the dying must train in advance, helped by a spiritual teacher, to face the clear light of the Void, reality itself, in such a way as to avoid REBIRTH or at least to ensure a human rebirth.

TIBETAN BUDDHISM/ VAJRAYANA/LAMAISM A mixture of BUDDHISM, TANTRISM and the ancient BÖN religion of Tibet. The two main groups are the RED HATS and the YELLOW HATS. (See also CHAKRAS; CHORTEN; DALAI LAMA; LAMA; MANDALA; PANCHEN LAMA; PRAYER WHEELS; TIBETAN BOOK OF THE DEAD.)

T'IEN ('Heaven') Chinese term sometimes used for the supreme GOD. From around 1000 BC the Chinese emperors were believed to rule by the mandate of heaven.

TILAK, B.G. (AD 1856–1920) Militant Hindu nationalist who wanted to turn India into a great HINDU nation. He provoked non-Hindus to violence, interpreting the BHAGAVAD GITA as a call to arms in the name of Hindu religion.

TIPITAKA The 'three baskets' of the BUDDHA's teaching, the canon of SCRIPTURE for THERAVADA Buddhists, comprising the VINAYA PITAKA, the SUTTA PITAKA and the ABIDHAMMA PITAKA.

TIPUNA Maori word for ancestors.

TIRTHANKARAS ('Ford-makers') The twenty-four great heros of JAIN belief who help others to cross the stream of existence to liberation. Huge statues of the Tirthankaras, who include PARSVA and MAHAVIRA, are to be found in southern India.

TIUHUANACO ('City of the dead') Centre of a South American civilization which flourished approximately AD 1000–1300. Its god was a weeping god. When the city was taken over by the INCAS, this god became associated with SUN GOD and the city came to be thought of as the holy city of VIRACOCHA.

TIXE Name for God in several Bantu languages of southern Africa.

TLALOC AZTEC god of rain and vegetation. His name means 'he who makes things sprout'. He is portrayed with long fangs and rings round his eyes.

TLOQUE NAHUAQUE Supreme god of the AZTECS. He was an abstract deity, remote from the everyday world. NEZAHUALCOYOTL worshipped him as the supreme god and tried to build a religious philosophy around him as 'the cause of all causes, the unknown god'.

TOHUNGA AHUREWA Maori specialist in the highest sacred knowledge.

TOHUNGA MATAKITE Maori term for a DIVINER.

TOHUNGA TAURA Maori word for a SORCERER, a specialist in the black arts.

TONGUES See GLOSSOLALIA.

TONALPOHUALLI AZTEC sacred almanac which was part of the calendar. It covered a period of 260 days; each day was distinguished by a name and a number, and the days were grouped into numbered weeks. Particular divinities presided over each group of days.

TORAH (1) The five books of the Law (the *Pentateuch*) revealed to MOSES; the first division of the HEBREW BIBLE. (2) 'The teaching', the correct response of ISRAEL to God, outlined in the rules for purity and social justice. It is God's gift to Israel and the way for Israel to fulfil God's call for holiness. (3) The cosmological principle of order which embraces moral and religious instruction as well as the physical ordering of the universe by God.

TORII Gateway to a SHINTO shrine which consists of two vertical posts supporting two horizontal bars, the higher of which is often curved at each end towards the sky.

TOTEMISM (From a North American Indian word meaning 'relative') The belief in some PRIMAL RELIGIONS that particular animals or sometimes plants or other objects have a special relationship with the tribal group and act as its guardians.

TOTEM POLES Tall decorated posts, found especially among North American Indians, which display tribal relationships with ancestors and guardian spirits.

TOWERS OF SILENCE Parsi mounds used for the disposal of corpses. In the belief of the PARSIS, sacred fire must not be polluted by contact with the dead. Corpses are exposed on the mounds where the flesh is eaten by vultures. The bleached bones are finally thrown down a well.

TRANSCENDENT That which is above or beyond common human experience or knowlege.

TRANSCENDENTAL MEDITATION/TM MEDITATION technique taught by Maharishi Mahesh Yogi which has flourished in the West since the 1960s. Practitioners need no religious beliefs. They are taught to meditate for fifteen to twenty minutes twice a day; this reduces stress and aids relaxation. In some states in the USA it has been ruled that Transcendental Meditation is a religion, of Hindu origin.

TRANSFIGURATION The occasion of CHRIST's appearance in glory to three of his disciples during his earthly ministry. It is celebrated as a feast in the Eastern Churches and by many in the West.

TRANSMIGRATION OF SOULS The belief held by some Hindus that souls are detached from their bodies at death and are attached to other human, animal or vegetable bodies. What the new body will be depends on the individual's KARMA.

TRIGLAV Slavic god with three heads.

TRINITY Christian doctrine of GOD as three Persons, equally God: the Father, the Son and the HOLY SPIRIT, constituting the divine unity.

TRIPITAKA (1) Sanskrit spelling of the (Pali) word TIPITAKA. (2) The SCRIPTURES of Chinese BUDDHISM which include translations of THERAVADA texts, SANSKRIT MAHAYANA texts and some Chinese additions and commentaries. Also called the *San Tsang*.

TRIPLE GEM The BUDDHA as teacher, his teaching and the SANGHA as the community who live by his teaching. The 'triple gem' is the core of the Buddhist faith.

TROMBA Madagascan term for possession by spirits.

TUAT The other world in Egyptian mythology, a land of gloom and darkness which is divided into twelve areas, one for each hour of the night. The souls of the dead have to cross this region to enter the judgement hall of OSIRIS.

TWELVERS The majority group among SHI'A Muslims who hold that the twelfth IMAN(2), Muhammad al-Mahdi, will reappear as the MAHDI on the last day. (See also ISMA'ILIS.)

TYLOR, Edward Burnett (AD 1832–1917) British anthropologist who believed that religion originated as 'the belief in spiritual beings'. He called this belief ANIMISM and summarized his arguments in *Primitive Culture* (1871).

TYR The oldest of the Norse gods. Originally a sky god like ZEUS or VARUNA, his attributes were taken over by ODIN. The Romans compared him with MARS because he became a war god, an inspirer of warriors. He is portrayed as having great strength and courage.

U

UFO ('Unidentified Flying Objects') The subject matter for many speculative cults and groups since the 1950s. Members consider the spiritual and practical significances of UFO sightings.

UGUNS MATE Latvian fire goddess.

'ULAMA' The doctors of the law in ISLAM. They are the interpreters of the SHARI'A and the upholders of Islamic orthodoxy. They exist in SUNNI and SHI'A communities.

'UMAR CALIPH after the death of ABU BAKR, from AD 634–644. His rule was a period of dramatic expansion for ISLAM, into Mesopotamia, Persia and Lower Egypt. He was murdered by a Christian slave in the MOSQUE of MEDINA.

UMAYYAD DYNASTY (AD 661–750) The Islamic dynasty based on the Meccan family Umayya. The caliphate was based in Damascus. Under the Umayyads ISLAM spread through North Africa to Spain and as far east as the Indus. There were eleven CALIPHS until the Umayyad period ended in military defeat and the succession of Abu'l 'Abbas as first caliph of the 'ABBASID DYNASTY.

UMMA The MUSLIM community, those who have received God's revelation through MUHAMMAD and live in submission to it.

UNDERWORLD The abode of spirits after the death of the body. In many religions the underworld is a shadowy half-real place presided over by a god of death. (See also DONN; HADES; HEL; HELL; KALUNGA; TUAT.)

UNIFICATION CHURCH Unorthodox sect founded in Korea in 1954 by Sun Myung MOON. Its teachings are ESOTERIC but certainly anti-communist. Its spiritual techniques and practices are controversial.

UNITARIANISM Dissenting movement which spread in England, Poland and Hungary from the sixteenth century. Unitarians reject the Christian doctrines of the TRINITY and INCARNATION and defend a reason-based ethical THEISM.

UNTOUCHABLES Indians who belong to no caste (see CASTE SYSTEM) and are therefore banished from normal social life. MAHATMA GANDHI called them 'children of God' and worked for their acceptance in Indian society.

UPANISHADS The last books of the Indian VEDAS which were written in SANSKRIT between 800 and 400 BC. They develop the concept of BRAHMAN as the holy power released in sacrifice to the point where it becomes the underlying reality of the universe. The soul, ATMAN, is identified with the holy power, Brahman. They include speculation on how the soul can realize its oneness with Brahman through contemplative techniques.

USINSH Latvian god of spring and patron of horses.

'UTHMAN Son-in-law of MUHAMMAD who succeeded 'UMAR as CALIPH in AD 644. He was regarded as weak and worldly and was murdered in 656 after a period of rebellion. Under his caliphate the final authoritative version of the QUR'AN was produced.

V

VAIROCANA A title for the sun in ancient HINDU mythology. In MAHAYANA Buddhism it became a title for one of the great Buddhas. He is regarded as supreme BUDDHA in Java and in the Japanese SHINGON sect. He was said to be identical with the SHINTO sun deity AMATERASU, an identification which helped the development of RYOBU SHINTO.

VAISHNAVISM Worship of, or devotion to, the Hindu god VISHNU. Devotees regard him as the sole deity of whom other gods are mere aspects.

VAISHYAS See CASTE SYSTEM.

VAJRAYANA ('Diamond vehicle') An expression sometimes used for Tibetan Buddhism, a form of MAHAYANA Buddhism which has distinctive doctrines and practices.

VALHALLA ('Hall of the slain') The part of ASGARD in Norse mythology reserved for dead heroes waiting for the final battle of RAGNARÖK. It had 540 doors and 800 men could march, shoulder to shoulder, out of each door. The dead heroes spent their time drinking, playing games and fighting.

VALKYRIES ('Choosers of the slain') Female servants of ODIN in Norse mythology who choose which side is to have victory and battle and which warriors are to die. They conduct the dead to VALHALLA and wait on them with food and drink. Some MYTHS portray them as witchlike beings, exulting in blood and death.

VAMPYR Spirit of a dead person in Slavic folklore who lives by sucking the blood of the living.

VANIR ('Shining ones') Divine beings of Norse mythology who at first fought with the AESIR and later allied with them and came to live in ASGARD.

VARANASI See BENARES.

VARUNA Indian sky god of the Vedic period (see VEDAS). He produced the cosmic order and was seen as a heavenly ruler and lawgiver as well as a moral guardian of the earth.

VATICAN COUNCILS The first was convened by POPE PIUS IX in AD 1869–70. It resulted in the dogma of Papal Infallibility and attacks on 'modern' thought. The second (1962–65) was called by John XXIII. It led to a drastic modernization of Roman Catholic worship and improved relations with other churches.

VEDANTA (1) 'The end of the VEDAS'. A name for the UPANISHADS, which close the period of HINDU revelation. (2) Indian philosophy based on the teachings of SHANKARA. Its basic tenet is that only BRAHMAN, the Absolute, is fully real. The world of sense experience is contradictory and dreamlike because it is spun from the illusions of MAYA. Release from illusion comes from recognizing the sole reality of Brahman.

VEDAS Scriptures which express the religion of the ARYAN people of India. They comprise HYMNS, instructions for RITUAL and cosmological speculations. There are four divisions: *Rig Veda*, hymns to the Aryan gods who are personifications of natural forces; *Sama Veda*, verses selected for chanting (see CHANT); *Yajur Veda*, prose instructions on matters of ritual; *Atharva Veda*, rites and SPELLS in verse, especially concerned with curing illness.

VENUS Roman goddess of love, identified with APHRODITE and thus honoured as the mother of the Roman people.

VESTA Roman goddess of the hearth and protectress of domestic life. She was regarded as the guardian of the Roman nation. Her cult was under the supervision of six Vestal Virgins who tended the undying flame (traditionally from Troy) which burned in her temple.

VESTMENTS Special garments worn by the Christian clergy during liturgical services (see LITURGY).

VIHARA A dwelling place for members of the Buddhist SANGHA. The term is also used today for any retreat house, temple or Buddhist monastery.

VINAYA PITAKA One of the oldest Buddhist scriptures consisting of the rules of discipline for the SANGHA, and related commentaries.

VIRACOCHA/HUIRACOCHA The uncreated creator god in the religion of the INCAS. He was god of the ancient city of TIUHUANACO and the giver of civilization. PACHACHUTEC, the ninth Inca, exalted him as supreme deity over even the SUN GOD.

VIRGINS OF THE SUN The *Aclla Cuna*, or 'chosen women' of the INCAS. They were selected at the age of ten to serve in the sun temples. Some became sacrificial victims, others wives of the Inca. They were ruled by a chief priestess, the Coya Pacsa, held to be the earthly consort of the SUN GOD.

VISHNU In HINDUISM, god as preserver and life-giver, the creator of the cosmos. He and SHIVA are the two great gods of Hindu devotion. As lawgiver and moral guardian, Vishnu appears on earth from time to time as an AVATAR to reawaken men to knowledge of truth.

VIVEKANANDA (about 1863–1902) Follower of RAMAKRISHNA, and founder of the RAMAKRISHNA MISSION in 1897. An apologist for VEDANTA, he criticized the dogmatism of CHRISTIANITY. Attending the World Parliament of Religions in Chicago in 1893, he commended Vedanta as the highest form of religion.

VOODOO Religion of ninety per cent of the people of Haiti (in spite of the official domination of Roman Catholicism) as well as others in the West Indies and parts of South America. The name derives from a West African word for GOD. In practice Voodoo is highly syncretistic: West African DIVINITIES are worshipped (see SHANGO), often as Christian SAINTS and their sanctuaries are closed during the Christian season of LENT.

W

WAHHABI MOVEMENT Puritanical Islamic movement founded by Al-Wahhab of Arabia (AD 1703–92). Wahhabi accept the authority only of the QUR'AN and the SUNNA. The movement has revived in the twentieth century and is the dominant religious influence in Saudi Arabia.

WAILING WALL See WESTERN WALL.

WANDERING ON In Buddhist thought the continual cycle by which the KARMA of past actions causes the coming-to-be of new mental and physical states which in turn produce more karma and further phases of existence.

WANDJINA Spirit beings of the Australian DREAMTIME who are

believed to have left their shadows on rock and cave walls in paintings and engravings. They are regarded as kindly beings who care for the people, ensure fertility and bring rain.

WEEKS/SHAVUOT Jewish feast celebrated seven weeks after PASSOVER. It has become associated with the giving of the Ten Commandments on Mt Sinai. Also known as PENTECOST(2).

WEREWOLF Human being who has been transformed into a wolf in Slavic folk tradition.

WESLEY, John (AD 1703–91) Founder of the METHODIST movement. He travelled through England on horseback preaching the 'new birth'. Although loyal to the Church of England, he was eventually forced to ordain his own ministers.

WESTERN WALL/WAILING WALL/KOTEL Site in JERUSALEM used by JEWS to lament the FALL OF JERUSALEM and the continuing suffering of the Jews and to pray for restoration. It is believed to be part of the original temple of Solomon, the only part of the temple left standing after the destruction of AD 70. (See TEMPLE OF JERUSALEM.)

WITCHCRAFT The practice of casting harmful SPELLS or charms. Witches are also widely believed to have the power of flying by night and to devour human souls.

WITCHDOCTOR/MEDICINE MAN A healer in PRIMAL RELIGIONS. The terms are rarely used today as they are felt to have misleading connotations.

WORLD COUNCIL OF CHURCHES Body including many Protestant and Orthodox Churches first constituted at Amsterdam in 1948 (see ECUMENICAL MOVEMENT).

WORLD FELLOWSHIP OF BUDDHISTS Society founded in 1950 in Ceylon (Sri Lanka) by G.P. Malalesekera to bring together Buddhists of all traditions and nations with the common intention of spreading Buddhist teaching throughout the world.

WORSHIP Reverence or homage to God or a god which may involve PRAYER, SACRIFICE, RITUALS, singing, dancing or chanting.

WOVOKA (AD 1856–1932) Paiute North American Indian PROPHET and MYSTIC who, reacting against white domination, urged his followers to live in peace, fighting the whites through the power of the GHOST DANCE. His hope of imminent regeneration spread among the Plains Indians. The movement was destroyed at the Battle of Wounded Knee in 1890.

WRATH The righteous anger of God against SIN.

WRITINGS The third and final division of the HEBREW BIBLE, comprising the Wisdom literature (such as Job and Proverbs), the Psalms and the later histories and other material.

WYCLIFFE, John (about 1329–84) English religious reformer who condemned the POPE as Antichrist and began the translation of the BIBLE into English.

XIPE TOTEC ('The flayed one') In Mexican mythology, the god of the west and of agriculture, who was skinned alive like the maize. He was represented by the mask of a skinned human face.

XIUHTECUHTLI ('Turquoise lord') The ancient Mexican fire god. His fire burned in every home and temple and he was regarded as a form of the supreme god.

YAHWEH See YHWH.

YAMA In the VEDAS the primordial man who crosses through death and becomes immortal. He is therefore god of death who judges men and consigns them to heaven or hell. His significance as judge faded as the pre-ARYAN doctrine of SAMSARA became established.

YASNA The form of public worship in ancient ZOROASTRIANISM, elements of which are retained by the PARSIS. Part of the AVESTA, it teaches the presence of the divine in all things and refers to many lesser divine beings alongside AHURA MAZDA.

YELLOW HATS Reformed branch of TIBETAN BUDDHISM whose leader is the DALAI LAMA. (See BUDDHISM.)

YGGDRASIL The great ash tree which unifies the creation according to Norse mythology. Its three roots reach ASGARD, MIDGARD and Niflheim, the UNDERWORLD. The tree holds together the nine worlds of giants, dwarfs, men, light elves, dark elves, AESIR, VANIR, the dead and the home of the world-destroyers. The tree of knowledge, it is simultaneously being nourished and destroyed. It is also a symbol of the generation of life: the first man in Norse myth is named Ash.

YHWH The 'tetragrammaton', the sacred name of the God of ISRAEL which was revealed to MOSES. The name means 'I am'. It could not be spoken and the HEBREW 'Adonai' ('the Lord') was substituted when the scriptures were read aloud. The MASORETES put the vowel points for Adonai into the name YHWH which gave rise to the malformation 'Jehovah'. YHWH was possibly pronounced 'Yahweh'.

YIN AND YANG The polarity of energies in Chinese philosophy. Yang is masculine, dynamic, bright and good; yin is feminine, passive, dark and bad. Their production and interplay is represented in a circular diagram (see T'AI CHI). Yin and Yang produce the elements and the cycle of the seasons. They also provided the theoretical basis for the Taoist practice of ALCHEMY (see TAOISM).

YOGA A way to union with GOD in HINDU philosophy. It also forms one of the six classical systems of Indian thought. Traditionally there are eight stages of yoga: restraint; discipline; posture; breathing; detachment; concentration; meditation, and trance. The four main styles of yoga correspond to different personality types: *Karma yoga*, the path of action; *Jnana yoga*, the path of knowledge; *Bhakti yoga*, the path of devotion; *Raja yoga*, the path of insight.

YOGI Indian holy man who has reached ENLIGHTENMENT through yogic practices (see YOGA). (See also TRANSCENDENTAL MEDITATION.)

YOM KIPPUR/DAY OF ATONEMENT Jewish day of FASTING and repentance, the most solemn day of the Jewish year. The liturgy includes a solemn chant, the *Kol Nidre*, which challenges Jews who have strayed from religion to return to faith.

YOUNG, Brigham See MORMONISM.

YUM KAAX Corn god of the MAYA. He is portrayed as a young god holding up a flowering plant.

ZADDIK Jewish teacher in the later Hasidist movement. The Zaddik was seen as the perfectly righteous man who was in mystical communion with God. The Zaddik's house became the meeting place for the HASIDIM(3).

ZAKAT Obligatory almsgiving, one of the FIVE PILLARS OF ISLAM. Originally it was for poor relief and for financing JIHAD. The proportion of the individual's income to be given has varied; at times it has come under state supervision and been levied as a tax, but modern MUSLIM states insist that zakat is quite separate from social welfare.

ZAMBE See NYAMBE.

ZANAHARY The creator god in Madagascan religion.

ZA-ZEN Japanese term for the form of MEDITATION practised in ZEN monasteries. It involves a sitting posture designed to accompany reflection on a KOAN.

ZEALOTS Jewish nationalistic party in Roman times who believed that the Roman presence was a defilement of the land and a flouting of TORAH. In AD 66 they revolted. The war which followed led to the destruction of JERUSALEM and her temple in AD 70. The last stand of the Zealots was at Masada, where 960 of them died in AD 73.

ZEMES DIEVS Latvian god of the farmstead. He is sometimes identified with PERKONS.

ZEMES MATE Latvian earth goddess.

ZEN Japanese Buddhist movement which developed from the Chinese CH'AN school in the thirteenth century AD. It is characterized by the teaching that ENLIGHTENMENT is a spontaneous event, totally independent of concepts, techniques or rituals. Zen aims at harmony in living and uses secular arts such as tea-making and calligraphy to develop effortless skills.

ZEUS Supreme ruler of the Greek gods. Described by HOMER as 'Father of gods and men', he may have originated as a storm god and continued to be regarded as controller of the weather. Although there were many MYTHS about him he did not appear in drama, which suggests that he was held in special awe. Sometimes the name Zeus stood simply for God, as supreme deity.

ZEUS KRETAGENES ('Cretan-born' Zeus) A dying and rising god whose cult flourished during and after the period of the Minoan civilization in Crete. He was associated with the bull and was the original son and consort of the MOTHER GODDESS.

ZEVI, Shabbetai (AD 1626–1716) Kabbalistic RABBI from Smyrna who became the centre of a Messianic movement which spread throughout the Jewish world (see KABBALAH). In 1665 he proclaimed himself MESSIAH. He was later imprisoned and, to the horror of his followers, converted to ISLAM. There were attempts to argue that the sin of the Messiah was a necessary part of redemption, but the movement disintegrated.

ZIGGURAT Ancient Babylonian TEMPLE in the form of a tower rising from a broad base to a narrow top.

ZIONISM The movement to establish a national and permanent homeland for JEWS. In 1897 the first Zionist Congress was organized in Basle by Theodore HERZL in the wake of a wave of European anti-Semitism. Gradually the movement became determined that Palestine was the only realistic place to establish the Jewish state and Jews were encouraged to emigrate and acquire property there. The majority of Jews today support Zionism to the extent that it is manifested in the modern state of ISRAEL.

ZOHAR Most important writing of the Jewish KABBALAH.

ZOMBIE Term used in Haiti and South America for the 'living dead'—those whose souls have been eaten by witches (see WITCHCRAFT).

ZOROASTER/ZARATHUSTRA Prophet and founder of ZOROASTRIANISM. He lived in Persia, either in the tenth and ninth centuries BC, or, more likely, in the seventh and sixth. At the age of thirty he had a revelation of AHURA MAZDA which drove him to preach against polytheism. According to tradition he died performing the fire sacrifice which was the central ceremony of the new faith.

ZOROASTRIANISM The religion of ancient Persia, founded by ZOROASTER, possibly related to the Vedic religion of India (see VEDAS). It was strongly ethical: Zoroaster taught that AHURA MAZDA would judge each individual soul after death. Later there developed a complex doctrinal system speculating about the inner nature of the universe. The expansion of ISLAM drove Zoroastrianism out of Persia (see also AVESTA; PARSIS; ZURVANISM).

ZURVANISM Zoroastrian heresy according to which an absolute being called Zurvan ('time') was the origin of good and evil and the source of the two spirits AHURA MAZDA and ANGRA MAINYU.

Index

Index / 439

Acknowledgements

Maps and charts
Roy Lawrance

Photographs
The photographs in this book are reproduced by permission of the following photographers and organizations.

Australian Information Service   149, 150 (both), back cover (right: aborigines)
Barnaby's Picture Library   87, 105, 139, 170–71, 175, 182, 186, 188 (below), 189, 191, 198, 203, 218, 230, 232, 235, 236, 250, 253 (below), 256, 259, 265, 273, 286, 295, 297, 299, 312, 318, 330, 347, front cover (left: Hindu Divali festival), cover spine
BBC Hulton Picture Library   16
Axel-Ivar Berglund   163
Barbara M. Boal   129, 134 (both), 135, 137
British Museum   123, 132, 140 (right), 316
Michael Cole   385 (all)
Douglas Davies   188 (above), 200(2)
Douglas Dickins   12, 21 (below), 53, 72 (above), 143, 181, 192 (above, both), 193, 194, 211, 214, 227, 229(3), 241, 260, 269, 308, 346, 374, front cover (right: funeral procession, Bali)
W. H. Edwards   21 (above)
Evangelical Union of South America   367, 387
Fritz Fankhauser   70, 76, 248, 254, 276–77, 305, 341, 361, 362, 366, 368–69, 382, 386 (both), front and back cover (main picture: Buddhist monks)
Werner Forman Archive   125
French Government Tourist Office   25

Sonia Halliday   298, 309, 313, 338, 344, 365, back cover (centre: stained glass)
John Hinnells   86
Hirmer Archive   92, 93
Michael Holford   45, 116
Alan Hutchison Library   title page, 43, 140 (left), 141, 144, 145 (left), 155, 156, 161, 167, 168, 321, 323, 350
Jewish Education Board   293
Lion Publishing, David Alexander   65, 91, 200(6), 279, 285, 288, 337, 356, 381; from the British Museum: 24, 60, 63, 68, 72 (below), 78 **Jon Willcocks**   29, 152, 153, 348, 353, 377
William Macquitty   10, 17, 19, 36, 51, 57, 73, 77(1,2,3), 82, 172, 185, 188 (centre), 196, 200(3,4), 202, 224, 229(2), 233, 240, 245, 247, 249, 257, 261, 263, 319, 328–29 (all), 332, 373, endpapers, front cover (centre: Japanese girl priest)
The Mansell Collection   89, 102 (both), 103 (both), 106, 107, 108, 290, 370
Wulf Metz   33, 77(5,6,7), 97, 130, 145 (right), 160, 180, 192 (below), 225, 229(1,4), 253 (above), 324, 326, 359
Middle East Photographic Archive   334
Open Doors   351, 383
Ann and Bury Peerless   176, 200(1,5), 205, 207, 209, 220 (both), back cover (left: Jain home shrine)
John Ruffle   62, 77(4), 81, 100
Len Scott   115, 119, 120
Silkeborg Museum, Denmark   114
Derek Swallow   371
Harold Turner   157

The article by the Rev. Robert Brow is reproduced from his book *Religion: Origins and Ideas* by kind permission of the publishers, Tyndale Press.